A Dictionary of
Law

Shelve in Nf.

Oxford Paperback Reference

The most authoritative and up-to-date reference books for both students and the general reader.

*forthcoming

A Dictionary of
Law

FIFTH EDITION

Edited by
ELIZABETH A. MARTIN

Oxford   New York

OXFORD UNIVERSITY PRESS

2002

OXFORD

UNIVERSITY PRESS

Great Clarendon Street, Oxford OX2 6DP

Oxford University Press is a deparment of the University of Oxford.
It furthers the University's objective of excellence in research, scholarship,
and education by publishing worldwide in

Oxford New York

Auckland Bangkok Buenos Aires Cape Town Chennai
Dar es Salaam Delhi Hong Kong Istanbul Karachi Kolkata
Kuala Lumpur Madrid Melbourne Mexico City Mumbai Nairobi
São Paulo Shanghai Singapore Taipei Tokyo Toronto

with an associated company in Berlin

Oxford is a registered trade mark of Oxford University Press
in the UK and in certain other countries

First published 1983 as *A Concise Dictionary of Law*
Second edition 1990
Third edition 1994
Reissued in new covers with corrections 1996
Fourth edition 1997
Fifth edition 2002

British Library Cataloguing in Publication Data

Data available

Library of Congress Cataloging in Publication Data

ISBN 0-19-860399-1

10 9 8 7 6 5 4 3

Typeset in Swift by Market House Books Ltd.

Printed in Great Britain by
Clays Ltd, St Ives plc

Preface

This dictionary has been written by a distinguished team of academic and practising lawyers. It is intended primarily for those without a qualification in law who nevertheless require some legal knowledge in the course of their work: chartered surveyors and accountants, civil servants and local-government officers, social workers and probation officers, as well as businessmen and legal secretaries are typical examples of those whose work often calls for a knowledge of the precise meaning (and spelling) of a legal term.

Each article, therefore, begins with a clear definition of the entry word (or words) and, in most cases, is followed by a more detailed explanation or description of the concepts involved.

Written in concise English, without the unnecessary use of legal jargon, the book will also be of considerable value to members of the public who come into contact with the law and lawyers – house buyers, motorists, and hire purchasers are among those who cannot escape the effects of legislation or the unique prose style in which it is usually expressed.

In the five years since the last edition of the dictionary was published there have been radical changes in the English legal system, most notably in the areas of civil procedure (resulting from the Access to Justice Act 1999 and the Civil Procedure Rules – the so-called 'Woolf Reforms') and human rights law (brought about by the Human Rights Act 1998). The new edition reflects these and many other changes. If any provisions of new legislation were not in force at the time of publication, the entries to which they apply will indicate the direction of the proposed changes.

An asterisk (*) placed before a word in a definition indicates that additional relevant information will be found under this article. Some entries simply refer the reader to another entry, indicating either that they are synonyms or abbreviations or that they are most conveniently explained, together with related terms, in one of the dictionary's longer articles. The use of the pronoun 'he' (rather than 'he or she') in entries has been adopted to simplify the construction of sentences; it does not imply that the subject matter relates exclusively to males.

E.A.M.
2001

Editor

Elizabeth A. Martin MA (Oxon)

Contributors for the Fifth Edition

Owain Blackwell BA, LLM (Nottm) *Senior Lecturer in Law, Buckinghamshire Chilterns University College*

Sandra Clarke MA (Oxon) *Barrister; Senior Lecturer in Law, University of Greenwich*

Kim Everett LLB *Senior Lecturer in Law, University of Greenwich*

Martin Fitzgerald MSc (Social Research), LLB, PGCE *Solicitor; Principal Lecturer in Law, University of Greenwich*

M. Gaborak LLM *Senior Lecturer in Law, University of Greenwich*

Sarah Greer MA (Cantab), ACA *Senior Lecturer in Law, University of Greenwich*

John Horder BSc, LLB, DPhil *Senior Lecturer in Law, University of Greenwich*

P. D. M. Jackson BSc *Barrister; Lecturer in Law, University of Greenwich*

Edward Phillips LLB (Mal), BCL (Oxon) *Principal Lecturer in Law, University of Greenwich*

Gary Shields BSc, ACII, LLM, CertEd *Principal Lecturer in Law, University of Greenwich*

Nicholas J. Simpson BA (Oxon) *Solicitor*

E. Susan Singleton LLB *Solicitor*

John Wadham BSc (London), MSc (Surrey) *Solicitor; Director of Liberty*

Margaret Whybrow LLB *Barrister, Senior Lecturer in Law, University of Greenwich*

Contributors for the First Edition

Martin R. Banham-Hall LLB *Solicitor*

Bernard Berkovits LLB *Lecturer in Law, University of Buckingham*

P. J. Clarke BCL, MA *Barrister; Fellow and Tutor in Law, Jesus College, Oxford*

Letitia Crabb LLB (Wales), LLM (London) *Solicitor; Lecturer in Law, University College of Wales, Aberystwyth*

J. W. Davies LLB, MA, BCL *Fellow of Brasenose College, Oxford*

B. Russell Davis MA, LLB *Barrister*

J. D. Feltham BA (Melb.), MA (Oxon) *Fellow of Magdalen College, Oxford*

Judith Lewis LLB *Solicitor*

Keith Uff MA, BCL (Oxon) *Lecturer in Law, University of Birmingham*

Contents

A

abandonment *n.* **1.** The act of giving up a legal right, particularly a right of ownership of property. Property that has been abandoned is *res nullius* (a thing belonging to no one), and a person taking possession of it therefore acquires a lawful title. An item is regarded as abandoned when it can be established that the original owner has discarded it and is indifferent as to what becomes of it: such an item cannot be the subject of a theft charge. However, property placed by its owner in a dustbin is not abandoned, having been placed there for the purpose of being collected as refuse. In marine insurance, abandonment is the surrender of all rights to a ship or cargo in a case of *constructive total loss. The insured person must do this by giving the insurer within a reasonable time a **notice of abandonment**, by which he relinquishes all his rights to the ship or cargo to the insurer and can treat the loss as if it were an actual total loss. **2.** In civil litigation, the relinquishing of the whole or part of the claim made in an action or of an appeal. Any claim is now considered to be abandoned once a *notice of discontinuance is served, according to rule 38(1) of the *Civil Procedure Rules. **3.** The offence of a parent or guardian leaving a child under the age of 16 to its fate. A child is not regarded as abandoned if the parent knows and approves steps someone else is taking to look after it. The court may allow a child to be adopted without the consent of its parents if they are guilty of abandonment.

abatement *n.* **1.** (of debts) The proportionate reduction in the payment of debts that takes place if a person's assets are insufficient to settle with his creditors in full. **2.** (of legacies) The reduction or cancellation of legacies when the estate is insufficient to cover all the legacies provided for in the will or on intestacy after payment of the deceased's debts. The Administration of Estates Act 1925 provides that general legacies, unless given to satisfy a debt or for other consideration, abate in proportion to the amounts of those legacies; specific and demonstrative legacies then abate if the estate is still insufficient to pay all debts, and a demonstrative legacy also abates if the specified fund is insufficient to cover it. For example, A's estate may comprise a painting, £300 in his savings account, and £700 in other money; there are debts of £100 but his will leaves the painting to B, £500 from the savings account to C, £800 to D, and £200 to E. B will receive the painting, C's demonstrative legacy abates to £300, and after the debts are paid from the remaining £700, D's and E's general legacies abate proportionately, to £480 and £120 respectively. When annuities are given by the will, the general rule is that they are valued at the date of the testator's death, then abate proportionately in accordance with that valuation, and each annuitant receives the abated sum. All these rules are subject to any contrary intention being expressed in the will. **3.** (in land law) Any reduction or cancellation of money payable. For example a lease may provide for an abatement of rent in certain circumstances, e.g. if the building is destroyed by fire, and a purchaser of land may claim an abatement of the price if the seller can prove his ownership of only part of the land he contracted to sell. **4.** (of nuisances) The termination, removal, or destruction of a *nuisance. A person injured by a nuisance has a right to abate it. In doing so, he must not do more damage than is necessary and, if removal of the nuisance requires entry on to the property from which it emanates, he may have to give notice to the wrongdoer. A local authority can issue an abatement notice to control statutory nuisances. **5.** (of proceedings) The termination of civil proceedings by operation of law, caused by a change of interest or status (e.g. bankruptcy or death) of one of the parties after the start but before the completion of the proceedings. An abatement did not prevent either of the parties from bringing fresh proceedings in respect of the same cause of action. Pleas in abatement have been abolished; in modern practice any change of interest or status of the parties does not affect the validity of the proceedings, provided that the cause of action survives.

abduction *n.* The offence of taking an unmarried girl under the age of 16 from the possession of her parents or guardians against their will. It is no defence that the girl looked and acted as if she was over 16 or that she was a willing party. No sexual motive has to be proved. It is also an offence to abduct an unmarried girl under the age of 18 or a mentally defective woman (married or unmarried) for the purpose of unlawful sexual intercourse. In this case a defendant can plead that he had reasonable grounds for believing that the girl was over 18, or that he did not know the woman was mentally defective, respectively. It is also an offence to abduct any woman with the intention that she should marry or have unlawful sexual intercourse with someone, if it is done by force or for the sake of her property. It is also an offence for a parent or guardian of a child under 16 to take or send him out of the UK without the consent of the other parent or guardians. Belief that the other person has or would have consented is a defence. It is also an offence for any other person to remove or keep such a child, without lawful authority or reasonable excuse, from the person with lawful control of him. Proof of belief that the child was 16 is a defence here. *See also* KIDNAPPING.

abet *vb. See* AID AND ABET.

abortion *n.* The termination of a pregnancy: a miscarriage or the premature expulsion of a foetus from the womb before the normal period of gestation is complete. It is an offence to induce or attempt to induce an abortion unless the terms of the Abortion Act 1967 and the Abortion Regulations 1991 are complied with. The pregnancy can only be terminated by a registered medical practitioner, and two registered medical practitioners must agree that it is necessary, for example because (1) continuation of the pregnancy would involve a risk to the life or physical or mental health of the pregnant woman (or of other children of hers) that is greater than the risk of terminating the pregnancy, or (2) that there is a substantial risk that the child will be born with a serious physical or mental handicap. However, doctors are not obliged to perform abortions if they can prove that they have a conscientious objection to so doing. A husband cannot prevent his wife having a legal abortion if she so wishes. *Compare* CHILD DESTRUCTION.

absconding *n.* The failure of a person to surrender to the custody of a court in order to avoid legal proceedings. *See also* SURRENDER TO CUSTODY.

absence *n.* (in court procedure) The nonappearance of a party to litigation or a person summoned to attend as a witness.

absent-mindedness *n. See* AUTOMATISM.

absent parent *See* NONRESIDENT PARENT; CHILD SUPPORT MAINTENANCE.

absolute assignment *See* ASSIGNMENT.

absolute discharge *See* DISCHARGE.

absolute privilege The defence that a statement cannot be made the subject of an action for *defamation because it was made in Parliament, in papers ordered to be published by either House of Parliament, in judicial proceedings or a fair and accurate newspaper or broadcast report of judicial proceedings, or in an official communication between certain officers of state. Under the Defamation Act 1996, the defence is also available for those reporting proceedings of the European Court of Justice. Under certain circumstances defined by the 1996 Act the absolute privilege accorded to statements or proceedings in Parliament may be waived (**waiver of privilege**) to permit evidence to be adduced in an action for defamation. *Compare* QUALIFIED PRIVILEGE.

absolute right A right set out in the European Convention on Human Rights that cannot be interfered with lawfully, no matter how important the public interest in doing so might be. Absolute rights include *freedom of thought, conscience, and religion and the prohibitions on *torture, *inhuman treatment or punishment, and *degrading treatment or punishment. *Compare* QUALIFIED RIGHT.

absolute title Ownership of a *legal estate in registered land with a guarantee by the state that no one has a better right to that estate. An absolute title to freehold land is equivalent to an estate in fee simple in possession in unregistered land. **Absolute leasehold title**, unlike *good leasehold title, guarantees that the lessor has title to grant the lease. (*Compare* POSSESSORY TITLE; QUALIFIED TITLE.) The title may be subject to (1) *encumbrances and other entries noted on the register by means of substantive registration (e.g. a registered legal charge or land charge); (2) minor interests, such as that of a beneficiary under a trust, which may be protected by means of "entry" on the register rather than by substantive registration; and (3) *overriding interests (which by their nature do not appear on the register and must be ascertained by search and enquiry). *See also* LAND REGISTRATION.

abstracting electricity The *arrestable offence, punishable with up to five years' imprisonment and/or a fine, of dishonestly using, wasting, or diverting electricity. This offence may be committed by someone who bypasses his electricity meter or reconnects a disconnected meter or who unlawfully obtains a free telephone call (though there is a more specific and potentially less serious offence to deal with this). Bypassing a gas or water meter could constitute *theft of the gas or water. Joyriding in a lift (or some similar abuse) might also constitute wasting electricity. Computer hackers were formerly charged with offences of abstracting electricity until the Computer Misuse Act 1990 made *hacking a specific criminal offence.

abstraction of water The taking of water from a river or other source of supply. It normally requires a water authority licence but there are exceptions; for example when less than 1000 gallons are taken, when the water is for domestic or agricultural use (excluding spray irrigation), or when it is removed in the course of fire-fighting or land drainage. It has been held not to include gravitational loss from a canal replacing water drawn from a connecting outfall channel.

abstract of title Written details of the *title deeds and documents that prove an owner's right to dispose of his land or an interest in this. An abstract generally deals only with the *legal estate and any equitable interests that are not *overreached. An owner usually supplies an abstract of title before *completion to an intending purchaser or mortgagee, who compares it with the original title deeds when these are produced or handed over on completion of the transaction. An abstract of title to registered land consists of *office copies of the entries in the register (together with an *authority to inspect the register) and details of any other documents necessary to prove the owner's title, such as a marriage certificate proving a woman's change of surname. For unregistered land, the abstract of title must usually trace the history of the land's ownership from a document at least 15 years old (the *root of title) and give details of any document creating encumbrances to which the land is subject. An abstract of title formerly comprised extracts, often in abbreviated note form, but now generally comprises duplicate copies of the relevant documents (an **epitome of title**). An abstract or epitome, with each copy document marked as examined against the original, may be sufficient in itself to deduce title; for instance, when a title is split into lots, the purchaser of each lot may be required to accept an examined abstract or epitome in lieu of the original title deeds, accompanied by an *acknowledgment and undertaking.

abuse of a dominant position Unlawful activities by large businesses, i.e. usually those having a market share of at least 40% in at least one EU state. Examples of such activities, which are contrary to *Article 82 of the Treaty of Rome and the UK Competition Act 1998, include refusing to supply an existing customer and engaging in *predatory pricing. The European Commission and the Office of Fair Trading can fine businesses up to 10% of annual worldwide turnover for breach of Article 82. The record individual fine, of 102M ECUs (now euros), was against Volkswagen in 1998; it was upheld on appeal in July 2000. Under the UK Competition Act 1998 a £3.21M penalty was imposed on Napp Pharmaceuticals. See ANTICOMPETITIVE PRACTICE.

abuse of process A tort where damage is caused by using a legal process for an ulterior collateral purpose. (See also MALICIOUS PROSECUTION.) Actions that are obviously frivolous, vexatious, or in bad faith can be stayed or dismissed by the court as an abuse of process.

abusive behaviour See THREATENING BEHAVIOUR.

ABWOR Advice by way of representation: assistance formerly given to a person by taking on his behalf any step in the institution or conduct of any proceedings before a court or tribunal under the provisions of the legal advice and assistance scheme. The legal aid scheme under which ABWOR was created was replaced by the *Community Legal Service from 1 April 2000. Under the new scheme, the authorization of legal representation for the purposes of a particular hearing is now in a form called **help at court**.

ACAS Advisory Conciliation and Arbitration Service: a statutory body that was established under the Employment Protection Act 1975; the composition and functions of ACAS are now governed by Parts IV and VI of the Trade Union and Labour Relations (Consolidation) Act 1992. ACAS was set up to promote the improvement of industrial relations and the development of *collective bargaining. In its conciliation function it may intervene, with or without the parties' consent, in a *trade dispute to offer facilities and assistance in negotiating a settlement. It employs **conciliation officers** who may assist parties to an application to an employment tribunal to reach a settlement. Earlier legislation removed the necessity for binding settlements of employment disputes to involve an ACAS conciliation officer: settlements can now be made when the invidual has had independent legal advice from a qualified lawyer.

    ACAS does not itself arbitrate in trade disputes, but with the consent of both parties it may refer a dispute to the *Central Arbitration Committee or to an independent arbitrator. ACAS may give free advice to employers, employees, and their respective representatives on matters of employment or industrial relations. It issues *codes of practice giving guidance on such matters as disciplinary procedures and *disclosure of information to trade unions. It may also conduct inquiries into industrial relations problems, either generally or in relation to particular businesses, and publish the results after considering the views of parties directly affected. ACAS can charge for its services when it considers that this is appropriate. The law on conciliation generally is contained in the Employment Tribunals Act 1996.

acceleration *n.* The coming into possession of a *future interest in any property at an earlier stage than that directed by the transaction or settlement that created the interest. For example, a landlord's interest in *reversion is accelerated if the tenant surrenders the lease before it has expired. When a will bequeaths an interest for life that lapses (e.g. because the legatee dies before the testator), the interest of the person entitled in *remainder is accelerated and takes effect immediately the testator dies.

acceptance *n.* Agreement to the terms of an *offer that, provided certain other requirements are fulfilled, converts the offer into a legally binding contract. If the method by which acceptance is to be signified is indicated by the offeror, that method alone will be effective. If it is not, acceptance may be either express (by word of mouth or in writing) or inferred from the offeree's conduct; for example, if he receives goods on approval and starts to make use of them. The acceptance must always, however, involve some action on the part of the person to whom the offer was made: the offeror cannot assert that his offer will be treated as accepted unless the offeree rejects it. The validity of an acceptance is governed by four principal rules. (1) It must take place while the offer is still in force, i.e. before it has lapsed (*see* LAPSE OF OFFER) or been revoked (*see* REVOCATION OF OFFER). (2) It must be on the same terms as the offer. An acceptance made subject to any variation is treated as a counteroffer. (3) It must be unconditional, thus an acceptance **subject to contract** is not a valid acceptance. (4) It must be communicated to the offeror. Acceptance by letter is treated as communicated when the letter is posted, but telex is equated with the telephone, so that communication takes place only on receipt. However, when the offer consists of a promise to confer a benefit on whoever may perform a specified act, the offeror waives the requirement of communication as a separate act. If, for example, he offers a reward for information, a person able to supply the information is not expected to accept the offer formally. The act of giving the information itself constitutes the acceptance, the communication of the acceptance, and the performance of the contract.

acceptance of a bill The written agreement by the person on whom a *bill of exchange is drawn (the **drawee**) that he will accept the order of the person who draws it upon him (the **drawer**). The acceptance must be written on the bill and signed. The signature of the drawee without additional words is sufficient, although generally the word "accepted" is used as well. Upon acceptance the drawee becomes the acceptor and the party primarily liable upon the bill. *See also* QUALIFIED ACCEPTANCE.

acceptance *supra protest* (acceptance for honour) A form of *acceptance of a bill of exchange to save the good name of the drawer or an endorser. If a bill of exchange has been either the subject of a *protest for dishonour by nonacceptance or protested for better security, and it is not overdue, any person who is not already liable on the bill may, with the consent of the holder, accept the bill *supra protest*. Such an acceptance must be written on the bill, indicate that it is an acceptance for honour, and be signed. The acceptor for honour engages that he will pay the bill on due presentment if it is not paid by the drawee, provided that it has been duly presented for payment and protested for nonpayment and that he receives notice of these facts. He is liable to the holder and to all parties to the bill subsequent to the party for whose honour he accepted.

access *n.* Formerly, the opportunity to visit a child that was granted (at the discretion of the court) to its parent when the other parent had the care and control of the child after divorce or when a custodianship order was in force. Since the Children Act 1989 came into force the concept of access has been replaced by that of *contact. *See also* SECTION 8 ORDERS.

accession *n.* **1.** The formal agreement of a country to an international *treaty. The term is applied to the agreement of a country to become a member state of the European Union. Member states accede to the Treaty of Rome or any other EU treaty by signing **accession agreements**. **2.** The process of a member of the royal family succeeding to the throne, which occurs immediately on the death or abdication of the previous sovereign.

access land Land to which the public will have access for the purposes of open-air recreation under the Countryside and Rights of Way Act 2000. It includes land shown as open country (mountain, moor, heath, or down) on a map in conclusive form issued by an appropriate countryside body (the Countryside Agency or the Countryside Council for Wales) or as common land, or land situated more than 600 metres above sea level, or land that has been dedicated as access land.

accessory *n.* One who is a party to a crime that is actually committed by someone else. An accessory is one who either successfully incites someone to commit a crime (**counsels or procures**) or helps him to do so (*aids and abets). The accessory is subject to the same punishments and orders as the principal (*see also* COMMON DESIGN). It is an offence to assist a person whom one knows has committed an arrestable offence with the intention of impeding his apprehension or prosecution. *See also* IMPEDING APPREHENSION OR PROSECUTION.

accessory liability If a stranger knowingly and dishonestly assists a trustee in a breach of trust he will be liable as an accessory. He will not usually have received any trust assets; however, in assisting in the breach he will be personally liable to account to the trust for any losses arising from his actions.

accident *n. See* FATAL ACCIDENTS; MISTAKE; ROAD TRAFFIC ACCIDENTS.

accident record book A record kept by the police of details of the accidents they have investigated. Access to this is usually requested by solicitors acting in subsequent litigation relating to *road traffic accidents. The Association of Chief Police Officers Traffic Committee has issued guidelines on charges for such reports.

accommodation bill A bill of exchange accepted by an **accommodation party**, i.e. a person who signs without receiving value and for the purpose of lending his name (i.e. his credit) to someone else. An accommodation party is liable on the bill to a *holder for value.

accomplice *n.* One who is a party to a crime, either as a *principal or as an *accessory. *See also* CORROBORATION.

accord and satisfaction The purchase by one party to a contract of a release from his obligations under it when the other party has already performed his side of the bargain. A release of this one-sided nature constitutes a **unilateral discharge** of the contract; unless granted by deed, it can at common law be effected only by purchase, i.e. by a fresh agreement (accord) for which new consideration (satisfaction) is given. If, for example, A is due to pay £1000 on a particular date to B for contractual services rendered, B might agree to accept £900 paid on an earlier date, the earlier payment constituting satisfaction. *Compare* BILATERAL DISCHARGE. *See also* (PROMISSORY) ESTOPPEL.

account *n.* A right at common law and later (more importantly) in equity, requiring one party to a relationship (e.g. a partnership) to account to the other or others for moneys received or due. An account may be: (1) **open** or **current**, where a balance has not been agreed or accepted by all parties; (2) **stated**, where a balance has been accepted as correct by all parties; or (3) **settled**, where a balance has been accepted and discharged.

accounting records *See* BOOKS OF ACCOUNT.

account of profits A remedy that a claimant can claim as an alternative to damages in certain circumstances, e.g. in an action for breach of *copyright. A successful claimant is entitled to a sum equal to the monetary gain the defendant has made through wronging the claimant.

accounts *pl. n.* A statement of a company's financial position. All registered companies must present accounts (in the form prescribed by the Companies Act 1985) annually at a *general meeting. These consist of a *balance sheet and a *profit-and-loss account with *group accounts (if appropriate) attached. They are accompanied by a directors' report and an auditor's report. All limited companies must deliver copies of their accounts to the *Companies Registry (where they are open to public inspection) but companies that are classified (on the basis of turnover, balance sheet total, and number of members) as "small" or "medium-sized" enjoy certain exemptions. Members are entitled to be sent copies of the accounts. *See also* ELECTIVE RESOLUTION; SUMMARY FINANCIAL STATEMENT.

accretion *n.* The process by which new land formations are legally assimilated to old by a change in the flow of a water channel. In contrast to *avulsion, this process involves a very slow, near imperceptible, natural action of water and other elements. It would include, for example, the natural diversion of a boundary river leaving an island, sandbank, or dry land where it previously flowed, the formation of islands at a river mouth, and additions to a delta by the deposit of sand and soil upon the shoreline. Accretion will allow the beneficiary state to legitimately claim title to the new land so created. *See also* THALWEG, RULE OF THE.

accumulation *n.* The continual addition of the income of a fund to the capital, so that the fund grows indefinitely. Before the Accumulation Act 1800 accumulation was permitted for the length of the perpetuity period (i.e. lives in being plus 21 years: *see* RULE AGAINST PERPETUITIES). The periods for which accumulation is now permitted are shorter; they are listed in the Law of Property Act 1925 and the Perpetuities and Accumulations Act 1964 and include a period of 21 years from the date of the disposition, the period of the life of the settlor, and the duration of the minority of any person mentioned in the disposition. Income is often directed to be accumulated if (for example) the beneficiary is a minor, or the interest in his favour is protected or contingent, or if the terms of a trust are discretionary.

accusatorial procedure (adversary procedure) A system of criminal justice in which conclusions as to liability are reached by the process of prosecution and defence. It is the primary duty of the prosecutor and defence to press their respective viewpoints within the constraints of the rules of evidence while the judge acts as an impartial umpire, who allows the facts to emerge from this procedure. Common-law systems usually adopt an accusatorial procedure. *See also* BURDEN OF PROOF. *Compare* INQUISITORIAL PROCEDURE.

acknowledgment *n.* **1.** The admission that a debt is due or a claim exists. Under the Limitation Act 1980, a written acknowledgment by a debtor or his agent causes the debt to be treated as if it had accrued on the date of the acknowledgment, provided that the limitation period is still current at that date. The result is that the limitation period of six years for bringing an action to recover the debt runs from the date of acknowledgment, rather than the date on which the debt in fact arose. *See also* LIMITATION OF ACTIONS. **2.** Confirmation by the signatory to a document that the signature on the document is his own. For example, the Wills Act 1837 requires that the testator's signature on the will be made or acknowledged in the presence of at least two witnesses present at the same time. Since January 1983 it has also been possible for a witness to acknowledge his signature in the presence of the testator.

acknowledgment and undertaking Confirmation in a *title deed that a person may see and have copies of relevant deeds not in his possession (acknowledgment), with a promise from the holder of them to keep them safely (undertaking). Thus when part of an owner's land is sold, he keeps his deeds to the whole but in the conveyance gives this acknowledgment and undertaking to the purchaser, who can then prove his title to the part from copies of the earlier deeds and by calling for production of the originals. In the majority of cases the vendor gives the purchaser all title documents relating solely to the land conveyed, and an acknowledgment and undertaking is only necessary when this does not happen. Note that personal representatives and fiduciary owners will normally give only an acknowledgment, no undertaking. Breach of an undertaking gives rise to an action in damages.

acknowledgment of service A response by a defendant to a claim. A defendant who intends to contest proceedings brought against him by a claimant must respond to the claim by filing an acknowledgment of service and/or by filing a *defence. Acknowledgments of service are used if the defendant is unable to file a defence within the required time or if the defendant intends to dispute the jurisdiction of the court. By acknowledging service a defendant is given an extra 14 days for filing the defence. In effect this means that the defendant has a 28-day period after service of the claim before the defence must be served. Once the defendant has returned the relevant section of the acknowledgment of service form, the court must notify the claimant in writing.

ACP states The African, Caribbean, and Pacific states that are associated with the European Union through the Lomé Convention. This convention, which was signed at Lomé (Togo) in 1975, provides for cooperation in matters of commerce between ACP states and EU states, including access to the EU market for products from the ACP countries. The Convention also provides for cooperation in industrial and financial matters.

acquiescence *n.* Express or implied *consent. In law, care must be taken to distinguish between mere knowledge of a situation and positive consent to it. For example, in the defence of *volenti non fit injuria* an injured party will not be regarded as having consented to a risk simply because he knew that the risk existed.

acquired rights *See* RELEVANT TRANSFER.

acquis communautaire [French] The body of *Community legislation by which all EU member states are bound.

acquittal *n.* A decision by a court that a defendant accused of a crime is innocent. A court must acquit a defendant following a verdict of *not guilty or a successful plea of *autrefois acquit* or *autrefois convict*. Once acquitted, a defendant cannot be retried for the same crime on fresh evidence, but an acquittal in a criminal court does not bind civil courts (for example, in relation to a libel charge against someone alleging the defendant's guilt).

action *n.* A proceeding in which a party pursues a legal right in a civil court. *See also* IN PERSONAM; IN REM.

active trust (special trust) A trust that imposes duties on the trustee other than that of merely handing over the trust property to the person entitled to it (*compare* BARE TRUST). These duties may impose a specific obligation on the trustee or confer a discretion on him.

act of God An event due to natural causes (storms, earthquakes, floods, etc.) so exceptionally severe that no-one could reasonably be expected to anticipate or guard against it. *See* FORCE MAJEURE.

Act of Parliament (statute) A document that sets out legal rules and has (normally) been passed by both Houses of *Parliament in the form of a *Bill and agreed to by the Crown (*see* ROYAL ASSENT). Under the Parliament Acts 1911 and 1949, however, passing of public Bills by the House of Lords can be dispensed with, except in the case of Bills to extend the duration of Parliament or to confirm provisional orders. Subject to these exceptions, the Lords can delay Bills passed by the House of Commons; it cannot block them completely. If the Commons pass a money Bill (for example, one giving effect to the Budget) and the Lords do not pass it unaltered within one month, it may be submitted direct for the royal assent. Any other Bill may receive the royal assent without being passed by the Lords if the Commons pass it in two consecutive sessions and at least one year elapses between its second reading in the first session and its third reading in the second.

Every modern Act of Parliament begins with a **long title**, which summarizes its aims, and ends with a **short title**, by which it may be cited in any other document. The short title includes the calendar year in which the Act receives the royal assent (e.g. The Competition Act 1998). An alternative method of citation is by the calendar year together with the Chapter number allotted to the Act on receiving the assent or, in the case of an Act earlier than 1963, by its regnal year or years and Chapter number. Regnal years are numbered from the date of a sovereign's accession to the throne, and an Act is attributed to the year or years covering the session in which it receives the royal assent. (*See also* ENACTING WORDS.) An Act comes into force on the date of royal assent unless it specifies a different date or provides for the date to be fixed by ministerial order.

Acts of Parliament are classified by the Queen's Printer as public general Acts, local Acts, and personal Acts. **Public general Acts** include all Acts (except those confirming provisional orders) introduced into Parliament as public Bills. **Local Acts** comprise all Acts introduced as private Bills and confined in operation to a particular area, together with Acts confirming provisional orders. **Personal Acts** are Acts introduced as private Bills and applying to private individuals or estates. Acts are alternatively classified as **public Acts** or **private Acts** according to their status in courts of law. A public Act is judicially noticed (i.e. accepted by the courts as a matter of general knowledge). A private Act is not, and must be expressly pleaded by the person relying on it. All Acts since 1850 are public unless they specifically provide otherwise. The printed version of an Act, rather than the version set out on the HMSO website, is the authentic text, although there are current proposals (2001) to alter this rule under the Electronic Communications Act 2000.

act of state An act, often involving force, of the executive of a state, or committed by an agent of a sovereign power with its prior approval or subsequent ratification, that affects adversely a person who does not owe allegiance to that power. The courts have power to decide whether or not particular conduct constitutes such an act, but if it does, they have no jurisdiction to award any remedy.

actual bodily harm Any hurt or injury calculated to interfere with the health or comfort of the victim. *Assault causing actual bodily harm is a summary or indictable offence carrying a maximum punishment of five years' imprisonment. The hurt need not be serious or permanent in nature, but it must be more than trifling. It is enough to show that pain or discomfort has been suffered, even though no bruising is evident. Hysteria brought on as a result of assault is sufficient for the offence to be proved.

actual military service *See* PRIVILEGED WILL.

actual notice Knowledge that a person has of rights adverse to his own. If a purchaser of unregistered land has actual notice of an interest that is not required to be registered as a land charge, and which will not be overreached on the sale to him, he will be bound by it. The doctrine of notice plays no part in registered land, where it has been replaced by the rules of registration. *See also* CONSTRUCTIVE NOTICE; IMPUTED NOTICE.

actual total loss (in marine insurance) A loss of a ship or cargo in which the subject matter is destroyed or damaged to such an extent that it can no longer be used for its purpose, or when the insured is irretrievably deprived of it. If the ship or cargo is the subject of a *valued policy, the measure of indemnity is the sum fixed by the policy; if the policy is unvalued, the measure of indemnity is the insurable value of the subject insured. *Compare* CONSTRUCTIVE TOTAL LOSS.

actus reus [Latin: a guilty act] The essential element of a crime that must be proved to secure a conviction, as opposed to the mental state of the accused (*see* MENS REA). In most cases the *actus reus* will simply be an act (e.g. appropriation of property is the act of theft) accompanied by specified circumstances (e.g. that the property belongs to another). Sometimes, however, it may be an *omission to act (e.g. failure to prevent death may be the *actus reus* of manslaughter) or it may include a specified consequence (death resulting within a year being the consequence required for the *actus reus* of murder or manslaughter). In certain cases the *actus reus* may simply be a state of affairs rather than an act (e.g. being unfit to drive through drink or drugs when in charge of a motor vehicle on a road).

actus reus non facit reum nisi mens sit rea [Latin: an act does not make a person guilty of his crime unless his mind be also guilty] The maxim that forms the basis for defining the two elements that must be proved before a person can be convicted of a crime (*see* ACTUS REUS; MENS REA).

ad colligenda bona [Latin] To collect the goods. The court may grant *letters of administration *ad colligenda bona* to any person to deal with specified property in an estate when that property might be endangered by delay. For example, if part of the estate consists of perishable goods the court may grant administration *ad colligenda bona* to any suitable person to allow him to sell or otherwise deal with those goods for the benefit of the estate. This is a limited grant only and ceases on the issue of a full grant of representation to the persons entitled to deal with the whole estate. In one case, such a grant was issued to the Official Solicitor on an application by the Inland Revenue when the executors of the deceased's will delayed applying for probate.

additional voluntary contribution (AVC) An additional payment that may be made by an employee to a pension scheme in order to increase the benefits available from their pension fund on retirement. AVCs can be paid into an employer's scheme or into a scheme of the employee's choice (a free-standing AVC); they can be made free of tax within Inland Revenue limits (*see* PENSION).

address for service The address, which a party to court proceedings gives to the court and/or the other party, to which all the formal documents relating to the proceedings should be delivered. Notices delivered at that address (which may be, for example, the address of his solicitors) are binding on the party concerned.

ademption *n.* The cancellation or reduction of a specific *legacy because the subject matter of the gift is no longer part of the testator's estate at his death, or the testator no longer has power to dispose of it, or there is nothing conforming to the description of it in the will. For example, if the will bequeaths a particular house that the testator sold during his lifetime, or if after making a will giving a legacy to his child the testator gives the child property constituting a *portion, the legacy is in each case adeemed. The gift of the house is cancelled and the child's legacy is reduced by the amount of the portion (*see also* SATISFACTION). Ademption need not occur by the testator's own deed; for example, an Act of Parliament that nationalized a company in which the testator had shares would cause a legacy of those shares to adeem.

ad idem [Latin: towards the same] Indicates that the parties to a transaction are in agreement. *See* CONSENSUS AD IDEM.

ADIZ *See* AIR DEFENCE IDENTIFICATION ZONE.

adjective law The part of the law that deals with practice and procedure in the courts. *Compare* SUBSTANTIVE LAW.

adjournment *n.* (in court procedure) The postponement or suspension of the hearing of a case until a future date. The hearing may be adjourned to a fixed date or *sine die* (without day), i.e. for an indefinite period. If an adjournment is granted at the request of a party the court may attach conditions, e.g. relating to the payment of any *costs thrown away.

adjudication *n.* **1.** The formal judgment or decision of a court or tribunal. **2.** A decision by the Commissioners of Inland Revenue as to the amount (if any) of *stamp duty payable on a written document.

adjudication order Formerly, a court order that made a debtor bankrupt. *See* BANKRUPTCY ORDER.

adjustment *n.* **1.** The determination of the amount due under a policy of insurance. **2.** The working out by an average adjuster of the rights and liabilities arising in a case of general *average.

ad litem [Latin] For the suit. A grant *ad litem* is the appointment by a court of a person to act on behalf of an estate in court proceedings, when the estate's proper representatives are unable or unwilling to act. For example, the Official Solicitor may be appointed administrator *ad litem* when a person wishes to claim under the Inheritance (Provision for Family and Dependants) Act 1975 (*see* FAMILY PROVISION) but the personal representatives are not willing to act, or nobody is entitled to a grant, or the only person entitled to a grant is the litigant himself. A guardian *ad litem* is the former name for a *children's guardian.

administration *n.* **1.** The collection of assets, payment of debts, and distribution to the beneficiaries of property in the estate of a deceased person. *See also* GRANT OF REPRESENTATION. **2.** The granting of *letters of administration to the estate of a

deceased person to an *administrator, when there is no executor under the will.
3. The process of carrying out duties imposed by a trust in connection with the property of a person of unsound mind or a bankrupt.

administration action Proceedings instituted in court by a personal representative or any other person interested in the estate of a deceased person to obtain a *grant of representation.

administration bond A guarantee by a third party, often an insurance company, to make good any loss arising if a person to whom letters of administration have been granted fails to deal properly with the estate. The court usually requires an administration bond as a condition of granting letters of administration only when the beneficiaries are considered to need special protection, e.g. when the administrator lives abroad or where there has been a dispute as to who should administer the estate.

administration of poison *See* POISON.

administration order **1.** An order made in a county court for the administration of the estate of a judgment debtor. The order normally requires the debtor to pay his debts by instalments: so long as he does so, the creditors referred to in the order cannot enforce their individual claims by other methods without the leave of the court. Administration orders are issued when the debtor has multiple debts but it is thought that his bankruptcy can be avoided.
2. An order made by the court under the Insolvency Act 1986, directing that, during the period for which it is in force, the affairs, business, and property of a company shall be managed by a person appointed by the court (known as the **administrator**). In order for the court to grant such an order it must be satisfied that the company cannot or is unlikely to be able to pay its debts when due *and* that the order is likely to allow (1) the survival of the company, or (2) the approval of a *voluntary arrangement, or (3) a more favourable realization of its assets than would be possible under a *winding-up or through an arrangement with creditors.

The Insolvency Act does not specify a period for the duration of the order: it remains in force until the administrator is discharged, by the court, having achieved the purpose(s) for which the order was granted or having decided that the purpose cannot be achieved.

While the order is in force the company may not be wound up; no steps may be taken to enforce any security over the company's property or to repossess goods in the company's possession, except with the leave of the court, and no other proceedings or other legal processes may be initiated or continued, against the company or its property, except with the court's leave.

administration pending suit Administration of a deceased person's estate by a person appointed by the High Court (the **administrator pending suit**) when legal proceedings are pending concerning the validity of the will or for obtaining, recalling, or revoking any grant. An administrator pending suit has all the rights, powers, and duties of a general administrator except that he may not distribute any part of the estate without the leave of the court.

administrative letter *See* COMFORT LETTER.

administrative powers Discretionary powers of an executive nature that are conferred by legislation on government ministers, public and local authorities, and other bodies and persons for the purpose of giving detailed effect to broadly defined policy. Examples include powers to acquire land compulsorily, to grant or refuse licences or consents, and to determine the precise nature and extent of services to be provided. Administrative powers are found in every sphere of public administration, including town and country planning, the regulation of public health and other environmental matters, the functioning of the welfare services, and the control of many trades, professions, and other activities. Their exercise is subject to judicial control by means of the doctrine of *ultra vires*.

administrative receiver A *receiver who, under the terms of a debenture secured by floating *charge, takes control of all (or substantially all) of a company's assets. *See also* INSOLVENCY PRACTITIONER.

administrative tribunal A body established by or under Act of Parliament to decide claims and disputes arising in connection with the administration of legislative schemes, normally of a welfare or regulatory nature. Examples are *employment tribunals and *rent assessment committees. They exist outside the ordinary courts of law, but their decisions are subject to judicial control by means of the doctrine of *ultra vires* and in cases of *error of law on the face of the record. *Compare* DOMESTIC TRIBUNAL. *See also* COUNCIL ON TRIBUNALS.

administrator *n.* **1.** A person appointed by the court to collect and distribute a deceased person's estate when the deceased died intestate, his will did not appoint an executor, or the executor refuses to act. An administrator's authority to deal with the estate does not begin until the court has granted *letters of administration. The Administration of Estates Act 1925 lays down the order in which people are entitled to a grant of representation. *Compare* EXECUTOR. **2.** *See* ADMINISTRATION ORDER.

Admiralty Court A court forming part of the *Queen's Bench Division of the High Court whose jurisdiction embraces civil actions relating to ships and the sea. *Puisne judges hear cases with the assistance of nautical assessors. The court's work includes cases about collisions, damage to cargo, prizes (*see* PRIZE COURT), and salvage, and in some cases *assessors may be called in to sit with the judge. The distinctive feature of the court's procedure is the action *in rem*, under which the property that has given rise to the cause of action (usually a ship) may be "arrested" and held by the court to satisfy the claimant's claim. In practice, it is usual for the owners of the property to give security for its release while the action is proceeding. If the claim is successful, the property held or the sum given by way of security is available to satisfy the judgment. Until 1971 the Admiralty Court was part of the *Probate, Divorce and Admiralty Division of the High Court. Since the Access to Justice Act 1999, all Admiralty proceedings will be allocated to the *multi-track.

admissibility of evidence The principles determining whether or not particular items of evidence may be received by the court. The central principle of admissibility is *relevance. All irrelevant evidence is inadmissible, but evidence that is legally relevant may also be inadmissible if it falls within the scope of one of the *exclusionary rules of evidence. *See also* CONDITIONAL ADMISSIBILITY; MULTIPLE ADMISSIBILITY.

admissibility of records In civil cases documents containing information (records) are admissible as evidence of the facts stated in them. Before the introduction of the Civil Evidence Act 1995, such documents and records were admissible only if they came within an exception to the rules prohibiting the use of hearsay evidence. Since 1995 the hearsay rules in civil cases have been abolished and accordingly these records are admissible. In criminal cases the hearsay rules in relation to business documents have been relaxed, although not completely abolished, by the Criminal Justice Act 1988. Under these provisions, such records are admissible if they have been compiled by someone acting in the course of a duty to do so.

admission *n.* **1.** In civil proceedings, a statement by a party to litigation or by his duly authorized agent that is adverse to the party's case. Admissions may be **informal** (i.e. in a document or by word of mouth) or **formal** (i.e. made in a statement of case or in reply to a request for further information). An admission may be related to the court by someone other than the person who made it under an exception to the rule against *hearsay evidence. **2.** In criminal proceedings, a statement admitting an offence or a fact that constitutes legally acceptable evidence of the offence or fact. Admissions may be informal or formal. An informal admission is called a *confession. A formal admission may be made either before or at the hearing, but if not made in court, it must be in writing and signed by the defendant or his legal adviser. An admission may be made in respect of any fact about which *oral evidence could be given and is *conclusive evidence of the fact admitted at all criminal proceedings relating to the matter, although it may be withdrawn at any stage with the permission of the court. A plea of guilty to a charge read out in court is a formal admission. *See also* CAUTION.

admonition *n.* A reprimand from a judge to a defendant who has been discharged from the further prosecution of an offence.

adoption *n.* **1.** The process by which a parent's legal rights and duties in respect of an unmarried minor are transferred to another person or persons. Adoption can only take place by means of an **adoption order** made by a magistrates' court (in the family proceedings court), county court, or the High Court (in the Children Branch of the Family Division). Adoption differs from fostering in that it affects *all* the parents' rights and duties and it is a permanent change. After adoption the natural parents are (except for the rules relating to *affinity and *incest) no longer considered in law to be the parents of the child, who is henceforth regarded as the legal child of the adoptive parents (*see also* ADOPTIVE RELATIONSHIP). However, the court may make a contact order (*see* SECTION 8 ORDERS) at the time the adoption order is made. Contact after adoption is becoming a contentious issue and recently the court has allowed a natural parent to seek permission to apply for a contact order in respect of an adopted child.

The first (but not the only) consideration in deciding whether or not a child should be adopted is whether the adoption would safeguard and promote the welfare of the child. The court must, if possible, try to ascertain the child's wishes and in addition take account of all the circumstances. This may involve consulting expert opinion (e.g. of psychiatrists or social workers). The court may also appoint a *children's guardian to act in the child's interests. There are many provisions in the Adoption Act 1976 as amended by the Children Act 1989 designed to make sure that an adoption would be in the child's best interests. Every local authority must set up an *adoption service, and *adoption societies are carefully controlled; in addition, the government is anxious to increase the adoption of children who are currently in the care of the local authority. There are rules as to who may adopt and who may be adopted and provisions for a probationary period, during which the child lives with the would-be adopter(s) and the court assesses whether he gets on well with them. One of the ways in which a commissioning couple may attain the legal status of parents in relation to a child born to a surrogate mother is by adopting the child; however, this is becoming less common now that the couple can apply for a *section 30 order (parental order) under the Human Embryology and Fertilization Act 1990. *See* SURROGACY; HUMAN ASSISTED REPRODUCTION.

Normally a child cannot be adopted without the consent of each of its parents or guardians, but in some cases the court may make an adoption order without the parents' consent (e.g. if they cannot be found or have ill-treated the child). If the court thinks that the parents are refusing unreasonably to agree to an adoption that would be in the child's best interests, it may make an adoption order against the parents' wishes. A parent may consent either to a specific adoption or to an order *freeing for adoption by whomever the court eventually decides is best suited to adopt the child. Since the Children Act 1989 the courts now have the option of making a section 8 order either instead of an adoption order, so that parental responsibility may be shared (e.g. a residence order), or in addition to it (e.g. a contact order). Adoption law is currently under review and there are recommendations to make it a duty of the court, when considering whether to make an adoption order, to consider alternative orders available under the Children Act, and to bring adoption law in line with the principles of the Act by making the child's welfare of paramount importance in adoption proceedings. In addition, a court will be able to dispense with parental consent if the welfare of the child demands this.

The Registrar General must keep a register containing details of all adoption orders, which any member of the public may consult. An adopted child over the age of 18 has a right to see a copy of his original birth certificate in order to find out who his natural parents are. Although natural parents can register their interest in contacting their children who have been adopted, they have no corresponding right to trace these adopted children.

2. Reliance by a court on a rule of international law that has not been expressly made part of the law of the land but is not inconsistent with it.

3. The decision of a local authority or similar body to bring into force in their area an Act of Parliament conferring powers on them at their option.

adoption agency A local authority or an approved *adoption society. Usually only adoption agencies may make arrangements for adoption.

Adoption Contact Register A register, maintained by the Registrar General, containing the names and addresses of all adopted persons who are over the age of 18, have a copy of their birth certificate, and wish to contact a relative, together with details of relatives who wish to make contact with an adopted person.

adoption order *See* ADOPTION.

adoption service Under the Adoption Act 1976, the different services, collectively, that local authorities must provide within their area in order to meet the needs of *adoption. These services include provision of accommodation for pregnant women and mothers, making arrangements for placing children with prospective adopters, and advising people with adoption problems.

adoption society A group of people organized to make arrangements for the *adoption of children. Adoption societies must be approved by the Secretary of State before acting as such.

adoptive leave *See* PARENTAL LEAVE.

adoptive relationship A legal relationship created as a result of an adoption order (*see* ADOPTION). A male adopter is known as the **adoptive father**, a female adopter as the **adoptive mother**, and other relatives as **adoptive relatives**. The laws of *affinity are, however, not altered by the new adoptive relationship.

ADR *See* ALTERNATIVE DISPUTE RESOLUTION.

ad referendum [Latin: to be further considered] Denoting a contract that has been signed although minor points remain to be decided.

adulteration *n.* The mixing of other substances with food. It is an offence of
*strict liability under the Food Act 1984 to sell any food containing a substance that
would endanger health. It is also an offence to mix dangerous substances into food
with the intention of selling the mixture.

adultery *n.* An act of sexual intercourse between a male and female not married
to each other, when at least one of them is married to someone else. Intercourse for
this purpose means penetration of the vagina by the penis; any degree of
penetration will suffice (full penetration is not necessary). Adultery is one of the
five facts that a petitioner may rely on under the Matrimonial Causes Act 1973 as
evidence to show that the marriage has irretrievably broken down. However, in
addition to the adultery, the petitioner must show that she or he finds it intolerable
to live with the respondent. *See* DIVORCE.

advance corporation tax (ACT) A form of *corporation tax payable by a
company on its qualifying distributions from April 1973 until April 1999, when it
was abolished.

advancement *n.* **1.** The power, in a trust, to provide capital sums for the benefit
of a person who is an infant or who may (but is not certain to) receive the property
under a settlement. The term is a shortened form of **advancement in the world**
and has the connotation of providing a single or lump sum from the trust fund for
a specific purpose of a permanent nature; examples include sums payable on
marriage, to buy a house for the beneficiary, or to establish the beneficiary in a
trade or profession. Before 1926, a power of advancement had to be specifically
included in any settlement; since 1925 a statutory power exists, subject to contrary
intention. No person may receive by way of advancement more than half that to
which he could ever become entitled. **2.** A presumption, arising in certain
circumstances, that if one person purchases property in the name of another, the
property is intended for the advancement of that other person and will be held
beneficially by that person and not on *resulting trust for the person who
purchases it. The presumption of advancement arises when a father or other person
in the position of a parent purchases property for a child. The presumption does not
automatically arise in the case of a mother because until 1882 a married woman
could not, during marriage, own property; her automatic exclusion from the
presumption now seems nonsensical (especially as a mother now has a statutory
duty to maintain her children), although she will in many cases be found to be "in
the position of a parent". A similar presumption has been held to exist when a
husband purchases property for his wife (though not *vice versa*), and occasionally a
man for his mistress, but the strength (and perhaps even the existence) of this
presumption is doubtful. The presumption may be rebutted by evidence that
advancement was not intended. This evidence may be parol evidence (i.e. given
orally).

adversary procedure *See* ACCUSATORIAL PROCEDURE.

adverse occupation Occupation of premises by a trespasser to the exclusion of
the owner or lawful occupier. *Trespass in itself is not usually a criminal offence,
but if the premises are residential and were being occupied, the trespasser (whether
or not he used force in order to enter) is guilty of an offence under the Criminal
Law Act 1977 if he refuses to leave when asked to do so by the displaced *residential
occupier or a protected intending occupier (or by someone acting on behalf of
them). A protected intending occupier includes a purchaser, someone let in by the
local authority, Housing Corporation, or a housing association with written evidence
of his claim to the premises, or someone holding a lease, tenancy, or licence with

two years to run. Under the Criminal Justice and Public Order Act 1994, such a person may obtain an interim possession order. This differs from an ordinary possession order in that it is much quicker, may be heard in the absence of those on the property, and involves the police in enforcement. It is only available for buildings and ancillary land and not against those, such as gypsies and New Age Travellers, who occupy open land. Once the proper procedure has been followed and the applicant has shown a good case for possession, an order will require those on the land to leave within 24 hours. Remaining on the premises or re-entry within 12 months is a *summary offence, punishable by a *fine on level 5 and/or six months' imprisonment. A uniformed constable has a power of *arrest. It is also an offence to make false or misleading statements in making or resisting such an order. Similar penalties apply on summary conviction, but on *indictment a maximum of two years' imprisonment and/or a fine may be imposed.

Usually it is a summary offence for a stranger or the landlord to use violence to gain entry to premises when it is known that there is someone on those premises opposed to such an entry. However, a displaced residential occupier or a protected intending occupier who has asked the person to leave may call on the police for assistance. A police constable may arrest anyone who refuses to leave for the *summary offence of adverse occupation of residential premises. Furthermore, it is not an offence if a constable, a displaced residential occupier, or a protected intending occupier (or their agents) uses force to secure entry. See FORCIBLE ENTRY.

adverse possession The occupation of land to which another person has title with the intention of possessing it as one's own. The adverse possessor must occupy the land as if he were entitled to it to the exclusion of all others, and must intend to occupy it as his own. Both these factors must be evidenced by the use made of the land; for example, cultivation, fencing, etc. Equivocal acts, such as use of the land for grazing animals from time to time or allowing children to play on the land, will not be sufficient. After 12 years' adverse possession, the original owner's title becomes statute-barred by the Limitation Act 1980, and he cannot recover his land from the adverse possessor. The adverse possessor becomes the lawful owner (a **squatter's title**), and is entitled to be registered as such. The law on adverse possession is frequently used to cure small discrepancies in the plan attached to a transfer of land, and the actual position of boundaries on the ground, but it can also be used to obtain ownership of large areas of land. See also POSSESSORY TITLE.

adverse witness A witness who gives evidence unfavourable to the party who called him. If the witness's evidence is merely unfavourable he may not be impeached (i.e. his credibility may not be attacked) by the party calling him, but contradictory evidence may be called. If, however, the witness is *hostile he may be impeached by introducing evidence that shows his untruthfulness.

advice on evidence The written opinion of counsel, usually prepared after *disclosure and inspection of documents, identifying the issues raised in the statements of case and advising counsel's instructing solicitor what evidence it will be necessary to call at the trial.

advisory jurisdiction The jurisdiction of the INTERNATIONAL COURT OF JUSTICE under which it can render legal opinions, similar in kind to declaration (see DECLARATORY JUDGMENT) under English municipal law. In contrast to the contentious jurisdiction of the Court, states are not parties to the proceedings and there is no claimant or defendant to the action. The Court proceeds by inviting states or international organizations to provide information to assist the Court in its determination of point of law at issue.

The authority of the International Court of Justice to give advisory opinions is found under Article 96 of the UN Charter. Under this Article the Court is empowered to give such opinions on legal questions at the request of the UN Security Council or the General Assembly. Moreover, the power to request advisory opinions on legal questions arising within the scope of their activities also resides in other organs of the United Nations and its specialized agencies if they have been authorized by the General Assembly to do so.

advocacy qualification A qualification authorizing a person to act as an *advocate under the provisions of the Courts and Legal Services Act 1990. There are separate qualifications for different levels of the court system, but the rights of those already entitled to appear as advocates at any level of the system at the time when the Act came into force are preserved.

advocate *n.* **1.** One who exercises a *right of audience and argues a case for a client in legal proceedings. In magistrates' courts and the county courts both *barristers and *solicitors have the right to appear as advocates. In most Crown Court centres, the High Court, the Court of Appeal, and the House of Lords barristers have exclusive rights of audience. However, the provisions of the Courts and Legal Services Act 1990 allows solicitors with appropriate experience to qualify for rights of audience similar to those of barristers and acquire *advocacy qualifications for the Crown Court, High Court, and Supreme Court. In many tribunals there are no rules concerning representation, and laymen may appear as advocates. Advocates no longer enjoy immunity from law suits for negligence in relation to civil or criminal litigation. **2.** In Scotland, a member of the Faculty of Advocates, the professional organization of the Scots Bar.

Advocate General An assistant to the judge of the *European Court of Justice whose function is to assist the court by presenting opinions upon every case brought before it. The Advocate General acts as an *amicus curiae* in putting forward arguments based upon his own view of the interests of the European Union, although it is not open to any of the parties to the legal action to submit observations on his opinion.

advowson *n.* A right of presenting a clergyman to an ecclesiastical living. The advowson is an incorporeal *hereditament that gives the owner (or patron) the right to nominate the next holder of a living that has fallen vacant. It may exist **in gross** (i.e. independently of any ownership of land by the person entitled) or may be **appendent** (i.e. annexed to land so that it may be enjoyed by each owner for the time being). The right is usually associated with the lordship of a manor.

aequitas est quasi aequalitas *See* EQUALITY IS EQUITY.

affidavit *n.* A sworn written statement used mainly to support certain applications and, in some circumstances, as evidence in court proceedings. The person who makes the affidavit must swear or *affirm that the contents are true before a person authorized to take oaths in respect of the particular kind of affidavit. *See also* ARGUMENTATIVE AFFIDAVIT.

affiliation order Formerly, an order of a magistrates' court against a man alleged to be the father of an illegitimate child, obliging him to make payments towards the upkeep of the child. Affiliation proceedings have been abolished by the Family Law Reform Act 1987 and financial provision for illegitimate and legitimate children is now the same (*see* CHILD SUPPORT MAINTENANCE).

affinity *n.* The relationship created by marriage between a husband and his wife's blood relatives or between a wife and her husband's blood relatives. Some categories of people related by affinity are forbidden to marry each other (*see* PROHIBITED DEGREES OF RELATIONSHIPS). The relationship of blood relatives is known as *consanguinity. *See also* INCEST.

affirm *vb.* **1.** To confirm a legal decision, particularly (of an appeal court) to confirm a judgment made in a lower court. **2.** To promise in solemn form to tell the truth while giving evidence or when making an *affidavit. Under the Oaths Act 1978, any person who objects to being sworn on *oath, or in respect of whom it is not reasonably practicable to administer an oath, may instead affirm. Affirmation has the same legal effects as the taking of an oath. **3.** To treat a contract as continuing in existence, instead of exercising a right to rescind it for *misrepresentation or other cause (*see* VOIDABLE CONTRACT) or to treat it as discharged by reason of repudiation or breach (*see* BREACH OF CONTRACT). Affirmation is effective only if it takes place with full knowledge of the facts. It may take the form of an express declaration of intention to proceed with the contract; alternatively, that intention may be inferred from conduct (if, for example, the party attempts to sell goods that have been delivered under a contract voidable for misrepresentation). Lapse of time without seeking a remedy may be treated as evidence of affirmation.

affirmative pregnant An allegation in a statement of case implying or not denying some negative. *Compare* NEGATIVE PREGNANT.

affirmative resolution *See* DELEGATED LEGISLATION.

affray *n.* The offence of intentionally using or threatening, other than by words alone, unlawful violence. The conduct must be such as would have caused a reasonable person to fear for his safety, though no such person need be present. The offence is found in the Public Order Act 1986, though it can be committed in private as well as in public places. It replaces the common-law offence of affray and is punishable on indictment with up to three years' imprisonment and/or a fine or, on summary conviction, by imprisonment for a term not exceeding six months or by a fine. A constable may arrest without warrant anyone he reasonable suspects is committing affray. *See also* ASSAULT; RIOT; VIOLENT DISORDER.

affreightment *n.* A contract for the carriage of goods by sea (the consideration being called **freight** and the carrier the **freighter**). It can be either a *charterparty or a contract whose terms are set out in the *bill of lading.

AG *See* ATTORNEY GENERAL.

agency *n.* **1.** The relationship between an *agent and his principal. **2.** The business carried on by an agent.

agent *n.* **1.** A person appointed by another (the **principal**) to act on his behalf, often to negotiate a contract between the principal and a third party. If an agent discloses his principal's name (or at least the existence of a principal) to the third party with whom he is dealing, the agent himself is not normally entitled to the benefit of, or be liable on, the contract. An **undisclosed principal** is one whose existence is not revealed by the agent to a third party; he may still be entitled to the benefit of, and be liable on, the contract, but in such cases the agent is also entitled and liable. However, an undisclosed principal may not be entitled to the benefit of a contract if the agency is inconsistent with the terms of the contract or if the third party shows that he wished to contract with the agent personally.

A **general agent** is one who has authority to act for his principal in all his business of a particular kind, or who acts for the principal in the course of his (the agent's) usual business or profession. A **special agent** is authorized to act only for a special purpose that is not in the ordinary course of the agent's business or profession. The principal of a general agent is bound by acts of the agent that are incidental to the ordinary conduct of the agent's business or the effective performance of his duties, even if the principal has imposed limitations on the agent's authority. But in the case of a special agent, the principal is not bound by acts that are not within the authority conferred. In either case, the principal may ratify an unauthorized contract. An agent for the sale of goods sometimes agrees to protect his principal against the risk of the buyer's insolvency. He does this by undertaking liability for the unjustifiable failure of the third-party buyer to pay the price of the goods. Such an agent is called a *del credere* **agent**. *See also* COMMERCIAL AGENT; MERCANTILE AGENT.

2. (in criminal law) *See* BUGGERY.

agent provocateur A person who actively entices, encourages, or persuades someone to commit a crime that would not otherwise have been committed for the purpose of securing his conviction (*see* ENTRAPMENT). In such a case the agent provocateur will be regarded as an accomplice in any offence that the accused commits as a result of this intervention.

age of consent The age at which a girl can legally consent to sexual intercourse, or to an act that would otherwise constitute an indecent assault. This age is 16. This minimum age limit does not apply to girls married under a foreign law that is recognized in English law. *See also* BUGGERY.

aggravated assault *See* ASSAULT.

aggravated burglary *See* BURGLARY.

aggravated damages *Damages that are awarded when the conduct of the defendant or the surrounding circumstances increase the injury to the claimant by subjecting him to humiliation, distress, or embarrassment, particularly in such torts as assault, false imprisonment, and defamation.

aggravated trespass *See* TRESPASS.

aggravated vehicle-taking An offence concerning **joyriding**, which was enacted in 1992. The offence arises when the accused has unlawfully taken a motor vehicle, driven it in a dangerous manner on a public road, and caused an accident resulting in injury to another person or to property. Any passenger in the vehicle who knows that it has been taken without the owner's consent is also guilty of the offence.

aggression *n.* (in international law) According to the General Assembly Resolution (3314) on the Definition of Aggression 1975, the use of armed force by one state against the sovereignty, territorial integrity, or political independence of another state or in any way inconsistent with the Charter of the United Nations. The Resolution lists examples of aggression, which include the following. (1) Invasion, attack, military occupation, or annexation of the territory of any state by the armed forces of another state. (2) Bombardment or the use of any weapons by a state against another state's territory. (3) Armed blockade by a state of another state's ports or coasts. (4) The use of a state's armed forces in another state in breach of the terms of the agreement on which they were allowed into that state. (5) Allowing one's territory to be placed at the disposal of another state, to be used by that state for committing an act of aggression against a third state. (6) Sending armed bands or guerrillas to carry out armed raids on another state that are grave enough to amount to any of the above acts.

The first use of armed force by a state in contravention of the UN Charter is prima facie evidence of aggression, although the final decision in such cases is left to the Security Council, who may also classify other acts as aggression. The Resolution declares that no consideration whatsoever can justify aggression, that territory cannot be acquired by acts of aggression, and that wars of aggression constitute a crime against international peace. *See also* HUMANITARIAN INTERVENTION; MARTENS CLAUSE; OCCUPATION; OFFENCES AGAINST INTERNATIONAL LAW AND ORDER; USE OF FORCE; WAR; WAR CRIMES.

agreement *n.* (in international law) *See* TREATY.

agreement for a lease A contract to enter into a *lease. Special rules govern the creation of such a contract. Before 27 September 1989, a contract to grant a lease was unenforceable unless it was evidenced in writing, or evidenced by a sufficient act of *part performance (such as entering onto the property and paying rent). Since 27 September 1989, a contract to grant a lease for not more than three years may be made orally or by any kind of written agreement. A contract to grant a longer lease must be in writing, incorporating all the terms of the agreement, and signed by the parties. A contract that does not comply with these requirements is wholly void and can no longer be evidenced by part performance.

agrément *n.* The formal diplomatic notification by a state that the diplomatic agent selected to be sent to it by another state has been accepted, i.e. is *persona grata* and can consequently become accredited to it. The *agrément* is the reply to a query by the sending state, which precedes the sent diplomat's formal nomination and accreditation. This type of mutual exchange by two states over their diplomatic representation is called **agréation**. *See also* PERSONA NON GRATA.

agricultural dwelling-house advisory committee (ADHAC) A committee that advises the local authority in its area on the agricultural need for *tied cottages. An owner of a tied cottage can apply to a local authority to rehouse a former worker who is occupying the cottage. The local authority has a duty to do this if the committee advises that possession is needed in the interests of efficient agriculture. *See also* ASSURED AGRICULTURAL OCCUPANCY.

agricultural holding A tenancy of agricultural land. Tenants have special statutory protection and there is a procedure to fix rent by arbitration if the parties cannot agree. The landlord normally has to give at least one year's notice to quit. The tenant can usually appeal to an *agricultural land tribunal to decide whether the notice to quit should operate. The landlord is entitled to compensation at the end of the tenancy if the holding has deteriorated and the tenant is at fault; the tenant can claim compensation at the end of the tenancy for disturbance and for improvements he has made. The Agricultural Holdings Act 1986 gives the security of tenure. Tenancies and licences to those working the land may give security of tenure under the Housing Act 1988 if the tenants are qualifying workers (working on the land as defined in the Act) and otherwise qualify. *See* ASSURED AGRICULTURAL OCCUPANCY.

agricultural land tribunal A tribunal having statutory functions in relation to tenancies of agricultural holdings. It normally consists of a legally qualified chairman, a representative farmer, and a representative landowner. Notice to quit a holding is in certain circumstances inoperative without a tribunal's consent, and on the death of a tenant the tribunal has power to direct that a qualifying member of his family is entitled to a new tenancy. Application may also be made to the tribunal for a certificate of bad husbandry.

aid and abet To assist in the performance of a crime either before or during (but not after) its commission. Aiding usually refers to material assistance (e.g. providing the tools for the crime), and abetting to lesser assistance (e.g. acting as a look-out or driving a car to the scene of the crime). Aiders and abettors are liable to be tried as *accessories. Mere presence at the scene of a crime is not regarded as aiding and abetting. It is unnecessary to have a criminal motive to be guilty of aiding and abetting: knowledge that one is assisting the criminal is sufficient. *See also* IMPEDING APPREHENSION OR PROSECUTION.

Air Defence Identification Zone (ADIZ) A zone, which can extend in some cases up to 300 miles beyond the territorial sea, established for security reasons by some states off their coasts. When entering the ADIZ all aircraft are required to identify themselves, report flight plans, and inform ground control of their exact position. *See also* AIRSPACE.

air-force law *See* SERVICE LAW.

air pollution *See* POLLUTION.

airspace *n.* In English law and international law, the ownership of land includes ownership of the airspace above it, by application of the maxim *cujus est solum ejus est usque ad coelum* (whose is the soil, his it is even to heaven); outer space, however, is not considered to be subject to ownership.

In English law an owner has rights in as much of the airspace above his land as is necessary for the ordinary use of his land and the structures on it. Within these limits a projection over one's land (such as a signboard) can be a trespass and pollution of air by one's neighbour can be a nuisance. Pollution of air is also controlled by various statutes. There is no natural right to the free flow of air from neighbouring land, but *easements for the flow of air through a defined opening (such as a window or a ventilator) can be acquired. Civil aircraft flying at a reasonable height over land do not commit trespass, but damages can be obtained if material loss or damage is caused to people or property.

In international law, national airspace, including airspace above the internal waters and the territorial sea, is under complete and exclusive sovereignty of the subjacent state. As a result, apart from aircraft in distress, any use of national airspace by non-national aircraft requires the official consent of the state concerned. This can be granted unilaterally or more commonly (in respect of commercial flights) through a bilateral treaty, usually on conditions of reciprocity. *See* TERRITORIAL WATERS.

alderman *n.* A senior member of a local authority, elected by its directly elected members. Active aldermanic rank now exists only in the *City of London, having been phased out elsewhere by the Local Government Act 1972. County, district, and London borough councils can, however, appoint past members to honorary rank in recognition of eminent service. The term was originally synonymous with 'elder' and is of Anglo-Saxon derivation.

alibi *n.* [from Latin: elsewhere] A defence to a criminal charge alleging that the defendant was not at the place at which the crime was committed and so could not have been responsible for it. If the defendant claims to have been at a particular place at the time of the crime, evidence in support of an alibi may only be given if the defendant has supplied particulars of it to the prosecution not later than seven days after committal, unless the Crown Court considers that there was a valid reason for not supplying them.

alien *n.* A person who, under the law of a particular state, is not a citizen of that state. Aliens are usually classified as **resident aliens** (domiciled in the host country) or **transient aliens** (temporarily in the host country on business, study, etc.). They are normally subject to certain civil disabilities, such as being ineligible to vote. For the purposes of UK statute law an alien is defined by the British Nationality Act 1981 (in force from 1 January 1983) as a person who is neither a Commonwealth citizen, nor a British protected person, nor a citizen of the Republic of Ireland. At common law, a distinction is drawn between friendly and **enemy aliens**. The latter comprise not only citizens of hostile states but also all others voluntarily living in enemy territory or carrying on business there; they are subject to additional disabilities. *See also* ALLEGIANCE; DUE DILIGENCE; JUS SANGUINIS.

alienable *adj.* Capable of being transferred: used particularly in relation to real property. *See also* RULE AGAINST INALIENABILITY.

alienation *n.* The transfer of property (particularly real property) from one person to another. *See also* RESTRAINT ON ALIENATION.

alieni juris [Latin: of another's right] Describing the status of a person who is not of full age and capacity. *Compare* SUI JURIS.

alimentary trust *See* PROTECTIVE TRUST.

alimony *n.* Formerly, financial provision made by a husband to his wife when they are living apart. Alimony is now known as *maintenance or *financial provision.

allegation *n.* Any statement of fact in a statement of case, *affidavit, or *indictment. In civil cases it is the duty of the party who makes an allegation to adduce evidence in support of it at trial, under the principle of "he who asserts must prove".

allegiance *n.* The duty of obedience owed to a head of state in return for his protection. It is due from all citizens of that state and its dependencies and also from any *alien present in the state (including enemy aliens under licence; for example, internees). A person who is declared by the British Nationality Act 1981 not to be an alien but who has a primary citizenship conferred by a state other than the UK is probably governed by the same principles as aliens so far as allegiance is concerned.

allocation *n.* The stage in civil litigation when a decision is made as to how the case is to be dealt with. After each of the parties has completed and filed an *allocation questionnaire, allocation is made to one of three **tracks**: (1) the *small claims track for cases worth less than £5000; (2) the *fast track for cases worth between £5000 and £15,000; and (3) the *multi-track for cases worth more than £15,000. After allocation has taken place, the court will proceed to give standard directions as to how the case should proceed. This stage was formerly (before the introduction of the Civil Procedure Rules in 1999) referred to as **setting down for trial**. *See also* CASE MANAGEMENT.

allocation questionnaire A questionnaire that (except in certain circumstances) is served on both parties in civil litigation when the defendant has filed a defence. The completion of this document enables the court to allocate the case to the most appropriate track (*see* ALLOCATION). The completed form will contain such information as the monetary value of the claim, the complexity of the case, the number of litigants involved, whether there are any counterclaims, the parties' track of choice, whether time is needed to allow for settlement (known as a 'stay'), and whether all or any applicable *pre-action protocols have been observed.

Failure to complete the questionnaire and return it to the appropriate place by the date specified may lead to the claim being struck out. On receipt, the court will allocate the case to a track, primarily based on the value of the claim but also considering the other information supplied in the questionnaire.

allotment *n.* A method of acquiring previously unissued shares in a *limited company in exchange for a contribution of capital. An application for such shares will often be made after the issue of a *prospectus on the *flotation of a *public company or on the privatization of a state-owned industry. The company accepts the application by dispatching a **letter of allotment** to the applicant stating how many shares he has been allotted; he then has an unconditional right to be entered in the *register of members in respect of those shares. If he has been allotted fewer shares than he has applied for, he receives a cheque for the unallotted balance (an application must be accompanied by a cheque for the full value of the shares applied for). *See also* AUTHORIZED CAPITAL; RETURN.

alteration *n.* A change that, when made in a legal document, may affect its validity. An alteration in a will is presumed to have been made after execution and will therefore be invalid. However, it will be valid if it is proved to have been made before execution or if it was executed in the same way as the will itself. If the alteration is duly attested by the testator and the witnesses placing their initials or signatures by it, it is presumed to be valid. If an invalid alteration completely obliterates the original words, it is treated as a blank space. If the original words can still be read, they remain effective. Alterations in deeds are presumed to have been made before execution. Alterations made after execution do not affect the validity of the deed if their purpose is to correct an obvious error. If, however, a material alteration is made to a deed after execution without the consent of the parties, the deed may become void in part. *See also* AMENDMENT.

alteration of share capital An increase, reduction (*see* REDUCTION OF CAPITAL), or any other change in the *authorized capital of a company. If permitted by the *articles of association, a limited company can increase its authorized capital as appropriate. It can also rearrange its existing authorized capital (e.g. by consolidating 100 shares of £1 into 25 shares of £4 or by subdividing 100 shares of £1 into 200 of 50p) and cancel unissued shares. These are reserved powers (*see* GENERAL MEETING), exercised – unless the articles of association provide otherwise – by an *ordinary resolution.

alternative dispute resolution (ADR) Any of a variety of techniques for resolving civil disputes without the need for conventional litigation. It may include **mini-trial** (a shortened and simplified form of court hearing), informal methods of *arbitration, and structured forms of conciliation using a specially trained mediator acting as a go-between (*see* MEDIATION).

Alternative Investment Market (AIM) *See* STOCK EXCHANGE.

alternative verdict A verdict of not guilty of the offence actually charged but guilty of some lesser offence not specifically charged. Such a verdict is only permitted when there is insufficient evidence to establish the more serious offence but the evidence given is sufficient to prove the lesser offence. If, for example, in a murder case there is evidence that the defendant lacked *malice aforethought, an alternative verdict of manslaughter may be returned.

ambiguity *n.* Uncertainty in meaning. In legal documents ambiguity may be patent or latent. A **patent ambiguity** is obvious to anyone looking at the document; for example, when a blank space is left for a name. A **latent ambiguity** at first appears to be an unambiguous statement, but the ambiguity becomes apparent in the light of knowledge gained other than from the document. An example is "I give my gold watch to X", when the testator has two gold watches. In general, *extrinsic evidence can be used to clarify latent ambiguities, but not patent ambiguities. Extrinsic evidence cannot be used to give a different meaning to words capable of ordinary interpretation.

ambulatory *adj.* (of a will) Taking effect not from when it was made but from the death of the testator. Thus descriptions of property bequeathed or of beneficiaries are taken to refer to property or persons existing at that time. The will remains revocable until death

ameliorating waste Alterations made by a tenant that improve the land he leases. *See* WASTE.

amendment *n.* **1.** Changes made to legislation, for the purpose of adding to, correcting, or modifying the operation of the legislation. **2.** Changes made to the *statement of case used in civil litigation. Changes in the parties' knowledge of the case as it proceeds may require alterations in the claim form, defence, or other documents. For example, an amendment will be necessary in order to add the name of a second defendant to the claim. On occasion, errors need to be corrected. The Civil Procedure Rules make clear that amendments may be allowed (1) with the consent of all parties, (2) with the permission of the court, or (3) in the absence of consent and without the court's permission, provided the amendment is made before the claim is served. The court may impose the penalty of costs on the party seeking the amendment if this has been made necessary by negligence. Not every minor development in the litigation, however, needs to be reflected in an amendment, only those changes that will have a real effect on the litigation. **3.** An alteration of a *treaty adopted by the consent of the *high contracting parties and intended to be binding upon all such parties. An amendment may involve either individual provisions or a complete review of the treaty.

a mensa et thoro [Latin] From board and bed. A decree of divorce *a mensa et thoro* was the forerunner of the modern judicial separation order. *See also* A VINCULO MATRIMONII.

amicus curiae [Latin: friend of the court] Counsel who assists the court by putting arguments in support of an interest that might not be adequately represented by the parties to the proceedings (such as the public interest) or by arguing on behalf of a party who is otherwise unrepresented. In modern practice, when a court requires the assistance of an *amicus curiae* it is customary to invite the *Attorney General to attend, either in person or by counsel instructed on his behalf, to represent the public interest, but counsel have been permitted to act as *amicus curiae* on behalf of professional bodies (e.g. the Law Society).

amnesty *n.* An act erasing from legal memory some aspect of criminal conduct by an offender. It is most frequently granted to groups of people in respect of political offences and is wider than a *pardon, which merely relieves an offender of punishment.

Amsterdam Treaty The EU treaty signed in Amsterdam in 1997 (in force from 1 May 1999), which amended provisions of the *Treaty of Rome (European Community Treaty) and the *Maastricht Treaty (Treaty on European Union). Among other effects, the Amsterdam Treaty increased the powers of the European Parliament by extending the *codecision procedure to all areas covered by qualified majority voting and enabled the *Social Chapter to be incorporated into the Treaty of Rome.

ancient lights An *easement acquired by lapse of time (*see* PRESCRIPTION) resulting from 20 years' continuous enjoyment of the access of light to the claimant's land without any written consent from the owner of the land over which the easement is claimed.

ancillary credit business A business involved in credit brokerage, debt adjusting, debt counselling, debt collecting, or the operation of a credit-reference agency. **Credit brokerage** includes the effecting of introductions of individuals wishing to obtain credit to persons carrying on a *consumer-credit business. **Debt adjusting** is the process by which a third party negotiates terms for the discharge of a debt due under *consumer-credit agreements or *consumer-hire agreements with the creditor or owner on behalf of the debtor or hirer. The latter may also pay a third party to take over his obligation to discharge a debt or to undertake any similar activity concerned with its liquidation. **Debt counselling** is the giving of advice (other than by the original creditor and certain others) to debtors or hirers about the liquidation of debts due under consumer-credit agreements or consumer-hire agreements. In **debt collecting**, someone other than the creditor takes steps to procure the payment of debts owing to him. A creditor may engage a debt collector for this purpose. A **credit-reference agency** collects information concerning the financial standing of individuals and supplies this information to those seeking it. The Consumer Credit Act 1974 provides for the licensing of ancillary credit businesses and regulates their activities.

ancillary probate A grant of probate to an executor appointed under a foreign jurisdiction to enable him to deal with assets of the deceased in the UK.

ancillary relief A court order incidental to another order or application. It usually refers to a *financial provision order or a *property adjustment order made in the course of proceedings for divorce, separation, or nullity under the Matrimonial Causes Act 1973. Such orders are made on or after granting the decree.

ancillary restraint A restriction that is imposed as part of a larger transaction. In relation to the EU *merger rules, there is a notice setting out for how long and on what terms ancillary restraints are permitted in the context of such arrangements.

angary *n.* The right of belligerent states to make use of (or destroy if necessary) neutral property on their own or on enemy territory or on the open sea, for the purpose of offence and defence. Traditionally, the right (*jus angariae*) was restricted to the belligerent laying an *embargo on and seizing neutral merchant ships in its harbours and compelling them and their crews to transport troops, ammunition, and provisions to certain places on payment of freight in advance. However, all sorts of neutral property, including vessels or other means of transport, arms, ammunition, provisions, or other personal property, may be the object of the modern right of angary, provided the articles concerned are serviceable to military ends and wants.

animals *pl. n. See* CLASSIFICATION OF ANIMALS.

animus *n.* [Latin] Intention. The term is often used in combination; for example, *animus furandi* – the intention to steal; *animus manendi* – the intention to remain in one place (for the purposes of the law relating to *domicile).

annexation *n.* (in international law) The acquisition of legal sovereignty by one state over the territory of another, usually by *occupation or conquest. Annexation is now generally considered illegal in international law, even when it results from a legitimate use of force (for example, in self-defence). It may subsequently become legal, however, by means of *recognition by other states. The annexing state is not bound by pre-existing obligations of the state annexed.

annual general meeting (AGM) A meeting of company members required by the Companies Act 1985 to be held each calendar year. Not more than 15 months should elapse between meetings, and 21 days' written notice (specifying the meeting as the annual general meeting) must usually be given. AGMs are concerned with the accounts, directors' and auditor's reports, dividends, the election of directors, and the appointment and remuneration of the auditor. Other matters are treated as *special business. *See also* ELECTIVE RESOLUTION; GENERAL MEETING.

annual return A document that registered companies are required by law to send to the *Companies Registry, usually each year. It includes information concerning the type of company and its business activities, the registered office, directors, company members, and certain company debts. It is open to public inspection. Failure to file the return is a criminal offence and may lead to the company being removed from the register and fined. *See* REGISTRATION OF A COMPANY.

annual value of land The annual rent that might reasonably be expected from letting land or buildings, if the tenant pays all usual rates and taxes while other expenses (including repairs) are borne by the landlord. It is used in assessing *rates. The Inland Revenue carries out the valuation.

annuity *n.* A sum of money payable annually for as long as the beneficiary (**annuitant**) lives, or for some other specified period (e.g. the life of another person (*pur autre vie*) or the minority of the annuitant). An annuity left by will is treated as a pecuniary legacy. An annuity may be charged on, or directed to be paid out of, a particular fund or it may be unsecured. A **joint annuity**, in which money is payable to more than one annuitant, terminates on the death of the last survivor. *See also* RENTCHARGE.

annulment *n.* **1.** A declaration by the court that a marriage was never legally valid. In all cases of nullity except nonconsummation, a decree of annulment will only be granted within three years after the celebration of the marriage. *See also* NULLITY OF MARRIAGE. **2.** The cancellation by a court of a *bankruptcy order, which occurs when it considers that the debtor was wrongly made bankrupt, when all the debts have been paid in full, or when the court approves a *voluntary arrangement. The power of annulment is discretionary. Annulment does not affect the validity of any sale of property or other action that has already taken place as a result of the bankruptcy order. **3.** The cancellation of *delegated legislation by resolution of either House of Parliament. **4.** The setting aside of legislation or other action by the *European Court of Justice.

annus et dies [Latin] A year and a day. At common law, the Crown was entitled to take possession of the lands of a person convicted of felony and to exploit them without reserve for a year and a day. This was known as the **right of year, day, and waste**.

answer *n.* **1.** A reply to a request for further information (*see* INTERROGATORY). **2.** A statement of case served by the respondent to a petition, e.g. an answer to a divorce petition. It is equivalent to the *defence served by the defendant in response to a claim form.

antecedents *pl. n.* An accused or convicted person's previous criminal record or bad character. Generally, the prosecution may not give evidence at the trial of the accused's bad character, as it might unduly prejudice the jury. But this rule is relaxed if previous conduct or a *previous conviction is in issue (for instance, when the crime is such that it could only have been committed by someone who had already been convicted of an offence or had misconducted himself in a particular way) or if the accused himself raises the matter by denying that he has a bad character or a criminal record. In such circumstances the prosecution may also use *similar-fact evidence. In cross-examination, the accused must not be asked questions tending to show that he has committed any previous offence or has a bad character unless proof of such matters is in issue or the accused has sought to establish his own good character, has cast aspersions on the character of the prosecution or their witnesses, or has given evidence against someone else charged with the same offence.

After conviction, however, the court may be given an **antecedents report** to assist in passing sentence. It should normally give details of the accused's age, education, employment, home circumstances, and previous convictions. It may contain statements that can be supported by first-hand evidence about the accused's reputation, although it may not contain general allegations. A copy of it is normally given to the accused.

antenuptial settlement *See* MARRIAGE SETTLEMENT.

anticipatory breach *See* BREACH OF CONTRACT.

anticompetitive practice An unfair practice by a business that is in breach of either the Chapter I prohibition of the Competition Act 1998 or *Article 81 of the Treaty of Rome. Examples of such practices include refusing to supply goods, operating discriminatory terms, and forcing purchasers to buy goods or services they do not want (tying clauses). Anticompetitive practices may be investigated by the *Director General of Fair Trading under the Competition Act 1998. Anticompetitive practice is an example of *abuse of a dominant position. Such practices, when carried out by companies in a dominant position, can lead to fines of 10% of the business's annual turnover under UK and EU competition law.

antidumping *n. See* DUMPING.

antitrust law *n. See* COMPETITION LAW.

Anton Piller order *See* SEARCH ORDER.

apology *n.* A defence to an action for *defamation (1) in cases of unintentional defamation, where the defendant innocently and without negligence defamed the claimant but has offered a suitable correction and apology and has paid compensation, or (2) in cases where a libel is published in a newspaper or periodical without malice or gross negligence and an apology is published before the start of the action. In addition to providing a defence in these cases, the fact that the defendant has made or offered to make an apology may always be taken into account in mitigation of damages.

a posteriori [Latin: from the later (i.e. from effect to cause)] Describing or relating to reasoning based on deductions from observation or known facts, i.e. inductive reasoning. *Compare* A PRIORI.

appeal *n.* An application for the judicial examination by a higher tribunal of the decision of any lower tribunal. In modern English practice most appeals are dealt with by way of *rehearing, in which the appellate tribunal notionally rehears the case tried before the lower tribunal, usually using a transcript or note of the evidence before the lower tribunal instead of hearing the witnesses in person. It may in general **make any order** that the lower tribunal could have made, but there are some statutory restrictions upon this power; for example, in criminal cases the Court of Appeal may not impose a more severe sentence than the trial court. Appellate tribunals are usually reluctant to overrule the decisions of lower tribunals on questions of fact even when they have the power to do so, and consequently most of the argument on appeals tends to be directed towards legal errors allegedly committed at the trial. In some cases (e.g. appeals by *case stated from magistrates' courts) the appeal may by law be confined to questions of law. Appeal may be contrasted with **review**, in which the higher tribunal is confined to an examination of the *record of the lower tribunal's proceedings. *See also* APPELLATE JURISDICTION.

appellant *n* A person who makes an *appeal to a court that has the jurisdiction to hear appeals, such as the Court of Appeal.

Appellate Committee *See* HOUSE OF LORDS.

appellate jurisdiction The power of a judge to hear *appeals from a previous court decision. Appellate jurisdiction in the criminal courts is determined by the nature of the criminal offence in question. Criminal appeals following *summary conviction are to the Crown Court for committals for sentencing and for appeals by the defendant against conviction and/or sentence. Appeals from magistrates' courts are to the High Court or Divisional Court of the Queen's Bench Division if an appeal by the prosecution or defence is by way of *case stated on a point of law. Appeals from the Crown Court can be by the prosecution or defence by way of case stated but only if the Crown Court had previously heard the appeal from the magistrates' court. Higher appeals are restricted to those from the High Court or Divisional Court of the Queen's Bench Division by either the prosecution or the defence on a point of law of general public importance and only with permission. Criminal appeals from trials on *indictment are to the Court of Appeal (Criminal Division) by the defendant against conviction and/or sentence. References to the Court of Appeal (Criminal Division) may also be made (1) by the Attorney General due to an unduly light sentence, (2) by the Attorney General on a point of law following acquittal (although the earlier acquittal will not be affected), or (3) by the Home Secretary for consideration following conviction. A further appeal to the House of Lords is only available by the defence or prosecution on a point of law of general public importance and with permission.

Appellate jurisdiction in the civil courts was substantially revised as a result of the Access to Justice Act 1999. Part IV of that Act requires anyone seeking to appeal to obtain permission to do so by the appropriate court. It also seeks to ensure that appeals are heard by the next most appropriate level of judge, rather than the next highest court, as was the position before the introduction of the *Civil Procedure Rules. The Lord Chancellor is able "by order" to vary routes of appeal if he considers it appropriate; such an order is now in place in the form of the Access to Justice Act 1999 (Destination of Appeals) Order 2000.

A circuit judge in the county court is now able to hear appeals from the *small claims track but under limited circumstances, provided that the judge sitting at first instance was a district judge. A single High Court judge is able to consider civil and criminal appeals in contempt of court cases; criminal appeals by way of case stated from magistrates' courts and the Crown Courts; and, subject to the *leapfrog procedure (Court of Appeal), civil appeals from High Court masters, district judges, and county court circuit judges. As an exception, civil appeals from High Court masters, district judges, and county court circuit judges will be to the Court of Appeal if the previous court matter was either (1) a final decision made in a *multi-track claim or in specialist proceedings or (2) an appeal itself from a county court judge. Where two or more High Court judges sit as a Divisional Court, appeals are permitted. In the Chancery Divisional Court, appeals may be heard from certain tribunals, e.g. the Inland Revenue Commissioners, and from the county courts for such matters as bankruptcy appeals. In the Family Divisional Court, appeals may be heard from the magistrates' courts and the county courts, typically in respect of financial provision under the Domestic Proceedings and Magistrates' Court Act 1978. In the Queen's Bench Divisional Court, appeals may be heard, when circumstances demand, from the magistrates' courts, the Crown Court, and various tribunals by way of case stated and in matters of *judicial review and *habeas corpus. The Court of Appeal (Civil Division) is able to hear appeals from the county courts (except in bankruptcy cases) by way of the leapfrog procedure (Court of Appeal), and appeals from the High Court and various tribunals. The House of Lords will hear appeals primarily from the Court of Appeal but can hear appeals from the High Court under the *leapfrog procedure (House of Lords).

applicable law The laws of a jurisdiction that apply to a particular transaction or agreement. Many countries are signatories of the international Rome Convention (1980; in force from 1 April 1991), which provides that the parties' choice of law will be respected and, in the absence of a term in the relevant agreement, the country's laws with the closest connection with the contract will apply.

applicant *n.* A person who applies for something, especially court relief.

applying the proviso *See* PROVISO.

appointed day The date specified in an Act of Parliament (or in a commencement order) for its coming into force.

appointee *n.* **1.** A person in whose favour a *power of appointment is exercised. **2.** A person selected for a particular purpose.

appointment *n. See* POWER OF APPOINTMENT.

appointor *n.* A person given a *power of appointment to exercise.

approbate and reprobate To accept and reject. A person is not allowed to accept the benefit of a document (e.g. a deed of gift) but reject any liabilities attached to it.

appropriation *n.* **1.** (in administrative law) The allocation of a sum of money to a particular purpose. The annual Appropriation Act authorizes the issue from the Consolidated Fund of money required to meet government expenditure and allocates it between departments and by reference to itemized heads of expenditure. **2.** (in criminal law) *See* THEFT.

appropriation of payments The allocation of one or more payments to one particular debt out of several owed by a debtor to the same creditor. The power of allocation belongs in the first instance to the debtor, but if he does not make an appropriation at the time of payment, then the creditor may do so. In the case of current accounts, in the absence of an express appropriation, payments are normally appropriated to the oldest outstanding debt.

appropriations in aid Day-to-day revenue received by government departments and retained to meet expenditure instead of being paid into the Consolidated Fund.

approximation of laws The process by which member states of the EU change their national laws to enable the free market to function properly. It is required by the Treaty of Rome. *Compare* HARMONIZATION OF LAWS.

appurtenant *adj.* Attached or annexed to land and enhancing the land or its use. An *easement* must be appurtenant to a *dominant tenement but a *profit à prendre* need not. Thus a right of way over land in Yorkshire granted to a Sussex landowner does not benefit his Sussex property and is not an easement, but a right to shoot game over the Yorkshire land could give a man in Sussex (whether landowner or not) a valid profit à *prendre*.

a priori [Latin: from the previous (i.e. from cause to effect)] Describing or relating to reasoning that is based on abstract ideas, anticipates the effects of particular causes, or (more loosely) makes a presumption that is true as far as is known, i.e. deductive reasoning. *Compare* A POSTERIORI.

arbitrary punishment *See* PUNISHMENT.

arbitration *n.* The determination of a dispute by one or more independent third parties (the **arbitrators**) rather than by a court. Arbitrators are appointed by the parties in accordance with the terms of the *arbitration agreement or in default by a court. An arbitrator is bound to apply the law accurately but may in general adopt whatever procedure he chooses and is not bound by the *exclusionary rules of the law of evidence; he must, however, conform to the rules of *natural justice. In English law, arbitrators are subject to extensive control by the courts, with respect to both the manner in which the arbitration is conducted and the correctness of the law that the arbitrators have applied, although this control was loosened to some extent by the Arbitration Act 1996. The judgment of an arbitrator is called his **award**, which can be the subject of an *appeal to the High Court on a question of law under the provisions of the Arbitration Act 1996. A 1979 Arbitration Act abolished the old *special case procedure. In some types of arbitration it is the practice for both parties to appoint an arbitrator. If the arbitrators fail to agree about the matter in dispute, they will appoint an **umpire**, who has the casting vote in making the award. English courts attach great importance to arbitration and will normally stay an action brought in the courts in breach of a binding arbitration agreement. *See also* ALTERNATIVE DISPUTE RESOLUTION.

The modern origins of international arbitration can be traced to the Jay Treaty (1784) between the USA and the UK, which provided for the determination of legal disputes between states by mixed commissions. The *Hague Conventions of 1899 and 1907 contained rules of arbitration that have now become part of customary international law. The 1899 Conventions created the Permanent Court of Arbitration, which was not strictly speaking a court but a means of providing a body of arbitrators on which the parties to a dispute could draw. Consent to arbitration by a state can be given in three ways: (1) by inclusion of a special arbitration clause in a treaty; (2) by a general treaty of arbitration, which arranges arbitration procedures for future disputes; and (3) by a special arbitration treaty designed for a current dispute.

arbitration agreement A contract to refer a present or future legal dispute to *arbitration. Such agreements are of two kinds: those referring an existing dispute to arbitration and those relating to disputes that may arise in the future. The second type is much more common. No particular form is necessary, but the agreement should name the place of arbitration and either appoint the arbitrator or arbitrators or (more usually) define the manner in which they are to be appointed in the absence of agreement between the parties. The agreement should also set out the procedure for appointing an umpire if two arbitrators are involved and they fail to agree.

arbitration clause An express term of a contract in writing (usually of a commercial nature) constituting an agreement to refer disputes arising out of the contract to *arbitration.

archipelago *n.* A collection of islands (including parts of islands, interconnecting waters, and other natural features) so closely interrelated that they form an intrinsic geographical, economic, and political entity, or which historically have been regarded as such. An example is the Galápagos Islands. In contrast, an **archipelagic state** has been defined by the Convention on the Law of the Sea (1982) as a state comprising one or more archipelagos; it may also include other islands. An example of an archipelagic state is the Bahamas. *See also* TERRITORIAL WATERS.

Area Child Protection Committee A committee that advises and reviews local practice and procedure for inter-agency cooperation and training with regard to children in need of protection by local authorities. It is made up of representatives from the various professions and agencies concerned with children.

argumentative affidavit An *affidavit containing not only allegations of fact but also arguments as to the bearing of those facts on the matter in dispute.

armchair principle A rule applied in the *interpretation of wills, enabling circumstances existing when the will was made to be used as evidence to elucidate the meaning of words appearing in the will. For example, such evidence may establish the identity of a beneficiary referred to in the will only by a nickname. The phrase originates from a well-known judicial observation that one may, when construing a will, "place [oneself] in the testator's armchair and consider the circumstances by which he was surrounded when he made his will".

arraign *vb.* To begin a criminal *trial on indictment by calling the defendant to the bar of the court by name, reading the indictment to him, and asking him whether he is guilty or not. The defendant then pleads to the indictment, and this completes the arraignment.

arrangement *n.* **1.** (in commercial and company law) *See* DEED OF ARRANGEMENT; SCHEME OF ARRANGEMENT; VOLUNTARY ARRANGEMENT. **2.** (in international law) *See* TREATY.

array *n.* *See* CHALLENGE TO JURY.

arrest *n.* The apprehension of a person suspected of criminal activities. Most arrests are made by police officers, although anybody may, under prescribed conditions, effect an arrest. In some cases the constable must have a *warrant of arrest signed by a magistrate, which must be shown to the accused (though not necessarily at the time of arrest). However, a warrant is not required for *arrestable offences. Further, a constable who reasonably suspects that a nonarrestable offence has been or is being committed may arrest the suspect if (1) he thinks that service of a *summons is impracticable or inappropriate because a "general arrest condition" is satisfied (for example, if he reasonably believes that arrest is necessary to prevent the suspect causing injury) or (2) he has specific statutory power to make the arrest without warrant (e.g. for *drunken driving or *soliciting) or common-law power (*see* BREACH OF THE PEACE). When an arrest is made, the accused must be told that he is being arrested and given the ground for his arrest. A policeman has power to search the person he is arresting for any property that may be used in evidence against him. Anyone making or assisting in an arrest may use as much force as reasonable in the circumstances. Resisting lawful arrest may involve the crime of *assault or *obstructing a police officer. A person who believes he has been wrongfully arrested may petition for *habeas corpus and may sue the person who arrested him for *false imprisonment. *See also* BAIL; CAUTION; DETENTION; REMAND.

arrestable offence An offence for which there is a fixed mandatory penalty or which carries a sentence of at least five years' imprisonment (e.g. theft). There are also some crimes that are specified to be arrestable offences even though they do not fulfil the usual conditions. For example, taking someone else's motor car for temporary use is arrestable even though it carries a maximum of only three years' imprisonment. Inciting, attempting, or conspiring to commit, or being an accessory to, an arrestable offence is also an arrestable offence. All other crimes are termed **nonarrestable offences**. Anyone may lawfully *arrest, without a *warrant, a person who is in the act of committing an arrestable offence or whom he reasonably suspects to be in the act of committing it. If an arrestable offence has been committed, anyone may subsequently arrest, without warrant, a person who is, or whom he reasonably suspects is, guilty of the offence. A constable who reasonably suspects that an arrestable offence has been committed may arrest anyone he reasonably suspects to be guilty of it. He may also arrest someone who is about to commit (or whom he reasonably suspects is about to commit) such an offence. A police officer may also enter and search any place he suspects is harbouring a person who may be arrested for an arrestable offence.

There are also special offences of *impeding apprehension or prosecution of persons guilty of an arrestable offence or concealing (for gain) information relating to such offences.

arrested development For the purposes of the Mental Health Act 1983, a form of *mental disorder comprising mental impairment and severe mental impairment. **Mental impairment** implies a lack of intelligence that does not amount to severe mental impairment but that nevertheless requires or will respond to medical treatment. **Severe mental impairment** is a lack of intelligence and social functioning associated with aggressive or severely irresponsible conduct.

arrest of judgment A motion by a defendant in criminal proceedings on indictment, between the conviction and the sentence, that judgment should not be given on the ground of some objection arising on the face of the *record, such as a defect in the indictment itself. Such motions are extremely rare in modern practice.

arrived ship *See* LAY DAYS.

arson *n.* The intentional or reckless destruction or damaging of property by fire without a lawful excuse. There are two forms of arson corresponding to the two forms of *criminal damage in the Criminal Damage Act 1971. Arson carries a maximum sentence of life imprisonment.

article *n.* A clause in a document. The plural, **articles**, is often used to mean the entire document, e.g. *articles of association.

Article 81 A provision of the Treaty of Rome that prohibits anticompetitive agreements the aim or effect of which is to restrict, prevent, or distort competition in the EU (*see also* COMPETITION LAW). Article 81 (formerly 85) applies directly in all member states (*see* COMMUNITY LEGISLATION) and is often used against *cartels; it only applies when the agreement affects trade between member states. Agreements that infringe the Article are void and unenforceable; third parties have the right to bring actions for damages if they have suffered loss through the operation of such agreements. Infringement of the Article may result in EU fines of up to 10% of annual worldwide turnover. In the UK there are very similar provisions in the Competition Act 1998, which prohibit anticompetitive agreements under Chapter I of that Act. *See also* BLOCK EXEMPTION.

Article 82 A provision of the Treaty of Rome, with direct effect throughout the

EU (*see* COMMUNITY LEGISLATION), that prohibits *abuses of a dominant position by businesses in the EU. Examples of breaches of Article 82 (formerly 86) include refusing to supply an existing customer (for example, when it has begun to operate in competition with the dominant company), selectively reducing prices to stop competition from competitors (*see* PREDATORY PRICING), unfair or excessive prices, tying clauses, and refusing to license *intellectual property rights. Article 82 only prohibits such conduct if the business is dominant, i.e. if it enjoys a market share of 40% or more in the EU (or a substantial part of it). The rules only apply when the conduct affects trade between member states. There is a very similar prohibition in the Chapter II prohibition of the Competition Act 1998, which holds that abuse of a dominant position will breach UK law if it has effects in the UK.

Article 234 Reference A provision of the Treaty of Rome entitling national courts to refer matters of EU law to the European Court of Justice for a determination. The case ultimately returns to the national court for a final judgment. Such a procedure is known as a "234 reference". Article 234 (formerly 177) is a provision of the Treaty that empowers the Court of Justice to decide such issues as how the Treaty of Rome should be interpreted and whether or not the European Commission or other bodies have acted properly.

articles of association Regulations for the management of registered companies (*see* TABLE A). They form, together with the provisions of the *memorandum of association, the company's constitution.

artificial insemination *See* HUMAN ASSISTED REPRODUCTION.

artificial person *See* JURISTIC PERSON.

ascertained goods *See* UNASCERTAINED GOODS.

assault *n.* An intentional or reckless act that causes someone to be put in fear of immediate physical harm. Actual physical contact is not necessary to constitute an assault (for example, pointing a gun at someone is an assault), but the word is often loosely used to include both threatening acts and physical violence (*see* BATTERY). Words alone cannot constitute an assault. Assault is a form of *trespass to the person and a crime as well as a tort: an **ordinary** (or **common**) **assault**, as described above, is a *summary offence punishable by a *fine at level 5 on the standard scale and/or up to six months' imprisonment. Certain kinds of more serious assault are known as **aggravated assaults** and carry stricter penalties. Examples of these are assault with intent to resist lawful arrest (two years), assault occasioning *actual bodily harm (five years), and assault with intent to rob (life imprisonment). *See also* AFFRAY; INDECENT ASSAULT.

Assembly of the European Communities *See* EUROPEAN PARLIAMENT.

assent *n.* A document by which personal representatives transfer property to a beneficiary under a will or on intestacy. Under the Administration of Estates Act 1925 they may transfer *real estate (including leaseholds) to beneficiaries by an assent in writing, which must be signed by the personal representatives. A beneficiary's title to the property is not complete until the assent has been effected. Personal representatives may also use an assent to vest land in trustees. An assent, once executed, relates back to the death of the deceased. Where an assent is made after 1998, it triggers registration of the land. If the land is already registered, the assent must be completed by registration. *See* LAND REGISTRATION.

assent procedure A procedure introduced by the Single European Act 1986 that gives greater powers to the *European Parliament over the unelected European

Commission. It applies when there is one reading of a new legislative measure in the Parliament: Parliament either assents by an absolute majority to the measure as presented to it or rejects it; it does not have a power to amend the measure. *Compare* CODECISION PROCEDURE; COOPERATION PROCEDURE.

assessment of costs The method by which the amount of costs payable by one party to another, or payable by a client to his solicitor, is determined by an officer of the court. Before the introduction of the *Civil Procedure Rules in 1999, this was called **taxation of costs**. Assessments may be summary or detailed. In a **summary assessment**, the court determines the amount payable immediately at the end of the hearing. In this instance, the court can call for whatever evidence is available at the time (e.g. brief fee) to determine the amount. This is the preferred method of assessment in *fast track trials. In contrast, a **detailed assessment** involves the quantification of costs to a *costs officer, who considers the amount at some stage after the hearing. Detailed assessments are mostly carried out by district judges in the county courts but there is a dedicated office, the Supreme Court Costs Office, for the High Court.

assessor *n.* A person called in to assist a court in trying a case requiring specialized technical knowledge. The High Court and the Court of Appeal have wide powers to appoint assessors to assist them in any action, but this power is rarely exercised except in Admiralty cases. Assessors will not give oral evidence and will not be open to cross-examination or questioning. In cases involving questions of navigation and seamanship, it is the invariable practice to appoint assessors who are Elder Brethren of Trinity House. In proceedings to review an *assessment of costs a practising solicitor and a *costs officer are usually appointed to assist the judge.

assets *pl. n.* Physical property and/or rights that have a monetary value and are capable of being those of a *juristic person or a natural person (i.e. a human being). They can comprise real assets (real property) and personal assets (personal property). In respect of a juristic person, such as a corporation, assets include fixed or capital assets (those identified as being held and used on a continuing basis in the business activity, e.g. machinery) and current or circulating assets (those not intended to be used on a continuing basis in the business activity but realized in the course of trading).
    In respect of a natural person who is deceased, assets comprise all real and personal property that forms part of the deceased's estate and is available for the payment of the deceased's debts and liabilities. *See also* FAMILY ASSETS; WASTING ASSETS.

assignee *n. See* ASSIGNMENT.

assignment *n.* **1.** The transfer of a *chose in action by one person (the **assignor**) to another (the **assignee**). By the rules of the common law, this was not permissible. If, for example, A was owed a contract debt by B, he could not transfer his right to C so as to enable C to sue B for the money owed. The assignment of certain choses in action is now authorized and governed by particular statutes. For example, the Companies Act 1985 allows shares in a company to be transferred in the manner prescribed by the company's articles of association. These, however, are special cases; in general, choses in action, whether legal (e.g. the benefit of a contract) or equitable (e.g. a right under a trust), can be transferred either by equitable assignment or, under the Law of Property Act 1925, by statutory assignment. For an **equitable assignment**, no formality is required. It is sufficient that the assignor shows a clear intention to transfer ownership of his right to the assignee. If, however, it is a legal chose that is assigned, the assignor must be made a party to any proceedings by the assignee to enforce the right. In the above example, C can sue B for the debt, but he must join A as co-claimant or (if A refuses to lend his name to the action in this way) as co-defendant. A **statutory assignment** under the Law of Property Act 1925 is sometimes referred to as a **legal assignment**, but since it may relate to an equitable chose in action as well as a legal one this is not wholly accurate. It enables the assignee to enforce the right assigned in his own name and without joining the assignor to the proceedings even if it is a legal chose. There are three requirements for its validity: it must be absolute; it must be in writing; and written notice of it must be given to the person against whom the right is enforceable. For these purposes, an **absolute assignment** is one that transfers the assignor's entire interest to the assignee unconditionally. If less than his entire interest (e.g. part of a debt) is transferred, or if any condition is attached to the transfer (e.g. that the consent of a third party be obtained), the assignment is not absolute. An assignment need not, however, be permanent to be absolute, and this is exemplified by the mortgage of a chose in action. If A, who owes money to C, assigns to C as security for that debt a debt due to him from B, with the proviso that C will reassign the debt if A settles what is due to him, the assignment is absolute despite the proviso for reassignment.

The assignment of contractual rights (which must be distinguished from *novation) is subject to certain restrictions. For reasons of public policy, the holder of a public office must not assign his salary nor a wife her right to maintenance payments awarded in matrimonial proceedings. Rights to the performance of personal services, as under contracts of employment, are also incapable of being assigned. *Intellectual property rights must be assigned or transferred by document in writing signed by the assignor. *Stamp duty is payable on assignments of property if the value transferred is over £60,000.

2. The transfer of the whole of the remainder of the term of a lease. A tenant may assign his lease unless there is a covenant against it: there is often a covenant against assignment without the landlord's consent. The landlord cannot charge a fee for giving his consent unless there is express provision for this in the lease and he may not withhold his consent unreasonably. Less commonly, a lease may contain a covenant that prohibits any assignment at all. Where a lease contains a covenant against assigning without the landlord's consent, such consent not to be unreasonably withheld, the landlord has certain statutory duties. These are: he must give the tenant notice of his decision within a reasonable time of the tenant requesting consent; the notice must give reasons for any refusal of consent, or conditions attached to acceptance (the conditions themselves must not be unreasonable); and the landlord cannot withhold consent unless the tenant would be in breach of covenant if he completed the transaction without consent. *See also* BUSINESS TENANCY.

assignor *n. See* ASSIGNMENT.

assize *n.* **1.** An assize court or council. In modern times assizes were sittings of High Court judges travelling on circuits around the country with commissions from the Crown to hear cases. These commissions were either of oyer, terminer, and general gaol delivery, empowering the judges to try the most serious criminal cases, or of *nisi prius*, empowering them to try civil actions. These assizes were abolished by the Courts Act 1971, and the criminal jurisdiction of assizes was transferred to the Crown Court. At the same time, the High Court was empowered to hear civil cases anywhere in England and Wales without the need for a special commission. **2.** A statute or ordinance, e.g. the Assize of Clarendon, Novel Disseisin.

association agreement An agreement between a member state of the European Union and a non-EU country or organization, as provided for in Article 310 of the

Treaty of Rome. The agreement, which may be with a country, a union of states, or an international organization, establishes an association involving reciprocal rights and obligations, common action, and special procedures.

assurance *n. See* INSURANCE.

assured agricultural occupancy A form of *assured tenancy in which the tenant is an agricultural worker living in a *tied cottage. This kind of tenancy replaced *protected occupancies from 15 January 1989. In certain circumstances a local authority may be required to rehouse assured agricultural occupants. *See* AGRICULTURAL DWELLING-HOUSE ADVISORY COMMITTEE.

assured shorthold tenancy A special kind of *assured tenancy at the end of which the landlord is entitled to recover possession without having to show one of the usual grounds for possession of an assured tenancy. This kind of tenancy was introduced by the Housing Act 1988, replacing **protected shorthold tenancies**. Under the 1988 Act the landlord was obliged to give the tenant notice before the grant of the tenancy that it was an assured shorthold tenancy. However, under the Housing Act 1996, from 28 February 1997 the requirement for the landlord to serve a notice is removed, and all new tenancies are automatically assured shortholds unless otherwise agreed. If a landlord wants to give the tenant security under an assured tenancy, this must be specifically created; if this is not done, the tenancy is an assured shorthold without *security of tenure. A tenant can apply to a rent assessment committee if he thinks the rent of the tenancy is excessive. The committee can fix a new rent if they think that the rent is significantly higher than that of other assured tenancies in the area. However, government regulations may restrict this right in certain areas or in certain circumstances.

The landlord may obtain possession at any time when he would have been entitled to do so contractually, by giving two months' notice and specifying that the tenancy is an assured shorthold tenancy. No order for possession may be made in the first six months of the tenancy.

assured tenancy A form of tenancy under the Housing Act 1988 that is at a market rent but gives *security of tenure. The premises may be furnished or unfurnished. This kind of tenancy replaces *protected tenancies except those in existence before the Housing Act 1988 came into force. Former assured tenancies under the Housing Act 1980 (where different provisions applied) are converted into the new kind of assured tenancy.

To qualify as an assured tenancy, the premises must be let as a separate dwelling, within certain rateable value limits. There are certain exceptions, such as when the landlord lives in another part of the same premises. Under the Housing Act 1996, from 28 February 1997 all new residential tenancies are *assured shorthold tenancies without security of tenure, unless a notice is specifically served stating that the parties are creating an assured tenancy.

The rent is an open market rent agreed between the landlord and tenant, and it is not registered. However, the landlord must give the tenant notice if he intends to increase the rent, and the tenant can then apply to a *rent assessment committee if he thinks the increase is excessive. The rent assessment committee determines the rent at the current market value. There are limits on the frequency of rent increases.

The landlord can only regain possession on certain statutory grounds. These include: nonpayment of rent; that the landlord formerly lived in the dwelling and requires it again for his own use; that the tenant is a *nuisance neighbour or may become a nuisance; and that alternative accommodation is available (the court has discretion in this last case).

When the tenant of an assured tenancy dies, his spouse has a right, in certain circumstances, to take over the tenancy as successor to the deceased tenant. An assured tenant cannot usually assign the tenancy without the landlord's consent. *See also* STATUTORY PERIODIC TENANCY.

asylum *n.* Refuge granted to an individual whose *extradition is sought by a foreign government. This can include refuge in the territory of a foreign country (**territorial asylum**) or in a foreign embassy (**diplomatic asylum**). The latter is particularly contentious as it is a derogation from the sovereignty of the territorial state; moreover, diplomatic asylum may only be granted in cases of an alleged political offence and not in cases involving common-law crimes. Diplomatic asylum is well recognized in Latin American states. Conventions relating to it include the Havana Convention of 1928, the Montevideo Convention of 1933, and the Caracas Convention of 1954. The UK Asylum and Immigration Act 1996 made it a criminal offence for employers to employ anyone subject to immigration control. *See* IMMIGRATION; POLITICAL ASYLUM.

at sea *See* PRIVILEGED WILL.

attachment *n.* A court order for the detention of a person and/or his property. Attachment can be used by the courts for the punishment of *contempt of court. However, the most common form of attachment is **attachment of earnings**, by which a court orders the payment of judgment debts and other sums due under court orders (e.g. maintenance) by direct deduction from the debtor's earnings. Payment is usually in instalments, and the debtor's employer is responsible for paying these to the court. *See also* GARNISHEE PROCEEDINGS.

attempt *n.* (in criminal law) Any act that is more than merely preparatory to the intended commission of a crime; this act is itself a crime. For example, shooting at someone but missing could be attempted murder, but merely buying a revolver would not. One may be guilty of attempting to commit a crime that proves impossible to commit (e.g. attempted theft from an empty handbag).

attendance centre A nonresidential institution run by a local authority at which offenders between the ages of 17 and 21 may be ordered by a youth court to attend if they have not previously been sentenced to prison or detention in a young offender institution. Attendance, which is outside normal school or working hours, is for periods of up to 3 hours each, to a maximum of 36 hours. Such orders are made when it is felt that a custodial order is not required but a fine or other order would be too lenient.

attestation *n.* The signature of witnesses to the making of a will or *deed. Under the Wills Act 1837 as amended the testator must acknowledge his signature (*see* ACKNOWLEDGMENT) in the presence of two witnesses who must each sign (attest) at the same time in the testator's presence. The signature of each party to a deed must be attested by one witness.

attorney *n.* A person who is appointed by another and has authority to act on behalf of another. *See also* POWER OF ATTORNEY.

Attorney General (AG) The principal law officer of the Crown. The Attorney General is usually a Member of Parliament of the ruling party and holds ministerial office, although he is not normally a member of the Cabinet. He is the chief legal adviser of the government, answers questions relating to legal matters in the House of Commons, and is politically responsible for the *Crown Prosecution Service, *Director of Public Prosecutions, Treasury Solicitor and *Serious Fraud Office. He is the leader of the English Bar and presides at its general meetings. The consent of the Attorney General is required for bringing certain criminal actions, principally ones relating to offences against the state and public order and corruption. The Attorney General sometimes appears in court as an *advocate in cases of exceptional public interest, but he is not now allowed to engage in private practice. He has the right to terminate any criminal proceedings by entering a *nolle prosequi. See also SOLICITOR GENERAL.

attornment n. **1.** An act by a bailee (see BAILMENT) in possession of goods on behalf of one person acknowledging that he will hold the goods on behalf of someone else. The attornment notionally transfers possession to the other person (constructive possession) and can thus be a delivery of goods sold. **2.** (largely historical) A person's agreement to hold land as the tenant of someone else. Some mortgages provide that the owner of the land attorns tenant of the mortgagee for a period of years that will be terminated when the debt is repaid.

auction n. A method of sale in which parties are invited to make competing offers (**bids**) to purchase an item. The auctioneer, who acts as the agent of the seller until fall of the hammer, announces completion of the sale in favour of the highest bidder by striking his desk with a hammer (or in any other customary manner). Until then any bidder may retract his bid and the auctioneer may withdraw the goods. The seller may not bid unless the sale is stated to be subject to the seller's right to bid. Merely to advertise an auction does not bind the auctioneer to hold one. However, if he advertises an auction without reserve and accepts bids, he will be liable if he fails to knock the item down to the highest outside bidder. An auctioneer who discloses his agency promises to a buyer that he has authority to sell and that he knows of no defect to the seller's title; he does not promise that the buyer of a specific chattel will get a good title.

auction ring A group of buyers who agree not to compete against each other at an auction with a view to purchasing articles for less than the open-market value. The profit earned thereby is shared among the members of the ring, or a second "knock-out" auction is held in private by the members of the ring with the article being sold to the highest bidder and the profit shared among the members. Under the Auctions (Bidding Agreements) Acts 1927 and 1969 it is a criminal offence for a dealer to participate in an auction ring and a seller is given the right to set aside the contract of sale if one of the purchasers is a dealer in a ring.

audi alteram partem See NATURAL JUSTICE.

Audit Commission See DISTRICT AUDITORS.

audit exemption Exemption from the requirement to file audited accounts, which (since 11 August 1994) can be claimed by small companies with a turnover of under £90,000 per annum and a balance-sheet total under £1.4M.

auditor n. A person appointed to examine the *books of account and the *accounts of a registered company and to report upon them to company members. An **auditor's report** must state whether or not, in the auditor's opinion, the accounts have been properly prepared and give a true and fair view of the company's financial position. The Companies Acts 1985 and 1989 set out the qualifications an auditor must possess and also certain rights to enable him to fulfil his duty effectively.

authentication *n.* A distinct procedural step at the conclusion of a *treaty at which the definitive text of the treaty is established as correct and authentic and not subject to further modification.

authority *n.* **1.** Power delegated to a person or body to act in a particular way. The person in whom authority is vested is usually called an *agent and the person conferring the authority is the principal. **2.** A governing body, such as a *local authority, charged with power and duty to perform certain functions. **3.** A judicial decision or other source of law used as a ground for a legal proposition. *See also* PERSUASIVE AUTHORITY.

authorized capital (nominal capital) The total value of the shares that a registered company is authorized to issue in order to raise capital. The authorized capital of a company limited by shares (*see* LIMITED COMPANY) must be stated in the memorandum of association, together with the number and nominal value of the shares (*see* CAPITAL). For example, an authorized capital of £20,000 may be divided into 20 000 shares of £1 (the **nominal value**) each. If the company has issued 10 000 of these shares, it is said to have an **issued capital** of £10,000 and retains the ability, without an increase in capital (*see* ALTERATION OF SHARE CAPITAL), to issue further shares in future. If the company has received the full nominal value of the shares issued, its *paid-up capital equals its issued capital. Where a company has not yet called for payment (*see* CALL) of the full nominal value, it has **uncalled capital**. **Reserve capital** is that part of the uncalled capital that the company has determined (by *special resolution) shall not be called up except upon a winding-up.

authorized investments Formerly, investments in which a trustee was permitted to invest trust property. Under the Trustee Investments Act 1961 (replacing earlier legislation, which did not give wide enough powers) trustees could invest not more than half the trust fund in shares in certain companies; the other half had to be invested in **authorized securities**, certain debentures, local authority loans, etc. A *general power of investment has now been given to trustees by the Trustee Act 2000.

authorized securities *See* AUTHORIZED INVESTMENTS.

automatic reservation A *reservation to the acceptance by a state of the compulsory jurisdiction of the INTERNATIONAL COURT OF JUSTICE. This is made under the *optional clause of the Statute of the Court, which permits an accepting state to unilaterally claim the right to determine the scope of its reservation.

automatism *n.* Unconscious *involuntary conduct caused by some external factor. A person is not criminally liable for acts carried out in a state of automatism, since his conduct is altogether involuntary. Examples of such acts are those carried out while sleepwalking or in a state of concussion or hypnotic trance, a spasm or reflex action, and acts carried out by a diabetic who suffers a hypoglycaemic episode. Automatism is not a defence, however, if it is self-induced (for example, by taking drink or drugs). When automatism is caused by a disease of the mind, the defence may be treated as one of *insanity. Mere absent-mindedness, even when brought about by a combination of, for example, depression and diabetes, is not regarded as a defect of reason under the defence of *insanity. It may, however, be grounds for concluding that the accused was not capable of having the necessary *mens rea at the time of the offence.

autopsy (post-mortem) *n.* The examination of a body after death in order to establish the cause of death. Autopsies are frequently requested by coroners (*see* INQUEST).

autrefois acquit [French: previously acquitted] A *special plea in bar of arraignment claiming that the defendant has previously been acquitted by a court of competent jurisdiction of the same (or substantially the same) offence as that with which he is now charged or that he could have been convicted on an earlier indictment of the same (or substantially the same) offence. When this plea is entered the judge determines the issue. If the plea is successful it bars further proceedings on the indictment. The plea may be combined with one of *not guilty. *See also* NEMO DEBET BIS VEXARI.

autrefois convict [French: previously convicted] A *special plea in bar of arraignment claiming that the defendant has previously been convicted by a court of competent jurisdiction of the same (or substantially the same) offence as that with which he is now charged or that he could have been convicted on an earlier indictment of the same (or substantially the same) offence. When this plea is entered the judge determines the issue. If the plea is successful it bars further proceedings on the indictment. The plea may be combined with one of *not guilty. *See also* NEMO DEBET BIS VEXARI.

autre vie *See* ESTATE PUR AUTRE VIE.

auxiliary jurisdiction The jurisdiction exercised by the *Court of Chancery to aid a claimant at common law; for example, by forcing a defendant to reveal documents and thus provide necessary evidence for his case. Auxiliary jurisdiction was rendered obsolete by the Judicature Acts 1873–75.

AVC *See* ADDITIONAL VOLUNTARY CONTRIBUTION.

average *n.* **1.** (in marine insurance) A loss or damage arising from an event at sea. **2.** A reduction in the amount payable under an insurance policy in respect of a partial loss of property. All marine insurance policies are subject to average under the Marine Insurance Act 1906; other policies may be subject to average if they contain express provision to that effect (an **average clause**).

In maritime law, the expression **general** (or **gross**) average is used in relation to certain acts, to the losses they cause, and to the rights of contribution to which they give rise. A **general-average act** consists of any sacrifice or expenditure made intentionally and reasonably to preserve property involved in a sea voyage. For example, the jettisoning of some of a ship's cargo to keep it afloat during a storm is a general-average act. The loss directly resulting from a general-average act is called **general-average loss** and is borne proportionately by all whose property has been saved. The owner of jettisoned cargo, for example, is entitled to a contribution from other cargo owners as well as the shipowners; such a contribution is called a **general-average contribution**. The principle of general average is common to the laws of all maritime nations, but the detailed rules are not uniform. To overcome conflict of law, a standard set of rules was agreed in the 19th century at international conferences of shipowners and others held at York and Antwerp. These, known as the **York–Antwerp rules**, do not have the force of law, but it is common practice to incorporate them (as subsequently amended) in contracts of *affreightment, thereby displacing national laws. The basic principle is that an insured who has suffered a general-average loss may recover the whole of it from his underwriters without enforcing his rights to contribution; these become enforceable by the underwriters instead.

By contrast, **particular average** (also called **simple** or **petty average**) relates purely to marine insurance. It consists of any partial loss that is not a general-average loss (for example, the damage of cargo by seawater). It is therefore borne purely by the person suffering it and is frequently covered by a policy only in limited circumstances.

A ship sold **free from average** is free from any claims whatsoever.

a vinculo matrimonii [Latin] From the bond of marriage. A decree of divorce *a vinculo matrimonii* allowed a spouse to remarry and was the forerunner of the modern divorce decree. *See also* A MENSA ET THORO.

avoid *vb.* To set aside a *voidable contract.

avoidance of disposition order An order by the High Court preventing or setting aside a transaction by a husband or wife that was made to defeat his (or her) spouse's claim to financial provision. A transaction, such as a gift, made within three years before the application is presumed to have been made in order to defeat the spouse's claim if its effect would be to defeat her claim. But a sale of property to a purchaser in good faith will not be set aside.

avulsion *n.* A sudden and violent shift in the course of a river that leaves the old riverbed dry. This could be caused by such natural forces as floods, tidal waves, or hurricanes. The alteration of territory by this means does not affect the title to territory; thus new claims by a state that would appear to benefit from the rapid geological change would be disbarred. *Compare* ACCRETION.

award *n. See* ARBITRATION.

B

backed for bail Describing a warrant for arrest issued by a magistrate or by the Crown Court to a police officer, directing him to release the accused, upon arrest, on bail under specified conditions. The police officer is bound to release the arrested person if his sureties are approved.

bail *n.* The release by the police, magistrates' court, or Crown Court of a person held in legal custody while awaiting trial or appealing against a criminal conviction. Conditions may be imposed on a person released on bail by the police. A person granted bail undertakes to pay a specified sum to the court if he fails to appear on the date set by the court (*see also* JUSTIFYING BAIL). This is known as **bail in one's own recognizance**. Often the court also requires guarantors (known as **sureties**) to undertake to produce the accused or to forfeit the sum fixed by the court if they fail to do so. In these circumstances the bailed person is, in theory, released into the custody of the sureties. Judges have wide discretionary powers as to whether or not bail should be granted, and for what sum. Normally an accused is granted bail unless it is likely that he will abscond, or interfere with witnesses, or unless he is accused of murder, attempted murder, manslaughter, rape, or attempted rape and has a previous conviction for such an offence. The accused, and the prosecution in limited circumstances, may appeal.

bailee *n. See* BAILMENT.

bail hostel Accommodation for persons of no fixed address who have been released on bail.

bailiff *n.* **1.** An officer of a court (usually a county court) concerned with the service of the court's processes and the enforcement of its orders, especially warrants of *execution authorizing the seizure of the goods of a debtor. The term is often loosely applied to a sheriff's officer. **2.** A judicial official in Guernsey (Royal Court Bailiff).

bailiwick *n.* The area within which a *bailiff or *sheriff exercises jurisdiction.

bailment *n.* The transfer of the possession of goods by the owner (the **bailor**) to another (the **bailee**) for a particular purpose. Examples of bailments are the hiring of goods, the loan of goods, the pledge of goods, and the delivery of goods for carriage, safe custody, or repair. Ownership of the goods remains in the bailor, who has the right to demand their return or direct their disposal at the end of the period (if any) fixed for the bailment or (if no period is fixed) at will. This right will, however, be qualified by any *lien the bailee may have over the goods. Bailment exists independently of contract. But if the bailor receives payment for the bailment (a **bailment for reward**) there is often an express contract setting out the rights and obligations of the parties. A bailment for which the bailor receives no reward (e.g. the loan of a book to a friend) is called a **gratuitous bailment**.

bailor *n. See* BAILMENT.

balance sheet A document presenting in summary form a true and fair view of a company's financial position at a particular time (e.g. at the end of its financial year). It must show the items listed in either of the two formats set out in the Companies Act 1985. Its purpose is to disclose the amount that would be available for the benefit of members if the company were immediately wound up and liabilities were discharged out of the proceeds of selling its assets. *See* ACCOUNTS; STATEMENTS OF STANDARD ACCOUNTING PRACTICE.

bank holidays Days that are declared holidays for the clearing banks and are kept as public holidays under the Banking and Financial Dealing Act 1971 or by royal proclamation under this Act. In England and Wales there are currently eight bank holidays a year: New Year's Day (or, if that is a Saturday or Sunday, the following Monday), Good Friday, Easter Monday, May Holiday (the first Monday in May), Spring Bank Holiday (the last Monday in May), Summer Bank Holiday (the last Monday in August), and Christmas Day and the following day (or, if Christmas Day is a Saturday or Sunday, the following Monday and Tuesday).

bankruptcy *n.* The state of a person who has been adjudged by a court to be insolvent (*compare* WINDING-UP). The court orders the compulsory administration of a bankrupt's affairs so that his assets can be fairly distributed among his creditors. To declare a debtor to be bankrupt a creditor or the debtor himself must make an application (known as a **bankruptcy petition**) either to the High Court or to a county court. If a creditor petitions, he must show that the debtor owes him at least £750 and that the debtor appears unable to pay it. The debtor's inability to pay can be shown either by: (1) the creditor making a formal demand in a special statutory form, and the debtor failing to pay within three weeks; or (2) the creditor of a *judgment debtor being unsuccessful in enforcing payment of a judgment debt through the courts. If the petition is accepted the court makes a *bankruptcy order. Within three weeks of the bankruptcy order, the debtor must usually submit a *statement of affairs, which the creditors may inspect. This may be followed by a *public examination of the debtor. After the bankruptcy order, the bankrupt's property is placed in the hands of the *official receiver. The official receiver must either call a creditors' meeting to appoint a *trustee in bankruptcy to manage the bankrupt's affairs, or he becomes trustee himself. The trustee must be a qualified *insolvency practitioner. He takes possession of the bankrupt's property and, subject to certain rules, distributes it among the creditors.

A bankrupt is subject to certain disabilities (*see* UNDISCHARGED BANKRUPT). Bankruptcy is terminated when the court makes an order of *discharge, but a bankrupt who has not previously been bankrupt within the preceding 15 years is automatically discharged after three years. *See also* VOLUNTARY ARRANGEMENT.

bankruptcy order A court order that makes a debtor bankrupt. When the order is made, ownership of all the debtor's property is transferred either to a court officer known as the *official receiver or to a trustee appointed by the creditors. It replaced both the former *receiving order and *adjudication order in bankruptcy proceedings. *See also* BANKRUPTCY.

bankruptcy petition An application to the High Court or a county court for a *bankruptcy order to be made against an insolvent debtor. *See* BANKRUPTCY.

banning order *See* FOOTBALL HOOLIGANISM.

banns *pl. n.* The public announcement in church of an intended marriage. Banns must be published for three successive Sundays if a marriage is to take place in the Church of England other than by religious licence or a superintendent registrar's certificate. *See also* MARRIAGE BY CERTIFICATE; MARRIAGE BY RELIGIOUS LICENCE.

bar *n.* **1.** A legal impediment. **2.** An imaginary barrier in a court of law. Only Queen's Counsel, officers of the court, and litigants in person are allowed between the bar and the *bench when the court is in session. **3.** A rail near the entrance to each House of Parliament beyond which nonmembers may not pass but to which they may be summoned (e.g. for reprimand).

Bar *n.* *Barristers, collectively. To be **called to the Bar** is to be admitted to the profession by one of the Inns of Court.

Bar Council (General Council of the Bar of England and Wales) The governing body of the barristers' branch of the legal profession. It regulates the activities of all barristers, maintains standards within the Bar, and considers complaints against barristers. *See also* COUNCIL OF THE INNS OF COURT.

bare licensee A person who uses or occupies land by permission of the owner but has no legal or equitable interest in it. Such permission is personal to him; thus he cannot transfer it. He cannot enforce it against a third party who acquires the land from the owner. His permission can be brought to an end at any time and he must leave the property with "all reasonable speed". If he does not do so he becomes a trespasser (*see* TRESPASS). *See also* LICENCE.

bare trust (naked trust, simple trust) A trust in which the trustee has no obligation except to hand over the trust property to a person entitled to it, at the latter's request. This will occur when the beneficiary is of full age and under no disability and the trustee has no duties in respect of the property. *Compare* ACTIVE TRUST.

barratry *n.* **1.** Any act committed wilfully by the master or crew of a ship to the detriment of its owner or charterer. Examples include scuttling the ship and embezzling the cargo. Illegal activities (e.g. carrying prohibited persons) leading to the forfeiture of the ship also constitute barratry. Barratry is one of the risks covered by policies of marine insurance. **2.** The former common-law offence (abolished by the Criminal Law Act 1967) of habitually raising or inciting disputes in the courts.

barring of entailed interest *See* ENTAILED INTEREST.

barrister *n.* A legal practitioner admitted to plead at the Bar. A barrister must be a member of one of the four *Inns of Court, by whom he is **called to the Bar** when admitted to the profession. Barristers normally take a three-year law degree at university, followed by a one-year course at Bar school after which they are called to the Bar. Thereafter they take a pupillage in chambers and then seek a permanent place as a "tenant". The primary function of barristers is to act as *advocates for parties in courts or tribunals, but they also undertake the writing of opinions and some of the work preparatory to a trial. Their general immunity from law suits in negligence for criminal and civil litigation has been abolished. With certain exceptions a barrister may only act upon the instructions of a *solicitor, who is also responsible for the payment of the barrister's fee. Barristers have the right of audience in all courts: they are either *Queen's Counsel (often referred to as **leaders** or **leading counsel**) or *junior barristers. *See also* ADVOCACY QUALIFICATION.

baseline *n.* The line forming the boundary between the INTERNAL WATERS of a state on its landward side and the territorial sea on its seaward side (*see* TERRITORIAL WATERS). Other coastal state zones (the contiguous zone, *exclusive economic zone, and exclusive fishing zone) are measured from the baseline.

basic award *See* COMPENSATION.

basic intent *See* INTENTION; INTOXICATION.

battered child A child subjected to physical violence or abuse by a parent, step-parent, or any other person with whom he is living. A battered child may be protected if the other parent (or person who is looking after him) applies for an injunction under the Family Law Act 1996, but only if the child is living, or might reasonably be expected to live, with the applicant. The Act applies to children under 18. When a child is suffering, or likely to suffer, significant harm, a local authority may apply for a *supervision order or *care order under the Children Act 1989. *See also* EMERGENCY PROTECTION ORDER.

battered spouse or cohabitant   A person subjected to physical violence by their husband, wife, or cohabitant (subsequently referred to as "partner" in this entry). Battered partners (or those afraid of future violence) may seek protection in a number of ways. Under the Family Law Act 1996 they can apply to the court for a *nonmolestation order, directing the other partner not to molest, annoy, or use violence against them, or for an *occupation order, entitling the applicant to remain in occupation of the matrimonial home and prohibiting, suspending, or restricting the abusive partner's right to occupy the house. Battered partners can apply for these orders if they are also applying for some other matrimonial relief (e.g. a divorce). The court must attach a power of arrest to a nonmolestation order or an occupation order if the abuser has used or threatened violence against his or her partner. This gives a constable the power to arrest without warrant the abuser if he or she is in breach of the order. In cases of emergency an injunction without notice may be granted. In theory, a criminal prosecution for *assault or for harassment under the Protection from Harassment Act 1997 could be brought, but in practice this is seldom used by victims of domestic violence. Under the Housing Act 1985, local authorities have a duty to supply emergency accommodation to those made homeless when they have left their homes because of domestic violence.

Those who have been subjected to continued beatings by their partners over a period of time may plead *provocation or *diminished responsibility if charged with the murder of their partner.

battery *n.* The intentional or reckless application of physical force to someone without his consent. Battery is a form of *trespass to the person and is a *summary offence (punishable with a *fine at level 5 on the standard scale and/or six months' imprisonment) as well as a tort, even if no actual harm results. If actual harm does result, however, the *consent of the victim may not prevent the act from being criminal, except when the injury is inflicted in the course of properly conducted sports or games (e.g. rugby or boxing) or as a result of reasonable surgical intervention. *Compare* ASSAULT; GRIEVOUS BODILY HARM.

bay *n.* A well-marked roughly semicircular indentation on a coastline. What does or does not constitute a bay can be of relevance in determining a state's control of its coastal waters. The test is a geographical one, taking into account relative dimensions and configuration. The following three considerations have been taken into account when making this determination: (1) the depth of the indentation relative to the width of its mouth; (2) the economic and strategic importance of the indentation to the coastal state; and (3) the seclusion of the indentation from the highway of nations on the open sea. *See also* TERRITORIAL WATERS.

bearer *n.* The person in possession of a bill of exchange or promissory note that is payable to the bearer.

beauty competition   A method used by an employer contemplating entering a *single-union agreement, in which a number of unions are invited to present proposals for collective bargaining arrangements within an establishment. After reviewing the proposals the company decides to recognize the union that best meets its criteria.

Beddoe order [from the case *re Beddoe* (1892)] An order made by the court granting trustees permission to bring or defend an action. The order protects the trustees against claims by the beneficiaries that the action should not have been brought and enables them to recover their costs from the trust property. If an order has not been obtained, these consequences may not follow, and the trustees may therefore have to compensate the beneficiaries for any loss and also may themselves have to pay any costs arising from the action.

belligerent communities, recognition of The formal acknowledgment by a state of the existence of a civil war between another state's central government and the peoples of an area within its territorial boundaries. Such recognition brings about the conventional operation of the rules of war, in particular those humanitarian restraints upon the combatants introduced by the international law of armed force. Another result of recognition of belligerency is that both the rebels and the parent central government are entitled to exercise belligerent rights and are subject to the obligations imposed on belligerents. Following recognition, third states have the rights and obligations of *neutrality. Compare INSURGENCY.

bench *n.* **1.** Literally, the seat of a judge in court. The bench is usually in an elevated position at one side of the court room facing the seats of counsel and solicitors. **2.** A group of judges or magistrates sitting together in a court, or all judges, collectively. Thus a lawyer who has been appointed a judge is said to have been **raised to the bench**.

Benchers (Masters of the Bench) *pl. n.* Judges and senior practitioners who form a governing body for each of the Inns of Court. They are recruited by co-option and elect one of their number annually to be the Treasurer. Benchers are responsible for admission of students and calls to the Bar and exercise disciplinary powers over the members of the Inn. Appeal from their decisions is to the Lord Chancellor and 'visitors' (i.e. High Court Judges sitting for the appeal).

bench warrant A warrant for the arrest of a person who has failed to attend court when summoned or subpoenaed to do so or against whom an order of committal for contempt of court has been made and who cannot be found. The warrant is issued during a sitting of the court.

beneficial interest The rights of a beneficiary in respect of the property held in trust for him. *See also* EQUITABLE INTERESTS.

beneficial owner An owner who is entitled to the possession and use of land or its income for his own benefit. Under the Law of Property Act 1925 a person who for valuable *consideration conveys land as beneficial owner gives implied covenants (1) that he has the right to convey it; (2) for quiet enjoyment (i.e. that the transferee takes possession free from adverse claims to the land); (3) that the land is free from encumbrances other than any specified in the conveyance; (4) for further assurance (i.e. that the transferor will do anything necessary to cure any defect in the conveyance); and (5) when the land is leasehold (a) that the lease is valid and subsisting and (b) that the convenants in the lease have been performed and the rent paid. When the owner of a legal estate is not the beneficial owner (e.g. a mortgagee, trustee, or personal representative) his only implied covenant in a conveyance of the land is that he has not himself created any encumbrance.

beneficiary *n.* **1.** A person entitled to benefit from a *trust. The beneficiary holds a *beneficial interest in the property of which a *trustee holds the legal *interest. A beneficiary was formerly known as the **cestui que trust**. **2.** One who benefits from a will.

benevolent purposes Purposes that are for the public good but not necessarily charitable. They are wider than *philanthropic purposes. *See* CHARITABLE TRUST.

Benjamin order [from the case *re Benjamin* (1902)] An order made by the court for the distribution of assets on death when it is uncertain whether or not a beneficiary is alive. The order authorizes the personal representatives of the deceased (who will be administering the estate) to distribute the property on the basis that the beneficiary is dead (or on some other basis); the personal representatives are therefore protected from being sued if the beneficiary is in fact alive and entitled. The beneficiary may, however, trace the trust property (*see* TRACING TRUST PROPERTY).

bequeath *vb.* To dispose by will of property other than land. *Compare* DEVISE.

bequest *n.* A gift by will of property other than land. *Compare* DEVISE. *See* LEGACY.

bereavement, damages for *See* FATAL ACCIDENTS.

bereavement benefit A benefit payable to widows and widowers, under the Welfare Reform and Pensions Act 1999, subject to certain conditions. It consists of a bereavement payment (made as a lump sum), a widowed parent allowance (where applicable), and a bereavement allowance.

Berne Convention The Berne Convention for the Protection of Literary and Artistic Works: an international convention of September 1886 that sets out ground rules for protection of *copyright at national level; it has since been amended several times. Many nations are signatories to the Convention, including the UK and, more recently, the United States. *See also* TRIPS.

best-evidence rule A rule requiring that a party must call the best evidence that the nature of the case will allow. Formerly of central importance, in modern law it is largely confined to a rule of practice, not a requirement of law, that the original of a private document must be produced in order to prove its contents; if it cannot be produced its absence must be explained.

bestiality *n.* Anal or vaginal intercourse by a man or a woman with an animal. Bestiality is a crime if penetration is proved. *See also* BUGGERY.

best value A requirement under the Local Government Act 1999 that *local authorities must have regard to economy, efficiency, and effectiveness when exercising their functions and must make arrangements to secure continuous improvement.

bias *n.* *See* NATURAL JUSTICE.

bid *n.* *See* AUCTION.

bigamy *n.* The act of going through a marriage ceremony with someone when one is already lawfully married to someone else. Bigamy is a crime, punishable by up to seven years' imprisonment; however, there is a defence if the accused honestly and reasonably believed that his or her first spouse was dead or that their previous marriage had been dissolved or annulled or was void. There is also a special defence if the accused's spouse has been absent for at least seven years, and is therefore presumed by the accused to be dead, even if he does not have positive proof of the death. Even though a person is found not guilty of the crime of bigamy, the bigamous marriage will still be void if that person had a spouse living at the time that the second marriage was celebrated.

bilateral contract (synallagmatic contract) A contract that creates mutual obligations, i.e. both parties undertake to do, or refrain from doing, something in exchange for the other party's undertaking. The majority of contracts are bilateral in nature. *Compare* UNILATERAL CONTRACT.

bilateral discharge The ending of a contract by agreement, when neither party has yet performed his obligations under it (an **executory contract**). Each party supplies consideration for the agreement to discharge by releasing the other from his existing obligations. *Compare* UNILATERAL DISCHARGE (*see* ACCORD AND SATISFACTION).

hill *n* **1.** Any of various written instruments; for example, a *bill of exchange, a *bill of indictment, or a *bill of lading. **2.** A written account of money owed; for example, a *bill of costs.

Bill *n.* A draft of a proposed *Act of Parliament, which must (normally) be passed by both Houses before becoming an Act. Bills are either public or private, and the procedure governing their passing by Parliament depends basically on this distinction. In general, a **public Bill** is one relating to matters of general concern; it is introduced by the government or by a private member (**private member's Bill**). In the House of Commons the government sets aside certain Fridays for debate on private member's Bills, and a ballot at the beginning of each session of Parliament determines the members whose Bills are to have priority on those days. A private member's Bill that is not supported by the government stands little chance of successfully completing all stages and becoming an Act. The government sometimes prefers a private member to sponsor a particularly controversial Bill that they themselves support; for example, the Abortion Act 1967 was introduced by a private member (David Steel) and was successful because it had the support of the government of the day. A public Bill, unless predominantly financial, can be introduced in either House (less controversial Bills are introduced in the Lords first). The Bill is presented by the minister or other member in charge, passed by being read three times, and then sent to the other House. Its first reading is a formality, but it is debated on second and third readings, between which it goes through a Committee stage and a Report stage during which amendments may be made. A Bill that has not become an Act by the end of the session lapses; if reintroduced in a subsequent session, it must go through all stages again.

A **private Bill** is one designed to benefit a particular person, local authority, or other body, by whom it is presented. It is introduced on a petition by the promoter, which is preceded by public advertisement and by notice to those directly affected. Its Committee stage in the first House is conducted before a small group of members, and evidence for and against it is heard. Thereafter, it follows the procedure for public Bills.

A **hybrid Bill** is a government bill that is purely local or personal in character and affects only one of a number of interests in the same class. For example, a government Bill to nationalize one only of several private-sector airlines would be hybrid. A hybrid Bill proceeds as a public Bill until after second reading in the first House, after which it is treated similarly to a private Bill.

bill of costs An account of *costs prepared by a solicitor in respect of legal services he has rendered his client. In general a solicitor may be required to furnish his client with a bill unless they have made an agreement in writing to the contrary. If no such agreement has been made the solicitor may not, without the permission of the High Court, sue for **recovery of costs** until one month after the bill of costs has been delivered. Any client dissatisfied with a bill can require his solicitor to obtain a **remuneration certificate** from the Law Society. The certificate will either say that the fee is fair and reasonable or it will substitute a lower fee. If the bill is endorsed with a notice saying that there is a right to ask for a remuneration certificate within one month, the client has one month from receipt of the bill to request the certificate. If the bill is not endorsed in this way, the client has a right to demand a remuneration certificate that lasts for one month from the time he was notified of this right. If the client requests a remuneration certificate, he must normally first pay half the bill and all the VAT on the bill and expenses and disbursements set out on the bill before the remuneration certificate is obtained, unless he has obtained permission from the Law Society to waive this requirement; this permission is given in exceptional circumstances. These rights are set out fully in the Solicitors (Non-Contentious Business) Remuneration Order 1994. In contentious (i.e. litigious) matters the bill is subject to *assessment of costs. *See also* COSTS DRAFTSMAN.

bill of exchange An unconditional order in writing, addressed by one person (the **drawer**) to another (the **drawee**) and signed by the person giving it, requiring the drawee to pay on demand or at a fixed or determinable future time a specified sum of money to or to the order of a specified person (the **payee**) or to the bearer. If the bill is payable at a future time the drawee signifies his *acceptance, which makes him the party primarily liable upon the bill; the drawer and endorsers may also be liable upon a bill. The use of bills of exchange enables one person to transfer to another an enforceable right to a sum of money. A bill of exchange is not only transferable but also negotiable, since if a person without an enforceable right to the money transfers a bill to a *holder in due course, the latter obtains a good title to it. Much of the law on bills of exchange is codified by the Bills of Exchange Act 1882 and the Cheques Act 1992.

bill of indictment A formal written accusation charging someone with an *indictable offence. The usual method of preferring a bill of indictment (i.e. bringing it before the appropriate court) is by committal proceedings before a magistrates' court (*see* COMMITTAL FOR TRIAL). *See also* INDICTMENT.

bill of lading A document acknowledging the shipment of a consignor's goods for carriage by sea (*compare* SEA WAYBILL). It is used primarily when the ship is carrying goods belonging to a number of consignors (a general ship). In this case, each consignor receives a bill issued (normally by the master of the ship) on behalf of either the shipowner or a charterer under a *charterparty. The bill serves three functions: it is a receipt for the goods; it summarizes the terms of the contract of carriage; and it acts as a document of title to the goods. A bill of lading is also issued by a shipowner to a charterer who is using the ship for the carriage of his own goods. In this case, the terms of the contract of carriage are in the charterparty and the bill serves only as a receipt and a document of title. During transit, ownership of the goods may be transferred by delivering the bill to another if it is drawn to bearer or by endorsing it if it is drawn to order. It is not, however, a *negotiable instrument. The responsibilities, liabilities, rights, and immunities attaching to carriers under bills of lading are stated in the **Hague Rules**. These were drawn up by the International Law Association meeting at The Hague in 1921 and adopted by an International Conference on Maritime Law held at Brussels in 1922. They were given effect in the UK by the Carriage of Goods by Sea Act 1924 and so became known in the UK as the Hague Rules of 1924. They were amended at Brussels in 1968, effect being given to the amendments by the Carriage of Goods by Sea Act 1971. The Rules, which are set out in a schedule to the Act, apply to carriage under a bill of lading from any port in Great Britain or Northern Ireland to any other port and also to carriage between any of the states by which they have been adopted. Every bill issued in Great Britain or Northern Ireland to which the Rules apply must state that fact expressly (the clause giving effect to this requirement is customarily referred to as the **paramount clause**). The Hague Rules were completely rewritten in 1978 in a new treaty known as the **Hamburg Rules**, which drastically alter the privileged position of a sea carrier as compared to other carriers, but they have not yet been generally adopted.

bill of sale　A document by which a person transfers the ownership of goods to another. Commonly the goods are transferred conditionally, as security for a debt, and a **conditional bill of sale** is thus a mortgage of goods. The mortgagor has a right to redeem the goods on repayment of the debt and usually remains in possession of them; he may thus obtain false credit by appearing to own them. An **absolute bill of sale** transfers ownership of the goods absolutely. The Bills of Sale Acts 1878 and 1882 regulate the registration and form of bills of sale.

bind over　To order a person to provide a bond or *recognizance by means of which he guarantees to carry out some act (e.g. to appear in court at the proper time if he has been granted bail) or not to commit some offence (such as causing a breach of the peace).

birth certificate　A certified copy of an entry of birth in the register of births, deaths, and marriages, which comprises evidence of the detail there stated. *See* REGISTRATION OF BIRTH.

blacklist　*n.* A list that contains details of members of trade unions, and in particular details of trade-union activists, compiled with a view to being used by outside bodies, usually employers and their associations, for the purpose of discrimination in relation to the recruitment and treatment of workers. The utilization of such lists is subject to the regulatory powers of the Secretary of State under section 3(2) of the Employment Relations Act 1999.

blackmail　*n.* The crime of making an unwarranted demand with menaces for the purpose of financial gain for oneself or someone else or financial loss to the person threatened. The menaces may include a threat of violence or of detrimental action, e.g. exposure of past immorality or misconduct. Blackmail is punishable by up to 14 years' imprisonment. As long as the demand is made with menaces, it will be presumed to be unwarranted, unless the accused can show both that he thought he was reasonable in making the demand and that he thought it was reasonable to use the menaces as a means of pressure. Under the Administration of Justice Act 1970, there is also a special statutory crime of *harassment of debtors. *See also* THREAT.

Black Rod, Gentleman Usher of the　An official of the House of Lords whose title derives from his staff of office – an ebony rod surmounted with a gold lion. The office originated as usher of the Order of the Garter in the 14th century; the parliamentary appointment dates from 1522. Black Rod is responsible for maintaining order in the House and summons members of the Commons to the Lords to hear a speech from the throne.

blasphemy　*n.* Statements or writings that deny – in an offensive or insulting manner – the truth of the Christian religion, the Bible, the Book of Common Prayer, or the existence of God. Blasphemy is a crime at common law, and if it is published there is no need to show an intention to shock or insult or an awareness that the publication is blasphemous. Prosecutions for blasphemy are now rare and it has been suggested that the crime be abolished.

blight notice A statutory notice by which an owner-occupier can require a public authority to purchase land that is potentially liable to compulsory acquisition by them and therefore cannot be sold at full value on the open market. The land may, for example, be shown in a development plan to be prospectively required for the authority's purposes or it may be designated in published proposals as the site of a future highway.

blockade *n.* The act of a belligerent power of preventing access to or egress from the ports of its enemy by stationing a ship or squadron in such a position that it can intercept vessels attempting to approach or leave such ports. A neutral merchant vessel trying to break through a blockade is liable to capture and condemnation by the captor's *prize court.

block exemption Exemption from *Article 81 of the Treaty of Rome for certain types of anticompetitive agreements that fall within the scope of special EU regulations that have direct effect in the EU (*see* COMMUNITY LEGISLATION). Block exemptions exist in a number of different areas, including *vertical agreements and agreements relating to motor-vehicle distribution, research and development, specialization, and *technology transfer. The regulations are published in the EU's *Official Journal*; any agreement that complies with the regulations will be exempt from Article 81. Many contracts in the EU are drafted to comply with the block exemption regulations by using the wording of those regulations in the agreements themselves. Block exemptions can also be issued under UK competition law. EU block exemptions provide an automatic exemption from the provisions of UK competition law in the Competition Act 1998.

blood relationship *See* CONSANGUINITY.

blood specimen *See* SPECIMEN OF BLOOD.

blood test **1.** An analysis of blood designed to show that a particular man could not be the father of a specified child (it cannot establish that the person *is* the father). The court may order blood tests in disputes about paternity, but a man cannot be compelled to undergo the test against his will. His refusal may, however, lead the court to draw adverse conclusions. Any attempt to take blood without consent would be trespass. *See also* DNA FINGERPRINTING. **2.** *See* SPECIMEN OF BLOOD.

blue book A form of government publication, such as a report of a committee, inquiry, or royal commission, published in blue covers. *See also* PARLIAMENTARY PAPERS.

board of inquiry A body convened by naval, army, or air force authorities to investigate and report upon the facts of any happening (e.g. the loss or destruction of service property), particularly for the purpose of determining whether or not disciplinary proceedings should be instituted.

bodily harm *See* ACTUAL BODILY HARM; ASSAULT; GRIEVOUS BODILY HARM.

body corporate *See* CORPORATION.

bomb hoax A deception in which one or more people are led to believe that an explosion is likely to occur that will cause physical injury or damage to property. A bomb hoax may constitute *blackmail (if accompanied by a demand), public nuisance, threats to damage property (an offence under the Criminal Damage Act 1971), or wasting the time of the police (under the Criminal Law Act 1967). Under the Criminal Law Act 1977 it is a special statutory offence, punishable by imprisonment for up to five years and/or a fine, to place or send an object anywhere with the intention of leading someone to believe that it is likely to explode and cause harm.

It is also an offence falsely to tell anyone that a bomb has been placed in a certain place or that some other object is liable to explode.

bona vacantia [Latin: empty goods] Property not disposed of by a deceased's will and to which there is no relation entitled on intestacy. Under the Administration of Estates Act 1925, such property passes to the Crown, the Duchy of Lancaster, or the Duke of Cornwall. In practice it is usually used to make *ex gratia* payments, at the discretion of the Crown, Duchy, or Duke, to any dependants of the deceased and anyone else for whom he might reasonably have been expected to provide.

bond *n.* **1.** A deed by which one person (the **obligor**) commits himself to another (the **obligee**) to do something or refrain from doing something. If it secures the payment of money, it is called a **common money bond**; a bond giving security for the carrying out of a contract is called a **performance bond**. **2.** A document issued by a government, local authority, company, or other public body undertaking to repay long-term debt with interest. **Bond issues** are issues of debt securities by a borrower to investors in return for the payment of a subscription price.

bonus issue (capitalization issue) A method of increasing a company's issued capital (*see* AUTHORIZED CAPITAL) by issuing further shares to existing company members. These shares are paid for out of undistributed profits of the company, the *share premium account, or the *capital redemption reserve. The bonus issue is made to shareholders in proportion to their existing shareholding (e.g. a 1 for 2 bonus issue means that shareholders receive an extra free share for every two shares they hold).

books of account (accounting records) Records that disclose and explain a company's financial position at any time and enable its directors to prepare its *accounts. The books (which registered companies are required to keep by the Companies Act) should reveal, on a day-to-day basis, sums received and expended together with details of the transaction, assets and liabilities, and (where appropriate) goods sold and purchased. Public companies must preserve their books for six years, private companies for three years. Company officers and *auditors (but not members) have a statutory right to inspect the books.

borough *n.* An area of local government, abolished as such (except in *Greater London) by the Local Government Act 1972. A *district may, however, be styled a borough by royal charter. Originally, a borough was a fortified town; later, a town entitled to send a representative to Parliament.

borough court An inferior *court of record for the trial of civil actions by charter, custom, or otherwise in a borough. All remaining borough courts were abolished in 1974 by the Local Government Act 1972.

borstal *n.* An institution to which young offenders (aged 15 to 20 inclusive) could be sent before June 1983 instead of prison. Sentence to borstal has been replaced by *detention in a young offender institution. *See also* JUVENILE OFFENDER.

bottomry *n.* *See* HYPOTHECATION.

boundary *n.* (in international law) An imaginary line that determines the territorial limits of a state. Such boundaries define the limitation of each state's effective *jurisdiction. They are three-dimensional in nature in that they include the *airspace and subsoil of the state, the *terra firma* within the boundary, and the maritime domain of the state's internal waters and territorial sea. *See also* ACCRETION; AVULSION; THALWEG, RULE OF THE.

boundary commissions Independent bodies established under the Parliamentary

Constituencies Act 1986 to carry out periodic reviews of parliamentary constituencies for the purpose of recommending boundary changes to take account of shifts in population. There are separate commissions for England, Wales, Scotland, and Northern Ireland. *Compare* LOCAL GOVERNMENT BOUNDARY COMMISSIONS.

breach of close Entry on another's land without permission: a form of *trespass to land. A close is a piece of land separated off from land owned by others or from common land.

breach of confidence **1.** The disclosure of confidential information without permission. **2.** Failure to observe an injunction granted by the court to prevent this. The injunction is most commonly granted to protect *trade secrets (except patents, registered designs, and copyrights, which are protected under statute), but may also be granted, for example, to protect the secrecy of communications made between husband and wife during marriage or, possibly, between cohabitants during their period of cohabitation. The laws protecting confidential information exist at common law and will only restrain the dissemination of truly confidential information. Information that has been disclosed anywhere in the world, unless it was disclosed under conditions (usually a contract) of confidence, cannot subsequently be prevented from disclosure by the courts.

breach of contract An actual failure by a party to a contract to perform his obligations under that contract or an indication of his intention not to do so. An indication that a contract will be breached in the future is called **repudiation** or an **anticipatory breach**, and may be either expressed in words or implied from conduct. Such an implication arises when the only reasonable inference from a person's acts is that he does not intend to fulfil his part of the bargain. For example, an anticipatory breach occurs if a person contracts to sell his car to A, but sells and delivers it to B before the delivery date agreed with A. The repudiation of a contract entitles the injured party to treat the contract as discharged and to sue immediately for *damages for the loss sustained. The same procedure applies to an actual breach if it amounts to breach of a *condition (sometimes referred to as **fundamental breach**) or breach of an *innominate term when the consequences of breach are sufficiently serious. In either an anticipatory or actual breach, the injured party may, however, decide to *affirm the contract instead. When an actual breach amounts to breach of a *warranty, or breach of an innominate term and the consequences of breach are not sufficiently serious to allow for discharge, the injured party is entitled to sue for damages only. However, most commercial agreements provide a right to terminate the agreement even when the breach is minor, thus overriding the common law principle described here. The process of treating a contract as discharged by reason of repudiation or actual breach is sometimes referred to as *rescission or repudiation, but this latter term is clearly confusing. Other remedies available under certain circumstances for breach of contract are an *injunction and *specific performance. *See also* PROCURING BREACH OF CONTRACT.

breach of privilege *See* PARLIAMENTARY PRIVILEGE.

breach of statutory duty Breach of a duty imposed on some person or body by a statute. The person or body in breach of the statutory duty is liable to any criminal penalty imposed by the statute, but may also be liable to pay damages to the person injured by the breach if he belongs to the class for whose protection the statute was passed. Not all statutory duties give rise to civil actions for breach. If the statute does not deal with the matter expressly, the courts must decide whether or not Parliament intended to confer civil remedies. Most actions for breach of statutory duty arise out of statutes dealing with *safety at work.

breach of the peace The state that occurs when harm is done or likely to be done to a person or (in his presence) to his property, or when a person is in fear of being harmed through an *assault, *affray, or other disturbance. At common law, anyone may lawfully arrest a person for a breach of the peace committed in his presence, or when he reasonably believes that a person is about to commit or renew such a breach. To breach the peace is a crime in Scotland; elsewhere, magistrates may *bind over a person to keep the peace. See also ARREST; OFFENCES AGAINST PUBLIC ORDER.

breach of trust Any improper act or omission, contrary to the duties imposed upon him by the terms of the trust, by a trustee or other person in a fiduciary position. A breach need not be deliberate or dishonest. In all cases the trustee is personally responsible to the beneficiaries and is liable for any loss caused to the trust. Any profit made by a trustee by virtue of his position must be handed to the trust, even when the trust has suffered no loss.

break clause A clause often contained in *fixed-term tenancy agreements that provides for an option to terminate the tenancy at a particular time or when a particular event occurs.

breakdown of marriage See MARITAL BREAKDOWN.

breathalyser n. A device, approved by the Secretary of State, that is used in the preliminary *breath test to measure the amount of alcohol in a driver's breath. Modern devices, such as the Lion Alcometer 7410, are battery-operated. The suspect blows through a tube and lights indicate when sufficient breath has been delivered and the range within which the alcohol level falls. Earlier devices were based on a tube attached to a balloon, which the suspect had to inflate in one breath: a change in the colour of crystals inside the tube indicated that there was alcohol in the breath. A breathalyser should not be used within 20 minutes after consuming alcohol or on a suspect who has just been smoking. Constables must give instructions; testing suspects who have difficulty with breathing requires special care.

breath specimen See SPECIMEN OF BREATH.

breath test A preliminary test applied by a uniformed police officer by means of a *breathalyser to a driver whom he suspects has alcohol in his body in excess of the legal limit, has committed a traffic offence while the car was moving, or has driven a motor vehicle involved in an accident. The test may be administered on the spot to someone either actually driving, attempting to drive, or in charge of a motor vehicle on a road or public place or suspected by the police officer of having done so in the above circumstances. If the test proves positive (see DRUNKEN DRIVING), the police officer may arrest the suspect without a warrant and take him to a police station, where further investigations may take place (see SPECIMEN OF BREATH). It is an offence to refuse to submit to a breath test unless there is some reasonable excuse (usually a medical reason), and a police officer may arrest without warrant anyone who refuses the test. The offence is punishable by a fine, endorsement (carrying 4 points under the *totting-up system), and discretionary disqualification. A police officer has the power to enter any place in order to apply the breath test to someone he suspects of having been involved in an accident in which someone else was injured or to arrest someone who refused the test or whose test was positive.

brewster sessions The annual meetings of licensing justices to deal with the grant, renewal, and transfer of licences to sell intoxicating liquor. *See* LICENSING OF PREMISES.

bribery and corruption Offences relating to the improper influencing of people in certain positions of trust. The offences commonly grouped under this expression are now statutory. Under the Public Bodies Corrupt Practices Act 1889 (amended by the Prevention of Corruption Act 1916) it is an offence, if done corruptly (i.e. deliberately and with an improper motive), to give or offer to a member, officer, or servant of a public body any reward or advantage to do anything in relation to any matter with which that body is concerned; it is also an offence for a public servant or officer to corruptly receive or solicit such a reward. The Prevention of Corruption Act 1906 (amended by the 1916 Act) is wider in scope. It relates to agents, which include not only those involved in the business of agency but also all employees, including anyone serving under the Crown or any public body. Under this Act it is an offence to corruptly give or offer any valuable consideration to an agent to do any act or show any favour in relation to his principal's affairs; like the 1889 Act, it also creates a converse offence of receiving or soliciting by agents.

bridle way Under the Highways Act 1980, a *highway over which the public has a right of way on foot and a right of way on horseback or leading a horse, with or without a right to drive animals along the highway. *See also* DRIFTWAY.

brief *n.* A document by which a solicitor instructs a barrister to appear as an advocate in court. Unless the client is receiving financial support from the Community Legal Service, the brief must be marked with a fee that is paid to counsel whether he is successful or not. A brief usually comprises a **backsheet**, typed on large brief-size paper giving the title of the case and including the solicitor's instructions, which is wrapped around the other papers relevant to the case. The whole bundle is tied up with red tape in the case of a private client and white tape if the brief is from the Crown.

British citizenship One of three forms of citizenship introduced by the British Nationality Act 1981, which replaced citizenship of the UK and Colonies. The others are *British Dependent Territories citizenship and *British Overseas citizenship.

On the date on which it came into force (1 January 1983), the Act conferred British citizenship automatically on every existing citizen of the UK and Colonies who was entitled to the right of abode in the UK under the Immigration Act 1971 (*see* IMMIGRATION). As from that date, there have been four principal ways of acquiring the citizenship – by birth, by descent, by registration, and by naturalization. A person acquires it by birth only if he is born in the UK and his father or mother is either a British citizen or settled in the UK (i.e. resident there, and not restricted by the immigration laws as to length of stay). If born outside the UK, he acquires it by descent if one of his parents has British citizenship (but not, normally, if that citizenship was itself acquired by descent). The British Nationality (Falkland Islands) Act 1983 makes special provisions to confer British citizenship on those people with connections with the Falkland Islands. The British Nationality (Hong Kong) Act 1997 gave additional rights to certain people from Hong Kong to acquire British citizenship "by descent" or "otherwise than with descent". Registration may be applied for by a minor, but adults are eligible only if they have particular links with the UK. In some cases (e.g. British Dependent Territories citizens, British Overseas citizens, British protected persons, and British subjects with certain residential qualifications), it is a right; in others, it is at the discretion of the Secretary of State.

Any adult may apply for naturalization but there are residential and other requirements (e.g. proof of good character), and its grant is always discretionary.

A registered or naturalized citizen may be deprived of his citizenship if he obtained it improperly, behaves disloyally, or is sentenced during the first five years to imprisonment exceeding one year.

British Commonwealth *See* COMMONWEALTH.

British Dependent Territories citizenship One of three forms of citizenship introduced by the British Nationality Act 1981 to replace citizenship of the UK and Colonies. The others are *British citizenship and *British Overseas citizenship. The dependent territories for the purposes of this form of citizenship are listed in a schedule to the Act; they include Bermuda and Gibraltar, among others.

On the date on which it came into force (1 January 1983), the Act conferred the citizenship automatically on a large number of existing citizens of the UK and Colonies on the grounds of birth, registration, or naturalization in a dependent territory or descent from a parent or grandparent who had that citizenship on one of those grounds. As from that date, acquisition (and deprivation in the case of registered or naturalized citizens) have been governed by principles similar to those applying to British citizenship, except that acquisition by registration relates almost exclusively to minors. A British Dependent Territories citizen can become entitled to registration as a British citizen by virtue of UK residence. On 1 July 1997, those who were British Dependent Territories citizens by virtue of a connection with Hong Kong ceased to be British Dependent Territories citizens. However, they were entitled to acquire a new form of British nationality, known as *British National (Overseas), by registration.

British National (Overseas) A form of British nationality that those who were *British Dependent Territories citizens by virtue of a connection with Hong Kong may acquire by registration. They ceased to be British Dependent Territories citizens on 1 July 1997.

British Overseas citizenship One of three forms of citizenship introduced by the British Nationality Act 1981 to replace citizenship of the UK and Colonies. On the date on which it came into force (1 January 1983), the Act conferred the citizenship automatically on every existing citizen of the UK and Colonies who did not qualify for either of the other new forms (*British citizenship and *British Dependent Territories citizenship). Acquisition as from that date has been by registration only, and this is confined almost completely to minors. A British Overseas citizen may become entitled to registration as a British citizen by virtue of UK residence.

British protected person One of a class of people defined as such by an order under the British Nationality Act 1981 or the Solomon Islands Act 1978 because of their connection with former protectorates, protected states, and trust territories. A British protected person may become entitled to registration as a British citizen by reason of UK residence.

British subject Under the British Nationality Act 1948, a secondary status that was common to all who were primarily citizens either of the UK and Colonies or of one of the independent Commonwealth countries. This status was also shared by a limited number of people who did not have any such primary citizenship, including former British subjects who were also citizens of Eire (as it then was) or who could have acquired one of the primary citizenships but did not in fact do so.

Under the British Nationality Act 1981 (which replaced the 1948 Act as from 1 January 1983), the status of British subject was confined to those who had enjoyed it under the former Act without having one of the primary citizenships; the expression *commonwealth citizen was redefined as a secondary status of more universal application. The Act provided for minors to be able to apply for registration as British subjects and for British subjects to become entitled to registration as British citizens by virtue of UK residence.

Broadmoor A *special hospital at Crowthorne, near Camberley, in Berkshire. It treats dangerous and violent patients (previously known as criminal lunatics) who are sent to it.

brothel n. A place used for the purpose of female or male *prostitution. A contract for the hiring or letting of a brothel is void (as being contrary to public policy) and under the Sexual Offences Act 1956 it is an offence for a landlord to let premises knowing that they are to be used as a brothel. It is also an offence for someone to help or manage a brothel or for a tenant or occupier of any premises to permit the premises to be used as a brothel.

Brussels Convention An international convention of 1968 that determines which courts will have jurisdiction in relation to international disputes (see FOREIGN JUDGMENTS). Generally, if a contract provides that a certain country's courts will hear any disputes that arise, this will be respected. The Convention also provides rules when the parties have not chosen a forum for their disputes. Many EU states are individually a party to the Convention; the UK signed up to it in 1978 and enacted it into national law in 1982.

Bryan Treaties (Bryan Arbitration Treaties) [named after William Jennings Bryan, US Secretary of State 1913–15] The series of treaties, signed at Washington in 1914, that established permanent commissions of inquiry. Such inquiries were designed to resolve differences between the United States of America and a large number of foreign states. The treaties were not all identical, but had the following key feature in common: the *high contracting parties agreed (1) to refer all disputes that diplomatic methods had failed to resolve to a Permanent International Commission for investigation and report, and (2) not to begin hostilities before the report was submitted. See also INQUIRY.

Budget n. See CHANCELLOR OF THE EXCHEQUER.

buggery (sodomy) n. Anal intercourse by a man with another man or a woman or *bestiality by a man or a woman. Except between consenting adults over 16 in private (see also HOMOSEXUAL CONDUCT), buggery is a crime if penetration is proved (it is not necessary for there to be ejaculation). The person effecting the intercourse is guilty as the **agent**, and the other party is called (and is guilty as) the **patient**. However, criminal proceedings are not brought without the consent of the *Director of Public Prosecutions against anyone under 16 for participating in buggery. It is also an offence (punishable by up to 10 years' imprisonment) to assault anyone with the intention of committing buggery. See also GROSS INDECENCY; INDECENCY; INDECENT ASSAULT.

bugging n. See ELECTRONIC SURVEILLANCE.

building lease A lease under which the tenant covenants to erect specified buildings on the land. Sometimes the lease only begins when the buildings have been erected. At the end of the lease the buildings generally become the property of the landlord. It used to be common for residential property to be built under a building lease, usually for 99 years, under which the landlord would let to a builder at a rent that ignored the value of the buildings (*ground rent), and the builder would sell the lease to a tenant. Under a lease of this kind, the tenant may acquire a statutory right to purchase the freehold under the Leasehold Reform Act 1967.

building preservation notice A notice by a local planning authority (*see* TOWN AND COUNTRY PLANNING) that places a building regarded as suitable for listing and in danger of demolition or alteration under temporary control as a *listed building, pending a decision on its listing by the Secretary of State.

building scheme A defined area of land sold by a single vendor in plots for (or following) development, each plot being sold subject to similar *restrictive covenants that are clearly intended to benefit the whole. For example, restrictive covenants prohibiting trade or excessive noise are frequently imposed on the sale of plots on a housing estate, to maintain the character of the estate as a whole. The law allows the owner of any plot in a building scheme to enforce such covenants against any other plot owner, even though neither was a party to the document that imposed the covenants.

building society A corporation established under the Building Societies Acts for the purpose of making loans to its members on the security of mortgages on their homes, out of funds invested by its members. Generally a building society's security must be a first legal mortgage on the borrower's home. However, the Building Societies Act 1986 now empowers societies to lend on the security of second mortgages and to provide a wide range of banking and other financial services.

Bullock order [from the case *Bullock* v *London General Omnibus Co.* (1907)] A form of order for the payment of costs in civil cases sometimes made when the claimant has, in the court's opinion, reasonably sued two defendants but has succeeded against only one of them. The order requires the claimant to pay the successful defendant's costs but allows him to include these costs in those payable to him by the unsuccessful defendant. It should be distinguished from a **Sanderson order** (from the case *Sanderson* v *Blyth Theatre Co.*, 1903), in which the unsuccessful defendant is ordered to pay the costs of the successful defendant directly. A Sanderson order is generally more advantageous to the claimant, but will not be ordered if, for example, the unsuccessful defendant is insolvent, because the successful defendant would thereby be deprived of his costs.

burden of proof The duty of a party to litigation to prove a fact or facts in issue. Generally the burden of proof falls upon the party who substantially asserts the truth of a particular fact (the prosecution or the claimant). A distinction is drawn between the **persuasive** (or **legal**) **burden**, which is carried by the party who as a matter of law will lose the case if he fails to prove the fact in issue; and the **evidential burden** (**burden of adducing evidence** or **burden of going forward**), which is the duty of showing that there is sufficient evidence to raise an issue fit for the consideration of the *trier of fact as to the existence or nonexistence of a fact in issue.

The normal rule is that a defendant is presumed to be innocent until he is proved guilty; it is therefore the duty of the prosecution to prove its case by establishing both the *actus reus* of the crime and the *mens rea*. It must first satisfy the evidential burden to show that its allegations have something to support them. If it cannot satisfy this burden, the defence may submit or the judge may direct that there is *no case to answer, and the judge must direct the jury to acquit. The prosecution may sometimes rely on presumptions of fact to satisfy the evidential burden of proof (e.g. the fact that a woman was subjected to violence during sexual intercourse will normally raise a presumption to support a charge of rape and prove that she did not consent). If, however, the prosecution has established a basis for its case, it must then continue to satisfy the persuasive burden by proving its case beyond reasonable doubt (*see also* PROOF BEYOND REASONABLE DOUBT). It is the duty of the judge to tell the jury clearly that the prosecution must prove its case and that it must prove it beyond reasonable doubt; if he does not give this clear direction, the defendant is entitled to be acquitted.

There are some exceptions to the normal rule that the burden of proof is upon the prosecution. The main exceptions are as follows. (1) When the defendant admits the elements of the crime (the *actus reus* and *mens rea*) but pleads a special defence, the evidential burden is upon him to create at least a reasonable doubt in his favour. This may occur, for example, in a prosecution for murder in which the defendant raises a defence of self-defence. (2) When the defendant pleads *coercion, *diminished responsibility, or *insanity, both the evidential and persuasive burden rest upon him. In this case, however, it is sufficient if he proves his case on a balance of probabilities (i.e. he must persuade the jury that it is more likely that he was insane than not). (3) In some cases statute expressly places a persuasive burden on the defendant; for example, a person who carries an *offensive weapon in public is guilty of an offence unless he proves that he had lawful authority or a reasonable excuse for carrying it.

burglary *n.* The offence, under the Theft Act 1968, of either entering a building, ship, or inhabited vehicle (e.g. a caravan) as a trespasser with the intention of committing one of four specified crimes in it (**burglary with intent**) or entering it as a trespasser only but subsequently committing one of two specified crimes in it (**burglary without intent**). The four specified crimes for burglary with intent are (1) *theft; (2) inflicting *grievous bodily harm; (3) causing *criminal damage; and (4) rape of a person in the building (*see also* ULTERIOR INTENT). The two specified offences for burglary without intent are (1) stealing or attempting to steal; and (2) inflicting or attempting to inflict grievous bodily harm. Burglary is punishable by up to 14 years' imprisonment. **Aggravated burglary**, in which the trespasser is carrying a weapon of offence, explosive, or firearm, may be punished by a maximum sentence of life imprisonment. The Crime (Sentences) Act 1997 provides for an automatic three-year minimum sentence for third-time burglars, although judges may give a lesser sentence if the court considers the minimum would be unjust in all the circumstances. *See also* REPEAT OFFENDER.

Business Expansion Scheme *See* ENTERPRISE INVESTMENT SCHEME.

business liability Liability (contractual or tortious) for a breach of obligations or duties arising in the course of a business (which can include the activities of a government department or local or public authority) or from the occupation of business premises. The Unfair Contract Terms Act 1977 and, for consumer contracts, the Unfair Terms in Consumer Contracts Regulations 1999 limit the extent to which a person may rely on terms in his contracts that attempt to exclude or restrict his business liability (*see* EXCLUSION AND RESTRICTION OF NEGLIGENCE LIABILITY).

business name The name, other than its own, under which a sole trader, partnership, or company carries on business. The choice of a business name is restricted by the Business Names Act 1985 and by the common law of *passing off. The true names and addresses of the individuals concerned must be disclosed in documents issuing from the business and upon business premises. Contravention of the Act may lead to a fine and to inability to enforce contracts. *See also* COMPANY NAME.

business tenancy A *tenancy of premises that are occupied for the purposes of a trade, profession, or employment. Business tenants have special statutory protection.

If the landlord serves a notice to quit, the tenant can usually apply to the courts for a new tenancy. If the landlord wishes to oppose the grant of a new tenancy he must show that he has statutory grounds, which may include breaches of the tenant's obligations under the tenancy agreement or the provision of suitable alternative accommodation by the landlord. Otherwise the court will grant a new tenancy on whatever terms the parties agree or, if they cannot agree, on whatever terms the court considers reasonable. When the tenancy ends, the tenant may claim compensation for any improvements he has made.

Under the Landlord and Tenant (Covenants) Act 1995, in force from 1 January 1996, when business tenancies are assigned the new tenant generally takes over the covenants (or promises and warranties) of the first tenant in the lease except when otherwise agreed. Previously the old tenant was always liable, even after *assignment, if a subsequent tenant defaulted on the lease

buyer n. The party to a contract for the sale of goods who agrees to acquire ownership of the goods and to pay the price. *See also* PURCHASER.

byelaw n A form of *delegated legislation, made principally by local authorities. District and London borough councils have general powers to make byelaws for the good rule and government of their areas, and all local authorities have powers to make them on a wide range of specific matters (e.g. public health). Certain public corporations (such as the British Airports Authority) also make byelaws for the regulation of their undertakings. A statutory power to make byelaws includes a power to rescind, revoke, amend, or vary them. By contrast with most other forms of delegated legislation, byelaws are not subject to any form of parliamentary control but take effect if confirmed by a government minister. It is common for central government to prepare draft byelaws that may be made by such authorities as choose to do so. Byelaws are, however, subject to judicial control by means of the doctrine of *ultra vires.

C

C *See* COMMAND PAPERS.

Cabinet *n.* A body of *ministers (normally about 20) consisting mostly of heads of chief government departments but also including some ministers with few or no departmental responsibilities; it is headed by the *Prime Minister, in whose gift membership lies. As the principal executive body under the UK constitution, its function is to formulate government policy and to carry it into effect (particularly by the initiation of legislation). The Cabinet has no statutory foundation and exists entirely by convention, although it has been mentioned in statute from time to time, e.g. in the Ministers of the Crown Act 1937, which provided additional salaries to "Cabinet Ministers". The Cabinet is bound by the convention of **collective responsibility**, i.e. all members should fully support Cabinet decisions; a member who disagrees with a decision must resign. If the government loses a vote of confidence, or suffers any other major defeat in the House of Commons, the whole Cabinet must resign.

cabotage *n.* Transport services provided in one member state of the EU by a carrier of another state. Article 71 (formerly 75) of the Treaty of Rome provides that the Council of the European Union may lay down proposals in relation to the conditions under which nonresident carriers may operate transport services within a member state.

CAC *See* CENTRAL ARBITRATION COMMITTEE.

Cafcass *See* CHILDREN AND FAMILY COURT ADVISORY AND SUPPORT SERVICE.

Calderbank letter (Calderbank offer) Formerly, a letter sent by one party to a civil action, in which a remedy other than debt or damages is claimed, to another offering to compromise the action on terms specified in the letter. The first such letter was sent in the case *Calderbank* v *Calderbank* (1976). Calderbank offers are now (since the introduction of the *Civil Procedure Rules in 1999) known as *Part 36 offers.

call *n.* **1.** A ceremony at which students of the Inns of Court become barristers. The name of the student is read out and he is "called to the Bar" by the Treasurer of his Inn. Call ceremonies take place four times a year, once in each dining term. **2.** A demand by a company under the terms of the articles of association or an ordinary resolution requiring company members to pay up fully or in part the nominal value of their shares. Unless the articles provide otherwise, calls must be made equally upon all shareholders of the same class. Calls should be distinguished from **instalments**, which become due upon a date predetermined at the time the shares were issued. *See also* PAID-UP CAPITAL.

calling the jury Announcing the names of those selected to serve on a jury as a result of a ballot of the jury panel.

Calvo clause [named after the Argentine jurist Carlos Calvo (1824–1906)] A clause in a contract stating that the parties to the contract agree to rely exclusively on domestic remedies in the event of a dispute. The insertion of such a clause in a contract was an attempt, originally by Latin American countries, to eliminate diplomatic intervention should a dispute arise with a foreign national: by making such a contract the foreign national was said to have renounced the protection of his government. The clause is in effect in most cases superfluous – firstly, because diplomatic intervention belongs to the state only, and thus cannot be renounced by an individual; and secondly, because the exhaustion of local remedies is always taken to be a *condition precedent to appealing for diplomatic intervention. Since the 1930s such clauses have not been used in international disputes.

cancellation *n.* **1.** (in equity) An order by the court that specified documents should no longer have effect. This may occur when a document has fulfilled its purpose but its continued existence could lead to improper claims against its maker. **2.** (in commercial law) The right to cancel a commercial contract after it has been entered into. The right to cancel exists generally for contracts concluded at a distance (*see* DISTANCE SELLING), such as mail order and Internet sales when the contract is with a *consumer, and in particular in such sectors as time-share sales and consumer credit.

cannabis *n.* A drug obtained from the crushed leaves and flowers of the hemp plant (*Cannabis sativa*); under the Misuse of Drugs Act 1971 cannabis is defined as a *controlled drug of Class B, but in October 2001 the Home Secretary announced a decision to reclassify it as a Class C drug. In addition to the offences applying to all controlled drugs, there is a specific offence applying only to cannabis and cannabis resin (and also to prepared opium): it is an offence for an occupier, landlord, or property manager to allow these substances to be smoked on the premises he occupies or manages.

cannon-shot rule The rule by which a state has territorial sovereignty of that coastal sea within three miles of land. Its name derives from the fact that in the 17th century this limit roughly corresponded to the outer range of coastal artillery weapons and therefore reflected the principle *terrae dominum finitur, ubi finitur armorium vis* (the dominion of the land ends where the range of weapons ends). The rule is now not widely recognized: many nations have established a 6- or 12-mile coastal limit. *See also* TERRITORIAL WATERS.

canonical disability *See* IMPOTENCE.

canon law (ecclesiastical law) Church law, such as the Roman Catholic Code of Canon Law and, in England, the law of the Church of England. Unless subsequently becoming *legislation or *custom, it is not part of the laws of England but is binding on the clergy and lay people holding ecclesiastical office, e.g. churchwardens. *See* ECCLESIASTICAL COURTS.

CAP *See* COMMON AGRICULTURAL POLICY.

capacity of a child in criminal law *See* DOLI CAPAX.

capacity to contract Competence to enter into a legally binding agreement. The main categories of persons lacking this capacity in full are minors, the mentally disordered, the drunk, and corporations other than those created by royal charter.

A minor is capable of making valid contracts for *necessaries and is also bound by any beneficial contract of service into which he enters (i.e. any contract of employment or training that is advantageous to him taken as a whole). Certain contracts of a proprietary nature (e.g. tenancy agreements, agreements to buy company shares, and partnership agreements) are voidable in that a minor may repudiate them either before he comes of age or within a reasonable time thereafter. If he fails to repudiate, he becomes fully bound. All other contracts made by a minor are unenforceable unless ratified by the minor when he comes of age (*see* RATIFICATION) unless the Minors Contracts Act 1987 applies. This Act gives the court the right to require the transfer of property acquired by a minor under a contract when it is just and equitable to do so and improves the rights of adults contracting with minors.

A contract made by a person who is mentally disordered or drunk is voidable if the other party knows that his disorder or drunkenness will prevent him from understanding what he is doing. This means that, subject to certain limitations, he can set the contract aside by *rescission.

A corporation incorporated by royal charter has full contractual capacity, but a statutory corporation has power to contract only for purposes connected with the objects for which it was incorporated. Other contracts are *ultra vires* and void.

capias *n.* [Latin: that you take] One of a group of writs of assistance conferring certain supplemental powers upon the sheriff in respect of the enforcement of judgment. Such writs are now obsolete.

capital **1. (share capital)** A fund representing the contributions given to the company by shareholders in return for their shares. These assets are intended to protect the interests of any creditors in the event of a *limited company encountering financial difficulties, and there are rules under the Companies Act 1985 to ensure that this fund is not reduced unless it is absolutely necessary. Each share is assigned a **nominal** or **par value** to enable each holder to measure his interest in and liability to the company. In a company limited by shares (*see* LIMITED COMPANY) the liability of a shareholder is limited to the unpaid purchase price of the share. If a company is able to command a market price for a share that is above the nominal value assigned to it, the difference is said to represent a **premium**. The total number of shares and their nominal values must be stated in the capital clause of the *memorandum of association and represents the company's **authorized share capital**. *See* AUTHORIZED CAPITAL. **2.** *See* LOAN CAPITAL.

capital allowance A tax allowance for businesses on capital expenditure on particular items. These include *machinery and plant, industrial buildings, agricultural buildings, mines and oil wells, energy-saving equipment, and scientific equipment. For other types of expenditure neither the capital cost nor the depreciation is allowable against tax. The percentage of the expenditure allowed varies (up to 100%) according to the type of expenditure. If a business's capital allowances exceed its profit, it may carry forward the balance for setting against future profits.

capital gains tax A tax charged on gains arising from the disposal of assets. The tax due is a proportion of the **chargeable gain**, which in general terms is the amount by which the proceeds of the disposal exceed the original cost of acquiring the asset. If the disposal results in a loss, this may be offset against other chargeable gains in the same year or subsequent years. Assets that may be taxed in this way include stocks, shares, unit trusts, land, buildings, machinery, jewellery, and works of art. There are, however, a number of exemptions, including private motor vehicles, an individual's *main residence, National Savings Certificates, and most personal chattels with an expected life of less than 50 years. Marketable government securities held for longer than 12 months are also exempt. Gains arising from the disposal of business assets may be offset against the cost of acquiring replacement assets. This is known as **roll-over relief**. Capital gains tax applies only to gains accruing since 31 March 1982. If the asset was held before this date, the gain is based on the asset's market value on 31 March 1982. The gain will be reduced by **taper relief** if the asset was held for more than one year. For example, a business asset owned for three years will have the gain reduced by 50%. The first £7500 (for

2001–02) of annual gains is exempt. The rate of tax is the taxpayer's marginal rate of income tax (10–40% in 2001–02).

capitalization issue See BONUS ISSUE.

capital money Money arising from certain transactions relating to *settled land or land held on a *trust of land. It may arise from sale, the granting of certain leases and similar transactions, borrowing on the security of a mortgage, and other circumstances in which the money should be treated as capital of the settlement, e.g. the proceeds of a fire insurance claim relating to the land. Generally capital money must be received by the trustees of the settlement, not the beneficiary. When the money is raised or paid for a specific purpose (e.g. for improvements authorized by the Settled Land Act 1925) it must be applied for that purpose. Otherwise, it is invested and held by the trustees on the same trusts as the land itself was held.

capital punishment Death (usually by hanging) imposed as a punishment for crime. Capital punishment for murder was abolished in the UK under the Murder (Abolition of Death Penalty) Act 1965. The death penalty continued to exist for a small number of offences, such as *piracy and *treason. The ratification by the UK of the Sixth Protocol of the European Convention on Human Rights and the introduction of the *Human Rights Act 1998 has meant that the death penalty is now completely abolished, apart from special provisions in respect of acts in times of war. Its reintroduction would be a violation of the Human Rights Act and, at an international level, a breach of a treaty obligation.

capital redemption reserve A fund established to protect creditors by ensuring that the assets representing a company's *capital are not reduced. In limited circumstances a company is permitted to buy back its own shares. If this is provided for by a term in the original share contract the company **redeems** its own shares. If no such term exists the company makes a **purchase of its own shares**. In either case the value of the capital sum will be reduced by the amount of the purchase or redemption unless an equal amount is transferred to a reserve that is subject to the same restrictions as the capital.

capital transfer tax (CTT) A tax formerly levied on property passing on death and on transfers of wealth during a person's lifetime. See INHERITANCE TAX.

capitulation n. **1.** An agreement under which a body of troops or a naval force surrenders upon conditions. The arrangement is a bargain made in the common interest of the contracting parties, one of which avoids the useless loss that is incurred in a hopeless struggle, while the other, besides also avoiding loss, is spared all further sacrifice of time and trouble. A capitulation must be distinguished from an **unconditional surrender**, which need not be effected on the basis of an instrument signed by both parties and is not an agreement. **2.** A system of extraterritorial jurisdiction, based partly upon custom and partly upon treaties of unilateral obligation, in which cases relating to foreign citizens were tried before diplomatic or consular courts operating in accordance with the laws of the states concerned. The practice is now obsolete, being a clear breach of the right of sovereign equality between states.

caravan n. For the purpose of collective *trespass and *powers of search in anticipation of violent disorder, any structure adapted for human habitation and capable of being moved from one place to another, either by being towed or being transported on a motor vehicle or trailer. See also UNAUTHORIZED CAMPING.

care and control Formerly, the right to the physical possession and control of the day-to-day activities of a minor. See PARENTAL RESPONSIBILITY; SECTION 8 ORDERS.

care contact order An order of the court allowing a local authority to restrict *contact with a child in care (*see* CARE ORDER). Under the Children Act 1989 there is a presumption that children in care will have reasonable contact with their parents (including unmarried parents) or those who have had care of them and a local authority must now seek a court order if it wishes to limit such contact.

careless and inconsiderate driving The offence of driving a motor vehicle on a road or other public place without due care and attention or without reasonable consideration for other road users. This is a *summary offence for which the maximum penalty is a *fine at level 4 on the standard scale and it carries 3–9 penalty points under the *totting-up system; *disqualification is discretionary. This offence, defined by the Road Traffic Act 1988 (in a section inserted by the Road Traffic Act 1991), replaces the former offences of careless driving and inconsiderate driving. *See also* CAUSING DEATH BY CARELESS DRIVING.

careless statement *See* NEGLIGENT MISSTATEMENT.

care or control Protection and guidance of a minor or the discipline of such a child. A court has authority to make orders in care proceedings only if it is satisfied that (in addition to other specified conditions) the child is in need of care or is beyond control. In this context it is not necessary to show that all his day-to-day needs are being neglected. *See* CARE ORDER.

care order A court order placing a child under the care of a local authority. Under the Children Act 1989 an application for a care order can only be made by a local authority, the NSPCC, or a person authorized by the Secretary of State. The court has the power to make a care order only when it is satisfied that a child is suffering or likely to suffer significant harm either caused by the care (or lack of care) given to it by its parents, or because the child is beyond parental control (the so-called **threshold criteria**). The phrase "significant harm", as defined in the Children Act, means ill treatment (including sexual abuse and forms of treatment that are not physical) or the impairment of health (either physical or mental) or development (whether physical, intellectual, emotional, social, or behavioural). Once the court is satisfied that the threshold criteria have been satisfied, it must decide whether a care order would be in the best interests of the child. In so doing, it should scrutinize the *care plan drawn up in respect of the child. The court may, instead of making a care order, make a *supervision order or a *section 8 order. Since the coming into force of the Human Rights Act 1998, the court must ensure that the granting of a care order will not be in breach of Article 8 (which guarantees a right to *family life); the court must be satisfied that any intervention by the state between parents and children is proportionate to the legitimate aim of protecting family life. A care order gives the local authority *parental responsibility for the child who is the subject of the order. Although parents retain their parental responsibility, in practice all major decisions relating to the child are made by the local authority. While the child is in care, the local authority cannot change the child's religion or surname or consent to an adoption order or appoint a guardian. There is a presumption that parents will have reasonable contact with their children while in care; if the local authority wishes to prevent this, it must apply for a court order to limit such contact. A parent with parental responsibility, the child itself, or the local authority may apply to discharge a care order. No care order can be made with respect to a child who is over the age of 16. A local authority can no longer use *wardship proceedings as an alternative means of obtaining a care order, nor may it take a child into care through administrative means. Before the Crime and Disorder Act 1998 came into force a care order could only be made if the threshold criteria were met. Now, however, the family proceedings court has the power to make a care order if a child is in breach of a *child safety order.

care plan A plan drawn up by a local authority in respect of a child it is looking after. The purpose of a care plan is to safeguard and promote the welfare of the child in accordance with the local authority's duties under the Children Act 1989. The plan will address such matters as where the child is be placed and the likely duration of such a placement, arrangements for contact between the child and its family, and what the needs of the child are and how these might be met. When a court is deciding whether or not to make a *care order or a *supervision order in respect of a child, the care plan is of crucial importance and must be scrutinized carefully.

care proceedings See CARE ORDER.

cargo *n.* Goods, other than the personal luggage of passengers, carried by a ship or aircraft. Normally (but not necessarily in relation to insurance) "cargo" denotes the whole of a ship's loading. Under a ship's charterparty, the freight payable to the shipowner is normally calculated at a rate per tonne of cargo. Unless otherwise agreed, the duty of the charterer is to provide a full and complete cargo: if he fails to do this, he is liable for damages known as **dead freight**.

carriage of goods by air The act of carrying goods by air, which is normally under a contract between the consignor and a *carrier. International carriage has been the subject of several international conventions: Warsaw (1929), The Hague (1955), Guadalajara (1961), Guatemala (1971), and Montreal (1975). The UK is party to a number of these Conventions, which have been given effect by the Carriage by Air Acts 1932, 1961, and 1962 and the Carriage by Air and Road Act 1979 (in part not yet in force). They deal with such matters as the nature and limit of the carrier's liability, who can sue and be sued, the right to stop in transit, the documentation of air carriage, and time limits for complaint.

carrier *n.* One who transports persons or goods from one place to another. Carriage is normally under a contract that may affect or limit the duties otherwise imposed by law, but such contracts may be subject to statutory control. Carriers of goods are bailees of the goods consigned. A **common carrier** is one who publicly undertakes to carry any goods or persons for payment on the routes he covers. A common carrier is subject to three common-law duties: (1) he must, if he has space, accept any goods of the type he carries or any person; (2) he must charge only a reasonable rate; and (3) he is strictly liable for all loss or damage to goods in the course of transit (*but see* INHERENT VICE). All other carriers are **private carriers**, and they owe only a duty of reasonable care.

carrier's lien The right of a common *carrier to retain possession of goods he has carried until he has been paid his freight or charge.

cartel *n.* **1.** An agreement between belligerent states for certain types of nonhostile transactions, especially the treatment and exchange of prisoners. **2.** A national or international association of independent enterprises formed to create a *monopoly in a given industry.

case *n.* **1.** A court *action. **2.** A legal dispute. **3.** The arguments, collectively, put forward by either side in a court action. **4. (action on the case)** A form of action abolished by the Judicature Acts 1873–75.

case law The body of law set out in judicial decisions, as distinct from *statute law. *See also* PRECEDENT.

case management Under the *Civil Procedure Rules (CPR), the new procedure for managing civil cases, as proposed in Lord Woolf's *Access to Justice* (Final Report) 1996. Under the new regime, the judge becomes the case manager. A case is allocated to one of three **tracks**, depending on the value of the dispute and the complexity of the case: the *small claims track, *fast track, or *multi-track. Each case is actively managed by the judge on a court-controlled timetable with the aims of encouraging and facilitating cooperation between the parties, identifying the areas in dispute, and encouraging settlement. The court can control progress and even 'strike out' an action. In considering the benefits of a particular way of hearing it can use a range of procedural devices to enforce discipline against lawyers not complying with CPR *pre-action protocols and/or *Practice Directions, including costs sanctions and refusing an extension of time.

case management conference Under the *Civil Procedure Rules, a central feature of *case management at which the judge reviews the progress of the case preparation, including the degree of compliance with *Practice Directions and *pre-action protocols. Legal representatives will attend, and the judge is able to make further directions as are considered necessary.

case stated A written statement of the facts found by a magistrates' court or tribunal (or by the Crown Court in respect of an appeal from a magistrates' court) submitted for the opinion of the High Court (Queen's Bench Divisional Court) on any question of law or jurisdiction involved. Any person who was a party to the proceedings or is aggrieved by the decision can request the court or tribunal to state a case; if it wrongly refuses, it can be compelled to do so by a *mandatory order.

casus belli [Latin: occasion for war] An event giving rise to war or used to justify war. The only legitimate *casus belli* now is an unprovoked attack necessitating self-defence on the part of the victim.

casus omissus [Latin: an omitted case] A case inadvertently not provided for in a defective statute.

catching bargain (unconscionable bargain) A contract on very unfair terms. An example is the sale of a future interest in property at a gross undervalue, made by someone with expectations to succeed to the property who is in immediate need of money. Such a contract may be set aside or modified by a court of equitable jurisdiction.

cattle trespass An early form of strict liability for damage done by trespassing cattle or other livestock (but not dogs or cats), replaced in England by the Animals Act 1971. Under the 1971 Act, the owner of livestock that strays on another's land and does damage to the land or any property on it is liable for the damage and any expenses incurred in keeping the livestock or ascertaining to whom it belongs. *See* CLASSIFICATION OF ANIMALS.

causa causans [Latin] The effective cause. *See* CAUSATION.

causation *n.* The relationship between an act and the consequences it produces. It is one of the elements that must be proved before an accused can be convicted of a crime in which the effect of the act is part of the definition of the crime (e.g. murder). Usually it is sufficient to prove that the accused had *mens rea* (intention or recklessness) in relation to the consequences; the *burden of proof is on the prosecution. In tort it must be established that the defendant's tortious conduct caused or contributed to the damage to the claimant before the defendant can be found liable for that damage. Sometimes a distinction is made between the effective or immediate cause (***causa causans***) of the damage and any other cause in the sequence of events leading up to it (***causa sine qua non***). Simple causation problems are solved by the "but for" test (would the damage have occurred but for the defendant's tort?), but this test is inadequate for cases of concurrent or cumulative causes (e.g. if the acts of two independent tortfeasors would each have been sufficient to produce the damage).

Sometimes a new act or event (***novus actus*** (or ***nova causa***) ***interveniens***) may break the legal chain of causation and relieve the defendant of responsibility. Thus if a house, which was empty because of a nuisance committed by the local authority, is occupied by squatters and damaged, the local authority is not responsible for the damage caused by the squatters. Similarly, if X stabs Y, who almost recovers from the wound but dies because of faulty medical treatment, X will not have "caused" the death. It has been held, however, that if a patient is dying from a wound and doctors switch off a life-support machine because he is clinically dead, the attacker, and not the doctors, "caused" the death. If death results because the victim has some unusual characteristic (e.g. a thin skull) or particular belief (e.g. he refuses a blood transfusion on religious grounds) there is no break in causation and the attacker is still guilty.

cause *n.* **1.** A court *action. **2.** *See* CAUSATION.

Cause Book The book recording the issue of claim forms in the *Central Office of the Supreme Court and certain later stages of the court proceedings.

Cause List A list of cases to be heard, displayed in the precincts of a court. The *Daily Cause List* lists all cases for trial in the Royal Courts of Justice and its outlying buildings. It also contains the **warned list** of cases about to be listed for hearing.

cause of action The facts that entitle a person to sue. The cause of action may be a wrongful act, such as *trespass; or the harm resulting from a wrongful act, as in the tort of *negligence.

causing death by careless driving The offence committed by someone whose driving while unfit through drink or drugs or driving over the prescribed limit (*see* DRUNKEN DRIVING) results in the death of another person. For this offence, which was created by the Road Traffic Act 1991, the driving must be judged careless (*see* CARELESS AND INCONSIDERATE DRIVING) rather than dangerous (*compare* CAUSING DEATH BY DANGEROUS DRIVING); the maximum punishment is five years' imprisonment and compulsory *disqualification.

causing death by dangerous driving The offence committed by someone guilty of *dangerous driving that results in the death of another person. The offence is defined by the Road Traffic Act 1991 and replaces the former offence of causing death by reckless driving (defined in the Road Traffic Act 1988). If the danger is such that there is an obvious and serious risk of injury to another person or significant damage to property – and the driver either recognizes the risk or fails to give any thought to the possibility that such a risk exists – this will constitute reckless *manslaughter in addition to causing death by dangerous driving. The maximum penalty for causing death by dangerous driving is ten years' imprisonment and compulsory *disqualification for not less than two years.

caution *n.* **1.** (in criminal law) **a.** A warning that should normally be given by a police officer, in accordance with a code of practice issued under the Police and Criminal Evidence Act 1984, when he has grounds for believing that a person has committed an offence and when arresting him. The caution is in the following terms: "You do not have to say anything. But it may harm your defence if you do not mention when questioned something which you later rely on in court. Anything you do say may be given in evidence." The caution must be given before any questions are put. If a person is not under arrest when a caution is given, the officer must say so; if he is at a police station the officer must also tell him that he is free to leave and remind him that he may obtain legal advice. The officer must record the caution in his pocket book or the interview record, as appropriate. *See* RIGHT OF SILENCE. **b.** A warning by a police officer, on releasing a suspect when it has been decided not to bring a prosecution against him, that if he is subsequently reported for any other offence, the circumstances relating to his first alleged offence may be taken into account. It is common practice for the police to give this type of caution, although the procedure has no statutory basis and there are no legal consequences if it is not followed. **2.** (in land law) A document lodged at the Land Registry by a person having an interest in registered land, requiring that no dealing with that land be registered until the cautioner has been notified, so that he may lodge an objection. For example, a caution might be lodged by someone who was induced by fraud to convey his land, in order to prevent the fraudulent transferee from registering his title. If a caution is lodged unreasonably the cautioner may be ordered to compensate anyone to whom it causes loss. The Land Registrar may order the caution to be vacated if he considers it to be unjust.

caveat *n.* [from Latin: let him beware] A notice, usually in the form of an entry in a register, to the effect that no action of a certain kind may be taken without first informing the person who gave the notice (the **caveator**). For example, a caveat may be filed in the Probate Registry by someone claiming an interest in a deceased person's estate. The caveat prevents anyone else from obtaining a *grant of representation without reference to the caveator, who may thus ensure that his claim is dealt with in the distribution of the estate.

caveat actor [Latin] Let the doer be on his guard.

caveat emptor [Latin: let the buyer beware] A common-law maxim warning a purchaser that he could not claim that his purchases were defective unless he protected himself by obtaining express guarantees from the vendor. The maxim has been modified by statute: under the Sale of Goods Act 1979 (a consolidating statute), contracts for the sale of goods have implied terms requiring the goods to correspond with their description and any sample and, if they are sold in the course of a business, to be of satisfactory quality and fit for any purpose made known to the seller. Each of these implied terms is a condition of the contract. However, in most commercial contracts the implied terms are excluded. This will usually be valid unless the exclusion is unreasonable or unfair under the law relating to unfair contract terms. These statutory conditions do not apply to sales of land, to which the maxim *caveat emptor* still applies as far as the condition of the property is concerned. However, a term is normally implied that the vendor must convey a good *title to the land, free from encumbrances that were not disclosed to the purchaser before the contract was made.

caveat subscriptor [Latin] Let the person signing (e.g. a contract) be on his guard.

caveat venditor [Latin] Let the seller be on his guard.

Cd *See* COMMAND PAPERS.

CE [French *Communauté européenne*: European Community] A marking applied to certain products, such as toys and machinery, to indicate that they have complied with certain EU directives that apply to them, including *electromagnetic compatibility. A CE marking is not a quality mark, but it indicates that health and safety and other legislation has been complied with. The manufacturer or first importer into the EU must apply the CE marking; fines can be levied for breach of the rules.

CELEX [Latin *Communitatis Europae Lex*: European Community Law] A database of EU material of a legislative nature, such as directives, regulations, and treaties, including national legislation. It is possible to access this electronically through the on-line data service EURIS.

Central Arbitration Committee (CAC) A statutory body, established under the Employment Protection Act 1975 (consolidated into the Trade Union and Labour Relations (Consolidation) Act 1992), that consists of a chairman and members appointed by the Secretary of State for Work and Pensions from persons nominated by *ACAS. The Committee determines disputes relating to. (1) arbitration in *trade disputes referred by ACAS with the consent of both parties; (2) *disclosure of information to trade unions; (3) the application of the Equal Pay Act 1970 (*see* EQUAL PAY) to collective agreements (*see* COLLECTIVE BARGAINING); (4) recognition of trade unions for the purpose of *collective bargaining (*see* RECOGNITION PROCEDURE); and (5) specified issues in relation to the introduction and operation of *European Works Councils.

When the Committee makes an award of pay and/or conditions of employment these generally become incorporated in the contracts of employment of individual employees and are enforceable in the courts.

Central Criminal Court The principal *Crown Court for Central London, usually known from its address as the **Old Bailey**. The Lord Mayor of London and any City aldermen may sit as judges with High Court or circuit judges or recorders. *See also* COMMON SERJEANT.

Central Office The administrative organization of the *Supreme Court of Judicature in London, from which claim forms are issued. Its business is superintended by the Queen's Bench Masters (*see* MASTERS OF THE SUPREME COURT), one of whom sits each day as **practice master** to give any directions that may be required on questions of practice and procedure.

certificate of incorporation A document issued by the Registrar of Companies after the *registration of a company, certifying that the company is incorporated (*see* INCORPORATION). For a *limited company, the certificate also certifies that the company members have limited liability, and for a *public company the fact that it is a public company. The validity of the incorporation cannot thereafter be challenged.

Certification Officer (CO) An official appointed by the Secretary of State for Work and Pensions (formerly Employment) under the Trade Union and Labour Relations (Consolidation) Act 1992, whose main duties concern the supervision of trade unions' and employers' associations' obligations as bodies corporate to keep accounting records and submit audited reports and accounts to him. He is also responsible for the certification of trade unions as independent in appropriate cases (*see* INDEPENDENT TRADE UNION). The powers of the CO were greatly increased by the Employment Relations Act 1999; in particular, the CO substantially took over the duties of both the Commissioner for the Rights of Trade Union Members and the Commissioner for the Protection Against Unlawful Industrial Action, which were abolished by that Act. *See* STRIKE; TRADE UNION.

certiorari *n.* [Latin: to be informed] *See* QUASHING ORDER.

certum est quod certum reddi potest [Latin] If something is capable of being made certain, it should be treated as certain. For example, a landlord can only distrain for rent (*see* DISTRESS) if the amount of rent is certain. However, if the amount of the rent is capable of being ascertained, it is treated as certain.

cessate grant A grant (e.g. of a lease) renewing a previous grant that has lapsed.

cesser *n.* The premature termination of some right or interest. For example, if land is held in trust for A for life so long as he does not marry and then for B, there is a cesser of A's life interest if he marries. A mortgage under which the mortgagor attorns tenant of the mortgagee (*see* ATTORNMENT) provides for cesser on redemption: thus the tenancy ends whenever the debt is repaid.

cesser clause A clause inserted in a charterparty when the charterer intends to transfer to a shipper his right to have goods carried. It provides that the shipowner is to have a lien over the shipper's goods for the freight payable under the charterparty, and that the charterer's liability for that freight will cease accordingly on shipment of a full cargo.

cession *n.* The transfer of sovereignty over a territory by means of a treaty. This may either be a peace treaty (e.g. the peace treaty between France and Germany in 1871 that made Alsace-Lorraine part of the German empire), a treaty to exchange territory (e.g. the treaty of 1890 whereby the UK ceded Heligoland to Germany in exchange for Zanzibar), or more rarely a treaty bestowing a gift. *See also* DERIVATIVE TITLE.

cestui que trust [Norman French, from *cestui à que trust*, he for whom is the trust] Formerly, a beneficiary under a trust.

cestui que use [Norman French, from *cestui à que use*, he to whose use] A person to whose use (i.e. for whose benefit) property was held by another. The modern equivalent is the *beneficiary. *See* USE.

cestui que vie [Norman French, from *cestui à que vie*, he for whose life] A person for whose life an interest in property is held by another person. *See* ESTATE PUR AUTRE VIE.

CET *See* COMMON EXTERNAL TARIFF.

CFP *See* COMMON FISHERIES POLICY.

CFSP (common foreign and security policy) *See* EUROPEAN UNION; MAASTRICHT TREATY.

chain of executorship (chain of representation) A rule under the Administration of Estates Act 1925 by which the executor of someone who was himself a sole or surviving executor stands, on the latter's death, in his place as executor of the testator who appointed him. Thus, if A appoints B as his only executor and B in turn appoints C as his own executor, on the death of A and B, C becomes the executor of both. The rule does not apply on intestacy or to an administrator, and the chain is broken by the failure of a testator to appoint an executor or a failure to obtain probate. *See also* DE BONIS NON ADMINISTRATIS.

challenge to jury A procedure by which the parties may object to the composition of a jury before it is sworn. Before the Criminal Justice Act 1988 came into force a challenge could be **peremptory** (i.e. with no reason for the challenge being given) or **for cause**. Peremptory challenges were abolished by the Criminal Justice Act 1988, but the prosecution can ask that a juror "stand by", in which case he rejoins the jury panel and may be challenged for cause when the rest of the panel has been gone through. Either party may challenge for cause. This may be **to the array**, in which the whole panel is challenged by alleging some irregularity in the summoning of the jury (e.g. bias or partiality on the part of the jury summoning officer); or **to the polls**, in which individual jurors may be challenged. Any challenge to jurors for cause is tried by the judge before whom the accused is to be tried.

chambers *pl. n.* **1.** The offices occupied by a barrister or group of barristers. (The term is also used for the group of barristers practising from a set of chambers.) **2.** The private office of a judge, master, or district judge. Most *interim proceedings are held in chambers (in private) and the public is not admitted, although judgment may be given in open court if the matter is one of public interest.

champerty *n.* *See* MAINTENANCE AND CHAMPERTY.

Chancellor of the Exchequer The minister who, as political head of the Treasury, is responsible for government monetary policy, raising national revenue (particularly through taxation), and controlling public expenditure in the UK. Each year he presents to Parliament a **Budget** (usually in March) proposing changes in revenue and taxation and a statement (in November) proposing government expenditure.

Chancery Division The division of the *High Court of Justice created by the Judicature Acts 1873–75 to replace the *Court of Chancery. The work of the Division is principally concerned with matters relating to real property, trusts, and the administration of estates but also includes cases concerned with company law, patents and other *intellectual property, and confidentiality cases. The effective head of the Division is the *Vice Chancellor, although the *Lord Chancellor is nominally its president. It may hear some *appeals. *See also* APPELLATE JURISDICTION; COMPANIES COURT.

Chancery Masters *See* MASTERS OF THE SUPREME COURT.

change of name A natural person (i.e. a human being) may change his or her *surname simply by using a different name with sufficient consistency to become generally known by that name. A change is normally given formal publicity (e.g. by means of a statutory declaration, deed poll, or newspaper advertisement), but this is not legally necessary. A woman can also change her surname through operation of law on getting married. A young child, however, has no power to change its surname, nor does one parent have such a power without the consent of the other. (An injunction may be sought to prevent a parent from attempting to change a child's name unilaterally.) When a mother has remarried after divorce or is living with another person, and wishes to change the name of the child to that of her new partner, a court order must be obtained and the welfare of the child will be the first and paramount consideration. A person's Christian name (i.e. a name given at baptism) can, under ecclesiastical law, be changed only by the bishop on that person's subsequent confirmation.

   A *juristic person may change its name but may be subject to formal procedure before the change of name takes effect; for example, for a company limited by shares, a change of name is possible only on the passing of a special resolution of the company at an extraordinary or annual general meeting.

Chapter VII The chapter of the United Nations Charter that is headed: "Action with respect to threats to the peace, breaches of the peace and acts of aggression" and includes Articles 39–51 of the Charter. Those who devised the UN Charter were acutely aware of the failure of the former Covenant of the League of Nations in respect of *collective security, namely (1) that it left it open to member states to respond, or not respond, to the call for military aid and (2) it provided no machinery or system for organizing League forces in advance or for coordinating such responses as members might make. Chapter VII addressed such problems by empowering the Security Council to orchestrate such collective actions under Articles 42 and 43. Under Articles 43–47 advance preparation of collective action was to be made through a *Military Staff Committee. Article 51 creates a right to *self-defence for member states; controversially, it is held to have preserved the wider scope of self-defence in customary international law. *See also* ENFORCEMENT ACTION.

character *n.* (in the law of evidence) **1.** The reputation of a party or witness. In civil cases the reputation of a party is not admissible unless it is directly in issue, as it may be in an action for *defamation. In criminal cases the accused may call evidence of his good character or give evidence to show the bad character of the witnesses for the prosecution. If he does so, the prosecution may call evidence in rebuttal, but any such evidence must be limited to evidence of reputation and not include opinions about the accused's *disposition. Evidence of the reputation for truthfulness of a witness may be given in both civil and criminal cases. **2.** Loosely, the disposition of a party.

charge *n.* **1.** A formal accusation of a crime, usually made by the police after *interrogation. *See also* INDICTMENT. **2.** Instructions given by a judge to a jury. **3.** A legal or equitable interest in land, securing the payment of money. It gives the creditor in whose favour the charge is created (the **chargee**) the right to payment from the income or proceeds of sale of the land charged, in priority to claims against the debtor by unsecured creditors. Under the Law of Property Act 1925 the only valid legal charges are: (1) a *rentcharge payable immediately and for a fixed period or in perpetuity; (2) a charge by way of legal *mortgage; and (3) certain charges arising under statute (e.g. under the Charging Orders Act 1979). All others take effect as equitable interests. All mortgages and charges over registered land must be registered to be enforceable against purchases of the land; both legal mortgages and *equitable charges over unregistered land must be registered as land charges unless the mortgagee or chargee holds the title deeds as security (*see* REGISTRATION OF ENCUMBRANCES). **4.** An interest in company property created in favour of a creditor (e.g. as a *debenture holder) to secure the amount owing. Most charges must be registered at the Companies Registry. A **fixed charge** is attached to specific assets (e.g. premises, plant and machinery) and while in force prevents the company from dealing freely with those assets without the consent of the lender. A **floating charge** does not immediately attach to any specific assets but 'floats' over all the company's assets until *crystallization. Until this point the company is free to deal freely with such assets; this type of charge is suitable for circulating assets (e.g. cash, stock in trade), whose values must necessarily fluctuate. In the event of the company not paying the debt the creditor can secure the amount owing in accordance with the terms of the charge. If the company goes into liquidation (*see* WINDING-UP) the order for repayment of debts laid down under the Insolvency Act 1986 is that fixed-charge holders are paid before floating-charge holders. A charge can also be created upon shares. For example, the articles of association usually give the company a *lien in respect of unpaid *calls, and company members may, in order to secure a debt owed to a third party, charge their shares, either by a full *transfer of shares coupled with an agreement to retransfer upon repayment of the debt or by a deposit of the *share certificate.

chargeable gain A profit made on the disposal of an asset, which may attract *capital gains tax or *corporation tax.

charge by way of legal mortgage *See* MORTGAGE.

charge certificate A certificate issued by the Land Registry to a legal mortgagee of registered land as evidence of his title. It will only be issued if the *land certificate is deposited at the Land Registry for the duration of the mortgage.

charge sheet A document in which an officer at a police station records an accusation against a suspect. It normally also gives details of his name and those of his accusers, who should sign the sheet.

charges register *See* LAND REGISTRATION.

charging clause A clause in a trust entitling a trustee to charge for his services. When a solicitor or some other professional person is appointed trustee, he is usually authorized to charge for his services. In the absence of such a clause neither he nor his firm is entitled to charge for his professional services, although he may recover expenses incurred during the course of his trusteeship.

charging order A court order obtained by a judgment creditor by which the judgment debtor's property (including money, land, and shares) becomes security for the payment of the debt and interest.

charitable trust A trust for purposes that the law regards as charitable. There is no statutory definition of 'charitable'. In a legal sense, a purpose is charitable only if it is for the furtherance of religion, for the advancement of education, for the relief of poverty, or for other purposes beneficial to the community. In every case the purpose must be for the benefit of the public or a section of it (though in cases of relief of poverty this is very easily satisfied); the precise meaning depends on the class of charity in question. The last class is taken to include every object of general utility to the public; it includes, for example, trusts for the protection of animals generally and for the provision of fire brigades. A trust cannot be charitable unless it is solely and exclusively for charitable purposes: **benevolent** and **philanthropic purposes** are not necessarily charitable. Trusts for purposes that are predominantly political are not charitable. A charitable trust has many advantages over a private noncharitable trust: its objects do not have to be certain; charitable trusts are not subject to the *rules against perpetuities or against perpetual trusts; if the objects are or have become impossible or impracticable, the trust may be saved by the *cy-près doctrine; and the trustees may act by a majority. The greatest benefit to a charitable trust is that it has fiscal advantages: a charity is either wholly or partially exempt from income tax, corporation tax, capital gains tax, inheritance tax, stamp duty, and council tax.

charity *n.* A body (corporate or not) established for one of the charitable purposes specified by statute (*see* CHARITABLE TRUST). A charity is subject to the control of the High Court in the exercise of its jurisdiction with respect to charities. With certain exceptions, all charities are required to be registered with the *Charity Commissioners.

Charity Commissioners A statutory body, now governed by the Charities Act 1993, generally responsible for the administration of charities. The Commissioners are responsible for promoting the effective use of charitable resources, for encouraging the development of better methods of administration, for giving charity trustees information and advice on matters affecting charity, and for investigating and checking abuses. The Commissioners maintain a register of charities and decide whether or not a body should be registered; an appeal from their decision may be made to the High Court. Their Annual Reports (published by the Stationery Office) indicate how the Commissioners operate and how they are allowing the law of charity to develop.

charter *n.* **1.** A document evidencing something done between one party and another. The term is normally used in relation to a grant of rights or privileges by the Crown; for example, the grant of a royal charter to a university. **2.** A constitution, e.g. the Charter of the United Nations.

charterparty *n.* A written contract by which a person (the **charterer**) hires from a shipowner, in return for the payment of freight, the use of his ship or part of it for the carriage of goods by sea. The hiring may be either for a specified period (a **time charter**) or for a specified voyage or voyages (a **voyage charter**), and the charterer may hire the ship for carrying either his own goods alone or the goods of a number of shippers, who may or may not include himself. A special but now rare type of charterparty is the **charter by demise**. It is analogous to a lease of land and gives the charterer full possession and control of the ship. The normal charterparty is a **simple charter**, under which the shipowner retains possession and control and the primary rights of the charterer are confined to placing goods on board and choosing the ports of call. A number of standard forms (known by codenames such as Austwheat and Shelltime) have been developed for use in particular trades. *See also* BILL OF LADING; CESSER CLAUSE.

chastisement *n.* Physical punishment as a form of discipline. A parent or guardian has the common-law right to inflict reasonable and moderate punishment on his children and may authorize someone *in loco parentis* to do so, such as a child carer, nanny, or school. State schools now prohibit this, although if parents have consented it is still lawful in private schools. A husband does not, however, have the right to chastise his wife, nor a wife her husband. Illegal chastisement may amount to one of the *offences against the person.

chattel *n.* Any property other than freehold land (*compare* REAL PROPERTY). Leasehold interests in land are called **chattels real**, because they bear characteristics of both real and personal property. Tangible goods are called **chattels personal**. The definition of "personal chattels" in the Administration of Estates Act 1925, for the purposes of succession on intestacy, excludes chattels used for business purposes at the intestate's death, money, and securities for money.

cheat *n.* A common-law offence, now restricted to defrauding the public revenue (e.g. the tax authorities). No act of deceit is required. It is enough if one dishonestly fails to make VAT or other tax returns and to pay the tax due.

check-off *n.* A system whereby a company deducts union membership fees from a member's wages during the calculation of those wages and pays them over to the union. Such deductions are regulated by the Deregulations (Deduction from Pay of Union Subscriptions) Order 1998. These require that an employer must obtain the workers' written authorization before making deductions; the authorization remains valid unless and until withdrawn.

cheque *n.* A *bill of exchange drawn on a banker payable on demand. Since a cheque is payable on demand it need not be presented to the drawee bank for acceptance. A cheque operates as a mandate or order to the drawee bank to pay and debit the account of its customer, the drawer. The Cheques Act 1992 gave legal force to the words "account payee" on cheques, making them nontransferable.

cheque card A card issued by a bank to one of its customers containing an undertaking that any cheque signed by the customer and not exceeding a stated sum will be honoured by the bank. This is normally subject to certain conditions; for example, the cheque must be signed in the presence of the payee, the signature must correspond with a specimen on the card, and the payee must write the card number on the reverse of the cheque. The bank thus undertakes to the payee of the cheque that the cheque will be honoured regardless of the state of the customer's account with the bank.

chief rent *See* RENTCHARGE.

child *n.* **1.** A young person. There is no definitive definition of a child: the term has been used for persons under the age of 14, under the age of 16, and sometimes under the age of 18 (an *infant). Each case depends on its context and the wording of the statute governing it. For the purposes of the Children Act 1989 and the Family Law Act 1996 a child is a person under the age of 18. **2.** An offspring of parents. In wills, statutes, and other legal documents, the effect of the Family Law Reform Act 1987 is that there is a presumption that (unless the contrary intention is apparent) the word "child" includes any illegitimate child (*see* ILLEGITIMACY). Adopted children are treated as the legitimate children of their adoptive parents. *See also* CHILD OF THE FAMILY; QUALIFYING CHILD.

child abuse Molestation of children by parents or others (*see* BATTERED CHILD). If the molestation is of a sexual nature, the offender may be guilty of *indecent assault or *gross indecency with children (*see also* PAEDOPHILE). It is an offence to take or allow the taking of indecent photographs of a child under the age of 16, to distribute or show such photographs, to advertise that one intends to distribute or show them, or simply to possess them without legitimate reason. Photographs on the Internet and computers have been held by the courts to fall within this legislation. *See also* OBSCENE PUBLICATIONS.

child assessment order An order of the court made when a local authority or the NSPCC has concerns for a child's welfare in circumstances when the child's parents are refusing to allow the child to be medically or otherwise examined. The order authorizes such an examination. If a local authority fears that a child is in immediate danger, or when it is denied access to a child, an *emergency protection order should be applied for rather than a child assessment order.

child being looked after by a local authority A child who is either the subject of a *care order or who is being provided with accommodation by the local authority on a voluntary basis (*see* VOLUNTARY ACCOMMODATION). In respect of such a child, the local authority must seek, where possible, to promote contact between the child and its parents, relatives, and others closely connected with the child. Accommodation should be near where the child lives, and siblings should be accommodated together. A written plan should be drawn up before a child is placed; all the people involved in the plan, including the child (so far as is consistent with his age and understanding), should be consulted.

child destruction An act causing a viable unborn child to die during the course of pregnancy or birth. (A foetus is generally considered to be viable, i.e. capable of being born alive, if the pregnancy has lasted at least 24 weeks.) If carried out with the intention of causing death, and if it is proved that the act was not carried out in good faith in order to preserve the mother's life, the offence is subject to a maximum punishment of life imprisonment. *Compare* ABORTION.

child employee A child of compulsory school age (i.e. between 5 and 16 years) who undertakes paid work. Subject to certain exceptions, such employment is prohibited in Britain, and any employment under the age of 13 years is completely prohibited. Children are prohibited from working in industrial undertakings, factories, or mines. There are narrow exceptions for work in theatres and films, sports, work experience and/or training, and light work, with strict conditions attached in each case. In many cases these exceptions require that prior authorization is obtained from a local authority with respect to the proposed work.

In particular, children falling within some of the above exceptions must not work for more than two hours on any school day (outside school hours) or for more than 12 hours a week during term times. Work must not start before 7 a.m. or after 7 p.m. These restrictions can be relaxed for working time during school holidays and for children between 13 and 15 years of age. Night work by children is prohibited between 8 p.m. and 6 a.m., and children working more than 4½ hours daily are entitled to a 30-minute break from work. Local authorities are also empowered to further regulate the employment of children under byelaws. Although byelaws can differ from authority to authority, the majority conform to guidance issued by the Department of Health and are subject to confirmation and deregulation by the Secretary of State for Health.

Workers aged between 15 and 18 are referred to as **young** or **adolescent workers**. Their employment is restricted. At present they are entitled to 12 consecutive hours' rest between each working day, two days' weekly rest, and a 30-minute rest break when working longer than 4½ hours. They are also entitled to four weeks' paid annual leave. The implementation of further restrictions relating to young workers, as required by the Young Workers Directive 94/33/EC, is currently under consideration. These restrictions are: (1) the limitation of the working day to 8 hours and the working week to 40 hours; (2) restriction of night work between midnight and 4 a.m.; (3) restriction of night work between 10 p.m. and 6 a.m. or 11 p.m. and 7 a.m.

child in care A child who is the subject of a *care order. It is important to note that not all children who are being looked after by a local authority are the subjects of care orders; some of these children may be being accommodated by the local authority on a voluntary basis (*see* VOLUNTARY ACCOMMODATION). *See also* CHILD BEING LOOKED AFTER BY A LOCAL AUTHORITY.

child of the family A person considered under the Matrimonial Causes Act 1973, the Domestic Procedures and Magistrates' Courts Act 1978, and the Children Act 1989 to be the child of a married couple, although not necessarily born to or adopted by them, on the grounds that he or she has been treated by them as their own child. Courts have powers to make orders in favour of children of the family in all *family proceedings.

child of unmarried parents *See* ILLEGITIMACY.

Child Protection Conference A conference that decides what action should be taken by the local authority in respect of a child believed to be at risk of suffering harm. The conference comprises representatives of those bodies concerned with the child's welfare, including the NSPCC, social services, the police, the health and education authorities, and the probation service. Parents have no absolute right to attend the Child Protection Conference but are usually excluded only in exceptional circumstances.

child protection in divorce The legal rules designed to safeguard the position of children of divorcees. In the past courts would routinely make orders for custody and access in respect of children on divorce. The Children Act 1989, however, introduced a presumption of non-interference; i.e. the court will assume that parents are able to make their own arrangements for their children and will only make an order if it is necessary to do so, for example when the parents are in disagreement. Divorce courts have wide powers to make financial provision and property adjustment orders in favour of *children of the family, as well as any *section 8 orders necessary to safeguard the child's welfare. A court is no longer able to make a care or supervision order during divorce proceedings. However, if it is concerned about the welfare of a child before it, the court may direct a local authority to investigate the child's circumstances with a view to determining whether intervention is necessary.

Children and Family Court Advisory and Support Service (Cafcass) An amalgamation of three former services, the Guardian ad Litem Service, the Family Court Welfare Service, and the Official Solicitor's children's department. Cafcass will provide courts with information about children coming before them.

children in care *See* CHILD IN CARE; CARE ORDER.

children in need Those children designated by the Children Act 1989 as being in need of special support and provision by the *local authority. They include disabled children and children who are unlikely to maintain a reasonable standard of health or development without the provision of these special services.

children's guardian A person appointed by the court to protect a minor's interests in proceedings affecting his interests (such as adoption, wardship, or care proceedings), formerly known as a **guardian *ad litem***. Since the Children Act 1989 came into force the role of guardians has increased and they must ensure that the options open to the court are fully investigated. However, if a child is deemed capable of instructing a solicitor on his own behalf, he may do so even if this conflicts with the interests of the guardian.

children's tax credit *See* INCOME TAX.

child safety order An order that enables local authorities and courts to intervene when a child under the age of 10 (who cannot be prosecuted in criminal proceedings by virtue of his age) behaves antisocially or disruptively. The order was introduced by the Crime and Disorder Act 1998 as part of a strategy to reduce youth crime and is founded on the belief that early intervention is more effective than waiting until a child is old enough to be dealt with under the youth justice system. Application for an order is made by a local authority on the grounds that the child has committed or is in danger of committing an offence, or is in breach of a local child curfew scheme, or has acted in a manner likely to cause harassment, alarm, or distress to a person not living in the same household as the child. The requirements imposed under the order are entirely a matter for the court and might include, for example, attendance at school or extracurricular activities, avoiding contact with disruptive and older children, and not visiting such areas as shopping centres unsupervised. The purpose of the requirements imposed is either to ensure that the child receives appropriate care, protection, and support and is subject to proper control, or to prevent the repetition of the kind of behaviour that led to the child safety order being made. Breach of the order may lead to the court making a *care order in respect of the child. *See also* PARENTING ORDER.

Child Support Agency (CSA) *See* CHILD SUPPORT MAINTENANCE.

child support maintenance The amount that a **nonresident parent** (i.e. one who does not live with the child concerned) must pay as a contribution to the upkeep of his or her *qualifying child to a **parent with care** (i.e. one with whom the child lives) or a person in whose favour a residence order is made (*see* SECTION 8

ORDERS). Since the Child Support Act 1991, responsibility for the assessment, review, collection, and enforcement of maintenance for children is supervised by the **Child Support Agency (CSA)**, an agency of the Department for Work and Pensions (formerly Social Security) established under the Act, rather than by the court. It is no longer possible for people who do not already have a court order for child maintenance to go to court to obtain an order for periodical payments other than on behalf of stepchildren. However, it is still possible to apply to the court to obtain property settlements or lump sums or when an absent parent does not live habitually in the UK. A child over the age of 12 who lives in Scotland and whose absent parent lives in the UK may apply directly to the Child Support Agency on his or her own behalf. The Agency has wide powers of enforcement: for example it can make an order for payment to be deducted directly from wages or salary (*see also* CLEAN BREAK). No distinction is made between married and unmarried parents, but when parentage is disputed the Agency has power to apply to the court for a declaration of parentage; if successful this will have effect only for the purposes of the Child Support Act.

Certain changes, contained in the Child Support, Pensions and Social Security Act 2000, have been (or will soon be) implemented; the most important of these is a change in the way in which the amount of maintenance payable by the nonresident parent is calculated. The original formula was extremely complex and took into account the income of the parent with care. The new formula is simply based on the following percentages of the net weekly income of the nonresident parent: 15% if there is one qualifying child; 20% if there are two qualifying children; and 25% if there are three or more. These amounts are reduced if the nonresident parent has one or more other children (for example, the children of a new partner) in his household and if he has staying contact with his child. Under the old system a married father was able to deny parentage, but there will now be a presumption of paternity in favour of both a married father and a person named as father on the child's birth certificate.

child witness *See* VIDEO EVIDENCE; WITNESS.

Chiltern Hundreds, stewardship of the An appointment that, as a nominal office of profit under the Crown, disqualifies its holder from membership of the House of Commons. Although the appointment has been a sinecure since the 18th century, it has been retained as a disqualifying office to enable members to give up their seats during the lifetime of a parliament (a member cannot by law resign his seat). After obtaining the stewardship (an application for which is never refused), the member resigns the office so as to make it available for re-use.

A second office used for the same purpose is the stewardship of the **Manor of Northstead**. The law relating to both these offices is now contained in the House of Commons Disqualification Act 1975.

chose *n.* A thing. Choses are divided into two classes. A **chose in possession** is a tangible item capable of being actually possessed and enjoyed, e.g. a book or a piece of furniture. A **chose in action** is a right (e.g. a right to recover a debt) that can be enforced by legal action.

Church of England The established Church in England, of which the sovereign is the supreme head. Structurally, the Church consists of the two provinces of Canterbury and York, which are divided into dioceses, and these into parishes. For each province there is an archbishop (that of Canterbury being Primate of All England, and that of York Primate of England), and for each diocese a bishop. A suffragan bishop has no diocese of his own but assists an archbishop or a diocesan bishop. The archbishops and other senior bishops are members of the House of Lords.

The governing body of the Church is the General Synod (formerly the Church Assembly, but renamed and reconstituted by the Synodical Government Measure 1969). It consists of a House of Bishops, a House of Clergy, and a House of Laity and has legislative functions. A **Measure** passed by each House and granted the royal assent following a resolution of each House of Parliament has the force of an Act of Parliament. There are also diocesan synods, and certain matters require the approval of a majority of these before they can be finally approved by the General Synod. The Dioceses Measure 1978 authorizes the reorganization of diocesan structure and the creation of area synods, to which diocesan synods may delegate functions. *See also* ECCLESIASTICAL COURTS.

c.i.f. contract (cost, insurance, freight contract) A type of contract for the international sale of goods by which the seller agrees not only to supply the goods but also to make a contract of carriage with a sea carrier, under which the goods will be delivered at the contract port of destination, and a contract of insurance with an insurer, to cover them while they are in transit. The seller performs his contract by delivering the relevant documents to the buyer: an invoice specifying the goods and their price, a *bill of lading evidencing the contract of carriage, a policy of insurance, and any other documents specified in the contract. The contract will normally provide for payment against documents. The risk of accidental loss or damage normally passes to the buyer on or as from shipment. c.i.f. is a defined *incoterm under *Incoterms 2000*.

circuit administrator A civil servant having responsibility for the administration of the courts within a circuit (*see* CIRCUIT SYSTEM). He liaises closely with the *presiding judge of the circuit in the allocation of resources and particularly the sittings of judges and recorders.

circuit judge Any of the judges appointed under the provisions of the Courts Act 1971 from among those who have had a ten-year Crown Court or county court *advocacy qualification, or who are *recorders, or who have held a full-time appointment of at least three years duration in one of the offices listed in the Courts Act 1971. They sit in the *county courts and the *Crown Court and may, by invitation of the Lord Chancellor, sit as High Court judges. All judges of county courts and other judges of comparable status were made circuit judges in 1971.

circuit system The system of dividing England and Wales into regional **circuits** for the purpose of court administration. It is based upon the traditional regional groupings adopted by the Bar and consists of the South-Eastern, Western, Midland and Oxford, Wales and Chester, Northern, and North-Eastern circuits. Each circuit is administered by a *circuit administrator and supervised by two *presiding judges. *See also* CIRCUIT JUDGE.

circumcision, female It is an offence, punishable with up to five years' imprisonment, to excise or otherwise mutilate the external genital organs of a woman, or to *aid and abet a woman mutilating herself in this way. Girls living in the UK who come from countries where female circumcision is the normal practice are, however, still sent abroad by their parents for such an operation. Male circumcision is lawful in the UK. *See also* CONSENT; WOUNDING.

circumstantial evidence (indirect evidence) Evidence from which the judge or jury may infer the existence of a fact in issue but which does not prove the existence of the fact directly. Case law has described circumstantial evidence as evidence that is relevant (and, therefore, admissible) but that has little probative value. *Compare* DIRECT EVIDENCE.

citation *n.* **1.** A notice, issued in the Probate Registry by an executor proving a will in solemn form (*see* PROBATE), calling upon persons to come forward if they object to the grant of probate to him. **2.** The quoting of a legal case or authority.

citizen's arrest An *arrest by anyone other than a police officer. Such an arrest is lawful. *See also* ARRESTABLE OFFENCE.

citizenship of the UK and Colonies A form of citizenship created by the British Nationality Act 1948. By the British Nationality Act 1981, it was replaced as from 1 January 1983 by *British citizenship, *British Dependent Territories citizenship, and *British Overseas citizenship.

City Code on Takeovers and Mergers A body of rules regulating those engaged in the conduct of *takeovers and *mergers of public companies. It is administered by a Panel representing the major City financial institutions, e.g. the *Stock Exchange and the Issuing Houses Association. The principal aim is to ensure that company members (rather than the directors) decide upon the merits of accepting a bid, that they are fully informed about what is going on, and that shareholders of the same class are treated equally in the event of a takeover or merger. The rules are not legally binding, but if they are contravened sanctions may be imposed on the company, including having the facilities of the securities markets withdrawn from them. Decisions of the Panel are subject to *judicial review.

City of London That part of *Greater London which, for local government purposes, is administered by the City of London Corporation. In addition to special powers under ancient royal charters, the Corporation has all the functions of a London borough council, which it exercises principally through a Court of Common Council consisting of the Lord Mayor, aldermen elected for life, and common council men elected annually. Limited governmental functions are exercised through a separate Court of Aldermen, and formal functions through a Court of Common Hall.

civil court A court exercising jurisdiction over civil rather than criminal cases. In England the principal civil *courts of first instance are the *county courts and the *High Court. *Magistrates' courts have limited civil jurisdiction, mainly confined to matrimonial proceedings.

civil defence Establishments and units organized or authorized by the competent authorities to carry out humanitarian tasks intended to protect the civilian population against the dangers of hostilities or disasters and to help it to recover from the immediate effects of these.

civil law **1.** The law of any particular state, now usually called *municipal law. **2.** Roman law. **3.** A legal system based on Roman law, as distinct from the English system of *common law. **4.** *Private law, as opposed to *public law, military law, and ecclesiastical law.

civil liability contribution The right of a person who is liable for damage to recover from any other person who is liable for the same damage a contribution to represent that person's share of responsibility for the damage. When two or more people are liable for causing the same damage, the injured person is entitled to recover full compensation for his losses from any one of them. The wrongdoer who is sued may then ask for contribution from the other wrongdoers. Since the Civil Liability (Contribution) Act 1978, the right to contribution is available in all forms of civil liability, whether tort, breach of contract, breach of trust, or otherwise. The court assesses the amount of contribution on the basis of what would be just and equitable, taking into account the parties' responsibility for the damage.

Civil List The sum authorized by statute to be paid annually out of the *Consolidated Fund for meeting the expenses of the royal household and for making allowances to certain members of the royal family. It may be increased in amount by Treasury order, but this is liable to annulment by the House of Commons. Certain members of the royal family have volunteered to be taxed on their Civil List allowances.

Civil Procedure Rules (CPR) The new procedural code, which was enacted in 1998 and revoked the *Rules of the Supreme Court with effect from 26 April 1999. The Rules, a result of the reforms proposed by Lord Woolf's *Access to Justice* (Final Report) 1996, now govern proceedings in the civil cases of the Court of Appeal (Civil Division), the High Court, and the county courts. The CPR have been supplemented by *Practice Directions and *pre-action protocols. They have no application in certain areas, including the Mental Health Act 1983 Part IV and family and adoption proceedings.

civil remedy *See* REMEDY.

Civil Service The body of *Crown servants that are employed to put government policies into action and are paid wholly out of money voted annually by Parliament. Civil servants include the administrative and executive staff of central government departments (e.g. the Home Office and Treasury) and the industrial staff of government dockyards and factories. Civil servants may serve in established or unestablished capacities, with effects on pension entitlement, etc. The police (not being Crown servants), the armed forces (not being civil), government ministers, and those (e.g. judges) whose salaries are charged on the Consolidated Fund are not civil servants.

civil wrong An infringement of a person's rights, for which the person wronged may sue for damages or some other civil remedy. Examples are *torts and *breaches of contract.

claim *n.* A demand for a remedy or assertion of a right, especially the right to take a particular case to court (right of action). The term is used in civil litigation. *See also* CLAIM FORM; PART 20 CLAIM.

claimant *n.* A person applying for relief against another person in an action, suit, petition, or any other form of court proceeding. Before the introduction of the *Civil Procedure Rules in 1999, a claimant was called a **plaintiff**. *Compare* DEFENDANT.

claim form (in civil proceedings) A formal written statement setting out details of the claimant, defendant, and the remedy being sought. The claim form may also contain details of the claim (the **particulars of claim**); alternatively, these can be served separately. Since the introduction of the Civil Procedure Rules in 1999, the usual method of initiating civil proceedings is by issuing a claim form; all previous methods (e.g. writ of summons, originating summons) have now been rendered obsolete. *See also* PART 8 CLAIM FORM; STATEMENT OF CASE.

claim of privilege *See* PRIVILEGE.

class gift A gift to people of a certain specified category (e.g. "to my daughters"), rather than to people named individually, (e.g. "to my daughters A and B").

classification of animals At common law animals were formerly classified as wild by nature (**ferae naturae**) or tame by nature (**mansuetae naturae**), referring to the species in general rather than the individual animal. The owner of a wild animal was strictly liable for any damage it caused. The owner of a tame animal was liable for damage it caused if he knew that it had a vicious tendency abnormal in the species (the **scienter rule**). Special rules applied to damage done by cattle (*see* CATTLE TRESPASS; DISTRESS DAMAGE FEASANT) and dogs. The common law classifications have been largely replaced by modern statutes.

For purposes of civil liability in England, animals are classified as belonging to a dangerous or a nondangerous species (Animals Act 1971). A dangerous species is one not commonly domesticated in the British Isles, fully grown members of which are likely to cause severe damage. The keeper of an animal of a dangerous species is strictly liable for any damage it causes. Liability for damage done by other animals arises either under the Animals Act, if the animal was known by its keeper to have characteristics not normally found in that species, or only normally found in particular circumstances, which made it likely to cause that kind of damage; or under ordinary rules of tort liability. Thus carelessly allowing a dog to stray on the highway can make the keeper liable in negligence if it causes an accident, and excessive smell from a pig farm can be an actionable nuisance. The Animals Act also imposes *strict liability for damage done by trespassing livestock, which includes cattle, horses, sheep, pigs, goats, and poultry. The keeper of a dog that kills or injures livestock is liable for the damage, except when the livestock was injured while straying on the keeper's land. If livestock is worried by a dog, the owner of the livestock (or the owner of the land on which the livestock lives) may kill or injure the dog to protect the livestock.

In Scotland, there is strict liability for damage caused by animals belonging to a species likely to kill or severely injure persons or animals or cause material damage to property under the Animals (Scotland) Act 1987. The Act also excuses the killing or injuring of an animal that attacks or harries people or livestock.

Dangerous wild animals may require a licence under the Dangerous Wild Animals Act 1976 (*see* DANGEROUS ANIMALS). Keeping dogs of a species bred for fighting is an offence under the Dangerous Dogs Act 1991. The use of *guard dogs is controlled by the Guard Dogs Act 1975. Other statutes protect various species, control importation of animals, and deal with animal diseases.

class rights Rights that attach to a clearly defined class of share (e.g. preference *shares) or are conferred upon a person for so long as he is a holder of any shares. In the latter case shareholders become a class in their own right. Typical class rights would relate to *dividends, return of capital on a *winding-up, or the right to appoint a director to the board. Class rights may only be altered either in accordance with a clause in the constitutional documents of the company (*see* ARTICLES OF ASSOCIATION) or with the consent of the class affected under the Companies Act 1985. Shareholders from the class affected who did not agree to the alteration may apply to court to have the change cancelled within 21 days.

clause *n.* **1.** A subdivision of a document. A clause of a written contract contains a term or provision of the contract. Clauses are usually numbered consecutively (1, 2, etc.); subclauses may follow a clause, numbered 1.1, 1.1.1, etc. **2.** A section of a *Bill.

clean break The principle that, upon divorce, spouses should try to settle their financial affairs in a final manner, by a lump sum order, rather than a continuous periodical payments order. Under the Matrimonial Causes Act 1973, the courts have a duty to consider whether they can achieve a clean break in their orders for financial relief even when there are children. However, the Child Support Act 1991 makes it possible for a parent with care of a child to apply directly to the Child Support

Agency for a maintenance assessment even when the divorce court has achieved a clean break (*see* CHILD SUPPORT MAINTENANCE).

clean hands A phrase from a *maxim of equity: he who comes to equity must come with clean hands, i.e. a person who makes a claim in equity must be free from any taint of fraud with respect to that claim. For example, a person seeking to enforce an agreement must not himself be in breach of it.

clearance *n.* **1.** A certificate acknowledging a ship's compliance with customs requirements. **2.** An indication from a taxing authority that a certain provision does not apply to a particular transaction. The procedure is laid down by statute in some cases.

clearance area Formerly, an area declared as such by a housing authority (usually a district or London borough council) on the ground that the houses in it were unfit for human habitation or otherwise dangerous or injurious to health and were best demolished. The authority must also have been satisfied that alternative accommodation existed and that its resources were sufficient; it then acquired the area and carried out the demolition. The power to designate a clearance area was abolished by the Housing Act 1974. *See also* REHABILITATION ORDER. *Compare* HOUSING ACTION AREA.

Clerk of the House The principal permanent officer of the House of Commons.

Clerk of the Parliaments The principal permanent officer of the House of Lords.

clerk to the justices (justices' clerk, magistrates' clerk) A person who has a five-year magistrates' court qualification, or a barrister or solicitor of not less than five years' standing as an assistant to a magistrates' clerk, who is appointed to assist magistrates in court, particularly by giving advice about law practice or procedure on questions arising in connection with the discharge of their or his functions. The clerk or one of his staff will sit in court with the justices in order to advise them, but should not retire with them when they consider their verdict. He may, however, advise them in private during their retirement, at their request, but should return to the court when his advice has been given. *See also* MAGISTRATES' COURT.

client *n.* A person who employs a solicitor to carry out legal business on behalf of himself or someone else. The relationship between a solicitor and his client is a *fiduciary one and any other transactions between them may be affected by *undue influence. A solicitor's client cannot consult a barrister directly but only through his solicitor: the solicitor is therefore the barrister's client.

clog on the equity of redemption Any provision in a *mortgage deed to prevent redemption on payment of the debt or performance of the obligation for which the security was given. Such provisions are void. An example is an option contained in the mortgage deed for the mortgagee to purchase the mortgaged property before or after the mortgage has been redeemed. **Unconscionable** provisions in a mortgage (for example, one to prevent redemption for 100 years) are also void. However, a company may issue irredeemable *debentures. A provision that would otherwise be unconscionable may be valid if the transaction containing it is a commercial arrangement rather than a mortgage. Thus, such provisions in mortgages of public houses or garages by their tenants or owners to breweries or oil companies will be upheld, provided that they do not infringe the contractual rules against *restraint of trade. Under the Unfair Terms in Consumer Contracts Regulations 1994 unfair redemption penalties may also be subject to challenge.

close *n.* Land that is enclosed.

close company A company under the control of its directors or five or fewer **participators**. The participators have or are entitled to acquire a share or interest in the capital or income of the company and can include *loan creditors. Special tax provisions apply to such companies.

closed-shop agreement A collective agreement requiring members of a particular group of employees to be or become members of a specified trade union. A **pre-entry agreement** is one that prohibits an employer from engaging a relevant employee unless he is already a member of the union concerned. A **post-entry agreement** requires employees to join the specified union within a certain time after the employment commences.

Under the Trade Union and Labour Relations (Consolidation) Act 1992, all employees are free to join a trade union or not, as they wish. If an employer takes action, short of dismissal, against an employee to enforce membership of a union, the employee can complain to an *employment tribunal, which can order the employer to pay him compensation. Dismissal for failure to belong to a trade union is automatically unfair (*see* INADMISSIBLE REASON). In this case there are special minimum rates of *compensation payable. If, as a result of trade union pressure, an employer dismisses an employee for failing to belong to a union, the employer can join the union as a party to the dismissal proceedings and pass the liability to pay compensation on to the union.

A union that attempts to enforce a closed shop by industrial action loses the immunity from legal action that it would otherwise have if the action was in furtherance of a *trade dispute.

The effect of these provisions is that, while closed-shop agreements are not in themselves illegal, they are unenforceable by either employers or unions.

close of pleadings Formerly, a stage in the course of pleading in an action in the High Court that occurred 14 days after service of the reply, defence to counterclaim, or defence. This stage has been taken over by the functions of *case management and track *allocation.

closing order An order made by a local housing authority under the Housing Act 1985 prohibiting the use of a house, which it considers unfit for human habitation, for any purpose not approved by the authority.

closure *n.* The curtailing of debate on a question, particularly in the House of Commons, by carrying a motion (which cannot itself be debated) "that the question be now put". The result is that a vote on the question under debate must be taken immediately. *Compare* GUILLOTINE.

club *n.* An association regulated by rules that bind its members according to the law of contract. Club property is either vested in trustees for the members (**members' club**) or owned by a proprietor (often a company limited by guarantee; *see* LIMITED COMPANY) who operates the club as a business for profit (**proprietary club**). The committee is usually liable for club debts in the case of a members' club; the proprietor in the case of a proprietary club.

Cmd *See* COMMAND PAPERS.

Cmnd *See* COMMAND PAPERS.

coastal waters *See* EXCLUSIVE ECONOMIC ZONE; FISHERY LIMITS; TERRITORIAL WATERS.

code *n.* A complete written formulation of a body of law, (e.g. the *Code Napoléon* in France). A code of English law does not exist, but a few specialized topics have been dealt with in this way by means of a *codifying statute (e.g. the Sale of Goods Act 1893, re-enacted with modifications by the Sale of Goods Act 1979).

codecision procedure A procedure introduced by the *Maastricht Treaty that gives the *European Parliament a power to veto certain legislative proposals. If the *Council of the European Union and the European Parliament fail to agree after a second reading of the proposal by the Parliament, a **conciliation committee** of the Council and Parliament will attempt to reach a compromise. If no compromise is reached, the Parliament can reject the measure by absolute majority voting. *Compare* ASSENT PROCEDURE; COOPERATION PROCEDURE.

code of practice A body of rules for practical guidance only, or that sets out professional standards of behaviour, but does not have the force of law, e.g. the Highway Code. Under the provisions of the Fair Trading Act 1973 the *Director General of Fair Trading has the duty of encouraging trade associations to prepare and distribute to their members codes of practice for guidance in safeguarding and promoting the interests of UK consumers. Several such codes have been approved by the Director General. Codes of practice have also been published by *ACAS, the Health and Safety, Equal Opportunities, and Racial Equality Commissions, and the Secretary of State for Work and Pensions, providing guidance to employers, employees, and their representatives on the fulfilment of their statutory obligations in relevant fields. Codes of practice under the Police and Criminal Evidence Act 1984 regulate searches and the *interrogation of suspects by the police.

Generally, failure to comply with a code of practice does not automatically expose the party in breach to prosecution or any civil remedy. It may, however, be relied on as evidence tending to show that he has not fulfilled some relevant statutory requirement.

codicil *n.* A document supplementary to a will, which is executed with the same formalities under the Wills Act 1837 (*see* EXECUTION OF WILL) and adds to, varies, or revokes provisions in the will. It must be proved with the will. A codicil confirming a will normally republishes the will (*see* REPUBLICATION OF WILL) and may revive a will that has been revoked if that is the testator's clear intention. If many changes are made to the will it is better to execute a new will.

codifying statute A statute that sets out the whole of the existing law (i.e. both statute law and common law) on a particular subject. Such statutes are extremely rare; an example is the Law of Property Act 1925. *Compare* CONSOLIDATING STATUTE. *See also* INTERPRETATION OF STATUTES.

coercion *n.* A defence available only to married women who have committed a crime (other than murder or treason) in the presence of, and under pressure from, their husbands. Its scope is unclear but may be wider than that of *duress in that it may cover economic and moral as well as physical pressure, though unlike duress it has to be proved (*see* BURDEN OF PROOF). If a wife is acquitted on grounds of coercion, her husband may be liable for the offence in question through his wife's innocent agency and/or for a crime involving a *threat.

cognates *pl. n.* Persons descended from a common ancestor.

cohabitants *pl. n. See* COHABITATION.

cohabitation *n.* Living together as husband and wife. Married persons generally have a right to expect their spouses to live with them. Unmarried people living together as husband and wife (**cohabitants**) do not usually have the status of a married couple (*see also* COMMON-LAW MARRIAGE). But under the **cohabitation rule** the resources and requirements of an unmarried couple living together are aggregated for the purposes of claiming social security benefits under the Social Security Acts even in the absence of a sexual relationship (*see* INCOME SUPPORT).

co-imperium *n.* Joint rule by two or more states of an entity that has a distinct international status (*compare* CONDOMINIUM). An example is the occupation and rule of Germany after 1945 by the four victorious powers.

collateral **1.** *adj.* Describing the relationship between people who share a common ancestor but are descended from him through different lines of descent. *See also* CONSANGUINITY. **2.** *adj.* Ancillary; subordinate but connected to the main subject, etc. **3.** *n.* Security that is additional to the main security for a debt (or an advantage to the mortgagee that is additional to the payment of interest). For example, a lender may require as collateral the assignment of an insurance policy in addition to the principal security of a mortgage on the borrower's home.

collateral benefits Benefits received from a third party by the victim of a tortious injury in consequence of the injury, such as insurance money, sick pay, disability pensions, loans, social security benefits, or gifts from a disaster appeal fund. Some collateral benefits are taken into account when assessing the damages to be paid by the person liable for the injury; others, such as insurance money and gifts, are not. Under the Social Security Administration Act 1992, the amount of social security benefits received by the victim for the first five years after the injury must, with a few exceptions, be deducted from the total damages and repaid to the Department for Work and Pensions by the person liable for the injury (or his insurer).

collateral contract A subsidiary contract that induces a person to enter into a main contract. For example, if X agrees to buy from Y goods made by Z, and does so on the strength of Z's assurance as to the high quality of the goods, X and Z may be held to have made a collateral contract consisting of Z's promise as to quality given in consideration of X's promise to enter into the main contract with Y.

collective agreement *See* COLLECTIVE BARGAINING.

collective bargaining Negotiations between trade unions (acting for their members) and employers about terms and conditions of employment. Under the Trade Union and Labour Relations (Consolidation) Act 1992, a **collective agreement** (an agreement between trade union and employer resulting from collective bargaining) is not legally binding unless it is in writing and specifically states the parties' intention to be bound. Unenforceable collective agreements frequently include terms (relating to pay, discipline, etc.) that will become incorporated in individual employees' binding contracts of employment. In these respects the written particulars of employees' contracts, which the employer must give under the Employment Rights Act 1996, must refer the employee to the collective agreement, which must be reasonably accessible to him. Terms of a collective agreement that discriminate on grounds of sex may be challenged by individuals in a court or employment tribunal on the ground that they contravene the principle of equal treatment. When a collective agreement provides that individual employees' contracts will circumscribe their right to strike, the employees will only be bound if their contracts contain that provision and the collective agreement was negotiated by an *independent trade union, is in writing, and is readily accessible to employees during working hours. The parties to a collective agreement containing procedures for determining complaints of unfair dismissal may apply to the Secretary of State for an order that those procedures be substituted for the statutory jurisdiction of employment tribunals. An order will only be made if the agreement was negotiated by an independent trade union, sufficiently identifies the employees affected, and gives them remedies as beneficial as the statutory scheme and a right to independent arbitration or adjudication. *See also* DISCLOSURE OF INFORMATION; RECOGNITION PROCEDURE.

collective redundancy The proposed dismissal as redundant by an employer of 20 or more employees. In such a situation the employer is required, under the Trade Union and Labour Relations (Consolidation) Act 1992, to disclose information (*see* DISCLOSURE OF INFORMATION) and to consult with elected workers' representatives or representatives of a recognized trade union with a view to reaching agreement about ways of avoiding the dismissals, reducing the numbers of employees to be dismissed, and mitigating the consequences of the dismissals. If the employer fails to comply with these requirements the union may complain to an employment tribunal who may, if the complaint is upheld, issue a *protective award. Employment tribunals have held that notification of impending redundancies must take place at the earliest opportunity in order that representations by the union may be taken into account.

collective responsibility *See* CABINET.

collective security The centralized system of international rules, now embodied in the Charter of the United Nations, that governs the collective resort to force under the authority of the United Nations for the purpose of maintaining or restoring international peace and security. An example is the action by the international community during the Gulf War of 1991. It should be noted that the precise legal justification of this conflict is uncertain, the UN Security Council Resolution 678 stating only that its legal basis was under *Chapter VII of the UN Charter. *See also* ENFORCEMENT ACTION.

collective trespass *See* TRESPASS.

collision clause (running-down clause) A clause in a marine insurance policy binding the underwriters to indemnify the insured in respect of any damages in tort he may be liable for as a result of his ship colliding with another. At common law, such a policy covers only the insured's physical losses. The clause is customarily restricted to three quarters of the damages in question. When two vessels collide, the damage done to each is added together and treated as a common loss. It is divided between insurers according to the proportion of blame attributable to each ship or, if this cannot be determined, equally.

collusion *n.* An improper agreement or bargain between parties that one of them should bring proceedings against the other. Collusion is no longer a bar to divorce or nullity proceedings, but it may affect the validity of a declaration of legitimacy.

colony *n.* A territory that forms part of the Crown's dominions outside the UK. Although it may enjoy internal self-government, its external affairs are controlled by the UK government.

colourable *adj.* Describing that which is one thing in appearance but another in substance; for example, a symbolic residence in a parish for the purpose of qualifying for marriage there.

comfort letter (administrative letter) A letter sent by the Competition Directorate of the European Commission following a notification for exemption or *negative clearance of a commercial agreement that may infringe EU *competition law. It is very rare for the Commission to issue a binding decision following such a notification. However, although a comfort letter does not have the force of a formal decision, it would be unusual for the Commission to fine a business in relation to an agreement that was notified and in relation to which a comfort letter was then issued.

comity (*comitas gentium*) *n.* Neighbourly gestures or courtesies extended from one state to another, or others, without accepting a legal obligation to behave in that manner. Comity is founded upon the concept of sovereign equality among states and is expected to be reciprocal. It is possible for such practices, over a period of time and with common usage, to develop into rules of customary international law, although this requires such behaviour to acquire a binding or compelling quality. *See* CUSTOM; OPINIO JURIS.

Command Papers Documents that the government, by royal command, presents to Parliament for consideration. They include **white papers** and **green papers**. The former contain statements of policy or explanations of proposed legislation; the latter are essentially discussion documents. For reference purposes they have serial numbers, with (since 1869) prefixes. The prefixes are **C** (1870–99), **Cd** (1900–18), **Cmd** (1919–56), and **Cmnd** (1957–   ).

commercial agent An *agent who solicits business from potential customers on behalf of a principal. In the EU the contracts of many commercial agents are governed by directive 86/653, which gives them substantial rights to claim compensation or an indemnity on termination of their agency agreement and implies other terms into their contracts; for example, in relation to payment of commission and notice periods for termination of the agreement. In the UK this directive is implemented by the Commercial Agents (Council Directive) Regulations 1993 as amended.

Commercial Court A court forming part of the *Queen's Bench Division of the High Court and specializing in the trial of commercial cases, mostly relating to shipping and commodity trading. Many of the court's cases arise from the awards of arbitrators (*see* ARBITRATION). The judges of the court are nominated by the Lord Chancellor from among the Queen's Bench *puisne judges who have special experience of commercial matters.

commission *n.* **1.** Authority to exercise a power or a direction to perform a duty; for example, a commission of a *justice of the peace. **2.** A body directed to perform a particular duty. Examples are the *Charity Commissioners and the *Law Commission. **3.** A sum payable to an *agent in return for his performing a particular service. This may, for example, be a percentage of the sum for which he has secured a contract of sale of his principal's property. The circumstances in which a commission is payable depend on the terms of the contract between principal and agent. The terms on which commission is paid to a *commercial agent are set down in the EU directive 86/653. **4.** Authorization by a court or a judge for a witness to be examined on oath by a court, judge, or other authorized person, to provide evidence for use in court proceedings. The procedure is used when the witness is unlikely to be able to attend the hearing (e.g. because of illness). If the witness is still unable to attend when the court hearing takes place the written evidence is read by the court.

Commissioner *n.* (in the EU) *See* EUROPEAN COMMISSION.

commissioner for oaths A person appointed by the Lord Chancellor to administer oaths or take affidavits. By statute, every solicitor who holds a *practising certificate has the powers of a commissioner for oaths, but he may not exercise these powers in a proceeding in which he is acting for any of the parties or in which he is interested. Thus when an affidavit must be sworn, the client cannot use his own solicitor but must go to another solicitor to witness the swearing.

Commissioner for the Protection Against Unlawful Industrial Action *See* CERTIFICATION OFFICER.

Commissioner for the Rights of Trade Union Members *See* CERTIFICATION OFFICER.

Commission for Health Improvement A body established under the Health Act 1999. Its remit includes providing advice to *Primary Care Trusts or *NHS Trusts for the purpose of monitoring and improving the quality of health care and reporting on the provision or quality of health care.

Commission for Racial Equality A body appointed by the Home Secretary under the Race Relations Act 1976 with the general function of working towards the elimination of *racial discrimination by promoting equality of opportunity and good relations between different racial groups. It keeps the working of the Act under review, investigates alleged contraventions and, when necessary, issues and applies for injunctions to enforce nondiscrimination notices.

Commission of the European Communities *See* EUROPEAN COMMISSION.

Commissions for Local Administration Two commissions, one each for England and Wales, that were established by the Local Government Act 1974 to investigate complaints by the public of injustice suffered through maladministration by local authorities, police authorities, the National Rivers Authority, and housing action trusts. The *Parliamentary Commissioner for Administration is a member of both commissions and there are three **Local Government Commissioners** (or **Ombudsmen**) for England and one for Wales. Certain matters (e.g. decisions affecting the public generally and the conduct of criminal investigations) are outside their competence. Complaints to a Commissioner must normally be made in writing through a member of the authority concerned, within one year of the date on which the matter first came to the complainant's notice, but if a complaint is not duly passed on it can be accepted directly by the Commissioner. Commissioners' reports are sent to the complainant and the authority concerned and are also made public.

committal for sentence The referring of a case from a magistrates' court to the Crown Court, which occurs when the magistrates have found the accused guilty and consider that their powers of sentencing are insufficient for the case.

committal for trial The referring of a case from a magistrates' court for trial at the Crown Court following a *preliminary investigation by the magistrates. The committal proceedings may consist of taking *depositions from all the witnesses in the form of oral evidence. Alternatively the committal may take a short form under section 6 of the Magistrates' Courts Act 1980. This occurs when the accused agrees that the prosecution should put all its evidence in writing; the justices may then commit for trial without considering the evidence. The accused does not have to disclose any defence that he intends to put forward at the trial, but must, not later than seven days after committal, give notice of any intended *alibi and details of the witnesses he is going to call in support of it. A committal without consideration of the evidence may only take place if the accused is legally represented. The press may normally only report certain limited facts about committal proceedings, such as the name of the accused and the charges. However, if the accused asks that reporting restrictions be lifted, the magistrates may allow publication of full details of the proceedings. Concern as to the effectiveness of committal proceedings in preventing weak cases going to trial led to provisions in the Criminal Justice and Public Order Act 1994, which have now created a new transfer for trial procedure, based upon consideration of case documents. The Criminal Procedure and Investigations Act 1996 lays down new committal procedures.

committal in civil proceedings A method of enforcing judgment by obtaining an order that a person be committed to prison. It is most commonly sought when the person has committed a *contempt of the court (e.g. by disobedience of an order of the court). In modern practice it is very occasionally available to enforce an order for the payment of a debt.

Committee of the whole House A committee of which all members of the House of Commons or the House of Lords are members. In the Lords it sits for the committee stage of all public Bills. In the Commons the committee stage is normally taken by a *standing committee, but major Bills (particularly if controversial) are sometimes referred instead to a whole House committee. Certain matters concerning expenditure and taxation were formerly considered by the whole House sitting as the **Committee of Supply** or the **Committee of Ways and Means**, but since 1967 they have been dealt with by the House sitting as such.

common *n.* A *profit *à prendre* enjoyed by a number of landowners over *common land. A right of common may be *appurtenant, in gross (i.e. independent of any *dominant tenement), or *pur cause de vicinage* ("by reason of neighbourhood": the right to allow animals grazing common land to stray onto adjoining common land). They generally comprise rights of pasture (grazing), piscary (fishing), turbary (rare; a right to take turf), *ferae naturae* (a right to take animals), *estovers, etc., and unless they exist in gross are usually limited to the reasonable needs of the dominant tenements.

Common Agricultural Policy (CAP) The agricultural policy of the EU as set out in Articles 32–38 of the Treaty of Rome. The overall aims of the CAP are to increase agricultural productivity, ensure a fair standard of living for the agricultural community, stabilize markets, assure the availability of supplies, and ensure that supplies reach consumers at a reasonable price. The Treaty is supplemented by a wide range of EU directives in this field. *See also* INTERVENTION.

common assault *See* ASSAULT.

Common Budget *See* COMMON EXTERNAL TARIFF.

common carrier *See* CARRIER.

common design The intention assumed to be shared by those engaged in a joint illegal enterprise: each party is liable for anything done during the pursuance of that enterprise, including any unexpected consequences that arise. If, however, one of the parties does something that was not agreed beforehand, the others may not be held responsible for the consequences of this act. *See also* ACCESSORY.

common duty of care The duty of an occupier of land or premises to take reasonable care to see that visitors will be reasonably safe in using the premises for the purposes for which they are invited or permitted to be there. *See* OCCUPIER'S LIABILITY.

Common External Tariff (CET) The tariff of import duties payable on certain goods entering any member state of the European Union from non-EU countries. The CET prevents the distortion of trade that would occur if member states set their own import duties on products coming into their state from outside the EU.

The Tariff contributes to the **Common Budget** of the EU, from which subsidies due under the *Common Agricultural Policy are paid.

Common Fisheries Policy (CFP) A fishing policy agreed between members of the European Community in 1983. It lays down annual catch limits (*quotas) for each state for major species of fish, a 12-mile exclusive fishing zone for each state, and an equal-access zone of 200 nautical miles from its coast, within which any member state is allowed to fish. There are some exceptions to these regulations. The CFP is handled by the European Commission's Fisheries Directorate General. It was reviewed in 1992 and is subject to a further review in 2002. *See also* FISHERY LIMITS.

common heritage of mankind principle The principle that areas of Antarctica, the sea bed, and outer space should not be monopolized for the benefit of one state or group of states alone, but should be treated as if they are to be used to the benefit of all mankind. For example, Article 4 of the Moon Treaty 1979 states that exploration "shall be the province of all mankind and shall be carried out for the benefit and in the interests of all countries, irrespective of their degree of economic or scientific development".

commonhold *n.* A third way of owning land, in addition to *freehold and *leasehold, that is expected to be introduced into England and Wales in accordance with the Commonhold and Leasehold Reform Bill. It is intended for developments in which individual properties, such as flats, houses, or shops, are owned and occupied by separate persons, but there are common parts, such as stairways and walkways, that need to remain in central ownership and to be maintained. Previously, such properties were usually held under long leases, but this had proved unsatisfactory.

Each separate property in a commonhold development will be a **unit**; the owner will be a **unit-holder**. The body owning the common parts will be the **commonhold association**, a private company limited by guarantee. Each unit-holder will be a member of that company. The company membership will be limited to the unit-holders, and the memorandum and articles of the company will be prescribed by the Lord Chancellor. The commonhold association will also need to create a **Commonhold Community Statement** (CCS) setting out the rules and regulations of the particular community. The commonhold association with its common parts and all the associated units will be registered at the Land Registry. It will be possible for leasehold developments to convert to commonhold, but only by the consent of all parties.

common land Land subject to rights of *common. The Commons Registration Act 1965 provides for the registration with local authorities of all common land in England and Wales, its owners, and claims to rights of common over it. Subject to the investigation by Commons Commissioners of disputed cases, and to exceptions for land becoming or ceasing to be common land, registration provides conclusive evidence that land is common land and also of the rights of common over it. Rights could be lost by failure to register.

common law 1. The part of English law based on rules developed by the royal courts during the first three centuries after the Norman Conquest (1066) as a system applicable to the whole country, as opposed to local customs. The Normans did not attempt to make new law for the country or to impose French law on it; they were mainly concerned with establishing a strong central administration and safeguarding the royal revenues, and it was through machinery devised for these purposes that the common law developed. Royal representatives were sent on tours of the shires to check on the conduct of local affairs generally, and this involved their participating in the work of local courts. At the same time there split off from the body of advisers surrounding the king (the *curia regis*) the first permanent royal court – the *Court of Exchequer, sitting at Westminster to hear disputes concerning the revenues. Under Henry II (reigned 1154–89), to whom the development of the common law is principally due, the royal representatives were sent out on a regular basis (their tours being known as circuits) and their functions began to be exclusively judicial. Known as *justiciae errantes* (wandering justices), they took over the work of the local courts. In the same period there appeared at Westminster a second permanent royal court, the *Court of Common Pleas. These two steps mark the real origins of the common law. The judges of the Court of Common Pleas so successfully superimposed a single system on the multiplicity of local customs that, as early as the end of the 12th century, reference is found in court records to the custom of the kingdom. In this process they were joined by the judges of the Court of Exchequer, which began to exercise jurisdiction in many cases involving disputes between subjects rather than the royal revenues, and by those of a third royal court that gradually emerged – the Court of King's Bench (*see* COURT OF QUEEN'S BENCH). The common law was subsequently supplemented by *equity, but it remained separately administered by the three courts of common law until they and the Court of Chancery (all of them sitting in Westminster Hall until rehoused in the Strand in 1872) were replaced by the *High Court of Justice under the Judicature Acts 1873–75. **2.** Rules of law developed by the courts as opposed to those created by statute. **3.** A general system of law deriving exclusively from court decisions.

common-law marriage 1. A marriage recognized as valid at common law although not complying with the usual requirements for marriage. Such marriages are only recognized today if (1) they are celebrated outside England and there is no local form of marriage reasonably available to the parties or (2) they are celebrated by military chaplains in a foreign territory (or on a ship in foreign waters), and one of the parties to the marriage is serving in the Forces in that territory. The form of marriage is a declaration that the parties take each other as husband and wife. **2.** Loosely, the situation of two unmarried people living together as husband and wife (*see* COHABITATION). In law such people are treated as unmarried, although recently they have been recognized as equivalent to married persons for purposes of protection against battering and for some provisions of the Rent Acts (such as succession to *statutory tenancies).

Common Market *See* EUROPEAN COMMUNITY.

common mistake *See* MISTAKE.

common money bond *See* BOND.

Common Serjeant The title held by one of the *circuit judges at the *Central Criminal Court. It was formerly an ancient office of the City of London, first mentioned in its records in 1291. Serjeants-at-law were the highest order at the English Bar from the 13th or 14th centuries until the King's Counsel took priority in the 17th century. Until 1873 the judges of the common law courts were appointed from the serjeants; the order of serjeants was dissolved in 1877. The title remains, however, for a circuit judge who has a ten-year Crown Court qualification and who has been appointed a Common Serjeant by the Crown.

Commonwealth (British Commonwealth) *n.* A voluntary association consisting of the UK and many of its former colonies or dependencies (e.g. protectorates) that have attained full independence and are recognized by international law as separate countries. The earliest to obtain independence (e.g. Canada and Australia) did so by virtue of the Statute of Westminster 1931, but the majority have been granted it individually by subsequent Independence Acts. Some (such as Canada and Australia) are still technically part of the Crown's dominions; others (e.g. India) have become republics. All accept the Crown as the symbol of their free association and the head of the Commonwealth.

commonwealth citizen Under the British Nationality Act 1948, a status synonymous with that of *British subject. By the British Nationality Act 1981 (which replaced the 1948 Act as from 1 January 1983 and gave the expression British subject a very limited meaning), it was redefined as a wide secondary status. It now includes every person who is either a British citizen, a British Dependent Territories citizen, a British National (Overseas), a British Overseas citizen, a British subject (in its current sense), or a citizen of one of the independent Commonwealth countries listed in a schedule to the 1981 Act.

commorientes *pl. n.* [Latin] Persons who die at the same time. Under the Law of Property Act 1925, when the order of death is uncertain commorientes are presumed (so far as the devolution of their property is concerned) to have died in order of seniority. Thus a bequest by the younger to the elder is treated as having lapsed. However, this rule may be displaced by a contrary intention expressed in a will, and under the Intestates' Estates Act 1952 the rule does not apply when intestate spouses die at the same time: it is assumed that neither spouse left the other surviving.

community *n.* A *local government area in Wales, as set out in the Local Government (Wales) Act 1994, consisting of a division of a *county or a county borough and equivalent to an English civil parish. All communities have meetings and many have an elected community council, which is a *local authority with a number of minor functions (e.g. the provision of allotments, bus shelters, and recreation grounds). A community council may by resolution call its area a town, itself a town council, and its chairman the town mayor, either in Welsh or in English.

community charge (poll tax) A former form of local tax levied on all adults (with some exceptions) to contribute to the cost of local government. It was introduced by the Local Government Finance Act 1988 to replace domestic *rates (i.e. rates paid by private householders) from April 1990 in England and Wales (it was introduced in Scotland in 1989). The tax proved unpopular and difficult to collect. It was abolished and replaced by the *council tax with effect from April 1993.

Community dimension (in EU mergers law) *See* MERGER.

community home An institution for the accommodation and maintenance of children and young persons in care. Community homes are provided by local authorities and voluntary organizations under the Children Act 1989. A local authority may be liable for the acts of children in community homes.

community land *See* DEVELOPMENT LAND.

Community law (EU law) The law of the European Union (as opposed to the national laws of the member states). It consists of the treaties establishing the EU (together with subsequent amending treaties), *Community legislation, and decisions of the *European Court of Justice. Any provision of the treaties or of Community legislation that is directly applicable or directly effective in a member state forms part of the law of that state and prevails over its national law in the event of any inconsistency between the two.

Community Legal Service The service that replaced the *legal aid scheme on 1

April 2000. The new service has many features similar to the legal aid scheme but has been redesigned to ensure that public funds are directed to those most in need. It does this by excluding more categories of potential applicant and also in prescribing new and stricter criteria for eligibility. The service is administered by the **Legal Services Commission** (which replaced the Legal Aid Board of the old scheme). There are various levels of service. They are: (1) **legal help**, which broadly replaces the *green form scheme; (2) **help at court**, which is similar to the previous *ABWOR; (3) **investigative help**, which provides the funding of investigation before assessment as to whether or not to proceed; (4) **full representation**, which is equivalent to the former full legal aid; (5) **support funding**, which provides partial funds to support high-cost claims but not the majority of the costs, which are met elsewhere; and (6) **specific directions**, by which the Lord Chancellor may authorize specific support for particular claims, e.g. test cases or class actions. Strict financial criteria are laid down for eligibility for each of these six levels of service, which reflect the requirements of the different levels of service. However, at the centre of such criteria is the cost-benefit criterion, under which funding will be refused if the benefit to be gained is considered not to justify the level of costs likely to be incurred.

Community legislation Laws made by the *Council of the European Union or the *European Commission. Each body has legislative powers, but most legislation is made by the Council, based on proposals by the Commission, and usually after consultation with the *European Parliament. The role of the Parliament in the legislative process was strengthened under the Single European Act 1986 and the Maastricht Treaty. Community legislation is in the form of regulations, directives, and decisions. **Regulations** are of general application, binding in their entirety, and directly applicable in all member states without the need for individual member states to enact these domestically (*see* COMMUNITY LAW). **Directives** are addressed to one or more member states and require them to achieve (by amending national law if necessary) specified results. They are not directly applicable – they do not create enforceable Community rights in member states until the state has legislated in accordance with the directive: the domestic statute then creates the rights for the citizens of that country. A directive cannot therefore impose legal obligations on individuals or private bodies, but by its **direct effect** it confers rights on individuals against the state and state bodies, even before it has been implemented by changes to national law, by decisions of the European court. **Decisions** may be addressed either to states or to persons and are binding on them in their entirety. Both the Council and the Commission may also make **recommendations**, give **opinions**, and issue *notices, but these are not legally binding.

community of assets (community of property) The sharing of ownership of matrimonial property, such as the home and furniture, as an automatic consequence of marriage. This is not a feature of English law. *See* FAMILY ASSETS.

community punishment order An order that requires an offender (who must consent and be aged at least 16) to perform unpaid work for between 40 and 240 hours under the supervision of a probation officer. Formerly known as a **community service order**, it has been renamed under the Criminal Justice and Court Services Act 2000. Such an order replaces any other form of punishment (e.g. imprisonment); it is usually based on a probation officer's report and is carried out within 12 months (unless extended). Breach of the order may be dealt with by fine or by revocation of the order and the imposition of any punishment that could originally have been imposed for the offence.

community rehabilitation order A court order, formerly known as a **probation order**, placing an offender under the supervision of a *probation officer for a period of between six months and three years, imposed (only with the consent of the offender) instead of a sentence of imprisonment. Such orders may be imposed on any offenders over the age of 16; they are most commonly imposed on first offenders, young offenders, elderly offenders in need of support, and offenders whose crimes are not serious. The order contains conditions for the supervision and behaviour of the offender during the rehabilitation period, including where he should live, when and how often he should report to his local probation officer, and a requirement that he should notify the probation officer of any change of address. The order may also require him to live in an approved probation hostel (for those offenders employed outside the hostel) or an approved probation home (for offenders not employed outside). An order may also be made that the offender should attend a specified **day-training centre**, designed to train him to cope with the strains of modern life, for a period of up to 60 days.

A community rehabilitation order has the same legal effect as a *discharge. If the offender is convicted of a further offence while undergoing community rehabilitation, he may be punished in the normal way for the original offence (for which the order was made) as though he had just been convicted of that offence. If he does not comply with the conditions specified in the community rehabilitation order, he may be fined or the court may make a *community punishment order or order for attendance at a day centre or it may punish him for the original offence as though he had just been convicted of it.

Community rehabilitation orders may also be imposed on offenders who, though not insane, are suffering from some mental problem. A medical practitioner or chartered psychologist may be specified in such orders.

Community Trade Mark (CTM) A *trade mark that is registered for the whole of the European Union. It can be obtained by application to national trade mark offices or the Community Trade Mark Office at Alicante, Spain. The European Commission adopted the Regulation for the Community Trade Mark, Regulation 40/94, on 20 December 1993; UK legislation was included in the Trade Marks Act 1994. Marks are registered for a period of ten years and may be renewed on payment of fees.

commutative contract *See* CONTRACT OF EXCHANGE.

Companies Court The collective name given to those judges forming part of the *Chancery Division of the High Court who deal with matters arising out of the Companies Acts, principally the formation, management, and winding-up of limited liability companies (*see* LIMITED COMPANY).

Companies House *See* COMPANIES REGISTRY.

companies register The official list of companies registered at the Companies Registry (*see* REGISTRATION OF A COMPANY).

Companies Registry (Companies House) The office of the Registrar of Companies (*see* REGISTRATION OF A COMPANY). Companies with a registered office in England or Wales are served by the registry at Cardiff; those in Scotland by the registry in Edinburgh. Certain documents lodged there are open to inspection. These documents include the *accounts of limited companies, the *annual return, any *prospectus, the *memorandum and *articles of association, and particulars of the directors, the secretary, the *registered office, some types of company *charge, and notices of liquidation.

company *n.* An association formed to conduct business or other activities in the name of the association. Most companies are incorporated (*see* INCORPORATION) and therefore have a legal personality distinct from those of their members. Incorporation is usually by registration under the Companies Act 1985 (*see* REGISTRATION OF A COMPANY) but may be by private Act of Parliament (*see* STATUTORY COMPANY) or by royal charter (**chartered company**). Shareholders and directors are generally protected when the company goes out of business. *See* FOREIGN COMPANY; LIMITED COMPANY; PRIVATE COMPANY; PUBLIC COMPANY; UNLIMITED COMPANY; WELSH COMPANY.

company meeting *See* GENERAL MEETING.

company member A person who holds *shares in a company or, in the case of a company that does not issue shares (such as a company limited by guarantee), any of those who have signed the *memorandum of association or have been admitted to membership by the directors. *See* LIMITED COMPANY.

company name The title of a registered company, as stated in its *memorandum of association and in the companies register. The names with which companies can be registered are restricted (*see also* BUSINESS NAME). The name must appear clearly in full outside the *registered office and other business premises, upon the company seal, and upon certain documents issuing from the company, including notepaper and invoices. Noncompliance is an offence and fines can be levied. Under the Insolvency Act 1986, it may be an offence for a director of a company that has gone into insolvent liquidation to re-use the company name. *See also* CHANGE OF NAME; LIMITED COMPANY.

company secretary An officer of a company whose role will vary according to the nature of the company but will generally be concerned with the administrative duties imposed upon the company by the Companies Act (e.g. delivering documents to the *Companies Registry). Under the Companies Act 1985 every company is required to have a company secretary. A sole *director cannot also be the company secretary, and in the case of a *public company the company secretary must be qualified to act as such.

compellable witness A person who may lawfully be required to give evidence. In principle every person who is competent to be a witness is compellable (*see* COMPETENCE). In criminal prosecutions the spouse of the accused is generally competent and, under the 1999 amendments to the Police and Criminal Evidence Act 1984, may in some circumstances be compellable; for example, when the offence charged is an assault upon the spouse or someone under the age of 16, the spouse is compellable as well as competent.

compensation *n.* Monetary payment to compensate for loss or damage. When someone has committed a criminal offence that caused personal injury, loss, or damage, and he has been convicted for this offence or it was taken into account when sentencing for another offence, the court may make a **compensation order** requiring the offender to pay compensation to the person suffering the loss (with interest, if need be). Magistrates' courts may make orders in respect of compensation. The court must take into account the offender's means and should avoid making excessively high orders or orders to be paid in long-term instalments. If the offender cannot afford to pay both a fine and compensation, priority should be given to payment of compensation. A compensation order may be made for funeral expenses or bereavement in respect of death resulting from an offence other than a death due to a motor-vehicle accident. Potential claimants and maximum compensation for bereavement are the same as those under the Fatal Accidents Act 1976 (see FATAL ACCIDENTS). An order may only be made in respect of injury, loss, or damage (other than loss suffered by a person's dependants in consequence of his death) due to a motor-vehicle accident if (1) it is for damage to property occurring while it was outside the owner's possession in the case of offences under the Theft Act 1968, or (2) the offender was uninsured to use the vehicle and compensation is not payable under the *Motor Insurers' Bureau agreement. A court that does not award compensation must give reasons. Victims of *criminal injury may apply for compensation under the *Criminal Injuries Compensation Scheme. Under the Theft Act 1968, a *restitution order in monetary terms may be made when the stolen goods are no longer in existence; this kind of order is equivalent to a compensation order. Compensation orders may be made in addition to, or instead of, other sentences. A court must order a parent or guardian of an offender under the age of 17 to pay a compensation order on behalf of the offender unless the parent or guardian cannot be found or it would be unreasonable to order him to pay it.

A person who has been wrongfully convicted of a criminal offence may apply to the Home Secretary for compensation, which is awarded upon the assessment of an independent assessor.

An *employment tribunal may order an employer to pay compensation to an employee who has been unfairly dismissed (see UNFAIR DISMISSAL). The compensation comprises a **basic award** of a sum equivalent to the *redundancy payment to which a redundant employee would be entitled (with a minimum of £3300 when dismissal is for trade union activity), and a **compensatory award** representing the loss that the employee suffers because of the dismissal (the compensatory award is subject to an upper limit of £51,700). This will include compensation for the loss of his earnings and other benefits of the former employment, and for the loss of his statutory rights in respect of unfair dismissal and redundancy in the initial period of any new employment he obtains (see CONTINUOUS EMPLOYMENT). Additional compensation may be awarded if the employer does not comply with an order by the tribunal to re-employ the employee; the additional award will be between 26 and 52 weeks' pay. Limits on the amount of weekly pay that can be used in these calculations are set by regulations made by the Secretary of State for Work and Pensions and reviewed annually. The tribunal may reduce any compensation by an appropriate proportion when the employee's conduct has contributed to his dismissal. The employee is under the same duty to mitigate his loss as someone claiming damages in the courts. Thus if he unreasonably refuses an offer of a new job he will not be compensated for his continued unemployment thereafter. If the employee was dismissed for his failure to enter into a *closed-shop agreement, following pressure by a trade union for his dismissal, the employer can pass on to the trade union the liability to pay compensation. Compensation may also be awarded by an employment tribunal when there is a finding of sexual or racial discrimination. In such cases the upper limit or financial cap on unfair dismissal damages has been removed, as the European Court of Justice has ruled that the cap is discriminatory and contrary to *equal treatment laws. This award can also include an amount for hurt feelings.

competence *n.* (of witnesses) The legal capacity of a person to be a *witness. Since the abolition in the 19th century of certain ancient grounds of incompetence, every person of sound mind and sufficient understanding has been competent, subject to certain exceptions. For example, a child may be sworn as a witness only if he understands the solemnity of the occasion and that the taking of an oath involves an obligation to tell the truth over and above the ordinary duty of doing so. However, under the Youth Justice and Criminal Evidence Act 1999, a child below the age of 14 years may only give *unsworn evidence. Since the Police and Criminal Evidence Act 1984 and the subsequent 1999 amendments, the spouse of an accused is generally a competent witness for the prosecution (subject to some exceptions) and compellable for the accused (subject to some exceptions).

competition law The branch of law concerned with the regulation of *anticompetitive practices, *restrictive trade practices, and *abuses of a dominant position or market power. Such laws prohibit *cartels and other commercial restrictive agreements. In the UK the Competition Act 1998 and the Fair Trading Act 1973 contain the legislative provisions. Throughout the EU, *Articles 81 and 82 of the Treaty of Rome and regulations made under those provisions contain the legal rules in this area, which constitute EU competition law. Under the *de minimis* principle, the European Commission has issued a notice that competition rules will be unlikely to apply to agreements affecting trade between member states when the parties to the agreement have a joint market share of 5% or less (10% for *vertical agreements, such as distribution contracts). In the USA competition law is known as **antitrust law**.

competitive tendering The introduction of competition into the provision of public services with the aim of improving the cost-effectiveness and quality of these services. It affected a wide range of public bodies, from local authorities to the prison service: public services were supplied by the body (usually a private-sector company) that submitted the most competitive tender for the service in question. Examples of services most commonly provided by this means were refuse collection, the provision of school meals, and residential care for the elderly. These rules were principally contained in the Local Government Acts 1988 and 1992. The Local Government Act 1999 abolished compulsory competitive tendering and replaced it with a duty to provide *best value, whereby authorities must have regard to economy, efficiency, and effectiveness when exercising their functions.

complainant *n.* A person who alleges that a crime has been committed. A complainant alleging rape, attempted rape, incitement to rape, or being an accessory to rape is allowed by statute to remain anonymous; evidence relating to her previous sexual experience cannot be given (unless the court especially rules otherwise).

complaint *n.* **1.** The initiating step in civil proceedings in the *magistrates' court, consisting of a statement of the complainant's allegations. The complaint is made before a *justice of the peace or, if the complaint is not required to be on oath, before a *clerk to the justices, who may then issue an originating *process directed to the defendant. **2.** An allegation of a crime. A complaint made by the victim of a sexual offence directly after the commission of the offence is admissible as evidence of the consistency of the complainant's story.

completely constituted trust *See* EXECUTED TRUST.

completion *n.* (in land law) The point at which ownership of land that is the subject of a contract for its sale changes hands. The purchaser hands over any unpaid balance of the price in exchange for the title deeds and a valid conveyance of the land to him if the land is unregistered. If the land is registered, the purchaser receives a simple form of transfer that must be lodged at the appropriate District *Land Registry with the *land certificate.

composition *n.* An agreement between a debtor and his creditors discharging the debts in exchange for payment of a proportion of what is due. The debtor may have

to register the agreement as a *deed of arrangement. *See also* SCHEME OF
ARRANGEMENT; VOLUNTARY ARRANGEMENT.

compound *vb.* **1.** To make a *composition with creditors. **2.** *See* COMPOUNDING AN
OFFENCE.

compounding an offence The offence of accepting or agreeing to accept
consideration for not disclosing information that might assist in convicting or
prosecuting someone who has committed an *arrestable offence (consideration here
does not include reasonable compensation for loss or injury caused by the offence).
There is also a special statutory offence of advertising a reward for stolen goods on
the basis that "no questions will be asked" or that the person producing the goods
"will be safe from inquiry".

compound settlement A settlement of land arising from a series of trust
instruments, e.g. a resettlement following the barring of an *entailed interest.
Under the Settled Land Act 1925 the trustees of the original settlement (or if there
are none, those of the resettlement) are treated as the trustees of the compound
settlement. Thus the tenant for life is always able to overreach the interests of all
other beneficiaries (*see* OVERREACHING).

compromis d'arbitrage [French] Agreements between states to submit disputes
between them to an arbitration tribunal. *See also* ARBITRATION.

compromise *n.* The settlement of a disputed claim by agreement between the
parties. Any court proceedings already started are terminated. The terms of the
settlement can be incorporated in a judgment by the court (called a **consent
judgment**) or the terms can form a contract between the parties.

compulsory purchase The enforced acquisition of land for public purposes, by
statutory authority and on payment of compensation. Authority may be given for a
specific acquisition, but public and local authorities have wide powers to acquire any
land required for particular functions, such as education. These powers are normally
exercised under the Acquisition of Land Act 1981, and compensation is assessed
under the Land Compensation Acts 1961 and 1973. A compulsory purchase order is
submitted for confirmation to the appropriate government minister, whose decision
is preceded by an inquiry into public objections. In most cases the procedure
includes the service of a *notice to treat on the landowner, who then negotiates
compensation. Any dispute about compensation is decided by the *Lands Tribunal.
See also SPECIAL PROCEDURE ORDERS.

compulsory winding-up A procedure for winding up a company by the court
based on a petition made under circumstances listed in the Insolvency Act 1986. The
main grounds for this type of petition are that the company is unable to pay its
debts or that the court is of the opinion that it is in the interests of the company
that a *just and equitable winding-up should be made. Any director, *contributory,
or creditor of the company, the supervisor of a *voluntary arrangement, or the
Secretary of State may make such a petition. The winding-up is conducted by a
*liquidator, who is supervised by the court, a *liquidation committee, and the
Department of Trade and Industry. *See also* WINDING-UP.

computer documents (in the law of evidence) In civil cases a document
produced by a computer is admissible under the general rules of evidence of any
fact recorded in it of which direct oral evidence would be admissible. In criminal
cases computer printouts are admissible as evidence by virtue of the amendments
introduced by the Youth Justice and Criminal Evidence Act 1999.

computer misuse *See* HACKING.

concealment *n*. *See* NONDISCLOSURE.

concealment of securities The offence (punishable by up to seven years' imprisonment) of dishonestly concealing, destroying, or defacing any **valuable security**, will, or any document issuing from a court or government department for the purpose of gain for oneself or causing loss to another. Valuable securities include any documents concerning rights over property, authorizing payment of money or the delivery of property, or evidencing such rights or the satisfying of any obligation.

concentration *n*. (in EU law) The technical term for a *merger.

concert party (consortium) An agreement (which may or may not be legally binding) between a number of people to acquire shares in a company in order to accumulate a significant holding of its voting shares. Under the Companies Act 1985 and rules administered by the Panel on Takeovers and Mergers anyone becoming interested in 3% or more of the voting shares of a public company must disclose this to the company; a member of a concert party is deemed to be interested not only in his own shares but also in those of other consortium members. Such disclosure may enable a company to counter a *takeover; it may also trigger rules relating to partial offers, which may make it necessary for the consortium to offer to buy the remaining shares. *See also* SARS. *Compare* DAWN RAID.

conciliation *n*. **1.** (in civil disputes) *See* ACAS; ALTERNATIVE DISPUTE RESOLUTION. **2.** A procedure of peaceful settlement of international disputes. The matter of dispute is referred to a standing or *ad hoc* commission of conciliation, appointed with the parties' agreement, whose function is to elucidate the facts objectively and impartially and then to issue a report. The eventual report is expected to contain concrete proposals for a settlement, which, however, the parties are under no legal obligation to accept. *See also* GOOD OFFICES; MEDIATION.

conciliation officer *See* ACAS.

conclusive evidence Evidence that must, as a matter of law, be taken to establish some fact in issue and that cannot be disputed. For example, the certificate of incorporation of a company is conclusive evidence of its incorporation.

concurrent interests Ownership of land by two or more persons at the same time; for example, *joint tenancy and *tenancy in common.

concurrent jurisdiction That part of the jurisdiction of the *Court of Chancery before the Judicature Acts 1873–75 that was enforced equally in the common law courts; equity usually took jurisdiction because the common law remedies were inadequate. Since the Judicature Acts the jurisdiction of all divisions of the High Court has been concurrent in name, but certain remedies (for example, specific performance and injunction) are more commonly sought in the Chancery Division. *Compare* EXCLUSIVE JURISDICTION.

concurrent lease A lease granted by a landlord to run at the same time as another lease of the same premises. The effect is that the lessee of the concurrent lease acquires the rights and duties of the landlord in relation to the other lease.

concurrent planning (twin-track planning) The planning involved in placing certain children who are in local-authority care with carers who are approved to both foster and adopt. Initially, the plan requires that the carers should work constructively to return the child to its parents. If it becomes apparent that this will not happen within a reasonable time, the carers will continue to look after the child and apply to adopt him. The aim of concurrent planning is to reduce the number of moves experienced by a child in care.

concurrent sentence A *sentence to be served at the same time as one or more other sentences, when the accused has been convicted of more than one offence. Concurrent sentences are usually terms of imprisonment, and in effect the accused serves the term of the longest sentence. Alternatively the court may impose **consecutive sentences**, which follow on from each other.

concurrent tortfeasors See JOINT TORTFEASORS.

condition n. **1.** A major term of a contract. It is frequently described as a term that goes to the root of a contract or is of the **essence of a contract** (see also TIME PROVISIONS IN CONTRACTS); it is contrasted with a **warranty**, which is a term of minor importance. Breach of a condition constitutes a fundamental breach of the contract and entitles the injured party to treat it as discharged, whereas breach of warranty is remediable only by an action for damages, subject to any contrary provision in a contract (see BREACH OF CONTRACT). A condition or a warranty may be either an *express term or an *implied term. In the case of an express term, the fact that the contract labels it a condition or a warranty is not regarded by the courts as conclusive of its status. See also INNOMINATE TERMS. **2.** A provision that does not form part of a contractual obligation but operates either to suspend the contract until a specified event has happened (a **condition precedent**) or to bring it to an end in certain specified circumstances (a **condition subsequent**). When X agrees to buy Y's car if it passes its MOT test, this is a condition precedent; a condition in a contract for the sale of goods that entitles the purchaser to return the goods if dissatisfied with them is a condition subsequent.

conditional admissibility The *admissibility of evidence whose *relevance is conditional upon the existence of some fact that has not yet been proved. The courts permit such evidence to be given conditionally, upon proof of that fact at a later stage of the trial. Such evidence is sometimes said to have been received *de bene esse.

conditional agreement An agreement that will take effect, if at all, upon the happening of some uncertain event.

conditional discharge See DISCHARGE.

conditional fee agreement An agreement, which must be in writing, between lawyer and client for legal services in litigation to be provided on the basis that payment is only due if the proceedings are successful ("no win, no fee"). In return for accepting the risk of no fee, the lawyer is entitled to charge a higher fee (by claiming a higher *uplift) if successful. If the claimant loses the case, he may have to pay the other party's costs. The litigation is therefore not entirely risk-free, although insurance, for which premiums are charged, can be taken out to accommodate this risk. The conditions on which a conditional fee agreement may be made (including the type of proceedings in which they are available and the maximum percentage increase in fees allowed) are prescribed by the Lord Chancellor under the Courts and Legal Services Act 1990 and the Access to Justice Act 1999. For most areas of law conditional fee agreements are unlawful, but they are allowed for certain limited categories of cases, including personal injury cases. See also CONTINGENCY FEE; MAINTENANCE AND CHAMPERTY.

conditional interest An interest that is liable to be forfeited, on the occurrence of a specified event, at the instance of the person who created it; for example, when

A conveys land to B in fee simple subject to a rentcharge and reserves a right of forfeiture for nonpayment. Under the Law of Property (Amendment) Act 1926 a conditional interest in land qualifies as a *fee simple absolute in possession and can therefore exist as a legal estate. *Compare* CONTINGENT INTEREST; DETERMINABLE INTEREST.

conditional sale agreement A contract of sale under which the price is payable by instalments and ownership is not to pass to the buyer (although he is in possession of the goods) until specified conditions relating to the payment of the price or other matters are fulfilled. The seller retains ownership of the goods as security until he is paid. A conditional sale agreement is a *consumer-credit agreement; it is regulated by the Consumer Credit Act 1974 if the buyer is an individual, the credit does not exceed £25,000, and the agreement is not otherwise exempt.

condition precedent *See* CONDITION.

condition subsequent *See* CONDITION.

condominium *n.* **1.** Joint sovereignty over a territory by two or more states (the word is also used for the territory subject to joint sovereignty). For example, the New Hebrides Islands in the South Pacific were a Franco-British condominium until 1980. Sovereignty is joint, but each jointly governing power has separate jurisdiction over its own subjects. *Compare* CO-IMPERIUM. **2.** Individual ownership of part of a building (e.g. a flat in a block of flats) combined with common ownership of the parts of the building used in common.

condonation *n.* Forgiving a matrimonial offence or turning a blind eye to it. Formerly a bar to divorce, it is no longer relevant in divorce proceedings.

confederation *n.* A formal association of states loosely bound by a treaty, in many cases one establishing a central governing mechanism with specified powers over member states but not directly over citizens of those states. In a confederation, the constituent states retain their national sovereignty and consequently their right to *secession. *Compare* FEDERAL STATE.

conference *n.* **1.** A meeting of members of the House of Lords and the House of Commons appointed to attempt to reach agreement when one House objects to amendments made to one of its Bills by the other. **2.** A meeting between counsel and a solicitor to discuss a case in which they are engaged. Conferences usually take place at counsel's chambers. If the barrister involved is a QC, the meeting is called a **consultation**.

confession *n.* An *admission, in whole or in part, made by an accused person of his guilt. At common law, confessions were admissible if made voluntarily, i.e. not obtained as a result of some threat or inducement held out by a person in authority (such as a police officer). They are now governed by the Police and Criminal Evidence Act 1984, which requires the prosecution, if called upon to do so, to prove beyond a reasonable doubt that the confession was not obtained by oppression of the person who made it or as a result of anything that was likely to render the confession unreliable. A confession may also be ruled to be inadmissible if the civil rights of the accused have been breached, for example if he has been denied access to legal advice.

confession and avoidance A pleading in the *defence that, while admitting or assuming the truth of the material facts alleged in the particulars of claim (the **confession**), seeks to avoid or destroy the legal consequences of those facts by alleging further facts constituting some defence to the claim (the **avoidance**). An example is a plea of self-defence to an action for assault.

confidential communication The mere fact that a communication is confidential does not in itself make it inadmissible; it will only be so if it is within the scope of an evidentiary *privilege, such as legal professional privilege or public-interest privilege.

confidential information *See* BREACH OF CONFIDENCE.

confiscation order An order that requires an offender convicted by the Crown Court of an *indictable offence, who has benefited by at least £10,000 from that offence (or an offence taken into consideration), to pay a sum that the court thinks fit. Magistrates may make such orders only in relation to a limited class of offences (e.g. offences relating to the supply of video recordings of unclassified work). The order is enforced like a *fine and is in addition to any other sentence. The High Court may make a restraint order prohibiting the transfer or disposal of realizable property held by a person when proceedings have been instituted against him for a relevant offence. *See also* CONTROLLED DRUGS.

conflict of laws *See* PRIVATE INTERNATIONAL LAW.

confusion of goods The mixing of goods of two or more owners in such a way that their original shares can no longer be distinguished. The owners hold the goods in common, in proportion to their shares. One owner may be awarded possession of the mixture, if he has best right to it, subject to him compensating the other owner for his proportion.

conjugal rights The rights of either spouse of a marriage, which include the right to the other's consortium (company), cohabitation (sexual intercourse), and maintenance during the marriage. There is, however, no longer any legal procedure for enforcing these rights. The old action for restitution of conjugal rights was abolished in 1971 and a husband insisting on sexual intercourse against the wishes of his wife may be guilty of *rape. *See also* CONSUMMATION OF A MARRIAGE.

connivance *n.* Behaviour of a person designed to cause his or her spouse to commit a matrimonial offence, such as adultery. Connivance is no longer an absolute bar to divorce, but may still be evidence that the marriage has not irretrievably broken down.

conquest *n.* The acquisition by military force of enemy territory followed by its formal annexation after the cessation of hostilities. It does not include the acquisition of land as a term of a peace treaty (*see* CESSION). The acquisition of territory after a war in the absence of any peace treaty, because the defeated state has ceased to exist, is known as **debellatio** or **subjugation**. Conquest is not now regarded as a legitimate means of acquiring territory, and hence conferring valid title, as Article 2(4) of the UN Charter expressly prohibits aggressive war and Article 5(3) of General Assembly Resolution 3314 (XXIX) of 1975 effectively nullifies any legal title acquired in this way.

consanguinity (blood relationship) *n.* Relationship by blood, i.e. by descent from a common ancestor. People descended from two common ancestors are said to be of the **whole blood**. If they share only one ancestor, they are of the **half blood**. *Compare* AFFINITY.

consecutive sentences *See* CONCURRENT SENTENCE.

consensus ad idem [Latin: agreement on the same thing] The agreement by contracting parties to identical terms that is necessary for the formation of a legally binding contract. *See* ACCEPTANCE; MISTAKE; OFFER.

consent *n.* Deliberate or implied affirmation; compliance with a course of proposed action. Consent is essential in a number of circumstances. For example, contracts and marriages are invalid unless both parties give their consent. Consent must be given freely, without duress or deception, and with sufficient legal competence to give it (*see also* INFORMED CONSENT). In criminal law, issues of consent arise mainly in connection with offences involving violence and *dishonesty. For public-policy reasons, a victim's consent to conduct which foreseeably causes him bodily harm is no defence to a charge involving an *assault, *wounding, or *homicide; in other cases the defendant should be acquitted if the magistrates or jury have a reasonable doubt not only as to whether the victim had consented but also as to whether he thought the victim had consented. *See also* AGE OF CONSENT; BATTERY; CONVEYANCE; RAPE.

conservation area An area designated as such by a local planning authority (*see* TOWN AND COUNTRY PLANNING) because it is of special architectural or historic interest the character of which ought to be preserved or enhanced. Each building in the area becomes protected as if it were a *listed building, and trees not protected by a *tree preservation order may only be lopped, felled, etc., after notice to the authority.

consideration *n.* An act, forbearance, or promise by one party to a contract that constitutes the price for which he buys the promise of the other. Consideration is essential to the validity of any contract other than one made by deed. Without consideration an agreement not made by deed is not binding; it is a *nudum pactum* (naked agreement), governed by the maxim *ex nudo pacto non oritur actio* (a right of action does not arise out of a naked agreement).

The doctrine of consideration is governed by four major principles. (1) A **valuable consideration** is required, i.e. the act, forbearance, or promise must have some economic value. **Good consideration** (natural love and affection or a moral duty) is not enough to render a promise enforceable. (2) Consideration need not be adequate but it must be sufficient. Not to be adequate in this context means that it need not constitute a realistic price for the promise it buys, as long as it has some economic value. If X promises to sell his £50,000 house to Y for £5000, Y is giving valuable consideration despite its inadequacy. £1 is often the consideration in commercial contracts. That it must be sufficient means sufficient in law. A person's performance of, or promise to perform, an existing duty usually cannot in law constitute consideration. (3) Consideration must move from the promisee. Thus if X promises to give Y £1000 in return for Y's promise to give employment to Z, Z cannot enforce Y's promise, for he has not supplied the consideration for it. (4) Consideration may be executory or executed but must not be past. A promise in return for a promise (as in a contract of sale) is **executory consideration**; an act or forbearance in return for a promise (as in giving information to obtain a reward) is **executed consideration**. However, a completed act or forbearance is **past consideration** in relation to any subsequent promise. For example, if X gives information to Y gratuitously and Y then promises to reward him this is past consideration, which does not constitute consideration.

consistory court *See* ECCLESIASTICAL COURTS.

Consolidated Fund The central account with the Bank of England maintained by the government for receiving public revenue and meeting public expenditure. Most payments from it are authorized annually by Consolidated Fund Acts, but some (e.g. judicial salaries) are permanent statutory charges on it.

consolidating statute A statute that repeals and re-enacts existing statutes relating to a particular subject. Its purpose is to state their combined effect and so simplify the presentation of the law. It does not aim to alter the law unless it is stated in its long title to be a consolidation with amendments. An example of a consolidating statute is the Trade Union and Labour Relations (Consolidation) Act 1992. *Compare* CODIFYING STATUTE. *See also* INTERPRETATION OF STATUTES.

consolidation of actions A procedure in civil cases by which two or more cases may be amalgamated. It is generally necessary to show that some common question of law or fact will arise in all the cases. The purpose of consolidation is to save costs and time.

consolidation of mortgages The right of a mortgagee who has taken mortgages on two or more properties from the same mortgagor to require the mortgagor to redeem all of the mortgages or none, provided that the contractual date of redemption (*see* POWER OF SALE) for all of them has passed. The right arose because it was considered unfair to a mortgagee to have one security redeemed when another, given by the same mortgagor, might be inadequate to secure that loan. Since 1881 at least one of the mortgage deeds must show an intent to allow consolidation for the mortgagee to exercise the right. *Compare* TACKING.

consortium *n.* **1.** The right of one spouse to the company, assistance, and affection of the other. Formerly, a husband could bring an action in tort (*per quod consortium amisit*) against anyone who, by a tortious act against his wife, deprived him of consortium. A wife had no corresponding action. The action for loss of consortium was abolished by the Administration of Justice Act 1982. **2.** *See* CONCERT PARTY.

conspiracy *n.* **1.** An agreement between two or more people to behave in a manner that will automatically constitute an offence by at least one of them (e.g. two people agree that one of them shall steal while the other waits in a getaway car). The agreement is itself a statutory crime, usually punishable in the same way as the offence agreed on, even if it is not carried out. *Mens rea*, in the sense of knowledge of the facts that make the action criminal, is required by at least two of the conspirators, even if the crime agreed upon is one of *strict liability. One may be guilty of conspiracy even if it is impossible to commit the offence agreed on (for example, when two or more people conspire to take money from a safe but, unknown to them, there is no money in it). A person is, however, not guilty of conspiracy if the only other party to the agreement is his (or her) spouse. Nor is there liability when the acts are to be carried out in furtherance of a trade dispute and involve only a summary and nonimprisonable offence. Incitement to conspire and attempt to conspire are no longer crimes.

Some forms of criminal conspiracy still exist at common law. These are now limited to: (1) conspiracy to *defraud (e.g. to commit fraud, theft, obtain property by deception, or infringe a copyright) or to cause an official to act contrary to his public duty; (2) conspiracy to corrupt public morals (*see* CORRUPTION OF PUBLIC MORALS); and (3) conspiracy to outrage public decency (this might include an agreement to mount an indecent exhibition).
2. A conspiracy to injure a third party is a tort if it causes damage to the person against whom the conspiracy is aimed. It is not necessary to prove that the conspirators used unlawful means. If unlawful means have not been used, conspiracy is not actionable if the predominant purpose of the conspirators was legitimate. Protection of one's own financial or trade interests is thus a legitimate

purpose provided no unlawful means are used; but retaliation for an insult to one's dignity is not. The operation of the tort in *trade disputes is limited by statute.

constable *n.* *See* POLICE OFFICER.

constituency *n.* An area of the UK for which a representative is elected to membership of the *House of Commons or the *European Parliament. *See also* BOUNDARY COMMISSIONS.

Constituency Members Members of the *London Assembly each of whom represents one of the 14 London constituencies. Constituency Members are elected every four years in May by voters in London, at the same time as *London Members and the *Mayor of London are elected. Each of the 14 London constituencies returns one member.

constitution *n.* The rules and practices that determine the composition and functions of the organs of central and local government in a state and regulate the relationship between the individual and the state. Most states have a written constitution, one of the fundamental provisions of which is that it can itself be amended only in accordance with a special procedure. The constitution of the UK is largely unwritten. It consists partly of statutes, for the amendment of which by subsequent statutes no special procedure is required (*see* ACT OF PARLIAMENT), but also, to a very significant extent, of *common law rules and *constitutional conventions.

constitutional conventions Practices relating to the exercise of their functions by the Crown, the government, Parliament, and the judiciary that are not legally enforceable but are commonly followed as if they were. One of the most important is that the Crown must exercise its constitutional powers only in accordance with the advice of ministers who collectively command the support of a majority of the House of Commons. There is no single reason why conventions are observed. For example, it is a very old convention that Parliament must be summoned at least once a year. If that were not to happen, there would be no annual Finance Act and the government would be able to function only by raising illegal taxation. By contrast, if the Crown broke the convention that the royal assent must not be refused to a Bill duly passed by Parliament, illegal conduct would not necessarily follow (although the future of the monarchy could well be at risk). The basic reason for obeying conventions is to ensure that the machinery of government should function smoothly; conventions have not been codified into law and therefore can be modified informally to meet changing circumstances.

constitutive theory The proposition that the existence of a state can only begin with its formal or implied *recognition by other states. The constitutive theory of recognition insists that only the positive act of recognition creates the new *international legal personality. *Compare* DECLARATORY THEORY.

construction *n.* *See* INTERPRETATION.

constructive *adj.* Describing anything that is deemed by law to exist or to have happened, even though that is not in fact the case.

constructive desertion Behaviour by one spouse causing the other to leave the matrimonial home. If the behaviour is so bad that the party who leaves is forced to do so, it is the spouse who stays behind who is considered, in law, to have deserted, and not the spouse who actually left. A petition for divorce may therefore be brought, after two years, on the ground of *desertion by the spouse who remained behind.

constructive dismissal Termination of a contract of employment by an employee because his employer has shown that he does not intend to be bound by some essential term of the contract. Although the employee has resigned, he has the same right to apply to an employment tribunal as one who has been unfairly dismissed by his employer. *See also* UNFAIR DISMISSAL.

constructive fraud (legal fraud) Any of certain forms of unintentional deception or misrepresentation (*compare* FRAUD). The concept is applied by equity to those cases in which the courts will not enforce or will set aside certain transactions (e.g. contracts) because it is considered unfair or unconscionable for a person to insist on the transaction being completed. This unfairness may be inferred from the terms of the transaction (when these are such that no person with proper advice would have entered the transaction) or from the relationship of the parties (for example, that of solicitor and client or of trustee and beneficiary).

constructive notice Knowledge that the law presumes a person to have even if he is actually ignorant of the facts. A purchaser of unregistered land has constructive notice of all matters that a prudent purchaser would discover on inspection of the property or proper investigation of the title. It has also been held that a purchaser has constructive notice of the rights of any person (such as a spouse) who may reside on the property but is not an owner of the legal estate and therefore does not appear on the title deeds. A purchaser of unregistered land is bound by all matters of which he has constructive, as well as actual, notice unless those matters are void against him for want of registration under the Land Charges Act 1972. Those dealing with registered companies have constructive notice of the contents of documents open to public inspection at the *Companies Registry. *See also* ACTUAL NOTICE; IMPUTED NOTICE.

constructive total loss A loss of a ship or cargo that is only partial but is treated for the purposes of a marine insurance policy as if it were an *actual total loss. This may occur when an actual total loss either appears unavoidable (e.g. when a perishable cargo becomes stranded indefinitely) or can only be prevented by incurring expenditure greater than the value of the ship or cargo. In estimating the cost of repairs for this purpose, general average contributions by other insurers are left out of account, but the expense of salvage operations is a relevant factor. The insured must serve a notice of *abandonment of the ship or cargo on the underwriters. This must be unconditional and served within a reasonable time of his learning of the loss; once accepted by the underwriters, it is irrevocable. The underwriters become liable to indemnify him as for a total loss and in return are entitled to all his rights in the ship or cargo.

constructive trust A *trust imposed by equity to protect the interests of the beneficiaries when a trustee or some other person in a fiduciary relationship gains an advantage through his position. It differs from an *implied trust in that no reference is normally made to the expressed or presumed intention of the parties. English law at present recognizes only the **institutional constructive trust**. This is a trust that automatically comes into being when certain circumstances arise; for example, when a person in a fiduciary position makes an unauthorized profit or when a stranger meddles in a trust. The concept is frequently used in commercial cases but not exclusively so. In a domestic setting, a constructive trust arises when a sole legal owner of property tries to exclude the rights of another person (usually a cohabitee) who has contributed to the purchase price of the property on the understanding that ownership of the property is to be shared, or when the sole legal owner tries to deny an express agreement to share ownership of the property.

Other Commonwealth jurisdictions recognize a **remedial constructive trust**: a trust imposed at the discretion of the court to remedy an injustice. This is not accepted by English courts, although recent case law has suggested that a development in this area is possible.

consul *n.* A *diplomatic agent commissioned by a sovereign state to reside in a foreign city, to represent the political and trading interests of the sending state, and to assist in all matters pertaining to the commercial relations between the two countries. *See also* DIPLOMATIC MISSION.

consumer *n.* A private individual acting otherwise than in a course of a business. Consumers are often given greater legal protection when entering into contracts, for example by having a right to avoid certain unfair terms or to cancel the contract (*see* CONSUMER PROTECTION; DISTANCE SELLING). Many regulations define "consumer" in a particular manner.

consumer-credit agreement A *personal-credit agreement in which an individual (the debtor) is provided with credit not exceeding £25,000. Unless exempted, consumer-credit agreements are regulated by the Consumer Credit Act 1974, which contains provisions regarding the seeking of business, entry into agreements, matters arising during the currency of agreements, default and termination, security, and judicial control. A loan to an individual businessman for business purposes can be a consumer-credit agreement.

consumer-credit business Any business that comprises or relates to the provision of credit under *consumer-credit agreements regulated by the Consumer Credit Act 1974. With certain exceptions, e.g. local authorities, a licence is required to carry on a consumer-credit business.

consumer-credit register The register kept by the Director General of Fair Trading, as required by the Consumer Credit Act 1974, relating to the licensing or carrying on of *consumer-credit businesses or *consumer-hire businesses. The register contains particulars of undetermined applications, licences that are in force or have at any time been suspended or revoked, and decisions given by the Director under the Act and any appeal from them. The public is entitled to inspect the register on payment of a fee.

consumer goods Goods normally supplied for private use or consumption. The Unfair Contract Terms Act 1977 provides that if consumer goods prove defective when used otherwise than exclusively for business purposes as a result of negligence of a manufacturer or distributor, that person's *business liability cannot be excluded or restricted by any guarantee under which the goods are sold. Under the Consumer Protection Act 1987, suppliers of all consumer goods must ensure that the goods comply with the *general safety requirement. Otherwise they commit a criminal offence.

consumer-hire agreement An agreement made by a person with an individual, a partnership, or with some other unincorporated body (the **hirer**) for the *bailment of goods to the hirer. Such an agreement must not be a *hire-purchase agreement, must be capable of subsisting for more than three months, and must not require the hirer to make payments exceeding £25,000. The concept thus does not include a hiring by a company. Consumer-hire agreements, unless exempted, are regulated by the Consumer Credit Act 1974. *Compare* CONSUMER-CREDIT AGREEMENT.

consumer-hire business Any business that comprises or relates to the bailment of goods under *consumer-hire agreements regulated by the Consumer Credit Act

1974. With certain exceptions, e.g. local authorities, a licence is required to carry on a consumer-hire business.

consumer protection The protection, especially by legal means, of consumers (those who contract otherwise than in the course of a business to obtain goods or services from those who supply them in the course of a business). It is the policy of current legislation to protect consumers against unfair contract terms. In particular they are protected against terms that attempt to exclude or restrict the seller's implied undertakings that he has a right to sell the goods, that the goods conform with either description or sample, and that they are of satisfactory quality and fit for their particular purpose (Unfair Contract Terms Act 1977). EU directive 93/13 renders unfair terms in consumer contracts void; it is implemented in the UK by the Unfair Terms in Consumer Contracts Regulations 1999. The Office of Fair Trading runs a special unfair terms unit, which investigates cases in this field. There is also provision for the banning of unfair *consumer trade practices (Fair Trading Act 1973). Consumers (including individual businessmen) are also protected when obtaining credit (Consumer Credit Act 1974) and there is provision for the imposition of standards relating to the safety of goods under the Consumer Protection Act 1987 and the General Product Safety Regulations 1994. There are, in addition, many legislative measures that are product-specific, such as toy safety regulations. For tort liability under the Consumer Protection Act, *see* PRODUCTS LIABILITY.

consumer trade practice Any practice carried on in connection with the supply of goods (by sale or otherwise) or services to consumers. These practices include the terms or conditions of supply and the manner in which they are communicated to the consumers, the promotion of the supply of goods or services, the methods of salesmanship employed in dealing with consumers, the way in which goods are packed, or the methods of demanding or securing payment for goods or services. Under the Fair Trading Act 1973, consumer trade practices are controlled by the Minister, the *Director General of Fair Trading, and the Consumer Protection Advisory Committee, who may ban any practice that adversely affects the economic interests of consumers in the UK.

consummation of a marriage The "completion" of a marriage by an act of sexual intercourse. It is defined for these purposes as complete penetration of the vagina by the penis (although ejaculation is not necessary). A marriage may be consummated despite the use of a contraceptive sheath. If a spouse is incapable of consummation or refuses without good reason to consummate the marriage, these may be grounds for *annulment of the marriage. If one of the partners refuses to arrange an additional marriage ceremony (e.g. in a church) without which he knows his spouse will not agree to have intercourse, this may be a good reason for the spouse's refusal to have intercourse. In this case it is the partner who refused to arrange the ceremony who is regarded as not having consummated the marriage, even though that partner is willing to have intercourse.

contact *n.* (in family law) The opportunity for a child to communicate with a person with whom that child is not resident. The degree of contact may range from a telephone call to a long stay or even a visit abroad, and the court may formalize such arrangements by making a contact order (*see* SECTION 8 ORDERS). A parent being visited by a child may exercise *parental responsibility during the child's visit. The question of contact after a child has been adopted is becoming a contentious issue. *See also* CARE CONTACT ORDER.

contact order *See* SECTION 8 ORDERS.

contemporanea expositio [Latin: contemporaneous interpretation] The interpretation of a document in the sense in which it would have been interpreted at the time of its making. This principle is applied particularly to the interpretation of ancient documents.

contempt of court 1. (civil contempt) Disobedience to a court judgment or process, e.g. breach of an injunction or improper use of discovered documents. If the injunction is served on the defendant with a **penal notice** attached, breach of the injunction can result in the defendant being jailed. **2. (criminal contempt)** Conduct that obstructs or tends to obstruct the proper administration of justice. At common law criminal contempt includes the following categories. (1) Deliberately interfering with the outcome of particular legal proceedings (e.g. attempting improperly to pressurize a party to settle legal proceedings) or bribing or intimidating witnesses, the jury, or a judge. (2) **Contempt in the face of the court**, e.g. using threatening language or creating a disturbance in court. (3) Scandalizing the court by "scurrilous abuse" of a judge going beyond reasonable criticism or attacking the integrity of the administration of justice. (4) Interfering with the general process of administration of justice (e.g. by disclosing the deliberations of a jury), even though no particular proceedings are pending.

Under the Contempt of Court Act 1981 it is a statutory contempt to publish to the public, by any means, any communication that creates a substantial risk that the course of justice in particular legal proceedings will be seriously impeded or prejudiced, if the proceedings are active. Such publications constitute **strict-liability contempt**, in which the intention to interfere with the course of justice is not required, but there are various special defences. It is also contempt under the Act to obtain or disclose any particulars of jury discussions and to bring into court or use a tape recorder without permission. The Act also protects (subject to certain exceptions) sources of information against disclosure in court. Contempt of court is a criminal offence punishable by a jail sentence and/or a fine of any amount ordered by the court.

contempt of Parliament *See* PARLIAMENTARY PRIVILEGE.

contemptuous damages A very small sum of *damages awarded when, although the claimant is technically entitled to succeed, the court thinks that the action should not have been brought. Contemptuous damages are sometimes awarded in "gold-digging" actions for defamation.

contentious business Business of a solicitor when there is a contest between the parties involved, especially litigation. It is important in relation to *costs, since different rules govern contentious and noncontentious costs.

contentious probate business Disputed applications to the court relating to the validity of wills and the administration of estates.

contiguous zone *See* TERRITORIAL WATERS.

continental shelf The sea bed and the soil beneath it that is adjacent to the coast of a maritime state and outside the limits of the state's territorial waters. The 1958 Geneva Convention on the Continental Shelf limits the extent of the shelf to waters less than 200 metres deep or, beyond that limit, to waters that are of such a depth that exploitation of the natural resources of the sea bed is possible. The coastal state is granted exclusive sovereign rights of exploitation over mineral resources and nonmoving species in its continental shelf, provided that this causes no unreasonable interference to navigation, fishing, or scientific research. The 1982 Conference on the Law of the Sea extends the continental shelf, in some cases, to a distance of 200 nautical miles from the baselines around the coast from which the breadth of the territorial sea is measured. It also makes special provisions for delimiting the continental shelf between states with adjacent or opposite coastlines, but does not lay down rules of law for such delimitation. Rocks that cannot sustain human habitation do not have a continental shelf. *See also* LAW OF THE SEA.

contingency fee Payment to a lawyer only if the case is won. Contingency fees are illegal in the UK but common in other countries, such as the United States. However, *conditional fee agreements are permitted for certain limited categories of cases.

contingent interest An interest that can only come into being upon the occurrence of a specified event (for example when A conveys land to B provided he marries). As a contingent interest can only come into being in the future, if at all, it cannot exist as a legal estate in land. Before 1997, such a transaction created a settlement to which the Settled Land Act 1925 applied. From 1997, such a transaction gives rise to a *trust of land under the Trusts of Land and Appointment of Trustees Act 1996. Contingent interests are consequently *equitable interests only. *Compare* CONDITIONAL INTEREST; DETERMINABLE INTEREST.

contingent legacy A bequest that only takes effect if a particular condition is fulfilled, e.g. a bequest "to A if he shall marry within five years".

continuous bail Bail granted by a magistrates' court directing the accused to appear at every time and place to which the proceedings may from time to time be adjourned, as opposed to a direction to appear at the end of a fixed period of remand.

continuous employment The period for which a person's employment in the same business has subsisted. Under the Employment Rights Act 1996, employees have the right to claim certain statutory remedies only if they have been continuously employed for certain minimum periods. The required period of continuous employment necessary to bring an *unfair dismissal action is currently one year. The right of employees to statutory redundancy payments and to *guarantee payments arises after two years' and one month's continuous employment, respectively. The minimum period of *notice to terminate an employee's contract also depends on his period of continuous employment in the business. When a business changes ownership as a going concern, the employee's period of continuous employment under both the old and the new employer counts in calculating the total (*see also* RELEVANT TRANSFER). When an employee is dismissed without notice, the minimum notice to which he was entitled is added to the actual period of employment in calculating whether or not he has served the minimum continuous period. Part-time employees (i.e. those whose normal working week is less than 16 hours) formerly had few statutory rights until they had completed five years' continuous employment in the business. However, the Employment Protection (Part-time Employees) Regulations 1995 now provide that part-timers, no matter what hours they work, will benefit in the same way as those who are employed full time.

Periods during which an employee was on strike do not break the continuity, but are excluded from his total period of continuous employment. Continuity is not broken when a woman is absent due to pregnancy or confinement, provided she takes up her right to return to work (*see* MATERNITY RIGHTS).

contraband *n.* **1.** Goods whose import or export is forbidden. **2. (contraband of war)** Goods (such as munitions) carried by a neutral vessel (ship or aircraft) during wartime and destined for the use of one belligerent power against the other (or capable of being so used). Arms and other goods of a military nature were traditionally referred to as **absolute contraband**, while goods having peaceful uses, but nevertheless of assistance to a belligerent, were **conditional contraband**. The distinction, though formally retained, has effectively been abolished. Belligerent states are expected to issue contraband lists in order to exercise the right of capture. Goods being carried to enemy territory in an enemy ship are contraband even if they belong to a neutral power. The other belligerent is entitled to seize and confiscate such goods. *See also* PRIZE COURT; SEARCH OF SHIP.

contra bonos mores [Latin] Against good morals. It is a matter of controversy to what extent the criminal law should, or does, prohibit immoral conduct merely on the ground of its immorality. The tendency in recent years has been to limit legal intervention in matters of morals to acts that cause harm to others. However, there are still certain offences regarded as essentially immoral (e.g. *incest and *buggery). There are also offences of conspiring to corrupt public morals (although *corruption of public morals is not in itself criminal) and of outraging (or conspiring to outrage) public decency, although the scope of these offences is uncertain. *See also* CONSPIRACY; OBSCENE PUBLICATIONS.

contract *n*. A legally binding agreement. Agreement arises as a result of *offer and *acceptance, but a number of other requirements must be satisfied for an agreement to be legally binding. (1) There must be *consideration (unless the contract is by deed). (2) The parties must have an intention to create legal relations. This requirement usually operates to prevent a purely domestic or social agreement from constituting a contract (*see also* HONOUR CLAUSE). (3) The parties must have *capacity to contract. (4) The agreement must comply with any formal legal requirements. In general, no particular formality is required for the creation of a valid contract. It may be oral, written, partly oral and partly written, or even implied from conduct. Certain transactions are, however, valid only if effected by deed (e.g. transfers of shares in British ships) or in writing (e.g. promissory notes, contracts for the sale of interests in land, and guarantees that can at law only be enforced if evidenced in writing). (5) The agreement must be legal (*see* ILLEGAL CONTRACT). (6) The agreement must not be rendered void either by some common-law or statutory rule or by some inherent defect, such as operative mistake (*see* VOID CONTRACT). Certain contracts, though valid, may be liable to be set aside by one of the parties on such grounds as misrepresentation or the exercise of undue influence (*see* VOIDABLE CONTRACT).

contract of employment (contract of service) A contract by which a person agrees to undertake certain duties under the direction and control of the employer in return for a specified wage or salary. The contract need not be in writing, but under the Employment Rights Act 1996 the employee must be given a *written statement of terms of employment. Implied in every contract of employment are a duty of mutual confidence and trust, the employer's duty to protect the employee from danger and risks to his health, and the employee's duty to do the work to the best of his ability. Employees who have been continuously employed in the same business for certain minimum periods (*see* CONTINUOUS EMPLOYMENT) have statutory rights, relating for example to *unfair dismissal and *redundancy, that do not apply to the self-employed. A self-employed person is engaged under a contract for services and owes his employer or customer no other duty than to complete the specified work in accordance with the terms of the individual contract; he is not otherwise under the direction or control of the employer as to how or when he works.

Termination of a contract of employment in breach of the terms of the contract is *wrongful dismissal and may be remedied in the county court or the High Court or by an employment tribunal. In such an action the court is not concerned with "fairness" but purely with compensating for a breach of the terms of the contract.

contract of exchange (commutative contract) A barter contract in which property is transferred from one party to the other in return for other property. No money passes from one party to the other. A contract of exchange of goods is not governed by the Sale of Goods Act 1979. *Compare* SALE OF GOODS.

contract of record A judgment or recognizance enrolled in the record of the proceedings of a *court of record, implying a debt that arises from the entry on the record and not from any agreement between the parties.

contract of sale *See* SALE; SALE OF GOODS.

contract of service *See* CONTRACT OF EMPLOYMENT.

contribution *n.* The payment made by each of two or more people in respect of damage or a loss for which they are jointly liable. In tort, when two or more people are jointly liable for the same damage and the person injured has recovered his losses from one of them, that person may seek contributions from the other tortfeasors (*see* CIVIL LIABILITY CONTRIBUTION; JOINT TORTFEASORS). In the case of a general-average loss (*see* AVERAGE), the person who has sustained the loss is entitled to contributions from others with an interest in the property. *See also* PART 20 CLAIM.

contributory *n.* Any of the past or present members of a company, who are potentially liable to contribute to the company's assets in the event of a *winding-up. The maximum liability is limited, in a company limited by shares (*see* LIMITED COMPANY), to the amount unpaid on shares (*see* CALL). A past member remains liable for this amount if *winding-up follows within one year.

contributory negligence A person's carelessness for his own safety or interests, which contributes materially to damage suffered by him as a result partly of his own fault and partly of the fault of another person or persons. Thus careless driving, knowingly travelling with a drunken driver, and failure to wear a seat belt are common forms of contributory negligence in highway accidents. The effect of contributory negligence is to reduce the claimant's damages by an amount that the court thinks just and equitable. The defence is most common in actions for negligence, but can be pleaded in some other torts, e.g. *nuisance, *Rylands* v *Fletcher*, *breach of statutory duty, or under the Animals Act 1971 (*see* CLASSIFICATION OF ANIMALS). Contributory negligence may also be a defence to some actions for breach of contract. It is not a defence to conversion or intentional trespass to goods.

controlled drugs Dangerous drugs that are subject to criminal regulation. In the Misuse of Drugs Act 1971 these are grouped in three classes: A, B, and C. Class A is the most dangerous and includes opium and its natural and synthetic derivatives (e.g. morphine and heroin), cocaine, and Ecstasy. Class B includes amphetamine and (as at October 2001) *cannabis, and C – the least dangerous class – includes anabolic steroids and benzodiazepine antidepressants. It is an offence to possess a controlled drug or to supply or offer it to another; possession of drugs of classes A or B is an *arrestable offence. In the case of an occupier or someone concerned in the management of premises, it is an offence (1) to allow the smoking of cannabis, cannabis resin, or prepared opium on the premises (but it is not an offence to allow the premises to be used for injecting heroin or consuming any other controlled drug); (2) to prepare opium for smoking; and (3) to produce or supply a controlled drug on the premises. The defendant is liable on a charge of possession for the minutest quantity of the drug and without proof of *mens rea, unless he can prove that he did not believe or suspect that it was a controlled drug.

Under the Drug Trafficking Offences Act 1986, the Crown Court must impose a *confiscation order when a person who has benefited from drug trafficking is sentenced for a related offence. The amount of the order is the proceeds of the offender's trafficking or, if less, the amount realizable from his property. Imprisonment follows any default. The Act also penalizes those assisting in the retention of drug trafficking proceeds or disclosing information likely to prejudice a drug trafficking investigation. Under the Crime (Sentences) Act 1997 there is an automatic seven-year minimum sentence on third-time dealers in Class A drugs. However, judges may give a lesser sentence if the court considers the minimum would be unjust in all the circumstances. *See also* REPEAT OFFENDER.

controlled tenancy A type of *protected tenancy that sometimes occurred with tenancies created before 6 July 1957. From 28 November 1980 all controlled tenancies were converted into *regulated tenancies.

controlled trust A trust of which one or more solicitors or their employees are sole trustees. Such trusts are subject to special accounts rules made under the Solicitors Act 1974; breaches of these rules may be reported to the Solicitors' Disciplinary Tribunal.

controller *n.* (in company law) Strictly, one who holds shares conferring a majority of the *voting power that can be exercised at a general meeting. In practice, effective control can often be exercised by a director with no voting power or a minority of it if he is able to manipulate *proxy voting. *See also* SUBSIDIARY COMPANY.

convention *n.* **1.** A *treaty, usually of a multilateral nature. The International Law Commission prepares draft conventions on various issues for the progressive development of international law. **2.** A written document adopted by international organizations for their own regulation. **3.** *See* CONSTITUTIONAL CONVENTIONS.

conversion *n.* **1.** (in tort) The tort of wrongfully dealing with a person's goods in a way that constitutes a denial of the owner's rights or an assertion of rights inconsistent with the owner's. Wrongfully taking possession of goods, disposing of them, destroying them, or refusing to give them back are acts of conversion. Mere negligence in allowing goods to be lost or destroyed was not conversion at common law, but is a ground of liability under the Torts (Interference with Goods) Act 1977. The claimant in conversion must prove that he had ownership, possession, or the right to immediate possession of the goods at the time of the defendant's wrongful act (*see also* JUS TERTII). Subject to some exceptions, it is no defence that the defendant acted innocently. **2.** (in equity) The changing (either actually or fictionally) of one kind of property into another. For example, if land is sold the interest of those entitled to the property changes from an interest in the land to an interest in the money that represents it. Before 1926 (and to a lesser extent thereafter) it was important to know whether a person entitled to property had interests in land or in the proceeds of its sale: to leave the determination of these rights to be decided by the precise moment of a sale could have led to uncertainty and injustice. The doctrine of conversion stated that if there was a **duty to convert** the property, equity would assume the property to have been converted forthwith: "equity looks on that as done which ought to have been done" (*see* MAXIMS OF EQUITY). This doctrine was abolished with effect from 1 January 1997 by the Trusts of Land and Appointment of Trustees Act 1996.

converted tenancy A tenancy that was converted from a *controlled tenancy into a *regulated tenancy. From 28 November 1980 all controlled tenancies were converted into regulated tenancies.

conveyance *n.* **1. a.** A document (other than a will) that transfers an interest in land. To convey a legal estate in land, the conveyance must be by deed. **b.** Transfer of an interest in land by means of this document. *See also* CONVEYANCING. **2.** Any vehicle, vessel, or aircraft manufactured or subsequently adapted to carry one or more people. It is a statutory offence (and also an *arrestable offence), punishable by up to six months' imprisonment and a fine, for anyone to take a conveyance for his own or someone else's use (albeit temporary) without permission or to drive or be transported in a conveyance knowing that it has been taken without authority. *See also* AGGRAVATED VEHICLE-TAKING; INTERFERING WITH VEHICLES.

conveyancing *n.* The procedures involved in validly creating, extinguishing, and transferring ownership of interests in land. Only a practising solicitor or *licensed conveyancer may charge a fee for undertaking the most essential parts of such transactions. Under the Law of Property (Miscellaneous Provisions) Act 1989 land contacts must be made in writing. Apart from preparing the deeds or other documents by which the transaction is effected, certain investigative steps are usually required. For example, the sale and purchase of a residential house in England or Wales will generally involve the following.
(1) Preparation of a contract by the vendor's solicitor defining the terms of the transaction, describing the property concerned, and disclosing *land charges and other interests in it that will affect the purchaser. In the case of registered land, this will be accompanied by *office copies of the registered title.
(2) Written inquiries by the purchaser's solicitor seeking assurances from the vendor that matters which may not be apparent from inspection of the site will not impose any unforeseen liability on the purchaser. These questions generally cover such potential problems as disputes over boundaries, the construction or treatment of buildings, compliance with planning and rating authorities' requirements, and liability for maintenance of shared facilities (such as boundary walls). If the Law Society's "Transaction" protocol is used, the vendor supplies a **Seller's Property Information Form**, which gives details of the property and replaces the standard *preliminary inquiries.
(3) *Official search by the purchaser's solicitor in the local land charges register to ensure there are no undisclosed charges of a local or environmental nature that could bind the purchaser. The local authority is also asked to disclose other information, such as proposals for building new roads near the property. Other searches may be carried out at this stage, for example commons registration searches. If the land appears to be unregistered, there will be an official search of the *index maps, to check that it has not, in fact, been registered.
(4) If the purchaser is raising a *mortgage loan towards the price, his solicitor or other agent will ensure that the funds will be available at the appropriate time and that any conditions imposed by the mortgagees can be satisfied.
(5) The purchaser's solicitor may then negotiate alterations to the draft contract with the vendor's solicitor, in order to ensure its compliance with the purchaser's requirements and to cover points arising from the earlier inquiries and search. For example, if an unforeseen local land charge has been discovered, a term may be inserted requiring the vendor to clear it before the transaction is completed.
(6) When there is a chain of sales and purchases dependent on one another, the solicitors for the parties involved liaise with one another through all steps of the transactions, particularly in arranging a date for completion, to ensure that the various completions coincide.
(7) The parties become legally committed to buy and sell respectively upon *exchange of contracts. It is then usual for the purchaser to pay a percentage of the price to the vendor's solicitor as stakeholder.

(8) The vendor's solicitor next prepares and delivers an epitome or *abstract of title to the purchaser's solicitor, who studies it to ensure that the vendor's title is proved in accordance with the contract. (It is increasingly common to deliver an epitome of title before exchange of contracts.) As final checks on the vendor's title, he conducts an official search in the *Land Charges Department (for unregistered land) or HM *Land Registry as appropriate, and raises *requisitions on title requiring the vendor to clear any defects or adverse interests revealed by the abstract or search. An official certificate of search from the Land Registry will reveal any entries on the vendor's title effected since the date on which the office copies were issued, and will give the purchaser priority against any further entries provided he registers his new title within the time shown on the certificate.

(9) The purchaser's solicitor prepares the deed (usually a conveyance, transfer, or assignment) by which the property is to be transferred to his client, and has its terms approved by the vendor's solicitor. He also ensures that the purchaser's mortgage deed (if any) is in order.

(10) In preparation for completion, the purchaser's solicitor arranges with the necessary parties for the funds to be available on the completion date and ensures that the necessary deeds will be executed by the time completion takes place.

(11) On completion, the purchaser's solicitor checks the vendor's original *title deeds against the epitome (or abstract) of title, and takes possession of them together with the deed of transfer. In the case of registered land, he will take the land certificate, or accept an undertaking from the vendor's solicitor to forward it when it is made available following redemption of any mortgage. He hands over the price, and the transaction is then legally completed.

(12) After completion, the transfer deed is produced to the Inland Revenue, and any stamp duty paid, by the purchaser's solicitor on his client's behalf. He also gives formal notice of the transaction when appropriate; for example, when a leasehold interest is purchased, the lessor must usually be notified. Whether or not land was registered before the transaction, it will need to be registered on completion. Therefore, the purchaser's solicitor lodges the relevant deeds with HM Land Registry for registration of his client's title, within the priority period conferred by the official search certificate.

These basic steps in respect of the sale and purchase of a house are common to many other conveyancing transactions, although the complexity of the particular requirements varies according to the nature of the transaction. *See also* ELECTRONIC CONVEYANCING.

conviction *n.* **1.** (for the purposes of the Bail Act 1976) In criminal proceedings, a finding of *guilty, or an acquittal on the ground of insanity. In a magistrates' court, a finding that the accused carried out the act for which he was charged (*see* SUMMARY CONVICTION). **2.** (for the purposes of the Rehabilitation of Offenders Act 1974) Any finding (except one of insanity), either in criminal proceedings or in care proceedings, that a person has committed an offence or carried out the act for which he was charged. *See also* SPENT CONVICTION.

cooperation procedure A procedure introduced by the *Single European Act 1986 that allows the *European Parliament to impede the adoption of proposed legislation by the *Council of the European Union; the *Maastricht Treaty extended the use of this procedure to cover new areas of policy. It applies when there is a second reading of a draft measure. If the Parliament takes no action for three months after receiving the proposal, it proceeds. However, if, after a second reading, Parliament votes by an absolute majority to reject the measure, this can only be overturned by a unanimous decision of the Council. *Compare* ASSENT PROCEDURE; CODECISION PROCEDURE.

copyhold *n.* Formerly, ownership of land enforceable only in the court of the lord of the manor and not protected by the sovereign's courts (*see* FEUDAL SYSTEM). The owner's title comprised a copy of an entry in the rolls of the lord's court. By the Law of Property Act 1922 copyhold tenure was abolished and existing copyholds were converted into freeholds.

copyright *n.* The exclusive right to reproduce or authorize others to reproduce artistic, dramatic, literary, or musical works. It is conferred by the Copyright, Designs and Patents Act 1988, which also extends to sound broadcasting, cinematograph films, and television broadcasts (including cable television). Copyright lasts for the author's lifetime plus 70 years from the end of the year in which he died; it can be assigned or transmitted on death. EU directive 93/98 requires all EU states to ensure that the duration of copyright is the life of the author plus 70 years. Copyright protection for sound recordings lasts for 50 years from the date of their publication; for broadcasts it is 50 years from the end of the year in which the broadcast took place. Directive 91/250 requires all EU member states to protect computer *software by copyright law. The principal remedies for breach of copyright (known as **piracy**) are an action for *damages and *account of profits or an *injunction. It is a criminal offence knowingly to make or deal in articles that infringe a copyright. *See also* BERNE CONVENTION; HACKING.

co-respondent *n.* In a petition of divorce under the Matrimonial Causes Act 1973, the party with whom a married person is alleged to have committed adultery and who, if named, is normally made a party to divorce proceedings.

coroner *n.* An officer of the Crown whose principal function is to investigate deaths suspected of being violent or unnatural. He will do this either by ordering an *autopsy or conducting an *inquest. The coroner also holds inquests on *treasure trove. Coroners are appointed by the Crown from among barristers, solicitors, and qualified medical practitioners of not less than five years' standing.

corporate personality *See* INCORPORATION.

corporate venturing scheme (CVS) A scheme designed to encourage established companies to invest in the full-risk ordinary shares of companies of the same kind as those qualifying under the *Enterprise Investment Scheme; the scheme encourages the investing and qualifying companies to form mutually beneficial corporate venturing relationships. Companies investing through the CVS may obtain *corporation tax relief (at 20%) on the amount invested provided that the shares are held for at least three years after issue or, if later, three years after the trade for which the money was raised begins. Investing companies also obtain relief for most allowable losses on the shares and deferral of corporation tax when a chargeable gain from the disposal of CVS shares is reinvested in a new CVS investment.

corporation (body corporate) *n.* An entity that has legal personality, i.e. it is capable of enjoying and being subject to legal rights and duties (*see* JURISTIC PERSON) and possesses the capacity of succession. A **corporation aggregate** (e.g. a *company registered under the Companies Acts) consists of a number of members who fluctuate from time to time. A **corporation sole** (e.g. the *Crown) consists of one member only and his or her successors. *See also* INCORPORATION.

corporation tax A tax on the worldwide profits of limited companies and certain other bodies resident or trading in the UK. Corporation tax started on 6 April 1966 (before this date companies paid income tax and profits tax). It applies to all bodies corporate and unincorporated associations, including limited companies, building societies, cooperative societies, unit trusts, and investment trusts, but excluding local authorities.

The tax is based on the profits shown in the company's audited accounts after adding back certain nonallowable deductions, which include depreciation of *machinery and plant, provisions for doubtful debts, and political contributions. However, *capital allowances are deductible for corporation tax purposes, as are losses carried forward from earlier years. From April 1973 until April 1999 a company was required to pay *advance corporation tax on its distributed profits, which was offset against its corporation tax liability. From 1999 larger companies pay corporation tax in instalments. Chargeable gains (see CAPITAL GAINS TAX) count as profits for corporation tax purposes but losses can be offset against any gains. The rates of corporation tax are (for 2001–02): 10% for profits up to £10,000; a 20% **small companies rate** for profits from £50,000 to £300,000, and a 30% **main rate** for profits over £1,500,000. There are sliding scales (**marginal relief**) for amounts between the different rates.

corporeal hereditament *See* HEREDITAMENT.

corroboration *n.* Evidence that confirms the accuracy of other evidence "in a material particular". In general, English law does not require corroboration and any fact may be proved by a single item of credible evidence. The obligation to warn the jury of the dangers of acting on uncorroborated evidence of accomplices or of complainants in cases of sexual offences has been abolished: the judge now has a discretion to indicate the dangers of a jury relying on particular evidence. Corroboration remains mandatory in cases of *treason and *perjury and for opinion evidence as to some matters, e.g. *speeding.

corrupt and illegal practices Offences defined by the Representation of the People Act 1983 in connection with conduct at parliamentary or local elections. Corrupt practices, which include bribery and intimidation, are the more serious of the two. The most frequent illegal practice is spending by a candidate in excess of the amount authorized for the management of his campaign.

corruption *n. See* BRIBERY AND CORRUPTION.

corruption of public morals Conduct "destructive of the [moral] fabric of society". It is uncertain if such acts are crimes, although those who published "directories" of prostitutes or magazine advertisements encouraging readers to meet the advertisers for homosexual purposes have been found guilty of conspiring to corrupt public morals. *See also* CONSPIRACY; CONTRA BONOS MORES.

cost, insurance, freight *See* C.I.F. CONTRACT.

costs *pl. n.* Sums payable for legal services. A distinction is drawn between **contentious** and **noncontentious costs** (broadly, the distinction between costs relating to litigious and nonlitigious matters). Solicitors' costs are normally divided into **profit costs** (representing the solicitor's profit and overheads) and **disbursements** (any out-of-pocket expenses he may have incurred in the conduct of the case).

In civil litigation the court has a wide discretion to make an award in respect of the costs of the case, but the general principle applied is that the loser of the case must pay the costs of the winner (this was previously known as **costs follow the event**). The court will order on what basis the costs will be assessed. In normal adversary litigation this is the **standard basis**, in which the loser pays a reasonable sum in respect of all costs reasonably incurred by the winning party (*see also* INDEMNITY BASIS). If the court does not make an order for payment of fixed costs (i.e. the amount allowed in respect of solicitors' charges), or fixed costs are not provided for, the amount of costs payable will be determined by the court or by a *costs officer (*see* ASSESSMENT OF COSTS). *See also* COSTS IN ANY EVENT; COSTS IN THE CASE; COSTS RESERVED.

costs draftsman A person (usually a legal executive rather than a qualified solicitor) who specializes in drawing up *bills of costs . Some work in solicitors' firms and some in independent firms of costs specialists.

costs in any event An order for costs made in *interim (interlocutory) proceedings by which the winner of the hearing in question shall be paid the costs of that stage in the proceedings whatever the outcome of the trial. *Compare* COSTS IN THE CASE.

costs in the case An order for costs made in *interim (interlocutory) proceedings by which the costs of the hearing in question are payable in accordance with the order for costs to be made at the trial. This will usually have the effect that they are paid by the overall loser of the litigation. *Compare* COSTS IN ANY EVENT.

costs officer The judge or officer of the court who determines the amount of costs payable in a detailed *assessment of costs. The costs officer may be a **costs judge** (an official of the Supreme Court, formerly known as a **taxing master**), a district judge, or an authorized officer of a county court, a district registry, the Principal Registry of the Family Division, or the Supreme Court Costs Office.

costs reserved An order for costs made in *interim (interlocutory) proceedings by which the costs of the hearing in question are reserved for the decision of the trial judge rather than decided by the master or district judge at the hearing itself.

costs thrown away Costs either unnecessarily incurred by a party as a result of some procedural error committed by the other party or properly incurred but wasted as a result of a subsequent act of the other party (e.g. by amending the claim form or statement of case).

council housing Residential accommodation provided for renting by local authorities (primarily by district and London borough councils, who, as housing authorities, have a general statutory duty to meet housing needs in their areas). Authorities may build new properties and acquire existing ones for the purpose. The allocation and management of housing stock is in general within their sole discretion, but statute does impose certain priorities (e.g. towards homeless persons) and the Housing Act 1980 (now repealed) gave their tenants a measure of security of tenure. There are also financial restraints, such as restrictions on the proportion of capital receipts available for house building, imposed by central government. Certain tenants of council housing have the right to purchase the freehold of a council house or a long lease of a council flat at a discount. The Housing Act 1988 introduced measures under which council housing can be transferred to the private rented sector if tenants so desire.

councillor *n.* (in local government) *See* LOCAL AUTHORITY.

Council of Europe A European organization for cooperation in various areas between most European (not just EU) states. The assembly of the Council of Europe elects the judges of the European Court of Human Rights.

Council of Legal Education A body established by the four *Inns of Court to supervise the education and examination of students for the Bar of England and

Wales. It administered the Inns of Court School of Law in Gray's Inn. In 1997 the **Inns of Court and Bar Educational Trust** was founded and took over responsibility of the Council.

Council of the European Union (Council of Ministers) The organ of the EU that is primarily concerned with the formulation of policy and (in conjunction with the *European Commission and *European Parliament) the adoption of *Community legislation. The Council consists of one member of government of each of the member states of the Community (normally its foreign minister, but other ministers may attend instead for the consideration of specialized topics), and its presidency is held by each state in turn for periods of six months. The Council is serviced by a Committee of Permanent Representatives (COREPER). This consists of senior civil servants of each state and its primary function is to clarify national attitudes for the assistance of the Council in reaching its decisions. It also disposes on behalf of the Council of matters that are not controversial. Decisions of the Council are taken by a unanimous vote (*see also* VETO) or, in most cases, by qualified majority voting. Each member state has a number of votes approximately proportional to the size of its population, with a total of 87 votes; in qualified majority voting a Commission proposal requires 62 votes to be passed. *Compare* EUROPEAN COUNCIL.

Council of the Inns of Court A body, comprising representatives of the four *Inns of Court, the *Bar Council, and the Inns of Court and Bar Educational Trust (*see* COUNCIL OF LEGAL EDUCATION), that coordinates the work of the three organizations represented. When the Council of the Inns of Court and Bar Council disagree, the latter's policy is implemented if it has the support of two-thirds of the profession.

Council on Tribunals A body appointed under the Tribunals and Inquiries Act 1971 to report on the functioning and advise on the procedure of the more important administrative tribunals. Appointment is by the Lord Chancellor and Lord Advocate, who may refer any matter concerning any tribunal for a special Council report.

council tax A form of local tax levied on all private households (with some exceptions) to contribute to the cost of local government. It was introduced by the Local Government Finance Act 1992 and took effect from April 1993, replacing the *community charge. The tax is based on the capital value of the dwelling owned or rented by the occupiers. Each dwelling is assessed to see which of eight bands (A to H) it falls within. For example, dwellings worth not more than £40,000 are placed in band A, dwellings worth between £68,000 and £88,000 in band D, and dwellings worth more than £320,000 in band H. A household living in a dwelling in band A will pay two-thirds of the amount paid by those living in a dwelling in band D, and one-third of the amount paid by those living in a dwelling in band H. The amount of the charge is set by the local council. In general, all the residents of a dwelling are jointly liable to pay the tax.

The amount payable can be reduced by discounts (e.g. there is a 25% discount where only one adult occupies the property), benefits for those on low incomes, and reductions for disabilities where homes are adapted for disabled persons.

counsel *n.* A barrister, barristers collectively, or anyone advising and representing litigants.

Counsellors of State Persons appointed under the Regency Acts 1937 to 1953 to exercise royal functions while the sovereign is ill (but not totally incapacitated, in which case the functions pass to a *regent) or temporarily absent from the UK. They are appointed by the sovereign by letters patent, which must specify the functions delegated to them. These must not include the function of dissolving Parliament, except on the sovereign's express instructions, or that of creating new peers. The persons to be appointed are the sovereign's spouse, the four next in line to the throne (omitting anyone not qualified to be Regent or intending to be abroad during the period of delegation), and Queen Elizabeth, the Queen Mother.

count *n.* See INDICTMENT.

counterclaim *n.* A cross-claim brought by a defendant in civil proceedings that asserts an independent cause of action but is not also a defence to the claim made in the action by the claimant. A counterclaim is an example of a *Part 20 claim, being a claim other than one made by the claimant against the defendant. See also SET-OFF.

countertrade *n.* A form of trading in which an exporter of goods or services undertakes to accept goods or services (rather than money) from the importer in exchange.

county *n.* A first-tier *local government area in England (outside Greater London) or Wales. The Local Government Act 1972 created 45 counties for England and 8 for Wales, dividing the former into 6 metropolitan and 39 nonmetropolitan counties. The metropolitan counties – Greater Manchester, Merseyside, South Yorkshire, Tyne and Wear, West Midlands, and West Yorkshire – were abolished and their functions transferred generally to district councils by the Local Government Act 1985. The Local Government (Wales) Act 1994 reorganized local government areas in Wales; on 1 April 1996 all the existing counties and *districts were replaced by 11 counties and 11 **county boroughs**, each administered by a single-tier (unitary) council. In some parts of England *unitary authorities have replaced *county councils; this has resulted in the reorganization of certain county areas. See also LOCAL GOVERNMENT COMMISSION FOR ENGLAND; PRESERVED COUNTY.

county council A *local authority whose area is a *county. A county council has certain exclusive responsibilities (e.g. education, fire services, highways, and refuse disposal) and shares others (e.g. recreation, town and country planning) with the councils of the districts in its area. The *Local Government Commission for England began work in 1992 on restructuring local government areas with a view to establishing single-tier local authorities (see UNITARY AUTHORITY), which has led to the abolition of certain county councils.

county court Any of the civil courts forming a system covering all of England and Wales, originally set up in 1846. The area covered by each court does not invariably correspond to the local government county boundary. Under Part 7 of the *Civil Procedure Rules, which sets out the rules for starting cases, the county court retains an unlimited jurisdiction for claims in contract and tort. It will hear some appeals (see APPELLATE JURISDICTION). Each court has a *circuit judge and a *district judge.

course of employment The scope of the work a person is employed to do. An employer may be held responsible under the principle of *vicarious liability for his employee's wrongful acts if they are necessarily incidental to his work, or authorized (expressly or by implication) by the employer, or, though not in any way authorized, are a wrongful way of doing something he was employed to do.

court *n.* **1.** A body established by law for the administration of justice by *judges or *magistrates. **2.** A hall or building in which a court is held. **3. a.** The residence of a sovereign. **b.** The sovereign and her (or his) family and attendants or officials of state.

Court for Consideration of Crown Cases Reserved A court created by the Crown Cases Act 1848 for considering questions of law arising out of the conviction of a person for treason, felony, or misdemeanour and reserved by the trial judge or justices for the consideration of the court. Its jurisdiction was exercised by the judges of the *High Court, at least five of whom had to sit together. The Court was abolished in 1907 and its jurisdiction transferred to the *Court of Criminal Appeal, which had wider powers.

court martial A court convened within the armed forces to try offences against *service law. It consists of a number of serving officers, who sit without a jury and are advised on points of law by a legally qualified *judge advocate. Army and air-force courts martial are similar. The Armed Forces Act 1996 (effective from 1 April 1997) updated the laws in this field; in particular, it reinforced the independence of courts martial. A **general court martial** must consist of a president of the rank of major/squadron leader or above and four members, at least two of whom must be of the rank of captain/flight lieutenant or above. Up to two members may be warrant officers (i.e. noncommissioned). A **district court martial** must consist of a president of the rank of major/squadron leader or above and two members, at least one of whom has held commissioned rank for at least two years. Up to one member may be a warrant officer. A **field general court martial** may only be convened in active service conditions, and may exceptionally consist of two officers. Naval courts martial must consist of between five and nine officers of the rank of lieutenant or above who have held commissioned rank for at least three years, although up to two members may be warrant officers. The members of the court may not all belong to the same ship or shore establishment. The president of a naval court martial must be of the rank of captain or above, and when a senior officer is to be tried there are further rules as to the court's composition. In all cases members of another branch of the armed forces of equivalent minimum rank may serve on army, air-force, or naval courts martial. Courts martial's findings of guilty, and their sentences, are subject to review by the Defence Council or any officer to whom they delegate. Since 1951 there has been a Courts-Martial Appeal Court, which consists of the Lord Chief Justice and other members of the Supreme Court. After first petitioning the Defence Council for the quashing of his conviction, a convicted person may appeal to the Court against the conviction and (from 1 April 1997) against sentence. Either he or the Defence Council may then appeal to the House of Lords.

When a member of the armed forces is charged in the UK with conduct that is an offence under both service law and the ordinary criminal law the trial must in certain serious cases (e.g. treason, murder, manslaughter, and rape) be held by the ordinary criminal courts (and is in practice frequently held by them in other cases). Provision exists to ensure that a person cannot be tried twice for the same offence. *See also* STANDING CIVILIAN COURT.

Court of Appeal A court created by the Judicature Acts 1873–75, forming part of the *Supreme Court of Judicature. The Court exercises *appellate jurisdiction over all judgments and orders of the High Court and most determinations of judges of the county courts. In some cases the Court of Appeal is the *court of last resort, but in most cases its decisions can be appealed to the *House of Lords, with permission of the Court of Appeal or the House of Lords. The Court is divided into a **Civil Division** (presided over by the *Master of the Rolls) and a **Criminal Division** (presided over by the *Lord Chief Justice). The ordinary judges of the Court are the

*Lords Justices of Appeal, but other specific office holders and High Court judges may, by invitation, also sit in the Court.

Court of Arches The ecclesiastical court of appeal from the consistory court (*see* ECCLESIASTICAL COURTS), which has the jurisdiction of the former provincial Court of Archbishop of Canterbury. The judge of the court, the **Dean of Arches**, hears appeals from bishops or their chancellors, deans and chapters, and archdeacons. The court's name is derived from its original location, the church of St Mary-le-Bow, whose steeple was erected upon arches.

Court of Chancery The original court of *equity, presided over by the *Lord Chancellor. By the Judicature Acts 1873–75 its jurisdiction was merged into that of the High Court, of which it became the *Chancery Division.

Court of Chivalry An ancient feudal court having jurisdiction over questions relating to armorial bearings and questions of precedence. It is not a *court of record.

Court of Common Pleas One of the three courts of *common law into which the *curia regis* was divided (the others being the *Court of Queen's Bench and the *Court of Exchequer) whose jurisdiction was merged into that of the High Court by the Judicature Acts 1873–75. It became the **Common Pleas Division**, which in 1880 was merged into the *Queen's Bench Division.

Court of Criminal Appeal A court created by the Criminal Appeal Act 1907 to take over the jurisdiction formerly exercised by the *Court for Consideration of Crown Cases Reserved. Its powers were greatly extended, particularly in considering questions of fact as well as law, but it was abolished by the Criminal Appeal Act 1966 and its jurisdiction transferred to that of the *Court of Appeal (Criminal Division).

Court of Ecclesiastical Causes Reserved A court created by the Ecclesiastical Jurisdiction Measure 1963 and having both original and appellate jurisdiction covering the provinces of Canterbury and York. Its original jurisdiction is to hear and determine proceedings in which a person in Holy Orders is charged with an offence against ecclesiastical law involving matters of doctrine, ritual, or ceremonial and all suits of *duplex querela*. Its appellate jurisdiction is in respect of appeals from decisions of consistory courts involving matters of doctrine, ritual, or ceremonial. The court comprises five judges and three diocesan or ex-diocesan bishops. *See also* ECCLESIASTICAL COURTS.

Court of Exchequer One of the three courts of *common law into which the *curia regis* was divided (the others being the *Court of Queen's Bench and the *Court of Common Pleas) whose jurisdiction was merged into that of the High Court by the Judicature Acts 1873–75. It became the **Exchequer Division**, which in 1880 merged into the *Queen's Bench Division. The judges of the Exchequer were known as **Barons**.

court of first instance 1. A court in which any proceedings are initiated. **2.** Loosely, a court in which a case is tried, as opposed to any court in which it may be heard on appeal.

Court of First Instance The first court of appeal from decisions of the European Commission. Established under powers conferred by the *Single European Act 1986, it started to operate at the end of October 1989. Appeals from the court are to the *European Court of Justice.

Court of Justice of the European Communities *See* EUROPEAN COURT OF JUSTICE.

court of last resort A court from which no appeal (or no further appeal) lies. In English law the *House of Lords is usually the court of last resort (although some cases may be referred to the *European Court of Justice). However, in some cases the *Court of Appeal is by statute the court of last resort.

Court of Probate A court created in 1857 to take over the jurisdiction formerly exercised by the ecclesiastical courts in relation to the granting of probate and letters of administration. By the Judicature Acts 1873–75 the jurisdiction of the court was transferred to the *Probate, Divorce and Admiralty Division of the High Court.

Court of Protection A court that administers the property and affairs of persons of unsound mind, formerly called the **Management and Administration Department**. The head of the court is called the **Master**.

Court of Queen's Bench Until 1875, one of the three courts of *common law into which the *curia regis* was divided (the others being the *Court of Common Pleas and the *Court of Exchequer). Its principal functions were the trial of civil actions in contract and tort and the exercise of supervisory powers over inferior courts. By the Judicature Acts 1873–75 its jurisdiction was transferred to the *Queen's Bench Division of the High Court. When the sovereign was a king, it was known as the **Court of King's Bench**.

court of record A court whose acts and judicial proceedings are permanently maintained and recorded. In modern practice the principal significance of such courts is that they have the power to punish for *contempt of court. *See also* CONTRACT OF RECORD.

Court of Session A Scottish court corresponding to the *Supreme Court of Judicature in England and Wales. It consists of an Outer House (corresponding to the *High Court) and an Inner House (corresponding to the *Court of Appeal).

court of summary jurisdiction *See* MAGISTRATES' COURT.

court order *See* ORDER.

covenant *n. See* DEED; LEASE; RESTRICTIVE COVENANT.

covenant running with the land **1.** A *restrictive covenant affecting freehold land and binding or benefiting third parties who acquire the land. A restrictive covenant runs with the land of the covenantee if it is intended to benefit, and is capable of benefiting, land owned by the covenantor (the *dominant tenement). A covenant created before 1926 will bind a purchaser **for value** of the legal estate in the *servient tenement if he has notice of it; a covenant created after 1925 will not bind a purchaser of the legal estate **for money or money's worth** unless it is registered (*see* REGISTRATION OF ENCUMBRANCES). A positive covenant (i.e. an obligation to perform an act) does not run with the land. **2.** In a lease, a covenant, either restrictive or positive, that "touches and concerns" the land, i.e. one that affects the nature, value, or enjoyment of the land, and will bind successors in title of the landlord and the tenant provided there is *privity of estate between them.

covenant to repair A clause contained in most *leases that sets out each party's obligations to carry out repairs. The standard of repair depends on the terms of the covenant and the kind of property. The general rule is that the property must be maintained in the condition that a reasonable tenant of that property would expect. The person carrying out the repairs must, so far as possible, restore the property to the condition it was in before the damage occurred. In the case of a block of flats or offices, the landlord is often responsible for external, and the tenant for internal, repairs. When one party alone is responsible for repairs, this is more likely to be the landlord in the case of a short lease and the tenant in the case of a longer lease. A landlord is liable by statute to repair the structure and exterior and the appliances for heating and sanitation in a dwelling house let for less than seven years.

If the tenant does not fulfil his repairing obligations the landlord's remedies are *forfeiture or suing the tenant for damages. If the landlord is in breach of covenant, the tenant's remedies are as follows: he can sue for damages equal to the difference between the value of the property as it is and the value it should have if repaired; he can sue for *specific performance, a court order to compel the landlord to carry out his obligations; or, if he is sure that the landlord is in breach of covenant and he has told the landlord about the breach, he can carry out the repairs himself and recover the cost from future rent.

coverture *n.* The status of a woman during, and arising out of, marriage. At common law a wife "lost" her own personality, which became incorporated into that of her husband, and could only act under his protection and "cover". Married women no longer suffer disabilities as a result of coverture. *See also* UNITY OF PERSONALITY.

CPR *See* CIVIL PROCEDURE RULES.

CPS *See* CROWN PROSECUTION SERVICE.

credit *n.* **1.** The agreed deferment of payment of a debt. Under the Consumer Credit Act 1974, credit also includes any other form of financial accommodation, including a cash loan. It does not include the charge for credit but does include the total price of goods hired to an individual under a *hire-purchase agreement less the aggregate of the deposit and the total charge for credit. **2.** (in the law of evidence) The credibility of a witness. It must be inferred by the *trier of fact from the witness's demeanour and the evidence in the case. A witness may be cross-examined as to credit (i.e. **impeached**) by reference to his *previous convictions, bias, or any physical or mental incapacity affecting the credibility of his evidence.

credit card A plastic card, issued by a bank or finance organization, that enables its holder to obtain credit when making purchases. The use of credit cards usually involves three contracts. (1) A contract between the company issuing the credit card and the cardholder whereby the holder can use the card to purchase goods and, in return, promises to pay the credit company the price charged by the supplier. The holder normally receives monthly statements from the credit company, which he may pay in full within a certain number of days with no interest charged; alternatively, he may make a specified minimum payment and pay a high rate of interest on the outstanding balance. (2) A contract between the credit company and the supplier whereby the supplier agrees to accept payment by use of the card and the credit company agrees to pay the supplier the price of the goods supplied less a discount. (3) A contract between the cardholder and the supplier, who agrees to supply the goods on the basis that payment will be obtained from the credit company.

credit limit **1.** The maximum credit allowed to a debtor. **2.** (under the Consumer Credit Act 1974) The maximum debit balance allowed on a running-account credit agreement during any period.

creditor *n.* **1.** One to whom a debt is owed. *See also* JUDGMENT CREDITOR; LOAN CREDITOR; SECURED CREDITOR; UNSECURED CREDITOR. **2.** (under the Consumer Credit Act 1974) The person providing credit under a *consumer-credit agreement or the person to whom his rights and duties under the agreement have passed by assignment or operation of law.

creditors' committee A committee that may be appointed by creditors to supervise the trustee appointed to handle the affairs of a bankrupt. A committee consists of between three and five creditors and their duty is to see that the distribution of the bankrupt's assets is carried out as quickly and economically as possible. *See also* BANKRUPTCY.

credit sale agreement A contract for the sale of goods under which the price is payable by instalments but the contract is not a *conditional sale agreement, i.e. ownership passes to the buyer. A credit sale agreement is a *consumer-credit agreement; it is regulated by the Consumer Credit Act 1974 if the buyer is an individual, the credit does not exceed £25,000, and the agreement is not otherwise exempt.

crime *n.* An act (or sometimes a failure to act) that is deemed by statute or by the common law to be a public wrong and is therefore punishable by the state in criminal proceedings. Every crime consists of an *actus reus* accompanied by a specified *mens rea* (unless it is a crime of *strict liability), and the prosecution must prove these elements of the crime beyond reasonable doubt (*see* BURDEN OF PROOF). Some crimes are serious wrongs of a moral nature (e.g. murder or rape); others interfere with the smooth running of society (e.g. parking offences). Most *prosecutions for crime are brought by the police (although they can also be initiated by private people); some require the consent of the *Attorney General. Crimes are customarily divided into *indictable offences (for trial by judge and jury) and *summary offences (for trial by magistrates); some are hybrid (*see* OFFENCES TRIABLE EITHER WAY). Crimes are also divided into *arrestable offences and nonarrestable offences. The *punishments for a crime include death (for treason), life imprisonment (e.g. for murder), imprisonment for a specified period, suspended sentences of imprisonment, conditional discharges, probation, binding over, and fines; in most cases judges have discretion in deciding on the punishment (*see* SENTENCE). Some crimes may also be civil wrongs (*see* TORT); for example, theft and criminal damage are crimes punishable by imprisonment as well as torts for which the victim may claim damages.

crimes against humanity *See* WAR CRIMES.

crimes against peace *See* WAR CRIMES.

criminal conviction certificate A certificate given to those who request details of information held about their criminal records. The certificate is obtained from the *Criminal Records Agency, which was set up under the Police Act 1997.

criminal court A court exercising jurisdiction over criminal rather than civil cases. In England all criminal cases must be initiated in the *magistrates' courts. *Summary offences and some *indictable offences are also tried by magistrates' courts; the more serious indictable offences are committed to the *Crown Court for trial.

criminal damage The offence of intentionally or recklessly destroying or damaging any property belonging to another without a lawful excuse. It is punishable by up to ten years' imprisonment. There is also an aggravated offence, punishable by a maximum sentence of life imprisonment, of damaging property (even one's own) in such a way as to endanger someone's life, either intentionally or recklessly. Related offences are those of threatening to destroy or damage property and of possessing anything with the intention of destroying or damaging property with it. *See also* ARSON.

Criminal Injuries Compensation Scheme A state scheme for awarding payments from public funds to victims who have sustained *criminal injury, on the same basis as civil damages would be awarded (*see also* COMPENSATION). Damage to property is not included in the scheme. The scheme is administered by a board that may refuse or reduce an award (1) if the claimant fails to cooperate in providing details of the circumstances of the injury or in assisting the police to bring the wrongdoer to justice, or (2) because of the claimant's activities, unlawful conduct, or conduct in connection with the injury. Dependants of persons dying after sustaining criminal injury may also claim awards. The board may apply for a county court order directing a convicted offender wholly or partly to reimburse the board for an award made. The Criminal Injuries Compensation Act 1995 (in force from 1 April 1996) set out new rules for payment. *See also* RIOT.

criminal injury For purposes of the *Criminal Injuries Compensation Scheme, any crime involving the use of violence against another person. Such crimes include rape, assault, arson, poisoning, and criminal damage to property involving a risk of danger to life; traffic offences other than a deliberate attempt to run the victim down are not included. The injury sustained includes pregnancy, disease, and mental distress attributable either to fear of immediate physical injury (even to another person) or to being present when another person sustained physical injury.

criminal libel *See* LIBEL.

Criminal Records Agency A state body that provides individuals with information about their criminal records in the form of a *criminal conviction certificate. The agency was set up under the Police Act 1997 and comes into operation in 1997. The Act also provides for full and enhanced checks to be undertaken on individuals with criminal records and for the information obtained to be passed, with their consent, to bodies registered for that purpose.

cross-appeals *pl. n.* Appeals by both parties to court proceedings when neither party is satisfied with the judgment of the lower court. For example, a defendant may appeal against a judgment finding him liable for damages, while the claimant may appeal in the same case on the ground that the amount of damages awarded is too low.

cross-examination *n.* The questioning of a *witness by a party other than the one who called him to testify. It may be **to the issue**, i.e. designed to elicit information favourable to the party on whose behalf it is conducted and to cast doubt on the accuracy of evidence given against that party; or **to credit**, i.e. designed to cast doubt upon the credibility of the witness. *Leading questions may be asked during cross-examination. *See also* CREDIT.

Crown *n.* The office (a *corporation sole) in which supreme power in the UK is legally vested. The person filling it at any given time is referred to as the **sovereign** (a **king** or **queen**: *see also* QUEEN). The title to the Crown is hereditary and its descent is governed by the Act of Settlement 1701 as amended by His Majesty's Declaration of Abdication Act 1936 (which excluded Edward VIII and his descendants from the line of succession). The majority of governmental powers in the UK are now conferred by statute directly on ministers, the judiciary, and other persons and bodies, but the sovereign retains a limited number of common law functions (known as *royal prerogatives) that, except in exceptional circumstances, can be exercised only in accordance with ministerial advice. In practice it is the minister, and not the sovereign, who today carries out these common law powers and is said to be the Crown when so doing.

At common law the Crown could not be sued in tort, but the Crown Proceedings Act 1947 enabled civil actions to be taken against the Crown (*see* CROWN PROCEEDINGS). It is still not possible to sue the sovereign personally.

Crown Agents for Overseas Governments and Administrations A body operating under the Crown Agents Act 1979 to provide commercial, financial, and professional services to overseas governments, international bodies, and public authorities. After the discovery of heavy financial losses between 1968 and 1974, the body was restructured by the 1979 Act and a tribunal of inquiry was set up to investigate its activities during those years.

Crown Court A court created by the Courts Act 1971 to take over the jurisdiction formerly exercised by *assizes and *quarter sessions, which were abolished by the same Act. It is part of the *Supreme Court of Judicature. The Crown Court has an unlimited jurisdiction over all criminal cases tried on *indictment and also acts as a court for the hearing of appeals from *magistrates' courts. Unlike the courts it replaced, the Crown Court is one court that can sit at any centre in England and Wales designated by the Lord Chancellor. *See also* THREE-TIER SYSTEM.

Crown Court rules Rules regulating the practice and procedure of the *Crown Court. The rules are made by the Crown Court Rule Committee under a power conferred by the Courts Act 1971.

Crown privilege The right of the Crown to withhold documentary evidence in any legal proceedings on the grounds that its disclosure would injure the public interest. It was expressly preserved by the Crown Proceedings Act 1947 (*see* CROWN PROCEEDINGS). In certain limited cases, however, the courts have demanded to inspect documents for which *privilege is claimed and rejected the claim as unwarranted.

Crown proceedings Actions against the Crown brought under the Crown Proceedings Act 1947. The prerogative of perfection (the King can do no wrong; *see* ROYAL PREROGATIVE) originally resulted in immunity from legal proceedings, not only of the sovereign personally but also of the Crown itself (including government departments and all other public bodies that were agencies of the Crown). It gradually became possible, however, to take proceedings against the Crown for damages for breach of contract or for the recovery of property. The form of the proceedings was a **petition of right** (not an ordinary action), and the procedure governing them was eventually regulated by the Petition of Right Act 1860. The Crown Proceedings Act 1947 replaced petitions of right by ordinary actions. It also made the Crown liable to action for the tort of any servant or agent committed in the course of his employment, for breach of its duties as an employer and as an occupier of property, and for breach of any statutory duty that is binding on the Crown. It does not affect the presumption of interpretation (*see* INTERPRETATION OF STATUTES) that statutes do not bind the Crown, nor does it affect *Crown privilege.

Formerly, members of the armed forces were unable to sue the Crown in tort for death or personal injury caused by a fellow member of the armed forces while on duty. This right was extended to them by the Crown Proceedings (Armed Forces) Act 1987, but controversially the right was not made retrospective.

Crown Prosecution Service (CPS) An organization created by the Prosecution of Offences Act 1985 to conduct the majority of criminal prosecutions. Its head is the *Director of Public Prosecutions, who is answerable to Parliament through the *Attorney General. The CPS is independent of the police and is organized on a regional basis, each region having a **Chief Crown Prosecutor**. It also advises police forces on matters related to criminal offences.

Crown servant Any person in the employment of the Crown (this does not include police officers or local government employees). The Crown employs its servants at will and can therefore dismiss them at any time. However, since 1971 statute has given civil servants the right to bring proceedings for *unfair dismissal before employment tribunals. A civil servant can bring proceedings against the Crown for arrears of pay but a member of the armed forces cannot. Crown servants are subject to the Official Secrets Act 1989. Since the 1980s the number of Crown servants has been reduced substantially, as the government has pursued a policy of *privatization of former public-sector functions. Some bodies have become *executive agencies.

cruelty *n.* Formerly, behaviour serious enough to injure a spouse's physical or mental health. Cruelty is no longer a basis in itself for granting a divorce or orders in magistrates' courts.

crystallization *n.* An event or a condition that is complied with, causing a floating *charge to stop 'floating' over a company's fluctuating assets (e.g. cash, stock-in-trade) and to fasten upon the existing assets (and value) at that time. This will occur when a *receiver has been appointed under the terms of the charge to arrange payment of the debt from assets subject to the charge. Alternatively, other events or conditions may be stated under the terms of the charge when created (e.g. that the company goes into liquidation (*see* WINDING-UP) or by notice to the company by the holder of the charge. Until crystallization the company is free to deal with assets subject to the charge as it wishes.

CSA Child Support Agency. *See* CHILD SUPPORT MAINTENANCE.

CTM *See* COMMUNITY TRADE MARK.

cum testamento annexo *See* LETTERS OF ADMINISTRATION.

cur. adv. vult (c.a.v.) [Latin *curia advisari vult*, the court wishes to consider the matter] An abbreviation in law reports indicating that the judgment of the court was delivered not extempore at the end of the hearing but at a later date.

curfew order A community order under the Criminal Justice and Public Order Act 1994 that requires an offender over 16 to remain at a specified place at particular times. The maximum duration of an order is six months. The periods of curfew must be specified; they must not be less than two hours or more than 12 hours.

curtain provisions Provisions in the Settled Land Act 1925 enabling the title of the *tenant for life of settled land to be proved by the deed that vests the fee simple in him. The trust instrument that declares the beneficial interests in the land is not revealed to a purchaser: as those interests are *overreached by the sale, they do not concern him.

custodian trustee A trustee who has care and custody of trust property; other trustees (the **managing trustees**) are responsible for its management.

custody *n.* **1.** Imprisonment or confinement. The current policy behind the use of custody was established in the Criminal Justice Act 1991 and has been consolidated by the Powers of Criminal Courts (Sentencing) Act 2000. There is a twin-track approach, under which long custodial sentences will be levied on very serious crimes, particularly those of violence, but custody may be replaced with "community penalties" (punishment in the community, e.g. reparation in the community) for the less serious ones. The Powers of Criminal Courts (Sentencing) Act 2000 establishes a framework for custodial sentencing that reflects this proportionality principle and includes a policy of reducing prison for non-serious offences. To this end, Section 79 of the Act introduces a "custody threshold" that has to be surmounted before any court can impose a custodial sentence, and section 80 imposes limits on the length of any custodial sentence given. **2.** (in family law) Formerly, the bundle of rights and responsibilities that parents (and sometimes others) had in relation to a child. "Custody", which featured in various statutes, has now been replaced by the concept of *parental responsibility introduced by the Children Act 1989.

custom *n.* A practice that has been followed in a particular locality in such circumstances that it is to be accepted as part of the law of that locality. In order to be recognized as customary law it must be reasonable in nature and it must have been followed continuously, and as if it were a right, since the beginning of legal memory. Legal memory began in 1189, but proof that a practice has been followed within living memory raises a presumption that it began before that date. Custom is one of the four sources of *international law. Its elaboration is a complex process involving the accumulation of state practice, i.e. (1) the decisions of those who advise the state to act in a certain manner, (2) the practices of international organizations, (3) the decisions of international and national courts on disputed questions of international law, and (4) the mediation of jurists who organize and evaluate the amorphous material of state activity. One essential ingredient in transforming mere practice into obligatory customary law is *opinio juris*.

customs duty A charge or toll payable on certain goods exported from or imported into the UK. Customs duties are charged either in the form of an *ad valorem* duty, i.e. a percentage of the value of the goods, or as a specific duty charged according to the volume of the goods. All goods are classified in the Customs Tariff but not all goods are subject to duty. The Commissioners of Customs and Excise administer and collect customs duties. Membership of the EU has required the abolition of import duties between member states and the establishment of a *Common External Tariff. *Compare* EXCISE DUTY.

CVS *See* CORPORATE VENTURING SCHEME.

cybercrime *n.* Crime committed over the Internet. No specific laws exist to cover the Internet, but such crimes might include *hacking, *defamation over the Internet, *copyright infringement, and *fraud.

cycle track A route over which riders of pedal cycles have a right of way. It is an offence under the Cycle Tracks Acts 1984 to place a motor vehicle on a cycle track.

cyngor *n.* The Welsh title for the council of a county or a county borough.

cy-près doctrine [French: *cy*, here; *près*, near] A doctrine that in some circumstances enables a gift to charity that would otherwise fail to be diverted to another related charitable purpose. If, for example, the purpose for which a charitable gift is made cannot be achieved in exactly the way intended, or if the funds available are more than sufficient to achieve the purpose, the court or the Charity Commissioners may make a scheme for the funds to be applied to a charitable purpose as close as possible to the original one. If the gift fails after it has come into effect, cy-près will operate automatically. If a gift fails at its inception, the application of the doctrine will depend on a court's perception of the settlor's intention; to apply the funds of cy-près, a general charitable intention must be found.

D

Daily Cause List *See* CAUSE LIST.

damage *n.* Loss or harm. Not all forms of damage give rise to a right of action; for example, an occupier of land must put up with a reasonable amount of noise from his neighbours (*see* NUISANCE), and the law generally gives no compensation to relatives of an accident victim for grief or sorrow, except in the limited statutory form of damages for bereavement (*see* FATAL ACCIDENTS). Damage for which there is no remedy in law is known as *damnum sine injuria*. Conversely, a legal wrong may not cause actual damage (*injuria sine damno*). If the wrong is actionable without proof of damage (such as trespass to land) and no damage has occurred, the claimant is entitled to nominal damages. Most torts, however, are only actionable if damage has been caused (*see* NEGLIGENCE). In *libel and some forms of *slander, damage to reputation is presumed.

damages *pl. n.* A sum of money awarded by a court as compensation for a tort or a breach of contract. Damages are usually a *lump-sum award (*see also* PROVISIONAL DAMAGES). The general principle is that the claimant is entitled to full compensation (*restitutio in integrum*) for his losses. **Substantial damages** are given when actual damage has been caused, but **nominal damages** may be given for breach of contract and for some torts (such as trespass) in which no damage has been caused, in order to vindicate the claimant's rights. Damages may be *aggravated by the circumstances of the wrong. In exceptional cases in tort (but never in contract) *exemplary damages may be given to punish the defendant's wrongdoing. Damages may be classified as unliquidated or liquidated. **Liquidated damages** are a sum fixed in advance by the parties to a contract as the amount to be paid in the event of a breach. They are recoverable provided that the sum fixed was a fair pre-estimate of the likely consequences of a breach, but not if they were imposed as a *penalty. **Unliquidated damages** are damages the amount of which is fixed by the court. Damages may also be classified as *general and special damages.

The purpose of damages in tort is to put the claimant in the position he would have been in if the tort had not been committed. Recovery is limited by the rules of *remoteness of damage. The claimant must take reasonable steps to mitigate his losses and so may be expected to undergo medical treatment for his injuries or to seek alternative employment if his injuries prevent him from doing his former job. Damages may also be reduced for the claimant's *contributory negligence. The purpose of damages in contract is to put the claimant in the position he would have been in if the contract had been performed, but, as in the case of damages in tort, recovery is limited by rules relating to remoteness of damage. Again as in the case of torts, the claimant is also under a duty to take all reasonable steps to mitigate his losses and cannot claim compensation for any loss caused by his failure to do this. If, for example, a hotel reservation is cancelled, the hotelier must make all reasonable attempts to relet the room for the period in question or as much of it as possible.

Damages obtained as a result of a cause of action provided by the *Human Rights Act 1998 will be provided on the basis of the principles of *just satisfaction developed by the European Court of Human Rights.

dangerous animals Animals the keeping or use of which is regulated by statute because of their propensity to cause damage. Under the Dangerous Wild Animals Act

1976, the keeping of apes, bears, crocodiles, tigers, venomous snakes, and other potentially dangerous animals requires a local-authority licence. The Dangerous Dogs Act 1991 made the breeding, sale, or possession of dogs belonging to a type bred for fighting (e.g. pit bull terriers) an offence, enabled similar restrictions to be imposed in relation to other dogs presenting a danger to the public, and made it an offence to let a dog get dangerously out of control in a public place. The use of *guard dogs is strictly controlled by the Guard Dogs Act 1975. *See also* CLASSIFICATION OF ANIMALS.

dangerous driving The offence of driving a motor vehicle in such a way as to fall far below the standard that would be expected of a competent and careful driver, or in a manner that would be considered obviously dangerous by a competent and careful driver. This offence is defined by the Road Traffic Act 1991 and has replaced the old offence of reckless driving (defined in the Road Traffic Act 1988). The maximum penalty is a *fine at level 5 on the standard scale or six months' imprisonment; *disqualification is compulsory. *See also* CAUSING DEATH BY DANGEROUS DRIVING.

dangerous machinery An employer is under a duty to safeguard employees from dangerous machinery. By the Factories Act 1961, all dangerous parts of machinery must be securely fenced, unless they are in such a position or of such construction that they are as safe as if they were securely fenced. The Mines and Quarries Act 1954 deals with the safety of machinery in mines and quarries, and the EU Machinery Directive also lays down rules in this field. The Health and Safety at Work Act 1974 contains general provisions on *safety at work. *See also* DEFECTIVE EQUIPMENT.

dangerous things *See* RYLANDS V FLETCHER, RULE IN.

database *n.* An organized collection of information held on a computer. Databases are usually protected by *copyright in the UK under the Copyright Designs and Patents Act 1988 and the EU directive 96/9 (implemented by the Copyright and Rights in Databases Regulations 1997). Copyright protects the structure, order, arrangement on the page or screen, and other features of the database in addition to the information in the database itself.

data protection Safeguards relating to personal data, i.e. personal information about individuals that is stored on a computer and on "relevant manual filing systems". The principles of data protection, the responsibilities of data controllers (formerly data users under the Data Protection Act 1984), and the rights of data subjects are governed by the Data Protection Act 1998, which came into force on 1 March 2000.

The 1998 Act extends the operation of protection beyond computer storage, replaces the system of registration with one of notification, and demands that the level of description by data controllers under the new Act is more general than the detailed coding system required under the Data Protection Act 1984. Under the 1998 Act, the eight principles of data protection are:

(1) The information to be contained in personal data shall be obtained, and personal data shall be processed, fairly and lawfully.

(2) Personal data shall be held only for specified and lawful purposes and shall not be used or disclosed in any manner incompatible with those purposes.

(3) Personal data held for any purpose shall be relevant to that purpose and not excessive in relation to the purpose(s) for which it is used.

(4) Personal data shall be accurate and, where necessary, kept up to date.

(5) Personal data held for any purpose shall not be kept longer than necessary for that purpose.

(6) Personal data shall be processed in accordance with the rights of data subjects.
(7) Appropriate technical and organizational measures shall be taken against unauthorized and unlawful processing of personal data and against accidental loss or destruction of, or damage to, personal data.
(8) Personal data shall not be transferred to a country or territory outside the European Community area unless that country or territory ensures an adequate level of protection for the rights and freedoms of data subjects in relation to the processing of personal data

Data controllers must now notify their processing of data (unless they are exempt) with the **Information Commissioner** via the telephone, by requesting, completing, and returning a notification form, or by obtaining such a form from the website (http://www.dpr.gov.uk/notify/1.html). Notification is renewable annually; a data controller who fails to notify his processing of data, or any changes that have been made since notification, commits a criminal offence.

The Information Commissioner can seek information (via an information notice) and ultimately take enforcement action (via an enforcement notice) against data controllers for noncompliance with their full obligations under the 1998 Act. Appeals against decisions of the Information Commissioner may be made to the **Data Protection Tribunal**, which comprises a chairperson and two deputies (who are legally qualified) and lay members (representing the interests of the data controllers and the data subjects). There are other strict liability criminal offences under the 1998 Act other than non-notification. They include (1) obtaining, disclosing (or bringing about the disclosure), or selling (or advertising for sale) personal data, without consent of the data controller; (2) obtaining unauthorized access to data; (3) asking another person to obtain access to data; and (4) failing to respond to an information and/or enforcement notice.

Data subjects have considerable rights conferred on them under the 1998 Act. They include: (1) the right to find out what information is held about them; (2) the right to seek a court order to rectify, block, erase, and destroy personal details if these are inaccurate, contain expressions of opinion, or are based on inaccurate data; (3) the right to prevent processing where such processing would cause substantial unwarranted damage or substantial distress to themselves or anyone else; (4) the right to prevent the processing of data for direct marketing; (5) the right to compensation from a data controller for damage or damage and distress caused by any breach of the 1998 Act; and (6) the right to prevent some decisions about data being made solely by automated means, where those decisions are likely to significantly affect them.

dawn raid **1.** An offer by a person or persons (*see* CONCERT PARTY) to buy a substantial quantity of shares in a public company at above the market value, the offer remaining open for a very short period (usually hours). Because of the speed required smaller shareholders may have little opportunity to avail themselves of the offer. Rules restrict the speed at which such acquisitions can be made. *See* SARS. **2.** An unannounced visit by officials of the European Commission or the UK Office of Fair Trading investigating cartels or other breaches of the competition rules under *Articles 81 and 82 of the Treaty of Rome or under the Competition Act 1998.

days of grace The three days that were added to the time of payment fixed by a *bill of exchange not payable on demand before the Banking and Financial Dealings Act 1971 came into force. A bill drawn on or after 16 January 1972 is payable in all cases on the last day of the time of payment fixed by the bill or, if that is a nonbusiness day, on the succeeding business day.

day-training centre A place that provides social education and intensive probation supervision. A court may order a person subject to a *community rehabilitation order to attend such a centre.

death *n.* *See* REGISTRATION OF DEATH.

death duties Taxes formerly charged on a person's property on his death. These have now been replaced by *inheritance tax.

death penalty *See* CAPITAL PUNISHMENT.

de bene esse [Latin: of well-being] Denoting a course of action that is the best that can be done in the present circumstances or in anticipation of a future event. An example is obtaining a *deposition from a witness when there is a likelihood that he will be unable to attend the court hearing.

debenture *n.* A document that acknowledges and contains the terms of a loan (usually to a company). The loan may be unsecured (a **naked debenture**). More usually, however, the debenture will be subject to a *charge and will contain the terms of the charge (e.g. the right to appoint a *receiver or a *crystallization event). Debentures may be issued to a single creditor or in a series to several creditors in order to raise finance for a company. In the case of the latter, a trust may be created and contained within the debenture in favour of such creditors. This enables the company to appoint a trustee for debenture holders to ensure that the financial activities of the company are managed in the interests of the group of creditors. Finance raised by the issue of debentures is known as *loan capital. This is contrasted with share *capital, the holders of which are *company members.

de bonis asportatis [Latin: of goods carried away] One form of trespass to goods (*see* TRESPASS), not distinguished in modern law from other direct interferences with the possession of goods.

de bonis non administratis [Latin: of unadministered goods] A grant of *letters of administration of the estate of a deceased person when administration has previously been granted to someone who has himself died before completing the administration of the estate leaving no executor, so that the chain of executorship is broken.

debt *n.* **1.** A sum of money owed by one person or group to another. **2.** The obligation to pay a sum of money owed.

debt adjusting *See* ANCILLARY CREDIT BUSINESS.

debt collecting *See* ANCILLARY CREDIT BUSINESS.

debtor *n.* **1.** One who owes a debt. *See also* JUDGMENT DEBTOR. **2.** (under the Consumer Credit Act 1974) The individual receiving credit under a *consumer-credit agreement or the person to whom his rights and duties under the agreement have passed by assignment or operation of law.

debtor-creditor agreement A *consumer-credit agreement regulated by the Consumer Credit Act 1974. It may be (1) a *restricted-use credit agreement to finance a transaction between the debtor and a supplier in which there are no arrangements between the creditor and the supplier (e.g. when a loan is paid by the creditor direct to a dealer who is to supply the debtor); (2) a restricted-use credit agreement to refinance any existing indebtedness of the debtor's to the creditor or any other person; or (3) an unrestricted-use credit agreement (e.g. a straight loan of money) that is not made by the creditor under arrangements with a supplier in the knowledge that the credit is to be used to finance a transaction between the debtor and the supplier.

debtor-creditor-supplier agreement A *consumer-credit agreement regulated by the Consumer Credit Act 1974. It may be (1) a *restricted-use credit agreement to finance a transaction between the debtor and the creditor, which may or may not form part of that agreement (e.g. a purchase of goods on credit); (2) a restricted-use credit agreement to finance a transaction between the debtor and a supplier, made by the creditor and involving arrangements between himself and the supplier; or (3) an unrestricted-use credit agreement that is made by the creditor under pre-existing arrangements between himself and a supplier in the knowledge that the credit is to be used to finance a transaction between the debtor and the supplier.

deceit n. A tort that is committed when someone knowingly or recklessly makes a false statement of fact intending that it should be acted on by someone else and that person does act on the false statement and thereby suffers damage. See FRAUD.

deception n. A false representation, by words or conduct, of a matter of fact (including the existence of an intention) or law that is made deliberately or recklessly to another person. Deception itself is not a crime, but there are six imprisonable crimes in which deception is involved: (1) Obtaining property. (2) Obtaining an overdraft, an insurance policy, an annuity contract, or the opportunity to earn money (or more money) in a job or to win money by betting. These two offences are punishable by up to ten years' imprisonment. (3) Obtaining any services (e.g. of a driver or typist or the hiring of a car). (4) Securing the remission of all or part of an existing liability to make payment (whether one's own or another's) with intent to make permanent default in whole or in part. (5) Causing someone to wait for or forego a debt owing to him. (6) Obtaining an exemption from or abatement of liability to pay for something (e.g. obtaining free or cheap travel by falsely pretending to be a senior citizen). It is not an offence, however, to deceive someone in any other circumstances, provided there is no element of *forgery or *false accounting.

decisions of the EU See COMMUNITY LEGISLATION.

declaration n. **1.** (in the law of evidence) An oral or written statement not made on oath. The term is often applied to certain types of out-of-court statement that are admissible as an exception to the rule against *hearsay evidence; for example, *declaration against interest, *declaration concerning pedigree, *declaration concerning public or general rights, and *declaration in course of duty. See also STATUTORY DECLARATION. **2.** A discretionary remedy involving a bare finding by the High Court as to a person's legal status, rights, or obligations. A declaration cannot be directly enforced, but is frequently sought both in private law (e.g. to answer a question as to nationality or rights under a will) and in public law (e.g. to test a claim that delegated legislation or the decision of some inferior court, tribunal, or administrative authority is *ultra vires). In both public and private law the applicant must show standing, i.e. that the issue affects him directly. Compare QUASHING ORDER. See also JUDICIAL REVIEW.

declaration against interest A *declaration by a person who has subsequently died which he knew, when he made it, would be against his pecuniary or proprietary interest. It may be tendered to the court as an exception to the rule against *hearsay evidence.

declaration concerning pedigree A *declaration made by a person who has subsequently died, or to be inferred from family conduct, concerning a disputed pedigree of a blood relation or the spouse of a blood relation. The declaration must have been made before the dispute in which it is tendered as evidence had arisen.

declaration concerning public or general rights A *declaration made by a person who has subsequently died concerning the reputed existence of a public or general right. **Public rights** affect everyone (e.g. a public *right of way) while **general rights** affect a class of people (e.g. a right of *common).

declaration in course of duty A *declaration by a person who has subsequently died made while pursuing a duty to record or report his acts.

declaration of incompatibility *See* HUMAN RIGHTS ACT.

declaration of intention *See* OFFER.

declaration of trust A statement indicating that property is to be held on trust. No specific words are necessary, as long as the intention to declare a trust is made clear. Once a declaration of trust is made, the person intended to be trustee still holds the property but is not entitled to hold it for his own benefit. A declaration of a trust where the trust property is land is subject to certain formalities, detailed in the Law of Property Act 1925 (s. 53).

declaratory judgment A judgment that merely states the court's opinion on a question of law or declares the rights of the parties, without normally including any provision for enforcement. A claim for declaration may, however, be combined with one for some substantive relief, such as damages.

declaratory theory The proposition that a state has capacity (and personality) in international law as soon as it exists in fact (that is, when it becomes competent in municipal law). This capacity is generated spontaneously from the assertion by the community that it is a judicial entity. When socially organized, the new state is internally legally organized, and hence competent to act in such a way as to engage itself in international responsibility. Thus, according to this theory, *recognition does not create any state that did not already exist. *See* INTERNATIONAL LEGAL PERSONALITY. *Compare* CONSTITUTIVE THEORY.

decompilation (reverse engineering) *n.* The process of taking computer *software apart. Under EU directive 91/250, computer software is protected by *copyright throughout the EU. However, a very limited right to decompilation is given in that directive for the defined purpose of writing an interoperable program, under certain very strict conditions. Any provision in a contract to exclude this limited right will be void. In the UK this directive is implemented by the Copyright (Computer Programs) Regulations 1992.

decree *n.* **1.** A law. **2.** A court order. *See also* DECREE ABSOLUTE; DECREE NISI.

decree absolute A decree of divorce, nullity, or presumption of death that brings a marriage to a legal end, enabling the parties to remarry. It is usually issued six weeks after the *decree nisi (unless there are exceptional reasons why it should be given sooner). A list of decrees absolute is kept at the Divorce Registry and access to it is open to the public.

decree nisi A conditional decree of divorce, nullity, or presumption of death. For most purposes the parties to the marriage are still married until the decree is made absolute. During the period between decree nisi and decree absolute the Queen's Proctor or any member of the public may intervene to prevent the decree being made absolute and the decree may be rescinded if obtained by fraud.

deductions *pl. n.* (in employment law) Sums deducted from an employee's wages. The Employment Rights Act 1996 provides strict rules on what can be deducted from wages. Permitted deductions include those for income tax, national insurance, and pension contributions (for employees who have agreed to be part of an employer's pension scheme). Deductions are also allowed when there has been an overpayment of wages or expenses in the past, when there has been a strike and wages are withheld, or when there is a court order, such as an order from the Child Support Agency or a court attachment of earnings order. There are special rules for those in retail employment. These provide, for example, that deductions of up to 10% may be made from gross wages for cash shortages or stock deficiencies.

deed *n.* A written document that must make it clear on its face that it is intended to be a deed and validly executed as a deed. Before 31 July 1990, all deeds required a seal in order to be validly executed, but this requirement was abolished by the Law of Property (Miscellaneous Provisions) Act 1989. A deed executed since that date by an individual requires only that it must be signed by its maker in the presence of a witness, or at the maker's direction and in the presence of two witnesses, and delivered. Deeds executed by companies require before delivery the signature of a director and secretary, or two directors, of the company; alternatively, if the company has a seal, the deed may be executed by affixing the company seal. If the deed is a contractual document, it is referred to as a **specialty**. A promise contained in a deed is called a **covenant** and is binding even if not supported by *consideration. Covenants may be either express or implied. A deed normally takes effect on delivery; actual delivery constitutes handing it to the other party; constructive delivery involved (in strict theory) touching the seal with the finger, and saying words such as "I deliver this as my act and deed". If a deed is delivered but is not to become operative until a future date or until some condition has been fulfilled, it is called an **escrow**. The **recitals** of a deed are those parts that merely declare facts and do not effect any of the substance of the transaction. They are usually inserted to explain the reason for the transaction. The **operative part** of a deed is the part that actually effects the objects of the deed, as by transferring land. The **testatum** (or **witnessing part**) constitutes the opening words of the operative part, i.e. "Now this deed witnesseth as follows". The **premises** are the words in the operative part that describe the parties and the transaction involved. The **parcels** are the words in the premises that describe the property involved. The **testimonium** is the concluding part, beginning "In witness whereof", and containing the signatures of the parties and witnesses. The *locus sigilli* is the position indicated for placing the seal. When a deed refers to itself as "these presents", "presents" means present statements. The advantage of a deed over an ordinary contract is that the limitation period is 12 rather than 6 years (*see* LIMITATION OF ACTIONS) and no *consideration is required for the deed to be enforceable. *See also* DEED POLL.

deed of arrangement A written agreement between a debtor and his creditors, when no *bankruptcy order has been made, arranging the debtor's affairs either for the benefit of the creditors generally or, when the debtor is insolvent, for the benefit of at least three of the creditors. A deed of arrangement is regulated by statute and must be registered with the Department of Trade and Industry within seven days. It may take a number of different forms: it may be a *composition, an *assignment of the debtor's property to a trustee for the benefit of his creditors, or an agreement to wind up the debtor's business in such a way as to pay his debts. The debtor usually agrees to such an arrangement in order to avoid bankruptcy. A similar arrangement can be agreed after a bankruptcy order is made, but this is regulated in a different way (*see* VOLUNTARY ARRANGEMENT).

deed of covenant A *deed containing an undertaking to pay an agreed amount over an agreed period. Certain tax advantages could be obtained through the use of covenants, particularly in the case of four-year covenants in favour of charities. This was superseded by *gift aid in April 2000.

deed of gift A *deed conveying property from one person (the **donor**) to another (the **donee**) when the donee gives no *consideration in return. The donee can enforce a deed of gift against the donor. Gifts made other than by deed are not generally enforceable (*but see* PART PERFORMANCE).

deed poll A *deed to which there is only one party; for example, one declaring a *change of name.

deemed *adj.* Supposed. In the construction of some documents (particularly statutes) an artificial construction is given to a word or phrase that ordinarily would not be so construed, in order to clarify any doubt or as a convenient form of drafting shorthand.

de facto [Latin: in fact] Existing as a matter of fact rather than of right. The government may, for example, recognize a foreign government *de facto* if it is actually in control of a country even though it has no legal right to rule (*see* RECOGNITION). *Compare* DE JURE.

defamation *n.* The *publication of a statement about a person that tends to lower his reputation in the opinion of right-thinking members of the community or to make them shun or avoid him. Defamation is usually in words, but pictures, gestures, and other acts can be defamatory. In English law, a distinction is made between defamation in permanent form (*see* LIBEL) and defamation not in permanent form (*see* SLANDER). This distinction is not made in Scotland. The remedies in tort for defamation are damages and injunction.

In English law, the basis of the tort is injury to reputation, so it must be proved that the statement was communicated to someone other than the person defamed. In Scottish law, defamation includes injury to the feelings of the person defamed as well as injury to reputation, so an action can be brought when a statement is communicated only to the person defamed. If the statement is not obviously defamatory, the claimant must show that it would be understood in a defamatory sense (*see* INNUENDO). It is not necessary to prove that the defendant intended to refer to the claimant. The test is whether reasonable people would think the statement referred to him, but the defendant may escape liability for **unintentional defamation** by making an offer of amends (*see* APOLOGY). Other defences are *justification, *fair comment, *absolute privilege, and *qualified privilege.

All those involved in the publication of a defamatory statement, such as printers, publishers, and broadcasting companies, are liable and every repetition of a defamatory statement is a fresh publication, giving rise to a new cause of action. A mere distributor of a book, newspaper, etc., is not liable if he did not know and had no reason to know of its defamatory contents. The Defamation Act 1996 put this defence on a statutory footing and generally speeded up procedures for defamation litigation, but it did not change the rule that the jury and not the judge decides on the damages in defamation cases.

default *n.* Failure to do something required by law, usually failure to comply with mandatory rules of procedure. If a defendant in civil proceedings is in default (e.g. by failing to file a defence), the claimant may obtain **judgment in default**. If the claimant is in default, the defendant may apply to the court to dismiss the action.

default notice A notice that must be served on a contract breaker before taking action in consequence of his breach. Under the Consumer Credit Act 1974 a default notice must be served on a debtor or hirer in breach of a regulated agreement before the creditor or owner is entitled to terminate the agreement; to demand earlier payment of any sum; to recover possession of any goods or land; to treat any right conferred on the debtor or hirer by the agreement as terminated, restricted, or deferred; or to enforce any security. The notice must specify the nature of the breach, what action (if any) is required to remedy it, and the date before which that action is to be taken. If the breach is not capable of remedy, the notice must specify the sum (if any) required in compensation and the date before which it is to be paid.

default summons Formerly, a summons used to initiate all proceedings in the county courts when the only relief claimed was the payment of money. Under the *Civil Procedure Rules, such claims are now made by *claim forms.

defect *n.* **1.** A fault or failing in a thing. The defect may be obvious (a **patent defect**) or it may not be apparent at first (a **latent defect**). In a sale of goods, the buyer usually has a legal remedy against a professional seller if the goods have a latent defect. If there is a patent defect he usually has no such remedy if he had an opportunity to inspect the goods before purchase. *See also* SATISFACTORY QUALITY.
2. (defect in a product) A fault in a product as defined in the Consumer Protection Act 1987. A defect exists in products under the Act when the safety of the products is not what people generally are entitled to expect. In determining what people are entitled to expect, reference should be made to the way in which the goods are marked, any warnings issued with them, and the time of supply. The Act implements EU directive 85/374 on *products liability.

defective equipment An employer's duty to provide his employees with a safe system of work, so far as is reasonably practicable, includes the provision and maintenance of safe tools and equipment (including materials) for the job. The employer is liable to an employee injured by a defect in the equipment he provides, even if the defect was due to the fault of some third party, such as the manufacturer of the equipment. *See also* SAFETY AT WORK.

defective premises Liability for defects in the construction of buildings can arise both at common law, in contract and tort, and by statute. In addition to any liability they may incur for breach of contract, builders, architects, surveyors, etc., are liable in tort on ordinary principles for *negligence and may also be in breach of statutory duties; for example, the duty imposed by the Defective Premises Act 1972, in respect of work connected with the provision of a dwelling, to see that the dwelling will be fit for habitation. A landlord who is responsible for repairs, or who has reserved the right to enter and carry out repairs, may be liable for damage caused by failure to repair not only to his tenants, but also to third parties who could be expected to be affected by the defects. For the liability of occupiers of premises, *see* OCCUPIER'S LIABILITY.

defective products *See* PRODUCTS LIABILITY.

defence *n.* **1.** The response by a defendant to service of a claim. Once a claim form or particulars of claim have been served on the defendant, he is under an obligation to respond. If he does not file a defence, judgment in default will be entered against him. Generally, a defence must be filed within 14 days of service of the claim. The defendant may obtain an extension of a further 14 days by filing an *acknowledgment of service. **2.** In civil and criminal proceedings, an issue of law or fact that, if determined in favour of the defendant, will relieve him of liability wholly or in part. *See also* GENERAL DEFENCES.

defence statement A document setting out the accused's *defence in criminal proceedings for initial hearings before trial. The Criminal Procedure and Investigations Act 1996 provides that, from 1 April 1997, the accused need not make a defence statement at all; however, an adverse inference may be drawn from a failure to give a statement in the *Crown Court. The statement should set out the nature of the defence in general terms (for example, mistaken identification, alibi), indicate the matters on which the accused takes issue with the prosecution, and set out in respect of each matter the reason why the accused takes issue. It must not contain any inconsistent defences and should not be different from the defence to be put forward at trial.

defendant *n.* A person against whom court proceedings are brought. *Compare* CLAIMANT.

deferred debt In bankruptcy proceedings, a debt that by statute is not paid until all other debts have been paid in full.

deferred sentence A *sentence imposed by a magistrates' court or the Crown Court after a period of up to six months from conviction for the offence. The court may postpone sentencing, if the convicted person agrees, if it wishes to assess any change in the offender's conduct or circumstances during that time.

defrauding *n.* Any act that deprives someone of something that is his or to which he might be entitled or that injures someone in relation to any proprietary right. It is a crime (a form of *conspiracy at common law) to conspire to defraud someone. *See also* CHEAT; DISHONESTY.

degrading treatment or punishment Treatment that arouses in the victim a feeling or fear, anguish, and inferiority capable of humiliating and debasing the victim and possibly breaking his physical or moral resistance. The prohibition on degrading treatment or punishment as set out in Article 3 of the European Convention on Human Rights is now part of UK law as a consequence of the *Human Rights Act 1998. This right is an *absolute right; such treatment can never be justified as being in the public interest, no matter how great that public interest might be. Public authorities have a limited but positive duty to protect this right from interference by third parties.

de jure [Latin] As a matter of legal right. *See* RECOGNITION. *Compare* DE FACTO.

***del credere* agent** [Italian: of trust] *See* AGENT.

delegated legislation (subordinate legislation) Legislation made under powers conferred by an Act of Parliament (an enabling statute, often called the parent Act). The bulk of delegated legislation is governmental: it consists mainly of *Orders in Council and instruments of various names (e.g. orders, regulations, rules, directions, and schemes) made by ministers (*see also* GOVERNMENT CIRCULARS). Its primary use is to supplement Acts of Parliament by prescribing the detailed and technical rules required for their operation; unlike an Act, it has the advantage that it can be made (and later amended if necessary) without taking up parliamentary time. Delegated legislation is also made by a variety of bodies outside central government, examples being *byelaws, the *Rules of the Supreme Court, and the codes of conduct of certain professional bodies (*see also* ORDERS OF COUNCIL).

Most delegated legislation (byelaws are the main exception) is subject to some degree of parliamentary control, which may take any of three principal forms: (1) a simple requirement that it be laid before Parliament after being made (thus ensuring that members become aware of its existence but affording them no special method or opportunity of questioning its substance); (2) a provision that it be laid and, for a specified period, liable to annulment by a resolution of either House (**negative resolution** procedure); or (3) a provision that it be laid and either shall not take effect until approved by resolutions of both Houses or shall cease to have effect unless approved within a specified period (**affirmative resolution** procedure). In the case of purely financial instruments, any provision for a negative or affirmative resolution refers to the House of Commons alone. (*See also* STATUTORY INSTRUMENT; SPECIAL PROCEDURE ORDERS.)

All delegated legislation is subject to judicial control under the doctrine of **ultra vires*. Delegated legislation is interpreted in the light of the parent Act, so particular words are presumed to be used in the same sense as in that Act. This rule apart, it is governed by the same principles as those governing the *interpretation of statutes.

See also SUBDELEGATED LEGISLATION.

delegation *n.* **1.** The grant of authority to a person to act on behalf of one or more others, for agreed purposes. **2.** *See* VICARIOUS LIABILITY.

delegatus non potest delegare |Latin| A person to whom something has been delegated cannot delegate further, i.e. one to whom powers and duties have been entrusted cannot entrust them to another. The rule applies particularly when the delegate possesses some special skill in the performance of the duties delegated, or when personal trust is involved. The rule does not apply if there is express or implied authority to delegate. Trustees, for example, have always been entitled to employ agents when this was necessary (for example, they can employ solicitors to do legal work). Since 1925, a trustee may delegate any business of the trust to an agent provided that he does so in good faith. Further, since 1971, any trustee may delegate, for a period not exceeding one year, any trusts, powers, or discretions he has; this delegation may be repeated.

de lege ferenda [Latin: of (or concerning) the law that is to come into force] A phrase used to indicate that a proposition relates to what the law ought to be or may in the future be.

de lege lata [Latin: of (or concerning) the law that is in force] A phrase used to indicate that a proposition relates to the law as it is.

delivery *n.* The transfer of possession of property from one person to another. Under the Sale of Goods Act 1979, a seller delivers goods to a buyer if he delivers them physically, if he makes **symbolic delivery** by delivering the document of title to them (e.g. a *bill of lading) or other means of control over them (e.g. the keys of a warehouse in which they are stored), or if a third party who is holding them acknowledges that he now holds them for the buyer. In **constructive delivery**, the seller agrees that he holds the goods on behalf of the buyer or the buyer has possession of the goods under a hire-purchase agreement and becomes owner on making the final payment.

demanding with menaces *See* BLACKMAIL.

de minimis non curat lex [Latin] The law does not take account of trifles. It will not, for example, award damages for a trifling nuisance. The *de minimis* rule applies in a number of other areas, including EU *competition law.

demise (in land law) **1.** *vb.* To grant a lease. **2.** *n.* The lease itself.

demise of the Crown The death of the sovereign. The Crown, in fact, never dies: the accession of the new sovereign takes place at the moment of the demise, and there is no interregnum.

demonstrative legacy *See* LEGACY.

demurrage *n.* Liquidated *damages payable under a charterparty at a specified daily rate for any days (**demurrage days**) required for completing the loading or discharging of cargo after the *lay days have expired. The word is also commonly used to denote the unliquidated damages to which the shipowner is entitled if, when no lay days are specified, the ship is detained for loading or unloading beyond a reasonable time.

departure *n.* The introduction of a new allegation of fact or the raising of a new ground or claim inconsistent with the party's earlier claim. Departure is not permitted by the Civil Procedure Rules, but it does not prevent the *amendment of documents used in litigation provided that the amended documents do not contain any departure. The principal effect of the rule is to prevent a claimant from setting up in his *reply a new claim that is inconsistent with the cause of action alleged in the particulars of claim.

dependant *n.* A person who relies on someone else for maintenance or financial support. On the death of the latter, the courts now have wide discretionary powers to award financial provision to dependants out of the estate of the deceased. The list of dependants includes not only spouses, former spouses, children, and children of the family, but anyone (e.g. a lover, housekeeper, or servant) who was being maintained to some extent by the deceased immediately before his death. *See also* REASONABLE FINANCIAL PROVISION.

dependent relative revocation The doctrine that if a testator revokes his will in the mistaken belief that a particular result will ensue, or that a particular set of facts exists when it does not, then the revoked will may still hold good. For example, if a testator destroys his will, in the mistaken belief that thereby an earlier will would be revived, the destroyed will will be held not to have been revoked. Similarly, a testator may revoke his will, intending to make another; the revoked will holds good if the testator subsequently makes no new will or an invalid one.

dependent state A member of the community of states with qualified or limited status. Such states possess no separate statehood or sovereignty: it is the parent state alone that possesses *international legal personality and has the capacity to exercise international rights and duties.

dependent territory A territory (e.g. a colony) the government of which is to some extent the legal responsibility of the government of another territory.

deportation *n.* The removal from a state of a person whose initial entry into that state was illegal (*compare* EXPULSION). In the UK this is authorized by the Immigration Act 1971 as amended by the Immigration and Asylum Act 1999 in the case of any person who does not have the right of abode there (*see* IMMIGRATION). He may be ordered to leave the country in four circumstances: if he has overstayed or broken a condition attached to his permission to stay; if another person to whose family he belongs is deported; if (he being 17 or over) a court recommends deportation on his conviction of an offence punishable with imprisonment; or if the Secretary of State thinks his deportation to be for the public good. The Act enables appeals to be made against deportation orders. Normally, they are either direct to the *Immigration Appeal Tribunal or to that tribunal after a preliminary appeal to an adjudicator. The Immigration Act 1988 restricts this right of appeal in the case of those who have failed to observe a condition or limitation on their leave to enter the UK. The Immigration and Asylum Act 1999 gives additional powers to order those present in the UK without permission to leave, either when they have overstayed or obtained leave to remain by deception or when they were never granted leave to remain. It also provides for the removal of asylum claimants under standing arrangements with other EU member states.

depose vb. To make a *deposition or other written statement on oath.

deposit n. **1.** A sum paid by one party to a contract to the other party as a guarantee that the first party will carry out the terms of the contract. The first party will forfeit the sum in question if he does not carry out the terms, even if the sum is in excess of the other party's loss. If the contract is completed without dispute the deposit becomes part payment. In land law a deposit is usually made by a purchaser when exchanging contracts (see EXCHANGE OF CONTRACTS) for the purchase of land. The contract stipulates whether the recipient (usually the vendor's solicitor or estate agent) holds the deposit as agent for the vendor, in which case the vendor can use the money pending *completion of the transaction, or as stakeholder, in which case the funds must remain in the stakeholder's account until completion or (in the case of a dispute) a court has decided who should have it. If the contract is rescinded the purchaser is entitled to the return of his deposit. **2.** The placing of title deeds with a mortgagee of unregistered land as security for the debt. A mortgagee not protected by deposit of title deeds (such as a second mortgagee of unregistered land) registers his mortgage (see REGISTRATION OF ENCUMBRANCES) and is then entitled to receive the title deeds from prior mortgagees after the redemption of their security. All mortgages of registered land must be registered to be binding on purchases of the land.

deposition n. A statement made on oath before a magistrate or court official by a witness and usually recorded in writing. In criminal cases depositions are taken during committal proceedings before the magistrates' court (see COMMITTAL FOR TRIAL). The usual procedure is that the prosecution witnesses give their evidence on oath and may be cross-examined by the accused or his legal advisers. The statement is then written down by the magistrates' clerk, read out to the witness in the presence of the accused, signed by the witness, and certified by the examining magistrate. The accused must be present throughout and be allowed to cross-examine. If these conditions are not fulfilled, both the committal proceedings and the subsequent trial will be null and void. There are special arrangements for depositions to be written down out of court if a witness is dangerously ill and cannot come to court, and also for depositions by children. Depositions made in committal proceedings are accepted as evidence at the trial if the witness is dead or insane, unfit to travel because of illness, or is being kept out of the way by the accused; they are also accepted to show a discrepancy between the deposition evidence and evidence given later on orally at the trial.

In civil cases the court may order an examiner of the court to take depositions from any witnesses who are (for example) ill or likely to be abroad at the time of the hearing. At the taking of the deposition the witness is examined and cross-examined in the usual way, and the examiner notes any objection to admissibility that may be raised. The deposition is not admissible at the trial without the consent of the party against whom it is given, unless the witness is still unavailable. See also LETTER OF REQUEST.

deprave vb. To make morally bad. The term is used particularly in relation to the effect of *obscene publications. A person is considered to have been depraved if his mind is influenced in an immoral way, even though this does not necessarily result in any act of depravity.

derecognition n. A process whereby notice is given to terminate union recognition in an establishment or company. Employees continue to have the right to belong to a trade union, but the employer no longer negotiates collectively: terms and conditions previously the subject of *collective bargaining are negotiated individually or with groups of employees unconnected with trade unions, resulting in a **personal contract**. *See also* RECOGNITION PROCEDURE.

deregulation *n.* **1.** The controls imposed by governments on the operation of markets, such as is allowed for under the Deregulation and Contracting Out Act 1990. **2.** A movement in the EU to reduce rules at Community level that could be better set at national level (*see* SUBSIDIARITY).

derivative action Civil proceedings brought by a minority of company members in their own names seeking a remedy for the company in respect of a wrong done to it. Such proceedings are exceptional; usually an action should be brought by the company (the injured party) in its own name. A derivative action will only be permitted when a serious wrong to the company is involved, which cannot be ratified by an ordinary resolution of company members (e.g. an **ultra vires* or illegal act or a case of **fraud on the minority) and the majority of members will not sanction an action in the company's name. *Compare* REPRESENTATIVE ACTION.

derivative deed A deed that is supplemental to another, whose scope it alters, confirms, or extends. An example is a deed admitting a new partner to a firm on terms set out in a principal deed executed by the original partners.

derivative title A claim of sovereignty over a territory, that territory having previously belonged to another sovereign state. Derivation of title to territory involves the transfer (**cession) of title from one sovereign state to another.

derivative trust *See* SUB-TRUST.

derogation *n.* Lessening or restriction of the authority, strength, or power of a law, right, or obligation. Specifically: **1.** (in the European Convention on Human Rights) A provision that enables a signatory state to avoid the obligations of some but not all of the substantive provisions of the rest of the Convention. This procedure is provided by Article 15 of the Convention and is available in time of war or other public emergency threatening the life of the nation. Although Article 15 is not brought into domestic law by the **Human Rights Act 1998, the Act exempts public authorities from compliance from any articles (or parts of articles) where a derogation is in place. **2.** (in EU law) An exemption clause that permits a member state of the EU to avoid a certain directive or regulation. Sometimes member states are allowed a longer than normal time to implement an EU directive.

desertion *n.* **1.** The failure by a husband or wife to cohabit with his or her spouse. Desertion usually takes the form of physically leaving the home, but this is not essential: there may be desertion although both parties live under the same roof, if all elements of a shared life (e.g. sexual intercourse, eating meals together) have ceased. Desertion must be a unilateral act carried out against the wishes of the other spouse, with the intention of bringing married life to an end (*animus deserendi*). If it is continuous for more than two years, it may be evidence that the marriage has irretrievably broken down and entitle the deserted spouse to a decree of **divorce. *See also* CONSTRUCTIVE DESERTION. **2.** An offence against service law committed by a member of the armed forces who leaves or fails to attend at his unit, ship, or place of duty. He must either intend at the time to remain permanently absent from duty without lawful authority or subsequently form that intention. One who absents himself without leave to avoid service overseas or service before the enemy is also guilty of desertion.

design right Legal protection for the external appearance of an article, including its shape, configuration, pattern, or ornament. A design right is distinct from a *patent, which protects the internal workings of the article. The right entitles the owner to prevent others making articles to the same design. Design rights in the UK are either registered (*see* REGISTERED DESIGN) or unregistered. Registered designs must have aesthetic appeal; they are protected under the Registered Designs Act 1949 as amended and last for a maximum of 25 years provided renewal fees are paid. Unregistered designs, which came into existence in 1989, are protected under the Copyright, Designs and Patents Act 1988. Unregistered design protection is for only 15 years. Design protection is not available for parts of articles that simply provide a fit or match to another article, such as a car-body panel.

de son tort *See* EXECUTOR DE SON TORT; TRUSTEE DE SON TORT.

detention *n.* Depriving a person of his liberty against his will following *arrest. The Police and Criminal Evidence Act 1984 closely regulates police powers of detention and detained persons' rights. Detention of adults without charge is allowed only when it is necessary to secure or preserve evidence or to obtain it by questioning; it should only continue beyond 24 hours (to 36 hours) in respect of serious arrestable offences (e.g. rape, kidnapping, causing death by dangerous driving) when a superintendant or more senior officer reasonably believes it to be necessary. Magistrates' courts may then authorize a further extension without charge for up to 36 hours, which can be extended for another 36 hours, but the overall detention period cannot exceed 96 hours.

If the ground for detention ceases, or if further detention is not authorized, the detainee must either be released or be charged and either released on *bail to appear before a court or taken before the next available court. An arrested person held in custody may have one person told of this as soon as practicable, though if a serious arrestable offence is involved and a senior police officer reasonably believes that this would interfere with the investigation, this can be delayed for up to 36 hours. The detainee has a broadly similar right of access to a solicitor. *Terrorism suspects may be detained for up to seven days on a magistrate's authority.

detention centre *See* DETENTION IN A YOUNG OFFENDER INSTITUTION.

detention in a young offender institution A custodial sentence that may be passed on a person aged 15 or over but under 21 (*see* JUVENILE OFFENDER). It combines the former **detention centre** orders (against male offenders aged 14 to 20) and **youth custody** sentences (for males and females aged 15 to 20). The offence must be so serious, by itself or with another offence, that detention is the only justifiable outcome; alternatively it must be a violent or sexual offence and detention in such an institution is the only way of protecting the public from further injury or death. The court may consider *mitigation and impose a noncustodial sentence.

The minimum detention period is 21 days and the maximum period is 24 months. Other custodial sentences include custody for life and secure training orders.

determinable interest An interest that will automatically come to an end on the occurrence of some specified event (which, however, may never happen). For example, if A conveys land to B until he marries, B has a determinable interest that would pass back to A upon his marriage. But if B dies a bachelor the *possibility of a reverter to A is destroyed and B's heirs acquire an absolute interest. An interest that must end at some future point (e.g. a *life interest) is not classified as a determinable interest, but one that could end during a person's life (for example a *protective trust) is so classified. A determinable legal estate in land prior to 1925 was known as a **determinable fee**, but under the Law of Property Act 1925 it can now exist only as an equitable interest. It is exceptionally difficult to distinguish between a determinable interest and a *conditional interest. *Compare* CONTINGENT INTEREST.

deterrence *n. See* PUNISHMENT.

detinue *n.* An action to recover goods, based on a wrongful refusal by the possessor of the goods to restore them to the owner. The old common law form of action was abolished by the Judicature Acts 1873–75 and detinue was abolished altogether by the Torts (Interference with Goods) Act 1977. Recovery of goods is now governed by the provisions of the 1977 Act.

devastavit *n.* [Latin: he has wasted] The failure of a personal representative to administer a deceased person's estate promptly and in a proper manner. For example, if he pays in full a legacy subject to the possibility of *abatement he is personally liable for the loss suffered by other beneficiaries and caused by his *devastavit*. He may also be liable if, for example, he disposes of an asset in the estate at an undervalue, even if acting in good faith.

development *n.* (in *town and country planning) Generally, the carrying out of any building or other operation affecting land and the making of any material change in the use of any buildings or land. Development does not include alterations to buildings not materially affecting their external appearance or changes of use that fall within certain **use classes** prescribed by statutory instrument. For example, office use is a use class and a mere change in the type of office business is not development. All development requires planning permission, other than "permitted development" under a general development order. The demolition of houses to provide car parking and a landscaped area is not development.

development land (community land) Under the Community Land Act 1975, land classified by a local authority as needed for commercial development and required to be brought first into public ownership, thus effectively nationalizing its development value. This Act was repealed by the Local Government, Planning and Land Act 1980.

development land tax A tax charged on the development value of land when the land was disposed of before 19 March 1985. It was abolished for all disposals after that date by the Finance Act 1985.

development plan *See* TOWN AND COUNTRY PLANNING.

deviation *n.* (in marine insurance) The departure of a ship from an agreed course. A ship must follow the course specified in a voyage or mixed insurance policy (*see* TIME POLICY); if no course is specified, the ship must follow the usual course for the voyage. Deviation discharges the underwriters from all liability for subsequent loss (even though it may not increase the risk) unless it is caused by circumstances beyond control or is justified on certain very limited grounds (e.g. to ensure the safety of the ship or to save human life, but not merely to save property). Unreasonable delay may also amount to deviation. Insurance cover does not revive when the ship rejoins the original course. Between the parties to a voyage charter, the possibility of deviation is normally the subject of an express deviation clause in the *charterparty. For goods carried under a *bill of lading, permitted deviation is dealt with by the Hague Rules.

devil 1. *n.* A junior member of the Bar who does work (usually settling statements of case or writing opinions) for a more senior barrister under an informal arrangement between them and without reference to the senior's instructing solicitor. The Junior Counsel to the Treasury is sometimes referred to as the **Attorney General's devil. 2.** *vb*. To act as a devil.

devise 1. *n*. A gift by will of *real property (*compare* BEQUEST; LEGACY); the beneficiary is called the **devisee**. A devise may be **specific** (e.g. "my house, Blackacre, to A"), **general** (e.g. "all my real property to B"), or **residuary** (e.g. after a specific devise "...and the rest of my real property to C"). **2.** *vb*. To dispose of real property by will.

devolution *n*. **1.** The delegation by the central government to a regional authority of legislative or executive functions (or both) relating to domestic issues within the region. The word is most commonly used in the context of such functions in Scotland, Wales, and Northern Ireland. For example, the Scotland Act 1998 devolved power to the *Scottish Parliament, enabling it to make certain Acts in some areas of policy and to alter income tax. However, the UK parliament reserved power to make laws for Scotland. The Government of Wales Act 1998 gave limited administrative powers to the *Welsh Assembly with the UK parliament continuing to legislate for Wales. The Northern Ireland Act 1998 established an elected *Northern Ireland Assembly but made devolution of power to the Assembly conditional on the decommissioning of arms by paramilitary groups. The Northern Ireland Act 2000 enables power to revert to the UK parliament upon failure to decommission arms, suspending the Northern Ireland Assembly until the Secretary of State makes a restoration order. **2.** The passing of property from one owner to another, which may occur on death or sale, as a gift, by operation of law, or in any other way.

dictum *n*. [Latin: a saying] An observation by a judge with respect to a point of law arising in a case before him. *See also* OBITER DICTUM.

digital signature Data appended to a unit of data held on a computer, or a cryptographic transformation of a data unit, that allows the recipient of the data unit to prove its source and integrity and protects against forgery. The International Standards Organization defined this means of identification and protection. An *electronic signature, as defined by the Electronic Communications Act 2000, has a similar effect in relation to a commercial agreement.

dilapidation *n*. A state of disrepair. The term is usually used in relation to repairs required at the end of a lease or tenancy.

diminished responsibility An abnormal state of mind that does not constitute *insanity but is a special defence to a charge of murder. The abnormality of mind (which need not be a brain disease) must substantially impair the mental responsibility of the accused for his acts, i.e. it must reduce his powers of control, judgment, or reasoning to a condition that would be considered abnormal by the ordinary man. It may be caused by disease, injury, or mental subnormality, and is liberally interpreted to cover such conditions as depression or *irresistible impulse. If the defendant proves the defence, he is convicted of *manslaughter. *See also* BATTERED SPOUSE OR COHABITANT.

diplomatic agent One of a class of state officials who are entrusted with the responsibility for representing their state and its interests and welfare and that of its citizens or subjects in the jurisdiction of another state or in international organizations. Diplomatic agents can be generally classified into two groups: (1) heads of mission and (2) members of the staff of the mission having diplomatic rank. *See also* DIPLOMATIC IMMUNITY; DIPLOMATIC MISSION.

diplomatic immunity The freedom from legal proceedings in the UK that is granted to members of diplomatic missions of foreign states by the Diplomatic Privileges Act 1964. This Act incorporates some of the provisions of the Vienna Convention on Diplomatic Relations (1961), which governs diplomatic immunity in international law. The extent of the immunity depends upon the status of the member in question, as certified by the Secretary of State. If he is a member of the mission's diplomatic staff, he is entitled to complete criminal immunity and to civil immunity except for actions relating to certain private activities. A member of the administrative or technical staff has full criminal immunity, but his civil immunity relates only to acts performed in the course of his official duties. For domestic staff, both criminal and civil immunity are restricted to official duties.

Similar immunities are granted to members of Commonwealth missions by the Diplomatic and other Privileges Act 1971, and to members of certain international bodies under the International Organisations Acts 1968 and 1981. Under the Diplomatic and Consular Premises Act 1987, the Secretary of State may remove diplomatic status from diplomatic or consular premises that are being misused.

diplomatic mission A body composed of government officers representing the interests and welfare of their state who have been posted abroad (by the sending state) and operate within the jurisdisdiction of another state (the receiving state). This mission will be accorded protection by the receiving state in accordance with the rules of *diplomatic immunity. *See also* DIPLOMATIC AGENT.

direct effect (in EU law) *See* COMMUNITY LEGISLATION.

direct evidence (original evidence) 1. A statement made by a witness in court offered as proof of the truth of any fact stated by him. *Compare* HEARSAY EVIDENCE. **2.** A statement of a witness that he perceived a fact in issue with one of his five senses or that he was in a particular physical or mental state. *Compare* CIRCUMSTANTIAL EVIDENCE.

direct examination *See* EXAMINATION-IN-CHIEF.

direction to jury The duty of a judge to instruct a jury on a point of law (e.g. the definition of the crime charged or the nature and scope of possible defences). Failure to carry out this instruction correctly may be grounds for an appeal if a miscarriage of justice is likely to have occurred as a result of the misdirection.

directives of the EU *See* COMMUNITY LEGISLATION.

Direct Labour Organization A local government division, staffed by local government employees, that submits bids for services in competition with private-sector companies when these services are put out to compulsory *competitive tendering.

directly applicable law Any provision of the law of the European Community that forms part of the national law of a member state. *See* COMMUNITY LAW; COMMUNITY LEGISLATION.

directly effective law *See* COMMUNITY LAW; COMMUNITY LEGISLATION.

director *n.* An officer of a company appointed by or under the provisions of the *articles of association. Directors may have a contract of employment with the company (**service directors** and *managing directors) or merely attend board meetings (**nonexecutive directors**). (*See also* SHADOW DIRECTOR.) Contracts of employment can be inspected by company members; long-term contracts may require approval by ordinary resolution. Usually, general management powers are vested in the directors acting collectively, although they may delegate some or all of these powers to the managing director. Directors act as agents of their company, to which they owe *fiduciary duties (in the performance of which they must consider the interests of both company members and employees) and a *duty of care. Transactions involving a conflict between their duty and their personal interests are regulated by the Companies Acts. Directors can be dismissed by *ordinary resolution despite the terms of the articles or any contract of employment, but dismissal in these circumstances is subject to the payment of damages for breach of contract. Under the Company Directors Disqualification Act 1986, directors may be disqualified for *fraudulent trading or *wrongful trading and conduct that makes them unfit to be concerned in the management of companies.

Remuneration of directors for their services may be due under a contract of employment or determined by the general meeting. Particulars appear in the *accounts.

Director General of Fair Trading The head of the Office of Fair Trading, who is appointed for a five-year term by the Secretary of State for Trade and Industry. He is responsible for reviewing the carrying on of commercial activities in the UK relating to the supply of goods or services supplied to consumers in the UK and for identifying situations relating to *monopolies and *anticompetitive practices.

Director of Public Prosecutions (DPP) The head of the *Crown Prosecution Service (CPS), who must be a lawyer of at least ten years' general qualification. The DPP is appointed by the *Attorney General and discharges his functions under the superintendence of the Attorney General. The DPP, through the CPS, is responsible for the conduct of all criminal prosecutions instituted by the police and he may intervene in any criminal proceedings when it appears to him to be appropriate. Some statutes require the consent of the DPP to prosecution.

disability discrimination *See* DISABLED PERSON.

disability living allowance A tax-free benefit payable to those under 65 who have had a disability requiring help for at least three months and are likely to need such help for at least a further six months. It has two components: a care component, payable at three rates to those needing help with personal care; and a mobility component, payable at two rates to those aged five or over who need help with walking. The rates depend on the level of help required.

disabled person Under the Disability Discrimination Act 1995, a person who has a physical or mental impairment that has a substantial and long-term effect on his abilities to carry out day-to-day activities. The Act makes it an offence to discriminate unjustifiably against anyone who is disabled. Discrimination occurs when a disabled employee (or interviewee) is treated less favourably by an employer (or potential employer) than someone without a disability, unless the employer can show that the difference in treatment is justified. Thus it is illegal for employers to refuse to employ someone qualified to do a job, simply because that person has, or has had, a physical or mental disability. In addition, employers have a duty to make alterations to premises to aid disabled employees. However, the law does not apply to employers with fewer than 15 employees (i.e. after all staff at all branches are aggregated).

On 5 March 2001 the government announced plans for significant changes to the Disability Discrimination Act. These include removal in 2004 of the small employers' exemption. The shape of any future proposal will be influenced by the need of the British government to comply with the recently issued EC Framework Directive 2000/78, which seeks to implement the extended role of the European Union with respect to the elimination of discrimination.

disabled person's tax credit An income-related benefit that, under the Tax

Credits Act 1999, replaced **disability working allowance** in October 1999. Administered by the Inland Revenue rather than the Benefits Agency, it is payable to those aged 16 or over who are working 16 or more hours a week, who have a disability that puts them at a disadvantage in obtaining employment, and whose income does not exceed an amount prescribed under statute.

disablement benefit *See* INDUSTRIAL INJURIES DISABLEMENT BENEFIT.

disabling statute A statute that disqualifies a person or persons of a specified class from exercising a legal right or freedom that he or they would otherwise enjoy.

disbar *vb.* To expel a barrister from his Inn of Court. The sentence of disbarment is pronounced by the *Benchers of the barrister's Inn, subject to a right of appeal to the judges who act as visitors of all the Inns of Court.

discharge *n.* Release from an obligation, debt, or liability, particularly the following. **1.** *Discharge of contract. **2.** The release of a debtor from all *provable debts (with minor exceptions) at the end of *bankruptcy proceedings. In certain circumstances discharge is automatic. In other cases, the debtor or the official receiver may apply to the court for an **order of discharge**. This may be subject to conditions, such as further payments by the debtor to his creditors out of his future income, or it may be suspended until the creditors receive a higher proportion of the amount due to them. After discharge the debtor is freed from most of the disabilities to which he was subject as an *undischarged bankrupt. **3.** The release of a convicted defendant without imposing a punishment on him. A discharge may be absolute or conditional. In an **absolute discharge** the defendant is not punished for the offence. His conviction may, however, be accompanied by a *compensation order or by *endorsement of his driving licence or *disqualification from driving. A **conditional discharge** also releases the defendant without punishment, provided that he is not convicted of any other offence within a specified period (usually three years). If he is convicted within that time, the court may sentence him for the original offence as well. Three conditions are required for the court to order a discharge: (1) that a community rehabilitation order is not appropriate; (2) that the punishment for the offence must not be fixed by law; and (3) that the court thinks it inadvisable to punish the defendant in the circumstances.

discharge of contract The termination of a contractual obligation. Discharge may take place by: (1) *performance of contract; (2) express agreement, which may involve either *bilateral discharge or unilateral discharge (*see* ACCORD AND SATISFACTION); (3) *breach of contract; or (4) *frustration of contract.

disclaimer *n.* The refusal or renunciation of a right, claim, or property. A beneficiary under a will that leaves him both a burdensome and a beneficial gift (e.g. a racehorse that never wins and £50) may disclaim the former and take the latter. A company's liquidator may disclaim the company's lease, to avoid liability for the rent and other "onerous" contracts. A trustee may disclaim a trust if he has not yet accepted it; once he has accepted his trusteeship he may no longer disclaim it but he may resign (*see* RETIREMENT OF TRUSTEES). Trusts and powers are normally disclaimed by deed.

disclosure *n.* **1.** (in contract law) *See* NONDISCLOSURE; UBERRIMAE FIDEI. **2.** (in company law) **a.** A method of protecting investors that relies on the company disclosing and publishing information, which is then evaluated by the investors, their advisers, and the press. *See also* STOCK EXCHANGE. **b.** A method of regulating the conduct of directors and promoters by requiring them, on *fiduciary principles or by statutory provisions, to disclose to the company any relevant information, e.g. an interest in a contract with the company.

disclosure and inspection of documents (in court proceedings) Disclosure by a party to civil litigation of the *documents in his possession, custody, or power relating to matters in question in the action and their subsequent inspection by the opposing party; before the introduction of the *Civil Procedure Rules in 1999, this procedure was called **discovery and inspection of documents**. For the purposes of disclosure, documents extend beyond paper to include anything upon which information is capable of being recorded and retrieved (e.g. tapes, computer disks). In *small claims track proceedings, the initial disclosure is by a **list of documents** that the party intends to rely upon. In *fast track and *multi-track proceedings, the lists must include all documents, both those that support the party making the list and those adversely affecting that party, which they would prefer not to disclose. Directions for disclosure generally take place at the *allocation stage or the *case management conference and, unless the court directs or the parties agree otherwise, there will normally be a direction for **standard disclosure**. This involves a reasonable search by the parties to disclose documents on which that party intends to rely, documents that may be adverse to their own case or another party's case, documents that support another party's case, and documents that are required to be disclosed by any relevant *Practice Direction. Some documents, although they must be disclosed in the list, may be privileged and thus exempted from the subsequent requirement to produce them for inspection (see PRIVILEGE). Once a party has served a list of documents, the other party, together with any co-defendants, must be allowed to inspect the (nonprivileged) documents referred to in the list within seven days of serving on the first party a written notice requesting inspection. If copies are needed, a further written notice must be served, with an undertaking to meet reasonable copying charges. In the absence of disclosure and/or inspection, the court has power to direct that **general** or **specific disclosure** and/or inspection be made. See also FAILURE TO MAKE DISCLOSURE; NONDISCLOSURE.

disclosure of information 1. (in employment law) The communication by an employer to employees and their trade-union representatives of information relevant to *collective bargaining, proposed *redundancies, and the preservation of employees' health and *safety at work. Under the Trade Union and Labour Relations (Consolidation) Act 1992, employers must disclose the following information to the representatives of a recognized *independent trade union. (1) Information that is essential for the maintenance of good industrial relations or for the formulation of wage and related demands. The duty to disclose this information only arises if the union requests the information. When disclosure would damage national security or harm the business (apart from its effect on collective bargaining), or the information is *sub judice* or relevant only to particular individuals, disclosure need not be given. Guidelines on disclosure are published by *ACAS (see also CODE OF PRACTICE). When an employer refuses to disclose essential information, the *Central Arbitration Committee is empowered on the application of the trade union to make awards of wages and conditions that are ultimately enforceable in the courts. (2) Details of any redundancies proposed by the employer. He must give the union 90 days' notice when 100 or more employees are to be made redundant over a period of 90 days or less, and 30 days' notice when between 20 and 99 redundancy dismissals are proposed within a 90-day period. The employer's notice must specify the reason for his proposals, the numbers and job descriptions of employees involved, the way in which employees have been selected for redundancy, and the procedures for their dismissal. He must consider any representations made by the union, but need not comply with its demands. If the employer fails to give the required notice, the union can apply to an employment tribunal, which may make a *protective award to the redundant employees. Under the Health and Safety at Work Act 1974, an employer must give his employees at large such information, instruction, and supervision as will ensure their health and safety so far as is reasonably practicable. He must also give copies of any relevant documents to safety representatives appointed by a recognized trade union. **2.** (in criminal proceedings) For criminal proceedings issued after 1 April 1997, the Criminal Procedure and Investigations Act 1996 sets out detailed rules on disclosures that the prosecution must make to the defence. It must disclose anything that might undermine its case and anything that might assist the defence, but the judgment of what undermines the prosecution or assists the defence remains with the prosecutor. Thus the Act enables the prosecution to decide what information they believe should be disclosed to the defence and, in particular, whether to disclose information about any weakness in their own investigation. **3.** *See* BREACH OF CONFIDENCE.

disclosure of interest The duty of local authority members to disclose (at the time or by prior notice to the authority) any pecuniary interest they or their spouses have in any matter discussed at a local authority meeting. They must also abstain from speaking and voting on it. Breach of the duty is a criminal offence.

discontinuance of action *See* NOTICE OF DISCONTINUANCE.

discovery *n.* (in international law) A method of acquiring territory in which good title can be gained by claiming previously unclaimed land (*terra nullius*). In the early days of European exploration it was held that the discovery of a previously unknown land conferred absolute title to it upon the state by whose agents the discovery was made. However, it has now long been established that the bare fact of discovery is an insufficient ground of proprietary right.

discovery and inspection of documents *See* DISCLOSURE AND INSPECTION OF DOCUMENTS.

discretion *n.* *See* JUDICIAL DISCRETION.

discretionary area of judgment A concept used in some cases in the domestic courts when reviewing decisions of public authorities under the *European Convention on Human Rights. The concept allows the courts to defer on democratic grounds to the decisions of elected bodies. It follows from the fact that the concept of the *margin of appreciation is not applicable in the domestic courts.

discretionary trust A trust under which the trustees are given discretion as to who, within a class chosen by the settlor, should receive trust property and how much each should receive. A settlor must give some indication as to the limits of the class of people he intends to benefit, but the trustees do not need to have an exhaustive list. A beneficiary under a discretionary trust has no enforceable right to any part of the property or its income, although the trustees must consider his claims together with those of the other beneficiaries. Such trusts are often very difficult to distinguish from *trust powers and *powers of appointment held by *trustees. Discretionary trusts have been invaluable in planning to mitigate liability to tax, but recent fiscal legislation has reduced their advantages.

discrimination *n.* Treating one or more members of a specified group unfairly as compared with other people. Discrimination may be illegal on the ground of sex, sexual orientation, race, religion, disability, or nationality. *See also* DISABLED PERSON; HUMAN RIGHTS ACT, POSITIVE DISCRIMINATION; RACIAL DISCRIMINATION; SEX DISCRIMINATION.

disentailing deed A deed used to bar (convert into a *fee simple) an *entailed interest.

disentailment *n.* The barring of an *entailed interest.

dishonesty *n.* An element of liability in *theft, *abstracting electricity, *deception, *handling stolen goods, and some related offences. To convict of such offences the magistrates or jury must be satisfied that what was done was dishonest by the standards of ordinary decent people and that the defendant realized this at the time.

dishonour *n.* (in commercial law) Failure to honour a bill of exchange. This may be by nonacceptance, when a bill of exchange is presented for *acceptance and this is refused or cannot be obtained (or when *presentment for acceptance is excused and the bill is not accepted); or by nonpayment, when the bill is presented for payment and payment is refused or cannot be obtained (or when presentment is excused and the bill is overdue and unpaid). In both cases the holder has an immediate right of recourse against the drawer and endorsers, but *foreign bills that have been dishonoured must first be protested (*see* PROTEST). *See also* NOTICE OF DISHONOUR.

dismissal *n.* (in employment law) The termination of an employee's contract of employment by the employer. An employer usually dismisses the employee by giving him the required period of *notice, but dismissal without notice may be justified in certain circumstances (e.g. for gross misconduct). An employer's failure to renew a fixed-term employment contract also counts as dismissal. An employee having the required length of service in the business (*see* CONTINUOUS EMPLOYMENT) can apply to an employment tribunal if he is unfairly dismissed (*see* UNFAIR DISMISSAL); the tribunal can order his *reinstatement or *re-engagement or can award him *compensation. An employee dismissed for *redundancy after two years' continuous employment in the business is entitled to a *redundancy payment under the Employment Rights Act 1996. An employee dismissed without due notice or before his fixed-term contract expires can also claim damages in the courts for *wrongful dismissal. *See also* STATEMENT OF REASONS FOR DISMISSAL.

dismissal of action The termination of a civil action in favour of the defendant. An order for dismissal of action may be made at the conclusion of the trial, but is usually made during the *interim (interlocutory) proceedings; for example, for breach of some rule of procedure. Dismissal for **want of prosecution** occurs if the claimant has been guilty of inordinate and inexcusable delay in circumstances in which there is a risk that a fair trial is no longer possible or in which there has been prejudice to the defendant. This type of dismissal is now rare under the heavily case-managed procedure prescribed by the Civil Procedure Rules.

dismissal procedures agreement A collective agreement containing provisions relating to the dismissal of employees and intended to replace the statutory provisions concerning *unfair dismissal. *See also* COLLECTIVE BARGAINING.

dismissal statement *See* STATEMENT OF REASONS FOR DISMISSAL.

disorderly house A *brothel or a place staging performances or exhibitions that tend to corrupt or deprave and outrage common decency. It is a misdemeanour at common law to keep a disorderly house.

disparagement of goods *See* SLANDER OF GOODS.

disposal of uncollected goods The sale by a bailee of goods in his possession or under his control when the bailor is in breach of an obligation to collect them (*see* BAILMENT). When the original contract does not require the bailor to collect the goods, the bailee may, by giving notice, impose such an obligation. The relevant statutory provisions in the Torts (Interference with Goods) Act 1977 lay down conditions relating to the giving of notice of the bailee's intention to sell, allowing the bailor a reasonable opportunity to collect. The bailee should adopt the best method of sale available and must account to the bailor for the proceeds of sale less any sum due before he gave notice of intention to sell. There is provision for a bailee to have a sale authorized by a court.

disposition n. **1.** (in land law) The transfer of property by some act of its owner, e.g. by sale, gift, will, or exchange. **2.** (in the law of evidence) The tendency of a party (especially the accused) to act or think in a particular way. Evidence of the accused's disposition may generally not be given unless it is based upon admissible evidence of character or admissible *similar-fact evidence. Evidence of *previous convictions, other than those admitted as similar-fact evidence or under the Criminal Evidence Acts, may tend to suggest to the *trier of fact that the accused has a particular disposition, but is technically admissible only on the question of his credibility. *See also* CHARACTER.

disqualification n. Depriving someone of a right because he has committed a criminal offence or failed to comply with specified conditions. Disqualification is usually imposed in relation to activities requiring a licence, and in particular for traffic offences. In the case of many traffic offences, the court has discretion to disqualify drivers for a stated period. There are also a number of traffic offences for which disqualification for at least 12 months is compulsory (unless the offender can show special reasons relating to the circumstances of the offence, not to his personal circumstances). These offences are: (1) manslaughter; (2) *causing death by dangerous driving (the minimum disqualification period here is two years); (3) *causing death by careless driving; (4) *dangerous driving; (5) driving or attempting to drive while unfit; (6) driving or attempting to drive with excess alcohol in the breath, blood, or urine (*see* DRUNKEN DRIVING); (7) failure (in certain cases) to provide a *specimen of breath, blood, or urine; (8) racing or speed trials on the highway.

If a person is convicted for a second time within ten years of a driving offence involving drink or drugs, he must be disqualified for at least three years. The courts may also disqualify anyone who commits an indictable offence of any kind involving the use of a car. There is also a *totting-up system of endorsements, which can result in disqualification. When someone is disqualified from driving, his licence will usually also be endorsed with details of the offence (but not with any penalty points for the purpose of totting up). The court may also make a *driving-test order. A person who has been disqualified from driving may apply to have the disqualification removed after two years or half the period of disqualification (whichever is longer) or, when he has been disqualified for ten years or more, after five years. *See also* DRIVING WHILE DISQUALIFIED.

dissolution n. **1.** The legal termination of a marriage; for example, by a decree of divorce, nullity, or presumption of death. **2.** The dissolving of a *registered company. This can be achieved by *winding-up or by the Registrar of Companies striking it off the companies register as "defunct", because he has reasonable cause to believe that the company is no longer carrying on business or has failed to file accounts. The company can be restored to register subsequently on application by petition and payment of the relevant fee. **3.** *See* PARLIAMENT.

distance selling The sale of goods or services to a consumer in which the parties do not meet, such as sale by mail order, telephone, digital TV, email, or the Internet. The EU distance selling directive 976/7, implemented from October 2000 in the UK by the Consumer Protection (Distance Selling) Regulations 2000, contains the relevant law. In particular, consumers have rights to certain information about the contract to be entered into and, in many cases the right to cancel the contract within a certain period, often seven working days from the day after receipt of the goods. The right applies whether the goods are defective or not, but it does not apply in certain important categories (such as auctions, betting, goods specifically made for a consumer, and food that will deteriorate).

distinguishing a case The process of providing reasons for deciding a case under consideration differently from a similar case referred to as a *precedent.

distortion of competition *See* ARTICLE 81.

distrain *vb*. To seize goods by way of *distress.

distress *n*. The seizure of goods as security for the performance of an obligation. The two principal situations covered by the remedy of distress are (1) between landlord and tenant when the rent is in arrears (*see* DISTRESS FOR RENT); and (2) when goods are unlawfully on an occupier's land and have done or are doing damage (*see also* DISTRESS DAMAGE FEASANT). In the latter case the occupier may detain the chattel until compensation is paid for the damage.

distress damage feasant A right to detain animals found doing damage on one's land as security for compensation. This right was abolished in England by the Animals Act 1971 and replaced by a statutory power to detain and ultimately to sell the animals. The statutory power is subject to detailed requirements of giving notice of detention and taking care of the animals.

distress for rent The seizing of a tenant's goods by the landlord to secure payment of rent arrears. If the tenant fails to pay the rent arrears after distress has been levied, the landlord may sell the goods and keep the amount due. In the case of an *assured, *protected, or *statutory tenancy the landlord must obtain a court's permission before levying distress. In 1986 the *Law Commission recommended abolition of distress.

distressing letters *See* SENDING DISTRESSING LETTERS.

distribution *n*. **1.** The process of handing over to the beneficiaries their entitlements under a deceased person's will or on his intestacy. **2.** Any payment made by a company to a shareholder out of its distributable profits in cash or kind. It does not include payments made in the course of a winding-up or repayments of the capital originally subscribed or subsequently received by the company. *See also* QUALIFYING DISTRIBUTION.

district *n*. A *local government area in England (outside Greater London) consisting of a division of a *county. The Local Government Act 1972 divided the 6 metropolitan and 39 nonmetropolitan counties in England into 36 metropolitan and 296 nonmetropolitan districts, respectively, and the 8 counties in Wales into 37 districts. The 6 metropolitan counties were abolished by the Local Government Act 1985 and their functions transferred generally to the metropolitan district councils, which became single-tier authorities. A district may be styled a borough by royal charter granted on the petition of the *district council. The Welsh counties and districts were abolished by the Local Government (Wales) Act 1994, being replaced on 1 April 1996 by 22 *unitary authorities (11 counties and 11 county boroughs). Unitary authorities have been phased in in certain nonmetropolitan areas of England. *See also* LOCAL GOVERNMENT COMMISSION FOR ENGLAND.

district auditors Civil servants who audited the accounts of all local authorities except those who chose audit by approved commercial accountants. Originally established under the Local Government Finance Act 1982 and now consolidated under the Audit Commission Act 1998, the **Audit Commission** was established to take responsibility for local authority audits. District auditors are now officials of the Audit Commission, but modern practice is to appoint independent approved auditors from private firms of accountants. If any transaction involved unlawful expenditure, they may obtain a court order for repayment by the persons responsible.

district council A *local authority whose area is a *district. A district council has certain exclusive responsibilities (e.g. housing and local planning) and shares others (e.g. recreation, town and country planning) with the council of the county to which the district belongs. Some responsibilities (e.g. education and the personal social services) belong to the district council if the district is metropolitan, but to the county council if it is not. If a district has the style of borough, its council is called a borough council and its chairman the mayor. The *Local Government Commission for England began work in 1992 on a review of local authorities with a view to establishing *unitary (single-tier) authorities. This has led to wider powers for district councils and to some amalgamations and boundary revision.

District Health Authorities *See* NATIONAL HEALTH SERVICE.

district judge In the county courts, a judicial officer appointed by the Lord Chancellor from solicitors of not less than seven years' standing. The district judge supervises interim (interlocutory) and post-judgment stages of the case, but can also try cases within a financial limit defined by statute. District judges were formerly known as **district registrars**.

district judge (magistrates' court) A barrister or solicitor of not less than seven years' standing, appointed by the Lord Chancellor to sit in a magistrates' court on a full-time salaried basis: formerly (before August 2000) called a **stipendiary magistrate**. Metropolitan district judges (magistrates' court) sit in magistrates' courts for Inner London; other magistrates sit in large provincial centres. They have power to perform any act and to exercise alone any jurisdiction that can be performed or exercised by two justices of the peace, except the grant or transfer of any licence. In other respects their powers are the same as other justices.

district registry An office of the High Court outside London, corresponding in function to the *Central Office; however, only a limited number of district registries exercise full powers in relation to proceedings in the *Chancery Division. There are district registries in all major towns and cities in England and Wales.

distringas *n.* [Latin: that you distrain] A writ, now obsolete, commanding the sheriff to distrain on a person for a certain purpose. In modern practice it has been replaced by a *stop notice, sometimes called a **notice in lieu of distringas**, which prevents dealings in securities that are subject to a *charging order.

disturbance *n.* **1.** The infringement of a right, e.g. the obstruction of a right of way. **2.** The removal of a person's rights under a statutory power. For example, compensation for disturbance may be payable to a landowner if his land is compulsorily acquired by a local authority.

dividend *n.* A payment declared either by the directors of a company (**interim dividend**) or at the *annual general meeting (**final dividend**) as being payable to shareholders from profits available for distribution. The payment is determined by reference to the terms of the *share contract; it is an agreed fixed rate for preference shares but will vary with the fortunes of the company for the holders of ordinary shares.

divisible contract *See* PERFORMANCE OF CONTRACT.

division *n.* The taking of a vote on any matter in either House of Parliament.

Divisional Court A court consisting of not less than two judges of one of the Divisions of the High Court. There are Divisional Courts of each of the Divisions. Their function is to hear appeals in various matters prescribed by statute; they also exercise the supervisory jurisdiction of the High Court over inferior courts. Most of this jurisdiction is exercised by the Queen's Bench Division, which also hears applications for *judicial review and appeals by *case stated from magistrates' courts. The Chancery Division hears appeals in *bankruptcy matters and the Family Division hears appeals from magistrates' courts in matters of family law.

Divisions of the High Court *See* CHANCERY DIVISION; FAMILY DIVISION; QUEEN'S BENCH DIVISION.

divorce *n.* The legal termination of a marriage and the obligations created by marriage, other than by a decree of nullity or presumption of death. The present law on divorce dates from 1969. Before this, the law required proof of a *matrimonial offence (adultery, cruelty, or desertion of three years). The current law is contained in the Matrimonial Causes Act 1973, which provides that there is only one ground for divorce, namely that the marriage has irretrievably broken down. Proceedings are initiated by either spouse filing a **petition for divorce**, stating the facts that have led to the marital breakdown and accompanied by a *statement of arrangement for children. (Divorce proceedings may not be started within the first year of a marriage.) Irretrievable breakdown of a marriage may only be evidenced by one of the following five facts: (1) that the respondent has committed *adultery and the petitioner finds it intolerable to live with the respondent; (2) that the respondent has behaved in such a way that the petitioner cannot reasonably be expected to live with the respondent (*see* UNREASONABLE BEHAVIOUR); (3) that the respondent has deserted the petitioner for at least two years (*see* DESERTION); (4) that the parties have lived apart for at least two years and the respondent consents to a divorce; or (5) that the parties have lived apart for at least five years. A respondent in a two-year separation case can apply for a postponement of the divorce until the court is satisfied that the petitioner has made fair and reasonable financial provision for the respondent. In a five-year separation case the court has the power to bar divorce if it believes that grave financial or other hardship would result from the dissolution and that it would be wrong to dissolve the marriage; however, this power is rarely exercised.

Divorce is a two-stage process. The first stage is the granting of a *decree nisi; six weeks later the petitioner may apply for a *decree absolute. The marriage is not terminated until the decree absolute has been granted. Uncontested divorce cases are heard under the *special procedure; the majority of cases are now dealt with in this way. Divorce courts have wide powers under the Matrimonial Causes Act 1973 to make orders in respect of children and to adjust financial and property rights. *See also* CHILD PROTECTION IN DIVORCE; FINANCIAL PROVISION ORDER; MAINTENANCE AGREEMENT; PROPERTY ADJUSTMENT ORDER.

Divorce Registry The section of the Family Division of the High Court with jurisdiction over divorce proceedings.

DNA fingerprinting (genetic fingerprinting) A scientific technique in which an individual's genetic material (DNA) is extracted from cells in a sample of tissue and analysed to produce a graphic chart that is unique to that person. The technique may be used as *evidence of identity in a criminal or civil case and has been notably successful in both paternity and rape cases. **DNA samples** (e.g. of hair) may be taken from suspects in accordance with the Police and Criminal Evidence Act 1984 and after conviction for any offence punishable by imprisonment.

dock brief The obsolete procedure by which a defendant to a criminal charge could, on indictment, select any barrister in the court who was not otherwise engaged to represent him, on payment of a nominal fee.

doctrine of incorporation The doctrine that rules of international law automatically form part of municipal law. It is opposed to the **doctrine of transformation**, which states that international law only forms a part of municipal law if accepted as such by statute or judicial decisions. It is not altogether clear which view English law takes with respect to rules of customary *international law. As far as international treaties are concerned, the sovereign has the power to make or ratify treaties so as to bind England under international law, but these treaties have no effect in municipal law (with the exception of treaties governing the conduct of war) until enacted by Parliament. However, judges will sometimes consider provisions of international treaties (e.g. those relating to *human rights) in applying municipal law. It has been said that directives of the European Community have the force of law in member states, but practice varies widely (*see* COMMUNITY LEGISLATION).

document *n.* Something that records or transmits information, typically in writing on paper. For the purposes of providing evidence to a court, documents include books, maps, plans, drawings, photographs, graphs, discs, tapes, soundtracks, and films (*see also* COMPUTER DOCUMENTS). Some legal documents are only valid if they meet certain requirements (*see* DEED; WILL). Documents that are to be used in court proceedings must be disclosed to the other party in a procedure known as *disclosure and inspection of documents. In court, the original of a document must be produced in most cases. In the case of a public document a particular kind of copy must be produced; for example, a copy of a statute must be a government printer's copy, and a copy of a byelaw must be certified by the clerk to the local authority concerned. The authenticity of private documents must be proved by the evidence of a witness. In practice this procedure is often avoided or simplified by each party admitting the authenticity of particular documents prior to the court hearing. *See also* PAROL EVIDENCE RULE; PRODUCTION OF DOCUMENTS.

documentary evidence Evidence in written rather than oral form. The admissibility of a document depends upon (1) proof of the authenticity of the document and (2) the purpose for which it is being offered in evidence. If it is being offered to prove the truth of some matter stated in the document itself it will be necessary to consider the application of the rule against hearsay (*see* HEARSAY EVIDENCE) and its many exceptions.

document of title to goods A document, such as a *bill of lading, that embodies the undertaking of the person holding the goods (the bailee) to hold the goods for whoever is the current holder of the document and to deliver the goods to that person in exchange for the document.

dogs *pl. n.* *See* CLASSIFICATION OF ANIMALS; DANGEROUS ANIMALS; GUARD DOG.

doli capax [Latin] Capable of wrong. A child under the age of 10 is deemed incapable of committing any crime. Above the age of 10 children are *doli capax* and are treated as adults, although they will usually be tried in special youth courts (with the exception of homicide and certain other grave offences) and subject to special punishments. Formerly, there was a rebuttable presumption that a child between the ages of 10 and 14 was also *doli incapax* (incapable of wrong). This presumption has now been abolished. *See* JUVENILE OFFENDER.

domain name An Internet address, which may be protected under *trade mark law.

domestic premises A private residence, used wholly for living accommodation, together with its garden, yard, and attached buildings (such as garages and outhouses).

domestic tribunal A body that exercises jurisdiction over the internal affairs of a particular profession or association under powers conferred either by statute (e.g. the disciplinary committee of the Law Society) or by contract between the members (e.g. the disciplinary committee of a trade union). The decisions of these tribunals are subject to judicial control under the doctrine of *ultra vires* and, if they are statutory, when there is an *error of law on the face of the record. *Compare* ADMINISTRATIVE TRIBUNAL.

domestic violence *See* BATTERED SPOUSE OR COHABITANT.

domicile *n.* The country that a person treats as his permanent home and to which he has the closest legal attachment. A person cannot be without a domicile and cannot have two domiciles at once. He acquires at birth a **domicile of origin**. Normally, if his father is then alive, he takes his father's domicile; if not, his mother's. He retains his domicile of origin until (if ever) he acquires a **domicile of choice** in its place. A domicile of choice is acquired by making a home in a country with the intention that it should be a permanent base. It may be acquired at any time after a person becomes 16 and can be replaced at will by a new domicile of choice. *See* LEX DOMICILII.

dominant tenement Land the ownership of which entitles the owner to rights comprising a legal or equitable interest (such as an easement or profit *à prendre*) in other land, called the **servient tenement**.

Dominions *pl. n.* Formerly, the group of UK colonies that, by virtue of the Statute of Westminster 1931, were the first to become fully independent. Certain of these, together with many other former colonies, are now collectively known as the *Commonwealth.

donatio mortis causa [Latin: a gift on account of death] An immediate gift of real or personal property made by a donor who expects to die in the near future. The gift must be made to take complete effect only on the death of the donor and there must be delivery of the property or something amounting to delivery. The latter requirement has been held to be satisfied by a transfer of the means or part of the means of obtaining the property or a transfer of the indications of title to the property (e.g. title deeds). The donor must make the transfer with the intention of relinquishing ownership of the property but may withdraw from that intention at any time prior to death and thereby defeat the gift. If the donor does not die the gift will be revoked.

double criminality The rule in *extradition procedures that, in order for the request to be complied with, the crime for which extradition is sought must be a crime in both the requesting state and the state to which the fugitive has fled. *See also* EXTRADITION TREATY; SPECIALITY.

double portions *pl. n. See* RULE AGAINST DOUBLE PORTIONS.

double probate A second grant of *probate in respect of the same estate in favour of an executor who was not a party to the first grant. This occurs when the executor has not renounced his executorship and has a power to apply for a grant of probate at a later time than the original grant.

DPP *See* DIRECTOR OF PUBLIC PROSECUTIONS.

draft *n.* **1.** An initial unsigned agreement, treaty, or piece of legislation, which is not yet in force. **2.** An order for the payment of money, e.g. a banker's draft.

Drago doctrine The doctrine that states cannot employ force in order to recover debts incurred by other states. Thus the fact that a state has defaulted on its debt to aliens or to another state does not legalize the use of military intervention by these creditors in order to reclaim monies they are owed.

driftway *n.* A *highway over which there exists a right to drive cattle, accompanied by persons either on foot or mounted.

driver *n.* For purposes of the Road Traffic Acts, anyone who uses the ordinary controls of a vehicle (i.e. steering and brakes) to direct its movement. This includes anyone steering a car when the engine is off or when being towed by another vehicle.

driving licence An official authority to drive a motor vehicle, granted upon passing a driving test. A renewable provisional driving licence, valid for 12 months, may be granted to learner drivers, but the holder of a provisional licence may not drive a motor car on a public road unless accompanied by a qualified driver and unless he displays 'L' plates on the front and rear of the vehicle.

A full licence may be obtained by anyone who has passed the Department of Transport driving test, which is carried out by the Driving Standards Agency (an executive agency) and is now preceded by a written test, or held a full licence issued in Great Britain, Northern Ireland, the Isle of Man, or the Channel Islands within ten years before the date on which the licence is to come into force. It is normally granted until the applicant's 70th birthday. After the age of 70, licences are granted for three-year periods. The applicant must disclose any disability and may be asked to produce his medical records or have a medical examination.

An applicant will not normally be granted a licence if he is suffering from certain types of disability, including epilepsy, sudden attacks of disabling giddiness or fainting, or a severe mental illness or defect. In the case of epilepsy, however, he may still be granted a licence if he can show that he has been free of all attacks for at least two years or that he has only had attacks during sleep for more than three years. If an applicant for a licence has diabetes or a heart condition, is fitted with a heart pacemaker, has been treated within the previous three years for drug addiction, or is suffering from any other disability (e.g. loss or weakness of a limb) that would affect his driving, the grant of a licence is usually discretionary.

It is an offence to knowingly make a false statement in order to obtain a driving licence, not to disclose any current *endorsements, or not to sign one's name in ink on the licence. A police officer may require a driver to show his driving licence or produce it personally at a specified police station within five days. He may also ask to see the licence of someone whom he believes was either driving a vehicle involved in an accident or had committed a motoring offence. Failure to produce one's licence in these circumstances carries a fine. *See also* DRIVING WITHOUT A LICENCE.

Under the Road Traffic (New Drivers) Act 1995, with effect from 1 June 1997, a driver who is convicted of an endorsable offence and who has accumulated 6 or more penalty points (*see* TOTTING UP) within two years of passing a driving test will have his licence revoked and must retake the test.

driving-test order An order by the court that a person who has been convicted of an offence that is subject to *disqualification should be disqualified from driving until he passes a test showing that he is fit to drive. The order should only be made where there is reason to suspect that the person is not fit to drive; for example, because he is very old or unwell, and has shown evidence of incompetence in his driving. It is not meant as a punishment but to protect the public.

driving while disqualified An offence committed by the *driver of a motor vehicle on a public road when he is disqualified from driving (see DISQUALIFICATION). This is an endorsable offence (carrying 7 penalty points under the *totting-up system) and the courts have discretion to impose a further period of disqualification.

driving while unfit See DRUNKEN DRIVING.

driving without a licence An offence committed by the *driver of a motor vehicle on a public road without a *driving licence or provisional driving licence valid for the vehicle he is driving. If the circumstances are such that he would in fact have been refused a licence had he applied for one, or if he fails to comply with the conditions applicable to a provisional licence, his licence (if he subsequently obtains one) will usually be endorsed (the endorsement carries 2 penalty points under the *totting-up system) and the court has discretion to order disqualification from driving (if he applies for a licence during the disqualification period). Otherwise this is not an endorsable offence.

driving without insurance An offence committed by a *driver who uses or allows someone else to use a motor vehicle on a public road without valid *third-party insurance. The offence is one of *strict liability (except when an employee is using his employer's vehicle) and applies even if, for example, the insurance company who issued the insurance suddenly goes into liquidation. The offence is punishable by a fine, endorsement (it carries 6–8 penalty points under the *totting-up system), and disqualification at the discretion of the court.

drugs *pl. n.* See CONTROLLED DRUGS.

drunken driving Driving (see DRIVER) while affected by alcohol. Drunken driving covers two separate legal offences.
(1) **Driving while unfit**. It is an offence to drive or attempt to drive a motor vehicle on a road or public place when one's ability to drive properly is impaired by alcohol or drugs. Drugs include medicines (such as insulin for diabetics), and the offence appears to be one of *strict liability. It is also an offence to be in charge of a motor vehicle on a road or in a public place while unfit to drive because of drink or drugs, but the defendant will be acquitted if he can show that there was no likelihood of his driving the vehicle in this condition (for example, if he arranged for someone else to drive him if he became drunk). A police officer can arrest without a warrant anyone whom he reasonably suspects is committing or has been committing either of these offences; he may also (except in Scotland) enter any place where he believes the suspect to be, using force if necessary.
(2) **Driving over the prescribed limit**. It is an offence to drive or attempt to drive a motor vehicle on a road or in a public place if the level of alcohol in one's breath, blood, or urine is above the specified prescribed limit (35 micrograms of alcohol in 100 millilitres (ml) of breath; 80 milligrams (mg) of alcohol in 100 ml of blood; 107 mg of alcohol in 100 ml of urine – roughly equivalent to 2½ pints of beer, or 5 glasses of wine, or 5 single whiskys). It is also an offence to be in charge of a motor vehicle on a road or in a public place when the proportion of alcohol is more than the prescribed limit, subject to the same defence as in being in charge while unfit. Both these offences are offences of strict liability: it is therefore not a defence to

show that one did not know that the drink was alcoholic or that it exceeded the prescribed limit. The normal way in which offences involving excess alcohol levels are proved is by taking a *specimen of breath for laboratory analysis, but this is not necessary if the offence can be proved in some other way (for example, by evidence of how much a person drank before driving). There is no power to arrest a person on suspicion of committing or having committed an offence of this sort before administering a preliminary *breath test.

Most charges involving drinking and driving are brought under the offence of driving over the prescribed limit rather than driving while unfit, but the powers to administer a breath test or to take a specimen of breath for analysis apply to both offences. The penalties for either of these offences are a fine and/or imprisonment, *endorsement, and obligatory *disqualification (in cases of driving or attempting to drive) or discretionary disqualification (in cases of being in charge). Under the *totting-up system, the discretionary disqualification offences carry 10 penalty points and the compulsory disqualification offences carry 3–11 penalty points (which are only imposed if there are special reasons preventing disqualification). *See also* CAUSING DEATH BY CARELESS DRIVING; OFFENCES RELATING TO ROAD TRAFFIC.

drunkenness *n.* *Intoxication resulting from imbibing an excess of alcohol. It is an offence to be drunk in a public place.

dualism *n. See* MONISM.

dubitante *adj.* [Latin] Doubting. The term is used in law reports in relation to a judge who is doubtful about a legal proposition but does not wish to declare it wrong.

duces tecum [Latin: you shall bring with you] *See* WITNESS SUMMONS.

due diligence The legal obligation of states to exercise all reasonable efforts to protect *aliens and their property in the host state. Such aliens must have been permitted entry into the host state. If there is a failure or lack of due diligence, the state in default is held responsible and liable to make compensation for injury to the alien or to the alien's estate. *See* STATE RESPONSIBILITY.

dum casta vixerit [Latin] As long as she lives chastely. A clause sometimes inserted in a separation agreement, freeing the husband from the terms of the agreement (e.g. maintenance obligations) if his wife commits adultery.

dumping *n.* The sale of goods abroad at prices below their normal value. Within the EU dumping regulations prohibit the sale of goods at below normal value. **Countervailing** (or **antidumping**) **duties** may be ordered on certain imported goods to prevent dumping.

dum sola [Latin] While single: the status of a single woman or widow.

duplex querela [Latin: double complaint] The procedure in ecclesiastical law for challenging a bishop's refusal to admit a presentee to a benefice.

durante absentia [Latin: during the absence of] Describing a grant of *letters of administration of a deceased's estate to some person interested in the estate while the personal representative is abroad. *See also* LIMITED ADMINISTRATION.

duress *n.* Pressure, especially actual or threatened physical force, put on a person to act in a particular way. Acts carried out under duress usually have no legal effect; for example, a contract obtained by duress is voidable (*see also* ECONOMIC DURESS; UNDUE INFLUENCE). In criminal law, when the defendant's power to resist is destroyed by a threat of death or serious personal injury, he will have a defence to a criminal charge, although he has the *mens rea* for the crime and knows that what he is doing is wrong. Duress is not a defence to a charge of murder as a principal (i.e. to someone who actually carries out the murder himself), although it is still a defence to someone charged with aiding and abetting murder. The threat need not be immediate; it is sufficient that it is effective; for example a threat in court to kill a witness may constitute duress and thus be a defence to a charge of perjury, even though it cannot be carried out in the courtroom. However, the defence is unavailable to someone who failed to take available alternative action to avoid the threat. *See also* COERCION; NECESSITY; SELF-DEFENCE.

during Her (or His) Majesty's pleasure A phrase colloquially used to describe the period of detention imposed upon a defendant found not guilty by reason of *insanity. Such a person was consequently known as a **pleasure patient**. The defendant must still be admitted to a hospital specified by the Home Secretary (either a local psychiatric hospital or a *special hospital) and remain there until otherwise directed, but the phrase "during Her Majesty's pleasure" is no longer used in the statute.

Dutch courage *See* INTOXICATION.

duty *n.* **1.** A legal requirement to carry out or refrain from carrying out any act. *Compare* POWER. **2.** A payment levied by the state, particularly on certain goods and transactions. Examples are *customs duty, *excise duty, and *stamp duty.

duty of care The legal obligation to take reasonable care to avoid causing damage. There is no liability in tort for *negligence unless the act or omission that causes damage is a breach of a duty of care owed to the claimant. There is a duty to take care in most situations in which one can reasonably foresee that one's actions may cause physical damage to the person or property of others. The duty is owed to those people likely to be affected by the conduct in question. Thus doctors have a duty of care to their patients and users of the highway have a duty of care to all other road users. But there is no general duty to prevent other persons causing damage or to rescue persons or property in danger, liability for careless words is more limited than liability for careless acts, and there is no general duty not to cause economic loss or psychiatric illness. In these and some other situations, the existence and scope of the duty of care depends on all the circumstances of the relationship between the parties. Most duties of care are the result of judicial decisions, but some are contained in statutes, such as the Occupiers' Liability Act 1957 (*see* OCCUPIER'S LIABILITY).

duty solicitors *Solicitors who attend by rota at magistrates' courts in order to assist defendants who are otherwise unrepresented.

duty to convert (in equity) *See* CONVERSION.

dying declaration An oral or written statement by a person on the point of death concerning the cause of his death. A dying declaration is admissible at a trial for the murder or the manslaughter of the declarant as an exception to the rule against *hearsay evidence, provided that he would have been a competent witness had he survived (*see* COMPETENCE). Case law requires that the person making the dying declaration must have had a "settled, hopeless expectation of death".

E

easement *n.* A right enjoyed by the owner of land (the **dominant tenement**) to a benefit from other land (the **servient tenement**). An easement benefits and binds the land itself and therefore continues despite any change of ownership of either dominant or servient tenement, although it will be extinguished if the two tenements come into common ownership (*compare* QUASI-EASEMENT). It may be acquired by statute (for example, local Acts of Parliament), expressly granted (e.g. by *deed giving a right of way), arise by implication (e.g. an easement of support from an adjoining building), or be acquired by *prescription. (*See also* PROFIT À PRENDRE.) An easement can exist as either a legal or an equitable interest in land. Only easements created by statute, deed, or prescription and held on terms equivalent to a *fee simple absolute in possession or *term of years absolute qualify as **legal easements** and are binding on all who acquire the unregistered servient tenement or any interest in it. Legal easements over registered land should be registered, but in practice will usually be binding without registration. All others are **equitable easements** and must generally be registered to be enforceable against a third party who acquires the servient tenement for value in money or money's worth. Under section 62 of the Law of Property Act 1925, when land is conveyed, all easements appertaining to it automatically pass with it without the necessity for express words in the conveyance. *See also* REGISTRATION OF ENCUMBRANCES.

easement of necessity An *easement arising by implication in favour either of a grantee of land over land retained by the grantor or, more rarely, of a grantor of land over land that he has granted, when access to any land granted or retained would otherwise be excluded by the operation of the grant. For example, if A, who owns a plot of land adjoining a highway, sells off the part of the plot immediately adjacent to the highway but retains the rest, an easement of necessity over the sold plot is implied if A has no other access to the plot he has retained. If there is any other right of access to the retained plot, there can be no easement of necessity, no matter how inconvenient that access proves to be. Any claimant must be able to prove that the land retained would be inoperative without the easement. The easement may be extinguished if alternative access becomes possible. The implication of necessity can be excluded by the terms of the grant; for example, when the grantor particularly wishes the land retained by him to remain inaccessible.

EAT *See* EMPLOYMENT APPEAL TRIBUNAL.

EBRD *See* EUROPEAN BANK FOR RECONSTRUCTION AND DEVELOPMENT.

EC *See* EUROPEAN COMMUNITY.

ecclesiastical courts Courts responsible for the administration of the ecclesiastical law of the Church of England. They comprise **consistory courts**, which are the courts of each diocese, for enforcing discipline among the clergy; the *Court of Arches and the **Chancery Court of York**, which hear appeals from consistory courts in their respective provinces; the *Judicial Committee of the Privy Council, which hears appeals from the provincial courts in matters not involving doctrine, ritual, or ceremonial; and the *Court of Ecclesiastical Causes Reserved.

ecclesiastical law *See* CANON LAW.

ECJ *See* EUROPEAN COURT OF JUSTICE.

ecolabel *n.* A label with the EU logo that is used on products that comply with environmental requirements in particular directives.

economic duress Historically within contract law, a claim that a contract was voidable for duress could only be successful if a threat to the person (i.e. physical duress) had induced the contract. Now, however, a contract may be voidable for economic duress. The essential elements are that an illegitimate threat is made (e.g. to breach an existing contract or to commit a tort) and that the injured party has no practical alternative to agreeing to the terms set out by the person making the threat. *See also* VOIDABLE CONTRACT.

e-conveyancing *n. See* ELECTRONIC CONVEYANCING.

ECSC *See* EUROPEAN COAL AND STEEL COMMUNITY.

ECU (European Currency Unit) *n.* A currency medium and unit of account of the *European Monetary System, which was replaced by the euro in 1999 (*see* EUROPEAN MONETARY UNION). Its value was calculated from the values of the currencies of individual member states of the European Union. The ECU was not a unit of currency as such, although some prices were quoted in ECU by the European Commission and other bodies. The ECU was used in the *Exchange Rate Mechanism, and some bonds were issued by member states in ECUs.

education authorities The authorities responsible for the statutory system of education introduced by the Education Act 1944, i.e. the Secretary of State for Education and Skills and local education authorities. In England and Wales the latter are county councils or unitary councils and, within *Greater London, the London borough councils. The Education Reform Act 1988 introduced measures under which schools could, with the approval of the Secretary of State, opt out of local education authority control to become grant-maintained schools, and many have done so. A new framework for schools has been introduced by the School Standards and Framework Act 1998.

EEA *See* EUROPEAN ECONOMIC AREA.

EEC (European Economic Community) *See* EUROPEAN COMMUNITY.

EEZ *See* EXCLUSIVE ECONOMIC ZONE.

effective date of termination The date on which a contract of employment comes to an end, i.e. the date of expiry of any *notice given or of a fixed-term contract or the date of the employee's dismissal or resignation if no notice is given. However, an employee dismissed without the statutory minimum notice is treated as having worked for that period after his dismissal for the purpose of calculating whether or not his length of service (*see* CONTINUOUS EMPLOYMENT) qualifies him to apply to an employment tribunal in respect of redundancy, unfair dismissal, etc.

effective remedy A right contained in Article 13 of the European Convention on Human Rights but not incorporated directly by the *Human Rights Act 1998. The Article stipulates that the state must provide systems that give effective remedies for violations and arguable claims of violations of the other rights contained in the Convention. This article requires that such systems can both determine such claims and provide for redress for those violations that are substantiated.

EFTA *See* EUROPEAN FREE TRADE ASSOCIATION.

eggshell skull rule The rule that a *tortfeasor cannot complain if the injuries he has caused turn out to be more serious than expected because his victim suffered from a pre-existing weakness, such as an unusually thin skull. A tortfeasor must take his victim as he finds him.

EIS *See* ENTERPRISE INVESTMENT SCHEME.

***ejusdem generis* rule** *See* INTERPRETATION OF STATUTES.

Elder Brethren *See* ASSESSOR.

election *n.* **1.** The process of choosing by vote a member of a representative body, such as the House of Commons or a local authority. For the House of Commons, a **general election** involving all UK constituencies is held when the sovereign dissolves Parliament and summons a new one; a **by-election** is held if a particular constituency becomes vacant (e.g. on the death of the sitting member) during the life of a Parliament. Local government elections (apart from those to fill casual vacancies) are held at statutory intervals (*see* LOCAL AUTHORITY). The conduct of elections is regulated by the Representation of the People Acts 1983 and 1985. The Representation of the People Act 2000 made some changes to electoral registration and absent voting and allowed for experiments involving innovative electoral procedures. Other changes make it easier for the disabled to vote and created an offence of supplying false particulars on a nomination form. Voting is secret and normally in person, but any elector can obtain a postal vote without having to specify a reason. The only requirement is that the applicant is included in the Register of Electors. Applications for a particular election must be received by the Electoral Registration Officer six working days before an election. Different rules apply in Northern Ireland. Any dispute as to the validity of the election of a Member of Parliament or a local government councillor is raised on an **election petition**, which is decided by an **election court** consisting of two High Court judges. **2.** A doctrine of equity, commonly applied to wills, based on the principle that a person must accept both benefits and burdens under one document, or reject both. It arises when there are two gifts in one document, one of A's (the creator's) property to B and one of B's property to C. B must choose whether to accept the gift of A's property to him and transfer his own property to C, or to reject both gifts.

election court *See* ELECTION.

election petition *See* ELECTION.

elective resolution A decision by all the members of a *private company (at a meeting called on at least 21 days' notice) to dispense with complying with specified provisions of the Companies Act 1985, for example holding the annual general meeting and laying the accounts before it or the annual appointment of auditors.

elector *n.* **1.** A person entitled to vote at an *election. For parliamentary and local government elections, a **register of electors** is maintained. A new register comes into force on 16 February each year and governs elections held during the following 12 months. It records electors by reference to their residence on the preceding 10 October (the qualifying date) and includes people who will become 18 (and so entitled to vote) in the year following its publication. Inclusion on the register is a requirement for voting. A person on it cannot be prevented from voting but incurs penalties if he votes without in fact being entitled to do so. *See* FRANCHISE. **2.** (in equity) One who makes an election.

electricity *n.* *See* ABSTRACTING ELECTRICITY.

electromagnetic compatibility The capability of electromagnetic products, such as computer equipment, machines, etc., to be used together without special modification. The EU electromagnetic compatibility directive, which is now part of English law, sets out the minimum requirements to ensure that the use of computers, etc., does not cause interference with other electromagnetic products. *See also* CE.

electronic conveyancing (e-conveyancing) The transfer of land by electronic means instead of by paper documents. The government has announced its intention to introduce such a method of transferring land, and the Electronic Communications Act 2000 paves the way for such transfers. It is already possible to discharge mortgages of registered land electronically. *Land registration (which is already computerized) has made electronic conveyancing and registration possible.

electronic data interchange (EDI) The use of electronic data-transmission networks to exchange information. Significant commercial contracts set out the terms on which such information is supplied, and much commerce is now done on this basis (known as **paperless trading**), either through a closed network called an **intranet**, to which only members of a limited group have access, or through an open network, i.e. the Internet. Some international legal rules have been agreed in this field, including the Uniform Rules of Conduct for Interchange of Trade Data by Teletransmission (*see* UNCID).

electronic signature An item of data incorporated into or associated with an electronically transmitted document or contract for use in establishing the authenticity of the communication. Under the Electronic Communications Act 2000 electronic signatures are recognized in legal proceedings and as having legal effect. An electronic signature can be purchased from such bodies as the Post Office and Chamber of Commerce on production of relevant identification documents. *See also* DIGITAL SIGNATURE.

electronic surveillance The use of *telephone tapping, hidden microphones (bugging) or cameras, or similar means to obtain evidence. The police and other state bodies may be permitted to use such devices provided that the Secretary of State has issued a warrant under the Interception of Communications Act 1985. Evidence obtained by electronic surveillance can usually be used in court proceedings: it has been compared with the evidence of an eavesdropper. The Police Act 1997 provides for a system in which independent commissioners of police oversee the arrangements and investigate complaints in relation to intrusive *surveillance operations.

eleemosynary corporation [from Latin: *eleemosyna*, alms] Originally, a lay (rather than an ecclesiastical) charity. An eleemosynary corporation is now a charity directed to the relief of individual distress.

embargo *n.* The detention of ships in port: a type of *reprisal. Ships of a delinquent state may be prevented from leaving the ports of an injured state in order to compel the delinquent state to make reparation for the wrong done. *See also* ANGARY.

embezzlement *n.* The dishonest appropriation by an employee of any money or property given to him on behalf of his employer. Before 1969 there was a special offence of embezzlement; it is now, however, classified as a form of *theft.

emblements *pl. n.* Cultivated crops that are normally harvested annually. A tenant for life of settled land may continue to harvest crops he has sown if his interest in the land ceases for any reason other than by his own act. For example, he may continue to harvest his crops if his interest ends on the death of another person but not if his interest was for life until remarriage and he remarries. When he dies, his personal representatives are entitled to reap for the benefit of his estate any crops sown by him before his death.

emergency powers Powers conferred by government regulations during a **state of emergency**. The existence of such a state is declared by royal proclamation under the Emergency Powers Acts 1920 and 1964. A proclamation, which lasts for one month but is renewable, may be issued whenever there is a threat (e.g. a major strike or natural disaster) to the country's essentials of life. The regulations made may confer on government departments, the armed forces, and others all powers necessary to secure the supply and distribution of necessities and the maintenance of public peace and safety.

emergency protection order A court order under the Children Act 1989 that gives a local authority or the NSPCC the right to remove a child to suitable accommodation for a maximum of eight days (with a right to apply for a seven-day extension) if there is reasonable cause to believe a child is suffering or is likely to suffer significant harm unless the order is made. The order gives the applicant *parental responsibility in so far as it promotes the *welfare of the child. In some cases it may be preferable to remove the abuser from the home rather than the child. The Children Act 1989 provides for the inclusion of an *exclusion requirement in an emergency protection order. The effect of this is to exclude the abuser from the family home. The order may only be made when another person in the same household as the child consents to the exclusion order and is able and willing to care properly for the child. *See also* SECTION 47 ENQUIRY.

eminent domain *See* EXPROPRIATION.

emoluments *pl. n.* A person's earnings, including salaries, fees, wages, profits, and benefits in kind (e.g. company cars). They are subject to *income tax under Schedule E in the Income and Corporation Taxes Act 1988.

empanel *vb.* To swear a jury to try an issue.

employee *n.* A person who works under the direction and control of another (the *employer) in return for a wage or salary. *See also* CHILD EMPLOYEE; CONTRACT OF EMPLOYMENT; EMPLOYER AND EMPLOYEE.

employees' inventions Products, equipment, or techniques invented by an employee in the course of his employment. Under the Patents Act 1977 these belong to the employer if the invention was made in the course of the employee's normal duties and these were likely to lead to an invention or in the course of any duties involving a special obligation to further the employer's business. These provisions cannot be changed in a contract of employment. The employee may, however, be awarded compensation by the Comptroller General of Patents, Designs and Trademarks if the invention is of outstanding benefit to the employer (this virtually never applies). Copyright works also belong to the employer if the employee produces them in the course of his employment.

employees' share scheme A method of sharing company profits with employees either by distributing shares already paid up by the company, either to the employees themselves or to trustees for them, or by conferring upon them options to acquire shares on favourable terms. Certain schemes carry tax concessions.

employer *n.* A person who engages another (the *employee) to work under his direction and control in return for a wage or salary (*see also* CONTRACT OF

EMPLOYMENT). Companies are **associated employers** if one of them controls the other or others or if they are themselves controlled by the same company.

employer and employee The relationship between the parties to a *contract of employment. (It was formerly known as **master and servant**.) The relationship is governed by the express and implied terms of the contract and by statutory rules that the contract cannot exclude. These relate, for example, to *unfair dismissal, *redundancy, *maternity rights, *trade union membership and activity, and health and *safety at work. On the principle of *vicarious liability, third parties may hold an employer responsible for certain wrongs committed by his employee in the course of his employment.

employers' association An organization whose members are wholly or mainly employers and whose principal purposes include the regulation of relations between employers and workers or trade unions. Under the Trade Union and Labour Relations (Consolidation) Act 1992, employers' associations have similar legal status to *trade unions, being immune from certain civil legal proceedings in tort relating to interference with contracts and restraint of trade.

employer's liability The liability of an employer for breach of his duty to provide for his employees competent fellow-workers, safe equipment, a safe place of work, and a safe system of work, including adequate supervision. Liability can be in tort for damages for *negligence and for *breach of statutory duty under statutes providing for *safety at work; there are also criminal penalties. *See* DANGEROUS MACHINERY; DEFECTIVE EQUIPMENT.

Employment Appeal Tribunal (EAT) A statutory body established to hear appeals from *employment tribunals. The EAT consists of a High Court judge as chairman and two or four lay members who have special knowledge or experience as employers' or employees' representatives. They can only hear appeals on questions of law, issues of fact being in the exclusive jurisdiction of employment tribunals. The EAT may allow or dismiss an appeal or, in certain circumstances, remit the case to the employment tribunal for further hearing. It does not generally order either party to pay the other's costs, except when the appeal is frivolous, vexatious, or improperly conducted. The parties may be represented at the hearing by anyone they choose, who need not have legal qualifications. The EAT cannot enforce its own decisions; thus, for example, when an employer fails to comply with an order for compensation that the EAT upholds, separate application must be made to the court to enforce the order. A party may appeal to the Court of Appeal from a decision of the EAT, but only with the leave of the EAT or the Court of Appeal. The Employment Tribunals Act 1996 (effective from 22 August 1996) sets out the jurisdiction of the EAT.

employment tribunal (ET) Any of the bodies established under the employment protection legislation, consolidated by the Employment (formerly Industrial) Tribunals Act 1996, to hear and rule on certain disputes between employers and employees or trade unions relating to statutory terms and conditions of employment. (Originally called **industrial tribunals**, they (and the 1996 Act) were renamed under the Employment Rights (Dispute Resolution) Act 1998.) The tribunals hear, inter alia, complaints concerning *unfair dismissal, *redundancy, *equal pay, *maternity rights, and complaints of unlawful deductions from wages under the Employment Rights Act 1996 (Part II). Tribunals sit in local centres in public and usually consist of a legally qualified chairman and two independent laymen, although chairmen are permitted to sit alone, without lay members, for certain types of case (e.g. deductions from wages claims), cases where the parties agree in writing, and uncontested cases. An ET differs from a civil court in that it cannot enforce its own awards (this must be done by separate application to a court) and it can conduct its proceedings informally. Strict rules of evidence need not apply and the parties can present their own case or be represented by anyone they wish at their own expense. The tribunal has wide powers to declare a dismissal unfair and to award *compensation, which is the usual remedy, but they also have power to order the *reinstatement or *re-engagement of a dismissed employee.

In cases involving allegations of sexual misconduct employment tribunals are empowered to make a **restricted reporting order**, which prevents identification of anyone pursuing or affected by the allegations until the tribunal's decision is promulgated. There is also a power to remove identifying information in such cases from the decisions and other public documents.

Before conducting a full hearing of the case, the tribunal may consider (on either party's application or on its own initiative) what the parties have said in the written complaint to the tribunal (the **originating application**) and the answer to it (the **notice of appearance**) in a **prehearing assessment**. If this assessment suggests that either party is unlikely to succeed, the tribunal may warn that party that he may be ordered to pay the other's costs if he insists on pursuing his case to a full hearing. When a full hearing takes place, the tribunal will not award costs to the successful party unless the other has been warned of this likelihood at a prehearing assessment or has acted vexatiously, frivolously, or unreasonably in bringing or defending the proceedings. An appeal on a point of law arising from any decision on an ET may be heard by the *Employment Appeal Tribunal.

EMS *See* EUROPEAN MONETARY SYSTEM.

EMU *See* EUROPEAN MONETARY UNION.

EN *See* EURO NORM.

enabling statute A statute that confers rights or powers upon any body or person.

enacting words The introductory words in an *Act of Parliament that give it the force of law. They follow immediately after the long title and date of royal assent, unless preceded by a preamble, and normally run: "Be It Enacted by the Queen's most Excellent Majesty, by and with the advice and consent of the Lords Spiritual and Temporal, and Commons, in this present Parliament assembled, and by the authority of the same, as follows...". A special formula is used in cases when the Parliament Acts 1911 and 1949 apply (*see* ACT OF PARLIAMENT).

enactment *n.* An Act of Parliament, a Measure of the General Synod (*see* CHURCH OF ENGLAND), an order, or any other piece of subordinate legislation, or any particular provision contained in any of these (e.g. a particular section or article). Delegated legislation is not an enactment for the purposes of the Local Government Act 1992.

encroachment *n.* The act of extending one's own rights at the expense of others, particularly by taking in adjoining land to make it appear part of one's own. If the encroachment is acquiesced in for 12 years, the land taken is considered to be annexed to the land of the person who made the encroachment.

encumbrance (incumbrance) *n.* A right or interest in land owned by someone other than the owner of the land itself; examples include easements, leases, mortgages, and restrictive covenants. When title to the land is registered (*see* LAND REGISTRATION), encumbrances other than minor and overriding interests are recorded in the Charges Register. Certain encumbrances affecting unregistered land will only be enforceable against third parties if registered at the Land Charges Registry. *See also* REGISTRATION OF ENCUMBRANCES.

endorsement *n*. **1.** The procedure in which the particulars of a driving offence are noted on a person's driving licence. When the court orders endorsement for an offence carrying obligatory or discretionary *disqualification but the driver is not disqualified, the endorsement also contains particulars of the number of penalty points imposed for the purposes of *totting up. When the court orders disqualification, only the particulars of the offence are noted. The courts can order endorsement upon a conviction for most traffic offences (the main exceptions being parking offences) and in many cases they must order an endorsement, unless there are special reasons (e.g. a sudden emergency) why they should not. A person whose licence is to be endorsed must produce it for the court; if he does not do so, his licence may be suspended. A driver whose licence has been endorsed may apply to have a new "clean" licence after a certain number of years has elapsed (usually 4 years, but 11 in the case of offences involving *drunken driving). Under the Road Traffic (New Drivers) Act 1995, with effect from 1 June 1997, a driver who is convicted of an endorsable offence and who has accumulated 6 or more penalty points within two years of passing a driving test has his licence revoked and must retake a driving test. **2.** The signature of the holder on a bill of exchange, which is an essential step in negotiating or transfering a bill payable to order. The endorsement must be completed by delivering the bill to the transferee. An **endorsement in blank** is the bare signature of the holder and makes the bill payable to bearer. A **special endorsement** specifies the person to whom (or to whose order) the bill is payable (e.g. "Pay X or order"). An endorser, by endorsing a bill, takes on certain obligations to the holder or a subsequent endorser. **3.** The noting on a document of details of a later transaction affecting the subject matter of that document. For example, a beneficiary in whose favour a personal representative executes an *assent of property may require details of the assent to be written (**endorsed**) on the document containing the *probate or *letters of administration. Equally, a purchaser of a plot forming part of a larger plot of land may require a note or memorandum of the conveyance to him to be endorsed on the title deeds relating to the whole plot.

endowment *n*. **1.** The provision of a fixed income for the support of a charity. **2.** Any property belonging permanently to a charity.

enforcement action Any action, authorized by the United Nations Security Council, to enforce *collective security under *Chapter VII (i.e. Articles 39–51) of the UN Charter. As such it stands as one of the very few legal justifications for *use of force in international law. Strictly, any enforcement action can only be justified under Article 42 of the Charter, which requires agreement by member states to place their armed forces at the disposal of the UN (*see* MILITARY STAFF COMMITTEE). However, although the theory of enforcement action would seem to be that of concerted action by members under Article 42, such a limitation is not expressly stated in the Charter. Article 39 was worded so widely as to allow the Security Council, using the implied powers allowed for by that Article, to bypass this problem and authorize that member states voluntarily furnish armed forces to be under the unified command of one member state. Upon the basis of such implied power, an enforcement action was justified under Security Council recommendations under Article 39 in order to defend Korea (1950).

enforcement notice A notice by a local planning authority (*see* TOWN AND COUNTRY PLANNING) that requires certain steps to be taken within a specified time to remedy an alleged breach of planning control. An example of such a breach would occur if development was carried out without planning permission or contrary to conditions attached to planning permission. A local planning authority that has notice of a breach of planning control has, however, a discretion as to whether to enforce against that breach. Appeal against the notice may be made to the Secretary of State on various grounds, including the ground that the development is one for which planning permission ought to be granted. *See also* STOP NOTICE.

enforcement of judgment The processes by which the orders of a court may be enforced. Orders for the payment of money may be enforced by a variety of methods, including a writ of **fieri facias* (in the county court, a warrant of execution), *garnishee proceedings, *charging orders, the appointment of a *receiver, a writ of *sequestration, and (rarely) an order of committal (*see* COMMITTAL IN CIVIL PROCEEDINGS). In the county court (and in the High Court in certain matrimonial proceedings only) *attachment of the debtor's earnings is also available.

Judgments for possession of land may be enforced by *writ of possession (in the county court, a warrant of possession). Judgments for delivery of goods may be enforced by *writ of delivery (in the county court, a warrant of delivery). Judgments relating to performance of or abstention from some act (e.g. an *injunction) may be enforced by order of committal or writ of sequestration.

enfranchise *vb.* **1.** To give to a person or class of people the right to vote at elections. **2.** To give to an area or a class of people the right to be represented on an elected body.

enfranchisement of tenancy A method for acquiring the freehold or an extended lease of a leasehold house. A tenant has a statutory right of enfranchisement when he has a long lease (exceeding 21 years) and the house has been his *main residence for at least three years. The valuation of the freehold, or rent of an extended lease, is based on the value of the land without the buildings on it.

The Leasehold Reform Act 1993 abolished the rateable value limits for houses and extended to flat leaseholders the right to acquire collectively the freeholds of their flats. From 1 April 1997 the Housing Act 1996 abolished in most cases an earlier requirement that enfranchisement only applied to leases at a low rent with a duration of over 35 years. This area of the law is currently under review, with a view to relaxing rules for qualification and residency.

engagement to marry An agreement, verbal or in writing, to marry at a future date. Such agreements are no longer treated as enforceable legal contracts, and no action can be brought for breach of such an agreement or to recover expenses incurred as a result of the agreement. Engagement rings are deemed to be absolute gifts and cannot be recovered when an engagement is broken. There is a special statutory provision that property rights between engaged parties (for example, in respect of a house purchased with a view to marriage) are to be decided in accordance with the rules governing property rights of married couples.

engross *vb.* To prepare a fair copy of a deed or other legal document ready for execution by the parties.

enlarge *vb.* (in land law) To acquire further rights in land, thereby increasing one's interest to some greater estate or interest. For example, a *tenant in tail may enlarge his interest into a fee simple by executing a disentailing deed (*see* ENTAILED INTEREST). A mortgagee in possession for 12 years may, by executing a deed, enlarge his interest into a fee simple free from the mortgage.

enrolment *n.* The registration of an act or document on an official record. It used to be obligatory to enrol many documents in the Enrolment Office, a department of the Chancery Division. Nearly all such obligations were abolished by the Judicature Acts 1873–75.

entailed interest An *equitable interest in land under which ownership is limited to a person and the heirs of his body (either generally or those of a specified class). Such heirs are still those who would inherit under the law of intestacy as it applied before the Administration of Estates Act 1925. Since 1997, no new entailed interests can be created. An attempt to do so creates an absolute interest instead.

enter *vb.* **1.** (in the law of *burglary) To make "an effective and substantial" entry as a trespasser. This does not necessarily require entry of the whole of the defendant's body. **2.** (in land law) *See* ENTRY INTO POSSESSION.

entering judgment A procedure in civil courts in which a judgment is formally recorded by the court after it has been given. In the Queen's Bench Division it is necessary for the party seeking to have judgment entered to draw up the judgment and present it to an officer of the court for entry together with the certificate of the associate (clerk of the court) and the statements of case. In the county court, the court itself draws up and enters the judgment.

Enterprise Investment Scheme (EIS) A scheme to encourage investment in unquoted companies; it replaced the similar **Business Expansion Scheme** on 1 January 1994. It gives income tax relief of 20% on investments to individuals who invest from £500 to £150,000 in any one year in shares issued by UK trading companies not quoted on the Stock Exchange. Shares issued under this scheme are also exempt from capital gains tax. Investors can hold paid directorships of the companies; there is also income and capital gains tax relief on losses. Companies providing private housing on assured tenancies are excluded from the scheme.

entire contract *See* PERFORMANCE OF CONTRACT.

entrapment *n.* Deliberately trapping a person into committing a crime in order to secure his conviction, as by offering to buy drugs. English courts do not recognize a defence of entrapment as such, since the defendant is still considered to have a free choice in his acts. Under the Police and Criminal Evidence Act 1984, entrapment may be a reason for making certain evidence inadmissible on the ground that the admission of the evidence would have such an adverse effect on the fairness of the proceedings that the court ought not to admit it. The question of the admissibility of evidence obtained through entrapment is in some doubt as a consequence of the cases now being decided under the *Human Rights Act 1998. Entrapment may also be used as a reason for mitigating a sentence. *See also* AGENT PROVOCATEUR.

entry into possession The act of going upon land to assert some right over it. For example, a lease usually gives the landlord the right to enter and take possession if the tenant fails to pay the rent or commits a breach of covenant. A mortgagee has the right to recover possession from a defaulting mortgagor who is in possession. In general, such rights of entry cannot be enforced unless the court orders the defaulter to give up possession.

entry without warrant Entry by a police officer onto private premises without the authority of a warrant. This is in general unlawful except with the occupier's consent (which is revocable), but it is permitted by statute for the purpose of arresting for certain offences (*see* ARRESTABLE OFFENCE) and in certain circumstances to search premises (*see* POWER OF SEARCH); it is also allowed at common law to stop an actual or apprehended breach of the peace.

epitome of title *See* ABSTRACT OF TITLE.

equality clause A clause in a contract of employment stipulating that if a woman is employed on similar work to that of a man in the same employment, or on work rated as equivalent or of like value to his, the terms of her contract must place her in no less favourable a position than the man. A contract not containing such a clause (either directly or as a result of some collective agreement) is deemed to include one by virtue of the Equal Pay Act 1970 as amended by the Sex Discrimination Acts 1975 and 1986 and by the Equal Pay (Amendment) Regulations 1983. However, the clause does not affect certain statutory requirements concerning the employment of women (e.g. with respect to health and safety requirements) or their *maternity rights. *See also* EQUAL PAY; SEX DISCRIMINATION.

equality is equity [from Latin: *aequitas est quasi aequalitas*] A *maxim of equity stating that if there are no reasons for any other basis of division of property, those entitled to it shall share it equally.

equality of arms A concept that has been created by the European Court of Human Rights in the context of the right to a *fair trial (Article 6). Equality of arms requires that there be a fair balance between the opportunities afforded the parties involved in litigation (for example, each party should be able to call witnesses and cross-examine the witnesses called by the other party). In some circumstances this may require the provision of financial support to allow a person of limited means to pay for legal representation.

Equal Opportunities Commission A body established by the Sex Discrimination Acts 1975 and 1986 to work towards eliminating discrimination on grounds of sex or marital status, to promote equality of opportunity between the sexes, and to keep the working of the Acts, and of the Equal Pay Act 1970, under review. It consists of 8–15 Commissioners. *See* SEX DISCRIMINATION.

equal pay The requirement of the Equal Pay Act 1970 that men and women in the same employment must be paid at the same rate for like work or work rated as equivalent or of equal value. They are in the same employment if they work at the same establishment (or if one works at an establishment that includes the other's) and they work for the same or an associated *employer. The establishments must also be those at which the terms and conditions of employment are observed generally or for employees of the relevant description. "Like work" is work that is broadly similar, where any differences between the man's work and the woman's are not of practical importance. Work is rated as equivalent when the employer has undertaken a study to evaluate his employees' jobs in terms of the skill, effort, and responsibility demanded of them and the woman's job is given the same grade as the man's. If the employer has no job-evaluation scheme, an independent expert is appointed by an employment tribunal to evaluate the two jobs to see if they are of equal value. Thus when the employer's job-grading system or the expert's report recognizes that the woman's job is as demanding as the man's, they are entitled to equal pay even though the nature of the work they do is very different. An employer's job-evaluation system can be challenged on the basis that it is discriminatory. *See also* EQUALITY CLAUSE.

The Code of Practice on Equal Pay, which was drafted by the Equal Opportunities Commission and applies to all employers, came into effect on 26 March 1997. The Code requires employers to review current pay structures and policy; introduce an equal-pay policy and ensure that pay structures and grades are transparent; change any rules of practice that are likely to result in discrimination in pay; establish a continuous monitoring procedure and on-going assessment so that bad practices do not develop; and assess whether there are any discrepancies in pay levels between male and female staff. The Code is admissible in evidence in any tribunal proceedings under the Sex Discrimination Act 1975 and the Equal Pay Act 1970.

equal treatment The requirement, enshrined in the Treaty of Rome, that nationals of one EU state moving to work in another EU state must be treated in the same way as those workers of the state to which they have moved. There must be *free movement of workers throughout the EU and no discrimination in relation to pay, social security, and tax benefits. *See also* EQUAL PAY.

equitable *adj.* **1.** Recognized by or in accordance with the rules of equity; applied to distinguish certain concepts used in both common or statute law and in equity. For example, assignments and mortgages can be either legal or equitable. **2.** Describing a right or concept recognized by the Court of Chancery. **3.** Just, fair, and reasonable. For example, a document may have two meanings, one strict and the other (the equitable construction) more benevolent.

equitable assignment *See* ASSIGNMENT.

equitable charge **1.** *See* EQUITABLE MORTGAGE. **2.** A *charge created by designating specific property for the discharge of some debt or other obligation. No special form of words is necessary to create an equitable charge, manifested intention being sufficient. *See* GENERAL EQUITABLE CHARGE.

equitable easement *See* EASEMENT.

equitable estate A right in property recognized by the Court of Chancery, as distinct from a *legal estate recognized in common law courts (*see* ESTATE). Equitable estates reflected legal interests but could be more flexible (*compare* SHIFTING USE; SPRINGING USE). Before 1926, most types of estate could exist either at law or in equity; since 1925 only a limited number of legal estates can exist; all other interests in land are called *equitable interests. The term equitable estate is now technically incorrect.

equitable estoppel *See* ESTOPPEL.

equitable execution Means of enforcing the judgment of a court when the judgment creditor cannot obtain satisfaction from the normal methods of *execution. For example, the creditor may appoint a receiver to manage the defendant's property or he may obtain an injunction to prevent the defendant from dealing with the property. These remedies are often regarded as relief granted by the court, rather than as execution.

equitable interests Interests in property originally recognized by the Court of Chancery, as distinct from legal interests recognized in the common-law courts. They arose in cases when it was against the principles of *equity for a person to enforce a legal right. Originally equitable rights (e.g. a trust, or the equity of redemption under a mortgage) were enforceable against the person with a legal right over property in question. Later, however, those who were given the property by the holder of the legal interests took it subject to equitable interests; later still, anyone who bought property knowing of the equitable interests was bound by them. In the developed law, everyone took property subject to equitable interests except those who bought it and neither knew nor ought to have known of the equitable interests (the doctrine of notice). Since 1925, equitable interests may be protected by the doctrine of *overreaching, under the system of *land charges, or by notice.

equitable lease An agreement for the grant of an interest in land on terms that correspond to a *legal lease but do not comply with the necessary formal requirements of a legal lease. For example, if L purports to grant T a lease for seven years but the transaction is effected by simple written contract to grant a lease rather than by deed, the court may enforce the contract to grant the lease between the parties. This follows the principle that "equity looks upon that as done which ought to be done" (*see* MAXIMS OF EQUITY). Further, T's rights under the contract could be registered as an *estate contract and thus bind any third party acquiring L's interest in the land.

equitable lien *See* LIEN.

equitable mortgage (equitable charge) A *mortgage under which the mortgagee does not obtain a legal estate in the land. An equitable mortgage may arise as follows:
(1) If the mortgagor has only an *equitable interest in the land, he can only grant an equitable mortgage. For example, a mortgage granted by a beneficiary under a *trust of land could only be equitable.
(2) An equitable mortgage will arise if the mortgage is made by deed (a requirement for legal mortgages). The contract for the mortgage must nevertheless be made in writing.

equitable presumptions *Presumptions assumed by equity in certain cases. The main examples are the presumption of *resulting trust, the presumption of *advancement, and the presumption of equality (*see* EQUALITY IS EQUITY).

equitable remedies Means granted by *equity to redress a wrong. Since the range of legal remedies was originally very limited, equity showed great flexibility in granting remedies, which were discretionary: the conduct of the parties, particularly that of the claimant, was taken into account (*see* CLEAN HANDS). The main equitable remedies are now *specific performance, *rescission, *cancellation, *rectification, *account, *injunction, and the appointment of a *receiver. These remedies may be sought in any division of the High Court or, in some instances, in the county courts; they are still discretionary in nature, although the discretion is often exercised on established lines.

equitable rights Rights recognized by *equity. *See* EQUITABLE INTERESTS; EQUITABLE REMEDIES.

equitable waste Alterations made by a tenant that cause serious damage to the leased property. *See* WASTE.

equity *n.* **1.** That part of English law originally administered by the *Lord Chancellor and later by the *Court of Chancery, as distinct from that administered by the courts of *common law. The common law did not recognize certain concepts (e.g. uses and trusts) and its remedies were limited in scope and flexibility, since it relied primarily on the remedy of damages. In the Middle Ages litigants were entitled to petition the king, who relied on the advice of his Chancellor, commonly an ecclesiastic ("the keeper of the king's conscience"), to do justice in each case. By the 15th century, petitions were referred directly to the Chancellor, who dealt with cases on a flexible basis: he was more concerned with the fair result than with rigid principles of law (hence the jurist John Selden's jibe that "equity varied with the length of the Chancellor's foot"). Moreover, if a defendant refused to comply with the Chancellor's order, he would be imprisoned for contempt of the order until he chose to comply (*see* IN PERSONAM). In the 17th century conflict arose between the common-law judges and the Chancellor as to who should prevail; James I resolved the dispute in favour of the Chancellor. General principles began to emerge, and by the early 19th century the Court of Chancery was more organized and its jurisdiction, once flexible, had ossified into a body of precedent with fixed principles. The Court of Chancery had varying types of jurisdiction (*see* AUXILIARY JURISDICTION; CONCURRENT JURISDICTION; EXCLUSIVE JURISDICTION) and many of its general principles were stated in the form of *maxims of equity; equity had (and still has) certain doctrines (*see* ELECTION; CONVERSION; RECONVERSION; PERFORMANCE OF CONTRACT; SATISFACTION). Under the Judicature Acts 1873–75, with the establishment of the High Court of Justice to administer both common law and equity, the Court of Chancery was abolished (though much of its work is still carried out by the *Chancery Division). The Judicature Acts also provided that in cases in which there was a conflict between the rules of law and equity, the rules of equity should prevail. The main areas of equitable jurisdiction now include *trusts, *equitable interests over property, relief against *forfeiture and penalties, and *equitable remedies. Equity is thus a regulated scheme of legal principles, but new developments are still possible ("equity is not past the age of child-bearing"): recent examples of its creativity include the *freezing injunction and the *search order. **2.** An equitable right or claim, especially an *equitable interest, or *equity of redemption, or *mere equity. **3.** A share in a limited company.

equity of redemption The rights of a mortgagor over his mortgaged property, particularly the right to redeem the property. This right of redemption allows a mortgagor to redeem the mortgaged property at any time on payment of principal, interest, and costs, even after the contractual date of redemption, as stated in the mortgage deed, has passed. Any *clogs on the equity of redemption are void, but the mortgagor's rights may be terminated under certain circumstances (*see* MORTGAGE).

Before 1926 a mortgage was commonly effected by the transfer of the mortgagor's interest in the property to the mortgagee, but the mortgagor's rights were recognized by equity. Since 1925 the mortgagor retains legal ownership of the property in all cases: the term equity of redemption is still used, however, although the right to redeem is no longer strictly an equitable interest.

***erga omnes* obligations** [Latin: towards all] (in international law) Obligations in whose fulfilment all states have a legal interest because their subject matter is of importance to the international community as a whole. It follows from this that the breach of such an obligation is of concern not only to the victimized state but also to all the other members of the international community. Thus, in the event of a breach of these obligations, every state must be considered justified in invoking (probably through judicial channels) the responsibility of the guilty state committing the internationally wrongful act. It has been suggested that an example of an *erga omnes* obligation is that of a people's right to *self-determination.

ERM *See* EXCHANGE RATE MECHANISM.

error *n.* A mistake of law in a judgment or order of a court or in some procedural step in legal proceedings. A **writ of error** was formerly used to instruct an inferior court to send records of its proceedings for review by a superior court. It was abolished in civil cases by the Judicature Acts 1873–75 and in criminal cases by the Criminal Appeal Act 1907 and replaced by the modern system of *appeal.

error of law on the face of the record A mistake of law that is made by an inferior court or tribunal in reaching a decision and is apparent from the record of its proceedings. The decision can be quashed by the High Court in *judicial review proceedings by the remedy of *quashing order except in the case of a *domestic tribunal with purely contractual powers. *See also* ULTRA VIRES.

escape *n.* The common-law offence of escaping from lawful custody. The custody may be in prison or a police station, or even in the open air. The escaper need not have been charged with any offence, provided his detention is lawful (e.g. he may be detained to provide a *specimen of breath). Nor is it necessary for him to commit any act of breaking out. It is also an offence to help the escape of a prisoner and to permit a prisoner who is detained in relation to a criminal matter to escape. If someone actually breaks out of a building in which he is lawfully confined he commits a separate offence of **prison breaking**.

escrow *n.* *See* DEED.

espionage *n.* *See* SPYING.

espousal of claim The action by which a state undertakes to gain redress of a grievance on behalf of one of its subjects or citizens. *See also* EXHAUSTION OF LOCAL REMEDIES.

essence of a contract *See* CONDITION.

estate *n.* **1.** (in land law) The character and duration of a person's ownership of land. For example, an estate in fee simple confers effectively absolute ownership; an estate for a term of years (called **leasehold**) or for life are lesser estates. Under the Law of Property Act 1925 only a *fee simple absolute in possession (called **freehold**) and a *term of years absolute can exist as legal estates in land. All other forms of ownership, e.g. an estate for life or an estate in fee simple coming into effect only on someone's death, are equitable only. **2.** (in revenue law) The aggregate of all the property to which a person is beneficially entitled. **Excluded property**, which includes most reversionary interests and certain foreign matters, is not taken into account for the death charge (*see* INHERITANCE TAX).

estate agent A person who introduces prospective buyers and sellers of property to each other. Such a person may be a member of a professional body but must, in any event, under the Estate Agents Act 1979, take out insurance cover to protect money received as deposits from clients. The Property Misdescription Act 1991 prohibits estate agents from making false or misleading statements about property in the course of their business; making such statements is punishable by a fine of up to £5000 or possibly by imprisonment. *See also* MISDESCRIPTION.

estate contract A contract in which the owner of land agrees to create or convey a legal estate in the land; for example, he may contract to grant a lease or to sell or he may grant a valid option to purchase. The contract confers on the purchaser an equitable interest that is enforceable against third parties if registered. *See* REGISTRATION OF ENCUMBRANCES.

estate duty An obsolete tax formerly levied on the value of property passing on death. *See* INHERITANCE TAX.

estate for years Ownership of land subsisting by reference to a period of time. *See* TERM OF YEARS.

estate owner The owner of a *legal estate in land.

estate *pur* (or *per*) *autre vie* [from Norman French: *autre vie*, other life] An interest in property for the lifetime of someone else. If A is given property for B's life, A is the tenant *pur autre vie* and will hold the property during the lifetime of B (the *cestui que vie*). If A dies before B, the persons entitled under A's will or on his intestacy will take the interest for the remainder of B's life; if B dies before A, A's interest thereupon terminates. The interest is a kind of *life interest and an estate of freehold, i.e. it could be inherited; since 1925 it has been an *equitable interest only.

estate rentcharge *See* RENTCHARGE.

estate subsisting at law *See* LEGAL ESTATE.

estoppel *n.* [from Norman French *estouper*, to stop up] A rule of evidence or a rule of law that prevents a person from denying the truth of a statement he has made or from denying facts that he has alleged to exist. The denial must have been acted upon (probably to his disadvantage) by the person who wishes to take advantage of the estoppel or his position must have been altered as a result. There are several varieties of estoppel. **Estoppel by conduct** (or *in pais*) arises when the party estopped has made a statement or has led the other party to believe in a certain fact. **Estoppel by deed** prevents a person who has executed a deed from saying that the facts stated in the deed are not true. **Estoppel by record** (or *per rem judicatam*) prevents a person from reopening questions that are *res judicata* (i.e. that have been determined against him in a previous legal proceeding). *See also* ISSUE ESTOPPEL.

There are two forms of **equitable estoppel** – promissory and proprietary. The doctrine of **promissory estoppel** applies when one party to a contract promises the other (by words or conduct) that he will not enforce his rights under the contract in whole or in part. Provided that the other party has acted in reliance on that promise, it will, though unsupported by consideration, bind the person making it: he will not be allowed subsequently to sue on the contract. When applicable, the doctrine thus modifies the common-law rules relating to *accord and satisfaction. Under the doctrine of **proprietary estoppel**, the courts can grant a discretionary remedy in circumstances where an owner of land has implicitly or explicitly led another to act detrimentally in the belief that rights in or over land would be acquired. The remedy may take the form of the grant of a *fee simple in the property at one extreme or the grant of a short-term occupational *licence at the other.

estovers *pl. n.* The right to cut timber for certain purposes from land not in one's own absolute ownership. The right arises in favour of a lessee or *tenant for life under a settlement of the land and it can exist as a *profit *à prendre*. Estovers comprise the right to take timber as: (1) **house bote**, for repairing a dwelling or for use as firewood in it; (2) **plough bote**, for repairing farm implements; and (3) **hay bote**, for repairing fences. In each case the lessee or tenant may take only sufficient timber for present needs and not for future requirements. Estovers as profits *à prendre* are usually *appurtenant.

Estrada doctrine The doctrine that *recognition of a government should be based on its *de facto* existence, rather than on its legitimacy. It is named after Don Genero Estrada, the Mexican Secretary of Foreign Affairs who in 1930 ordered that Mexican diplomats should issue no declarations that amounted to a grant of recognition: he felt that this was an insulting practice and offended against the sovereignty of other nations. In 1980 the UK, USA, and many other states adopted the Estrada doctrine. *Compare* TOBAR DOCTRINE.

estreat [from Old French *estrait*] **1.** *n.* an extract from a record relating to *recognizances and fines. **2.** *vb.* To forfeit a recognizance, especially one given by the surety of someone admitted to bail, or to enforce a fine.

ET *See* EMPLOYMENT TRIBUNAL.

ethnic cleansing *See* ETHNIC MINORITY.

ethnic minority A group numerically inferior to the rest of the population of a state whose members are nationals of that state and possess cultural, religious, or linguistic characteristics distinct from those of the total population and show, if only implicitly, a sense of solidarity, directed towards preserving their own social customs, religion, or language. The attempted extirpation of an ethnic minority by the forces of the majority within a state (known as **ethnic cleansing**) can be regarded as a crime against humanity (*see* WAR CRIMES) justifying humanitarian intervention.

ETSI *See* EUROPEAN TELECOMMUNICATIONS STANDARDS INSTITUTE.

EU *See* EUROPEAN UNION.

EU law *See* COMMUNITY LAW.

Euratom *See* EUROPEAN ATOMIC ENERGY COMMUNITY.

euro *See* EUROPEAN MONETARY UNION.

Euro Norm (EN) A European standard adopted by European standards bodies, such as CEN (the European Standardization Committee) and CENELEC (the European Electrotechnical Standardization Committee), in place of a national standard, such as those produced in the UK by the British Standards Institution (BSI).

European Atomic Energy Community (Euratom) The organization set up under the Treaty of Rome (1957) by the six members of the *European Coal and Steel Community and effective from 1 January 1958. Euratom was formed to create the technical and industrial conditions necessary to establish the nuclear industries and direct them to peaceful use to obtain a single energy market. *See* EUROPEAN COMMUNITY.

European Bank for Reconstruction and Development (EBRD) An intergovernmental bank set up in 1990 to provide loans for industrial and commercial projects in the countries of central and eastern Europe. Membership includes all the countries of the European Union and the Organization for Economic Cooperation and Development, as well as the central and eastern European countries. The EU provided 51% of the initial capital. The bank's headquarters are in London.

European Central Bank (ECB) A central bank of the *European Union to which member states who have adopted *European Monetary Union (EMU) are committed by the *Maastricht Treaty. The ECB was set up in 1998 and became active in 1999, as the governor of economic and monetary policy throughout the Union. It works closely with the central banks of the states participating in EMU.

European Coal and Steel Community (ECSC) The first of the European Communities, established by the *Paris Treaty (1951) and effective from 1952. The ECSC created a common market in coal, steel, iron ore, and scrap between the member states, and it coordinates policies of the member states in these fields. The original members were Belgium, France, West Germany, Italy, Luxembourg, and the Netherlands. These six countries, in 1957, signed the *Treaty of Rome setting up the European Economic Community. *See* EUROPEAN COMMUNITY.

European Commission (Commission of the European Communities) An organ of the European Union formed in 1967, having both executive and legislative functions. It is composed of 20 **Commissioners**, who must be nationals of member states and are appointed by member states by mutual agreement (two Commissioners each from the five largest member states – France, Germany, Italy,

Spain, and the UK; one each from the remaining members); their appointment must be approved by the *European Parliament. Each Commissioner assumes responsibility for a particular field of activity and oversees the department (**Directorate General**) devoted to that field (see Appendix II). Once appointed, the Commissioners must act in the interests of the EU; they are not to be regarded as representatives of their countries and must not seek or take instructions from any government or other body. Each Commissioner is appointed for a (renewable) four-year period. The Commission's executive functions include administration of Community funds and ensuring that Community law is enforced (*see* EUROPEAN COURT OF JUSTICE). Its legislative functions consist primarily of submitting proposals for legislation to the *Council of the European Union, in some cases on the orders of the Council and in others on its own initiative (*see also* EUROPEAN PARLIAMENT). It also has legislative powers of its own, partly under the Treaty of Rome and partly by virtue of delegation by the Council, but only on a limited range of subjects (*see* COMMUNITY LEGISLATION).

European Community (EC) An economic and political association of European states that originated as the **European Economic Community (EEC)**. It was created by the *Treaty of Rome in 1957 with the broad object of furthering economic development within the Community by the establishment of a **Common Market** and the approximation of the economic policies of member states. Its more detailed aims included eliminating customs duties internally and adopting a common customs tariff externally, the following by member states of common policies on agriculture and transport, promoting the free movement of labour and capital between member states, and outlawing within the Community all practices leading to the distortion of competition (*see* ARTICLE 81). Two of its institutions, the *European Parliament and the *European Court of Justice, were shared with the *European Coal and Steel Community (established in 1951) and the *European Atomic Energy Community (Euratom; established in 1957); the separate executive and legislative bodies of these three **European Communities** were merged in 1967 (*see* EUROPEAN COMMISSION; COUNCIL OF THE EUROPEAN UNION).

The *Single European Act 1986, given effect in the UK by the European Communities (Amendment) Act 1986, contains provisions designed to make "concrete progress" towards European unity, including measures to establish a *Single Market for the free movement of goods, services, capital, and persons within the Community: the Single Market came into operation on 1 January 1993. In February 1992 the member states signed the Treaty on European Union (*see* MAASTRICHT TREATY). This amended the founding treaties of the Communities by establishing a *European Union based upon the three Communities; renamed the EEC the European Community; and introduced new policy areas with the aim of creating closer economic, political, and monetary union between member states. The Treaty came into force on 1 November 1993; it was amended by the *Amsterdam Treaty.

The original members of the EC were Belgium, France, Germany, Italy, Luxembourg, and the Netherlands. The UK, the Republic of Ireland, and Denmark joined in 1972, Greece in 1981, and Spain and Portugal in 1986, and Austria, Sweden, and Finland in 1995 (in 1994 Norway voted by referendum not to join). The changes in UK law necessary as a result of her joining were made by the European Communities Act 1972.

European Community Treaty *See* TREATY OF ROME.

European company A proposed type of company to be incorporated under European *Community law rather than under the national law of a member state. European companies would be recognized by all member states and would facilitate mergers between two or more limited companies each incorporated under the national law of a member state.

European Convention on Human Rights A convention, originally formulated in 1950, aimed at protecting the *human rights of all people in the member states of the Council of Europe. Part 1 of the Convention, together with a number of subsequent protocols, define the freedoms that each signatory state must guarantee to all within its jurisdiction, although states may derogate from the Convention in respect of particular activities (*see* DEROGATION). The Convention established a **Commission on Human Rights** and a **Court of Human Rights** in Strasbourg. The Commission may hear complaints (known as **petitions**) by one state against another. It may also hear complaints by an individual, group, or nongovernmental organization claiming to be a victim of a breach of the Convention, provided that the state against which the complaint has been made declares that it recognizes the authority of the Commission to receive such petitions. The Commission cannot deal with any complaint, however, unless the applicant has first tried all possible remedies in the national courts (in England he must usually first appeal to the House of Lords). All complaints must be made not later than six months from the date on which the final decision against the applicant was made in the national courts. The Commission will only investigate a complaint if it is judged to fulfil various conditions that make it admissible. If the Commission thinks there has been a breach of the Convention, it places itself at the disposal of the parties in an attempt to achieve a friendly settlement. If this fails, the Commission sends a report on the case to the Committee of Ministers of the Council of Europe. The case may then be brought before the Court within three months by either the Commission or one of the states concerned (an individual victim cannot take the matter to the Court himself). No case can be brought before the Court, however, unless the state against which the complaint is made has accepted the Court's jurisdiction. The Court then has power to make a final ruling, which is binding on the parties, and in some cases to award compensation. If the matter is not taken to the Court, a decision is made instead by the Committee of Ministers.

The Convention has established a considerable body of jurisprudence. As of 2 October 2000 the Convention and its terms were transformed into English law as the *Human Rights Act 1998.

European Convention on State Immunity An international convention of 1972 setting out when and how member states of the European Community (now the European Union) may sue or be sued (by other states or by individuals). It is in force only in those EU states that have signed up to the convention. *See also* IMMUNITY.

European Council A body consisting of the heads of government of the member states of the European Union. It is not a formal organ of the EU (*compare* COUNCIL OF THE EUROPEAN UNION), but meets three times a year to consider major developments of policy. It inspired, for example, the *European Monetary System.

European Court of Human Rights *See* EUROPEAN CONVENTION ON HUMAN RIGHTS.

European Court of Justice (ECJ, Court of Justice of the European Communities) An institution of the European Union that has three primary judicial responsibilities. It interprets the treaties establishing the European Community; it decides upon the validity and the meaning of *Community legislation; and it determines whether any act or omission by the European Commission, the Council of the European Union, or any member state constitutes a breach of *Community law.

The Court sits at Luxembourg. It consists of 15 judges appointed by the member states by mutual agreement and assisted by six *Advocates General. Proceedings before the Court involve written and oral submissions by the parties concerned. Proceedings against the Commission or the Council may be brought by the other of these two bodies, by any member state, or by individual persons; proceedings to challenge the validity of legislative or other action by either Commission or Council are known as proceedings for **annulment**. Proceedings against a member state may be brought by the Commission, the Council, or any other member state. Appeals from the *Court of First Instance go to the ECJ. The decisions of the Court are binding and there is no appeal against them.

The Court also has power, at the request of a court of any member state, to give a preliminary ruling on any point of Community law on which that court requires clarification.

European Currency Unit *See* ECU.

European Economic Area (EEA) A free-trade area encompassing the 15 member states of the *European Union and the member states (excluding Switzerland) of the *European Free Trade Association (EFTA), i.e. Norway, Iceland, and (from 1 May 1995) Liechtenstein. The EEA Agreement, which contains many provisions similar to the *Treaty of Rome, was signed in 1992 and came into force on 1 January 1994. The EEA has its own institutions, such as the EFTA Court of Justice and the EFTA Surveillance Authority (ESA), and many of the EU *Single Market directives and other legislative measures apply within it, although it does not have a budget.

European Economic Community *See* EUROPEAN COMMUNITY.

European Free Trade Association (EFTA) A trade association formed in 1960 between Austria, Denmark, Norway, Portugal, Sweden, Switzerland, and the UK. Finland, Iceland, and Liechtenstein joined later. The UK, Denmark, Portugal, Austria, Finland, and Sweden left on joining the *European Union (or its earlier communities). EFTA is a looser association than the EU, dealing only with trade barriers rather than generally coordinating economic policy. EFTA is governed by a council in which each member has one vote; decisions must normally be unanimous and are binding on all member countries. EFTA has bilateral agreements with the EU. All tariffs between EFTA and EU countries were abolished finally in 1984 and a free-trade area now exists between EU and EFTA member states (*see* EUROPEAN ECONOMIC AREA).

European Monetary System (EMS) A financial system formed in March 1979 to develop closer cooperation in monetary policy among members of the European Community in advance of the liberalization of capital. It included the *Exchange Rate Mechanism (ERM) to stabilize exchange rates between member states as a precursor to *European Monetary Union. Directive 88/361 removed restrictions on the movement of capital between people resident in the member states. Article 102A of the Single European Act 1986 inserted a new Article (now called Article 98) into the Treaty of Rome to refer to the EMS. The UK has been a party to the EMS since its inception and participated in the ERM from 1990 to 1992.

European Monetary Union (EMU) The establishment of a common currency for member states of the European Union. The *Maastricht Treaty specified three stages for achieving EMU, starting with participation in the *Exchange Rate Mechanism. The second stage created the European Monetary Institute, which coordinated the economic and monetary policy of member states. The third stage, achieved by January 1999, locked member states into a fixed exchange rate, activated the

*European Central Bank, and introduced the single currency, the **euro** (divided into 100 cents), for all noncash transactions (national currencies continued in use for cash transactions). From 2002 euro notes and coins will be in circulation in those states within the system (i.e. all member states except the UK, Denmark, and Sweden) and national currencies of those states will cease to be legal tender.

European Parliament An institution of the EU, formerly called the **Assembly of the European Communities**. Members of the European Parliament (**MEPs**) are drawn from member states of the EU but group themselves politically rather than nationally. There are 626 seats of which the UK has 87. In the case of the UK, MEPs are elected under the European Assembly Elections Act 1978 for constituencies comprising two or more UK parliamentary constituencies.

The European Parliament's power and influence derive chiefly from its power to amend, and subsequently to adopt or reject, the EU's budget. The Parliament is consulted by the *Council of the European Union on legislative proposals put to the Council by the *European Commission; it gives opinions on these after debating reports from specialist committees, but these opinions are not binding. However, its powers in the legislative process were extended under the Single European Act 1986 and the Maastricht Treaty by the introduction of the *cooperation, *codecision, and *assent procedures. The Parliament may also put questions to the Council and the Commission and, by a motion of censure requiring a special majority, can force the resignation of the whole Commission (but not of individual Commissioners). Under the Maastricht Treaty it can now veto the appointment of a new Commission.

The European Parliament holds its sessions in Strasbourg, but its Secretariat-General is in Luxembourg and its committees meet in Brussels. The elected Parliament serves a term of five years, after which elections are held.

European Telecommunications Standards Institute (ETSI) The organization that sets standards for the telecommunications industry throughout Europe. Established in 1988, it is made up of representatives of the telecommunications industry.

European Union (EU) The 15 nations (Belgium, Denmark, France, Germany, Greece, Ireland, Italy, Luxembourg, the Netherlands, Portugal, Spain, the UK, Austria, Finland, and Sweden) that have joined together to form an economic community with common monetary, political, and social aspirations. The EU came into being on 1 November 1993 according to the terms of the *Maastricht Treaty. It comprises the three European Communities (*see* EUROPEAN COMMUNITY), extended by the adoption of a common foreign and security policy (CFSP), which requires cooperation between member states in foreign policy and security, and cooperation in justice and home affairs.

European Works Council (EWC) A council, set up by a special negotiating body, consisting of both employee and management representatives established at European level for the purpose of informing and consulting with employees. The requirement to set up such councils originated from the European Works Council Directive. The Directive was implemented by the UK through the Transnational Information and Consultation of Employees Regulations 1999, which came into force in January 2000. The Regulations apply to undertakings or groups with at least 1000 employees across member states and at least 150 employees in each of two or more of those member states. The Regulations set out the procedures for negotiating an EWC agreement, the enforcement mechanisms, provisions on confidentiality, and statutory protections for employees who are members of such a group when asserting their rights or performing duties under the Regulations. Disputes over procedural matters in setting up an EWC are heard by the *Central Arbitration Committee. Complaints of a failure to establish an EWC, or a failure to operate the system properly once set up, are heard by the *Employment Appeal Tribunal. Employment protection disputes with respect to individual employees go to an *employment tribunal.

eurotort *n.* A directly effective rule of European Community law (*see* COMMUNITY LEGISLATION), breach of which gives the person injured a remedy in British courts in the form of an action in tort. *See also* COMMUNITY LAW.

eviction *n.* The removal of a tenant or any other occupier from occupation. Under the Protection from Eviction Act 1977 the eviction of a *residential occupier, other than by proceedings in the court, is a criminal offence. It is also an offence to harass a residential occupier to try to persuade him to leave (*see* HARASSMENT OF OCCUPIER). Note that it has recently been confirmed that if it is possible for a mortgagee to recover possession peaceably, no court order is necessary. Many tenants have statutory protection and the landlord must prove to a court that he has appropriate grounds for possession. Under the Housing Act 1988 a tenant may claim damages for unlawful eviction. *See also* AGRICULTURAL HOLDING; ASSURED SHORTHOLD TENANCY; ASSURED TENANCY; BUSINESS TENANCY; LONG TENANCY; PROTECTED TENANCY; SECURE TENANCY; RESTRICTED CONTRACT; TRESPASS.
    The Protection from Harassment Act 1997 allows the court to impose a restraining order against a tenant who is harassing a neighbour, which might require the harasser to be evicted (*see* NUISANCE NEIGHBOURS).

evidence *n.* That which tends to prove the existence or nonexistence of some fact. It may consist of *testimony, *documentary evidence, *real evidence, and, when admissible, *hearsay evidence. The law of evidence comprises all the rules governing the presentation of facts and proof in proceedings before a court, including in particular the rules governing the *admissibility of evidence and the *exclusionary rules. *See also* CIRCUMSTANTIAL EVIDENCE; CONCLUSIVE EVIDENCE; DIRECT EVIDENCE; EXTRINSIC EVIDENCE; PRIMARY EVIDENCE; SECONDARY EVIDENCE; VIDEO EVIDENCE.

evidenced in writing *See* UNENFORCEABLE CONTRACT.

evidence in rebuttal Evidence offered to counteract (**rebut**) other evidence in a case. There are some restrictions on the admissibility of evidence in rebuttal, for example if it relates to a collateral question, such as the *credit of a witness.

evidence obtained illegally Evidence obtained by some means contrary to law. At common law, if evidence was obtained illegally (e.g. as a result of a search of premises without a search warrant), it was not inadmissible but the court might exclude it as a matter of discretion. The Police and Criminal Evidence Act 1984 provides that the court may refuse to allow evidence on which the prosecution proposes to rely if the admission of the evidence would have such an adverse effect on the fairness of the proceedings that the court ought not to admit it. The *Human Rights Act 1998 and the cases now being decided under its provisions have left the previous law in some doubt. *See also* CONFESSION.

evidence of character *See* CHARACTER.

evidence of disposition *See* DISPOSITION.

evidence of identity That which tends to prove the identity of a person. A person's identity may be proved by *direct evidence (even though it may involve an expression of *opinion) or by *circumstantial evidence. *Secondary evidence of an out-of-court identification by a witness (e.g. that he picked the accused out of an identification parade) may also be given to confirm the witness's testimony. In criminal cases, if the evidence of identity is wholly or mainly based on visual identification the jury must be specially warned of the danger of accepting the evidence; any *corroboration must be pointed out to them by the judge. In criminal cases this issue must be dealt with under the detailed provisions of the appropriate Code of Practice under the Police and Criminal Evidence Act 1984. Failure to follow this procedure and its accompanying safeguards will render the evidence of identity inadmissible. *See also* DNA FINGERPRINTING.

evidence of opinion *See* OPINION EVIDENCE.

evidence of user Evidence of the manner in which the parties to a contract have acted. In a limited number of circumstances, evidence of user is admissible to assist the court in resolving a dispute between the parties as to their precise obligations. It may, for example, help to clarify an ambiguity in the wording of the contract or an allegation that written terms have been varied by oral agreement.

EWC *See* EUROPEAN WORKS COUNCIL.

ex aequo et bono [Latin] As a result of fair dealing and good conscience, i.e. on the basis of *equity. The phrase refers to the way in which an international tribunal can base its decision not upon conventional law but on what is just and fair to the parties before it. Article 38(2) of the Statute of the International Court of Justice specifically authorizes settlement of disputes based upon *ex aequo et bono* should both parties give their consent, although the Court has not yet given any judgment on this basis.

examination *n.* The questioning of a witness on oath or affirmation. In court, a witness is subject to *examination-in-chief, *cross-examination, and *re-examination. In some circumstances a witness may be examined prior to the court hearing (*see* COMMISSION).

examination-in-chief (direct examination) The questioning of a witness by the party who called him to give evidence. *Leading questions may not be asked, except on matters that are introductory to the witness's evidence or are not in dispute or (with permission of the judge) when the witness is *hostile. The purpose of examination-in-chief is to elicit facts favourable to the case of the party conducting the examination. It is followed by a *cross-examination by the opposing party.

examined copy *See* ABSTRACT OF TITLE.

examining justices Justices of the peace sitting upon a preliminary inquiry into whether or not there is sufficient evidence to commit an accused person from the magistrates' court to the Crown Court for trial on indictment.

excepted perils Risks expressly excluded from the cover given by an insurance policy.

exchange of contracts The point at which a purchaser of land exchanges a copy of the sale contract signed by him for an identical copy signed by the vendor. At that point the contract becomes legally binding on both parties and the purchaser acquires an *equitable interest in the land.

exchange of medical reports The exchange of medical reports in personal injury actions in the hope that they can be agreed before the hearing of the case, thus saving time and expense. The exchange of reports that are intended to be relied on at the hearing is compulsory, unless the court's permission not to disclose is obtained. The court also has power to order disclosure of medical reports by persons not party to the proceedings, such as a hospital authority.

Exchange Rate Mechanism (ERM) A component of the *European Monetary System under which the central banks of participating countries could not allow their currencies to fluctuate more than a certain percentage above (the ceiling rate) or below (minimum rate) a central rate, which was set in *ECUs. The system was intended as a precursor to full *European Monetary Union (EMU). The ERM linked currencies with the aim of ensuring their stability. From 1999, states wishing to participate join **ERM II**, which is based on the euro and supervised by the *European Central Bank.

Exchequer *n.* The department within Government that receives and controls the national revenue. *See* CHANCELLOR OF THE EXCHEQUER; COURT OF EXCHEQUER.

excise duty A charge or toll payable on certain goods produced and consumed within the UK. Payments for licences, e.g. for the sale of spirits, are also classed as excise duty. *Compare* CUSTOMS DUTY.

exclusion and restriction of contractual liability *See* EXEMPTION CLAUSE.

exclusion and restriction of negligence liability The Unfair Contract Terms Act 1977 provides that a person cannot exclude or restrict his *business liability for death or injury resulting from negligence. Nor can he exclude or restrict his liability for other loss or damage arising from negligence, unless any contract term or notice by which he seeks to do so satisfies the requirement of reasonableness (as defined in detail in the Act). For the purposes of this provision, negligence means the breach of any contractual or common-law duty to take reasonable care or exercise reasonable skill or of the *common duty of care imposed by the Occupiers' Liability Acts 1957 and 1984. There are similar provisions in relation to consumer contracts in the Unfair Terms in Consumer Contracts Regulations 1999.

exclusionary rules Rules in the law of evidence prohibiting the proof of certain facts or the proof of facts in particular ways. Although all irrelevant evidence must be excluded, the rules are usually restricted to relevant evidence, e.g. the rule against *hearsay evidence. Exclusionary rules may be justified in various ways; for example, by the desirability of excluding material that is of little evidentiary weight or may be unfairly prejudicial to an accused person.

exclusion order An order of the Secretary of State under the Prevention of Terrorism (Temporary Provisions) Act 1989 (now repealed) excluding a named person from Great Britain, Northern Ireland, or the UK in order to prevent terrorist acts aimed at influencing policy or opinion concerning Northern Ireland. *See also* TERRORISM.

exclusion requirement A requirement in an *emergency protection order or an interim care order that a person who is suspected of having abused a child is excluded from the child's home. A *power of arrest may be attached to the order.

exclusive economic zone (EEZ) A zone defined by Articles 55–75 of the UN Convention on the Law of the Sea as comprising that area of sea adjacent to a coastal state not exceeding 200 miles from the *baseline of the territorial sea. The state shall have sovereign rights over the zone for the purpose of exploring and exploiting, conserving, and managing the living and nonliving resources of the sea, seabed, and subsoil within it. *See also* HIGH SEAS; LAW OF THE SEA; TERRITORIAL WATERS.

exclusive jurisdiction 1. That part of the jurisdiction of the *Court of Chancery that belonged to the Chancery alone. The jurisdiction ceased after the Judicature

Acts 1873–75, but the matters under exclusive jurisdiction (e.g. trusts, administration of estates) are now dealt with in the Chancery Division. *Compare* CONCURRENT JURISDICTION. **2.** A clause in a commercial agreement providing that only the English, Scottish, or other courts will be entitled to determine disputes between the parties. Normally agreements provide that the parties agree to submit to either the exclusive or the nonexclusive jurisdiction of particular courts. If no such clause is included, international conventions, such as the Brussels and Lugano conventions, determine which courts have jurisdiction. EU regulation 44/2001 contains provisions in this area applicable from January 2001. In particular, customers are given a right to bring proceedings in their home state.

excusable homicide The killing of a human being that results in no criminal liability, either because it took place in lawful *self-defence or by misadventure (an accident not involving gross negligence).

ex debito justitiae [Latin] As a matter of right. The phrase is applied to remedies that the court is bound to give when they are claimed, as distinct from those that it has discretion to grant.

executed *adj.* Completed. A contract that has been carried out by both parties is said to have been executed, and *consideration that has been actually given for a contract is described as **executed consideration**. *See also* EXECUTED TRUST. *Compare* EXECUTORY.

executed trust (completely constituted trust, perfect trust) A trust that is complete and enforceable by the beneficiaries without further acts by the settlor. *Compare* EXECUTORY TRUST.

execution *n.* **1.** The process of carrying out a sentence of death imposed by a court. *See also* CAPITAL PUNISHMENT. **2.** The enforcement of the rights of a judgment creditor (*see also* ENFORCEMENT OF JUDGMENT). The term is often used to mean the recovery of a debt only, especially by seizure of goods belonging to the debtor under a writ of *fieri facias or a warrant of execution. In the case of property not subject to ordinary forms of execution, e.g. an interest under a trust, judgment is enforced by means of *equitable execution. **3.** The completion of the formalities necessary for a written document to become legally valid. In the case of a *deed, for example, this comprises the signing and delivery of the document. *See also* EXECUTION OF WILL.

execution of will The process by which a testator's will is made legally valid. Under the Wills Act 1837 the will must be signed at the end by the testator or by someone authorized by him, and the signature must be made or acknowledged (*see* ACKNOWLEDGMENT) by the testator in the presence of at least two witnesses, present at the same time, who must themselves sign the will or acknowledge their signatures in the testator's presence. A will witnessed by a beneficiary or the beneficiary's spouse is not void, but the gift to that beneficiary or spouse is void.

executive agency An independent agency, operating under a chief executive, that is responsible for delivering a service according to the policy of a central government department. Examples are the Benefits Agency and the Passport Agency. The intention is that central government should become purely policy-making, the services it is responsible for being delivered by executive agencies.

executor *n.* A person appointed by a will to administer the testator's estate. A deceased person's property is vested in his executors, who are empowered to deal with it as directed by the will from the time of the testator's death. They must, however, usually obtain a grant of *probate from the court in order to prove the will and their right to deal with the estate. Appointment as an executor confers only the power to deal with the deceased's property in accordance with his will, and not beneficial ownership, although an executor may also be a beneficiary under the will. *Compare* ADMINISTRATOR.

executor *de son tort* [French: by his own wrongdoing] A person who deals (intermeddles) with a deceased person's assets without the authority of the rightful personal representatives or of the court. He is answerable to the rightful personal representatives and to the creditors of the estate for any acts done without such authority and for any assets of the estate that come into his hands.

executor's year The period of a year, starting from the death of the deceased, within which nobody can compel his personal representatives to distribute the estate, even if the testator has directed payment of a legacy before the expiry of that period (Administration of Estates Act 1925).

executory *adj.* Remaining to be done. A contract that has yet to be carried out is said to be an **executory contract**, and *consideration that has still to be given for a contract is described as **executory consideration**. *See also* EXECUTORY INTEREST; EXECUTORY TRUST. *Compare* EXECUTED.

executory interest (mainly historical) An interest in property that arises or passes to a particular person on the occurrence of a specified event. For example, when property is settled in trust "for A, but for B if he marries Mary", then B has an executory interest. Under the Law of Property Act 1925 executory interests in land can only exist as equitable interests. *Compare* REMAINDER; REVERSION.

executory trust (imperfect trust, incompletely constituted trust) A trust that is incomplete, i.e. one that the beneficiaries are unable to enforce until some further act is done by the settlor or a third party. *Compare* EXECUTED TRUST.

exemplary damages (punitive damages, vindictive damages) Damages given to punish the defendant rather than (or as well as) to compensate the claimant for harm done. Such damages are exceptional in tort, since the general rule is that damages are given only to compensate for loss caused. They can be awarded in some tort actions: (1) when expressly authorized by statute; (2) to punish oppressive, arbitrary, or unconstitutional acts by government servants; (3) when the defendant has deliberately calculated that the profits to be made out of committing a tort (e.g. by publishing a defamatory book) may exceed the damages at risk. In such cases, exemplary damages are given to prove that "tort does not pay". Exemplary damages cannot be given for breach of contract.

exemption clause A term in a contract purporting to exclude or restrict the liability of one of the parties in specified circumstances. The courts do not regard exemption clauses with favour. If such a clause is ambiguous, they will interpret it narrowly rather than widely. If an exclusion or restriction is not recited in a formal contract but is specified or referred to in an informal document, such as a ticket or a notice displayed in a hotel, it will not even be treated as a term of the contract (unless reasonable steps were taken to bring it to the notice of the person affected at the time of contracting). The Unfair Contract Terms Act 1977 and Unfair Terms in Consumer Contracts Regulations 1999 contain complex provisions limiting the extent to which a person can exclude or restrict his *business liability towards consumers. In addition, the 1977 Act subjects certain types of exemption clause to a test of reasonableness, even in a business-to-business transaction. The Office of Fair Trading runs an unfair terms unit to monitor such clauses and enforce the 1999 Regulations. Other statutes forbidding the exclusion or restriction of particular forms of liability are the Defective Premises Act 1972, the Consumer Protection Act 1987, and the Road Traffic Act 1988. *See also* EXCLUSION AND RESTRICTION OF NEGLIGENCE LIABILITY; INTERNATIONAL SUPPLY CONTRACT.

exempt supply A supply that is outside the scope of *value-added tax. Examples include sales of land, the supply of certain financial and insurance services, and the services performed in the course of employment. *See also* ZERO-RATED SUPPLY.

exequatur *n.* A certificate issued by a host state that admits and accords recognition to the official status of a *consul, authorizing him to carry out consular functions in that country. The sending state grants the consular official a commission or patent, which authorizes the consul to represent his state's interests within the host state.

ex gratia [Latin] Done as a matter of favour. An *ex gratia* payment is one not required to be made by a legal duty.

exhaustion of local remedies The rule of customary international law that when an *alien has been wronged, all municipal remedies available to the injured party in the host country must have been pursued before the alien appeals to his own government to intervene on his behalf. This is a customary precondition to any *espousal of claim by a state on behalf of a national based upon foreign soil.

exhaustion of rights A free-trade principle which holds that, once goods are put on the market, owners of *intellectual property rights in those goods, who made the goods or allowed others to do so under their rights, may not use national intellectual property rights to prevent an import or export of the goods. Within the EU these rules derive from Articles 28–30 (formerly 30–36) of the Treaty of Rome. *See also* FREE MOVEMENT.

exhibit 1. *n.* A physical object or document produced in a court, shown to a witness who is giving evidence, or referred to in an *affidavit. Exhibits are marked with an identifying number, and in jury trials the jury is normally permitted to take exhibits with them when they retire to consider their verdict. Physical objects produced for the inspection of the court (e.g. a murder weapon) are referred to as *real evidence. **2.** *vb.* To refer to an object or document in an *affidavit.

ex nudo pacto non oritur actio *See* CONSIDERATION.

ex officio [Latin] By virtue of holding an office. Thus, the Lord Chief Justice is *ex officio* a member of the Court of Appeal.

ex officio information A criminal information laid by the Attorney General on behalf of the Crown. It was abolished in 1967. *See* LAYING AN INFORMATION.

ex officio magistrate A magistrate by virtue of holding some other office, usually that of mayor of a city or borough. Most *ex officio* magistrateships were abolished by the Justices of the Peace Act 1968 and the Administration of Justice Act 1973, but High Court judges are justices of the peace *ex officio* for the whole of England and Wales and the Lord Mayor and aldermen are justices *ex officio* for the City of London.

ex parte [Latin] **1.** On the part of one side only. Since the introduction of the *Civil Procedure Rules in 1999, this phrase is no longer used in civil proceedings, having been replaced by **without notice**. *See* WITHOUT NOTICE APPLICATION. **2.** On behalf of. This term is used in the headings of law reports together with the name of the person making the application to the court in the case in question.

expatriation *n.* A person's voluntary action of living outside his native country, either permanently or during his employment abroad, whereby he renounces or loses allegiance to his former state of nationality. *Compare* DEPORTATION.

expectant heir A person who has an interest in remainder or in reversion in property or a chance of succeeding to it (interest in expectancy). An unconscionable contract with an expectant heir (e.g. in which he sells his inheritance at an undervalue in order to raise cash) may be set aside by the court.

expert opinion *See* OPINION EVIDENCE.

Expiring Laws Continuance Acts Statutes formerly passed annually to continue in force for a further year a number of miscellaneous Acts that were originally stated to remain in force for one year only. The renewal of temporary statutes is now effected individually.

explosive *n.* Any substance made in order to achieve an explosion that causes damage or destruction or intended to be used in that way by a person who possesses it. If someone committing *burglary has an explosive with him, he is guilty of aggravated burglary, punishable with a maximum of life imprisonment. The Explosive Substances Act 1883 creates special offences of (1) causing an explosion that is likely to endanger life or cause serious damage to property (even if no harm or damage is actually done); (2) attempting to cause such an explosion; and (3) making or possessing an explosive with the intention of using it to endanger life or to seriously damage property. Under the Offences Against the Person Act 1861, it is an offence to injure anyone by means of an explosion, to send or deliver an explosive to anyone, or to place an explosive near a building, ship, or boat with the intention of causing physical injury. These crimes cover most acts of *terrorism.

export bans *Anticompetitive practices that have the effect of banning the resale of products from one EU territory in another state of the EU. Export bans have long been held to infringe the competition rules in *Article 81 of the Treaty of Rome; they can lead the European Commission to levy fines of up to 10% of annual worldwide group turnover. Examples of practices that infringe the rules include clauses in contracts banning exports; an export ban in a written contract will be void when Article 81 applies. However, when the *vertical agreements regulation 2790/99 applies it is permitted to restrict an exclusive distributor from actively soliciting sales outside its territory. It is not permissible to prevent a distributor from advertising on a website as this is regarded as 'passive' rather than 'active' selling. In addition, practices that have the effect of bolstering or imposing an export ban are forbidden, including buying up all *parallel imports, marking products solely for the purposes of tracing them to stop parallel importation, and sending faxes to, or otherwise putting pressure on, dealers not to engage in parallel importation.

ex post facto [Latin: by a subsequent act] Describing any legal act, such as a statute, that has retrospective effect.

expressio unius est exclusio alterius *See* INTERPRETATION OF STATUTES.

express term A provision of a contract, agreed to by the parties, that is either written or spoken. Such a provision may be classified as a *condition, a *warranty, or an *innominate term. *Compare* IMPLIED TERM.

express trust A trust created expressly by the settlor, i.e. by stating directly his intention to create a trust. There is no need for formal words provided that the intention to create a trust is clear from the documents or from the oral statements of the settlor, but most express trusts are contained in documents that have been professionally drafted. *Compare* IMPLIED TRUST.

expropriation *n.* The taking by the state of private property for public purposes, normally without compensation (*compare* COMPULSORY PURCHASE, which carries with it a right to compensation). The right to expropriate is known in some legal systems as the right of **eminent domain**. In the UK, expropriation requires statutory authority except in time of war or apprehended war (*see* ROYAL PREROGATIVE).

ex proprio motu (ex mero motu) [Latin: of his own motion] Describing acts that a court may perform on its own initiative and without any application by the parties.

expulsion *n.* The termination by a state of an alien's legal entry and right to remain. This is often based upon the ground that the alien is considered undesirable or a threat to the state. *Compare* DEPORTATION.

extended sentence A sentence longer than the maximum prescribed for a particular offence, which was formerly imposed on persistent offenders under certain circumstances. The power to impose extended sentences was abolished by the Criminal Justice Act 1991.

extinguishment *n.* The cessation or cancellation of some right or interest. For example, an *easement is extinguished if the dominant and servient tenements come into the same ownership. Mere *non-user of an easement, however, will not cause it to be extinguished unless an intention to abandon it can be shown.

extortion *n.* A common-law offence committed by a public officer who uses his position to take money or any other benefit that is not due to him. If he obtains the benefit by means of menaces, this may also amount to blackmail.

extradition *n.* The surrender by one state to another of a person accused of committing an offence in the latter. Extradition from the UK relates to surrender to foreign states (*compare* FUGITIVE OFFENDER) and is governed by the Extradition Act 1989. There must be an *extradition treaty between the UK and the state requiring the surrender. The offence alleged must be a crime in the UK as well as in the requesting state, it must be both covered by the treaty and within the list of extraditable offences contained in the Act itself, and it must not be of a political character. *See also* DOUBLE CRIMINALITY.

extradition treaty A treaty under the terms of which a state agrees to deport a fugitive criminal (or suspect) to the state where the offence was committed or to the fugitive's state of nationality (*see* EXTRADITION). In the latter case the crime in question must be one that is a breach of the municipal law of the national committed outside the territorial boundaries of the state of which he is a citizen. Extradition treaties are bilateral in character and there is a lack of uniformity in their provisions and in their interpretation. However, they invariably contain the following three features: (1) the state that has custody will not surrender the fugitive unless *prima facie* evidence of his guilt is submitted to them; (2) no political offenders will be surrendered; (3) no surrender will be made unless adequate assurances are given that the accused will not on that occasion be tried for any offence other than the crime for which he is surrendered.

extrajudicial divorce A divorce granted outside a court of law by a nonjudicial process (such as a *ghet or a *talaq). An extrajudicial divorce will not be recognized in the UK if it takes place in the UK, Channel Islands, or Isle of Man. *See also* OVERSEAS DIVORCE.

extraordinary general meeting Any meeting of company members other than the *annual general meeting (*see also* GENERAL MEETING). Except when the meeting is for the passing of a *special resolution, 14 days' written notice must be given (7 days suffices in the case of an unlimited company). Only *special business can be transacted. Such a meeting can be convened by the directors at their discretion or by company members who either hold not less than 10% of the paid-up voting shares (*see* CALL) or, in companies without a share capital (*see* LIMITED COMPANY; UNLIMITED COMPANY), represent not less than 10% of the voting rights.

extraordinary resolution A decision reached by a majority of not less than 75% of company members voting in person or by proxy at a general meeting. It is appropriate in situations specified by the Companies Act 1985, e.g. *voluntary winding-up. At least 14 days' notice must be given of the intention to propose an extraordinary resolution; if the resolution is to be proposed at the annual general meeting, 21 days' notice is required.

extraterritoriality *n.* A theory in international law explaining *diplomatic immunity on the basis that the premises of a foreign mission form a part of the territory of the sending state. This theory is not accepted in English law (thus a divorce granted in a foreign embassy in England is not obtained outside the British Isles for purposes of the Recognition of Divorces Act 1971). Diplomatic immunity is based either on the theory that the diplomatic mission personifies – and is entitled to the immunities of – the sending state or on the practical necessity of such immunity for the functioning of diplomacy.

extrinsic evidence Evidence of matters not referred to in a document offered in evidence to explain, vary, or contradict its meaning. Its admissibility is governed by the *parol evidence rule.

ex turpi causa non oritur actio [Latin: no action can be based on a disreputable cause] The principle that the courts may refuse to enforce a claim arising out of the claimant's own illegal or immoral conduct or transactions. Hence parties who have knowingly entered into an *illegal contract may not be able to enforce it and a person injured by a fellow-criminal while they are jointly committing a serious crime may not be able to sue for damages for the injury.

F

fact *n.* An event or state of affairs known to have happened or existed. It may be distinguished from law (as in **trier of fact) or, in the law of evidence, from opinion (*see* OPINION EVIDENCE). The **facts in issue** are the main facts that a party carrying the persuasive **burden of proof must establish in order to succeed; in a wider sense they may include subordinate or collateral facts, such as those affecting the **credit of a witness or the **admissibility of evidence. *See also* FACTUM.

factor *n.* An agent entrusted with the possession of goods (or documents of title representing goods) for the purposes of sale. A factor is likely to fall within the definition of a **mercantile agent in the Factors Act 1889 and to have the powers of a mercantile agent. A factor has a **lien over the goods entrusted to him that covers any claims against the principal arising out of the agency.

factum *n.* [Latin] **1.** A **fact or statement of facts. For example, a ***factum probans*** (*pl.* ***facta probantia***) is a fact offered in evidence as proof of another fact, and a ***factum probandum*** (*pl.* ***facta probanda***) is a fact that needs to be proved. **2.** An act or deed. *See also* NON EST FACTUM.

failure to maintain The failure of either spouse to provide reasonable maintenance for the other or to make a proper contribution towards the maintenance of any children of the family during the subsistence of the marriage. Upon proof of such failure, magistrates' courts have jurisdiction to make orders for unsecured periodical payments and for lump-sum orders not exceeding £1000. The divorce county courts and High Court have power to make orders for periodical payment (which may also be secured by a charge on the property of the respondent spouse) and for lump-sum orders (of any sum). It is no longer necessary to prove **wilful neglect to maintain** (i.e. deliberate withholding of maintenance). Under the Child Support Act 1991, application for periodical payments for children can now usually be made directly to the Child Support Agency (*see* CHILD SUPPORT MAINTENANCE) rather than the court.

failure to make disclosure Failure of a party to disclose documents as required by a disclosure direction (*see* DISCLOSURE AND INSPECTION OF DOCUMENTS). This will lead to an application to the court for an order compelling disclosure. The court will most likely consider an **unless order with some sanction for noncompliance, e.g. dismissal of action, striking out of the defence.

fair comment The defence to an action for **defamation that the statement made was fair comment on a matter of public interest. The facts on which the comment is based must be true and the comment must be fair. Any honest expression of opinion, however exaggerated, can be fair comment, but remarks inspired by personal spite and mere abuse are not. The judge decides whether or not the matter is one of public interest. *See also* ROLLED-UP PLEA.

fair dismissal **Dismissal of an employee when a tribunal decides that an employer has acted reasonably in dismissing the employee and that the dismissal was for a lawful reason, i.e. on the grounds of the employee's capability, qualifications, or conduct; redundancy; the fact that it would be illegal to continue employing the employee; or some other sufficient and substantial reason. *Compare* UNFAIR DISMISSAL.

fair rent Rent fixed by a rent officer or rent assessment committee for the holder of a *protected or *statutory tenancy. The rent is registered in relation to the property. When fixing the rent, no account is taken of the scarcity of rented property and therefore the rent is often lower than a market rent. The rent of *assured tenancies is fixed by agreement between the landlord and tenant. The tenant can apply to a *rent assessment committee to determine the rent if the landlord wishes to increase it. The committee must fix the rent at the amount the landlord could obtain on the open market. There is no registration of rent for assured tenancies, but the rents determined by rent assessment committees are recorded and this information is available to the public.

fair trading *See* DIRECTOR GENERAL OF FAIR TRADING.

fair trial A right set out in Article 6 of the European Convention on Human Rights and now part of UK law as a consequence of the *Human Rights Act 1998. The right to a fair trial applies in civil and criminal proceedings and includes the right to a public hearing (subject to some exceptions) by an independent and impartial tribunal established by law. In criminal cases there are the following specified rights: the *presumption of innocence; the right to be told the details of the case; to have time and facilities to prepare a defence and to instruct lawyers (with financial support where necessary); to call witnesses and examine the witnesses for the prosecution; and to have the free assistance of an interpreter. *See also* EQUALITY OF ARMS.

fairway *n.* The mid-channel of a navigable river, extending as near to the shore as there is sufficient depth of water for ordinary navigation.

fair wear and tear A phrase often found in repairing covenants in leases. When a tenant is not obliged to repair fair (reasonable) wear and tear occurring during his tenancy, he must nevertheless do any repairs to prevent consequential damage resulting from the original wear and tear. For example, if a slate blows off a roof the tenant is not liable to repair it, but he ought to prevent the rain entering through the hole and doing more damage.

false accounting An offence, punishable by up to seven years' imprisonment, committed by someone who dishonestly falsifies, destroys, or hides any account or document used in accounting or who uses such a document knowing or suspecting it to be false or misleading. The offence must be committed for the purpose of gain or causing loss to another. There is also a special offence (also punishable by up to seven years' imprisonment) committed by a company director who publishes or allows to be published a written statement he knows or suspects is misleading or false in order to deceive members or creditors of the company. *See also* FORGERY.

false imprisonment Unlawful restriction of a person's freedom of movement, not necessarily in a prison. Any complete deprivation of freedom of movement is sufficient, so false imprisonment includes unlawful arrest and unlawfully preventing a person leaving a room or a shop. The restriction must be total: it is not imprisonment to prevent a person proceeding in one direction if he is free to leave in others. False imprisonment is a form of *trespass to the person, so it is not necessary to prove that it has caused actual damage. It is both a crime and a tort. Damages, which may be *aggravated or *exemplary, can be obtained in tort and the writ of *habeas corpus is available to restore the imprisoned person to liberty.

false plea (sham plea) A statement of case that is obviously frivolous or absurd and is made only for the purpose of vexation or delay. A court may order a statement of case that would adversely affect the fair trial of a case to be struck out or amended.

false pretence The act of misleading someone by a false representation, either by words or conduct. The former offence of obtaining property by false pretences is now known as obtaining property by *deception.

false statement *See* PERJURY.

false trade description A description of goods made in the course of a business that is false in respect of certain facts (*see* TRADE DESCRIPTION). Under the Trade Descriptions Acts 1968 and 1972 it is an offence to apply a false trade description to goods either directly, by implication, or indirectly (e.g. by tampering with a car's mileometer or painting over rust on the bodywork). It is also an offence to supply or offer to supply goods to which a false trade description is attached. These offences are triable either summarily or on indictment (in which case they carry a maximum two years' prison sentence). They are offences of *strict liability, although certain specified defences are allowed (e.g. that the defendant relied on information supplied by someone else). The Acts are supplemented by the Fair Trading Act 1973.

falsification of accounts *See* FALSE ACCOUNTING.

family *n.* A group of people connected by a close relationship. For legal purposes a family is usually limited to relationships by blood, marriage, or adoption, although sometimes (e.g. for social security purposes) statute expressly includes other people, such as common-law wives (*see* COMMON-LAW MARRIAGE). The courts have interpreted the word "family" to include unmarried couples living as husband and wife in permanent and stable relationships. In the past, gay couples have always been excluded from the definition. However, in a recent case the court interpreted the word "family" in the Rent Act 1977 to include the gay partner of a deceased tenant.

family assets Property acquired by one or both parties to a marriage to be used for the benefit of the family as a whole. Typical examples are the *matrimonial home, furniture, and car. There is no special body of law dealing with family assets as such, but the courts have wide discretion to make orders in relation to such assets upon dissolution of the marriage and have developed flexible guidelines to apply in the case of family assets. Thus, one spouse will often acquire a share in the home owned by the other, by reason of his or her contributions to the welfare of the family and its finances.

family assistance order A court order under the Children Act 1989 that a probation officer, or an officer of a local authority, should advise, assist, and befriend a particular child or a person closely connected with the child (such as a parent) in order to provide short-term support for the family. The order can only be made with the consent of the person it concerns (other than the child) and has effect for up to six months.

family credit *See* WORKING FAMILIES TAX CREDIT.

Family Division The division of the *High Court concerned with *family proceedings and noncontentious probate matters. Until 1971, it was known as the *Probate, Divorce and Admiralty Division. It may hear some appeals (*see* APPELLATE JURISDICTION). The chief judge of the Division is called the **President**.

Family Health Services Authority (FHSA) *See* HEALTH AUTHORITY; NATIONAL HEALTH SERVICE.

family life A right set out in Article 8 of the European Convention on Human Rights and now part of UK law as a consequence of the *Human Rights Act 1998. The right to family life extends beyond formal relationships and legitimate arrangements. This right is a *qualified right; as such, the public interest can be used to justify an interference with it providing that this is prescribed by law, designed for a legitimate purpose, and proportionate. Public authorities have a limited but positive duty to protect family life from interference by third parties. The right to found a family (the right to procreation) is contained in Article 12 of the Convention.

family name *See* SURNAME.

family proceedings All court proceedings under the inherent jurisdiction of the High Court that deal with matters relating to the *welfare of children. Before 1989 the court's powers to make orders concerning children varied, depending on the level of the court and the proceedings involved. The Children Act 1989, together with the Family Proceedings Rules 1991, rationalized the court's powers and created a unified structure of the High Court, county courts, and magistrates' courts. The ambit of family proceedings is very wide, including proceedings for *divorce, domestic violence (*see* BATTERED SPOUSE OR COHABITANT), children in care (*see* CARE ORDER), *adoption, and *wardship and applications for a parental order under section 30 of the Human Fertilization and Embryology Act 1990 (*see* SECTION 30 ORDER).

family provision Provision made by the courts out of the estate of a deceased person in favour of his family or *dependants. The court may award a family provision if it is satisfied that the provision made for the applicant either by the deceased person or by the law of intestacy is, in the circumstances, unreasonable.

Farrand Committee A governmental committee set up in 1984 to consider (1) what tests were needed for non-solicitor conveyancers, and what other requirements should be imposed on them to ensure adequate consumer protection; and (2) the scope for simplifying conveyancing practice and procedure in England and Wales. *Licensed conveyancers were created in response to the committee's recommendations on (1), and the Conveyancing Standing Committee was set up to advise the Law Commission on (2).

fast track The track to which a civil case is allocated when the amount claimed exceeds £5000 but is less than £15,000 (*see* ALLOCATION). The fast track provides a streamlined procedure in order to ensure that any legal and other costs remain proportionate to the amount claimed. It achieves this through the use of standard directions by the court, a fixed timetable of about 30 weeks between directions and trial, a trial of one day only, no oral expert evidence to be used in trial, and costs being fixed dependent on the level of advocacy used.

fatal accidents Formerly, at common law, the death of either party extinguished the right to bring an action in tort. In addition, a person who caused death was not liable to compensate the deceased's relatives and others who suffered loss because of the death. Both rules have now been abolished by statute.

By the Law Reform (Miscellaneous Provisions) Act 1934, a right of action by (or against) a deceased person survives his death and can be brought for the benefit of (or against) his estate. Thus if a person is killed in a motor accident due to the negligence of the driver, an action can be brought against the driver in the name of the deceased; any damages obtained become part of the deceased's estate. Actions for defamation of a deceased person and claims for certain types of loss are excluded from the Act and do not survive death.

The Fatal Accidents Act 1976, amended by the Administration of Justice Act 1982, confers the right to recover damages for loss of support on the dependants of a person who has been killed in an accident, if the deceased would have been able to recover damages for injury but for his death. The class of dependants who may sue is defined by statute and includes such persons as spouses, former spouses, parents, children, brothers, and sisters. The main purpose of the action is to compensate dependants for loss of the financial support they could have expected to receive from the deceased. However, **damages for bereavement** may be claimed, on the death of a spouse or an unmarried minor child, by the surviving spouse of the former or the parents of the latter; other relatives have no claim. The amount awarded is currently fixed at £7500. Funeral expenses can be recovered if incurred.

federal state A state formed by the amalgamation or union of previously autonomous or independent states. A newly created federal state is constitutionally granted direct power over the subjects or citizens of the formerly independent states. As such, the new federal state becomes a single composite international legal person. Those former entities that comprise it have consented to subsume their former sovereignty into that of the federal state, although they retain their identity in municipal law. Examples of federal states include the USA and Switzerland. *Compare* CONFEDERATION.

fee *n.* A legal estate (other than leasehold) in land that is capable of being inherited. Since the Law of Property Act 1925 the term's only modern significance is in the phrase *fee simple absolute in possession. All other such estates that formerly existed in fee are now equitable interests only.

fee farm rent *See* RENTCHARGE.

fee simple absolute in possession One of only two forms of ownership of land that, under the Law of Property Act 1925, can exist as a legal estate (*see also* TERM OF YEARS ABSOLUTE). All others take effect as equitable interests. **Fee simple** indicates ownership that is not liable to end upon any person's death, with the expiration of time, or on the failure of a particular line of heirs. **Absolute** means that the owner's rights are not conditional or liable to terminate on the occurrence of any event (except the exercise of a right of *re-entry – Law of Property (Amendment) Act 1926). **In possession** means that the owner's rights are immediate, thus future interests do not qualify, but possession need not imply actual physical occupation (for instance, a person in receipt of rents and profits can be said to be in possession).

fee tail A legal estate in land that was abolished by the Law of Property Act 1925. It can now exist only as an equitable *entailed interest, and no new entailed interests can be created since 1997.

felony *n.* Formerly, an offence more serious than a *misdemeanour. Since 1967 the term has been abandoned (although it is retained in pre-1967 statutes that are still in force) and the law formerly relating to misdemeanours now applies to felonies. *See also* ARRESTABLE OFFENCE; INDICTABLE OFFENCE; SUMMARY OFFENCE.

feme covert [Anglo-French] A married woman, under the *coverture of her husband.

feme sole [Anglo-French] An unmarried woman. The term includes a widow or divorcée or a woman whose marriage has been annulled.

ferae naturae *See* CLASSIFICATION OF ANIMALS.

ferry *n.* A public highway by boat across water connecting places where the public have rights (usually of way) granted by royal charter or acquired by *prescription.

feudal system A political, economic, and social system in which the main social bond was the relationship between the Lord and others and in which this personal relationship was inseparable from a proprietary relationship that existed between them. It was introduced into England as a result of the Norman Conquest (1066). At its centre was the doctrine of **tenures**. All the land in the country was regarded as being owned by William I as the result of his conquest, and thereafter only the Crown could own land. The subject could merely hold it on a tenure, either directly from the Crown or indirectly through an intermediate superior. Such lands as William did not retain in his own possession he parcelled out to his barons. Holding directly from him, they were known as **tenants-in-chief**, and the tenures on which they held were **knight service** (which involved a duty to render military service for a specified number of days in each year), **sergeanty** (the performance of personal services), or **frankalmoign** (services of a religious character). Tenants-in-chief subgranted portions of their lands to lesser men to hold by tenure from them, the lesser men did likewise, and so on. The process of subgranting was called **subinfeudation**, and a man's immediate superior was known as his **mesne lord**. The principal tenures by which land was held through subinfeudation were knight service, frankalmoign, and **socage** (the rendering of agricultural or other services of a fixed nature, including the payment of money). All these tenures were free tenures. Much land was, however, held by unfree tenure, known as *copyhold: its tenant (a villein) was required to give any type of labour demanded of him.

The system of tenures did not continue as an active force for more than a few centuries. The services to be performed were gradually commuted to money payments (**quit rents**), tenures were virtually reduced to socage and copyhold by the Statute of Military Tenures (or Tenures Abolition Act) 1660, and copyhold was converted into socage by the Law of Property Act 1922. However, the theory that the subject cannot own the land itself remains at the roots of land law; what he can own is an *estate in land, which entitles him to enjoy the land as much as if he did own it.

fiction *n.* An assumption that something is true irrespective of whether it is really true or not. In English legal history fictions were used by the courts during the development of forms of court action. They enabled the courts to avoid cumbersome procedures, to make remedies available when they would not be otherwise, and to extend their jurisdiction. For example, the action of *trover was originally based on the defendant's finding the claimant's goods and taking them for himself. In time, it became unnecessary to prove the "finding": a remedy was granted on the basis only of proving that the goods were the claimant's and that the defendant had taken them.

fiduciary [from Latin: *fiducia*, trust] **1.** *n.* A person, such as a trustee, who holds a position of trust or confidence with respect to someone else and who is therefore obliged to act solely for that person's benefit. **2.** *adj.* In a position of trust or confidence. Fiduciary relationships include those between trustees and their beneficiaries, company promoters and directors and their shareholders, solicitors and their clients, and guardians and their wards.

fieri facias (fi. fa.) [Latin: you should cause to be done] A writ of execution to enforce the payment of a debt when judgment has been entered against the debtor. The writ can also be used to enforce a judgment for payment of damages. The writ is addressed to the *sheriff requiring him to seize the property of the debtor in order to pay the debt, interest, and costs.

fieri feci [Latin: I have caused to be done] The report of the *sheriff or other appropriate officer saying how much he has recovered by levying execution under a writ of *fieri facias*.

fi. fa. *See* FIERI FACIAS.

final act A document containing a formal summary of the proceedings of an international conference. The signature appended to the final act is not regarded as binding on the signatory state with regard to the treaties it refers to. For the document to be binding, a separate signature is required followed by *ratification. In rare circumstances, the final act can constitute a *treaty.

final judgment The *judgment in civil proceedings that ends the action, usually the judgment of the court at trial. Appeal against a final judgment may be made without leave of the court. *Compare* INTERIM JUDGMENT.

final process A *writ of execution on a judgment or decree.

Finance Bill A parliamentary Bill dealing with taxation matters, usually introduced each year to enact the Budget proposals.

financial assistance (in company law) A loan, guarantee, security, indemnity, or gift by a registered company or any of its subsidiaries made for the purpose of assisting someone to acquire its shares. Under the Companies Act 1985, this is unlawful unless it can be shown that the company's principal purpose for giving the assistance was not to finance the acquisition of its shares or that the assistance was an incidental part of another, larger, purpose of the company. A *private company may make such transactions, however, if the directors make a declaration, supported by the company's auditors, to the effect that the company is able to pay all its debts for at least one year following the assistance being given. In addition, the Companies Act 1985 lays down a strict timetable for providing the assistance, which must be complied with by the private company.

financial provision order An order for periodical payments or a lump sum made for the purpose of adjusting the financial position of the parties to a marriage and any children of the family. Such orders may be made on or after the granting of a decree of divorce, nullity, or judicial separation or when one party to the marriage has failed to provide, or to make a proper contribution towards, reasonable maintenance for the other or a child of the family. On divorce, judicial separation, or nullity, the court also has the power to make *property adjustment orders. In determining whether to make financial provision orders, the court has a very wide discretion under section 25 of the Matrimonial Causes Act 1973. It has an overriding duty to give first consideration to the welfare of any child under the age of 18 years and to try to achieve a *clean break wherever possible. The Act lists seven matters that the court must take into account as part of the circumstances it is to consider. These include: the financial resources and needs each of the parties has or is likely to have in the foreseeable future; the age of the parties and the length of the marriage; the standard of living enjoyed by the family before the breakdown of the marriage; the contributions that each of the parties has made to the welfare of the family, which include looking after the home or caring for the family; and the conduct of the parties, but only where it would be very unjust to ignore such conduct. A recent landmark case in this area made it clear that the implicit objective of section 25 is to achieve a fair outcome and that there should be no discrimination between husbands and wives and their respective roles (i.e. if one spouse stays at home while the other goes out to work, this fact is immaterial). A starting point should be that assets are equally divided, unless there is a good reason for not doing so. *See also* MAINTENANCE PENDING SUIT; PROPERTY ADJUSTMENT ORDER.

financial relief Any or all of the following: *maintenance pending suit orders, *financial provision orders, *property adjustment orders, and court orders for maintenance during the marriage and for the maintenance of children (*see* CHILD SUPPORT MAINTENANCE). The court has powers to set aside transactions made by a husband or wife with the intention of preventing a spouse from making a claim for financial relief, or to prevent such a transaction from taking place (*see* AVOIDANCE OF DISPOSITION ORDER). Financial relief provisions for children, other than in matrimonial proceedings, are consolidated in the Children Act 1989; for example, it is possible for unmarried parents and those in whose favour a residence order is made to obtain financial relief. In addition, children over the age of 18 have an independent right to seek financial relief from their parents.

financial year For statutes referring to finance, the period fixed by a statute of 1854 as the 12 calendar months ending on 31 March. Annual public accounts are made up for this period. For income-tax purposes, the year runs to 5 April. Companies and other bodies are free to choose their own financial years for accounting purposes. *See also* TAX YEAR.

fine *n.* **1.** A sum of money that an offender is ordered to pay on conviction. Most *summary offences are punishable by a fine with a fixed maximum, in accordance with a standard scale of five levels. These are currently (2001) as follows: level 1 – £200; level 2 – £500; level 3 – £1000; level 4 – £2500; level 5 – £5000. Under the Criminal Justice Act 1991, before fixing a fine, a court must enquire into the financial circumstances of the offender and the amount of the fine fixed by the court should, in addition, reflect the seriousness of the offence. Sometimes provision is made for imprisonment in cases of failure to pay the fine. A fine may also be imposed instead of, or in addition to, any other punishment for someone convicted on indictment (except in cases of murder). This fine is **at large**, i.e. the amount is at the discretion of the judge. Fines are often imposed upon companies for breach of statutory obligations; although the sums may be relatively small, companies will try to avoid being fined because of the bad publicity this may cause.

When imposing a fine on an offender under the age of 16 (*see* JUVENILE OFFENDER), the court is not normally empowered to order the offender to pay the fine himself unless his parent or guardian cannot be found or it would be unreasonable in the circumstances to expect his parent or guardian to pay it. Otherwise the offender pays unless payment by the parent or guardian is more appropriate.
2. A lump-sum payment by a tenant to a landlord for the grant or renewal of a lease. *See also* PREMIUM.

firearm *n.* For the purposes of the Firearms Act 1968, any potentially lethal weapon with a barrel that can fire a shot, bullet, or other missile or any weapon classified as a *prohibited weapon (even if it is not lethal). The Act creates various offences in relation to firearms. The main offences include: (1) buying or possessing a firearm without a licence; (2) buying or hiring a firearm under the age of 17 or selling a firearm to someone under 17 (similar offences exist under the Crossbows Act 1987 in relation to crossbows); (3) possessing a firearm under the age of 14; (4) supplying firearms to someone who is drunk or insane; (5) carrying a firearm and suitable ammunition in a public place without a reasonable excuse; (6) trespassing with a firearm; (7) possessing a firearm with the intention of endangering life; (8) using a firearm with the intention of resisting or preventing a lawful arrest; (9) having a firearm with the intention of committing an indictable offence; (10) possessing a firearm or ammunition after having previously been convicted of a crime; and (11) having a firearm in one's possession at the time of committing or being arrested for such offences as rape, burglary, robbery, and certain other offences. The Firearms Act 1982 extends the provisions of the 1968 Act to imitation firearms that can be easily converted to firearms and a 1988 Act strengthened controls over some of the more dangerous types of firearms, shotguns, and ammunition.

The Firearms (Amendment) Act 1997 bans all handguns above .22 calibre. The public may own and use less powerful pistols in secure gun clubs. The pistols may not be removed from the clubs without prior permission of the police. The Act also provided for the establishment of licensed gun clubs, tightened police licensing procedures, and introduced stronger police powers to suspend or revoke certificates. Anyone who uses a handgun must have a licence. The police have powers to revoke certificates when good reasons for possessing the gun no longer exist. Illegal possession of a prohibited weapon carries a maximum sentence of 10 years' imprisonment. The government proposes to extend the ban to include *all* privately owned handguns; legislation is expected to be in force by the end of 1997.

Under the Theft Act 1968 someone who has with him a firearm or imitation firearm while committing *burglary is guilty of aggravated burglary. For the purposes of this Act, a firearm may include an airgun, air pistol, or anything that looks like a firearm. *See also* OFFENSIVE WEAPON; REPEAT OFFENDER.

fire damage An occupier of land or buildings is not liable for a fire that begins there accidentally (Fires Prevention (Metropolis) Act 1774). Liability is imposed if the fire is caused by negligence, nuisance, or a non-natural user of the land or if the fire, having started accidentally, is negligently allowed to spread.

first offender A person with no previous conviction by a criminal court. A court of summary jurisdiction (*see* MAGISTRATES' COURT) is not empowered to send a person to prison for a first offence, unless it is satisfied that there is no other appropriate method of dealing with that person. *See also* SENTENCE.

fiscal year *See* TAX YEAR.

fishery *n. See* PISCARY.

fishery limits The area of sea over which a state claims exclusive fishing rights, except as agreed in treaties with other states. British fishery limits extend to 200 nautical miles from the baselines used for measuring the *territorial waters. Fishery limits may be limited or restricted by bilateral or multilateral fishing treaties or agreements, such as the EU's *Common Fisheries Policy. The UK Merchant Shipping Act 1988 preventing "quota hopping" (*see* QUOTA) in British waters by non-UK EU vessels, such as Spanish and Dutch vessels, was held unlawful by the European Court of Justice in 1996. *See also* EXCLUSIVE ECONOMIC ZONE.

fit for habitation A statutory implied covenant applied to certain tenancies at a very low rent. Premises are regarded as not reasonably fit for habitation if they are defective in one or more of the following: repair, stability, freedom from damp, natural lighting, ventilation, water supply, drainage and sanitary conveniences, facilities for cooking and for storage and preparation of food, and disposal of waste water. These provisions are currently under review. A landlord normally has no obligation to see that premises are fit for habitation when the statutory provisions do not apply. There is an implied term that furnished tenancies are fit for habitation at the commencement of the tenancy.

fitness for purpose A standard that must be met by one who sells goods in the course of a business. When the buyer makes known to the seller any particular purpose for which the goods are being bought, there is an implied condition that the goods are reasonably fit for that purpose, except when the circumstances show that the buyer does not rely (or that it is unreasonable for him to rely) on the skill or judgment of the seller.

fixed charge *See* CHARGE.

fixed-date summons Formerly, a summons in the county courts used to initiate actions in which a claim was made for any relief other than the payment of money. Such a claim is now made by means of a *claim form.

fixed penalty notice A notice given to a person who has committed a traffic offence entitling that person to discharge any liability to conviction by payment of a prescribed amount of money in accordance with the Road Traffic Offenders Act 1988.

fixed-sum credit Any facility (other than *running-account credit) under a *personal-credit agreement by which the debtor is entitled to receive credit, either in one amount or by instalments.

fixed term A tenancy or lease for a fixed period. The date of commencement and the length of a lease must be agreed before there can be a legally binding lease. It may take effect from the date of the grant, an earlier date, or a date up to 21 years ahead. At the end of the fixed term, the lease or tenancy comes to an end automatically: there is no need for a notice to quit. However, if the tenancy is an *assured tenancy, it will continue at the end of the term as a *statutory periodic tenancy unless it is brought to an end by *surrender of tenancy or a court order. *See also* HALF A YEAR; LONG TENANCY.

fixture *n.* A chattel that has been annexed to land or a building so as to become a part of it, in accordance with the maxim *quicquid plantatur solo, solo cedit* (whatever is annexed to the soil is given to the soil). Annexation normally involves actual affixation, but a thing resting on its own weight can be regarded as annexed if it can be shown that it was intended to become part of the land or to benefit it. Fixtures become the property of the freeholder, subject to certain rights of removal (as, for example, in the case of *trade fixtures and certain agricultural fixtures). A vendor of land may retain the right to fixtures as against the purchaser by express provision in the contract.

flag of convenience The national flag of a state flown by a ship that is registered in that state but is owned by a national of another state. A state whose law allows this practice can grant, in return for financial considerations, nationality and the right to fly its national flag to virtually any ship without stipulating any requirements, such as those relating to the safety of the ship and crew, the nationality of the vessel's owner, or the country of construction. Before a state is justified in extending its nationality to a ship, or permitting a ship to fly its flag, it seems that there must be some effective link connecting the ship with the state. Hence a flag of convenience may only be validly granted when a genuine link exists, though what constitutes such a link remains unclear. *See also* FLAG STATE JURISDICTION.

flagrante delicto [Latin] In the commission of an offence. Certain types of *arrest can only be made when a person is in the act of committing an offence (*see* ARRESTABLE OFFENCE). The phrase is most commonly applied to the situation in which a person finds his or her spouse in the act of committing adultery. Someone who kills his or her spouse in this situation may have a defence of *provocation.

flag state jurisdiction The rule whereby, exceptions applying, a ship on the *high seas is subject only to the jurisdiction of the flag state, i.e. that state permitting it the right to sail under its flag (see FLAG OF CONVENIENCE).

floating charge See CHARGE.

flotation n. A process by which a public company can, by an issue of securities (shares or debentures), raise capital from the public. It may involve a **prospectus issue**, in which the company itself issues a *prospectus inviting the public to acquire securities; an **offer for sale**, in which the company sells the securities on offer to an **issuing house**, which then issues a prospectus inviting the public to purchase the securities from it; or a **placing**, whereby an issuing house arranges for the securities to be taken up by its own or another's clients in the expectation that they will ultimately become available to the public on the open market. See also RIGHTS ISSUE; TENDER OFFER; UNDERWRITER.

f.o.b. contract (free on board contract) A type of contract for the international sale of goods in which the seller's duty is fulfilled by placing the goods on board a ship. There are different types of f.o.b. contract: the buyer may arrange the shipping space and the procurement of a bill of lading and nominate the ship to the seller; he may nominate a general ship and leave it to the seller to place the goods on board and to procure a bill of lading; or the seller may be asked to make all the shipping arrangements for which the buyer will pay. The risk of accidental loss or damage normally passes to the buyer when the goods are loaded onto the ship. Insurance during the sea transit is the responsibility of the buyer. f.o.b. is a defined *incoterm in *Incoterm 2000*.

following trust property See TRACING TRUST PROPERTY.

football hooliganism The Sporting Events (Control of Alcohol etc.) Act 1985 contains finable offences of possessing alcohol, being drunk, or causing or permitting the carriage of alcohol on trains and vehicles capable of carrying nine or more passengers; the vehicle must be carrying two or more passengers to or from a "designated sporting event" (mainly Football League club and international fixtures), and normal scheduled coach or train services are excluded. A constable who reasonably suspects that a relevant offence is being or has been committed may stop the vehicle or train and search it or the suspected offender. It is also an offence to be drunk or to possess alcohol or (unless lawful authority is proved) fireworks and similar objects (but not matches or lighters) in the viewing area within two hours before, during, or one hour after the event, or while trying to enter. Under the Public Order Act 1986, persons convicted of the above alcohol-related offences, or offences committed at the football ground, can be excluded by the courts from football matches. Admission to a designated football match is controlled under the Football Spectators Act 1989 and is subject to the control of disorderly behaviour there under the Football (Offences) Act 1991. Under the Football Spectators Act 1989, a **banning order** may be made to prohibit an offender from attending a football match in England and Wales. Such an order may also require that the offender surrender his passport to prevent him travelling to a football match abroad. See also OFFENCES AGAINST PUBLIC ORDER.

footpath n. Under the Highways Act 1980, any *highway (other than a *footway) over which the public have a right of way on foot only.

footway n. Under the Highways Act 1980, any way over which the public have a right of way on foot only and which is part of a highway that also comprises a way for the passage of vehicles. *Compare* FOOTPATH.

forbearance n. A deliberate failure to exercise a legal right (e.g. to sue for a debt). A forbearance to sue at a debtor's request may be *consideration for some fresh promise by the debtor. A promise not to enforce a claim that is bad in law may still be consideration if the claim is believed to be valid. A requested forbearance, even if it is not binding, may have more limited effects either at common law or in equity (e.g. in certain circumstances it may not be revoked without reasonable notice).

force majeure [French] Irresistible compulsion or coercion. The phrase is used particularly in commercial contracts to describe events possibly affecting the contract and that are completely outside the parties' control. Such events are normally listed in full to ensure their enforceability; they may include *acts of God, fires, failure of suppliers or subcontractors to supply the supplier under the agreement, and strikes and other labour disputes that interfere with the supplier's performance of an agreement. An express clause would normally excuse both delay and a total failure to perform the agreement.

forcible entry A common-law offence (as amended by various statutes) that applied under certain circumstances when force was used to gain entry to premises. The common-law offence has been replaced by a statutory *arrestable offence of using or threatening violence against people or property in order to secure entry into premises (Criminal Law Act 1977). The offence only applies if there is someone present on the premises who is opposed to the entry and the offender knows of this. The fact that the offender is the legal owner or occupier of the premises is not in itself a defence. However, there is a special defence if the offender can prove that he was at the relevant time a displaced *residential occupier or protected intending occupier who requires the property for his residence and has a qualifying freehold or leasehold interest, tenancy, or licence and was seeking to gain entry or to pass through premises that form an access to his own place of residential occupation. These provisions do not apply to landlords seeking to regain possession and it is a summary offence to make false statements when claiming to be a protected occupier. It is not an offence, however, for a person unlawfully evicted from his own home to use force to re-enter, subject to the common-law rule that the force must not be excessive. The police may use force to enter with lawful authority. *See also* ADVERSE OCCUPATION.

foreclose down *See* REDEEM UP, FORECLOSE DOWN.

foreclosure n. A remedy available to a mortgagee when the mortgagor has failed to pay off a *mortgage by the contractual date for redemption. The mortgagee is entitled to bring an action in the High Court, seeking an order fixing a date to pay off the debt; if the mortgagor does not pay by that date he will be foreclosed, i.e. he will lose the mortgaged property. If, after this order (a foreclosure order nisi) is made, the mortgagor does not pay on the date and at the place (usually a room in the Royal Courts of Justice) named, the foreclosure is made absolute and the property thereafter belongs to the mortgagee. However, the court has discretion to allow the mortgagor to reopen the foreclosure and thereby regain his property. The remedy is unpopular: the mortgagee's *power of sale may be more useful; moreover, if the mortgaged property is worth less than the loan, the mortgagee cannot sue for the balance, a point that has recently re-acquired significance. *See also* REPOSSESSION.

foreign agreement An agreement or contract the proper law of which is the law of some country other than England and Wales, Northern Ireland, or Scotland. *See* FOREIGN LAW; PROPER LAW OF A CONTRACT.

foreign bill Any bill of exchange other than an *inland bill. The distinction is relevant to the steps taken when the bill has been dishonoured (*see* DISHONOUR).

foreign company A company incorporated outside Great Britain but having a place of business within Great Britain. Foreign companies are subject to provisions of the Companies Acts relating to registration, accounts, name, etc. *See* OVERSEA COMPANY.

foreign enlistment The offence under the Foreign Enlistment Act 1870 of enlisting oneself or others (except with the licence of the Crown) for armed service with a foreign state that is at war with a state with which the UK is at peace. A foreign state for this purpose includes part of a province or persons exercising or assuming powers of government. It is also an offence under the Act (again, except with licence) to build or equip any ship for such service or to fit out any naval or military expedition for use against a state with which the UK is at peace.

foreign judgments The *judgment of a foreign court may be enforced in England provided that the foreign court was competent and that the judgment is for a definite sum and is final and conclusive. At common law a foreign court is regarded as competent if (1) the judgment debtor, being a defendant in the original court, submitted to the jurisdiction of that court by voluntarily appearing in the proceedings otherwise than for the purpose of either protecting or obtaining the release of property seized (or threatened with seizure) in the proceedings or of contesting the jurisdiction of that court; (2) the judgment debtor was claimant in or counterclaimed in the proceedings in the original court; (3) the judgment debtor, being a defendant in the original court, had agreed before the proceedings commenced to submit to the jurisdiction of that court or of the courts of that country; or (4) the judgment debtor, being a defendant in the original court, was resident in the country of that court when the proceedings were instituted (or, in the case of a corporation, had its principal place of business in that country).

In addition to the common-law rule, foreign judgments may be registered for enforcement by the English courts under a number of statutory powers, notably those contained in the Foreign Judgments (Reciprocal Enforcement) Act 1933 and the Civil Jurisdiction and Judgments Act 1982, which derive from such international conventions as the *Brussels Convention and the Lugano Convention.

foreign law For the purposes of *private international law, any legal system other than that of England. A foreign legal system may be the system of a foreign state (one recognized by public *international law) or of a law district. Thus the law of Scotland, Northern Ireland, the Channel Islands, and Isle of Man and the law of each of the American or Australian states or Canadian provinces is a separate foreign law. When an element of foreign law arises in an English court, it is usually treated as a question of fact, which must be proved (usually by expert evidence) in each case. The English courts retain an overriding power to refuse to enforce (or even to recognize) provisions of foreign law that are against English public policy, foreign penal or revenue laws, or laws creating discriminatory disabilities or status. *See also* COMMUNITY LAW.

foresight *n.* Awareness at the time of doing an act that a certain consequence may result. In the case of some crimes (e.g. *wounding with intent) an *intention by the accused to bring about a certain consequence must be proved before he can be found guilty; foresight is not enough (*see also* ULTERIOR INTENT). However, conviction for many crimes (including *wounding) requires only that the accused foresaw a specified consequence as likely or possible. In all cases where foresight suffices for liability, the court may not assume that the defendant had foresight merely because the particular consequence that occurred was the natural and likely consequence of his acts. *See also* RECKLESSNESS.

forfeiture *n.* Loss of property or a right as a consequence of an offence or of the breach of an undertaking. There are three main situations in which the courts may order forfeiture of property. (1) Property that is illegally possessed is subject to forfeiture. (2) Any property relating to an offence under the Misuse of Drugs Act 1971 or the Drug Trafficking Offences Act 1986 (*see* CONTROLLED DRUGS) may be forfeited and either destroyed or dealt with as the court sees fit (this includes the proceeds of the sale of drugs). (3) Property may be forfeited if it is legally possessed but used (or intended to be used) to commit a crime (e.g. a getaway car) when the owner has previously been convicted of an offence. Property confiscated under this heading is held by the police for six months and then disposed of.

Most *leases provide for the landlord to terminate the lease when the tenant is in breach of his covenants. The landlord must follow a particular procedure before effecting forfeiture. From 24 January 1996 a freeholder cannot forfeit a lease for nonpayment of a service charge unless the lessee accepts the charge or the *leasehold valuation tribunal agrees. In the case of forfeiture for nonpayment of rent, the landlord must make a formal demand for the rent unless the lease exempts him from the need to do this. When other covenants have been breached, the landlord must serve a statutory notice on the tenant specifying the breach, requiring him to put it right where this is possible, and requiring compensation in money if appropriate. If the tenant fails to comply with the notice the landlord may proceed with forfeiture. This may be done through court proceedings for possession or, more rarely, by *re-entry. A landlord loses his right of forfeiture if he treats the lease as continuing when he is entitled to forfeit it. This is known as **waiver of forfeiture**. *See also* CONFISCATION ORDER; RACIAL HATRED; RELIEF FROM FORFEITURE.

forgery *n.* The offence of making a "false instrument" in order that it may be accepted as genuine, thereby causing harm to others. Under the Forgery and Counterfeiting Act 1981, an "instrument" may be a document, a stamp issued by the Post Office or the Inland Revenue, or any device (e.g. magnetic tape) in which information is recorded or stored. An instrument is considered to be "false" if, for example, it purports to have been made or altered (1) by or on the authority of someone who did not in fact do so; (2) on a date or at a place when it was not; or (3) by someone who is nonexistent. In addition to forgery itself, it is a criminal offence under the Act to copy or use a false instrument, knowing or believing it to be false. It is also an offence merely to have in one's possession or control any one of certain specified false instruments with the intention of passing them off as genuine. It is also an offence to make or possess any material that is meant to be used to produce any of the specified false instruments. These specified instruments include money or postal orders, stamps, share certificates, passports, cheques, cheque cards and credit cards, and copies of entries in a register of births, marriages, or deaths. All the above offences are punishable on indictment by up to ten years' imprisonment and upon summary trial to a *fine at level 5 on the standard scale and/or six months' imprisonment.

The Act also deals with the offences of **counterfeiting currency** (notes or coin), with or without the intention of passing it off as genuine; possessing counterfeit currency; passing it off; making or possessing anything which can be used for counterfeiting; and importing or exporting counterfeit currency. It is also an offence to reproduce any British currency note (e.g. to photocopy a £5 note), even in artwork, and, under certain circumstances, to make an imitation British coin. Some of these offences are subject to the same penalties as forgery.

forum *n.* [from Latin: public place] The place or country in which a case is being heard. If a case involving a foreign element is brought in the English courts, the forum is England. *See* LEX FORI.

forum non conveniens [Latin: not in agreement with the judicial forum] A doctrine that permits a court to decline to accept jurisdiction over a case, so that the case may be tried in an alternative forum (i.e. a foreign court). Such decisions are almost entirely at the court's discretion, except that the party seeking a *forum non conveniens* decision must submit to the effective jurisdiction of the alternative court. The stay will be granted by the court if it is satisfied that a foreign court having competent jurisdiction is available and that the case may be tried more suitably for the interests of all the parties and the ends of justice in that court. The factors that courts generally consider in making this decision include the location of witnesses, exhibits, and documents, the language of the witnesses and documents, the citizenship of the claimants, and the law applicable to the dispute.

In general, the burden of proof rests on the defendant to persuade the court to exercise its discretion to grant a stay, but if the court is satisfied that another court is available, the burden will then shift to the claimant to show that there are special circumstances requiring that the trial should nevertheless take place in the first court.

forum prorogatum [Latin] Prorogated jurisdiction, which occurs when a power is conferred – by the consent of the parties and following the initiation of proceedings – upon the International Court of Justice, which otherwise would not have adjudicated. Such consent can be indicated in an implied or informal way or by a succession of acts.

forum rei [Latin: forum of the thing] The court of the country in which the subject of a dispute is situated.

forum shopping The practice of choosing a country in which to bring a legal case through the courts on the basis of which country's laws are the most favourable. In some instances there is a choice of jurisdiction.

foster child A child who is cared for by someone other than its natural or adopted parents or a person having parental responsibility (*see* FOSTER PARENT). Local authorities are obliged by law to supervise the welfare of foster children within their area and to inspect and control the use of premises as foster homes. Foster children do not include children who are looked after by relatives or guardians or boarded out by a local authority or voluntary organization.

foster parent A person looking after a *foster child. Foster parents have no legal rights over the children they foster, who may be removed from their care by their parents or legal guardian. They may, however, apply to have the child made a ward of court or apply for a residence order (*see* SECTION 8 ORDERS) when a child has lived with them for three years (or within that period if the local authority gives its consent), which will invest them with parental responsibility. If the child has been living with them for at least 12 months they may apply to adopt him.

four-day order A supplemental order of a civil court fixing the time for the performance of an act in cases in which no time has been fixed by the principal order. In the Chancery Division this is known as a four-day order although four days is not invariably the time fixed.

four unities *See* JOINT TENANCY.

franchise *n.* **1.** (in constitutional law) A special right conferred by the Crown on a subject. Also known as a **liberty**, it is exemplified by the right to hold a market or fair or to run a ferry. **2.** (in constitutional law) The right to vote at an election. To qualify to vote at a parliamentary or local-government election, a person must be a *commonwealth citizen or a citizen of the Republic of Ireland, must be aged 18 or over, must be shown on the register of electors governing the election (*see* ELECTOR) as resident on the qualifying date in the parliamentary constituency or local government area concerned, and must not be subject to any legal incapacity to vote. Those incapacitated are peers and peeresses in their own right (for parliamentary elections only, and not including peers of Ireland), persons serving sentences of imprisonment, persons convicted during the preceding five years of certain offences relating to elections or to the bribery of public officials, and persons who are incapable of understanding the nature of their acts. **3.** (in commercial law) A licence given to a manufacturer, distributor, trader, etc., to enable them to manufacture or sell a named product or service in a particular area for a stated period. The holder of the licence (**franchisee**) usually pays the grantor of the licence (**franchisor**) a royalty on sales, often with a lump sum as an advance against royalties. The franchisor may also supply the franchisee with a brand identity as well as finance and technical expertise. Franchises are common in the fast-food business, petrol stations, travel agents, etc. A franchise contract in the EU must comply with regulation 4087/88, which sets out which provisions are permitted and which are banned under EU *competition law.

franked income Formerly, income that a person or a company received on which *advance corporation tax had been paid. In the case of an individual the tax paid was imputed (*see* IMPUTATION SYSTEM) to the basic income-tax liability of the recipient. In the case of a company, it was imputed to its own liability to corporation tax.

fraud *n.* A false representation by means of a statement or conduct made knowingly or recklessly in order to gain a material advantage. If the fraud results in injury to the deceived party, he may claim damages for the tort of *deceit. A contract obtained by fraud is voidable on the grounds of fraudulent *misrepresentation. *See also* CONSTRUCTIVE FRAUD. In relation to crime, *see* CHEAT; CONSPIRACY; CYBERCRIME; DEFRAUDING; DISHONESTY; FALSE PRETENCE; FORGERY.

fraud on a power An exercise of a *power of appointment that, although made to an object within the class chosen by the donor, was made in circumstances that render it void. Examples are when the appointor intended to obtain a benefit for himself or another or when there was a deliberate intention to defeat the intentions of the donor of the power.

fraud on the minority An improper exercise of voting power by the majority of members of a company. It consists of a failure to cast votes for the benefit of the company as a whole and makes a resolution voidable. Examples are the ratification of an expropriation of company property by the directors (themselves the majority shareholders) and alteration of the articles of association to allow the compulsory purchase of members' shares when this is not in the company's interests. Actual or threatened fraud on the minority may give rise to a *derivative action.

fraudulent conveyance A transfer of land made without valuable *consideration and with the intent of defrauding a subsequent purchaser. An example of fraudulent conveyance is when A, who has contracted to sell to B, conveys the land to his associate C in order to escape the contract with B. Under the Law of Property Act 1925, B is entitled to have the conveyance to C set aside by the court.

fraudulent misrepresentation *See* MISREPRESENTATION.

fraudulent trading Carrying on business with the intention of defrauding creditors or for any other fraudulent purpose, e.g. accepting advance payment for goods with no intention of either supplying them or returning the money. Such conduct is a criminal offence and the court may order those responsible to contribute to the company's assets on a *winding-up. *See also* WRONGFUL TRADING.

freeboard *n.* Under the Merchant Shipping (Safety and Load Line Conventions) Act 1932, the vertical distance measured amidships from the upper edge of the deck line to the upper edge of the load line mark.

freedom from encumbrance The freedom of property from the binding rights of parties other than the owner. In contracts for the sale of goods, unless the seller makes it clear that he is contracting to transfer only such title as he or a third person may have, there is an implied *warranty that the goods are free from any charge or encumbrance not disclosed or known to the buyer before the contract was made.

freedom of association A right set out in Article 11 of the European Convention on Human Rights and now part of UK law as a consequence of the *Human Rights Act 1998. This right protects **freedom of peaceful assembly**, including the right to form and join trade unions and similar bodies. It is a *qualified right; as such, the public interest can be used to justify an interference with it providing that this is prescribed by law, designed for a legitimate purpose, and proportionate. The right of those in the armed forces, the police, and the administration of the state is protected only to the extent that any interference with this right must be prescribed by law.

freedom of expression A right set out in Article 10 of the European Convention on Human Rights and now part of UK law as a consequence of the *Human Rights Act 1998. "Freedom of expression constitutes one of the essential foundations of a democratic society, one of the basic conditions for its progress and for the development of every man...it is applicable not only to 'information' or 'ideas' that are favourably received or regarded as inoffensive or as a matter of indifference, but also to those that offend, shock or disturb...such are the demands of that pluralism, tolerance and broadmindedness without which there is no 'democratic society'." Convention jurisprudence gives different weight to different kinds of expression. The most important expression – political speech – therefore is likely to be protected to a much greater extent than the least important – commercial speech.

Freedom of expression is a *qualified right; as such, the public interest can be used to justify an interference with it providing that this is prescribed by law, designed for a legitimate purpose, and proportionate.

freedom of testation A person's right to provide in his will for the distribution of his estate in whatever manner he wishes. The principle is restricted by the powers of the court to set aside a will made by a person of unsound mind (*see* TESTAMENTARY CAPACITY) and to award *reasonable financial provision from an estate to certain relatives and dependants of the deceased under the Inheritance (Provision for Family and Dependants) Act 1975.

freedom of thought, conscience, and religion A right set out in Article 9 of the European Convention on Human Rights and now part of UK law as a consequence of the *Human Rights Act 1998. While freedom of thought itself is an *absolute right, and as such not subject to public-interest limitations, the right to manifest one's beliefs or religion is a *qualified right; therefore the public interest can be used to justify an interference providing that this is prescribed by law, designed for a legitimate purpose, and proportionate.

free elections A right set out in Article 3 of the First Protocol to the European Convention on Human Rights and now part of UK law as a consequence of the *Human Rights Act 1998. The state has a duty to hold free elections at reasonable intervals by secret ballot, under conditions that will ensure the free expression of the opinion of the people in the choice of the legislature. This duty does not apply to local elections (local authorities are not the legislature but the European Parliament is), and there is no duty to use any particular system of voting (proportional representation or first past the post).

free from average *See* AVERAGE.

freehold *n.* The most complete form of ownership of land: a legal estate held in *fee simple absolute in possession.

freeing for adoption Giving consent in general terms to the *adoption of one's child, as opposed to consenting to an adoption by particular prospective adopters. The procedure is used by an *adoption agency in cases in which the parents freely agree that the child may be adopted, or their consent is dispensed with by the court on one of the statutory grounds. Once an order is made, the parental rights and duties are transferred to the adoption agency, who may then proceed to arrange for the child's adoption without asking the parents' consent or notifying them who the adopters are. Adoption law is currently under review: if recommendations are adopted, freeing orders will be abolished.

free movement The movement of goods, persons, services, and capital within an area without being impeded by legal restrictions. This is a basic principle of the *European Community, whose treaty insists on the free movement of goods (involving the elimination of customs duties and quantitative restrictions between member states and the setting up of a *Common External Tariff) as well as the free movement of services, capital, and persons (including workers and those wishing to establish themselves in professions or to set up companies). *See also* EXHAUSTION OF RIGHTS.

free on board *See* F.O.B. CONTRACT.

freezing injunction An injunction, now consolidated in statute, that enables the court to freeze the assets of a defendant (whether resident within the jurisdiction of the English court or not). This prevents the defendant from removing his assets abroad and thus makes it worthwhile to sue such a defendant. The remedy is draconian and has become very popular, both in the commercial world and outside it; any person seeking the remedy, however, must himself disclose all material information to the court. Before the introduction of the Civil Procedure Rules in 1999, freezing injunctions were known as **Mareva injunctions**, from the case *Mareva Compania Naviera S.A. v International Bulkcarriers S.A.* (1975).

freight *n.* **1.** The profit derived by a shipowner or hirer from the use of the ship by himself or by letting it to others, or for carrying goods for others. **2.** The amount payable under a contract (of affreightment) for the carriage of goods by sea.

frustration of contract The unforeseen termination of a contract as a result of an event that either renders its performance impossible or illegal or prevents its main purpose from being achieved. Frustration would, for example, occur if the goods specified in a sale of goods contract were destroyed (impossibility of performance); if the outbreak of a war caused one party to become an enemy alien (illegality); or if X were to hire a room from Y with the object (known to Y) of viewing a procession and the procession was cancelled (failure of main purpose). Unless specific provision for the frustrating event is made, a frustrated contract is automatically discharged and the position of the parties is, in most cases, governed by the Law Reform (Frustrated Contracts) Act 1943. Money paid before the event can be recovered and money due but not paid ceases to be payable. However, a party who has obtained any valuable benefit under the contract must pay a reasonable sum for it. The Act does not apply to certain contracts for the sale of goods, contracts for the carriage of goods by sea, or contracts of insurance.

fugitive offender A person present in the UK who is accused of committing an offence in a Commonwealth country or a dependent territory of the UK and is liable to be surrendered for trial under the Fugitive Offenders Act 1967. The requirements for surrender are similar to those for *extradition to a foreign state, except that no treaty is involved.

full age *See* MAJORITY.

full powers A document produced by the competent authorities of a state designating a person (or body of persons) to represent the state for negotiating, adopting, or authenticating the text of a *treaty, for expressing the consent of the state to be bound by a treaty, or for accomplishing any other act with respect to a treaty. *See also* SIGNATURE OF TREATY.

full representation *See* COMMUNITY LEGAL SERVICE.

fully mutual housing association A housing association whose rules restrict membership to people who are tenants or prospective tenants of the association and prevent the granting or assigning of tenancies to those who are not members. Fully mutual housing associations are exempt from the *assured tenancy provisions.

fundamental breach *See* BREACH OF CONTRACT; INNOMINATE TERMS.

funeral expenses The reasonable cost of a deceased person's burial, which is the first priority for payment from his estate.

furnished tenancy *See* ASSURED TENANCY; PROTECTED TENANCY.

future goods Goods to be manufactured or acquired by a seller after a contract of sale has been made. Future goods must be distinguished as the subject of a contract of sale from existing goods, which are owned or possessed by a seller.

future interest Any right to property that does not take effect immediately. An example is B's interest in property held in trust for A for life and then for B. Under the Law of Property Act 1925 future interests in land (with the exception of *future leases) can exist as equitable interests only and not as legal estates.

future lease A lease that confers on the tenant the right to possession of land only from a specified future time. A lease, or contract to grant a lease, that is made in consideration of a capital payment or a rent and will take effect more than 21 years after its commencement is void under the Law of Property Act 1925. Subject to this, a future lease can qualify as a legal estate in land.

game *n.* Wild animals or birds hunted for sport or food. The Game Acts define these as including hares, pheasants, partridges, grouse, heath or moor game, black game, and bustards. The right to game belongs basically to the occupier, although in leases it is frequently reserved to the landlord rather than the tenant. *See also* POACHING.

gaming (gambling) *n.* Playing a game in order to win money or anything else of value, when winning depends on luck. There are various restrictions upon gaming, depending on whether it takes place in controlled (i.e. licensed or registered) or uncontrolled premises. If the premises are uncontrolled, it is illegal to play a game that involves playing against a bank or a game in which each player does not have an equal chance or the chance of winning is weighted in favour of someone other than the players (e.g. a promoter or organizer), unless the game takes place in a private house in the course of ordinary family life. Thus one cannot play roulette with a zero in uncontrolled premises, but one may play such games as bridge, whist, poker, or cribbage. It is also illegal (subject to one or two exceptions) to game when a charge is made for the gaming or a levy is charged on the winnings. Gaming in any street or any place to which the public has access is illegal, except for dominoes, cribbage, or any game specially authorized in a pub (provided the participants are over 18). If the premises are controlled (either by the grant of a licence or by registration as a gaming club), the restrictions applying to uncontrolled premises apply unless they have been permitted by regulation. Thus casino-type games may be played on controlled premises for commercial profit if permission has been obtained, but only by members of licensed or registered clubs and their guests. There are also restrictions relating to playing on Sundays, and no one under 18 may be present when gaming takes place. It is illegal to use, sell, or maintain gaming machines without a certificate or licence.

gaming contract A contract involving the playing of a game of chance by any number of people for money or money's worth. A **wagering contract** is one involving two parties only, each of whom stands to win or lose something of value according to the result of some future event (e.g. a horse race) or to which of them is correct about some past or present fact; neither party can have any interest in the contract except his stake. In general, gaming and wagering contracts are by statute null and void and no action can be brought to recover any money paid or won under them.

garden leave clause A clause in an employment contract that provides for a long period of notice by the employer, during which the employee will be remunerated in full but will not be required to attend at the workplace. The use of such clauses is increasing by employers wishing to safeguard trade secrets or, more importantly, prevent a highly skilled employee from leaving to undertake work for a rival firm. An employee wishing to leave, or one who has been head-hunted, could be required to serve 'garden leave' for a period of up to one year in order to lawfully terminate his existing contract. Throughout the period of garden leave an employee will be subject to all the normal contractual restraints. Management sees the use of such clauses as an expensive, but reliable and enforceable, alternative to traditional *restraint of trade clauses. Moreover, these clauses may be enforced by way of injunction without encountering the difficulties that arise with respect to restraint of trade clauses, which are notoriously difficult to draft and enforce.

garnishee *n.* A person who has been warned by a court to pay a debt to a third party rather than to his creditor. *See* GARNISHEE PROCEEDINGS.

garnishee proceedings A procedure by which a judgment creditor may obtain a court order against a third party who owes money to, or holds money on behalf of, the judgment debtor. The order requires the third party to pay the money (or part of it) to the judgment creditor. For example, if the judgment debtor has £1000 in a bank account and judgment has been entered against him for £500, the court may order the bank to pay £500 direct to the judgment creditor.

GATT *See* GENERAL AGREEMENT ON TARIFFS AND TRADE.

gazumping *n.* The withdrawal by a vendor from a proposed sale of land in the expectation of receiving a higher price elsewhere after agreeing the price with a purchaser but before a legally binding contract has been made (*see* EXCHANGE OF CONTRACTS). The first prospective purchaser has no legal right either to compel the vendor to sell to him or to recover his wasted expenditure (such as surveyor's and solicitor's charges) unless an agreement, such as a *lock-out agreement, has been signed.

GBH *See* GRIEVOUS BODILY HARM.

gender reassignment A physiological and ultimately surgical procedure, under medical supervision, for the purpose of changing a person's sexual characteristics. The process is undertaken by *transsexuals (estimated to number some 5000 in the UK). Initially discrimination in the workplace with respect to a person's sexual orientation or transsexualism was outside the ambit of the Sex Discrimination Act 1975 (*see* SEX DISCRIMINATION). The definition of sex within that Act referred to discrimination on grounds of biological gender and hence covered discrimination only between men and women. As a result of a series of test cases taken before both the European Court of Justice and the European Court of Human Rights, the UK Sex Discrimination Act must now be construed to include both sexual orientation and transsexualism within its definition. However with respect to transsexualism, as gender reassignment is an ongoing process, it was necessary to introduce supporting regulations, to clarify the protections to be given at the workplace to a transsexual undergoing this process. The Sex Discrimination (Gender Reassignment) Regulations 1999 bring UK law into line with the decision of the European Court of Justice in *P v S and Cornwall County Council* 1996, the case in which discrimination on grounds of gender reassignment was ruled to be contrary to European Community law.

The Regulations provide protection against discrimination by employers at all stages of the reassignment process, starting when an individual indicates an intention to begin reassignment. The Regulations also cover recruitment procedures, vocational training, and discrimination with respect to pay (*see* EQUAL PAY). The Sex Discrimination Act as amended by the Regulations outlaws direct discrimination and provides for employees who are absent from work to undergo treatment to be treated no less favourably than they would be if the absence was due to sickness or personal injury. The protection is extended to postoperative treatment on a transsexual's return to work. A defence to a claim of unlawful treatment is also provided in relation to the employment in question, if being a man or woman is a genuine occupational qualification for the job. This could arise, for example, if an employee recruited to a sex-specific post begins the gender reassignment process, or if the job involves the holder of the post to perform intimate physical body searches, or if the nature or location of the establishment makes it impracticable for the holder of the job to live elsewhere than on the premises provided by the employer and the issue of decency and privacy must be taken into consideration.

The Department for Work and Pensions (formerly Employment) has produced a guide to the implementation of these Regulations. It offers further assistance to employers on such issues as: whether or not an employee should be redeployed following treatment, the amount of time off necessary for surgical procedures, and the expected point or phase of change of name and personal details and the required amendments to records and systems. Further assistance given relates to confidentiality issues: informing line managers, colleagues, and clients. The guide also offers advice on agreeing a procedure between the employee and employer regarding a changing in dress code and agreeing when individuals will start using single-sex facilities at the workplace in their new gender.

general act *See* TREATY.

general agent *See* AGENT.

General Agreement on Tariffs and Trade (GATT) An international treaty signed in 1947 to provide for some measure of world free trade with the aim of reducing high tariffs on goods. Its objectives in extending free trade have been achieved in a series of eight negotiations (rounds); the last of these, the Uruguay Round (1986–94), led to the establishment of the *World Trade Organization and further agreement to ensure more free trade around the world.

general and special damages A classification of *damages awarded for a tort or a breach of contract, the meaning of which varies according to the context. **1.** General damages are given for losses that the law will presume are the natural and probable consequence of a wrong. Thus it is assumed that a libel is likely to injure the reputation of the person libelled, and damages can be recovered without proof that the claimant's reputation has in fact suffered. Special damages are given for losses that are not presumed but have been specifically proved. **2.** General damages may also mean damages given for a loss that is incapable of precise estimation, such as *pain and suffering or loss of reputation. In this context special damages are damages given for losses that can be quantified, such as out-of-pocket expenses or earnings lost during the period between the injury and the hearing of the action.

General Assembly (of the UN) *See* UNITED NATIONS.

general average *See* AVERAGE.

General Council of the Bar of England and Wales *See* BAR COUNCIL.

general defences Common-law defences to any common-law or statutory crimes; with one exception (*insanity), these defences relate to *involuntary conduct. A defendant should be acquitted when the magistrates or jury have a reasonable doubt as to whether he was entitled to a general defence. By contrast, **special defences** are confined to individual offences, are usually of statutory origin, and usually place a *burden of proof on the defendant to show that he acted reasonably. *See also* AUTOMATISM; IMPOSSIBILITY; MISTAKE; SELF-DEFENCE.

general equitable charge A class of *land charge, registrable under the Land Charges Act (*see* REGISTRATION OF ENCUMBRANCES), that affects a *legal estate in land but neither arises under a trust nor is secured by deposit of the title deeds.

general improvement area A predominantly residential area in which a housing authority considers that it should improve or help to improve living conditions by improving dwellings or amenities (or both). *See also* HOUSING ACTION AREA; PRIORITY NEIGHBOURHOOD.

general issue A plea in which every allegation in the opposite party's pleading is denied. In civil proceedings it is no longer permitted. Instead, each allegation must be specifically admitted or denied. In criminal cases the defendant pleads the general issue by pleading *not guilty and cannot generally be required to disclose the nature of his defence until his own case is presented (*but see* ALIBI).

general legacy *See* LEGACY.

general lien *See* LIEN.

general meeting A meeting of company members whose decisions can bind the company. Certain **reserved powers**, specified by the Companies Act, can only be exercised by a general meeting. These include alteration of the memorandum and articles of association, removal of a director before his term of office has expired, *alteration of share capital, the appointing of an auditor other than upon a casual vacancy, and putting the company into voluntary winding-up. Powers may also be reserved by the articles of association of a particular company. Powers other than reserved powers are usually delegated in the articles to the directors. The general meeting can overrule the directors' decision in relation to these delegated powers by *special resolution, but this will not affect the validity of acts already done; it could also, while exercising reserved powers, dismiss the directors or alter the articles and thus the delegation. General meetings are either *annual general meetings or *extraordinary general meetings. Unless the articles of association provide or the court orders otherwise, at least two company members must be present personally.

general participation clause A clause in the *Hague Conventions of 1899 and 1907. The clause, concerning the conduct of hostilities, stipulates that the Conventions shall be binding upon the belligerents only so long as all belligerents are parties to the Convention. The effect of this clause was to significantly weaken the effectiveness of the Hague Convention rules.

general power *See* POWER OF APPOINTMENT.

general power of investment A power, introduced by the Trustee Act 2000, that allows a trustee to make any kind of investment that he could make if he were absolutely entitled to the assets of the trust fund. Previously, trustees were only permitted to make certain *authorized investments. This much wider general power of investment may be expressly excluded in the trust instrument. There are still some restrictions on investments in land. In exercising the general power of investment, the trustees are required by the Act to consider criteria relating to the suitability of the proposed investment to the trust and the need for diversification of investment within the unique circumstances of the trust. Trustees are also required by the Act to review the investments from time to time with the same standard criteria in mind. Before investing, the trustee must obtain and consider proper advice, unless he reasonably considers it unnecessary or inappropriate to do so.

general principles of law According to the Statute of the *International Court of Justice, the source for rules of international law can be found in what it terms "General Principles of Law". The majority of Western jurists consider that these principles should be based on those underlying the municipal legal systems of civilized states, especially those of Europe and the USA. These jurists also consider the general principles to be a law-creating source that is independent of either treaties or custom. Due to their possible bias towards certain Western capitalist countries, these propositions have proved highly contentious in the Third World and Socialist countries, which have endeavoured to limit the scope of the principles.

general safety requirement A standard of safety that consumer goods must meet in order to comply with the Consumer Protection Act 1987 and the General Product Safety Regulations 1994. The goods are required to be reasonably safe having regard to all the circumstances, e.g the way the goods are marketed, including any instructions or warnings about their use; their compliance with published safety standards for goods of that kind; and whether reasonable steps could be taken to make them safer. Suppliers of consumer goods who fail to meet the safety requirement commit an offence.

general verdict 1. (in a civil case) A *verdict that is entirely in favour of one or other party. 2. (in a criminal case) A verdict either of *guilty or *not guilty. *Compare* SPECIAL VERDICT.

general warrant A warrant for arrest that does not name or describe the person to be arrested, or a search warrant that does not specify the premises to be searched or the property sought. Such warrants are usually illegal, although they may sometimes be expressly authorized by statute (*see* POWER OF SEARCH). Someone arrested under an illegal general warrant can claim damages for *false imprisonment. Sometimes, however, Parliament grants a general power of arrest while searching premises with a search warrant, e.g. under the Betting, Gaming and Lotteries Act 1963.

general words Words in a *conveyance describing rights and benefits that are incidental to the land (such as easements and profits *à prendre*) and that are conveyed with it. Under the Law of Property Act 1925 such words are no longer necessary, since a conveyance of land is deemed to include all such ancillary rights unless a contrary intention is expressed in the document.

genetic fingerprinting *See* DNA FINGERPRINTING.

Geneva Conventions A series of international conventions on the laws of war, the first of which was formulated in Geneva in 1864. The 1864 and 1906 Conventions protect sick and wounded soldiers; the Geneva Protocol of 1925 prohibits the use of gas and bacteriological warfare; the three Conventions of 1929 and the four Conventions of 1949 protect sick and wounded soldiers, sailors, and prisoners of war, and the 1949 Conventions protect, in addition, certain groups of civilians. The First Protocol of 1977 supplements the 1949 Conventions, extending protection to wider groups of civilians, regulating the law of bombing, and enlarging the category of wars subject to the 1949 Conventions (to include, for example, civil wars). The 1949 Conventions are accepted by many states and are generally considered to embody customary international law that relates to war. *See also* HAGUE CONVENTIONS; MARTENS CLAUSE.

genocide *n.* Conduct aimed at the destruction of a national, ethnic, racial, or religious group. Genocide, as defined in the United Nations Convention on the Prevention and Punishment of the Crime of Genocide 1948, includes not only killing members of the group, but also causing them serious physical or psychological harm, imposing conditions of life that are intended to destroy them physically or measures intended to prevent childbirth, or forcibly transferring children of the group to another group, if these acts are carried out with the intention of destroying the group as a whole or in part. Destruction of a cultural or political group does not amount to genocide. The Genocide Convention 1948 declares that genocide is an international crime; the parties to the Convention undertake to punish not only acts of genocide committed within their jurisdiction but also complicity in genocide and conspiracy, incitement, and attempts to commit genocide. The Convention has been enacted into English law by the Genocide Act 1969. It is generally considered that the Convention embodies principles of customary international law that bind all nations, including those that are not parties to the Convention. *See also* WAR CRIMES; HUMANITARIAN INTERVENTION.

ghet *n.* A Jewish religious divorce, executed by the husband delivering a bill of divorce (which must be handwritten according to specific detailed rules) to his wife in the presence of two witnesses. In theory a ghet does not require a court procedure, but in practice it is usually executed through a court because of the many complexities of the relevant religious law. *See also* EXTRAJUDICIAL DIVORCE.

gift *n.* A gratuitous transfer or grant of property. A legally valid gift must normally be effected by deed, by physical delivery in the case of chattels, or by **donatio mortis causa*; the donor must intend ownership to pass as a gift. However, an **imperfect gift** (i.e. one for which the legal formalities have not been observed) may be treated as valid in equity in certain circumstances (*see, for example,* (PROPRIETARY) ESTOPPEL). A gift by will takes effect only on the death of the testator.

gift aid A system for individuals and companies to donate money to charities and for the charities to recover the tax paid on these donations (thus increasing the value of the donation by 28% in 2001–02). The taxpayer must make a **gift aid declaration** to the charity, stating that the payment is to be treated as gift aid. This system was first introduced in 1990, but tax relief was subject to the donation being of a minimum value, most recently £250. From April 2000, the system was extended to gifts of any value, including regular and one-off payments. It replaces the **deed of covenant in favour of charities from that date, although existing covenants remain valid.

gift over A provision in a will or other settlement enabling an interest in property to come into existence on the termination or failure of a prior interest.

gipsy (gypsy) *n.* A person of a nomadic way of life with no fixed abode. Formerly, local authorities had a duty to provide sites for gipsies resorting to their areas. (The strict definition of gipsy as a member of the Romany race did not apply for this purpose, but the term did not include travelling showmen or New Age travellers.) Under the Criminal Justice and Public Order Act 1994 this duty is abolished, although local authorities may provide sites if they wish. *See also* TRESPASS; UNAUTHORIZED CAMPING.

glue sniffing *See* INTOXICATION.

going public The process of forming a **public company or of reregistering a **private company as a public company.

golden handshake A payment, usually very large, made to a director or other senior executive who is forced to retire before the expiry of an employment contract (e.g. because of a takeover or merger) as compensation for loss of office. It is made when a contract does not allow payment in lieu of notice. The first £30,000 is often tax-free.

golden hello A lump-sum payment to entice an employee of senior level to join a new employer. Whether or not the payment is tax-free depends on the nature of the payment.

golden rule *See* INTERPRETATION OF STATUTES; INTERPRETATION OF WILLS.

golden share See SHARE.

good behaviour A term used in an order by a magistrate or by a Crown Court upon sentencing. The person named in the order should "be of good behaviour" towards another person (the complainant). The court may order that the person named enter into a *recognizance, and if he does not comply with the order he may be imprisoned for up to six months. The procedure may be used against anyone who has been brought before the court if there is a fear that he may cause a breach of the peace or if he is the subject of a complaint by someone (which need not be based on the commission of a criminal offence).

good consideration See CONSIDERATION.

good faith Honesty. An act carried out in good faith is one carried out honestly. Good faith is implied by law into certain contracts, such as those relating to commercial agency. See also UBERRIMAE FIDEI.

good leasehold title A form of title to registered leasehold land (see LAND REGISTRATION) that is equivalent to absolute leasehold title (see ABSOLUTE TITLE) except that the landlord's right to grant the lease is not guaranteed. Good leasehold title usually occurs when the lease appears valid on the face of it but the documents proving the landlord's title, or any superior lessor's title, have not been registered at the Land Registry.

good offices A technique of peaceful settlement of an international dispute, in which a third party, acting with the consent of the disputing states, serves as a friendly intermediary in an effort to persuade them to negotiate between themselves without necessarily offering the disputing states substantive suggestions towards achieving a settlement. See also CONCILIATION; MEDIATION.

goods *pl. n.* Personal chattels or items of property. Land is excluded, and the statutory definition in the Sale of Goods Act 1979 also excludes *choses in action and money. It includes *emblements and things attached to or forming part of land that are agreed to be severed before sale or under a contract of sale.

goodwill *n.* The advantage arising from the reputation and trade connections of a business, in particular the likelihood that existing customers will continue to patronize it. Goodwill is a substantial item to be taken into account on the sale of a business; it may need to be protected by prohibiting the vendor from setting up in the same business for a stated period in competition with the business he has sold.

government circulars Documents circulated by government departments on behalf of ministers, setting out principles and practices for the exercise of ministerial powers delegated to others. These may provide mere administrative guidelines or they may be intended to have legislative effect (i.e. as *delegated legislation), in which case any purported exercise of the delegated powers is invalid unless it complies with them. See ULTRA VIRES.

government department An organ of central government responsible for a particular sphere of public administration (e.g. the Treasury). It is staffed by permanent civil servants and is normally headed by a minister who is politically responsible for its activities and is assisted by one or more junior ministers, usually responsible for particular aspects of departmental policy.

government-in-exile *n.* A government established outside its territorial jurisdiction. Following the German defeat of Poland in 1939, the Polish government transferred its operations to London and thereby became a government-in-exile.

Grand Committees, Scottish and Welsh Committees of the House of Commons involved with matters relating to Scotland and Wales, respectively. The former consists of the 72 members representing Scottish constituencies and 10–15 other members. A Bill certified by the Speaker as relating exclusively to Scotland may by standing orders of the House be referred to the Committee for its second reading, and the Committee also debates other purely Scottish matters. The Welsh Grand Committee, which consists of the 38 members representing Welsh constituencies and up to 5 others, is purely deliberative. It considers matters relating exclusively to Wales but is not empowered to undertake second readings.

grant *n.* **1.** The creation or transfer of the ownership of property (e.g. an estate or interest in land) by written instrument; for example, the grant of a lease. *See also* LIE IN GRANT. **2.** A *grant of representation. **3.** The allocation of money, powers, etc., by Parliament or the Crown for a specific purpose.

grant of representation Authority granted by the court to named individuals or to a *trust corporation to administer the estate of a deceased person. The grant is of *probate when the will is proved by the executors named in it or of *letters of administration when the deceased died intestate, the deceased's will did not appoint executors, or the executors named do not prove the will.

grants in aid Central government grants towards local authority expenditure, comprising specific grants for particular services (e.g. the police) and rate support grants to augment income generally.

grave hardship (in divorce proceedings) If a divorce petition is based on a five-year separation, the respondent may oppose the grant of the *decree nisi on the ground that the dissolution of the marriage will result in grave financial or other hardship and that it would be wrong in all the circumstances to dissolve the marriage. Such applications rarely succeed. *See also* DIVORCE.

Gray's Inn One of the four *Inns of Court, situated in Holborn. The earliest claims for its existence are *c.* 1320.

Greater London A local government area consisting of the 32 **London boroughs** (12 inner, and 20 outer), the *City of London, and the Inner and Middle Temples. A Greater London Council was established by the Local Government Act 1972 but abolished by the Local Government Act 1985 with effect from 1 April 1986. London borough councils, which are unitary (single-tier) authorities, are elected every fourth year, counting from 1982 (*see also* LOCAL AUTHORITY). In 1998 Londoners voted in favour of government proposals to elect a *Mayor of London and a *London Assembly to operate from 2000; the Great London Authority Act 1999 enacted these proposals (*see also* GREATER LONDON AUTHORITY). The City of London is distinct in both constitution and functions. The Temples have limited independent functions (e.g. public health), but are administered in many respects by the City's Common Council.

Greater London Authority A body created by the Greater London Authority Act 1999 and consisting of the *Mayor of London and the *London Assembly. Its principal purposes are to promote economic development and wealth creation, social development, and the improvement of the environment in Greater London. The *London Development Agency was created to further the first of these aims.

green form Under the Legal Aid Act 1988, the form upon which an application for legal advice and/or legal assistance could be made by those within the financial limits on eligibility. Persons receiving certain specified social security allowances automatically qualified for green form advice. The name referred to the colour of the application form used. As from 1 April 2000, the *legal aid scheme was replaced by differing levels of legal service provided by the *Community Legal Service, under which the service offered by the green form scheme is most broadly covered by the level of service entitled **legal help**.

green paper *See* COMMAND PAPERS.

grievous bodily harm (GBH) Serious physical injury. Under the Offences Against the Person Act 1861 there are several offences involving grievous bodily harm. It is an offence, punishable by up to five years' imprisonment, to inflict (by direct acts) grievous bodily harm upon anyone with the intention of harming them (even only slightly); if the intention was merely to frighten the victim the defendant is guilty of *assault and *battery. It is an offence, punishable by a maximum sentence of life imprisonment, to cause grievous bodily harm to anyone with the intention of seriously injuring them or of resisting or preventing lawful arrest. "Causing" in this offence includes indirect acts, such as pulling a chair away from a person so that he falls and breaks his arm. If a person intends to cause grievous bodily harm but his victim actually dies, he is guilty of murder, even though he did not intend to kill him. Causing grievous bodily harm may also be an element in some other offence, e.g. *burglary. The courts have said that judges should not attempt to define grievous bodily harm for the jury, but should leave it to them, in every case, to decide whether the harm caused was really serious. *See also* WOUNDING WITH INTENT.

gross *See* IN GROSS.

gross indecency A sexual act that is more than ordinary *indecency but falls short of actual intercourse. It may include masturbation and indecent physical contact, or even indecent behaviour without any physical contact. It is an offence for a man to commit an act of gross indecency with another man unless both parties are over 18, consent to the act, and it is carried out in private. This is punishable by up to two years' imprisonment or, if one of the parties is under 18, by up to five years' imprisonment. It is also an offence to cause or arrange for a man to commit an act of gross indecency with another man, even if the act is carried out in private and between consenting adults. It is an offence, punishable by up to two years' imprisonment, to commit an act of gross indecency with or towards a child (of either sex) under the age of 14 or to incite a child to commit such an act.

gross negligence A high degree of *negligence, manifested in behaviour substantially worse than that of the average reasonable man. Causing someone's death through gross negligence could be regarded as *manslaughter if the accused appreciated the risk he was taking and intended to avoid it, but showed an unacceptable degree of negligence in avoiding it.

ground rent A rent reserved by a long lease of land. For example when a house or flat is sold on a lease for 99 years, the lessor may reserve a small annual rent payable throughout the term as well as the capital price payable on the grant of the lease. In essence, a ground rent ignores the value of the buildings on the land. *Building leases are sometimes granted in return for a ground rent rather than a capital sum.

group accounts *Accounts required by law to be prepared by a registered company that has a *subsidiary company. Group accounts deal with the financial position of the company and its subsidiaries collectively.

group action A procedure in which a large number of claims arising out of the same event, or against the same defendant, are dealt with together (e.g. proceedings by the victims of a plane crash for damages for personal injury). The court exercises more direct control over the *interim (interlocutory) proceedings in such cases than is normal. *Compare* REPRESENTATIVE ACTION.

guarantee *n.* **1.** A secondary agreement in which a person (the **guarantor**) is liable for the debt or default of another (the principal debtor), who is the party primarily liable for the debt. A guarantee requires an independent *consideration and must be evidenced in writing. A guarantor who has paid out on his guarantee has a right to be indemnified by the principal debtor. *Compare* INDEMNITY. **2.** *See* WARRANTY.

guarantee company *See* LIMITED COMPANY.

guarantee payment Under the Employment Rights Act 1996, the sum that an employer must pay to an employee for whom he is unable to provide work during the whole of any working day or shift. However, an employee is not entitled to a guarantee payment if he is laid off because of industrial action affecting his own or an associated employer, if he unreasonably refuses other suitable work, or if he fails to comply with the employer's reasonable requirements for ensuring that he is available for work if and when needed. Generally, employees only become entitled to a guarantee payment after four weeks' *continuous employment in the business; one employed for a specific task that is not expected to last more than 12 weeks and one having a fixed-term employment contract of a year or less do not qualify at all. The payment is limited to the employee's basic wage for the relevant shift, subject to a maximum prescribed by regulations made by the Secretary of State for Work and Pensions and reviewed annually. An employee is not entitled to more than five guarantee payments in any period of three months. The statutory payment is offset by any amount payable to the employee under his employment contract while he is laid off. An employee may complain to an employment tribunal if his employer fails to pay him any sum due as a guarantee payment, and the tribunal can order the employer to pay the sum due.

guard dog A dog kept specifically for the purpose of protecting people, property, or someone who is guarding people or property. Under the Guard Dogs Act 1975 it is a summary offence punishable by fine to use a guard dog, or to allow its use, unless either it is secured and cannot roam the premises freely or a handler is controlling it. The Act does not, however, affect civil liability for injuries or damage caused by the dog, which depends on the law of tort (*see* CLASSIFICATION OF ANIMALS). In some cases the owner may be criminally liable for injury caused by a guard dog; for example, if it kills someone, the owner may be guilty of manslaughter by gross negligence or of constructive *manslaughter. *See also* DANGEROUS ANIMALS.

guardian *n.* One who is formally appointed to look after a child's interests when the parents of the child do not have *parental responsibility for him or have died. Appointment can be made either by the courts during *family proceedings, if it is considered necessary for the child's welfare, or privately by any parent with parental responsibility. Under the Children Act 1989 a private appointment does not have to be by deed or will but merely made in writing, dated, and signed by the person making it. A guardian automatically assumes parental responsibility for the child.

guardian *ad litem* *See* CHILDREN'S GUARDIAN.

guardianship order An order, made under the Mental Health Act 1983, placing a person over the age of 16 who has been convicted of an offence and who is suffering from any of certain types of mental illness under the guardianship of a local social services authority or an approved person. It has been proposed by the Law

Commission that it should no longer be possible to appoint an individual as guardian.

guillotine *n.* A House of Commons procedure for speeding up the passing of legislation: a means whereby government can control the parliamentary timetable and limit debate. The number of days allowed for a Bill's Committee and Report stages is limited by an allocation-of-time order moved by the government; the total time available is then allotted between particular portions of the Bill. When the time limit for any portion is reached, debate on it ceases and all outstanding votes are taken forthwith. *Compare* CLOSURE.

guilty *adj.* **1.** An admission in court by an accused person that he has committed the offence with which he is charged. If there is more than one charge he may plead guilty to some and *not guilty to others. **2.** A *verdict finding that the accused has committed the offence with which he was charged or some other offence of which he can be convicted on the basis of the evidence in the case. *See also* CONVICTION.

guilty knowledge The knowledge of facts or circumstances required for a person to have *mens rea* for a particular crime. Knowledge is usually actual knowledge, but when a person deliberately ignores facts that are obvious, he is sometimes considered to have "constructive" knowledge.

guilty mind *See* MENS REA.

gunboat diplomacy The settling of disputes with weaker states by the threat of *use of force. The phrase derives from the Victorian colonial empire, in which gunboats and other naval vessels were often utilized in order to coerce local rulers to accept the terms and trade of British merchants.

gypsy *n. See* GIPSY.

habeas corpus A prerogative writ used to challenge the validity of a person's detention, either in official custody (e.g. when held pending deportation or extradition) or in private hands. Deriving from the royal prerogative and therefore originally obtained by petitioning the sovereign, it is now issued by the Divisional Court of the Queen's Bench Division, or, during vacation, by any High Court judge. If on an application for the writ the Court or judge is satisfied that the detention is prima facie unlawful, the custodian is ordered to appear and justify it, failing which release is ordered.

habitual residence The place or country in which a person has his home. Habitual residence is necessary in order to establish *domicile.

hacking *n.* Gaining unauthorized access to a computer system. This is a summary offence under the Computer Misuse Act 1990. Under this Act it is also an offence, triable summarily or on indictment, to engage in hacking with the intention of committing another offence (e.g. theft, diverting funds), or to destroy, corrupt, or modify computer-stored information or programs while hacking. This offence can be committed either through using one computer to gain access to another computer or simply by gaining access to one computer only. *Copyright protection applies. *See also* DATA PROTECTION.

Hague Conventions The Hague Conventions for the Pacific Settlement of International Disputes: a series of international conventions on the laws of war (3 in 1899 and 13 in 1907). The 1899 Conventions established a *Permanent Court of Arbitration, which was active before the Permanent Court of International Justice and the *International Court of Justice functioned. The Hague Conventions are still in force but their provisions are often inapplicable to modern warfare. *See also* GENERAL PARTICIPATION CLAUSE; GENEVA CONVENTIONS; MARTENS CLAUSE.

Hague Rules *See* BILL OF LADING; INTERNATIONAL CARRIAGE.

half a year (in a lease) A *fixed term that begins on a quarter day and ends on the next but one quarter day.

half blood *See* CONSANGUINITY.

half-pay A method of remunerating officers who are retained on the active list but are not for the time being required to perform military or naval duties. It is now only applicable to field marshalls.

half-secret trust (semi-secret trust) A trust whose existence is disclosed on the face of the will or other document creating it but the beneficiaries of which are undisclosed, though known to the secret trustee(s). *See also* SECRET TRUST.

Hamburg Rules *See* BILL OF LADING; INTERNATIONAL CARRIAGE.

handguns *See* FIREARM.

handling stolen goods Dishonestly receiving goods that one knows or believes to be stolen or undertaking, arranging, or assisting someone to retain, remove, or dispose of stolen goods. Under the Theft Act 1968, this is an offence subject to a maximum sentence of 14 years' imprisonment. "Stolen goods" include not only goods that have been the subject of theft but also anything that has been obtained by *blackmail or *deception. The theft or other crime may have occurred at any time and anywhere in the world, provided the handling occurs in England or Wales. There is also a provision to extend the concept of stolen goods to the proceeds of their sale. Thus if A steals goods, sells them for £3000, and gives part of the money to B, B is guilty of handling if he knows the money represents the proceeds of the sale of stolen goods. If A then buys a car with the rest of the £3000 and C agrees to dispose of the car for A, knowing or believing that it was bought with the proceeds of sale of stolen goods, C will also be guilty of handling, since he has "undertaken to dispose of stolen goods". The crime is therefore very widely defined; it also covers, for instance, forging or providing new documents and number plates for stolen cars and contacting and negotiating with dealers in stolen property (fences). *See also* DISHONESTY.

Hansard *n.* The name by which the Official Report of Parliamentary Debates is customarily referred to (after the Hansard family, who – as printers to the House of Commons – were concerned with compiling reports in the 19th century). Reporting was taken over by the government in 1908, and separate reports for the House of Commons and the House of Lords are published by The *Stationery Office in daily and weekly parts. They contain a verbatim record of debates and all other proceedings (e.g. question time). Members of Parliament have the right to correct anything attributed to them, but may not make any other alterations. In certain circumstances Hansard may be used to discover the will of Parliament, as an aid to judicial statutory interpretation when legislation is unclear. *Compare* JOURNALS.

harassment *n.* Under amendments made in 1994 to the Public Order Act 1986, an offence is committed when harassment, alarm, or distress is caused to the victim. *See* HARASSMENT OF DEBTORS; HARASSMENT OF OCCUPIER; NUISANCE NEIGHBOURS; RACIST ABUSE; SEX DISCRIMINATION; STALKING; THREATENING BEHAVIOUR.

harassment of debtors Behaviour designed to force a debtor or one believed to be a debtor to pay his debt. This is a criminal offence, punishable by fine, if the debt is based on a contract and the nature or frequency of the acts subject the debtor (or members of his household) to alarm, distress, or humiliation. Harassment also includes false statements that the debtor will face criminal proceedings or that the creditor is officially authorized to enforce payment and using a document that the creditor falsely represents as being official. The offence may overlap with the crime of *blackmail, but it will also cover cases in which the creditor believes he is entitled to act as he does (which might not amount to blackmail).

harassment of occupier The offence of a landlord (or his agent) using or threatening violence or any other kind of pressure to obtain possession of his property from a tenant (the residential occupier) without a court order. The offence is found in the Protection from Eviction Act 1977 and includes interfering with the tenant's peace or comfort (or that of the tenant's household), withdrawing or not providing services normally required by the tenant (e.g. cutting off gas or electricity, even when the bills have not been paid), and preventing the tenant from exercising any of his rights or taking any legal or other action in respect of his tenancy. The Act does not apply, however, to a displaced residential owner, as opposed to a landlord (*see also* FORCIBLE ENTRY). The Protection from Harassment Act 1997 prohibits harassment; the offence is punishable with a jail sentence of up to five years. *See also* NUISANCE NEIGHBOURS.

harbouring *n.* Hiding a criminal or suspected criminal. This will normally constitute the offence of *impeding apprehension or prosecution. *See also* ESCAPE.

hard law *See* SOFT LAW.

harmonization of laws The process by which member states of the EU make changes in their national laws, in accordance with *Community legislation, to produce uniformity, particularly relating to commercial matters of common interest. The Council of the European Union has, for example, issued directives on the harmonization of company law and of units of measurement. *Compare* APPROXIMATION OF LAWS.

hay bote *See* ESTOVERS.

headings *pl. n.* Words prefixed to sections of a statute. They are treated in the same way as *preambles and may be used to assist in resolving an ambiguity.

Health and Safety Commission A body responsible for furthering the general purposes of the Health and Safety at Work Act 1974, for example by advising and promoting research and training. It also appoints a Health and Safety Executive, which shares with local authorities responsibility for enforcing the Act and operates for this purpose through such inspectorates as the Factories and Nuclear Installations Inspectorates. *See also* SAFETY AT WORK.

Health Authority A body through which the health service is administered and supplied at district level. Health Authorities came into being in April 1996 with the merger of the District Health Authorities and the Family Health Service Authorities (*see* NATIONAL HEALTH SERVICE), with the aim of ensuring better coordination of purchasing across primary and secondary health care. They are responsible for developing strategies to improve health and for securing a wide range of health-care services for their populations.

health records Records kept by the National Health Service about patients. Under the Access to Health Records Act 1990, from 1 November 1991 most patients were given the right to see their health records. The patient does not have to give a reason for wanting access and can authorize someone else, such as his solicitor, to obtain access on his behalf. It is a policy of the Department of Health that individuals are permitted to see what has been written about them and that health-care providers should make arrangements to allow patients to see, if they wish, records other than those covered by the 1990 Act. This Act has been amended by the Data Protection Act 1998 (*see also* DATA PROTECTION).

Health Service Commissioners Commissioners (one each for England and Wales) instituted by the National Health Service Reorganization Act 1973. They investigate complaints by members of the public of hardship or injustice suffered through failure in a health-care service and other cases of maladministration by a *Health Authority. They also now investigate complaints about general practitioners, dentists, pharmacists, and opticians. Complaints must be made directly to a Commissioner within one year of the date on which the matter first came to the complainant's notice. Certain matters (e.g. alleged professional negligence) are excluded from investigation. Both offices are in practice held by the *Parliamentary Commissioner for Administration.

hearing *n.* The trial of a case before a court. Hearings are usually in public but the public may be barred from the court in certain circumstances (*see* IN CAMERA).

Hearing Officer An officer of the *European Court of Justice whose role was established in 1982 after criticism of the administrative nature of the decision-making process of the Commission in *competition law cases. His terms of reference were published in the Commission's XXth Report on Competition Policy.

He organizes and chairs hearings, decides the date, duration, and place of hearings, seeks to ensure protection of the interests of defendants, and supervises the preparation of minutes of hearings. He will, in addition, prepare his own report of a hearing and make recommendations as to the future conduct of the matter.

hearsay evidence Evidence of the statements of a person other than the witness who is testifying and statements in documents offered to prove the truth of what was asserted. In general, hearsay evidence is inadmissible (the **rule against hearsay**) but this principle is subject to numerous exceptions. In civil cases, the Civil Evidence Act 1995 abolished the rule against hearsay. The 1995 Act provides that what in civil litigation would formerly have been called "hearsay evidence" may be used when a notice of the intention to reply on that evidence is given. It is for the court to decide at trial what weight to put on any particular evidence, whether it is hearsay or not. At common law, there are numerous exceptions applicable to both civil and criminal cases, e.g. *declarations of deceased persons, evidence given in former trials, *depositions, *admissions, and *confessions. Some exceptions apply only to criminal cases, e.g. *dying declarations and statements admitted under the Criminal Justice Act 1988 (which makes most first-hand hearsay and certain business documents admissible). *See also* ADMISSIBILITY OF RECORDS; ORIGINAL EVIDENCE.

hedgerow *n.* A row of shrubs or small trees bordering a field or lane. Hedging of ancient origin is protected under the Hedgerow Regulations 1997. Farmers are required to notify local authorities of their intention to uproot a hedgerow, allowing time for a protection order to be issued; the notification period is currently 42 days. Failure to comply with the regulations is punishable by an unlimited fine.

heir *n.* Before 1926, the person entitled under common law and statutory rules to inherit the freehold land of one who died intestate. The Administration of Estates Act 1925 abolished these rules of descent and the concept of heirship, except that *entailed interests and in certain rare cases the property of mental patients devolve according to the old rules. In addition, the Law of Property Act 1925 provides that a conveyance of property in favour of the heir of a deceased person conveys it to the person who would be the heir under the old rules. Where these exceptions apply, an **heir apparent** is the person (e.g. an eldest son) who will inherit provided that he outlives his ancestor; an **heir presumptive** is an heir (e.g. a daughter) whose right to inherit may be lost by the birth of an heir with greater priority (e.g. a son). *See also* HEIRS OF THE BODY.

heir apparent *See* HEIR.

heirloom *n.* A *chattel that, by custom or close association with land, passed on the owner's death with his house to his heir and did not form part of his residuary estate. Heirlooms now pass to the deceased's personal representatives unless special provision is made for them to pass to the heir direct. When heirlooms are held, together with land, under a settlement, the *tenant for life is entitled under the Settled Land Act 1925 to sell the heirlooms. The price is payable to the trustees as *capital money.

heir presumptive *See* HEIR.

heirs of the body Lineal descendants who were entitled to inherit freehold land under the rules applying on intestacy before the Administration of Estates Act 1925. A conveyance of land "to A and the heirs of his body" creates an *entailed interest that devolves to descendants only, according to the old rules. Thus (1) males are first in priority and the principle of primogeniture applies, e.g. an older son is preferred to a younger; (2) in the absence of male heirs, females in equal degree share the land equally; and (3) lineal descendants of an heir represent him, thus the son of an older son who dies will inherit to the exclusion of a younger son.

Helms-Burton Act The Cuban Liberty and Democratic Solidarity (Libertad) Act 1996: an Act of the US Congress under which nationals of third states dealing with US property expropriated by the Cuban revolutionary state, using such property, or benefiting by it may be sued for damages before American courts and even face being barred from entry into the United States.

help at court *See* COMMUNITY LEGAL SERVICE; ABWOR.

hereditament *n.* **1.** Historically, any real property capable of being passed to an *heir. **Corporeal hereditaments** are tangible items of property, such as land and buildings. **Incorporeal hereditaments** are intangible rights in land, such as easements and profits *à prendre*. **2.** A unit of land that has been separately assessed for rating purposes.

Her Majesty's Stationery Office (HMSO) The government's official publisher, which was privatized on 1 October 1996. Most of its functions were taken over by The *Stationery Office; however, certain of its functions have been retained. These include administration of Crown and Parliamentary copyright, overseeing the functions of the Queen's Printer in relation to Acts of Parliament, statutory instruments, and some other material of an official or legislative nature, the administration of the library subsidy, and provision of official publications to members of the European Parliament. It operates as part of the Office of Public Services in the Cabinet Office. The Copyright Unit of Her Majesty's Stationery Office handles day-to-day administration in this area.

high contracting parties The representatives of states who have signed or ratified a *treaty. From the point of view of international law it is immaterial where the treaty-making power resides (e.g. in a head of state, a senate, or a representative body): this is a question determinable by the constitutional law of the particular contracting state concerned. Other nations are entitled only to demand from those with whom they contract a *de facto* capacity to bind the society that they represent. The House of Lords has held that the determination of who the high contracting parties are is to be based upon the terms of the individual treaty in question. Thus the signatories, as well as the parties, can be considered to be high contracting parties.

High Court of Justice A court created by the Judicature Acts 1873–75, forming part of the *Supreme Court of Judicature. Under Part 7 of the *Civil Procedure Rules, which sets out the rules for starting proceedings, the High Court is restricted to (1) personal injury claims of £50,000 or more, (2) other claims exceeding £15,000, (3) specialist High Court claims that are required to be placed on a specialist list (e.g. the Commercial List), and (4) claims that are required by statute to be commenced in the High Court. The High Court has *appellate jurisdiction in civil and criminal matters. It is divided into the three Divisions: the *Queen's Bench Division, *Chancery Division, and *Family Division.

high seas The seas beyond *territorial waters, i.e. the seas more than 12 miles from the coasts of most countries. The English courts have jurisdiction to try offences committed by anyone anywhere on the high seas in a British ship. They also have jurisdiction to try offences committed anywhere in the world on board a British-controlled aircraft while it is in flight. Sometimes these offences amount to the special crimes of *hijacking or *piracy.

The high seas as defined by Article 86 of the UN Convention on the Law of the Sea 1982 exclude the *exclusive economic zone. However, the freedoms of all states to fly over, navigate, lay submarine cables, etc., in the exclusive economic zone, as stated in the earlier Geneva Convention on the High Seas 1958, have been preserved in Article 58 (1) of the UN Convention. *See also* LAW OF THE SEA.

highway *n.* A road or other way over which the public may pass and repass as of right. Highways include *footpaths, *bridle ways, *driftways, carriage ways, and cul-de-sacs. Navigable rivers are also highways. A highway is created either under statutory powers or by dedication (express or implied) by a landowner and acceptance (by use) by the public. Once a highway has been created, it does not cease to be a highway by reason of disuse. Obstructing a highway is a public nuisance (*see also* OBSTRUCTION), and misuse of the public right to pass and repass over a highway is a trespass against the owner of the subsoil of the highway.

hijacking *n.* Seizing or exercising control of an aircraft in flight by the use or threat of force (the term derives from the call "Hi Jack," used when illegal alcohol was seized from bootleggers during Prohibition in the United States). Hijacking is prohibited in international law by the Tokyo Convention 1963, which defines the conditions under which jurisdiction may be assumed over hijackers, but does not oblige states to exercise such jurisdiction and does not create an obligation to extradite hijackers. There is also a Hague Convention of 1970 and a Montreal Convention of 1971 creating the offences of unlawfully seizing or exercising control of an aircraft by force or threats and of sabotaging aircraft; these conventions provide for compulsory jurisdiction as well as extradition. In English law, hijacking and similar offences are governed by the Hijacking Act 1971, the Protection of Aircraft Act 1973, and the Aviation Security Act 1982.

hire **1.** *vb.* To enter into a contract for the temporary use of another's goods, or the temporary provision of his services or labour, in return for payment. In the case of goods, the person hiring them is a bailee (*see* BAILMENT). **2.** *n.* **a.** The act of hiring. **b.** The payment made under a contract of hire.

hire purchase A method of buying goods in which the purchaser takes possession of them as soon as he has paid an initial instalment of the price (a **deposit**) and obtains ownership of the goods when he has paid all the agreed number of subsequent instalments and exercises his option to purchase the goods. A **hire-purchase agreement** differs from a *credit sale agreement and a sale-by-instalments contract because in these transactions ownership passes when the contract is signed. It also differs from a contract of *hire, because in this case ownership never passes. Hire-purchase agreements were formerly controlled by government regulations that stipulated the minimum deposit and the length of the repayment period. These controls were removed in July 1982. Hire-purchase agreements were also formerly controlled by the Hire Purchase Act 1965, but most are now regulated by the Consumer Credit Act 1974. In this Act a hire-purchase agreement is regarded as one in which goods are bailed in return for periodical payments by the bailee; ownership passes to the bailee if he complies with the terms of the agreement and exercises his option to purchase.

A hire-purchase agreement often involves a finance company as a third party. The seller of the goods sells them outright to the finance company, which enters into a hire-purchase agreement with the hirer. In this situation there is generally no direct contractual relationship between the seller and the buyer.

historic buildings *See* BUILDING PRESERVATION NOTICE; LISTED BUILDING.

HM Procurator General *See* TREASURY SOLICITOR.

HMSO *See* HER MAJESTY'S STATIONERY OFFICE.

holder *n.* The person in possession of a *bill of exchange or promissory note. He may be the payee, the endorsee, or the bearer. A holder may sue on the bill in his own name. When value (which includes a past debt or liability) has at any time been given for a bill, the holder is a **holder for value**, as regards the acceptor and all who were parties to the bill before value was given. A **holder in due course** is one who has taken a bill of exchange in good faith and for value, before it was overdue, and without notice of previous dishonour or of any defect in the title of the person who negotiated or transferred the bill. He holds the bill free from any defect of title of prior parties and may enforce payment against all parties liable on the bill.

holding company *See* SUBSIDIARY COMPANY.

holding out Conduct by one person that leads another to believe that he has an authority that does not in fact exist. By the doctrine of *estoppel, the first person may be prevented from denying that the authority exists. For example, a person who wrongly represents himself as being a partner in a firm will be as liable as if he were in fact a partner to anyone who gives credit to the firm on the faith of the representation.

holding over The action of a tenant continuing in occupation of premises after his lease has expired. If this is without the landlord's consent, the landlord may claim damages from the tenant. If, however, a landlord accepts rent from a tenant who is holding over, a new tenancy is created.

holograph *n.* A document written completely by the hand of its author; for example, a will in the testator's own handwriting.

homeless person Under the Housing Act 1996, one who has no living accommodation that he is entitled to occupy, or is unlawfully excluded from his own living accommodation, or whose accommodation is mobile and cannot be placed in a location where he is permitted to reside in it. Certain homeless people (e.g. the elderly or infirm or those with dependent children) have a statutory right to permanent local-authority accommodation or, if they became homeless intentionally, to temporary accommodation.

home-loss payment Additio..al compensation paid under the Land Compensation Act 1973 to a person on the compulsory acquisition of his property if he has occupied it as his principal residence throughout the preceding five years.

Home Secretary The minister in charge of the Home Office, who is responsible throughout England and Wales for law and order generally (including matters concerning the police and the prison and security services) and for a variety of other domestic matters, such as nationality, immigration, race relations, extradition, and deportation. He also advises the sovereign on the exercise of the *prerogative of mercy.

homicide *n.* The act of killing a human being. **Unlawful homicide**, which constitutes the crime of *murder, *manslaughter, or *infanticide, can only be committed if the victim is an independent human being (*see* ABORTION), the act itself causes the death (*see* CAUSATION), and the victim dies within a year after the act alleged to have caused the death. A British citizen may be tried for homicide committed anywhere in the world. **Lawful homicide** occurs when somebody uses reasonable force in preventing crime or arresting an offender, in self-defence or defence of others, or (possibly) in defence of his property, and causes death as a result. *See also* EXCUSABLE HOMICIDE.

homosexual conduct Sexual behaviour between persons of the same sex. The acts of *buggery and *gross indecency are not crimes if the act is committed in private and both parties are over the age of 16 and consent to the act. Lesbianism is not a criminal act.

honorarium *n.* A payment or reward made to a person for services rendered by him voluntarily.

honour clause An express statement in a *contract that an agreement is intended to be binding in honour only. The courts will usually allow it to take effect and so will not enforce the agreement.

horizontal agreements Agreements between companies at the same level of trade; for example, agreements between two or more manufacturers or wholesalers, rather than between a manufacturer and a distributor (*compare* VERTICAL AGREEMENTS). Horizontal agreements that restrict competition may infringe the competition provisions of *Article 81 of the Treaty of Rome and the Chapter I prohibition in the Competition Act 1998. Most *cartels are horizontal agreements.

hospital order An order of the Crown Court or a magistrates' court authorizing the detention in a specified hospital (for a period of 12 months, renewable by the hospital managers) of a convicted person suffering from *mental disorder. Unless a *restriction order has also been made, discharge while an order is in force may be authorized by the managers or the doctor in charge or directed by a *Mental Health Review Tribunal.

hostage *n.* A person who is held as a security. Under the Taking of Hostages Act 1982, it is an offence, punishable in the English courts by a maximum sentence of life imprisonment, to take anyone as a hostage against his will anywhere in the world and to threaten to kill, injure, or continue to hold him hostage in order to force a state, international governmental organization, or person to do or not to do something. This is an extraditable offence, but prosecutions may only be brought with the consent of the Attorney General. *See also* HIJACKING; KIDNAPPING; TERRORISM.

hostile witness An *adverse witness who wilfully refuses to testify truthfully on behalf of the party who called him. A hostile witness may, with the permission of the court, be cross-examined by that party, for example by putting to him a *previous statement that is inconsistent with his present testimony.

hotchpot *n.* The bringing into account, on distribution of an intestate's estate, of certain benefits separately conferred on the beneficiaries. In the case of total intestacy, the Administration of Estates Act 1925 expressly brings the *rule against double portions into operation. It provides that property given by the intestate during his lifetime to any of his children must be brought into account, unless a contrary intention is expressed or appears from the circumstances. Thus if A gives £10,000 to his son B, and dies intestate leaving an estate worth £50,000 to which his children B and C are entitled equally, B will in fact receive £20,000 and C £30,000. The rule applies only to lifetime gifts made by way of advancement (i.e. as permanent provision and not for maintenance or temporary purposes). In the case of partial intestacy, benefits conferred by the will on a surviving spouse and on the deceased's issue (i.e. his children, grandchildren, and remoter direct descendants) are also brought into account.

hot pursuit, right of The right of a coastal state to pursue a foreign ship within its *territorial waters (or possibly its contiguous zone) and there capture it if the state has good reason to believe that this vessel has violated its laws. The hot pursuit may – but only if it is uninterrupted – continue onto the *high seas, but it must terminate the moment the pursued ship enters the territorial waters of another state, as such pursuit would involve an offence to the other state; in these circumstances *extradition should be employed instead.

house bote *See* ESTOVERS.

housebreaking *n.* Forcing one's way into someone else's house. If this is carried out with the intention of committing certain specified crimes in the house, or if, after breaking into a house, certain crimes then take place, the housebreaking amounts to *burglary. It is also a statutory offence, which is punishable by up to three years' imprisonment, if a person has with him any article that he intends to use in connection with burglary, theft, or criminal deception. In addition to the usual housebreaking implements, this includes such things as rubber gloves to conceal fingerprints.

House of Commons The representative chamber of *Parliament (also known as the **Lower House**), composed of 659 **Members of Parliament (MPs)** elected for 529 single-member constituencies in England, 72 in Scotland, 40 in Wales, and 18 in Northern Ireland (*see* ELECTION; FRANCHISE). The total number of MPs may within certain limits be varied as a result of constituency changes proposed by the *boundary commissions.

A number of people are disqualified from membership. They include those under 21, civil servants, the police and the regular armed forces, most clergy (but not Nonconformist ministers), aliens, those declared bankrupt, convicted prisoners and people guilty of corrupt or illegal practices, the holders of most judicial offices (but not lay magistrates), and the holders of a large number of public offices listed in the House of Commons Disqualification Act 1975. Public offices that disqualify include stewardship of the *Chiltern Hundreds and the Manor of Northstead. The number of members who may hold ministerial office is limited to 95. The House of Lords Act 1999 removed an earlier disqualification on hereditary peers from voting and from being elected members of the House of Commons. The Removal of Clergy Disqualification Bill, when enacted, will permit all clergy to be MPs.

The House is presided over by the **Speaker**, who is elected from among themselves by the members at the beginning of each Parliament. The Speaker is responsible for the orderly conduct of proceedings, which must be supervised with complete impartiality, and is the person through whom the members may collectively communicate with the sovereign. The **Leader of the House** is a government minister responsible for arranging the business of the House in consultation with the Opposition.

House of Commons Commission A body established in 1978 to supervise the staffing of the House. It consists of the Speaker, the Leader of the House, and four other members, one of whom is appointed by the Leader of the Opposition.

House of Lords The second chamber of *Parliament (also known as the **Upper House**), which scrutinizes legislation and has judicial functions. The House of Lords Act 1999 substantially changed the constitution of the House by excluding hereditary peers from a place in the House as of right, although for a transitional period 92 were allowed to remain on merit. Of these, 75 were elected by their own political party or by cross-bench (usually non-party-political) groups. A further 15 hereditary peers were elected to act as Deputy Speakers or Committee chairmen. Two hereditary royal appointments were also retained: the Earl Marshal and the

Lord Great Chamberlain. The other members of the Lords are (as at July 2001) life
peers (592) or bishops (26), comprising the Archbishops of Canterbury and York, the
Bishops of London, Durham, and Winchester, and 21 other Anglican bishops selected
according to seniority of appointment. Long-term reform of the Lords is currently
being debated; a white paper published in November 2001 proposed the following
composition of the Lords: 120 members to be elected by the public, 120 non-party-
political members to be selected by the *House of Lords Appointments Commission,
up to 332 members to be nominated by party leaders, and 16 bishops.

The House is presided over by the *Lord Chancellor and its business is arranged, in
consultation with the Opposition, by a government minister appointed **Leader of
the House**. The Lords is the final court of appeal in the UK in both civil and
criminal cases, although it refers some cases to the *European Court of Justice for a
ruling. In its judicial capacity the Lords formally adopts opinions delivered by an
Appellate Committee (of which there are two), and it is a constitutional convention
that the only peers who may participate in the proceedings of the committee are
the Lord Chancellor, the *Lords of Appeal in Ordinary, and others who have held
high judicial office.

House of Lords Appointments Commission A body that recommends people
for appointment as non-party-political life peers and vets all nominations for
membership of the House of Lords. Set up by the Government following the House
of Lords Act 1999, which modernizes the Lords, the Commission is an independent
nondepartmental public body staffed by civil servants.

housing action area An area declared to be such by a housing authority on the
grounds that living conditions in it are unsatisfactory and should be dealt with
comprehensively over a five-year period. This is done by special measures to improve
the standards and management of accommodation and the well-being of the
inhabitants. A housing action area may incorporate a *general improvement area. *See
also* PRIORITY NEIGHBOURHOOD. *Compare* CLEARANCE AREA.

housing action trust (HAT) A statutory trust set up for a particular area with
the objects to secure: the repair and improvement of housing in the area; its proper
and effective management; greater diversity of kinds of tenure of the housing; and
the improvement of social and living conditions in the area generally. In their areas,
housing action trusts can be given power to exercise most of the functions of a
housing authority and the planning control and public-health functions of local
authorities. Local authority housing can be transferred to a housing action trust by
government order if a majority of the tenants agree. A housing action trust must
achieve its objects as quickly as possible and is then dissolved and its property
disposed of. Housing action trusts were introduced by the Housing Act 1988.

housing association A non-profit-making organization whose main purpose is to
provide housing. A *fully mutual housing association is excepted from the *assured
tenancy provisions. The *Housing Corporation can make grants to housing
associations registered by them.

housing association tenancy A tenancy in which the landlord is a housing
association, a housing trust, or the Housing Corporation. The Housing Act 1996 gave
certain housing association tenants a right to buy their homes, and they may be able
to obtain a grant towards the purchase price.

housing benefit A benefit payable by local authorities to those with no or very
low incomes who pay rent for their housing. There are two types: *rent rebates,

paid to the local authority's own needy tenants, and rent allowances, paid to tenants other than their own (e.g. Housing Association tenants).

Housing Corporation A body with functions under the Housing Associations Act 1985 and the Housing Act 1988. These include maintaining a register of *housing associations, promoting and assisting the development of – and making and guaranteeing loans to – registered housing associations and unregistered *self-build societies, and providing dwellings for letting or sale.

Housing for Wales A body set up under the Housing Act 1988, having the functions of the *Housing Corporation in respect to property and housing associations in Wales. It was abolished by the Government of Wales Act 1998, its functions being transferred to the Secretary of State pending transfer of powers to the Welsh Assembly (1999).

Housing Ombudsman An official appointed, under the Housing Act 1996, to deal with complaints against registered social landlords (not including local authorities). The first Housing Ombudsman was appointed with effect from 1 April 1997; he is in charge of the *Independent Housing Ombudsman.

housing subsidy An annual contribution from central government funds, payable under the Housing Act 1985, towards the provision of housing by local authorities and new town corporations.

housing trust A trust set up to provide housing, or whose funds are devoted to charitable purposes and which in fact uses most of its funds for the provision of housing. If it is a *fully mutual housing association, it is exempted from the *assured tenancy provisions. *See also* HOUSING ACTION TRUST.

human assisted reproduction Techniques to bring about the conception and birth of a child other than by sexual intercourse between the parties. It includes artificial insemination by the husband (AIH) or by a donor (DI), in vitro fertilization (IVF), and egg and embryo donation. Such methods mean it is no longer possible to base legal parentage solely on genetic links. Under terms of the Human Fertilization and Embryology Act 1990, the legal mother is the woman who has given birth to the child, regardless of genetic parentage, unless the child is subsequently adopted or a *section 30 order is made. However, the Act is not retrospective and the position of children conceived or born before the Act came into force has yet to be resolved. The legal father is generally the genetic father except when the latter is a donor whose sperm is used for licensed treatment under the 1990 Act, or when the donor's sperm is used after his death. If a wife conceives as a result of assisted reproduction, her husband may be regarded as the child's legal father, even if he is not the genetic father, as long as he consented to her treatment. However, this does not hold for all purposes. For example, in a recent case it was ruled that a peer's "son" born by donor insemination could not inherit his father's title when it was found after the peer's death that his wife had been impregnated by sperm from a third party (rather than from her husband) at the relevant clinic.

It is an offence to use female germ cells from an embryo or fetus, or to make use of embryos created from such germ cells, for the purpose of providing a fertility service. Such practice is already banned by the *Human Fertilization and Embryology Authority. The offence is triable only on *indictment and is punishable with up to ten years' imprisonment.

Human Fertilization and Embryology Authority A body, established under the Human Fertilization and Embryology Act 1990, that monitors, controls, and reviews research involving the use of embryos and issues licences for such research and for treatment in *human assisted reproduction. It must also maintain a register of persons whose gametes are kept or used for such purposes and of children born as a result. Children over the age of 18 can apply to the Authority for information concerning their ethnic and genetic background.

humanitarian intervention The interference of one state in the affairs of another by means of armed force with the intention of making that state adopt a more humanitarian policy, usually the protection of human rights of minority groups. Despite debate, such intervention is not recognized as legal under the UN Charter. However, states continue to rely on humanitarian grounds as justification for military action; examples of humanitarian intervention include Vietnam's invasion of Cambodia (1978), the declaration by the USA, the UK, Russia, and France of an air exclusion zone in southern Iraq in an effort to protect the Shia Marsh Arabs (1992), and military actions to protect the Muslim population of Kosovo (1999).

human rights Rights and freedom to which every human being is entitled. Protection against breaches of these rights committed by a state (including the state of which the victim is a national) may in some cases be enforced in international law. It is sometimes suggested that human rights (or some of them) are so fundamental that they form part of *natural law, but most of them are best regarded as forming part of treaty law.

The United Nations Universal Declaration of Human Rights (1948) spells out most of the main rights that must be protected but it is not binding in international law. There are two international covenants, however, that bind the parties who have ratified them: the 1966 International Covenant on Civil and Political Rights and International Covenant on Economic, Social and Cultural Rights. The United Nations has set up a Commission on Human Rights, which has power to discuss gross violations of human rights but not to investigate individual complaints. The Human Rights Committee, set up in 1977, has power to hear complaints from individuals, under certain circumstances, about alleged breaches of the 1966 Covenant on Civil and Political Rights. There are also various regional conventions on human rights, some of which have established machinery for hearing individual complaints. The best known of these is the *European Convention on Human Rights (enacted in English law as the *Human Rights Act 1998) and the Inter-American Convention on Human Rights (covering South America).

Human Rights Act Legislation, enacted in 1998, that brought the *European Convention on Human Rights into domestic law for the whole of the UK on 2 October 2000. In the past the use of the Convention was limited to cases where the law was ambiguous and public authorities had no duty to exercise administrative discretion in a manner that complied with the Convention.

The Act creates a statutory general requirement that all legislation (past or future) be read and given effect in a way that is compatible with the Convention. Section 3 provides that all legislation, primary and secondary, whenever enacted, must be read and given effect in a way that is compatible with Convention rights *wherever possible*.

The Act requires public authorities – including courts – to act compatibly with the Convention unless they are prevented from doing so by statute. This means that the courts have their own primary statutory duty to give effect to the Convention unless a statute positively prevents this. Section 7 gives the *victim of any act of a public authority that is incompatible with the Convention the power to challenge the authority in court using the Convention, to found a cause of action or as a defence. The Act introduces a new ground of illegality into proceedings brought by way of judicial review, namely, a failure to comply with the Convention rights protected by the Act, subject to a 'statutory obligation' defence. Secondly, it will create a new cause of action against public bodies that fail to act compatibly with the Convention. Thirdly, Convention rights will be available as a ground of defence or appeal in cases brought by public bodies against private bodies (in both criminal and civil cases). Section 7(5) imposes a limitation period of one year for those bringing proceedings.

However, only persons classified as "victims" by the Act are able to enforce the duty to act compatibly with the Convention in proceedings against the authority, and only victims will have standing to bring proceedings by way of judicial review. Most private litigants, at least in private law proceedings, will count as victims.

The Convention rights that have been incorporated into the Act are: Articles 2 to 12, 14, 16, 17, 18; Articles 1 to 3 of the First Protocol; and Articles 1 and 2 of the Sixth Protocol (individual rights are subjects of entries in this dictionary). *See* ABSOLUTE RIGHT; QUALIFIED RIGHT.

The Act requires any court or tribunal determining a question that has arisen in connection with a Convention right to take into account the jurisprudence of the Strasbourg organs (the European Court and Commission of Human Rights and the Committee of Ministers). This jurisprudence must be considered "so far as, in the opinion of the court or tribunal, it is relevant to the proceedings in which that question has arisen", whenever the judgment, decision, or opinion to be taken into account was handed down.

Section 19 provides that when legislation is introduced into Parliament for a second reading, the introducing minister must make a statement, either (1) to the effect that, in his view, the legislation is compatible with the Convention, or (2) that although the legislation is not compatible with the Convention, the government still wishes to proceed. If it is not possible to read legislation so as to give effect to the Convention, then the Act does not affect the validity, continuing operation, or enforcement of the legislation. In such circumstances, however, section 4 empowers the high courts to make a **declaration of incompatibility**. Section 10 and schedule 2 provide a 'fast-track' procedure by which the government can act to amend legislation in order to remove incompatibility with the Convention when a declaration of incompatibility has been made.

The Act gives a court a wide power to grant such relief, remedies, or orders as it considers just and appropriate, provided they are within its existing powers. Damages may be awarded in civil proceedings, but only if necessary to afford *just satisfaction; in determining whether or not to award damages and the amount to award, the court must take account of the principles applied by the European Court of Human Rights.

Sections 12 and 13 provide specific assurances as to the respect that will be afforded to *freedom of expression and *freedom of thought, conscience, and religion: these are 'comfort clauses' for sections of the press and certain religious organizations.

The Act does not make Convention rights directly enforceable against a private litigant, nor against a quasi-public body with some public functions if it is acting in a private capacity. But in cases against a private litigant, the Act still has an effect on the outcome, because the court will be obliged to interpret legislation in conformity with the Convention wherever possible; must exercise any judicial discretion compatibly with the Convention; and must ensure that its application of common law or equitable rules is compatible with the Convention.

hybrid Bill *See* BILL.

hybrid power *See* POWER OF APPOINTMENT.

hypothecation *n.* **1.** A mortgage granted by a ship's master to secure the repayment with interest, on the safe arrival of the ship at her destination, of money borrowed during a voyage as a matter of necessity (e.g. to pay for urgent repairs). The hypothecation of a ship itself, with or without cargo, is called **bottomry**; that of its cargo alone is *respondentia*. It is effected by a bond, and the bondholder is entitled to a maritime *lien. **2.** An authority given to a banker, usually as a **letter of hypothecation**, to enable the bank to sell goods or property that have been pledged to it as security for a loan. It applies only when the goods remain in the possession of the pledgor.

identity *n.* (in the law of evidence) *See* EVIDENCE OF IDENTITY.

ignorance of the law *See* MISTAKE.

ignorantia juris non excusat [Latin] Ignorance of the law is no excuse, i.e. no defence against criminal or other proceedings arising from its breach. The Statutory Instruments Act 1946 modifies the rule slightly (*see* STATUTORY INSTRUMENT). *See also* MISTAKE.

ignoring traffic signals Failing to comply with traffic signs, traffic lights, or road markings. A number of different offences are included in this category, all concerned with breaches of the rules relating to traffic signals as laid down in the Highway Code. All these offences are subject to a fine, *endorsement (carrying 3 penalty points under the *totting-up system), and *disqualification at the discretion of the court. Sometimes charges may also be brought under the head of *careless and inconsiderate driving or *dangerous driving, depending on the circumstances. It is also an offence not to comply with road directions given by a uniformed police officer acting in the course of his duties or engaged in a traffic census or survey.

 Prosecutions for ignoring traffic signals or police directions are subject to a *notice of intended prosecution.

ILC *See* INTERNATIONAL LAW COMMISSION.

illegal contract A contract that is prohibited by statute (e.g. one between traders providing for minimum resale prices) or is illegal at common law on the grounds of *public policy. An illegal contract is totally void, but neither party (unless innocent of the illegality) can recover back any money paid or property transferred under it (*see* EX TURPI CAUSA NON ORITUR ACTIO). Related transactions may also be affected. A related transaction between the same parties (e.g. if X gives Y a promissory note for money due from him under an illegal contract) is equally tainted with the illegality and is therefore void. The same is true of a related transaction with a third party (e.g. if Z lends X the money to pay Y) if the original illegality is known to him. In certain circumstances, illegal contracts may be saved by *severance.

illegal practices *See* CORRUPT AND ILLEGAL PRACTICES.

illegal trust A trust that contravenes statute, morality, or public policy. Such a trust is void and of no effect.

illegitimacy *n.* The status of a child born out of wedlock. Although evidence of illegitimacy is readily available from the entry in the birth register relating to the child's parents, it is usual for a short form of birth certificate to be issued, which makes no mention of the parents. Entry in the register of the name of a man who is not married to the mother (which may only be done with the consent of the mother) is evidence of his paternity.

 The effect of the Family Law Reform Act 1987 is that, for nearly all purposes, children are to be treated alike, whether or not their parents are married to one another. The parents of illegitimate children have much the same rights, duties, and responsibilities in relation to them as they have for their legitimate children. The father of an illegitimate child is under a duty to maintain the child in the same way as his duty to maintain legitimate children (*see* CHILD SUPPORT MAINTENANCE), but does not automatically have *parental responsibility for that child. Illegitimate children are able to inherit property under wills (unless the contrary intention is apparent) and on intestacy in the same way as if they were legitimate. However, the Family Law Reform Act 1987 did not remove all distinctions between legitimate and illegitimate children, notably in relation to entitlement to British citizenship and succession to the throne of England and to titles of honour.

It is now becoming more usual to use the term "child of unmarried parents" for children born out of wedlock, rather than "illegitimate child".

illusory appointment The giving of property under a *power of appointment that confers little or no benefit to one or more objects of the power. Before 19th-century legislation such appointments were void; they are now valid.

illusory trust A conveyance by a debtor to a trustee on trust for his creditors, which in some cases may be revoked. This is contrary to the normal rule that an *executed trust is irrevocable.

immigration *n.* The act of entering a country other than one's native country with the intention of living there permanently. Immigration into the UK is subject to control under the Immigration Acts 1971 and 1988, as amended by the Immigration and Nationality Act 1999. This control extends to all potential entrants except those to whom the Act gives the **right of abode** in the UK and except citizens of the Republic of Ireland. Nationals of other member states of the EU will also be exempted from control as from a date to be set by the Secretary of State. As originally enacted, the Act gave the right of abode to all citizens of the UK and Colonies who either owed their status to their own (or a parent's or grandparent's) birth, registration, or naturalization in the UK or were or became at any time settled in the UK and had at that time been ordinarily resident there for at least five years. Commonwealth citizens had the right of abode if one of their parents was a citizen of the UK and Colonies by reason of birth in the UK. A person having the right of abode was termed a **patrial**. As from 1 January 1983 the Act was amended by the British Nationality Act 1981 to confine the right of abode to British citizens as defined by that Act (*see* BRITISH CITIZENSHIP) and to *commonwealth citizens enjoying it before the Act came into force; the term patrial was discarded. With minor exceptions, a person subject to immigration control may not enter or remain in the UK except with leave, which may be granted either indefinitely or for a limited period; if leave is granted for a limited period, an immigrant is subject to further conditions (e.g. conditions restricting employment). The 1971 Act itself gave indefinite leave to stay to those not entitled to the right of abode but who were lawfully settled in the UK when it came into force. Whether or not leave is needed, whether it should be granted, and whether a time limit and any other conditions should be imposed are decided initially by immigration officers acting in accordance with immigration rules made by the Secretary of State. Appeals against the decisions of immigration officers are made to adjudicators at the ports of entry, and thence to the Immigration Appeal Tribunal.

Under the Immigration (Carriers' Liability) Act 1987, the owners of ships and aircraft are liable to pay a penalty of £1000 in respect of any person who arrives in the UK on their ship or aircraft and who seeks leave to enter the UK without proper documents (e.g. passport or visa). Under the Asylum and Immigration Act 1996, from 27 January 1997 it has been a criminal offence for an employer to employ anyone subject to immigration control. Breach of this Act leads to fines of up to £5000. Employers must ask new employees taken on or re-employed after that date for evidence of residential status, such as national insurance documents and EU passports; this request must be made in a nondiscriminatory way, which does not breach racial discrimination legislation.

Immigration Appeal Tribunal A tribunal appointed by the Lord Chancellor, under the Immigration Act 1971, to hear appeals against immigration and deportation decisions. It has a legally qualified chairman and is subject to the supervision of the *Council on Tribunals.

immoral contract A contract based on sexual immorality, such as a contract of prostitution. Such contracts are *illegal contracts on the grounds that they contravene *public policy.

immovables *pl. n.* Tangible things that cannot be physically moved, particularly land and buildings.

immunity *n.* Freedom or exemption from legal proceedings. Examples include the immunity of the sovereign personally from all legal proceedings (*see* ROYAL PREROGATIVE); the immunity of members of the House of Commons and the House of Lords from proceedings in respect of words spoken in debate (*see* PARLIAMENTARY PRIVILEGE); *judicial immunity; and the immunity from the jurisdiction of national courts enjoyed by members of diplomatic missions and by foreign sovereigns (*see* DIPLOMATIC IMMUNITY; SOVEREIGN IMMUNITY).

imparlance *n.* Permission given to a defendant to delay his answer to the claimant's claim, to enable him to attempt to settle the claim amicably.

impeachable waste *Waste that results in liability on the part of the person who commits it. Thus when a tenant commits impeachable waste his landlord may sue him for damages or obtain an injunction to prevent him committing any further waste.

impeding apprehension or prosecution Giving assistance to a person one knows to be guilty of an *arrestable offence with the intention of preventing or delaying his arrest or prosecution (e.g. providing a hiding place or destroying evidence). There are also special offences of (1) agreeing not to disclose information that might help to convict or prosecute a criminal (*see* COMPOUNDING AN OFFENCE), (2) refusing to aid a police officer when asked to help stop a breach of the peace, (3) *obstructing a police officer, and (4) *wasting police time by giving them misleading information. *See also* ESCAPE.

imperfect gift *See* GIFT.

imperfect trust *See* EXECUTORY TRUST.

impersonation *n.* Pretending to be another person. It is an offence to impersonate a woman's husband in order to persuade her to have sexual intercourse (rape), to impersonate the holder of a Crown office in order to gain access to prohibited places, and to impersonate a police officer, a variety of public officials, a voter, or a juror. Obtaining property, services, or certain financial advantages through impersonation may amount to a crime of *deception.

implementation *n.* The process of bringing any piece of legislation into force. EU directives, which are not directly applicable (*see* COMMUNITY LEGISLATION), are implemented at national level by member states by Act of Parliament or regulation. In the UK this may be done by statute or by statutory instrument or regulation.

implied condition A term or obligation implied by law in a contract, any breach of which will entitle the innocent party not only to damages but to treat the contract as discharged (*see* CONDITION). In a contract of sale of goods there are

implied conditions that the seller has the right to sell the goods, that the goods will
correspond with the contract description, and, in the case of sales in the course of
business, that the goods are of *satisfactory quality and fit for the buyer's declared
purpose.

implied contract A contract not created by express words but inferred by the
courts either from the conduct of the parties or from some special relationship
existing between them.

implied malice *Mens rea* that the law considers sufficient for a crime, although
there is no intention to commit that crime. The term is usually now used only in
relation to murder, referring to the intention to cause *grievous bodily harm (*see*
MALICE AFORETHOUGHT).

implied term A provision of a contract not agreed to by the parties in words but
either regarded by the courts as necessary to give effect to their presumed
intentions or introduced into the contract by statute (as in the case of contracts for
the sale of goods; *see* CAVEAT EMPTOR). An implied term may constitute either a
*condition of the contract or a warranty; if it is introduced by statute it often
cannot be expressly excluded. *Compare* EXPRESS TERM.

implied trust A trust that arises either from the presumed but unexpressed
intention of the settlor or by operation of law. Equity imposes an obligation to
create such trusts by inference from the facts, including the conduct or relationship
of the parties. An implied trust may be subdivided into or overlap with *resulting
trusts and *constructive trusts.

implied use *See* RESULTING USE.

impossibility *n.* A *general defence that arises when compliance with the
criminal law is physically impossible. This is most likely to arise in the context of
crimes of omission. Thus one cannot be found guilty of failing to report a road
traffic accident of which one was unaware. However, under the Criminal Attempts
Act 1981 one may be convicted of attempting the impossible (*see* ATTEMPT).

impossibility of performance The impossibility of carrying out a contract,
which occurs, for example, when it relates to subject matter that does not exist. The
event making fulfilment impossible may arise either before or after the contract is
made. In the former case (e.g. if X agrees to sell Y a horse that, unknown to either, is
already dead) the contract is void for *mistake. In the latter case (e.g. if the horse
dies between contract and performance) the contract will be discharged under the
doctrine of *frustration of contract.

impotence *n.* The inability of either partner to have normal sexual intercourse (*see
also* CONSUMMATION OF A MARRIAGE). In the case of a married couple this is sometimes
called **canonical disability** (i.e. a disability recognized by canon law, including that
of the Roman Catholic Church, as a ground for annulment of the marriage). If the
impotence is permanent and incurable, the marriage is voidable and either party
may apply for a nullity decree. Impotence must be distinguished from *wilful
refusal to consummate.

imprisonment *n. See* CUSTODY; SENTENCE; FALSE IMPRISONMENT; LIFE IMPRISONMENT.

improvement *n.* (of rented premises) An addition or alteration that improves the
premises from the tenant's point of view; it does not necessarily have to increase the
value of the premises. In the case of a lease that contains an obligation by the tenant
to obtain the landlord's consent before making improvements, the landlord cannot
withhold his consent unreasonably. He can, however, claim from the tenant any

expense or loss he suffers as a result and he can require the tenant, at the end of the tenancy, to put the premises back into the condition they were in before the improvement was carried out. When rented dwellings lack certain basic amenities, such as a bath, the local authority can require the landlord to provide these amenities and carry out other repairs and improvements after service of an *improvement notice. In the case of business tenancies and agricultural holdings, the tenant can claim compensation for improvements.

improvement notice 1. A local-authority notice requiring a person to provide a dwelling under his control with certain standard amenities (e.g. a bath). If he fails to do this the authority may do so at his expense. **2.** A notice requiring any person responsible for a breach of the Health and Safety at Work Act 1974 (or associated legislation) to take steps to remedy the breach or prevent its repetition. *Compare* PROHIBITION NOTICE.

imputability *n.* The principle that internationally illegal acts or omissions contributing to the damage to foreign property, and caused in some way by organs of the state apparatus, are attributable to the state and therefore incur that state's responsibility. Thus, there must have been state participation in the act before there can be *state responsibility for it.

imputation *n.* An allegation of misconduct or bad character made by an accused against the prosecutor or one of his witnesses. When this occurs the accused may (under the Criminal Evidence Act 1898), with *leave of the court, be cross-examined about his own *previous convictions and bad character. Under the Criminal Justice and Public Order Act 1994 allegations made against the character of a deceased victim may lead to cross-examination of the accused as to his character.

imputation of unchastity A statement imputing unchastity or adultery to a woman or girl, which is defamatory and actionable whether or not it has caused actual financial or material loss. *See* SLANDER; DEFAMATION.

imputation of unfitness or incompetence A statement calculated to disparage someone in his office, profession, calling, trade, or business, which is defamatory and actionable whether or not it has caused actual financial or material loss. *See* SLANDER; DEFAMATION.

imputation system Formerly, a system of taxation applying to the payment of *corporation tax on the distributed profits of a company. In this system, which came into force in the UK in April 1973, that part of the tax paid by the company as *advance corporation tax (ACT) was imputed to the shareholders and their dividends are franked (*see* FRANKED INCOME) accordingly. ACT was abolished in April 1999.

imputed notice An *agent's knowledge of facts that the law presumes the person employing him (the *principal) to have, irrespective of his actual knowledge of those facts. A purchaser of land has imputed notice of all matters relating to the purchase of which his agent (e.g. a solicitor) has (or ought reasonably to have) knowledge. *See also* ACTUAL NOTICE; CONSTRUCTIVE NOTICE; NOTICE.

inadmissible reason (in employment law) A reason for dismissing an employee that is based on his membership or participation in the activities of an *independent trade union or his refusal to become or remain a member of a union. Dismissal for an inadmissible reason is always treated as *unfair dismissal, and the employee may apply to an *employment tribunal regardless of his age and length of continuous employment. *See also* COMPENSATION.

inalienability *n. See* RULE AGAINST INALIENABILITY.

in camera [Latin: in the chamber] In private. A court hearing must usually be public but the public may be barred from the court or the hearing may continue in the judge's private room in certain circumstances; for example, when it is necessary for public safety or when a child gives evidence in a case involving indecency.

incapacity (incompetence) *n.* A lack of full legal competence in any respect; for example, the incapacity of mentally disordered persons to conclude valid contracts (*see* CAPACITY TO CONTRACT). A person suffering from incapacity is frequently referred to as a **person under disability**.

incapacity benefit A state benefit that replaced invalidity benefit and sickness benefit in April 1995. It is paid at three basic rates, the two highest of which are taken into account as taxable income. Short-term incapacity benefit is payable at the lower rate for the first 28 weeks of incapacity and at the higher rate for the 29th–52nd weeks. Long-term benefit is payable, at the highest rate, after 52 weeks. Those claiming the benefit must complete a questionnaire about the activities they can engage in; after 28 weeks they must undergo a medical test to assess their capacity for work-related activities as well as submitting a questionnaire. Doctors must certify in all cases the material supplied.

incest *n.* Sexual intercourse between a man and his mother, daughter, sister, half-sister, or granddaughter or between a woman over the age of 16 and her father, son, brother, half-brother, or grandfather. Even if both parties consent, incest is a criminal offence if the parties know of their relationship. It is punishable by up to seven years' imprisonment (or, with a girl under the age of 13, by a maximum sentence of life imprisonment), but no prosecution may be brought without the consent of the Director of Public Prosecutions. The relationships listed above include illegitimate relationships. It is a statutory offence for a man to incite a girl under the age of 16 to have incestuous intercourse with him, but being under 16, she would not be guilty of any crime if intercourse took place.

Inchmaree clause A clause frequently inserted in marine insurance policies to provide cover for a variety of risks that are not covered as *perils of the seas. It provides protection against such events as accidents in loading or discharging cargo or taking on fuel, bursting of boilers, breakage of shafts, and explosions on board ship or elsewhere. It also provides cover for negligence of the ship's master, officers, or crew.

inchoate *adj.* Incomplete. Certain acts, although not constituting a complete offence, are nonetheless prohibited by the criminal law because they constitute steps towards the complete offence. These inchoate offences include *incitement, *attempt, and *conspiracy. One may be guilty of inciting someone to commit the crime of incitement or of attempting to incite, but one cannot be guilty of incitement to conspire or of attempting to conspire.

incitement *n.* Persuading or attempting to persuade someone else to commit a crime. If the other person then actually carries out the criminal act, the inciter becomes a participator in the crime and is guilty of aiding and abetting it. If the other person does not carry out the crime, the person who attempted to persuade him to do so may nonetheless be guilty of the crime of incitement. Incitement may be by means of suggestion, persuasion, threats, or pressure, by words or by implication; for example, advertising an article for sale to be used to commit an offence may constitute incitement to commit that offence.

incitement to racial hatred *See* RACIAL HATRED.

income support An income-related benefit payable under the Social Security Acts to persons over 16 whose income and savings do not exceed a prescribed amount, and who are not working 16 or more hours a week, and (if applicable) whose spouses or cohabitants (*see* COHABITATION) are not working 24 hours or more a week, and who are incapable of or unavailable for work (for example, because they are disabled or a lone parent). It replaced supplementary benefit from April 1988. Since October 1996 the unemployed who would formerly have been recipients of income support have received instead a *jobseeker's allowance.

income tax A tax on a person's wages or salary and on most other sources of income, including unearned income and the profits from an unincorporated business. The amount of tax is based on a person's entire income for the year, less certain allowances, on a progressive scale. The effect is that those with higher incomes pay higher rates of tax.

The allowances (for 2001–02) include a personal allowance of £4535; a **children's tax credit** of £5200, which may be shared between a child's parents; and pension contributions. The children's tax credit is restricted to 10%. Other reliefs are available to older taxpayers (over 65) and the blind.

The first £1880 of taxable income is charged at 10% (this is known as the **starting rate**). Taxable income from £1881 to £29,400 is charged at 22% (the **basic rate**). Any income over £29,400 is charged at 40% (the **higher rate**). Although assessed annually, in many cases tax is deducted at source, in particular by employers under the *Pay As You Earn (PAYE) system. Nonresidents in the UK are subject to income tax if their income originates in the UK, as are UK residents who receive income from abroad. However, there are agreements with many countries to give relief against double taxation. Certain income is exempt from tax, including interest on national savings certificates, some social security benefits, and redundancy payments up to £30,000.

Income tax was introduced as a temporary measure in 1799. It is renewed annually in a Finance Act, which traditionally enacts the Chancellor of the Exchequer's Budget proposals. The types of taxable income are set out in the Income and Corporation Taxes Act 1988 under five schedules:
A: income from UK land;
C: public revenue dividends;
D: profits or gains from trades, professions, and vocations; interests, annuities and annual payments; income from securities and possessions outside the UK;
E: *emoluments from offices and employments; pensions;
F: dividends and distributions from UK companies.

incompetence *n. See* INCAPACITY.

incompletely constituted trust *See* EXECUTORY TRUST.

inconsiderate driving *See* CARELESS AND INCONSIDERATE DRIVING.

incorporation *n.* **1.** The formation of an association that has **corporate personality**, i.e. a personality distinct from those of its members. A corporation (such as a company) has wide legal capacity (subject to the doctrine of *ultra vires*): it can own property and incur debts. Company members have no liability to company creditors for such debts (though they may be under some liability to their company). An incorporated company has its own rights and liabilities and legal proceedings in respect of them should be brought by and against it in its own name (*but see* DERIVATIVE ACTION). It can be convicted of crimes; when *mens rea* is a requirement of the offence, the *mens rea* of the officers responsible may be attributed to the company. A company is usually incorporated by *registration under the Companies

Act 1985 but there are other methods (e.g. by royal charter or private Act of Parliament). *See also* CERTIFICATE OF INCORPORATION; LIFTING THE VEIL. **2.** *See* DOCTRINE OF INCORPORATION.

incorporation by reference 1. Reference in a will to another document without which the will cannot be understood (the document then forms part of the will). For example, a will leaving a specified sum "to each of the persons listed in my notebook" incorporates the notebook. The document must be clearly identified in the will, in existence at the date of the will, and clearly referred to as being in existence at that date. **2.** Reference to named contract terms, for example on the back of a railway ticket, saying where the terms can be seen for those who want to read them. This will often be sufficient to incorporate the terms by reference into the contract, although the other party may not have taken the opportunity to read the terms. However, there are risks in incorporation; for example, it is harder to enforce an exclusion of liability clause (*see* EXEMPTION CLAUSE) if the terms are merely incorporated by reference.

incorporeal hereditament *See* HEREDITAMENT.

incoterm *n.* An international trade term. Incoterms, the best known of which are *c.i.f. and *f.o.b., are used as an international shorthand in commercial agreements. A glossary of these terms, the latest edition of which is **Incoterms 2000**, is published by the International Chamber of Commerce. It sets out definitions of the various incoterms, which deal with such matters as which party to a contract is responsible for transport of the goods, who insures them in transit, and who arranges payment of customs duties.

incriminate *vb.* **1.** To charge with a criminal offence. **2.** To indicate involvement in the commission of a criminal offence. A witness in court need not answer a question if, in the judge's opinion, the answer might expose him to the danger of criminal prosecution. A witness does not have this protection when his answer might lead only to civil action against him.

incumbrance *n. See* ENCUMBRANCE.

indecency *n.* Conduct that the average man would find shocking or revolting. There are common-law offences of outraging public decency and conspiring to outrage public decency (*see* CONSPIRACY); examples might include staging an indecent exhibition, keeping a *brothel, or *indecent exposure. Indecency is a question of fact that is left in each case to the jury to decide. *See also* GROSS INDECENCY.

indecent assault An *assault or *battery in circumstances of indecency. Indecent assult is punishable by up to ten years' imprisonment. *Consent is normally a defence, except when the victim is under the age of 16. Touching or attempting to touch the genitals of another person without their consent would constitute an indecent assault. *See also* DOLI CAPAX; GROSS INDECENCY; INDECENT EXPOSURE.

indecent exposure Exposing one's body in public in a way that outrages public decency. When the exposure (by a man or woman) goes far beyond the generally accepted standards of decency and at least two people could have seen it, it amounts to a common-law offence, even if no one was actually disgusted or upset; such conduct is also punishable under the Vagrancy Act 1824. If a man exposes his genitals to a woman, even in private, with the intention of insulting her, he is guilty of a statutory offence and is liable to imprisonment. Such conduct, if threatening or frightening, may also amount to an *indecent assault.

indefeasible *adj.* Incapable of being made *void.

indemnity *n.* An agreement by one person (X) to pay to another (Y) sums that are owed, or may become owed, to him by a third person (Z). It is not conditional on the third person defaulting on the payment, i.e. Y can sue X without first demanding payment from Z. If it is conditional on the third person's default (i.e. if Z remains the principal debtor and must be sued for the money first) it is not an indemnity but a *guarantee. Unlike a guarantee, an indemnity need not be evidenced in writing.

An **indemnity insurance** policy is taken out for the benefit of a mortgagee (lender) when a high proportion (often 80%) of the purchase price for a domestic property is borrowed. Such indemnity policies have been held by the courts not normally to be for the benefit of the mortgagor (borrower), although the mortgagor pays the premiums on the policy; only the mortgagee can make a claim. *See also* INSURANCE.

indemnity basis A basis of *assessment of costs under which the receiving party recovers all costs incurred except any that have been unreasonably incurred or are of an unreasonable amount. The receiving party is given the benefit of any doubt on questions of reasonableness.

indenture *n.* (mainly historical) A deed, generally one creating or transferring an estate in land (e.g. a conveyance or a lease).

independent contractor A person or firm engaged to do a particular job of work, as opposed to a person under a *contract of employment. An independent contractor is his own master, bound to do the job he has contracted to do but having a discretion as to how to do it. A taxi-driver, for example, is the independent contractor of the passenger who hires him. A person who uses an independent contractor is not generally vicariously liable for torts committed by the contractor, but may be in exceptional cases; situations in which *vicarious liability may be incurred include those in which the contractor is employed in particularly hazardous activities, or to perform statutory duties, or to work on or over (but not merely near) the highway, or is specifically authorized to commit a negligent act.

Independent Housing Ombudsman A body set up under the Housing Act 1996, under the control of the *Housing Ombudsman, to ensure protection for housing association tenants against landlord mismanagement and to attempt to resolve disputes for housing association tenants.

independent trade union A trade union holding a certificate of independence issued by the *Certification Officer. A certificate will only be issued if the union is not under the domination or control of any employer, group of employers, or employers' association and is not liable to any interference from them tending towards such control. A union that is refused a certificate of independence may appeal to the *Employment Appeal Tribunal. Trade unions that do not hold a certificate of independence cannot conclude a collective agreement restricting employees' rights to strike and have no statutory right to certain information that employers must disclose to recognized independent trade unions (*see* DISCLOSURE OF INFORMATION). Only officials of independent trade unions have a statutory right to time off work to pursue union activities and duties. Rules regarding the dismissal of an employee for an *inadmissible reason and rules that prohibit employers from taking other action to deter employees from participating in a union only apply if the union holds a certificate of independence.

index maps Maps kept in the Land Registry showing the position and extent of every registered estate in land. The index maps can be searched to find out if a particular piece of land has an estate registered in respect of it.

indictable offence An offence that may be tried on *indictment, i.e. by jury in the Crown Court. Most serious common-law offences are indictable (e.g. murder, rape) and many are created by statute. When statute creates an offence without specifying how it is to be tried, it is automatically an indictable offence. An attempt to commit an indictable offence is itself an indictable offence; the same is not true for a *summary offence. Some indictable offences, if not very serious, may be tried either by magistrates or on indictment (*see* OFFENCES TRIABLE EITHER WAY).

indictment *n.* A formal document accusing one or more persons of committing a specified *indictable offence or offences. It is read out to the accused at the trial. An indictment is in a particular form. It is headed with the name of the case and the place of trial. There is then a statement of offence, stating what crime has allegedly been committed, followed by particulars of offence, i.e. such details as the date and place of the offence, property stolen, etc. If the accused is charged with more than one offence, each allegation and charge appears in a separate paragraph called a **count**. Counts may, however, be **framed in the alternative**, i.e. two or more counts may charge different offences arising out of the same allegation of fact but the defendant may be convicted of only one of them; for example, when a defendant is charged as a principal in one count and as an accessory in another in respect of the same incident. *See also* BILL OF INDICTMENT; TRIAL ON INDICTMENT.

indigenous peoples Those peoples and nations that have a historical continuity with pre-invasion and pre-colonial societies that developed on their territories and consider themselves distinct from other sectors of the societies now prevailing in those territories (or parts of them). Forming a non-dominant sector of the prevailing society, they exhibit a determination to preserve, develop, and transmit to future generations their ancestral territories, and their ethnic identity, as the basis of their continued existence as peoples, in accordance with their own cultural patterns, social institutions, and legal systems. Examples of indigenous peoples include the Sami (Lapps) in Scandinavia and the Cymry (Welsh) in the United Kingdom.

indirect evidence *See* CIRCUMSTANTIAL EVIDENCE.

Individual Savings Account (ISA) A type of savings account on which no tax is payable. There are three main types of property (components) that can be included in an ISA: cash, stocks and shares, and life assurance policies. These can be included all in one ISA – a **maxi-ISA**, or separately in **mini-ISAs**. In each tax year a taxpayer can invest in either one maxi-ISA (which must include stocks and shares) or up to three mini-ISAs – one each for cash, stocks and shares, and life assurance. No tax is payable on any of the income from ISA savings and investments, including dividends, interest, and bonuses, and no capital gains tax is payable on gains arising on ISA investments. The ISA manager will arrange for tax credits attached to dividends from UK companies to be paid into the ISA until 5 April 2004. The insurer does not have to pay tax on income or capital gains on investments (including claiming tax credits on dividends from UK companies) used to back ISA life assurance policies; no tax is payable when the policy pays out. Money can be withdrawn at any time without losing tax relief. The maximum that may be invested in ISAs in the tax year 2001–02 is £7000.

indivisible contract *See* PERFORMANCE OF CONTRACT.

indorsement *n.* *See* ENDORSEMENT.

inducement *n.* **1.** The promise of some advantage (e.g. bail) held out by a person in authority in relation to a prosecution to a person suspected of having committed a criminal offence. At common law a confession made after an inducement was inadmissible. It may now render the confession unreliable, and therefore inadmissible, under the terms of the Police and Criminal Evidence Act 1984. **2.** *See* MISREPRESENTATION.

inducing breach of contract *See* PROCURING BREACH OF CONTRACT.

industrial death benefit A state pension formerly payable to the widow of a man who had died from injuries sustained in the course of his employment or from a prescribed industrial disease. The system came to an end in April 1988. However, widows whose husbands die after that date as a result of an industrial accident or disease are entitled to widows' benefit and retirement pensions, their husbands being deemed to have satisfied the contribution conditions in full.

industrial democracy Participation in company management by employees. This may take the form of including directors elected by employees on the board of directors. *See also* EMPLOYEES' SHARE SCHEME.

industrial dispute *See* TRADE DISPUTE.

industrial injuries disablement benefit A pension or lump sum payable by the state to a person disabled by injury or a prescribed industrial disease sustained or contracted in the course of his employment. The benefit is payable as a weekly amount. The amount of the benefit depends on the degree of disablement, which is assessed by a specialist or a board of two doctors. To be entitled to benefit, the disablement must be assessed as being at least 14% of total disability (1% in the case of pneumoconiosis, byssinosis, and diffuse mesothelioma). The benefit is payable if the claimant is still suffering disability 15 weeks or more after the date of the accident or onset of the disease. It is payable for a period assessed as the time for which the claimant is likely to suffer the disability. The assessment can be reviewed if the claimant's condition deteriorates or if he is still disabled at the end of the period of assessment.

industrial tribunal *See* EMPLOYMENT TRIBUNAL.

inevitable accident An accident that could not have been prevented by the exercise of ordinary care and skill.

infant (minor) *n.* Since 1969, a *child under the age of 18. Certain rights (such as rights of parental responsibility, the right to make a child a ward of court, and the right to withhold consent to marriage) only apply to infants. Other rights (such as the right to marry with consent) are governed by different age limits, often 16. Infants have a limited *capacity to contract.

infanticide *n.* The killing of a child under 12 months old by its mother. If the mother can show that the balance of her mind was disturbed because of the effects of the childbirth or lactation, she will be found guilty of infanticide, rather than murder, and punished as though she was guilty of *manslaughter. Most cases of infanticide are dealt with by probation or discharge. *See also* DIMINISHED RESPONSIBILITY.

inferior court Any of the courts that are subordinate to *superior courts, having a jurisdiction limited to a particular geographical area, size of claim, or type of case. Their decisions are normally subject to appeal to a superior court, and the exercise of their jurisdiction may be subject to control by a superior court. In England and Wales, *county courts and *magistrates' courts are inferior courts.

information *n.* *See* LAYING AN INFORMATION.

informed consent The doctrine that determines the information to be disclosed to a patient to render his consent to treatment lawful. In the USA, the doctrine is based upon the "prudent patient" criterion, i.e. the nature, depth, and amount of information is judged by the physician as that required by a prudent patient. In the UK the doctrine is based upon the "prudent physician" criterion, i.e. the nature, depth, and amount of information is judged by the physician as that which is necessary for the patient. Failure to disclose such information will render any treatment unlawful.

informer *n.* A person who gives information to the police about crimes committed by others. An informer who is himself involved in the crimes may sometimes receive a lighter sentence in return for cooperation with the police that leads to the conviction of other offenders. However, the police may not employ their own informers to participate in crimes and then arrest the criminals, and a police informer who pretends to join a plot to commit a crime may himself be guilty of *conspiracy. It is nevertheless generally thought that if a police informer pretends to help in committing a crime with the intention of frustrating it, he will not be considered an *accessory if he fails to prevent the crime taking place.

in gross Absolute, i.e. existing in its own right and not as ancillary to land or any other thing. For example a profit *à prendre* can exist in gross, conferring rights on persons whether or not they own land capable of benefiting. An easement cannot exist in gross since there must be a dominant tenement.

inherent vice An inherent defect in certain goods that makes them liable to damage. Some fibres, for example, are liable to rot during shipment. If a carrier or insurer of such goods has not been warned of the inherent vice, he will not be liable for damage resulting directly from the defect.

inheritance *n.* **1.** The devolution of property on the death of its owner, either according to the provisions of his will or under the rules relating to intestacy contained in the Administration of Estates Act 1925 as amended. **2.** Property that a beneficiary receives from the estate of a deceased person.

inheritance tax A tax introduced by the Finance Act 1986 to replace capital transfer tax. The tax is payable on the value of a person's estate on death added to the value of lifetime gifts in the seven years preceding death and on certain other lifetime gifts. At present (2001–02) there are two rates of tax: nil on estates up to £242,000; 40% on estates over that figure. The tax charged on lifetime gifts made within the seven years before the death of the donor is reduced on a sliding scale according to how long before death the gift was made. Other lifetime gifts are charged at half the death rate. There are a number of exemptions, including gifts between husband and wife, gifts to charities and political parties, and gifts for national purposes or for the public benefit.

inhibition *n.* (in land law) An entry in the proprietorship register relating to registered land (*see* LAND REGISTRATION) that prohibits the registration of any dealing with the land (such as a transfer or mortgage) for a specified time or until a specified event occurs or until further order or entry. An inhibition may be registered on the application of any person having a sufficient interest; for example, when the owner of land claims that another has become registered as proprietor by fraud. The Chief Land Registrar has total discretion whether to make or cancel any order or entry, but an inhibition must be registered when a receiving order in bankruptcy is made against the proprietor or when registered land is transferred to the incumbent of a benefice.

inhuman treatment or punishment Treatment that causes intense physical and mental suffering. The prohibition on inhuman treatment or punishment as set out in Article 3 of the European Convention on Human Rights is now part of UK law as a consequence of the *Human Rights Act 1998. This right is an *absolute right; inhuman treatment or punishment can never be justified as being in the public interest, no matter how great that public interest might be. Public authorities have a limited but positive duty to protect this right from interference by third parties.

injunction *n.* A remedy in the form of a court *order addressed to a particular person that either prohibits him from doing or continuing to do a certain act (a **prohibitory injunction**) or orders him to carry out a certain act (a **mandatory injunction**). For example, a prohibitory injunction may be granted to restrain a nuisance or to stop the infringement of a copyright or trademark. A mandatory injunction may be granted to order a person to demolish a wall that he has built in breach of covenant. The remedy is discretionary and will be granted only if the court considers it just and convenient to do so; it will not be granted if damages would be a sufficient remedy.

Injunctions are often needed urgently. A temporary injunction (**interim** or **interlocutory injunction**) may therefore be granted at a special hearing pending the outcome of the main hearing of the case. If it is granted, the claimant must undertake to compensate the defendant for any damage he has suffered by the grant of the injunction if the defendant is successful in the main action. If judgment is given for the claimant in the main action, a **perpetual injunction** is granted. A person who fails to abide by the terms of an injunction is guilty of *contempt of court. *See also* FREEZING INJUNCTION; QUIA TIMET.

injurious falsehood *See* MALICIOUS FALSEHOOD.

injury *n.* **1.** Infringement of a right. **2.** Actual harm caused to people or property.

inland bill A *bill of exchange that is (or on the face of it purports to be) both drawn and payable within the British Islands or drawn within the British Islands upon some person resident there. All other bills are foreign bills. Unless the contrary appears on the face of a bill, the holder may treat it as an inland bill. The distinction is relevant to the steps taken when a bill has been dishonoured (*see* DISHONOUR).

Inland Revenue, Board of The body responsible for the care, management, and collection of most taxes within the UK. The officials of which it is made up are the Commissioners. The day-to-day administration is carried out by civil servants. Inspectors of Taxes are responsible for assessing taxes, which are collected by Collectors of Taxes (*see also* SELF-ASSESSMENT). A taxpayer can appeal against an inspector's assessment either to the General Commissioners for his district (lay persons appointed to hear appeals) or to a Special Commissioner (a full-time official appointed by the Treasury to hear appeals).

in limine [Latin] Preliminary: used, for example, to describe an objection or pleading.

in loco parentis [Latin] In place of a parent: used loosely to describe anyone looking after children on behalf of the parents, e.g. foster parents or relatives. In law, however, only a guardian or a person in whose favour a residence order is made stands *in loco parentis*; their rights and duties are determined by statutory provisions.

Inner Temple An *Inn of Court situated in the Temple between the Strand and the Embankment. The earliest recorded claim for its existence is 1440. Its Hall and Library were destroyed by bombing in World War II but have since been rebuilt.

innocent misrepresentation *See* MISREPRESENTATION.

innocent passage *See* TERRITORIAL WATERS.

innominate terms (intermediate terms) Terms of a contract that cannot be classified as *conditions or *warranties. The parties to a contract may label the terms of the contract as either conditions or warranties and those labels will usually be respected by the courts provided that the result is reasonable. Similarly, certain terms have traditionally been treated as conditions or warranties even though they have not been labelled as such (for example, time clauses in mercantile contracts are to be treated as conditions). Innominate terms are those that will not fit the above categories. The remedy for breach of an innominate term will depend on whether or not the breach is of a **fundamental** nature, i.e. that the injured party has been deprived of substantially the whole of the benefit of the contract. If the injured party has been so deprived, he will be entitled to treat the contract as repudiated and claim damages. If not, he will be entitled to damages only. *See also* BREACH OF CONTRACT.

Inns of Chancery Formerly, Inns similar but subordinate to the *Inns of Court, to which they were attached (for example, Staple Inn and Barnard's Inn were attached to Gray's Inn). Originally they were societies in which students prepared for admission to the Inns of Court; later they became societies of attorneys. They were dissolved in the late 19th century.

Inns of Court Ancient legal societies situated in central London; every *barrister must belong to one of them. These voluntary unincorporated associations have the exclusive right of call to the Bar. The early history of the Inns is disputed, but they probably began as hostels in which those who practised in the common law courts lived. These hostels gradually evolved a corporate life in which *Benchers, barristers, and students lived together as a self-regulating body. From an early date they had an important role in legal education. In modern times four Inns survive: *Gray's Inn, *Inner Temple, *Lincoln's Inn, and *Middle Temple.

Inns of Court and Bar Educational Trust *See* COUNCIL OF LEGAL EDUCATION.

innuendo *n.* In an action for *defamation, a statement in which the claimant explains the defamatory meaning of apparently innocent words that he alleges are defamatory. The claimant must set out in his particulars of claim the facts or circumstances making the words defamatory.

in personam [Latin: against the person] Describing a court action or a claim made against a specific person or a right affecting a particular person or group of people (*compare* IN REM). The *maxim of equity "equity acts *in personam*" refers to the fact that the Court of Chancery issued its decrees against the defendant himself, who was liable to imprisonment if he did not enforce them.

inquest *n.* An inquiry into a death the cause of which is unknown. An inquest is conducted by a *coroner and often requires the decision of a jury of 7–11 jurors. It must be held in the case of a sudden death whose cause is unknown or suspicious, a death occurring in prison, or when the coroner reasonably suspects that the death was caused by violent or unnatural means. Inquests are not, however, criminal proceedings; witnesses are usually cross-examined only by the coroner and the strict laws of evidence do not apply. If unlawful *homicide is suspected, and criminal proceedings are likely, the coroner will usually adjourn the inquest (and must do so if requested to by a chief police officer). If the inquest jury find that a particular person caused the death in circumstances amounting to homicide, that person may stand trial. It is an offence to dispose of a body with the intention of preventing an inquest being held.

inquiry *n.* (in international law) An attempt to discover the facts surrounding an international incident that is the subject of a dispute between two or more parties by means of an impartial investigative body. Such an investigation is intended to promote a successful resolution of the dispute. In treaty law each of the *Bryan Treaties and a number of other treaties between South and Central American states provided for the establishment of permanent commissions of inquiry. In 1967, the UN General Assembly adopted a resolution supporting the institution of such impartial fact-finding and requested the Secretary-General to establish a register of experts whose services could be used by states in specific disputes. *See also* CONCILIATION; GOOD OFFICES; MEDIATION.

inquisition *n.* A document containing the verdict of a coroner's *inquest. It consists of the **caption** (details of the coroner, jury, and the inquest hearing), the **verdict** (identification of the body and probable cause of death), and the **attestation** (signatures of the coroner and jurors). An **open verdict** may be recorded when there is insufficient evidence of the cause of death.

inquisitorial procedure A system of criminal justice, in force in some European countries but not in England, in which the truth is revealed by an inquiry into the facts conducted by the judge. In this system it is the judge who takes the initiative in conducting the case, rather than the prosecution or defence; his role is to lead the investigations, examine the evidence, and interrogate the witnesses. *Compare* ACCUSATORIAL PROCEDURE.

in re [Latin: in the matter of] A phrase is used in the headings of law reports, together with the name of the person or thing that the case is about (for example, cases in which wills are being interpreted). It is often abbreviated to *re*, in which form it is used in headings to letters, etc.

in rem [Latin: against the thing] **1.** Describing a right that should be respected by other people generally, such as ownership of property, as distinct from a right *in personam*. **2.** Describing a court action that is directed against an item of property, rather than against a person or group of people. Actions *in rem* are a feature of the *Admiralty Court.

insanity *n.* (in criminal law) A defect of reason, arising from mental disease, that is severe enough to prevent a defendant from knowing what he did (or what he did was wrong). A person accused of a crime is presumed sane and therefore responsible for his acts, but he can rebut this presumption and escape a conviction if he can prove (*see* BURDEN OF PROOF) that at the time of committing the crime he was insane. For purposes of this defence, insanity is defined by the **McNaghten Rules**. These were formulated by judges after the trial of Daniel McNaghten (1843), who killed the Prime Minister's secretary by mistake for the Prime Minister, under the delusion that the government was persecuting him, and was acquitted on the grounds of insanity. According to the rules, the defendant must show that he is suffering from a defect of reason arising out of "a disease of the mind". This would usually include most psychoses, paranoia, and schizophrenic diseases, but psychopaths and those

suffering from neuroses or subnormality would not normally fall within the terms
of the rules. The defendant must also show that, as a result of the defect of reason,
he either did not know the "nature and quality" of his acts, i.e. he did not know
what he was doing (for example, if he put a child on a fire, thinking it was a log of
wood) or he did not know that his acts were wrong, even if he knew their nature
and quality (for example, if he knew he was murdering, but did not know that this
was wrong). If the defendant is suffering from an insane delusion, he is treated as
though the delusion was true and will have a defence if there would normally be
one on those facts (for example, if he kills someone under the insane delusion that
he is acting in self-defence, since self-defence is a defence). Medical evidence may be
brought, but the jury are entitled to form their opinion on the facts. If found to be
insane the defendant is given a **special verdict** of "not guilty by reason of insanity"
and may be admitted to hospital. In cases of homicide, the accused must be sent to
hospital (usually a *special hospital, such as Broadmoor). Because of the consequences
of successfully pleading it, in practice insanity was usually only pleaded to avoid the
death penalty. However, a defendant who puts his mental state in issue (e.g. by
raising a defence of *diminished responsibility on a murder charge) might have to
change his plea to guilty to avoid being treated as pleading insanity (though he is
entitled to appeal against an insanity verdict).

Magistrates' courts are not empowered to return a special verdict. They will either
grant a complete acquittal, if the defendant's evidence of mental abnormality
amounts to a denial that he had any necessary *mens rea for the crime, or they may
make a *hospital order, if the crime with which he is charged is one for which they
could usually imprison him.

If someone in custody for trial is suffering from mental illness or severe
subnormality, he may be detained in hospital and not brought to trial until he is fit.
A person who is insane at the time of his trial, in the sense that he does not
understand the charge and cannot properly instruct his lawyers, may be found
*unfit to plead.

See also GENERAL DEFENCES; IRRESISTIBLE IMPULSE.

insider dealing Taking advantage of specific unpublished price-sensitive
information to deal in *securities to make a profit or avoid a loss. Under the
Criminal Justice Act 1993, dealings by insiders and those who have acquired
information from insiders may be a criminal offence. Improperly disclosing such
information or encouraging others to deal is also prohibited.

insolvency practitioner A person appointed to officiate in the *winding-up of a
company or in *bankruptcy proceedings. The Insolvency Act 1986 requires the
appointment of a qualified practitioner to act as a *liquidator, an *administrative
receiver, the supervisor of a *voluntary arrangement, or a *trustee in bankruptcy.
Under the Act, a person is only authorized to act in such a capacity if he has met
certain statutory requirements, including membership of an approved professional
body (such as the Institute of Chartered Accountants of England and Wales or the
Insolvency Practitioners Association).

inspection by judge *See* VIEW.

inspection of documents *See* DISCLOSURE AND INSPECTION OF DOCUMENTS.

inspection of property (in court procedure) The High Court or the county
courts may order the inspection, photographing, preservation, custody, and
detention of any property that is (or may become) the subject matter of proceedings
or in respect of which any questions may arise in proceedings. Such an order may be
made before the issue of proceedings, in respect of any property that may become

the subject matter of subsequent proceedings. Once proceedings have started, an order may be made in respect of property in the possession of a party, provided that the application is in respect of a physical thing (not details of a manufacturing process, for example), and an order may be made if the property is in the possession of a non-party. In each instance, the order is sought by isuing an application notice supported by evidence.

instant committal A short committal under section 1 of the Criminal Justice Act 1967. *See* COMMITTAL FOR TRIAL.

institutional constructive trust *See* CONSTRUCTIVE TRUST.

instrument *n.* A formal legal document, such as a will, deed, or conveyance, which is evidence of (for example) rights and duties. The *European Convention on Human Rights is a **living instrument** in that it must be interpreted in the light of present-day conditions rather than by trying to ascertain the meaning of those who drafted it over fifty years ago. *See also* STATUTORY INSTRUMENT.

insufficient evidence A direction by a judge to a jury that, as a matter of law, the evidence does not entitle them to make a certain finding. For example, if there is insufficient evidence for a conviction, the judge may direct the jury to return a verdict of not guilty.

insulting behaviour *See* THREATENING BEHAVIOUR.

insurable interest An interest (financial or otherwise) in the subject matter of a contract of *insurance, which provides the person insured with the right to enforce the contract. An insurable interest (e.g. ownership of goods insured) distinguishes a contract of insurance from a wager or bet. An interest is required by statute for various types of insurance contract (e.g. life insurance).

insurance *n.* A contract in which one party (the **insurer**) agrees for payment of a consideration (the **premium**) to make monetary provision for the other (the **insured**) upon the occurrence of some event or against some risk. For such contracts to be enforceable, there must be some element of uncertainty about the events insured against and the insured must have an *insurable interest in the subject matter of the contract. (The term **assurance** has the same meaning as insurance but is generally used in relation to events that will definitely happen at some time or another (especially death), whereas insurance refers to events that may or may not happen.) There are two types of insurance: **indemnity insurance**, which provides an indemnity against loss and in which the measure of the loss is the measure of payment (e.g. a fire policy); and **contingency insurance**, which involves payment on a contingent event and in which the sum paid is not measured by the loss but stated in the policy (e.g. a life policy). A contract of insurance is one requiring the utmost good faith (*see* UBERRIMAE FIDEI) and is voidable if a party fails in preliminary negotiations to disclose a fact material to the risk (*see* NONDISCLOSURE; VOIDABLE CONTRACT). Innocent or fraudulent *misrepresentation may also render the contract voidable, or the contract may be terminated for breach of an essential term (*see* WARRANTY). Particular types of insurance include *life assurance, fire insurance, motor-vehicle insurance (*see* THIRD-PARTY INSURANCE), *marine insurance, liability insurance, and guarantee insurance. There is considerable statutory regulation of insurance business.

Insurers are either **insurance companies** or *Lloyd's underwriters. Insurance companies are regulated by statute, aimed, among other things, at ensuring the insurance companies have sufficient funds to meet all claims made on them. **Insurance brokers** negotiate insurance contracts with insurance companies or

Lloyd's underwriters on a commission basis and usually handle claims on their clients' behalf. In the event of a claim the insured receives either the amount agreed in the policy or an appropriate sum that is calculated by an independent **insurance assessor**.

insurance broker *See* INSURANCE.

insurance company *See* INSURANCE.

insurance policy A formal document issued by an insurer setting out the terms of a contract of *insurance. Insurance contracts are not required by law to be in writing. Before the issue of a policy an insurer may issue a **cover note**, which is itself a temporary contract of insurance.

Insurgency *n.* A state of revolt against constituted authority by rebels who are not recognized as *belligerent communities. Hence, recognition by nation X of a state of insurgency in nation Y means that while the former nation acknowledges a state of rebellion or revolt in nation Y, it is not yet prepared to extend recognition of a state of belligerency to that nation. Such a decision is based upon the relative proportion and success of the rebellion or revolt within state Y.

intangible property *Property that has no physical existence: *choses in action and incorporeal *hereditaments.

intellectual property Intangible property that includes *patents, *trade marks, *copyright, and registered and unregistered *design rights.

intention *n.* The state of mind of one who aims to bring about a particular consequence. Intention is one of the main forms of *_mens rea_, and for some crimes the only form (for example, in the crime of threatening to destroy someone's property, with the intention that he should fear that the threat will be carried out). A person is assumed to intend those consequences of his acts that are inevitable but cannot be presumed to intend a consequence merely because it is probable or natural. In the latter case, the jury must decide, on all the available evidence, whether or not in fact the accused did intend the consequences. For purposes of the law of murder, however, a person is presumed to intend to cause death if he foresees that it is a highly likely consequence of his acts. This is sometimes known as **oblique intention**. Intention is often contrasted with *recklessness and should not be confused with *motive. For some purposes, offences are divided into crimes of **basic intent** or **specific intent** (*see* INTOXICATION). *See also* ULTERIOR INTENT.

Intention to injure is also a constituent element of some torts, particularly those dealing with business relations (e.g. *conspiracy, *intimidation, *procuring breach of contract).

intention of testator The meaning that a testator intends his will to have. In interpreting a will, the court seeks to give effect to the intention of the testator as expressed in the will, even if capricious or eccentric. If the intention of the testator is to be challenged, this can only be done by an application under the Inheritance (Provision for Family and Dependants) Act 1975 (*see* FAMILY PROVISION). There are rules of construction to enable the testator's intention to be ascertained where it is not clear from the face of the will (*see* ARMCHAIR PRINCIPLE; INTERPRETATION OF WILLS).

interest *n.* (in land law) A right in or over land. It may comprise equitable ownership of the land (such as the interest of the tenant for life under a settlement), where the legal estate is owned by trustees; or the benefit of some other right over the land of another, such as an easement or rentcharge. Interests of the latter type can be legal or equitable, but under the Law of Property Act 1925 only interests owned on terms equivalent to a *fee simple absolute in possession or a *term of years absolute qualify as legal interests. A person interested in land is one who has rights in it. *See also* EQUITABLE INTERESTS.

interest in expectancy Any future interest in property.

interfering with subsisting contract *See* PROCURING BREACH OF CONTRACT.

interfering with trade or business The tort of deliberately interfering with the trade or business of another person by unlawful means, thereby causing damage to that person. Liability in this tort is wider than in the tort of *procuring breach of contract, since it is not necessary to show that an existing contract has been interfered with or broken. The operation of the tort in *trade disputes is limited by statute.

interfering with vehicles Under the Criminal Attempts Act 1981, it is an offence, punishable with up to three months' imprisonment and/or a fine, for a person to interfere with a vehicle or anything it carries with the intention that he or someone else will steal the vehicle or any of its contents or take the vehicle without the owner's consent. The offence was introduced when the *sus law was abolished. A constable may arrest anyone he reasonably suspects of this offence. It is also a *summary offence, under the Road Traffic Act 1988, to get onto a vehicle on a road or local authority car park or to tamper with its brakes or other part of its mechanism without lawful authority or reasonable cause. *See also* CONVEYANCE.

interfering with witnesses Attempting to prevent a witness from giving evidence or to influence the evidence he gives. Making improper threats against witnesses may amount to the common-law offence of *perverting the course of justice; persuading a witness to tell a lie constitutes – in addition to this – the offence of subornation of *perjury. It is also perverting the course of justice to put pressure upon a witness to give evidence or to pay him money to testify in a particular way. Sometimes interfering with witnesses may also amount to *contempt of court. There is also a separate common-law offence of **tampering with witnesses** when one uses threats to persuade them not to give evidence. *See also* INTIMIDATION.

interim *See* INTERLOCUTORY.

interim appeal (interlocutory appeal) An appeal against an order made during the pre-trial stage of civil litigation. Appeals from district judges and masters are to the High Court or a county court circuit judge, and appeals from a decision of a county court circuit judge or a High Court judge are to the Court of Appeal (Civil Division). Any appeal can only be made if permission to appeal is granted.

interim injunction (interlocutory injunction) *See* INJUNCTION.

interim judgment (interlocutory judgment) A decision by the court in civil proceedings that only deals with part of the matter in dispute. *Compare* FINAL JUDGMENT.

interim measures (in competition law) Temporary sanctions that the European Commission and the UK Office of Fair Trading have powers (by decision and under the Competition Act 1998, respectively) to impose on businesses that are in breach of the competition rules, pending a final decision. This ensures that permanent damage is not done to the party who has complained of a breach of the rules. The interim measures may consist of requiring the offending company to resume supplies of goods to the complainant or to remedy the conduct of which complaint has been made in some other way. *See also* INTERIM RELIEF.

interim payment Payment on account by a defendant of any damages, debt, or other sum (excluding costs) that he is liable to pay to the claimant. The High Court (but not the county courts) may order a defendant to make an interim payment. When damages are claimed, it is necessary to show that (1) the defendant has admitted liability; or (2) the claimant has already obtained judgment for damages to be assessed; or (3) if the action proceeded to trial the claimant would obtain judgment for substantial damages.

interim proceedings (interlocutory proceedings) The preliminary stages in civil proceedings, such as statements of case and disclosure of documents, which occur between the issue of the claim form and the trial. Their principal functions are to define the issues that will have to be decided at the trial and to prevent *surprise

interim relief (interlocutory relief) A temporary remedy, such as an interim *injunction or *interim payment, granted to a claimant by a court pending the trial.

interim rent Rent that a landlord can request a court to fix for a *business tenancy when he has given the tenant notice to quit or when the tenant has applied for a new tenancy.

interlineation *n.* Writing between the lines of a document. The effect is the same as that of an *alteration.

interlocutory *adj.* During the course of proceedings. Before the introduction of the Civil Procedure Rules in 1999, the term was applied to certain processes in civil proceedings occurring between initiation of the action and the final judgment (e.g. interlocutory injunction, interlocutory proceedings). Under the Rules, it has been replaced by the term **interim**.

intermediate terms *See* INNOMINATE TERMS.

internal waters All rivers, canals, lakes (excluding international ones), and landlocked seas, the waters of ports, bays, and roadsteads, and the waters on the landward side of the *baseline of the territorial sea. Within its internal waters, a coastal state exercises civil and criminal jurisdiction over foreign merchant ships and also administrative functions, such as enforcing customs and fishing regulations. *Compare* TERRITORIAL WATERS.

International Bank for Reconstruction and Development (IBRD; World Bank) A specialized agency of the United Nations. It developed from the international monetary and financial conference held at Bretton Woods, New Hampshire, in 1944 and was established by 44 nations in 1945. Its central purpose is to spur economic growth in developing states through the provision of loans and technical assistance to their respective governments. The IBRD currently has 181 members.

international carriage The carriage of persons or goods between two or more nations, which is regulated by various international conventions. The international carriage of goods by sea is governed by the **Hague Rules** (1924), the **Hague–Visby Rules** (1968), and the **Hamburg Rules** (1978, not yet in force); that of goods by road by the Geneva Convention (1956); and that of goods by rail by a convention of 1980. (*See also* CARRIAGE OF GOODS BY AIR.) There are also conventions regulating the international carriage of passengers by sea, rail, and road. The UK is a party to various of these conventions and has legislated to give them legal effect; for example, the Carriage of Goods by Sea Act 1971 covers the Hague–Visby Rules.

International Court of Justice A court at The Hague, consisting of 15 judges elected for 9-year terms of office, that has power to determine disputes relating to international law. It was set up by the United Nations in succession to the Permanent Court of International Justice, and all members of the UN are automatically parties to the Statute of the Court. No state may be brought before the Court in contentious proceedings unless it has accepted its jurisdiction, either by agreement in a particular case or by recognition of the authority of the Court in general, in respect of any dispute with another state accepting the general jurisdiction of the Court (the **principle of reciprocity**; *see also* OPTIONAL CLAUSE). The Court may also give advisory opinions (*see* ADVISORY JURISDICTION), which do not bind the parties but are of great *persuasive authority.

International Criminal Court A permanent court to try individuals for the most serious offences of global concern. In July 1998, 160 nations decided to establish this court; the Statute of the Court will enter into force after 60 countries have ratified it. Crimes within the jurisdiction of the Court are genocide, war crimes, and crimes against humanity, such as widespread or systematic extermination of civilians, enslavement, torture, rape, forced pregnancy, persecution on political, racial, ethnic, or religious grounds, and enforced disappearances. The Court's Statute lists and defines all these crimes to avoid ambiguity. The seat of the Court will be at The Hague, in the Netherlands, but it will be authorized to try cases in other venues when appropriate.

international law (*jus gentium*, law of nations) The system of law regulating the interrelationship of sovereign states and their rights and duties with regard to one another. In addition, certain international organizations (such as the *United Nations), companies, and sometimes individuals (e.g. in the sphere of *human rights) may have rights or duties under international law. International law deals with such matters as the formation and recognition of states, acquisition of territory, war, the law of the sea and of space, treaties, treatment of aliens, human rights, international crimes, and international judicial settlement of disputes. The usual sources of international law are (1) *conventions and *treaties; (2) international *custom, in so far as this is evidence of a general practice of behaviour accepted as legally binding (*see* OPINIO JURIS); (3) the *general principles of law recognized by civilized nations.

International law is also known as **public international law** to distinguish it from *private international law, which does not deal with relationships between states.

International Law Commission (ILC) A body established in 1947 by General Assembly Resolution 174 (II) and acting under Article 13 of the United Nations Charter. The ILC consists of 25 members of recognized competence in international law who are elected for five-year periods by the General Assembly from a list of candidates nominated by the member states of the UN. The mission of the ILC is to promote the progressive development of international law by preparing draft conventions on subjects that have not yet been regulated by international law and by codifying the law. It produces annual reports of current problems.

international legal personality In the international community, entities who are endowed with rights and obligations under public international law are said to have international legal personality. The entities with this legal personality include states, international organizations, *nongovernmental organizations, and to some limited extent private individuals and corporations within a state.

international minimum standard (in international law) A minimum standard of treatment that must always be observed with regard to the treatment of foreign nationals. This standard consists of at least the right to life, liberty, and free access to the courts and to the protection of property (especially fair compensation for the nationalization of property). The international minimum standard has proved to be contentious with developing countries and Socialist states, who believe that it merely advances Western economic imperialism. *See also* ESPOUSAL OF CLAIM; EXPROPRIATION; STATE RESPONSIBILITY. *Compare* NATIONAL TREATMENT STANDARD.

International Sea Bed Authority A body, based in Jamaica, that is charged with responsibility for the 1982 Convention on the Law of the Sea. *See* LAW OF THE SEA.

international supply contract A contract for the sale of goods made by parties whose places of business (or habitual residences) are in the territories of different states. The limitations imposed by the Unfair Contract Terms Act 1977 on the extent to which a person may exclude or restrict his liability (e.g. by an *exemption clause) do not apply to such a contract if (1) when it is made, the goods are in carriage (or due to be carried) from one state to another; (2) the offer and its acceptance take place in different states; or (3) the goods are to be delivered in a state other than that in which the offer and acceptance take place. However, other statutes may apply to such contracts, and in many countries the Vienna Convention on the International Sales of Goods and world trade rules under the *General Agreement on Tariffs and Trade (GATT) and the *World Trade Organization (WTO) will apply.

interpleader *n.* A procedure used to decide how conflicting claims against the same person should be dealt with. It applies when there are two or more claims against the applicant (whether or not court proceedings have been issued) that conflict with each other; for example, when two or more people claim the same goods that are being held by the applicant. The court decides how the matter should be dealt with; it may, for example, direct that there should be a court action between the rival claimants.

Interpleader can be of two types. A **stakeholder's interpleader** applies to any person holding any debt, goods, or chattels in respect of which there are rival claims. A **sheriff's interpleader** applies when the applicant is the *sheriff, who has to deal with rival claims after execution of a writ of *fieri facias* when a third party (e.g. a television rental company) claims that the goods seized belong to him. In the county courts, special forms of summons are prescribed irrespective of whether proceedings have commenced or not. In the High Court, the application is by *claim form if proceedings have yet to start, and by ordinary application notice if proceedings have already been issued.

interpretation (construction) *n.* The process of determining the true meaning of a written document. It is a judicial process, effected in accordance with a number of rules and presumptions. So far as is relevant, the rules and presumptions applicable to Acts of Parliament (*see* INTERPRETATION OF STATUTES) apply equally to private documents, such as deeds and wills.

Interpretation Act An Act of 1978 (originally 1889) that defines a number of common words and expressions and provides that the same definitions are to apply in all other Acts except those specifically indicating otherwise. For example, "person" includes (in addition to an individual) any body of persons corporate or unincorporate.

interpretation clause A clause in a written document that defines words and phrases used in the document itself. In an Act of Parliament it is called an **interpretation section**. *See also* INTERPRETATION ACT.

interpretation of statutes The judicial process of determining, in accordance with certain rules and presumptions, the true meaning of Acts of Parliament. The principal rules of statutory interpretation are as follows.

(1) An Act must be construed as a whole, so that internal inconsistencies are avoided.

(2) Words that are reasonably capable of only one meaning must be given that meaning whatever the result. This is called the **literal rule**.

(3) Ordinary words must be given their ordinary meanings and technical words their technical meanings, unless absurdity would result. This is the **golden rule**.

(4) When an Act aims at curing a defect in the law any ambiguity is to be resolved in such a way as to favour that aim (the **mischief rule**).

(5) The *ejusdem generis* **rule** (of the same kind): when a list of specific items belonging to the same class is followed by general words (as in "cats, dogs, and other animals"), the general words are to be treated as confined to other items of the same class (in this example, to other *domestic* animals).

(6) The rule *expressio unius est exclusio alterius* (the inclusion of the one is the exclusion of the other): when a list of specific items is not followed by general words it is to be taken as exhaustive. For example, "weekends and public holidays" excludes ordinary weekdays.

The House of Lords has ruled against the existence of an alleged **social policy rule**, which would enable an ambiguous Act to be interpreted so as to best give effect to the social policy underlying it. Ambiguities may occasionally be resolved by referring to external sources; for example, the intention of Parliament in regard to a proposed Act, as revealed by ministers during its passage through Parliament, may be discovered by reference to *Hansard.

There are some general presumptions relating to the interpretation of statutes. They are presumed (1) not to bind the Crown (including the sovereign personally); (2) not to operate retrospectively so far as substantive (but not procedural) law is concerned; (3) not to interfere with vested rights (particularly without compensation); (4) not to oust the jurisdiction of the courts; and (5) not to derogate from constitutional rights or international law. But clear words or necessary implication may override these presumptions. A consolidating statute is presumed not be intended to alter the law, but this does not apply to codifying statutes, which may be concerned with clarifying law that was previously unclear. Penal and taxing statutes are subject to **strict construction**, i.e. if after applying the normal rules of interpretation it is still doubtful whether or not a penalty or tax attaches to a particular person or transaction, the ambiguity must be resolved in favour of the subject.

See also INTERPRETATION ACT; INTERPRETATION CLAUSE.

interpretation of wills The process of determining the true meaning of wills to give effect, as far as possible, to the testator's intention expressed in the will (*see* INTENTION OF TESTATOR). Generally the words used are given their ordinary grammatical meaning. If the words used are ambiguous, either in themselves or in the light of surrounding circumstances, extrinsic evidence may be admitted to assist in ascertaining the testator's intention. The process of construing a will by reference to the circumstances surrounding the testator when he made his will is commonly known as the *armchair principle. Such evidence may not be used to contradict a clear expression in the will. The **golden rule** is to adopt a construction that will avoid an *intestacy, on the basis that if the testator went to the trouble of making a will, he presumably did not intend to die intestate. There are also many detailed rules relating to the meaning of particular phrases and to imprecise gifts for charitable purposes.

interregnum *n.* **1.** The period between the death of a sovereign and the accession of his or her successor. **2.** Temporary rule exercised during such a period. In the UK a sovereign's death does not result in an interregnum (*see* DEMISE OF THE CROWN).

interrogation *n.* The questioning of suspects by the police. Suspects are not obliged to answer such questions (*see* RIGHT OF SILENCE), and the right of the police to question suspects is governed by the Police and Criminal Evidence Act 1984 and the Codes of Practice made under it. The Codes deal with such matters as the rights of the suspect to communicate with third parties, rights to legal advice and to medical treatment, and advice to the police on the administering of a *caution, the provision of interpreters, and the keeping of records concerning all these matters. There are special provisions relating to the interrogation of juveniles, the mentally ill, and the mentally handicapped. The provisions of the 1984 Act and its Codes must now be read subject to the requirements of the *Human Rights Act 1998. *See also* CONFESSION.

interrogatory *n.* Formerly, a formal written question submitted by one party to civil litigation to another party and required to be answered on oath. Since the introduction of the Civil Procedure Rules in 1999, this procedure has been replaced by a **request for further information**.

in terrorem [Latin] Intimidating. The doctrine of *in terrorem* applies to conditions attached to gifts of personal property in wills or elsewhere. Such conditions are *in terrorem* if it is apparent that the donor does not really intend the recipient to lose the gift, but is merely making an idle threat; for example, when a donor makes a gift subject to a condition against marriage without another person's consent but does not make provision for the disposal of the gift if the recipient does not comply with the condition. Such conditions are void.

interstate trade Trade between states. EU competition rules (*see* COMPETITION LAW) apply only when an anticompetitive agreement or *abuse of a dominant position will affect trade between member states. Whether or not interstate trade is affected is therefore crucial to any competition analysis. Agreements relating to imports or exports are most likely to affect interstate trade, but so might an agreement between two businesses situated in one member state, depending on the terms or effect of the agreement.

intertemporal law The law that international courts apply when a long time has elapsed since the conclusion of a treaty, to take into account changes that have taken place in international law since the treaty was formulated and changes in the meaning of the expressions in the treaty. The existence of a right (e.g. to a territorial claim) should be based not only on the law in effect at the time the right was created, but also on the international law as applied to the continued existence of that right. The legitimacy of a title to territory must be renewed by the claimant state.

intervention *n.* Action taken to intervene in markets, for example to support prices, in the EU or within similar trading groups throughout the world. In the EU it occurs in relation to the *Common Agricultural Policy. The European Commission buys surplus produce at an agreed **intervention price**; the produce may be stored until prices alter. This practice formerly led to butter or meat "mountains", but goods held in intervention in this way have now largely been dissipated.

intestacy *n.* The state in which a person dies without having made a will disposing of all his property. A **total intestacy** occurs when the deceased leaves no will at all or a will that only appoints executors but does not dispose of any property; a **partial intestacy** arises when a will deals with only part of the testator's estate. The Administration of Estates Act 1925 as amended and orders made under it govern the manner in which an intestate estate is to be administered, the persons entitled to inherit, and the amounts and proportions of the estate they receive. The rules relating to intestacy reflect the importance accorded to familial relationships: the surviving spouse is given the larger share of the estate.

intimidation *n.* **1.** The act of frightening someone into doing something. Intimidation is not in itself a crime, but it may constitute part of a crime. For example, it is a crime to have sexual intercourse with a woman if her agreement was obtained by intimidation. It is a crime to intimidate a juror or witness in relation to proceedings with which he is connected (*see* CONTEMPT OF COURT). If one intimidates someone into handing over money or property, this may amount to theft, and in some cases to blackmail. There are also special statutory offences of threatening to destroy or damage someone else's property and threatening to kill someone. A person who commits a crime when intimidated by others may sometimes have a defence of *duress. See also* THREAT.

Under the Criminal Justice and Public Order Act 1994 it is also an offence to intimidate a person whom the offender believes to be a potential or actual witness or juror. The offender must, however, have an intention to obstruct an investigation or the course of justice although this will be presumed where it is proved that he did an act that intimidates with that intention. Similar offences exist with regard to reprisals against potential witnesses or jurors. On *summary conviction the maximum penalty is six months' imprisonment and/or a fine up to the statutory maximum of £5000, and on *indictment it is five years' imprisonment and/or an unlimited fine.

2. A tort in which A, with the intention of injuring B, either directly threatens B with some unlawful act or threatens C with an unlawful act in order to make him cause damage to B. Thus if A threatens to do an unlawful act to B's employer (C) unless he dismisses B, and C succumbs to the threat, B has an action for intimidation against A for causing the loss of his job. It is irrelevant that C was entitled to dismiss B and did not act unlawfully: the essence of the tort is A's unlawful threat. The operation of the tort in *trade disputes is limited by statute.

intoxicating liquor For the purposes of the Licensing Act 1964, spirits, wine, beer, porter, cider (including perry), and any other fermented, distilled, or spirituous liquor. *See also* LICENSING OF PREMISES.

intoxication *n.* The condition of someone who is drunk or under the influence of drugs. Although intoxication itself is not an offence (*but see* DRUNKENNESS), it is an element in a number of offences. These include *drunken driving, being found drunk in a public place, being drunk and disorderly in a public place, and being drunk in a public place while possessing a loaded firearm. It is also an offence to supply or offer to supply to a person under 18 a substance (e.g. a glue or solvent) whose fumes are likely to be inhaled by that person for the purpose of causing intoxication.

When a person is so intoxicated that he is incapable of forming the *mens rea* required to be guilty of a particular crime, he is usually entitled to be acquitted if the crime is one that requires a specific intention (but not if it requires a basic intention). A crime is one of **basic intent** if the *mens rea* required does not go beyond the *actus reus* of the crime (for example, rape, in which the *actus reus* is sexual intercourse without the woman's consent and the *mens rea* is intention to have sexual intercourse without her consent, or recklessness whether she consents or not). A crime is one of **specific intent** if the *mens rea* required goes beyond the *actus reus* (for example, theft, in which the *actus reus* is merely appropriating someone else's property, but the *mens rea* – in addition to the intention of appropriating it – requires an intention to deprive the owner of it for good). Intoxication will not be a defence, however, if the crime is one of specific intent that can be committed by being reckless and the indictment is framed in terms of recklessness. For example, if a drunken person sets fire to a building and endangers the lives of people in it, he may be guilty of destroying property being reckless as to whether life would be endangered, even though he was unaware of the risk. He could not, however, be guilty of damaging property intending to endanger life. Intoxication is not a defence if a person deliberately drinks or takes drugs in order to give himself **Dutch courage** to commit a crime.

intra vires [Latin: within the powers] Describing an act carried out by a body (such as a public authority or a company) that is within the limits of the powers conferred on it by statute or some other constituting document (such as the memorandum and articles of association of a company). Compare ULTRA VIRES.

introductory tenancy A tenancy granted by a local authority or housing action trust that is intended as a probationary tenancy for 12 months. This will not be a *secure tenancy until the end of the 12 months. If the landlord wishes to seek possession during the introductory tenancy, he must serve notice on the tenant, who has 14 days to seek a review. After the review has been completed, the landlord must notify the tenant of the decision and give reasons if the decision to evict stands.

invalid care allowance A taxable benefit under the Social Security Acts, payable in certain circumstances to a person of working age who is not gainfully employed because he (or she) is regularly and substantially engaged in caring for a severely disabled relative. Those earning over £72 per week (2001) cannot claim.

invalidity benefit A former benefit under the Social Security Acts that replaced sickness benefit after 28 consecutive six-day weeks. From April 1995 sickness and invalidity benefits were replaced by *incapacity benefit.

inventory *n.* A detailed list of assets or property. A lease of furnished premises or a contract for the sale of chattels will usually contain an inventory from which the particular items can be identified. Under the Administration of Estates Act 1925, personal representatives must produce on oath an inventory of the deceased's estate when called upon by the court (this duty is effectively discharged by lodging an Inland Revenue account).

investigation of a company An inquiry into the running of a company made by inspectors appointed by the Department of Trade and Industry acting under Part XIV of the Companies Act 1985 or the Financial Services Act 1986. It may be ordered by the Secretary of State, on his own initiative or upon application by the shareholders or the company itself, or by the court. Such an inquiry may be held to supply company members with information or to investigate fraud, *unfair prejudice, nominee shareholders, or *insider dealing. The inspectors' report is usually published.

investigative help *See* COMMUNITY LEGAL SERVICE.

investment company A public listed company with a business of investing its funds mainly in securities in order to spread investment risk and give company members the benefit derived from the management of its funds. Investment companies must give notice in prescribed form to the Companies Registry. Under the Companies Act 1985 they are subject to special provisions in relation to dividends.

invitation to treat *See* OFFER.

invitee *n.* A person permitted to enter land or premises for a purpose in which the occupier of the land has a material interest. An example of an invitee is a customer in a shop. *See* OCCUPIER'S LIABILITY.

in vitro fertilization (IVF) *See* HUMAN ASSISTED REPRODUCTION.

involuntary conduct Conduct that cannot be controlled because one is suffering from a physical or mental condition or is acting under *duress. Involuntary conduct will often give rise to a defence of *automatism, although it may not be a defence if one is aware of one's condition or induced it oneself. Sometimes conduct may be regarded as involuntary if one is in control of one's faculties; for example, when the brakes of a car suddenly fail; this will also afford a defence to a driving offence charge.

IR35 A rule introduced with effect from 6 April 2000 that requires an individual who provides services to an employer through an intermediary (such as a limited company) to be taxed on the basis that he is an employee rather than self-employed. This requires deduction of tax at source under the PAYE (*Pay As You Earn) rules and gives less favourable treatments for the deduction of expenses than formerly.

irrebuttable presumption *See* PRESUMPTION.

irresistible impulse An uncontrollable urge to do something. Irresistible impulse is not usually a defence in law and it will not afford a defence of *insanity, unless it arises out of a disease of the mind as defined by the McNaghten Rules. When, however, an impulse is irresistible in that the body reacts in an instinctive way to it, there may be a defence of *involuntary conduct. An irresistible impulse may also constitute *diminished responsibility. *See also* PROVOCATION.

irretrievable breakdown (of a marriage) *See* MARITAL BREAKDOWN; DIVORCE.

irrevocable *adj.* Incapable of being revoked. For example, *powers of appointment may be made irrevocable. On the other hand, a testator of sound mind can revoke his will at any time.

ISA *See* INDIVIDUAL SAVINGS ACCOUNT.

issue *n.* **1.** The matter in dispute in a court action. **2.** The children or other lineal descendants of a person. **3.** The total of bank notes in circulation within a country.

issued capital *See* AUTHORIZED CAPITAL.

issue estoppel *Estoppel arising in relation to an issue that has previously been litigated and determined between the same parties or their predecessors in title. The issue must be an essential element of the claim or defence in both sets of proceedings. Unlike estoppel *per rem judicatam*, it does not prevent fresh evidence from being introduced in relation to the issue previously determined. This type of estoppel does not arise in criminal cases and its scope in civil cases is uncertain.

itemized pay statement The written statement that, under the Employment Rights Act 1996, an employer must provide for every employee who works eight or more hours a week, on or before each occasion wages or salaries are paid. The statement must contain the following information: (1) the employee's gross pay for the period; (2) the amounts and reason for any deductions; (3) the net amount paid; and (4) the method of calculating the net pay when different parts are calculated differently (e.g. if the pay is partly a basic wage and partly a commission or bonus payment). The statement need not contain details of fixed deductions if it contains an aggregate amount of these deductions and the employer has given the employee, either before or at the time of payment, a standing written statement of fixed deductions that contains the following particulars of each deduction: (1) the amount; (2) the intervals at which the deduction is made; (3) the purpose for which it is made. The standing statement of fixed deductions must be reissued within 12 months of its first being issued and not more than every 12 months after that and it must incorporate any amendments. An employee can apply to an *employment tribunal if his employer fails to provide the statutory statement or reason for deductions. The tribunal can order the employer to provide statements and also to refund any unexplained deductions in respect of a period up to 13 weeks before the application.

IVF In vitro fertilization. *See* HUMAN ASSISTED REPRODUCTION.

J

jactitation of marriage A false assertion that one is married to someone to whom one is not in fact married. Proceedings for jactitation were abolished by the Family Law Act 1986 but an injunction may be sought to restrain such claims being made and may be useful in preventing a presumption of marriage from arising.

Jobseeker's Agreement An agreement that must be signed by a claimant for the *jobseeker's allowance and his Employment Service adviser. The agreement sets out any restrictions on the claimant's availability for work and outlines the type of work being sought and the plans the claimant has made for seeking work.

jobseeker's allowance (JSA) A taxable benefit that replaced both unemployment benefit and income support for jobseekers from 7 October 1996. Those with national insurance contributions can claim contribution-based JSA, which is paid for up to six months. Those without NI contributions can claim income-based JSA, which is payable for as long as the claimant satisfies the rules. JSA is only paid to those who are available for work, are actively seeking work, and who have signed a *Jobseeker's Agreement.

joinder of causes of action The combination in one action of several causes of action against the same defendant. Although any number of causes of action may be joined in the first instance, the court may order that they be severed if the joinder would cause procedural difficulties.

joinder of charges The joining of more than one charge of a criminal offence together in the same *indictment. This may be done when the charges are based on the same facts or are part of a series of offences of the same or similar character.

joinder of defendants Mentioning two or more defendants in one count of an *indictment and trying them together. It is possible to join two or more defendants even if one of them is the principal offender and the other an accessory; if they are separately indicted, however, they cannot subsequently be tried together. Sometimes (e.g. in cases of conspiracy) it is usual to join two or more defendants; one may be convicted even if all his co-conspirators named in the count are acquitted and even though conspiracy by definition requires more than one participant. Two or more defendants may also be joined in one indictment if they are charged with different offences, if the interests of justice require this; for example, if two witnesses commit perjury in relation to the same facts in the same proceedings. Defendants who have been jointly indicted will normally only be tried by separate trials if a joint trial might prejudice one or more of them; for example, when evidence against one accused is not admissible against the other or when the prosecution wish to call one of the defendants to give evidence against another.

joinder of documents The connecting together of two or more documents so that, jointly, they fulfil statutory requirements when one of the documents alone would be insufficient.

joinder of parties The combination as claimants or defendants of two or more persons in a single action. Joinder may take place with the permission of the court or when separate actions would result in some common question of law or fact arising in all the actions, and all claims in the action are in respect of or arise out of the same transaction or series of transactions. *See also* JOINDER OF DEFENDANTS.

joint and several Together and in separation. If two or more people enter into an obligation that is said to be joint and several, their liability for its breach can be enforced against them all by a joint action or against any of them by individual action. *See also* JOINT TORTFEASORS.

Joint Committee on Statutory Instruments (Joint Scrutiny Committee) A committee of both Houses of Parliament whose function is to examine most delegated legislation (particularly *statutory instruments of a general character) and to draw Parliament's attention to it on a number of specified grounds; for example, if it imposes a tax, has retrospective effect, has been unduly delayed in publication, or is badly drafted. The Committee consists of seven members appointed by each House.

Joint Scrutiny Committee *See* JOINT COMMITTEE ON STATUTORY INSTRUMENTS.

joint tenancy Ownership of land by two or more persons who have identical interests in the whole of the land (*compare* TENANCY IN COMMON). A joint tenancy can only arise when four conditions (the **four unities**) are satisfied. (1) Each joint tenant must be entitled to possession at the same time. (2) The estate or interest each has in the land must be identical; each joint tenant is entitled to the whole property and has no exclusive entitlement to any separate part of it (*see* UNDIVIDED SHARES). (3) Each must have the same *title to the land, i.e. their ownership must be traced from the same instrument, such as a conveyance "to A and B as joint tenants". (4) Each joint tenant's interest must *vest at and subsist for the same time. Under a joint tenancy the **right of survivorship** applies: thus ownership of the entire interest in the property passes automatically on the death of one joint tenant to the survivor(s). The last survivor becomes the sole and absolute owner.

Under the Law of Property Act 1925 a distinction is made between a legal and an equitable joint tenancy. When two or more persons hold the *legal estate, they invariably hold it as joint tenants, and the right of survivorship applies. When the conveyance to them contains no words indicating that they are entitled to the property in *undivided shares (words of *severance), they hold as joint tenants in equity and the right of survivorship again applies. However, when they take distinct and separate shares, or when the equitable joint tenancy has been terminated (as by notice of severance, *partition, etc.), the equitable interest is held by them as tenants in common. However the equitable (or beneficial) interests are structured, the legal estate is always held by joint tenants as trustees upon a statutory *trust of land (Trust of Land and Appointment of Trustees Act 1996; TOLATA), and the trustees are accountable to those who hold the equitable interests – in the proportions to which they are entitled if they are tenants in common – for the property. The owners in equity have many rights under the trust of land, such as the right to be consulted and the right to occupy the property. Any joint tenant may apply to the court under section 14 of TOLATA for an order relating to the exercise by the trustees of any of their functions, including sale of the property. The court may make such order as it thinks fit.

joint tortfeasors Two or more people whose wrongful actions in furthering a common design cause a single injury. For example, if two men searching for a gas leak both applied a naked light to a gas pipe and caused an explosion, they are joint tortfeasors. But if a single injury is caused by several people acting without a common design they are not joint, but **concurrent tortfeasors**. An example of concurrent tortfeasors would be two motorists in separate cars, both driving negligently and causing a collision in which a pedestrian is injured. In both cases, the injured claimant is entitled to sue any or all of the tortfeasors for his whole loss; if he obtains a judgment against one tortfeasor that is not satisfied, he may proceed against the others. A tortfeasor liable for damage may recover contribution from other tortfeasors (whether joint or concurrent) liable for the same damage. *See* CIVIL LIABILITY CONTRIBUTION.

joint venture A commercial undertaking entered into by two or more parties, often by setting up a separate joint-venture company in which all partners have shares, to enable resources and skills to be shared. Joint ventures are defined in a European Commission *notice of 31 December 1994 as "undertakings which are jointly controlled by two or more other undertakings." In practice joint ventures encompass a broad range of operations, from merger-like operations to cooperation for particular functions, such as research and development, production, or distribution. A Commission notice of 23 December 1992 sets out how cooperative joint ventures are treated under the EU competition rules.

joint will A will comprising a single document executed by two or more persons as the will of all of them. It is treated as the separate will of each testator, and probate will be granted separately on the death of each. A joint testator may revoke the will only insofar as it applies to himself. A joint will is a convenient instrument for the exercise of a power conferred on persons jointly to appoint by will (*see* POWER OF APPOINTMENT) but has no other practical benefit. *Compare* MUTUAL WILLS.

Journals *pl. n.* The authentic record of proceedings in Parliament, as opposed to the verbatim record of debates (*see* HANSARD). There are two series published annually: *Journals of the House of Lords* (beginning in 1509) and *Journals of the House of Commons* (beginning in 1547).

joyriding *n. See* ABSTRACTING ELECTRICITY; AGGRAVATED VEHICLE-TAKING.

JP *See* JUSTICE OF THE PEACE.

judge *n.* A state official with power to adjudicate on disputes and other matters brought before the courts for decision. In English law all judges are appointed by the Crown, on the advice of the Lord Chancellor in the case of *circuit judges and High Court *puisne judges and on the advice of the Prime Minister in the case of judges of the *Court of Appeal and the *Lords of Appeal in Ordinary. All judges are experienced legal practitioners, mostly barristers, but solicitors can be appointed if they possess the relevant *advocacy qualification. The independence of the higher judiciary is ensured by the principle that they hold office during good behaviour and not at the pleasure of the Crown (with the exception of the Lord Chancellor). They can only be removed from office by a resolution of both Houses of Parliament assented to by the Queen. Their salaries are a charge on the *Consolidated Fund and are not voted annually. Circuit judges may be removed by the Lord Chancellor for incapacity or misbehaviour. All judicial appointments are pensionable and there is a compulsory retirement age of 70 years, but this can be extended to 75 if considered to be in the public interest. *See also* JUDICIAL IMMUNITY. *Compare* MAGISTRATE.

judge advocate A barrister or solicitor who advises a *court martial on questions of law. He is appointed by the Judge Advocate-General's Department or, in the case of naval courts martial, by the Judge Advocate of the Fleet. At the conclusion of the evidence the judge advocate sums up the case to the members of the court.

Judge Advocate-General's Department A department that advises the Secretary of State for Defence and the Defence Council on matters relating to the administration of military law and reviews proceedings of army and air-force courts martial.

judge in his own cause *See* NATURAL JUSTICE.

Judges' Rules Formerly, rules of practice drawn up by the High Court governing the questioning and charging of suspects by the police. They were replaced by a *code of practice issued under the provisions of the Police and Criminal Evidence Act 1984. *See also* INTERROGATION.

judgment *n.* **1.** A decision made by a court in respect of the matter before it. Judgments may be **interim (interlocutory)**, deciding a particular issue prior to the trial of the case; or **final**, finally disposing of the case. They may be *in personam*, imposing a personal liability on a party (e.g. to pay damages); or *in rem*, determining some issue of right, status, or property binding people generally. **2.** The process of reasoning by which the court's decision was arrived at. In English law it is the normal practice for judgment to be given in open court or, in some appellate tribunals, to be handed down in printed form. If the judgment contains rulings on important questions of law, it may be reported in the *law reports. *See also* ENFORCEMENT OF JUDGMENT; FOREIGN JUDGMENTS.

judgment creditor The person in whose favour a court judgment is made against a debtor.

judgment debtor A person against whom a court judgment has been entered, ordering him to pay money that he owes (the **judgment debt**). *See also* ENFORCEMENT OF JUDGMENT.

judgment in default *See* DEFAULT.

judgment summons A summons, issued on the application of a person entitled to enforce a judgment, that requires a judgment debtor to appear and be examined on oath as to his means. If it can be shown that the debtor had the means to pay the debt but has failed to do so the judge may make an order committing him to prison, suspended for as long as specified instalments are paid. Since the virtual abolition of imprisonment for debt, this procedure has been available only in respect of certain *maintenance orders and judgments for payment of certain taxes and state contributions.

judicial cognizance *See* JUDICIAL NOTICE.

Judicial Committee of the Privy Council A tribunal, created by the Judicial Committee Act 1833, consisting of the Lord Chancellor, Lord President of the Council and ex-Lords President, Lords of Appeal in Ordinary, and other members of the *Privy Council who have been Lords of Appeal in Ordinary or who have held high judicial office. Certain judges of Commonwealth countries who are Privy Counsellors are also members. The Committee's jurisdiction is to hear appeals from courts in dependent territories and those Commonwealth countries that have retained appeals to the Privy Council since attaining independence; it also hears appeals under certain statutes. The Committee's decisions are not technically judgments but merely advice to the Crown: they do not become final until incorporated into an *Order in Council. For this reason also, until 1966 dissenting opinions were not disclosed. The Committee's decisions are not binding as precedents upon English courts but are merely of *persuasive authority.

judicial dictum *See* OBITER DICTUM.

judicial discretion The power of the court to take some step, grant a remedy, or admit evidence or not as it thinks fit. Many rules of procedure and evidence are in discretionary form or provide for some element of discretion. In criminal cases, under the provisions of the Police and Criminal Evidence Act 1984, the court may exclude prosecution evidence if its admission would have such an adverse effect on the fairness of the proceedings that the court ought not to admit it. The *Court of Appeal is reluctant to review the exercise of discretion by trial judges.

judicial immunity The exemption of a *judge or *magistrate from personal actions for damages arising from the exercise of his judicial office. The immunity is absolute in respect of all words or actions of the judge while acting within his *jurisdiction and extends to acts done without jurisdiction provided that they were done in good faith.

judicial notice (judicial cognizance) The means by which the court may take as proven certain facts without hearing evidence. **Notorious facts** (i.e. matters of common knowledge) may be judicially noticed without inquiry; some other facts (e.g. matters that can easily be checked in a standard work of reference and are reasonably indisputable) may be noticed after inquiry. When judicial notice has been taken, *evidence in rebuttal is not permitted.

judicial precedent *See* PRECEDENT.

judicial review The simplified procedure by which, since 1977, prerogative and other remedies have been obtainable in the High Court against inferior courts, tribunals, and administrative authorities. On an application for the judicial review of a decision, the Court may grant a *quashing order, *mandatory order, *prohibition order, *declaration, or *injunction; it may also award damages.

judicial separation order An order by the courts that a husband and wife do not have to cohabit. The order does not terminate the marriage but it does free the parties of marital obligations. Judicial (*or* legal) separation is appropriate when there are religious objections to divorce or when the parties have not finally decided upon divorce. The grounds for separation are the same as those for *divorce. The courts have the same powers in relation to financial orders and children as they do when granting a divorce.

judicial trustee A trustee appointed by the court under the Judicial Trustee Act 1906, either as sole trustee or as co-trustee. He is an officer of the court, is subject to the court's control, and is entitled to such remuneration as the court allows. In practice, the *Public Trustee has replaced a trustee appointed under the Act.

junior barrister Any barrister who is not a *Queen's Counsel. The word "junior" does not necessarily imply youth or lack of seniority: many members of the Bar remain juniors throughout their careers.

jure gestionis [Latin] Describing commercial transactions by bodies that are owned by the state but are not regarded as organs of the state. In international law the state accepts responsibility for such transactions and does not claim immunity. *Compare* JURE IMPERII.

jure imperii [Latin] Describing transactions by state bodies or representatives, such as diplomats. In international law the state maintains immunity from such transactions. *Compare* JURE GESTIONIS.

juridical *adj.* Relating to judicial proceedings or the law. Juridical days were days on which legal business could be transacted.

jurisdiction *n.* **1.** The power of a court to hear and decide a case or make a certain order. (For the limits of jurisdiction of individual courts, see entries for those courts.) **2.** The territorial limits within which the jurisdiction of a court may be exercised. In the case of English courts this comprises England, Wales, Berwick-upon-

Tweed, and those parts of the sea claimed as *territorial waters. Everywhere else is said to be **outside the jurisdiction**. **3.** The territorial scope of the legislative competence of Parliament. *See* SOVEREIGNTY OF PARLIAMENT.

In international law, jurisdiction can be exercised on a number of grounds, based on the following principles: (1) the territorial principle (that the state within whose boundaries the crime has taken place has jurisdiction, irrespective of the nationality of the transgressor); (2) the nationality principle (that a state has the power of jurisdiction over one of its nationals for an offence he has committed in another state); (3) the protective principle (that a potentially injured state can exercise jurisdiction in all cases when its national security is threatened); (4) the passive personality principle (that a state has jurisdiction if the illegal act has been committed against a national of that state); and (5) the universality principle (when the accused has committed a crime in breach of a rule of *jus cogens*, i.e. a crime against humanity, any party having custody of the alleged lawbreaker is permitted to bring criminal proceedings against him).

juris et de jure [Latin] Of law and from law: an irrebuttable *presumption is so described.

juristic person (artificial person) An entity, such as a *corporation, that is recognized as having legal personality, i.e. it is capable of enjoying and being subject to legal rights and duties. It is contrasted with a human being, who is referred to as a **natural person**.

juror *n.* A member of a *jury. Each juror must swear that he will faithfully try the case and give a true verdict according to the evidence; failure to do so is contempt of court. Jurors are chosen from the electoral register; they must be aged between 18 and 70 and must have been resident in the UK for a period of at least five years since the age of 13. The following are ineligible for jury service: (1) past and present holders of any judicial office; (2) solicitors, barristers, members of a court staff, police officers, and others concerned with the administration of justice, if they have held the office within the preceding 10 years; (3) clergymen; and (4) the mentally ill. Members of Parliament, full-time members of the armed forces, and practising doctors, chemists, and vets may claim excusal from jury service and there are also special categories of discretionary excusal. A practising member of a religious society or order the tenets or beliefs of which are incompatible with jury service are excused from service as of right. Anyone who has ever been imprisoned for five years or more, or who has been imprisoned for more than three months within the preceding 10 years, or who is on bail, is disqualified from jury service.

A defendant is entitled to challenge individual jurors (*see* CHALLENGE TO JURY); if he succeeds in his challenges, another person takes the place of the challenged juror. A person who appears to be suffering from a disability that could impair performance of their duties as juror must now be brought before the judge so that he may form an opinion as to their suitability.

jury *n.* A group of *jurors (usually 12) selected at random to decide the facts of a case and give a verdict. Most juries are selected to try crimes but juries are also used in coroner's *inquests and in some civil cases (e.g. defamation actions). The judge directs the jury on points of law (*see* DIRECTION TO JURY) and sums up the evidence of the prosecution and defence for them, but he must leave the jury to decide all questions of fact themselves. He must also make it clear to them that they are the only *triers of fact and must acquit the defendant unless they feel sure that he is guilty beyond reasonable doubt. The verdict of a jury should, if possible, be unanimous, but when there are at least 10 people on the jury and they cannot reach a unanimous verdict, a *majority verdict is acceptable. Many offences must be tried by a jury; many others may be tried by a jury or by magistrates (*see* INDICTABLE OFFENCE). *See also* CHALLENGE TO JURY.

It is a criminal offence to attempt to influence a jury's discussions or to question them about their discussions when the case is over. *See also* CONTEMPT OF COURT; INTIMIDATION.

jus *n.* [Latin] A law or right.

jus accrescendi [Latin] *See* RIGHT OF SURVIVORSHIP. locum non habet

jus accrescendi inter mercatores pro beneficio commercii locum non habet [Latin: for the advancement of commerce there is no place for the right of survivorship between merchants] A maxim stating the principle that equity will treat as tenants in common (*see* TENANCY IN COMMON) those in partnership whose interest in partnership property is at common law a *joint tenancy. Thus on the death of a partner his interest in the partnership property is part of his estate rather than belonging to the surviving partners.

jus civile [Latin: civil law] **1.** *Municipal law. **2.** The whole body of Roman law.

jus cogens [Latin: coercive law] A rule or principle in international law that is so fundamental that it binds all states and does not allow any exceptions. Such rules (sometimes called **peremptory norms**) will only amount to *jus cogens* rules if they are recognized as such by the international community as a whole. A treaty that conflicts with an existing *jus cogens* rule is void, and if a new *jus cogens* rule emerges, any existing treaty that conflicts with it automatically becomes void. States cannot create regional customary international law that contradicts *jus cogens* rules. Most authorities agree that the laws prohibiting slavery, genocide, piracy, and acts of aggression or illegal use of force are *jus cogens* laws. Some suggest that certain human rights provisions (e.g. those prohibiting racial discrimination) also come under the category of *jus cogens*.

jus gentium [Latin: the law of peoples] *See* INTERNATIONAL LAW.

jus in re aliena [Latin] A right in the property of another (*see* ENCUMBRANCE). It is contrasted with **jus in re propria** – a right in one's own property.

jus naturale [Latin: natural law] The fundamental element of all law. *See* NATURAL LAW.

jus sanguinis [Latin: law relating to blood] The principle that the nationality of children is the same as that of their parents, irrespective of their place of birth. This contrasts with *jus soli*, whereby nationality is dependent on place of birth. In states in which the *jus sanguinis* principle applies (i.e. France and Germany), a conflict of jurisdiction may arise when a child is born of parents who are citizens of another state. For example, a child born in the United States of French parents is an American citizen *jure soli*, but a French citizen *jure sanguinis*. His effective citizenship will depend upon the jurisdiction within which he happens to be in; in the United States he is a US citizen; in France, a Frenchman; in any other country he is both.

Conflicts resulting from the simultaneous presence of these contrasting claims of allegiance are generally settled between states by deferring *jus sanguinis* to *jus soli* when the state asserting its primary claim of allegiance has *de facto* jurisdiction of the individual in question. Most jurisdictions (including the United Kingdom and the United States) now adopt within their nationality law a combination of *jus soli* and *jus sanguinis*.

jus soli [Latin: law relating to the soil (of one's country)] The rule by which birth in a state is sufficient to confer nationality, irrespective of the nationality of one's parents (*compare* JUS SANGUINIS). The United Kingdom and the United States originally adhered to a strict version of this principle. Thus the children of an *alien, born on the territory of the host state, would from their birth adopt the nationality of that state. Most jurisdictions (including the United Kingdom and the United States) now adopt a combination of *jus soli* and *jus sanguinis.*

just and equitable winding-up A *compulsory winding-up on grounds of fairness. This may occur, for example, when the purpose of the company cannot be achieved, when the management is deadlocked or has been guilty of serious irregularities, or, in small companies run on the basis of mutual trust between members, when the majority have exercised their legal rights in breach of a common understanding between the members when the company was formed. No order will be made if another form of *minority protection would be more appropriate. *See also* UNFAIR PREJUDICE.

jus tertii [Latin: right of a third party] A defence raised by a party who is sued in respect of property alleging that some third party has a better claim to the property than the claimant. The Torts (Interference with Goods) Act 1977 provides that this is a good defence to an action in *conversion, but a special procedure is laid down for the joinder of the third party in the action.

justice *n.* A moral ideal that the law seeks to uphold in the protection of rights and *punishment of wrongs. Justice is not synonymous with law – it is possible for a law to be called unjust. However, English law closely identifies with justice and the word is frequently used in the legal system; for example, in justice of the peace, Royal Courts of Justice, and administration of justice.

justice of the peace (JP) A person holding a commission from the Crown to exercise certain judicial functions for a particular **commission area**. JPs are appointed on behalf of and in the name of the Queen by the Lord Chancellor and may be removed from office in the same way. On reaching the age of 70 they are placed on a supplemental list and cease to be able to exercise any judicial functions. Their principal function is to sit as *magistrates in the *magistrates' courts but they may also sit in the *Crown Court when it is considering committals for sentence and appeals from magistrates' courts, sign warrants of arrest and search warrants, and take statutory declarations. All High Court judges are *ex officio* justices of the peace for the whole of England and Wales.

justices' clerk *See* CLERK TO THE JUSTICES.

justification *n.* **1.** The defence to an action for *defamation that the defamatory statement made was true. Truth is a complete defence to a civil action for defamation, except where true statements about *spent convictions are proved to have been made maliciously. **2.** The defence that interference with the contractual or business relations of another was justified. The scope of the defence is uncertain, but the fact that the wages of chorus girls were so low that they were compelled to resort to prostitution has been held to justify a theatrical performers' protection society inducing theatre owners to break their contracts with the girls' employer (*Brimelow* v *Casson* 1924). *See* PROCURING BREACH OF CONTRACT.

justifying bail Demonstrating to a court granting bail that one is capable of meeting the surety specified in the bail (for example, disclosing one's financial resources). A person standing surety for bail must be able to provide the bail out of his own resources. It is a criminal offence (**bail-bonding**) for a defendant who is granted bail to agree to indemnify his surety against any loss arising out of standing surety.

just satisfaction The basis for damages awarded by the European Court of Human Rights (and thus in respect of claims under the *Human Rights Act 1998). In many cases where the Court finds a violation it has declined to award any damages on the basis that this finding is in itself sufficient just satisfaction. Subject to this discretion, damages can be obtained for pecuniary loss, nonpecuniary loss, and costs and expenses.

juvenile court *See* YOUTH COURT.

juvenile offender A person between the ages of 10 and 17 who has committed a crime (*see* DOLI CAPAX); an offender between the ages of 14 and 17 is known as a **young offender**. A child (aged between 10 and 14) cannot normally be tried on indictment (even for an *indictable offence) except when charged with homicide. A young offender may be tried on indictment when charged with homicide or an offence for which an adult could be sentenced to at least 14 years' imprisonment or if he is jointly charged with someone aged 18 or over and it is felt to be necessary that they be tried together. In all other cases, juvenile offenders must be tried summarily by a magistrates' court or a *youth court; they can be "found guilty" of an offence but may not be described as "convicted".

A juvenile offender cannot be sentenced to imprisonment; instead he may be sentenced to *detention in a young offender institution. If found guilty of murder or some other grave crime he must be detained in a place and on such conditions as the Home Secretary may determine. The Crime (Sentences) Act 1997 provides that the Parole Board, rather than the Home Secretary, has responsibility for the release of juveniles convicted of murder. Under the Criminal Justice and Public Order Act 1994 it is possible to sentence an offender aged 12 to 14 who has been convicted of a serious offence punishable in an adult by imprisonment to custody under a **secure training order** for a period of six months to two years. A juvenile offender may not be sentenced to do community service or put on probation before the age of 16. He may be fined (*see* FINE), made the subject of a supervision or hospital order, or required to attend an *attendance centre. He could also be discharged (absolutely or conditionally). The procedures for dealing with juvenile offenders have now been amended in some respects by the Youth Justice and Criminal Evidence Act 1999.

K

keeping *n.* (of property) *See* THEFT.

keeping term *See* TERM.

keeping the peace Behaving in such a way as not to cause or threaten a breach of the peace, i.e. a disturbance of public order. Magistrates' courts have very wide powers to *bind over people to keep the peace or to make them enter into *recognizances (either personally or through a surety) to pay a sum of money into court if they fail to keep the peace. The order may be made against a defendant on a criminal charge or merely upon complaint by a member of the public (if there is some evidence that a *breach of the peace may occur). A person may be bound over for any sum of money or any period of time; if he refuses to be bound over or to enter into the recognizance, he may be sentenced immediately to imprisonment (even if he has committed no criminal offence).

kerb crawling The offence by a man of *soliciting a woman for prostitution in a street or public place either from a motor vehicle or having just alighted from one, when the soliciting is persistent or likely to cause annoyance to the woman or nuisance to other people in the vicinity.

kidnapping *n.* Carrying a person away, without his consent, by means of force, threats, or fraud. Kidnapping is a common-law offence punishable with a maximum sentence of life imprisonment. A man may be guilty of kidnapping his wife. Disputes between parents about the right to their children are dealt with in family proceedings. A parent with care of the child may obtain a warrant for the arrest of the other parent if he or she takes the child away. Failure to comply with an order for the return of the child amounts to contempt of court. *See also* ABDUCTION; HOSTAGE.

kleptomania *n.* A mental disorder leading to the *irresistible impulse to steal.

knock-out agreement An agreement by dealers not to bid against each other at an auction. Such an agreement is illegal (*see* AUCTION RING).

knowhow *n.* Technical information often exploited in conjunction with a *patent. EU regulation 240/96 governs the terms that may or may not be included in a knowhow licence agreement. *See* TECHNOLOGY TRANSFER.

knowing receipt If a stranger receives trust property knowing it to be in breach of trust, he will be liable to account to the beneficiaries for that property or for the proceeds of it (*see* TRACING TRUST PROPERTY).

laches *n.* [from Norman French *lasches*, slackness, negligence] Neglect and unreasonable delay in enforcing an equitable right. If a claimant with full knowledge of the facts takes an unnecessarily long time to bring an action (e.g. to set aside a contract obtained by fraud) the court will not assist him; hence the maxim "the law will not help those who sleep on their rights" and "equity aids the vigilant". The defence of laches is only allowed if there is no statutory limitation period. If there is such a period, the claimant can bring an action at any time up to the expiry of the time stated. *See* ACQUIESCENCE; WAIVER.

Lady Day *See* QUARTER DAYS.

land *n.* Those parts of the surface of the earth that are capable in law of being owned and are within the court's jurisdiction. Generally, ownership of land includes the *airspace above it and the subsoil below. For the purposes of land law, the Law of Property Act 1925 defines land as including mines and minerals (whether or not owned separately from the surface), buildings, and most interests in land. Chattels fixed to the land so that they become part of it are also treated in law as land, under the maxim *quicquid plantatur solo, solo cedit* (*see* FIXTURE).

land certificate A document issued by the Land Registry to the proprietor of registered land as proof of his ownership of it. *See* LAND REGISTRATION.

land charge An interest in *unregistered land that imposes an obligation on the landowner in favour of some other person (the **chargee**). If validly created and registered where appropriate under the Land Charges Act 1972 at the *Land Charges Department (*see* REGISTRATION OF ENCUMBRANCES), land charges will normally bind purchasers of the land. Important examples of land charges created by act of the parties include mortgages not protected by deposit of title deeds, binding contracts for sale (including options and rights of pre-emption), *restrictive covenants that affect freehold land, and equitable *easements. Some land charges arise under statute; for example, a spouse's right to occupy the matrimonial home under the Matrimonial Homes Act 1983 (a Class F land charge) and the Inland Revenue charge for unpaid inheritance tax (a Class D land charge). **Local land charges**, which arise in favour of local authorities from the exercise of their statutory powers, are registered by the local authority itself and apply to *registered land as well as to unregistered land.

Land Charges Department A department of the Land Registry, maintained under the Land Charges Act 1972 to keep registers of certain interests affecting the rights of persons owning *unregistered land (called **estate owners**). For the interests capable of being registered, *see* REGISTRATION OF ENCUMBRANCES. Registration of land charges against the name of the estate owner constitutes notice to everyone of their existence and generally renders them binding upon purchasers of any interest or estate in the land affected. A person contemplating taking such an interest may apply to the Department for an *official search certificate, which will reveal all interests registered against the estate owner's name.

landlord *n.* A person who grants a lease or tenancy. He need not be the outright owner of the tenanted premises (he may, for example, be a lessee himself or even a licensee). A landlord may be an individual, a local authority, a trustee, a personal representative, or a corporation (such as a company). A landlord may provide services to the tenant, such as heating, lighting, and porterage. There are statutory controls on the amount that a landlord can charge for such services and procedures for consultation with the tenants. The person who receives the rent is obliged to reveal the landlord's identity on the tenant's request. When there is a change of ownership the new landlord must inform the tenant within two months or when rent is next due, whichever is the later. The kind of security of tenure a tenant has is affected by who his landlord is. *See* ASSURED TENANCY; PROTECTED TENANCY; SECURE TENANCY; RESTRICTED CONTRACT.

land registration The system of registering, at local branch offices of HM Land Registry, certain legal estates or interests in land. Under the Land Registration Act 1925 compulsory registration was to be introduced in a specified area by Order in Council: registration has now been extended to the whole of England and Wales, and over 90% of all land in England and Wales is now registered land. There is, however, no obligation on existing owners to register, but most transactions in land, including sale, gift, legal mortgage, etc., now trigger registration by the new or existing owner. If he fails to do so he does not acquire the legal estate and therefore runs the risk that the vendor or landlord may sell to someone else who can acquire a better title by registration. Existing owners or tenants under a lease having at least 21 years to run may register their titles if they wish.

Upon registration of a title the Land Registry allocates a title number. Evidence of title is provided by the issue of a **land certificate** to the owner (who is known as the **registered proprietor**) or, if the land is in mortgage, a **charge certificate** to the mortgagee. The certificate represents the registered title, which is in three parts, comprising:

(1) The **property register**. This describes the land and any additional rights incidental to it, such as rights of way over adjoining land. The **filed plan** shows the location of the land, usually with a general indication of the position of the boundaries. Registration of precise boundaries is possible under a special procedure involving notice to adjoining owners and hearing their objections.

(2) The **proprietorship register**. This names the registered proprietor(s) of the land and notes any restriction on their powers to dispose of it (for example, *restrictions, *inhibitions, *cautions, etc.). The register also states the nature of the title, which may be *absolute, *qualified, *possessory, or *good leasehold.

(3) The **charges register**. This details interests adverse to the proprietor, such as mortgages, restrictive covenants, or easements to which the land is subject.

The land certificate fulfils a similar function to title deeds to unregistered land, but if a more up-to-date record of the state of the registered title is required (for example, by a prospective purchaser or mortgagee), the Land Registry will issue *office copies or a certificate of *official search on application by the registered proprietor or any person with his authority to inspect the register. A registered proprietor's title is guaranteed by the state subject to *overriding interests, which are not registrable in the charges register. The extent of the guarantee depends on the nature of the title. The register can be rectified by the court in certain circumstances to correct a mistake; compensation is generally paid by the government to a party who suffers loss as a result.

Land Registry A statutory body established under the Land Registration Act 1925 to maintain registers of certain legal estates in land. *See also* LAND REGISTRATION.

Lands Tribunal A tribunal established by the Lands Tribunal Act 1949 to decide disputes concerning compensation for the compulsory acquisition of land and similar questions involving land valuation. It also determines disputes as to the value of land or buildings for inheritance-tax purposes. Its members, who must be legally qualified or experienced in valuation, are appointed by the Lord Chancellor, and it is subject to the supervision of the *Council on Tribunals.

lapse *n.* The cancellation of a bequest when the beneficiary dies before the testator. Thus, in general, if A's will leaves property to B but B predeceases A, the bequest does not take effect. The property becomes part of A's residuary estate and is distributed to his residuary beneficiaries. This rule is subject to the following exceptions.
(1) When property is bequeathed to two or more persons as joint tenants, those who survive the testator take the property.
(2) The Wills Act 1837 provides that when property is bequeathed to a child or remoter descendant of the testator who predeceases him but leaves descendants of his own who are alive at the testator's death, those descendants take the property (subject to a contrary intention being expressed in the will). A similar rule applies when property is left in tail (*entailed interest).
(3) Some gifts to charities that cease to exist before the testator's death may be applied *cy-près.
(4) Most importantly, the testator may stipulate what is to happen to the gift if the beneficiary predeceases him.

lapse of offer The termination of an *offer as a result of the passage of time, death, or the nonfulfilment of a condition. An offer made subject to a specified time limit lapses after that time has passed; all other offers lapse after a reasonable time. Death of the offeree causes an offer to lapse, but death of the offeror does not always do so. The offer remains available for acceptance if the death is unknown to the offeree and the resulting contract could be performed by the offeror's personal representatives. An offer lapses if one or more conditions are not fulfilled. An offer to buy goods, for example, is made on the assumption that they will remain in the same condition until acceptance; it lapses if that ceases to be the case. *See also* REJECTION OF OFFER; REVOCATION OF OFFER.

larceny *n.* Formerly (before 1969), *theft. Larceny was more limited than theft and required an **asportation** (carrying away of the property).

latent ambiguity *See* AMBIGUITY.

latent defect *See* DEFECT.

law *n.* **1.** The enforceable body of rules that govern any society. *See also* COMMON LAW; NATURAL LAW. **2.** One of the rules making up the body of law, such as an *Act of Parliament.

Law Commission A body established by the Law Commissions Act 1965 to take and keep the law under review with a view to systematically developing and reforming it. In particular, it considers the codification of the law, the elimination of anomalies, the repeal of obsolete and unnecessary enactments, a reduction in the number of separate enactments, and simplification and modernization generally. The Commission consists of a chairman and four other members, appointed by the Lord Chancellor from among the holders of judicial office, barristers, solicitors, and academic lawyers. There is a separate Commission for Scotland.

Law Lords *See* LORDS OF APPEAL IN ORDINARY.

law merchant The international practice of merchants relating to commercial and maritime matters. In early times it influenced Admiralty law and the law administered in local courts. Parts of the law merchant were absorbed into the common law of England (e.g. that relating to negotiable instruments and the transfer of bills of lading).

law officers of the Crown The *Attorney General, *Solicitor General, *Lord Advocate, Solicitor General for Scotland, and Attorney General for Northern Ireland.

law of nations *See* INTERNATIONAL LAW.

law of the sea The rules of international law governing rights over the seas. The seas are divided into several different areas. (1) The internal waters of a state (e.g. rivers, lakes, ports, and harbours). A state may usually apply its laws to any merchant ship within its internal waters. It may also apply navigation or health regulations to foreign warships in such waters and exclude foreign warships from its ports. (2) The *territorial waters. (3) The *high seas, beyond the territorial waters, which are open to all nations for such purposes as navigation, fishing, laying of submarine cables, and over-flying. Ships on the high seas are usually subject only to international law (for example, in relation to acts of piracy) and the law of the flagstate (usually dependent on registration in that state). There is also a limited right of *hot pursuit. (4) The *continental shelf, which – although geographically part of the high seas   is subject to specific rules.

The law of the sea is contained in customary international law and in the four Geneva Conventions of 1958. Since 1982, when the United Nations Convention on the Law of the Sea came into force, there is a comprehensive code governing the whole of this law, which includes some completely new rules. To date (2001), 135 countries have established their consent to be bound by this Convention; the UK acceded to the treaty on 25 July 1997. In addition, many nations have subscribed to the related 1994 Agreement Regarding the United Nations Convention on the Law of the Sea. Even though some states chose not to ratify the 1982 Convention, many of the Convention's principles have now passed into the corpus of customary international law.

Law Reform Committee A body established by the Lord Chancellor to consider particular areas of law that may need reform.

law reports Reports of cases decided by the courts, comprising a statement of the facts of every case and the reasons the court gave for judgment. The earliest reports were contained in the *Year Books*, which were published annually between 1283 and 1535. Their authors were anonymous and may have been student lawyers. The *Year Books* were superseded by personalized reports, i.e. reports written privately by lawyers (e.g. Chief Justice Coke) who appended their names to them. In 1865 was established the Incorporated Council of Law Reporting, a semiofficial body that publishes *The Weekly Law Reports* (formerly *Weekly Notes*). These are reports of important cases selected by the Council, written by lawyers, and approved by the judges involved. There are in addition still a number of commercially published reports, e.g. the *All England Law Reports*, but the Court of Appeal and the House of Lords will cite the reports of the Incorporated Council in preference to other reports where there is a choice.

law sittings *See* SITTINGS.

Law Society The professional body for solicitors in England and Wales, incorporated by royal charter in 1831. The Society exists both to further the professional interests of solicitors and to discharge important statutory functions in relation to the admission to practice, the conduct, and discipline of solicitors. It issues annual *practising certificates to solicitors, without which they may not practise, and through its disciplinary committee may strike a solicitor's name off the roll or take other disciplinary action, subject to an appeal to the High Court. The Society is responsible for the examination of intending solicitors and organizes educational and training courses both through the College of Law and recognized universities.

lay days (lying days) The number of days specified in a charterparty to enable the charterer to load or discharge cargo. They begin to run as soon as the ship is an **arrived ship**, i.e. has reached the berth or mooring specified in the charterparty. If only a port is specified, the ship must have reached a position within that port at which it is at the immediate and effective disposition of the charterer (the **Reid test**). The charterparty may provide for the payment of dispatch money when the charterer saves days in loading or discharging the cargo. Unless the charterparty provides otherwise (e.g. by restricting them to good-weather working days), lay days are **running days**, i.e. they run consecutively, without any break. *See also* DEMURRAGE.

laying an information Giving a magistrate a concise statement (an **information**), verbally or in writing, of an alleged offence and the suspected offender, so that he can take steps to obtain the appearance of the suspect in court. Information can be laid by any member of the public, although it is usually done by the police. If an arrest warrant is required, the information must be in writing and on oath. Objections cannot normally be made to information laid, on the grounds of formal defects or discrepancies between it and the prosecution's subsequent evidence. But if the defect is fundamental to the charge the information will be dismissed, and if the defendant was misled by a discrepancy, he may be granted an adjournment of the trial.

LCJ *See* LORD CHIEF JUSTICE.

leader *n.* A *Queen's Counsel or any barrister who is the senior of two counsel appearing for the same party.

Leader of HM Opposition The leader in the House of Commons of the party in opposition to the government that has the greatest numerical strength in the House. By statute a salary is payable to him (in addition to his salary as an MP); any doubt as to his identity is resolved by the Speaker.

Leader of the House *See* HOUSE OF COMMONS; HOUSE OF LORDS.

lead evidence To call or adduce evidence.

leading case A case, the legal reasoning in which establishes an important principle of law. *See* PRECEDENT.

leading question A question asked of a witness in a manner that suggests the answer sought by the questioner (e.g. "You threw the brick through the window, didn't you?") or that assumes the existence of disputed facts to which the witness is to testify. Leading questions may not be asked during *examination-in-chief (except relating to formal matters, such as the witness's name and address) but may normally be asked in *cross-examination.

leapfrog procedure 1. (House of Lords) The procedure for appealing direct to the House of Lords from the High Court or a Divisional Court, bypassing the Court of Appeal. The procedure is only allowed in exceptional cases. All parties must consent and the case must raise a point of law of public importance, which either relates wholly or partly to the interpretation of a statute or of a statutory instrument or is one in respect of which the trial judge is bound by a previous decision of the Court of Appeal or the House of Lords. The trial judge must certify that he is satisfied as to the importance of the case and the House of Lords must give permission to appeal in this way. **2. (Court of Appeal)** The procedure by which a High Court judge or the Master of the Rolls may transfer an appeal from a decision of a district judge or master to the Court of Appeal. Under the Access to Justice Act 1999 and the *Civil Procedure Rules, which substantially revised *appellate jurisdiction in the civil courts, such an appeal would normally be to a circuit judge or a High Court judge. However, if the appeal is considered to raise an important point of principle or practice, or if there is some other compelling reason for the Court of Appeal to hear it, it may be transferred.

lease *n.* A contract under which an owner of property (the *landlord or **lessor**) grants another person (the *tenant or **lessee**) exclusive possession of the property for an agreed period, usually (but not necessarily) in return for rent and sometimes for a capital sum known as a *premium. Unless it satisfies the conditions for a *parol lease, a lease must be made by a formal document (a *deed), which is itself called a lease. If this is not done, however, there may still be an *agreement for a lease. The lessee must have exclusive possession, i.e. the right to control the property and to exclude everyone else from it (subject to any rights of entry or re-entry reserved to the landlord). If possession is not exclusive, there is no lease but there may be a *licence. A lease must be for a definite period, which may be a *fixed term or by way of a *periodic tenancy. *See also* EQUITABLE LEASE; LEGAL LEASE.

The deed that creates the lease sets out the terms, which include the parties, the property, the length of the lease, the rent, and other obligations (**covenants**), particularly concerning repairs, insurance, and parting with possession. Certain covenants are implied in all leases (though the lease may vary or exclude them). In the case of the lessor these are: (1) not to derogate from his grant (i.e. he must not do anything that would make the property unfit for the purpose for which it was let); (2) *quiet enjoyment; and, in certain cases, (3) to ensure that the premises are *fit for habitation. In the case of the tenant, the implied covenants are: (1) to pay the rent; (2) to pay all ordinary rates and taxes; (3) not to commit *waste; and (4) to use the property in a tenant-like manner, i.e. to do the sort of small maintenance jobs that any reasonable tenant would be expected to do (he is not, however, responsible for *fair wear and tear or other disrepair that is not his fault). *See also* ASSIGNMENT; COVENANT TO REPAIR.

leasehold *adj.* Held under a *lease, i.e. for a period of fixed minimum duration. *See* TERM OF YEARS ABSOLUTE.

leasehold ownership Ownership of property under a *lease. The period of ownership depends on the terms of the lease: it may vary from a very short time, such as a week, to a very long period, such as 999 years. The tenant's ownership is also restricted by the terms of the lease. Under the Leasehold Reform Act 1967, holders of long leases (over 21 years) for houses may have a statutory right to purchase the freehold or extend the existing lease by 50 years (*see* ENFRANCHISEMENT OF TENANCY). The Leasehold Reform Act 1993 granted a similar right to leaseholders of flats.

leasehold valuation tribunal A body that handles disputes over service charges and over the purchase of leasehold property by tenants holding long leases; it also appoints managers of leasehold properties when the landlords' managers are not acceptable. Leasehold valuation tribunals started operating in 1997.

leave *n.* Permission given by the court to take some procedural step in litigation. Situations in which permission is required include *service out of the jurisdiction and appeals to higher civil courts (*see* APPELLATE JURISDICTION). Some items of evidence may be admissible only upon permission being granted by the trial judge.

leave to defend An order of the High Court on a summons for *summary judgment, granting the defendant leave to continue with his defence to the action. The leave may be **conditional** (e.g. subject to the defendant paying the whole or part of the claimant's claim into court) or **unconditional**.

legacy *n.* A gift of personal property effected by will (*compare* DEVISE). A **general legacy** is a gift of property not identifiable with a specific asset or fund; for example, a simple legacy of "£1000 to A" or "my shares to B". A **specific legacy** is a particular identifiable object, for example a named painting. It is liable to *ademption but is otherwise payable by the deceased's personal representatives in priority to general legacies. A **demonstrative legacy** is payable from a specified fund; for example, "£500 from the £1000 kept under my bed". Such a legacy is not adeemed if the testator disposes of the fund during his lifetime and is payable in priority to general legacies. **Pecuniary legacies** (i.e. gifts of cash) carry interest from one year after the testator's death. A **residuary legacy** is one that disposes of the whole of the testator's personal property after payment of debts and specific, demonstrative, and general legacies.

legal aid scheme A scheme under the Legal Aid Act 1988 whereby the payment of legal costs was made out of public funds for those unable to meet the costs themselves, provided that the person qualified under the financial and merits tests laid down under the scheme. There were separate provisions for civil and criminal cases. Civil legal aid had two components: legal advice and assistance (sometimes known as the *green form scheme) and legal aid. Under the former, payment was made to qualified lawyers under the scheme who provided legal advice and help preliminary to litigation. Under legal aid, payment was made for the provision of legal advice and assistance at all stages of litigation, including appeals. In criminal cases, the court determined whether or not legal aid was granted and made a legal aid order if it considered legal aid desirable in the interest of justice.

The legal aid scheme was replaced in April 2000 by the *Community Legal Service. Under this new scheme of legal aid and assistance, the green form scheme was replaced by the legal help scheme and legal aid was replaced by full representation; there are, in addition, intermediate levels of service.

legal assignment *See* ASSIGNMENT.

legal easement *See* EASEMENT.

legal estate Ownership of land or an interest in land either in *fee simple absolute in possession or for a *term of years absolute. Under the Law of Property Act 1925 these are the only forms of ownership that can exist as legal estates in land. All other forms, e.g. life interests and entailed interests, are equitable only.

legal fiction *See* FICTION.

legal fraud *See* CONSTRUCTIVE FRAUD.

legal help *See* COMMUNITY LEGAL SERVICE; GREEN FORM.

legal lease A contract or grant that creates an estate in land for a *term of years absolute. A legal lease must normally be created by deed; however, there are no formal requirements for the creation of a legal lease for a term that takes effect in possession and does not exceed three years at a full market rent without a premium. Under the Law of Property Act 1925, the *assignment of a legal lease of whatever duration must be effected by deed, otherwise it may only take effect as a contract to assign the term. A legal lease for more than 21 years must be registered at the Land Registry (*see* LAND REGISTRATION). *Compare* EQUITABLE LEASE.

legal memory The period over which the law's recollection extends. Its commencement was arbitrarily fixed at 1189 by the Statute of Westminster I 1275. Time before legal memory is referred to as **time immemorial**. *Compare* LIVING MEMORY.

legal mortgage *See* MORTGAGE.

legal person A natural person (i.e. a human being) or a *juristic person.

legal rights 1. Rights recognized by the common law courts, as distinct from *equitable rights or interests recognized by the Court of Chancery. In their developed form, legal rights affect everyone whether or not they know (or ought to know) of their existence (hence the expression "legal rights bind the world"). **2.** Generally, all rights recognized by the law (both common law and equity) as having legal existence and effect, as distinguished from moral rights.

legal separation *See* JUDICIAL SEPARATION ORDER.

Legal Services Commission *See* COMMUNITY LEGAL SERVICE.

Legal Services Ombudsman An official, appointed by the Lord Chancellor under the Legal Services Ombudsman (Jurisdiction) Order 1990, who is responsible for hearing complaints against solicitors, barristers, and licensed conveyancers made by their professional bodies.

legal year The period made up, in any year, of the four court *sittings.

legatee *n.* The person to whom a *legacy is given.

legislation *n.* **1.** The whole or any part of a country's written law. In the UK the term is normally confined to *Acts of Parliament, but in its broadest sense it also includes law made under powers conferred by Act of Parliament (*see* DELEGATED LEGISLATION), law made by virtue of the *royal prerogative, and Measures (*see* CHURCH OF ENGLAND). **2.** The process of making written law.

legislature *n.* The body having primary power to make written law. In the UK it consists of Parliament, i.e. the Crown, the House of Commons, and the House of Lords.

legitimacy *n.* The legal status of a child born to parents who were married at the time of his conception or birth (or both). (*See also* LEGITIMATION.) There is a **presumption of legitimacy** in all cases when the mother is married, so that children of the marriage are presumed to be the offspring of the mother's husband. This may be rebutted, however, either by showing that the husband was impotent or absent on the date on which the child must have been conceived or by *blood tests showing that he could not be the father. Children born of a voidable marriage annulled since 1949 are legitimate; those born of such a marriage annulled between 1937 and 1949 are legitimate only if the grounds of nullity were that the other spouse was of unsound mind or epileptic or suffering from a communicable venereal disease. Since 1959, children born of a void marriage are treated as legitimate if at the time of their conception or insemination at least one of their parents reasonably thought the marriage was valid and the father was domiciled in England at the time of the child's birth. The Family Law Reform Act 1987 provides that a child conceived, by a party to a marriage, through artificial insemination by a donor, is to be treated as a legitimate child of that marriage.

Under certain conditions (specified in the Family Law Act 1986) a person may seek a court declaration of his legitimacy. *See also* ILLEGITIMACY.

legitimate aim A prerequisite for interference with a *qualified right as set out in the European Convention on Human Rights: a signatory state will be able to interfere with a qualified right only if that interference is designed to pursue a legitimate aim and the interference is a proportionate one (*see* PROPORTIONALITY). Legitimate aims include national security, public order, the prevention of crime, etc.

legitimation *n.* The process of replacing the status of illegitimacy by that of legitimacy. A living child may be legitimated if his parents marry one another, provided that the father is domiciled in England or Wales at the date of the marriage. Evidence that the husband recognized the child as his own may be sufficient to establish his paternity for purposes of legitimation. Legitimation takes effect from the date of the marriage and the child is treated thereafter as if he had been born legitimate. Under the Family Law Act 1986, a person may seek a court declaration that he is a legitimated person.

lessee *n.* The person to whom a *lease is granted. *See also* TENANT.

lessor *n.* The person by whom a *lease is granted. *See also* LANDLORD.

letter of attorney *See* POWER OF ATTORNEY.

letter of credence (*lettre de créance*) A formal document by which the head of an accredited state presents its newly appointed diplomatic agent to the head of state of the host country.

letter of credit A document whereby a bank, at the request of a customer, undertakes to pay money to a third party (the **beneficiary**) on presentation of documents specified in the letter (e.g. bills of lading and policies of insurance). The obligation of the bank to pay is independent of the underlying contract of sale and so is not affected by any defects in the goods supplied under the contract of sale. A contract of sale of goods may require the buyer to open an **irrevocable letter of credit** in favour of the seller. This cannot be revoked by the issuing bank or the purchaser of the goods before its expiry date, without the consent of the beneficiary. A **confirmed letter of credit** is one in which the negotiating bank guarantees payment to the beneficiary should it not be honoured by the issuing bank.

letter of request (rogatory letter, letter rogatory) A letter issued to a foreign court requesting a judge to take evidence from a specific person within that court's jurisdiction. The resulting *deposition may be read at a subsequent court hearing.

letters of administration Authority granted by the court to a specified person to act as an *administrator of a deceased person's estate when the deceased dies intestate. Letters of administration *cum testamento annexo* (with the will annexed) are granted when the deceased's will does not appoint executors or when the executors named do not prove the will. In certain circumstances, letters of administration may be granted for limited purposes to persons not entitled to deal with the whole estate (*see* AD COLLIGENDA BONA; DURANTE ABSENTIA). *See also* DE BONIS NON ADMINISTRATIS.

lex causae [Latin: the law of the case] In *private international law, the system of law (usually foreign) applicable to the case in dispute, as opposed to the *lex fori.

lex domicilii [Latin] The law of *domicile. In *private international law, the law of the country of domicile determines such matters as capacity to make a will in respect of personal property, the validity of such a will, succession to personal property, consent to marriage, and the proper law of a marriage contract or settlement (*see* PROPER LAW OF A CONTRACT).

lex fori [Latin] The law of the *forum. In *private international law, the law of the forum governs matters of procedure, the mode of trial, most matters relating to evidence, the nature of the remedy available, and most matters of *limitation of actions based on time bars.

lex loci actus [Latin] The law of the place where a legal act takes place. In *private international law, this law governs such questions as whether or not property in a bill of exchange or promissory note passes to the transferee and the formal validity of an assignment of an intangible movable (e.g. a share in a trust fund). *See also* LEX LOCI CELEBRATIONIS; LEX LOCI CONTRACTUS.

lex loci celebrationis [Latin] The law of the place of celebration of a marriage. In *private international law, this law governs such questions as the formalities required for a marriage (subject to four special exceptions), whether or not such a marriage is monogamous or polygamous, and possibly what law governs impotence or wilful refusal to consummate a marriage.

lex loci contractus [Latin] The law of the place where a contract was made. In *private international law, this law governs such matters as the formal requirements of a contract and the capacity to incur liability as a party to a bill of exchange. Most other matters relating to contracts are governed by the *proper law of the contract.

lex loci delicti commissi [Latin] The law of the place in which a delict (tort) is committed. In *private international law as applied in most countries in Europe, this law governs liability for torts. In some cases, however, it may be difficult to establish where the tort was committed (for example, when goods negligently manufactured in one country are distributed in another) or the place may be a matter of mere chance (for example, when an aeroplane crashes and lands). For these reasons, England does not accept the theory that liability in tort is governed by the *lex loci delicti.*

lex loci situs [Latin] The law of the place where an object is situated. In *private international law, this law usually governs such matters as succession to, title to, and the right to possession of immovables and the essential validity of trusts of immovables (for example, what estates can be created and whether or not gifts to charities are valid).

lex loci solutionis [Latin] The law of the place where a contract is to be performed or a debt is to be paid. In *private international law as applied in England, the *lex loci solutionis* governs the due date for payment of a *bill of exchange but does not usually govern matters relating to the law of contract.

liability *n.* **1.** An amount owed. **2.** A legal duty or obligation. *See* BUSINESS LIABILITY; OCCUPIER'S LIABILITY; PARENTS' LIABILITY; PRODUCTS LIABILITY; STRICT LIABILITY; VICARIOUS LIABILITY.

libel *n.* A defamatory statement made in permanent form, such as writing, pictures, or film (*see* DEFAMATION). Radio and television broadcasts, public performance of plays, and statements posted on the Internet are treated as being made in permanent form for the purposes of the law of defamation. A libel is actionable in tort without proof that its publication has caused special damage (actual financial or material loss) to the person defamed. Libel can also be a crime (**criminal libel**). Proof of publication of the statement to third parties is not necessary in criminal libel and truth is a defence only if the statement was published for the public benefit.

liberty and freedom from arbitrary detention A right set out in Article 5 of the European Convention on Human Rights and now part of UK law as a consequence of the *Human Rights Act 1998. All detentions must be prescribed by law and detentions must only be for one of the specified purposes set out in Article 5. Those detained must promptly be given reasons for their detention and then at regular intervals have access to a court to test the lawfulness of their continued detention. Those remanded in custody pending a criminal trial must be released on bail unless their detention is justified and they shall be entitled to trial within a reasonable time. There is an enforceable right to compensation for unlawful detention.

licence *n.* **1.** Formal authority to do something that would otherwise be unlawful. Examples include a *driving licence, a licence for selling intoxicating liquor (*see* LICENSING OF PREMISES), and a licence by the owner of a patent to manufacture the patented goods. **2.** (in land law) Permission to enter or occupy a person's land for an agreed purpose. A licence does not usually confer a right to exclusive possession of the land, nor any estate or interest in it: it is a personal arrangement between the licensor and the licensee. A **bare licence** (i.e. gratuitous permission to enter or occupy the licensor's land) can be revoked at any time and cannot be assigned by the licensee to a third party (*see* BARE LICENSEE). A **contractual licence** cannot be revoked during the period the parties intended it to last. Neither type is by itself binding on third parties acquiring the land from the licensor. However, if the licence is **coupled with a grant** of property or of an interest in land, the licence may be irrevocable and binding on the licensor's successors in title. For example, if A grants to B the right to catch and remove fish from water on his land, a licence to enter A's land to take up this *profit à prendre* is necessarily implied and will be irrevocable for the duration of the profit. The profit, as a legal interest over A's land, will bind A's successors in title, as will the licence that is irretrievably bound up with it. A bare or contractual licence may become irrevocable by the licensor or binding on a third party acquiring the land from the licensor if the circumstances give rise to a proprietary *estoppel or a *constructive trust.

licensed conveyancer A person, other than a solicitor, who is qualified to practise *conveyancing. Entry to this profession, which was created in 1985 in response to recommendations by the *Farrand Committee, is by examination; the level of competence required, ethics, and professional conduct are regulated by the Council for Licensed Conveyancers. The Solicitors Act 1974 makes it an offence for an "unqualified person" (i.e. a non-solicitor) to undertake conveyancing for reward, but from May 1987, the Administration of Justice Act 1985 made an exception in the case of licensed conveyancers.

licensee *n.* **1.** A person who has been granted a licence, most commonly used of one who has been granted a licence by a magistrates' court to sell intoxicating liquor (*see* LICENSING OF PREMISES) or one who has been granted a licence to use intellectual property, such as *patents. **2.** A person with permission to do what would otherwise be unlawful. In relation to land, a licensee is one who enters land with the express or implied permission of the occupier. *See* LICENCE; OCCUPIER'S LIABILITY.

licensing of premises The granting of a justices' licence authorizing the sale by retail of *intoxicating liquor either for consumption on or off the premises (an **on-licence**) or for consumption off those premises only (an **off-licence**). Licensing justices deal with the grant, renewal, and transfer of licences at a general annual licensing meeting (the **brewster sessions**) in the first fortnight of every February and at regular licensing sessions thereafter.

lie in grant   To be capable of being transferred by deed. Land and interests in it lie in grant; property that can be transferred by physical delivery **lies in livery**.

lie in livery   *See* LIE IN GRANT.

lien *n*. [via Old French from Latin *ligamen*, a binding] *n*. The right of one person to retain possession of goods owned by another until the possessor's claims against the owner have been satisfied. The lien may be **general**, when the goods are held as security for all outstanding debts of the owner, or **particular**, when only the claims of the possessor in respect of the goods held must be satisfied. Thus an unpaid seller may in some contracts be entitled to retain the goods until he receives the price (*see also* UNPAID VENDOR'S LIEN), a carrier may have a lien over goods he is transporting, and a repairer over goods he is repairing. Whether a lien arises or not depends on the terms of the contract and usual trade practice. A lien may be waived and can be lost, for example when an owner in possession sells goods to a buyer ignorant of a third party's lien. This type of lien is a **possessory lien**, but sometimes actual possession of the goods is not necessary. In an **equitable lien**, for example, the claim exists independently of possession. If a purchaser of the property involved is given notice of the lien it binds him; otherwise he will not be bound. Similarly a **maritime lien**, which binds a ship or cargo in connection with some maritime liability, does not depend on possession and can be enforced by arrest and sale (unless security is given). The lien accordingly travels with the ship or cargo when possession changes, and is good against a *bona fide* purchaser without notice. Examples of maritime liens are the lien of a salvor, that of seamen for their wages and of masters for their wages and outgoings, that of a bottomry or respondentia bondholder (*see* HYPOTHECATION), and that over a ship at fault in a collision in which property has been damaged. A maritime lien is enforceable by proceedings *in rem. *See also* SOLICITOR'S LIEN.

life assurance   *Insurance providing for the payment of a sum on the occurrence of an event that is in some way dependent upon a human life. In **endowment assurance** the insurer is liable to pay a fixed sum either at the end of a fixed period or at death if the insured should die in the meantime. **Whole-life assurance** provides for the payment of a fixed sum on the death of the insured. **Term** (or **temporary**) **assurance** provides for a fixed sum to be paid in the event of the death of the insured within a specified period.

life estate   *See* LIFE INTEREST.

life imprisonment   Punishment of a criminal by imprisonment for the rest of his life. The only crime that always carries a sentence of life imprisonment is murder, but there are many crimes (e.g. arson, manslaughter, wounding with intent, and rape) that carry a maximum penalty of life imprisonment, which is imposed in serious cases, and the Crime (Sentences) Act 1997 provides for a mandatory sentence of life imprisonment for those convicted for a second time for certain of these crimes (*see* REPEAT OFFENDER). In practice the imprisonment may often not be for life: the Home Secretary may order the release of a life prisoner on licence, on the advice of the Parole Board (*see* PAROLE) and after consulting the Lord Chief Justice (and, if possible, the trial judge). The Crime (Sentences) Act 1997 provides that the Parole Board has responsibility for the release of juveniles convicted of murder, rather than the Home Secretary. When imposing life imprisonment for murder, the judge may make a recommendation that the defendant should serve a **minimum term**

(number of years), which is usually not less than 12 years and up to 35 years. This recommendation is not legally binding on the Home Secretary, but in practice he will almost always follow it. Judges are also empowered to make a private representation to the Home Secretary, when imposing a life sentence, pointing out any special mitigating factors that might induce him to release the prisoner at an early date.

life interest (life estate) An interest in property subsisting only during the lifetime of the person to whom it was granted (e.g. "to A for life") or of some other person (e.g. "to A during the life of B"). The latter type is called an *estate (or interest) *pur autre vie*. Under the Law of Property Act 1925 a life interest in land cannot exist as a legal estate, only as an *equitable interest. Until 1997 the creation of a life interest in land created a settlement, governed by the Settled Land Act 1925. Since that date it creates a *trust of land, governed by the Trusts of Land and Appointment of Trustees Act 1996. *See* SETTLED LAND.

life peerage A nonhereditary peerage of the rank of baron or baroness created by the Crown by letters patent under the Life Peerages Act 1958. The purpose of the Act was to strengthen the composition of the House of Lords, and there is no limit to the number of peerages that may be created. The peerage of a Lord of Appeal in Ordinary is also for life but is not customarily included among life peerages.

life policy A policy providing a formal embodiment of a contract of *life assurance. The benefit of a life policy can be assigned to a third party.

life tenant *See* TENANT FOR LIFE.

lifting the veil The act of disregarding the veil of *incorporation that separates the personality of a corporation from the personalities of its members. This exceptional course is occasionally sanctioned by statute, for example in relation to *wrongful trading or *fraudulent trading and inaccurate use of company names, when it may result in members of a limited company losing their limited liability. It is also employed by the courts, for example if incorporation has been used to perpetrate fraud or gives rise to unreal distinctions between a company and its subsidiary companies, but never so as to defeat limited liability. Very occasionally the courts openly disregard corporate personality but more often they evade its inconvenient consequences by deciding that the acts were performed by the corporation acting as agent or trustee for the company members, to whom therefore they should be attributed.

limitation of actions Statutory rules limiting the time within which civil actions can be brought. Actions in simple contract and tort must be brought within six years of the accrual of the *cause of action (in the case of contracts, within six years of the date of the contract). In actions in respect of land and of contracts made by deed the period is 12 years from the accrual of the cause of action. Time does not run against a party under a disability until the disability ceases.

Special rules apply in the following cases. (1) If the claim is for damages for personal injury or death caused by negligence, nuisance, or breach of duty, the limit is three years from the accrual of the cause of action or (if later) from the date when the claimant knew of the relevant circumstances, but the court has a discretion to extend the period. (2) In other tort actions for negligence the period is six years from when the cause of action accrued or (if later) three years from the date when the claimant knew or should have known the material facts about the damage, but no action may be brought more than 15 years after the date of the defendant's alleged negligence. Changes in ownership of the property damaged do not extend the period. Each owner can sue but once time has started to run against one owner, it continues to run against his successors. (3) In strict liability actions for defective products (*see* PRODUCTS LIABILITY), the period is three years from accrual of the cause of action or (if later) the date when the claimant knew or should have known the material facts, but not later than ten years from when the product was put into circulation.

The present law is contained in the Limitation Act 1980, the Latent Damage Act 1986, and the Consumer Protection Act 1987.

limited administration (special administration) The administration of a deceased person's estate for restricted purposes specified by the court in the *letters of administration. Examples of such grants include grants *ad colligenda bona* and *durante absentia* and grants for the administration of an estate during the minority of a child appointed as executor by the will.

limited company A type of company incorporated by registration under the Companies Act whose members have a limited liability towards their company. Most companies are in this category. In a company limited by *shares, members must pay the nominal value (*see* AUTHORIZED CAPITAL) of their shares either upon *allotment or subsequently (*see* CALL). In a company limited by guarantee (a **guarantee company**) members must pay an agreed nominal amount (the guarantee), usually £1 £5, to their company in the event of a winding-up. The guarantee fund is intended to be for the benefit of company creditors when the company is wound up and members' liability to contribute to it cannot be reduced or extinguished by the company. Because payment of the guarantee is postponed guarantee companies often lack a working capital and are therefore more appropriate for charitable or social purposes than for trading.

The name of a limited company must end with the words "Limited" (or "Ltd.") in the case of a private company and "public limited company" (or "plc") in the case of a public company (or their Welsh equivalents; *see* WELSH COMPANY) as a warning to creditors of the limit upon members' liability. *See also* CHANGE OF NAME. *Compare* UNLIMITED COMPANY.

limited executor A person appointed by a will to deal only with specified property, not the whole of the deceased's estate. *Compare* LIMITED ADMINISTRATION.

limited liability partnership A legally recognized entity defined under the Limited Liability Partnership Act 2000, which is capable of entering into contracts in its own right and is correspondingly liable for debts under those contracts. Any two or more persons associated for carrying on a lawful business with a view to profit may set up such a partnership under the Act. This type of business organization is intended to combine the flexibility of a traditional *partnership with the corporate notion of limited liability. Under the provisions of the Act there is power to apply sections from both the Partnership Act 1890 and the Companies Act 1985, as appropriate, when dealing with the internal relations of the partners and limited liability, respectively. Persons intending to set up a limited liability partnership must register it with the *Companies Registry. There are also several disclosure requirements that are similar in nature to those required by companies.

limited owner A *tenant for life or a *statutory owner of land comprised in a settlement.

limited owner's charge An equitable charge on land securing repayment to a *limited owner of inheritance tax paid by him to the Inland Revenue on the acquisition of his interest. The tax is normally payable out of the trust property but if the limited owner pays it personally (e.g. to avoid having to sell land when the trust money is insufficient to cover the tax) the charge arises to secure his reimbursement. The charge is registrable (*see* REGISTRATION OF ENCUMBRANCES).

limited partnership *See* PARTNERSHIP.

Lincoln's Inn An *Inn of Court situated between Carey Street and Holborn. The records of the Inn, the *Black Books*, survive in a continuous series from 1422 to the present. By tradition, barristers practising in the *Chancery Division of the High Court normally belong to Lincoln's Inn.

linked transaction (under the Consumer Credit Act 1974) A transaction (except one for the provision of security) that is linked to, but not part of, a *regulated agreement (the **principal agreement**) and is entered into by a debtor or hirer with any other person. A linked transaction may comply with a term of the principal agreement (e.g. if the principal agreement requires that the goods be insured with X) or it may be financed by the principal agreement if the latter is a *debtor-creditor-supplier agreement. Alternatively it may be suggested by a creditor or owner to the debtor or hirer. The latter then enters into the linked transaction either to induce the creditor or owner to enter into the principal agreement, or for some other purpose related to the principal agreement, or – when the principal agreement is a *restricted-use credit agreement – for a purpose related to a transaction financed by the principal agreement.

liquidated damages *See* DAMAGES.

liquidated demand A demand for a fixed sum, e.g. a debt of £50. Such a demand is distinguished from a claim for unliquidated *damages, which is the subject of a discretionary assessment by the court.

liquidation *n. See* WINDING-UP.

liquidation committee A committee set up by creditors of a company being wound up in order to consent to the *liquidator exercising certain of his powers. When the company is unable to pay its debts, the committee is usually composed of creditors only; otherwise it consists of both creditors and *contributories. *See also* COMPULSORY WINDING-UP; VOLUNTARY WINDING-UP.

liquidator *n.* A person who conducts the *winding-up of a company. Unless he is the *official receiver, he must be a qualified *insolvency practitioner. *See also* COMPULSORY WINDING-UP; LIQUIDATION COMMITTEE; PROVISIONAL LIQUIDATOR; VOLUNTARY WINDING-UP.

lis alibi pendens [Latin] A suit pending elsewhere. The fact that there is already litigation pending between the same parties in respect of the same subject matter in another jurisdiction may give the defendant a ground on which he can obtain a *stay of proceedings. However, he must show that the continuance of the English action would cause an injustice to him and would not cause injustice to the claimant.

lis mota [Latin] A court action that has been set in motion.

lis pendens [Latin] A *pending action.

listed building A building of special architectural or historic interest specified on a list compiled or approved by the Secretary of State. Listed buildings are graded according to their importance. It may be demolished or altered in character only with listed-building consent granted by the local planning authority (*see* TOWN AND

COUNTRY PLANNING) or the Secretary of State. *See also* BUILDING PRESERVATION NOTICE; CONSERVATION AREA.

listed company A company that has satisfied the **listing rules** of the *Stock Exchange and whose shares may therefore be quoted and traded on the Listed Market. Listed companies are subject to continuing obligations of disclosure to the Stock Exchange.

Listed Market *See* STOCK EXCHANGE.

lists *pl. n.* Calendars of cases awaiting trial. A court may maintain several lists comprising different types of case. Thus in the High Court there is the Queen's Bench nonjury list, the jury list, the *short cause list, etc. A case enters the list after it has been allocated for trial.

literal rule *See* INTERPRETATION OF STATUTES.

litigant *n.* A person who is a party to a court action. A litigant may present his case personally to the court. If he does so, he may be assisted by a friend who can take notes and advise but cannot assist in the actual presentation of the case (a **McKenzie friend**). Alternatively, a litigant may be represented by a *barrister or, where appropriate, a *solicitor. A successful litigant can usually claim his legal *costs from his opponent. If the litigant did not have legal representation he may claim costs for the work he has done himself that would otherwise have been carried out by a lawyer.

litigation *n.* **1.** The taking of legal action by a *litigant. **2.** The field of law that is concerned with all contentious matters.

litigation friend An adult responsible for the conduct and cost of legal proceedings instituted on behalf of, or against, a child or a mentally disordered person. Before the introduction of the Civil Procedure Rules in 1999 such a person was called a **next friend**. *See also* OFFICIAL SOLICITOR.

lives in being *See* RULE AGAINST PERPETUITIES.

livestock *See* CLASSIFICATION OF ANIMALS.

living apart The condition required to establish *desertion or separation as evidence that a marriage has irretrievably broken down (*see* DIVORCE). A couple may be living apart for divorce purposes even when living under the same roof, if they are living in separate households. In order to satisfy this test, all form of common life between the parties must have ceased.

living instrument *See* INSTRUMENT.

living memory The period over which the recollection of living people extends. *Compare* LEGAL MEMORY.

living on immoral earnings Using money obtained from prostitution for one's livelihood or upkeep. It is an offence punishable by up to seven years' imprisonment for a man (but not for a woman) to knowingly live on the proceeds of female prostitution. The offence is normally committed by a man who lives with a prostitute and is wholly or mainly kept by her or by a man who runs a *brothel or in any other way forces or helps a prostitute to commit prostitution. In all these cases he is assumed to be knowingly living on her immoral earnings unless he can prove that he is not. The offence also covers supplying goods or services that relate only to prostitution (e.g. advertising for pay the names and addresses of prostitutes or driving them and their clients to places where they might have intercourse). The offence does not include selling ordinary items to prostitutes or renting them accommodation (unless this is used only for prostitution or a higher rent is charged because they are prostitutes). It is also an offence for either a man or a woman to knowingly live on the proceeds of male prostitution, and it is an offence for one woman to force another into prostitution or to aid her prostitution for financial gain.

living together *See* COHABITATION.

LJ *See* LORD JUSTICE OF APPEAL.

Lloyd's A society of *underwriters that was incorporated by Act of Parliament in 1871. Originally Lloyd's only provided marine insurance but they now also provide other kinds. The *insurance is undertaken by syndicates of private underwriters (**names**), each of which is managed by a professional underwriter; since 1992 limited companies have been allowed to become names. Each name underwrites a percentage of the business written by the syndicate and has to deposit a substantial sum with the corporation before being admitted as an underwriter. The public deals with the underwriters only through Lloyd's brokers.

loan capital Money raised by a company issuing *debentures. The aggregate amount borrowed by the company with each issue is sometimes referred to as **stock**.

loan creditor A creditor of a company, such as a person who holds redeemable *loan capital issued by the company. For the purposes of tax law, loan creditors (other than banks) are participators in *close companies.

local Act *See* ACT OF PARLIAMENT.

local authority A body of **councillors** elected by the inhabitants of a local government area (*see* FRANCHISE) to exercise local government functions. In England (except *Greater London and the metropolitan county areas) county areas are governed either by *county councils and *district councils (in a two-tier system) or by *unitary authorities (single-tier system); this mixed system of local government was introduced between 1996 and 1998, which resulted in the reorganization of some local government areas. There are in addition *parish councils for parishes with 200 or more electors. In Wales the local authorities are the county council, the county borough council, and the *community council. The Welsh county and county borough councils are unitary authorities.

All councillors are elected for four years. County councillors are elected every fourth year counting from 1981, and parish and community councillors every fourth year from 1979. Metropolitan district councillors are elected by thirds, one in each year other than a former county council year, and other district councillors according to whether their council has opted for this method or for simultaneous election in every fourth year from 1979. A candidate for election to any local authority must be over 21 and a commonwealth citizen or citizen of the Republic of Ireland, must have sufficient local connection (e.g. residence, local employment, or voting rights), and must not be disqualified (e.g. by reason of being a bankrupt or holding paid employment under the authority).

Local authorities and children. Local authorities have statutory responsibilities for children in their area. The Children Act 1989 requires local authorities to provide services for *children in need so that wherever possible they may be brought up by their own families, thus avoiding the need for instituting care proceedings. The Act specifies certain services that local authorities must provide. These include: appropriate day care provision for under fives and after school and holiday activities for children of school age; advice, guidance, and counselling; home help; transport or assistance with travel expenses in order to use any of the services provided and assistance with holidays; and family centres for all children in their area. Local authorities are also under a duty to provide accommodation for children whose parents are unable to do so (*see* VOLUNTARY ACCOMMODATION). An important objective of the Children Act is to promote the provision of these services as positive help for children in need. Emphasis is placed on the need for local authorities and families to work in partnership and often on the basis of written agreements. Local authorities also have a duty to investigate when they suspect that children in their area are being ill treated or neglected. If their suspicions are confirmed they must apply for a *care order, an *emergency protection order, or a *supervision order, as appropriate (*see also* SECTION 47 ENQUIRIES). In relation to adoption, local authorities are obliged to maintain an *adoption service and to report to the court in respect of non-agency adoption applications.

local government A form of government in which responsibility for the regulation of certain matters within particular localities (*local government areas) is delegated by statute to locally elected councillors (*see* LOCAL AUTHORITY).

local government area An area constituting a unit for local government purposes. The local government areas in England (except *Greater London) are the *county, the *district, and the *parish. In certain parts of England *unitary authorities replaced nonmetropolitan county and district councils between 1996 and 1998, which resulted in the reorganization of some local government areas. In Wales the areas are the county, the county borough, and the *community; counties and county boroughs, which are administered by unitary authorities, replaced the two-tier system of counties and districts in April 1996.

local government boundary commissions Two bodies established by the Local Government Act 1972 to undertake regular reviews of local government areas in England and Wales, respectively, and to propose alterations designed to improve the effectiveness and convenience of local government. Under the Local Government Act 1992 they were replaced by the *Local Government Commission for England and the Local Boundary Commission for Wales.

Local Government Commissioners *See* COMMISSIONS FOR LOCAL ADMINISTRATION.

Local Government Commission for England A body, established under the Local Government Act 1992, consisting of a Chairman and Chief Executive appointed by the Secretary of State for the Environment; the Chairman is empowered to appoint staff. The Commission was charged with the review of *local government areas in accordance with the directions of the Secretary of State. It can recommend structural changes – the replacement in any nonmetropolitan area of the two principal tiers of local government with a single tier (*see* UNITARY AUTHORITY); boundary changes; and electoral changes, such as changes in the number of councillors of the council for that area and the name of the area.

local land charge *See* LAND CHARGE; REGISTRATION OF ENCUMBRANCES.

local land charges register *See* REGISTRATION OF ENCUMBRANCES.

local laws Laws applying in only one locality, such as the area of a local authority (*see* BYELAW). In 1996 the Law Commission published a four-volume Chronological Table of Local Legislation to help those wanting to find out whether a local Act has been passed that affects them or their property. The table lists all 26,500 or so local

Acts passed since 1797 and states whether or not they are in force and how they have been amended.

local lottery *See* LOTTERY.

lock-out agreement A contract between a potential purchaser and the vendor of a property in which the vendor agrees that for a fixed period, such as two weeks, he will take the house off the market and not accept any other offers. Meanwhile the purchaser moves towards a quick *exchange of contracts, with the aim of securing the sale within that period. If the vendor breaches the agreement by accepting another offer, he can be sued for *breach of contract. Many vendors will not accept such agreements and some lawyers have argued they are unenforceable.

locus sigilli [Latin: place of the seal] *See* DEED.

locus standi [Latin: a place to stand] The right to bring an action or challenge some decision. Questions of *locus standi* most often arise in proceedings for *judicial review.

lodger *n.* A person who is given occupation of part of a house in return for rent, where the premises remain under the close control of the owner. A lodger normally has a mere *licence rather than a tenancy.

loitering *n. See* SUS LAW.

London *See* CITY OF LONDON; GREATER LONDON.

London Assembly A component of the *Greater London Authority, created by the Greater London Authority Act 1999, consisting of 25 members, of whom 14 are *Constituency Members and 11 are *London Members. The principal functions of the Assembly are to review and investigate actions and decisions of the *Mayor of London and to submit proposals to the Mayor. It may amend the Mayor's budget and it provides members to serve on the Metropolitan Police Authority, the London Fire and Emergency Planning Authority, and the London Development Agency.

London borough *See* GREATER LONDON.

London Development Agency A body created by the Greater London Authority Act 1999 to further the economic development of London, by promoting business efficiency and investment.

London Members Members of the *London Assembly who jointly represent the "Londonwide" constituency. The 11 London Members are elected every four years in May by voters in London, at the same time as *Constituency Members and the *Mayor of London are elected.

long tenancy For statutory purposes, a *fixed-term tenancy for a period exceeding 21 years. Where the rent is less than two-thirds of the property's rateable value, the tenancy is excluded from being an *assured tenancy. However, it will qualify for special protection if it would have been a *protected tenancy had the rent not been a low one. This allows the tenant to continue the tenancy beyond the fixed term. In such cases, if the landlord wishes to terminate the tenancy at the end of the fixed term, he must serve a statutory notice at least 6 months, but not more than 12 months, before the end of the tenancy. In this notice he can either propose a *statutory tenancy (the terms of which must be agreed with the tenant or settled by a court) or he can claim the right to resume possession of the premises. In the latter case he must have statutory grounds for possession, which correspond to those required for possession of a protected tenancy. If the tenant contests this notice, the landlord must apply for a court order for possession. If this is refused, the tenant will be entitled to a statutory tenancy. Long tenancies made after the coming into force of the Housing Act 1988 are not protected in this way because no new protected tenancies can be made after that date. *See also* ENFRANCHISEMENT OF TENANCY.

long title *See* ACT OF PARLIAMENT.

Long Vacation A *vacation of the Supreme Court lasting from 1 August to 30 September. During the Long Vacation only certain kinds of urgent business (called **vacation business**) can be transacted. It was formerly the rule in the High Court that statements of case could not be served during the Long Vacation, but this rule has now been abolished.

Lord Advocate The chief law officer of the Crown in Scotland, corresponding to the *Attorney General in England. He has ultimate responsibility for criminal prosecutions in Scotland, being assisted by a Solicitor General, advocates depute, and *procurators fiscal. He is normally a supporter of the ruling party and resigns his office upon a change of government, but he is not always a Member of Parliament.

Lord Chancellor The head of the judiciary, a government minister (in charge of the Lord Chancellor's Department), and Speaker of the House of Lords. He thus combines judicial, executive, and legislative functions. He is entitled to preside over the House when it sits as a final court of appeal; he appoints magistrates, makes recommendations for higher judicial appointments, and oversees such matters as the administration of the courts, the Community Legal Service, law reform, data protection, and human rights. As **Speaker**, he normally presides from the Woolsack over legislative proceedings but is free to vacate his seat and take part in debates and divisions. He is appointed by the Crown on the advice of the Prime Minister and (since 1974) may be a Roman Catholic. Conduct

Lord Chancellor's Advisory Committee on Legal Education and Conduct A committee established by the Courts and Legal Services Act 1990 to assist in the maintenance and development of standards in the education, training, and conduct of those offering legal services. It consists of a senior member of the judiciary as chairman, practising and academic lawyers, and lay members.

Lord Chief Justice (LCJ) The chief judge of the *Queen's Bench Division of the High Court. He ranks second only to the Lord Chancellor in the judicial hierarchy. It was formerly the practice to appoint the Attorney General when a vacancy in the office occurred but this practice has now been abandoned and recent LCJs have been either *Lords Justices of Appeal or *Lords of Appeal in Ordinary on appointment. The LCJ is *ex officio* a member of the Court of Appeal and is President of its Criminal Division.

Lord Justice of Appeal (LJ) An ordinary judge of the *Court of Appeal. The Lord (and Lady) Justices (LJJ) are normally appointed from those holding the post of a High Court judge or those possessing a ten-year High Court qualification under the Courts and Legal Services Act 1990. They become members of the Privy Council on appointment.

Lords, House of *See* HOUSE OF LORDS.

Lords of Appeal in Ordinary (Law Lords) Up to 11 persons, holders of high judicial office or practising barristers of at least 15 years' standing, who are appointed to life peerages under the Appellate Jurisdiction Act 1876 to carry out the judicial functions of the *House of Lords.

loss leader A product or service offered for sale by an organization at a loss in order to attract customers. The Competition Act 1998 prohibits *predatory pricing by dominant companies, as does Article 82 of the Treaty of Rome. Nondominant companies, however, are largely free to set their own resale pricing policy. *See also* RESALE PRICE MAINTENANCE.

loss of amenity Loss or reduction of a claimant's mental or physical capacity to do the things he used to do, suffered as a result of personal injuries. In actions for personal injuries the claimant may recover damages for loss of the amenities of life, in addition to his financial losses and an award for *pain and suffering. Thus loss of the ability to play games or a musical instrument, if these were the claimant's hobbies, will be taken into account in fixing damages. The assessment is based on an objective view of the value of the loss of these amenities to the claimant.

loss of services An action in tort (*per quod servitium amisit*) could formerly be brought against someone who had caused a parent to be deprived of the services of a child or a master to be deprived of the services of a menial servant. Both forms of action were abolished by the Administration of Justice Act 1982.

lost modern grant A legal fiction by which a court will uphold a claim to an easement over another's land by presuming it to have been created by a formal *grant (i.e. a deed) that has been lost, if the claimant can show 20 years' uninterrupted exercise of the easement as of right (i.e. other than as a *licensee). The claim can be defeated only by proof that the grant could not have been made at any time during the period of use; for example, if the *servient tenement was at all relevant times owned by someone with no power to grant easements. The doctrine may only be pleaded if something prevents the plea of common law *prescription.

lottery *n.* A game of chance in which the participants buy numbered tickets and the prizes are distributed by drawing lots. Under the Lotteries and Amusements Act 1976, lotteries are usually illegal (*see also* GAMING) unless they are: (1) on behalf of registered charities or sports, (2) restricted to members of a private club, (3) **local lotteries**, promoted in accordance with schemes approved by local authorities and registered with the Gaming Board, or (4) small lotteries that take place as part of an entertainment (e.g. in a bazaar or at a dance). The **National Lottery** was established by statute (the National Lottery Act 1993).

lump-sum award The form in which damages are given by a court. The award covers both past losses (up to the time of judgment) and losses likely to be suffered in the future. The general rule is that only one award of damages may be made, unless the wrong is a continuing one (such as continuing trespass or nuisance). However, *interim payments can be ordered pending the final estimation of damages, and in actions for personal injuries in which the claimant may develop some serious disease or suffer some serious deterioration in his condition, *provisional damages may be given. This enables the claimant to come back for further damages at a future date if the disease or deterioration occurs. Settlements of personal injury cases out of court can include periodic payments as well as a lump sum as part of a *structured settlement.

M

Maastricht Treaty The Treaty on European Union, which was signed at Maastricht (in the Netherlands) in February 1992 and came into force on 1 November 1993. The Treaty amended the founding treaties of the three *European Communities by establishing a *European Union based on these Communities. It required the defining and eventual implementation of a common foreign and security policy (CFSP), cooperation in justice and home affairs, and – under certain conditions – the introduction of a single currency (see EUROPEAN MONETARY UNION). It also introduced the principle of *subsidiarity and increased the powers of the *European Parliament. It has since been amended by the *Amsterdam Treaty.

machinery and plant The machines, parts of machines, and all other apparatus used for carrying on a business, but excluding stock in trade. Capital expenditure on machinery and plant is eligible for *capital allowances.

McKenzie friend [from the case *McKenzie* v *McKenzie* (1971)] A person who sits beside an unrepresented *litigant in court and assists him by prompting, taking notes, and quietly giving advice.

McNaghten Rules (M'Naghten Rules) *See* INSANITY.

magistrate *n.* A *justice of the peace sitting in a *magistrates' court. Most magistrates are lay persons and have no formal legal qualifications: they receive no payment for their services but give their time voluntarily. There are also, however, *district judges (magistrates' court) (formerly called stipendiary magistrates) in London and other major cities.

magistrates' clerk *See* CLERK TO THE JUSTICES.

magistrates' court A court consisting of between two and seven *magistrates or a single *district judge (magistrates' court) (formerly called stipendiary magistrate) exercising the jurisdiction conferred by the Magistrates' Courts Act 1980 and other statutes. The principal function of magistrates' courts is to provide the forum in which all criminal prosecutions are initiated. In the case of an *indictable offence or an *offence triable either way for which the defendant elects *trial on indictment, the court sits as *examining justices to consider whether or not there is sufficient evidence to justify committing the defendant to the *Crown Court. For a *summary offence or an offence triable either way in which the defendant elects *summary trial, the court sits as a **court of summary jurisdiction**, i.e. as a criminal court of trial without a jury in which justices, assisted by the *clerk to the justices, decide all questions of law and fact.

Magistrates' courts also have a limited jurisdiction in civil matters relating to debt and matrimonial proceedings. Each magistrates' court sits for a **petty-sessions area** and its jurisdiction is generally confined to that area, although it may in some cases extend beyond. A magistrates' court may sit on any day of the year, including (if the court thinks fit) Christmas Day, Good Friday, or any Sunday, but in practice it is unusual for magistrates' courts to sit on public holidays or at weekends.

Magna Carta The Great Charter of Runnymede, acceded to by King John in 1215 after armed rebellion by his barons. It guaranteed the freedom of the church, restricted taxes and fines, and promised justice to all. Confirmed frequently by subsequent feudal kings, it has since been largely repealed as having only symbolic significance.

main purpose rule *See* REPUGNANCY.

main residence For the purposes of *enfranchisement of a tenancy, a dwelling in which the tenant has lived for at least the last three years or for periods amounting to three years in the last ten years. Whether or not the dwelling has in fact been his main residence is also considered in each case. For the purposes of *capital gains tax there is an exemption for gains on the disposal of owner-occupied homes. If an individual has more than one residence he may nominate the one that he wishes to qualify for exemption.

maintenance *n.* The provision of food, clothing, and other basic necessities of life. A husband or wife is obliged to maintain his or her spouse (*see* FAILURE TO MAINTAIN). Parents are bound at common law to maintain their minor children, and since the Family Law Reform Act 1987 and the Child Support Act 1991 both parents, whether married or not, have a legal responsibility to support their children financially if they can afford to do so (*see* CHILD SUPPORT MAINTENANCE). Neglect or refusal to provide this maintenance is a criminal offence.

Before 1881 it was common for settlements to include a power for the trustees to maintain and educate minors. Since then, a statutory power has existed enabling trustees to pay money for the maintenance, education, or benefit of a minor; this power is subject to any contrary provision in the settlement.

The obligation after a divorce of one spouse to support another or of a parent to support a child of the family is often referred to as maintenance; this is more correctly known as financial provision or *financial relief.

maintenance agreement An agreement between spouses concerning their financial obligations to one another. Maintenance agreements are governed by the provisions of the Matrimonial Causes Act 1973. Any clause that attempts to deny the right of either spouse to apply to a court for financial relief will be void, and the county courts and High Court (and, to a more limited extent, the magistrates' courts) have wide powers to vary the terms of maintenance agreements (*see also* MARRIAGE SETTLEMENT). When one party has died the other spouse may apply to the court, under the special provisions for *dependants, to have the terms of the agreement altered, but only if it was in writing.

maintenance and champerty The promotion or support of litigation by a third party who has no legitimate interest in the proceedings (**maintenance**) and the support of litigation by a third party in return for a share of the proceeds (**champerty**, an aggravated form of maintenance). The old crimes and torts of maintenance and champerty were abolished by statute in 1967 but a champertous agreement may still be treated as contrary to public policy and so unlawful. An agreement by a lawyer to receive payment in the form of a share of the client's damages (if successful) is regarded as champertous in England, but a modified form of "no win, no fee" agreement was legalized by the Courts and Legal Services Act 1990, although it is authorized only for certain categories of cases (*see* CONDITIONAL FEE AGREEMENT).

maintenance order A court order providing for payment of sums for the maintenance of a spouse or a child of the family. Strictly speaking the term now applies only to *maintenance agreements incorporated into a court order; orders in the magistrates' courts or High Court on the ground of *failure to maintain and orders in the divorce courts for maintenance are now called *financial provision orders. Power to order payment by direct debit or standing order was introduced by the Maintenance Enforcement Act 1991.

Spouses may try to evade their financial obligations to each other or their children by emigrating. In such cases the Domestic Proceedings and Magistrates' Courts Act 1978 and the Maintenance Orders (Reciprocal Enforcement) Act 1972 grant powers to obtain maintenance from emigrant spouses in certain designated ("convention") countries. For these purposes maintenance orders include any order providing for periodical payments to a person whom the payer is liable to maintain, including children of unmarried parents. The Child Support Act 1991 has greatly curtailed the power of the court to make, vary, or revise maintenance orders; application solely for *child support maintenance must now usually be made to the Child Support Agency rather than the court.

maintenance pending suit A court order for temporary periodical payments during the hearing of a petition for divorce, nullity, or judicial separation.

majority (full age) *n.* The age of 18 years. The state of being below that age is a state of **minority** (*see* INFANT). The age of majority was originally 21 years, but was reduced to 18 by the Family Law Reform Act 1969. This majority applies for the purposes of any relevant legal rule and for the interpretation of any relevant statute, whenever it was made. It does not apply, however, to deeds, wills, and other private documents made before 1969, in which reference is made to majority or minority.

majority rule The principle by which the majority of company members has the power to control the company through voting at a company meeting. There are various ways to safeguard the minority (*see* MINORITY PROTECTION). The rule does not apply when the actions taken by those in control of the company (e.g. *directors) require more than a simple majority vote to authorize them; for example, altering the *articles of association, which requires approval by 75% of shareholders who attend a *general meeting and who are entitled to vote (*see* ORDINARY RESOLUTION; SPECIAL RESOLUTION). *See also* FRAUD ON THE MINORITY.

majority verdict The verdict of a *jury reached by a majority. The verdict need not be unanimous if there are no fewer than 11 jurors and 10 of them agree on the verdict or if there are 10 jurors and 9 of them agree on the verdict. The jury must be given at least two hours in which to reach a unanimous verdict and the foreman of the jury must state in open court the number of jurors who respectively agreed to and dissented from the majority verdict. Majority verdicts can be taken in both criminal and civil cases.

making off without payment Leaving without paying for goods or services received and with the intention of avoiding payment, when payment on the spot is expected. This is now an offence punishable by up to two years' imprisonment, but it must be proved that the person who made off knew that payment on the spot was expected. It will usually cover such behaviour as walking out of a restaurant after having had a meal, without paying (even if there was originally no intention not to pay for the meal, and therefore no theft, and no *deception when the meal was ordered); taking a taxi and disappearing without paying; and collecting any items from a shop that has repaired or cleaned them, without paying. *See also* SHOPLIFTING.

male issue Direct descendants through the male line, e.g. sons and sons of sons (but not sons of daughters).

malfeasance *n.* An unlawful act. *Compare* MISFEASANCE; NONFEASANCE.

malice *n.* **1.** (in criminal law) A state of mind (*see* MENS REA) usually taken to be equivalent to *intention or *recklessness: it does not require any hostile attitude. Malice is said to be **transferred** when someone intends to commit a crime against one person but in fact commits the same crime against someone else (for example, if he intends to shoot X but misses, and instead kills Y). Malice is **universal** (or **general**) when the accused has no particular victim in mind (for example, if he shoots into a crowd intending to kill anyone). In both cases this constitutes *mens rea.* **2.** (in tort) A constituent element of certain torts. In the English law of tort, the general rule is that a malicious motive cannot make conduct unlawful if it would otherwise be lawful. For example, a right to take water from under one's own land can lawfully be exercised solely in order to cause damage to a neighbour. However, in some cases malice can be relevant. An action for *malicious prosecution requires proof that the prosecution was instigated maliciously, i.e. without reasonable and probable cause. In *defamation, a malicious motive invalidates the defences of fair comment and qualified privilege. Malice is also relevant to liability for *conspiracy to injure someone.

malice aforethought The *mens rea* (state of mind) required for a person to be guilty of murder. It is unnecessary for there to be any element of hostility (*see* MALICE) or for the intention to kill to be "forethought" (i.e. premeditated). The term covers (1) intention to kill (**direct express malice aforethought**), (2) intention to cause *grievous bodily harm (**direct implied malice aforethought**), (3) realizing while doing a particular act that death would almost certainly or very probably result (**indirect express malice**), and (4) realizing that grievous bodily harm would very probably result from the act, e.g. shooting at someone without intending to kill him, but realizing that he may at least suffer a serious injury (**indirect implied malice**). The prosecution must prove one of these four types of malice aforethought to secure a conviction of murder.

malicious damage Formerly (before 1971), *criminal damage.

malicious falsehood (injurious falsehood) A false statement, made maliciously, that causes damage to another. The oldest forms of this tort are *slander of title and *slander of goods, but other false and malicious statements (e.g. that a businessman has ceased to trade) can also give rise to an action in tort. Usually actual damage must be proved. Malicious falsehood can overlap with *defamation, but mainly protects property and business interests.

malicious prosecution The malicious institution of legal proceedings against a person. Malicious prosecution is only actionable in tort if the proceedings were initiated both maliciously and without reasonable and probable cause and they were unsuccessful. No one who has been convicted of a criminal charge can sue for malicious prosecution. Making unjustified threats of infringement of trade mark or other *intellectual property rights is also a statutory offence; the person accused of this can apply to the court for a *declaration that they do not infringe these rights.

malicious wounding *See* WOUNDING.

management order A court order to appoint a manager for which certain tenants of flats have the right to apply if the court is satisfied that mismanagement has taken place. There are proposals for this right to be extended to tenants even where there is no mismanagement if at least two-thirds of the tenants in a block of flats wish to create a private limited company (an **RTM company**) to manage the block instead of the landlord.

managing director A *director to whom management powers have been delegated, either absolutely or subject to supervision, by the other directors of the company under the terms of the articles of association. Managing directors are agents of the company and have wide authority to act on its behalf.

managing trustee *See* CUSTODIAN TRUSTEE.

mandate *n.* **1.** (in private law) An authority given by one person (the **mandator**) to another to take some course of action. A mandate is commonly revocable until acted upon and is terminated by the death of the mandator. A cheque is a mandate from the customer to his bank to pay the sum in question and to debit his account. **2.** (in international law) The system by which dependent territories (such as the former German colonies in Africa) were placed under the supervision (but not the sovereignty) of mandatory powers by the League of Nations after World War I. After World War II, all remaining mandated territories became *trust territories under the United Nations with the exception of South-West Africa (now Namibia) and a strategic trust area consisting of a number of Pacific Islands north of the equator, which were administered by the USA. The mandate over Namibia was terminated by the General Assembly of the UN in 1966, which placed the territory under the direct responsibility of the United Nations; it became an independent state in 1990. The Pacific Islands territories are also now independent states.

mandatory injunction *See* INJUNCTION.

mandatory order A *prerogative order from the High Court instructing an inferior tribunal, public official, corporation, etc., to perform a specified public duty relating to its responsibilities (*see also* JUDICIAL REVIEW); for example, an instruction to a statutory tribunal to hear a particular dispute. Formerly called **mandamus** (from Latin: we command), it was renamed in 1999 under Part 54.1 of the Civil Procedure Rules.

Manor of Northstead *See* CHILTERN HUNDREDS, STEWARDSHIP OF THE.

mansion house *See* PRINCIPAL MANSION HOUSE.

manslaughter *n.* Homicide that does not amount to the crime of murder but is nevertheless neither lawful nor accidental. Manslaughter may be committed in several ways. It may arise if the accused is charged with murder and had the *mens rea* required for murder (*see* MALICE AFORETHOUGHT), but mitigating circumstances (*diminished responsibility, a *suicide pact, or *provocation) reduce the offence to manslaughter; this is known as **voluntary manslaughter**. It may also be committed when there was no *mens rea* for murder in one of two situations: (1) if the accused committed an act of *gross negligence or (2) if the act, although not negligent, was criminally illegal and also involved an element of danger to the victim. For example, it would be manslaughter to knock some bricks off a bridge into the path of a train (*criminal damage), killing the driver, even if one had no idea that there was a train in the area. Such cases are known as **involuntary manslaughter**. There are generally four types of involuntary manslaughter, although the distinction between them remains unclear: **negligent manslaughter**, **constructive manslaughter**, **reckless manslaughter**, and **corporate manslaughter**. The maximum punishment for manslaughter is life imprisonment, although this is rarely imposed; however, the Crime (Sentences) Act 1997 provides for a mandatory life sentence for those convicted of manslaughter for a second time (*see* REPEAT OFFENDER). Most cases of *causing death by dangerous driving and *causing death by careless driving are usually not charged as manslaughter but as special statutory offences under the Road Traffic Act 1991. However, in certain circumstances causing death by dangerous driving may amount to reckless manslaughter.

mansuetae naturae *See* CLASSIFICATION OF ANIMALS.

Mareva injunction *See* FREEZING INJUNCTION.

margin of appreciation A concept created by the European Court of Human Rights to allow a certain amount of freedom for each signatory state to regulate its own activities and its application of the *European Convention on Human Rights without being subject to review by the Court. This freedom is not available to national courts when considering Convention issues arising within their own countries. However, in some cases the domestic courts, when reviewing decisions of public authorities under the Convention, may defer on democratic grounds to those elected bodies (*see* DISCRETIONARY AREA OF JUDGMENT).

marine insurance A form of *insurance in which the insurer undertakes to indemnify the insured against loss of the ship (**hull insurance**), the cargo, any sums paid in freight (**freight insurance**), or any liability to a third party occurring during a sea voyage. A marine insurance contract may be extended to losses on inland waters or to risks on land that may be incidental to a sea voyage. The risks listed in marine insurance policies include *perils of the seas, fire, war perils, pirates, seizures, restraints, jettisons, and *barratry, and the cover may be for a particular voyage, or for a specified time, or both (*see* TIME POLICY). In marine insurance a distinction is made between an *actual total loss and a *constructive total loss; partial loss is subject to *average. The law relating to marine insurance is codified by the Marine Insurance Act 1906. Under this Act marine insurance contracts that are by way of being wagering or *gaming contracts are void; these include contracts in which the insured has no insurable interest as defined in the Act.

mariner's will *See* PRIVILEGED WILL.

marital breakdown The deterioration of a marriage to such an extent that the court will grant a *divorce. The breakdown must be **irretrievable**. Under the Matrimonial Causes Act 1973 this can be evidenced only by *adultery, *desertion, *living apart, or *unreasonable behaviour.

marital privileges Privileges protecting information given by one spouse to the other from disclosure in court. In general, the privilege has now been abolished in both civil and criminal proceedings. However, in civil proceedings a person may still not be compelled to disclose a statement made by his (or her) spouse with a view to effecting a reconciliation between them. Nor may someone be compelled to give evidence that could incriminate his (or her) spouse, subject to some exceptions.

maritime lien *See* LIEN.

market *n.* A facility for the sale and purchase of goods. The concept of an **available market** is important in deciding the amount of damages for breach of contracts of sale of goods: it assumes that goods of the contract description can be sold at a market price fixed by supply and demand. The disappointed buyer or seller will usually, upon breach, make a substitute purchase or sale on the market and his damages will be the difference between the contract price and the market price. *See also* MARKET OVERT.

market maker *See* STOCK EXCHANGE.

market overt An open, public, and legally constituted market or fair. When goods were sold in market overt according to the usage of the market, the buyer acquired a good title to the goods, provided he bought them in good faith and without notice of any defect in the seller's title. This was one of the exceptions to the general principle of *nemo dat quod non habet*, but it was abolished from 3 January 1995 by the Sale of Goods (Amendment) Act 1994.

market testing Testing a particular service to see which supplier – in-house or external – offers the best combination of value for money and quality of service for the user. Launched in 1991, it affects all public services, including the health-care, magistrates', and prison services. Under the Local Government Act 1999, certain authorities are designated as *best value authorities, including the police and fire authorities. Under the Act, these authorities must have regard to economy, efficiency, and effectiveness when exercising their functions.

marriage n. **1.** The relationship between husband and wife. **2.** A ceremony, civil or religious, that creates the legal status of husband and wife and the legal obligations arising from that status (*see* MARRIAGE CEREMONY). All marriages must be registered by an authorized marriage registrar. The minimum age for marriage is 16 with parental consent (18 without), and capacity to marry in general is governed by the law of *domicile of both parties before the marriage. Relationships within which marriage is prohibited are specified in the Marriage Act 1949, as amended by the Marriage (Prohibited Degrees of Relationship) Act 1986 (*see* PROHIBITED DEGREES OF RELATIONSHIPS). Parties to a marriage must be respectively male and female as determined at birth (sex-change operations have no legal effect), must not be already married to someone else (*see* BIGAMY; POLYGAMY), and must enter into the marriage freely. *See also* MARRIAGE BY CERTIFICATE.

marriage articles The clauses setting out the terms of a *marriage settlement.

marriage brokage contract A contract in which one person undertakes, for financial gain, to arrange a marriage for another. Such contracts are void because they contravene *public policy.

marriage by certificate Marriage authorized by a certificate issued by the Superintendent Registrar of Births, Deaths, and Marriages. All marriages other than those solemnized in the Church of England must be authorized by a certificate (or certificate and licence – *see* MARRIAGE BY CERTIFICATE AND LICENCE); marriages solemnized in the Church of England may be authorized either by a certificate or by a religious procedure (e.g. *banns, common licence, or special licence – *see* MARRIAGE BY RELIGIOUS LICENCE). Notice must be given of the intended marriage to the Superintendent Registrar of the district(s) in which the parties have lived for seven days previously, together with a declaration that there are no lawful obstacles to the marriage and that all necessary consents have been obtained. This notice is made public for 21 days, to give members of the public the opportunity to point out the existence of a lawful obstacle, after which the Registrar must issue a certificate. The marriage must take place within three months from the day the notice was entered in the notice book.

marriage by certificate and licence Marriage authorized by a certificate and licence issued by the Superintendent Registrar. The main difference between this procedure and that of *marriage by certificate alone is its speed – the marriage may take place any time after 24 hours have elapsed from the day of giving notice. This procedure may also be used when only one party has been resident in the district (although the minimum period of residence is 15 days), and the notice of intended marriage need not be publicly displayed. The procedure costs more than marriage by certificate.

marriage by Registrar-General's licence Marriage authorized by a licence issued by the Registrar-General of Births, Deaths, and Marriages. Marriage outside a register office or registered building may now take place in certain other licensed venues, such as stately homes.

marriage by religious licence A marriage in the Church of England based on the grant of an ecclesiastical licence, rather than on publication of *banns. A **common licence** may be granted if one of the parties swears an affidavit that he believes there is no lawful impediment, that at least one of the parties has been resident in the parish for at least 15 days previously (or usually worships at the church), and that (in the case of a minor) the consent of each parent with *parental responsibility (or a person in whose favour a residence order is made) has been obtained. If no caveat is issued against the grant of a licence, the ecclesiastical judge will grant a licence and the marriage may take place immediately. The Archbishop of Canterbury may also grant a **special licence** authorizing a marriage at any time of the day or night in any church, chapel, or other convenient place (even if unconsecrated).

marriage ceremony The ceremony creating the status of marriage. There are four main types of marriage ceremony (excluding marriage in military chapels). In a civil marriage, the ceremony takes place in a register office or other registered venue, with open doors, in the presence of the Superintendent Registrar (who conducts the ceremony), a registrar (who supervises registration formalities), and at least two witnesses. Under the Marriage Act 1983, housebound and detained persons may get married where they reside.

In a Church of England marriage, the ceremony usually takes place in church and is celebrated by a clergyman in the presence of at least two witnesses according to the rite of the Book of Common Prayer (or any alternative authorized form of service). A clergyman may refuse to solemnize the marriage of anyone whose former marriage has been dissolved if the former spouse is still living, or whose marriage would have been void for *affinity of the parties before the passing of the Marriage (Prohibited Degrees of Relationship) Act 1986. The marriage ceremony in Quaker and Jewish marriages is governed by the rules of those religions and need not be celebrated in a registered building, or by an authorized person, or in public. All other religious marriage ceremonies must be celebrated in a registered building designated as a place of meeting for religious worship, with open doors, and in the presence of at least two witnesses and a registrar or previously notified authorized person.

marriage settlement A *settlement made between the parties to a marriage. A settlement made before the marriage ceremony is called an **antenuptial settlement**; that made after the marriage is a **postnuptial settlement**. The purpose of a marriage settlement is to provide an income for one spouse or the children, while securing the capital for the other spouse. The courts have power when giving decrees of divorce, nullity, or judicial separation either to order property owned by one spouse to be settled for the benefit of the other spouse and children or to vary the terms of any existing ante- or postnuptial settlement. This power is often used to retain the use of the matrimonial home until the children are independent, as well as to retain the parents' financial investment.

marshalling of assets A process in which the claims of different creditors are directed towards different funds of the same debtor in an attempt to reach a fair result. When there are two creditors and two funds, and one has a claim exclusively on one fund but the other can claim against either fund, the rule of marshalling requires the latter to claim against the fund from which the former is excluded. The aim is, so far as possible, to allocate the assets so as to satisfy all the creditors.

marshalling of securities An application of *marshalling of assets. If A mortgages two properties to B and then mortgages one of the properties in addition to C (who may or may not know of B's mortgage) B, as first mortgagee, may obtain his money from whichever mortgaged property he chooses. However, if he chooses to obtain his money from the property mortgaged to C, C may if necessary obtain his money from the other property. This right cannot be exercised when a purchaser has obtained the property without knowing of the facts giving rise to the right to marshal.

Martens clause A clause that was included in the Hague Conventions of 1899 and 1907 by the Russian delegate, Friedrich von Martens (1845–1909), and has since then been included in many other treaties. It states that anything not proscribed by the regulations of the treaty will be subject to the international law and will therefore not necessarily be permissible; it also allows the regulations of the treaty to keep pace with the consequences of modern developments in warfare.

martial law Government by the military authorities when the normal machinery of government has broken down as a result of invasion, civil war, or large-scale insurrection. The constitution of the UK does not provide for a declaration (with specified consequences) of martial law: it is no more than a situation capable of arising. While the military authorities are restoring order, their conduct could not be called into question by the ordinary courts of law. After the restoration of order, the legality of their actions would be theoretically capable of examination, but the standards that would be applied by the courts are unknown. Martial law should not be confused with military law (*see* SERVICE LAW); any courts held by the military authorities to try civilians during a state of martial law would not enjoy the status of courts martial.

master *n.* **1.** One of the *Masters of the Supreme Court or the Masters of the Bench (*see* BENCHERS). **2.** The person having command or charge of a vessel. **3.** Formerly, an *employer. *See also* EMPLOYER AND EMPLOYEE.

Master of the Rolls (MR) The judge who is president of the Civil Division of the *Court of Appeal. The office is an ancient one and was originally held by the keeper of the public records. Later the holder was a judge of the Court of Chancery and assistant to the Lord Chancellor, with his own court, the **Rolls Court**. Since 1881 he has been a judge of the Court of Appeal only, but retains important duties in relation to public records. He also admits solicitors to practice.

Masters of the Bench *See* BENCHERS.

Masters of the Supreme Court Inferior judicial officers of the *Queen's Bench and *Chancery Divisions of the High Court. Their principal function is to supervise *interim (interlocutory) proceedings in litigation and (especially in the Chancery Division) to take accounts. By convention, Chancery Masters are usually solicitors and Queen's Bench Masters are usually barristers. In the provinces a comparable jurisdiction is exercised by *district judges of the High Court. *See also* DISTRICT REGISTRY.

matching broker *See* STOCK EXCHANGE.

material facts See STATEMENT OF CASE.

maternity leave See MATERNITY RIGHTS.

maternity pay See MATERNITY RIGHTS.

maternity rights The rights a woman has against her employer when she is absent from work wholly or partly because of her pregnancy or confinement. The current law is contained in the Employment Rights Act 1996 as supplemented by the Maternity and Parental Leave Regulations 1999. The provisions with respect to maternity pay are governed by the Social Security Contributions and Benefits Act 1992 and its supporting regulations. It is possible for an employer to agree contractually to more generous maternity leave provisions than the statutory minimum. There are currently seven statutory rights:

(1) All pregnant employees are entitled to reasonable time off work, with pay, for antenatal care, but an employer is entitled to ask for evidence of appointments. An employee who is unreasonably refused time off may complain to an *employment tribunal.

(2) An employee is entitled not to be dismissed because of pregnancy or any reason connected with it. She is treated as having been unfairly dismissed if the principal reason for the dismissal is that she is pregnant, or that she has given birth, or that she has taken maternity leave.

(3) A pregnant employee who meets certain qualifying conditions based on her length of service and average earnings is entitled to receive **statutory maternity pay** from her employer for up to 18 weeks (to be increased to 26 weeks from April 2003). To qualify for statutory maternity pay a pregnant employee must have been working for the same employer continuously for at least 26 weeks ending in the 15th week before the week the baby is due, must have been paying national insurance, and must leave work between the 11th and 6th week before the expected date of confinement. If she can satisfy these conditions, she will receive 90% of salary for six weeks followed by a fixed statutory rate for the remaining 12 weeks (set at £75 from April 2002 and £100 from April 2003). An employee who does not qualify for statutory maternity pay but who earns at least £30 per week on average may be entitled to claim the state maternity allowance from the Benefits Agency. Employers can recover 92% of such payments by setting the amount against their national insurance payments. They can require the employee to provide them with evidence of the baby's birth.

(4) An employee who continues to be employed by her employer until the beginning of the 11th week before the expected week of confinement is entitled to **maternity leave**. All pregnant employees are entitled to at least 18 weeks' maternity leave (to be increased to 26 weeks from April 2003). **Additional maternity leave** of up to 29 weeks from the actual birth of a child is also available to employees who have completed a minimum of one year's service by the 11th week before the expected week of confinement. An employee must inform her employer, at least 21 days before her absence begins (or as soon as reasonably practicable), that she intends to be absent because of maternity leave and that she intends to return to work (if she wishes to exercise that right); this notice must also state the expected week of confinement, for which she may be required by her employer to produce evidence. Women entitled to additional maternity leave in effect enjoy a maximum of 40 weeks' maternity leave, but this maximum can only be achieved by taking 11 weeks before and 29 weeks after the expected week of confinement.

(5) An employee entitled to maternity leave is also entitled to return to work with her employer after taking such leave, either in the job in which she was employed

or in suitable alternative employment, provided that the employer employs more than five people. If a woman wishes to return to work before her statutory maternity leave period has expired she may do so providing she informs her employer 21 days in advance of her proposed return. If the employer refuses to allow her to return, the employee is treated as having been continuously employed up to the intended date of her return and as having been dismissed on that date for the reason for which she was not allowed to return. If she complains to an employment tribunal that she has been unfairly dismissed (see *unfair dismissal), the dismissal will be treated as fair if the employer shows that it was not reasonably practicable to allow her to return, that the dismissal would have been reasonable if she had not been absent, or that in any event she would properly have been made redundant during her absence.

(6) Throughout the maternity leave period the employee is entitled to continue to benefit from all contractual terms of her employment with the exception of remuneration (money payment). These entitlements may include such things as pension contributions from her employer, company car and personal petrol allowance, and private health insurance. The maternity leave period begins either on the date that the employee notifies her employer that she intends to begin her leave (she must give 21 days' notice, or as much notice as is reasonably practicable) or the first day on which she is absent from work because of pregnancy or childbirth, if this date is earlier than the notified date (in which case the employer must be notified of the reason for the absence as soon as is reasonably practicable and this must be in writing if the employer requests it).

(7) Pregnant women, and women who have recently given birth or who are breastfeeding, have the right to be offered any suitable alternative work, rather than being suspended on maternity-related health and safety grounds. If there is no suitable alternative work available and the employee is suspended because of her condition, then she is entitled to receive the same remuneration that she would have received had she not been suspended.

matrimonial causes *See* MATRIMONIAL PROCEEDINGS.

matrimonial home The home in which a husband and wife have lived together. When only one of the spouses owns the matrimonial home the Family Law Act 1996 gives the nonowner certain *matrimonial home rights, which may be enforced by court order (*see* OCCUPATION ORDER). These rights include a right to live in the matrimonial home while still married. They will bind third parties (such as banks and building societies) if they are registered as a Class F land charge (in the case of previously unregistered land) or if they are protected by a notice (in the case of registered land) – *see* REGISTRATION OF ENCUMBRANCES. In Scotland similar rights have been granted (for a limited period only) to unmarried cohabitants, under the Matrimonial Homes (Financial Provision) (Scotland) Act 1981. When the legal estate is registered under the Land Registration Act and the wife is in actual occupation, she may also be protected against eviction by a third party if she has an interest in the land, even though she has not registered a notice or caution. Such an interest may be acquired by virtue of her contributions to the mortgage payments or, sometimes, to household expenses, as well as by making improvements in the matrimonial home.

Upon divorce, nullity, or separation the court has wide powers to make orders transferring the matrimonial home from one party to the other or altering their rights in it, in particular to provide for dependent children. County courts and magistrates' courts have powers to grant matrimonial injunctions excluding a spouse from the matrimonial home (*see* BATTERED SPOUSE OR COHABITANT) as well as making an order for sale of the matrimonial home in order to redistribute resources.

matrimonial home rights   The rights of a spouse who is not a co-owner of the *matrimonial home to live in the home. A spouse who is in occupation of the home has a right not to be evicted from it, and a spouse who is not in occupation has a right to enter and occupy the home. *See also* OCCUPATION ORDER.

matrimonial injunctions   *See* BATTERED SPOUSE OR COHABITANT.

matrimonial offence   Misbehaviour, such as adultery, desertion, or cruelty, by a party to a marriage. Formerly (before 1969), proof of matrimonial offences provided grounds for divorce and was important in applications in magistrates' courts for financial relief during the marriage.

matrimonial order   Formerly, an order made by magistrates under the 1960 Matrimonial Proceedings and Magistrates' Courts Act for periodical payments, custody of children, or noncohabitation clauses. However, both the grounds on which magistrates may exercise jurisdiction and the type of orders they may make are now governed by the 1978 Domestic Proceedings and Magistrates' Courts Act.

matrimonial proceedings (matrimonial causes)   Proceedings for *divorce, *judicial separation, or *nullity of marriage. All matrimonial proceedings must be heard in a divorce county court or the Divorce Registry in London. The proceedings may be transferred from the county court to the High Court, and vice versa, at the court's discretion. *See also* FAMILY PROCEEDINGS.

maturity *n.*   The time at which a *bill of exchange becomes due for payment. When a bill is payable at a fixed period after date, after sight, or after the happening of a specified event, the date of payment is determined by excluding the day from which the time is to begin to run and including the day of payment. When a bill is payable at a fixed period after sight, the time begins to run from the date of *acceptance if the bill is accepted and from the date of noting or *protest if the bill is noted or protested for nonacceptance.

maxims of equity   Short pithy statements used to denote the general principles that are supposed to run through *equity. Although often inaccurate and subject to exceptions, they are commonly used to justify particular decisions and express some of the basic principles that have guided the development of equity. The main maxims are as follows:
equity acts *in personam*;
equity acts on the conscience;
equity aids the vigilant;
equity will not suffer a wrong without a remedy (i.e. equity will not allow a person whom it considers as having a good claim to be denied the right to sue);
equity follows the law (i.e. equity follows the rules of common law unless there is a good reason to the contrary);
equity looks at the intent not at the form (i.e. equity looks to the reality of what was intended rather than the way in which it is expressed);
where the equities are equal, the earlier in time prevails (i.e. where rights are equal in worth or value, the earlier right created takes precedence over the later);
he who seeks equity must do equity;
he who comes to equity must come with *clean hands (*see* EQUITABLE REMEDIES);
*equality is equity;

equity looks on that as done which ought to be done (*see* CONVERSION);
equity imputes an intent to fulfil an obligation (*see* SATISFACTION);
equity will not assist a volunteer (*see* VOLUNTARY SETTLEMENT).

Mayor of London The head of the *Greater London Authority, elected every four
years by the voters in London; the office was created under the Greater London
Authority Act 1999. The responsibilities of the Mayor include the promotion of
cultural, economic, and social development and improvement of the London
environment by use of strategies to reduce air pollution and waste

Mayor's and City of London Court A court formed in 1922 by the
amalgamation of the Mayor's Court and the City of London Court. It had an
unlimited civil jurisdiction over matters arising within the City. The Court was
abolished by the Courts Act 1971, but the name is retained by the *county court for
the City of London, which has normal county court jurisdiction.

Measure *n.* *See* CHURCH OF ENGLAND.

measure of damages The principle that determines the amount of *damages
awarded for a tort or a breach of contract.

mediation *n.* **1.** A form of *alternative dispute resolution in which an
independent third party (**mediator**) assists the parties involved in a dispute or
negotiation to achieve a mutually acceptable resolution of the points of conflict. The
mediator, who may be a lawyer or a specially trained nonlawyer, has no decision-
making powers and cannot force the parties to accept a settlement. In family law,
for example, mediators assist spouses to resolve disputes that have arisen as a
consequence of the breakdown of their marriage by reaching agreement or reducing
conflict over future arrangements for children or their finances. Mediation, which is
designed to avoid the need to take cases to court, is likely to be extended to many
other areas of the law since the publication of Lord Woolf's *Access to Justice* (Final
Report) 1996 and the introduction of the *Civil Procedure Rules, in which it is
actively encouraged. **2.** (in international law) A method for the peaceful settlement
of an international dispute in which a third party, acting with the agreement of the
disputing states, actively participates in the negotiating process by offering
substantive suggestions concerning terms of settlement and, in general, by trying to
reconcile the opposing claims and appeasing any feeling of resentment between the
parties involved. *See also* CONCILIATION; GOOD OFFICES.

Member of Parliament (MP) *See* HOUSE OF COMMONS.

Members' interests Interests of Members of Parliament that might affect their
conduct as MPs; for example, employments, company directorships, shareholdings,
substantial property holdings, and financial sponsorships. By a 1975 resolution of the
House, these must be registered for public information. After various allegations of
Members not disclosing financial rewards received from outside parties in return
for asking questions in the House ("cash for questions"), the rules on disclosure were
tightened in 1996, when the Code of Conduct for Members of Parliament with a
Guide to the Rules Relating to the Conduct of Members were published.

memorandum in writing Under former provisions of the Law of Property Act
1925, written evidence of a contract for the sale or other disposition of land or of
any interest in it. The Act provided that such a contract could not be enforced
unless it, or some memorandum or note evidencing the parties' agreement
(identifying the parties, the property, the price, and other essentials), was in writing
and signed by the party to be held liable on the contract. In practice, a contract

would usually be in writing, but a signed memorandum showing that the parties had been bound from the time of an earlier oral agreement was equally acceptable as evidence to support any claim to enforce the contract.

However, the Law of Property (Miscellaneous Provisions) Act 1989 now insists that such a contract can only be made in writing that sets out in one document (or incorporates by reference to other existing documents) all the terms the parties have expressly agreed; the contract must be signed by both parties. A mere memorandum or note evidencing the terms of the agreement will no longer suffice unless it is incorporated in the contract by reference.

memorandum of association A constitutional document of a *registered company that must be drawn up by the person(s) wishing to set it up. Under the Companies Act 1985 certain compulsory clauses must be inserted into the memorandum. These clauses deal with and outline the company's identity (**names clause**); its registered address (**registered office clause**); the amount of its authorized share *capital (**capital clause**); the purpose(s) for which the company has been formed (**objects clause**); and (if applicable) whether it is a *limited company or a *public company. The Companies Act 1985 contains specimen examples of such clauses for different types of company. The memorandum is said to be the "superior constitutional document" of the company; in the event of a conflict between it and the *articles of association, the memorandum prevails.

menace *n. See* THREAT.

mensa et thoro *See* A MENSA ET THORO.

mens rea [Latin: a guilty mind] The state of mind that the prosecution must prove a defendant to have had at the time of committing a crime in order to secure a conviction. *Mens rea* varies from crime to crime; it is either defined in the statute creating the crime or established by *precedent. Common examples of *mens rea* are *intention to bring about a particular consequence, *recklessness as to whether such consequences may come about, and (for a few crimes) *negligence. Some crimes require knowledge of certain circumstances as part of the *mens rea* (for example, the crime of receiving stolen goods requires the knowledge that they were stolen). Some crimes require no *mens rea*; these are known as crimes of *strict liability. Whenever *mens rea* is required, the prosecution must prove that it existed at the same time as the *actus reus* of the crime (coincidence of *actus reus* and *mens rea*). A defendant cannot plead ignorance of the law, nor is a good *motive a defence. He may, however, bring evidence to show that he had no *mens rea* for the crime he is charged with; alternatively, he may admit that he had *mens rea*, but raise a general defence (e.g. duress) or a particular defence allowed in relation to the crime.

mental disorder For the purposes of the Mental Health Act 1983, mental illness, incomplete or *arrested development of mind, *psychopathic disorder, and any other disorder or disability of mind. A person suffering (or appearing to be suffering) from mental disorder can be detained in hospital either for assessment or for treatment. Detention for assessment normally takes place on an application for his admission made by his nearest relative or an approved social worker. This is supported in either case by the recommendation of two doctors that it is desirable in the interests of the patient's own health and safety or for the protection of others. The application authorizes detention for up to 28 days. In a case of emergency, however, detention may be for up to 72 hours on an application supported by one doctor only and made by an approved social worker or the patient's nearest relative. The procedure for detention for treatment is the same as the normal procedure for detention for assessment. The application authorizes detention for six months, renewable for a further six months, initially, and then for periods of one year on a report to the hospital managers by the doctor in charge. Discharge of a person detained may be effected by the managers or the doctor in charge and, within certain limits, the nearest relative; in the case of detention for treatment, discharge may also be directed by a *Mental Health Review Tribunal. The National Health Service and Community Care Act 1990 provided for more care in the community for patients who previously may have been treated in secure hospitals. *See also* HOSPITAL ORDER; SPECIAL HOSPITAL.

Mental Health Act Commission A regulatory body established in 1983 to monitor the operation of the Mental Health Act 1983. Its members, appointed by the Secretary of State for Health, include psychiatrists, nurses, lawyers, members of other clinical professions, and lay people. Commissioners are responsible for regularly visiting patients detained under the Act, reviewing psychiatric care, investigating certain complaints, and advising ministers.

Mental Health Review Tribunal A tribunal, constituted under the Mental Health Act 1983, to which applications may be made for the discharge from hospital of a person detained there for assessment or treatment of *mental disorder or under a *hospital order or a *guardianship order. When a patient is subject to a restriction order or direction an application may only be made after his first six months of detention. Such tribunals include legally and medically qualified members appointed by the Lord Chancellor and are under the supervision of the *Council on Tribunals.

mental impairment *See* ARRESTED DEVELOPMENT.

MEP Member of the European Parliament. *See* EUROPEAN PARLIAMENT.

mercantile agent A commercial *agent who has authority either to sell goods, to consign goods for the purpose of sale, to buy goods, or to raise money on the security of goods on behalf of his principal.

mercenary *n.* A person who is paid to serve with armed forces other than those of the state of which he is a national. British officers undertaking such service (e.g. in Oman) were commonly known as **contract officers**. *See also* FOREIGN ENLISTMENT.

merchantable quality An *implied condition now replaced by *satisfactory quality.

merchant shipping registration *See* SHIP.

mercy *n.* *See* PREROGATIVE OF MERCY.

mere equity A right affecting property that is less significant than an *equitable right or a *legal right; it does not affect anyone except the parties to the transaction in which it is contained. An example is the right to rectify a document.

merger *n.* **1.** An amalgamation between companies of similar size in which either the members of the merging companies exchange their shares for shares in a new company or the members of some of the merging companies exchange their shares for shares in another merging company. It is usually effected by a *takeover bid. Under current EU mergers law, mergers with a **Community dimension**, i.e. a combined Community-wide turnover of at least 250M euros and a combined worldwide turnover of over 500M euros, must be notified to the EU Mergers Secretariat. However, if each of the merging companies derives two-thirds of its EU business from one and the same member state, the merger does not have to be notified. *Compare* TAKEOVER. **2.** The extinguishing of a lesser interest in land when it comes into the same ownership as a greater one. For example, if a freehold owner acquires the unexpired leasehold estate, the latter may merge into the freehold. Whether or not merger occurs depends on the circumstances of the transaction (thus a leasehold that is subject to a subsisting mortgage will not normally merge with the freehold) and the intention of the parties.

mesne profits Money that a landlord can claim from a tenant who continues to occupy property after his tenancy ends, the amount being equivalent to the current market rent of the property. This may be more than the rent that the tenant was paying before the tenancy ended. If the landlord continues to accept the original rent from the tenant at the end of the tenancy, a new tenancy may be created.

messuage *n.* A house and its associated garden, outbuildings, and orchard.

Michaelmas Day *See* QUARTER DAYS.

micro-state *n.* A state with an area of less than 500 square miles and a population under 100,000. Examples of micro-states include Andorra, Antigua and Barbuda, Grenada, and Monaco, all of which have been admitted to membership of the United Nations. Although the UN membership of such small states was contentious, ultimately the principle of universality of membership of states, whatever their size, prevailed over the issue of whether or not they were capable of fulfilling their obligations as members. *See also* RECOGNITION.

Middle Temple One of the four *Inns of Court, situated in the Temple between the Strand and the Embankment. The earliest recorded claim for its existence is 1404.

Midsummer Day *See* QUARTER DAYS.

military court A *court martial or the *Court of Chivalry.

military law *See* SERVICE LAW. *Compare* MARTIAL LAW.

Military Staff Committee A committee established under Article 47 of the United Nations Charter. Articles 43–47 of the Charter (within *Chapter VII) envisage, through the Military Staff Committee, advance military cooperation for UN collective military security. This body is to advise the Security Council on all questions relating to armed forces placed at the disposal of the latter. It consists of the chiefs of staff of the permanent members of the Security Council, although other members of the United Nations may be invited to sit with it when the efficient discharge of the Committee's responsibilities so requires.

Due to deadlock, principally among the permanent members of the Security Council, the Committee declared that it could make no further progress on the matter of military cooperation for UN collective security measures. Although the Committee still formally exists it has had no real function to perform since its establishment in October 1945. *See also* COLLECTIVE SECURITY; ENFORCEMENT ACTION.

military stores Any chattel belonging to the Crown that is issued, or stored for the purpose of being issued when required, for military purposes. *Compare* NAVAL PROPERTY.

military testament *See* PRIVILEGED WILL.

minerals *pl. n. See* MINING LEASE.

minimum term *See* LIFE IMPRISONMENT.

minimum wage The lowest rate of remuneration that an employer may pay. The National Minimum Wage's adult hourly rate from October 2001 is £4.10; this will increase to £4.20 in October 2002. The youth rate for 18–21-year-olds is (from October 2001) £3.50 per hour.

mining lease A lease granting a tenant the right to extract minerals from the land for a specified period in return for a rent (which may vary in accordance with the amount or value of minerals extracted). The Settled Land Act 1925 allows the tenant for life of settled land to grant mining leases for up to 100 years whether or not he is liable for any *waste committed by him, and whether or not the mine is already open. As a general rule, and subject to any contrary intention expressed in the settlement, the tenant for life is entitled to three-quarters of the rent, but if he is liable for waste in respect of minerals, he is only entitled to one-quarter of the rent. In either case, the balance must be paid as *capital money to the trustees of the settlement. The Act defines minerals for these purposes as all substances in or under the land that can be extracted by underground or surface working.

minister *n.* A person (by *constitutional convention a member of either House of Parliament) appointed to government office by the Crown on the advice of the Prime Minister. He may be a senior minister in charge of a department (normally styled Secretary of State but sometimes Minister), a senior minister without specific departmental responsibilities (e.g. the Lord Privy Seal or a Minister without Portfolio), or a junior minister assisting in departmental business (a Minister of State or a Parliamentary Secretary or Under-Secretary). In the Treasury the ministerial ranks are *Chancellor of the Exchequer, Chief Secretary, Financial Secretary, and Ministers of State.

ministerial responsibility The responsibility to Parliament of the Cabinet collectively and of individual ministers for their own decisions and the conduct of their departments. A minister must defend his decisions without sheltering behind his civil servants; if he cannot, political pressure may force his resignation.

mini-trial *n.* *See* ALTERNATIVE DISPUTE RESOLUTION.

minor *n.* *See* INFANT.

minor interests Interests in *registered land that cannot be created or transferred by registered disposition, are not *overriding interests, and could be overridden by a registered proprietor unless protected by registration. Such interests include the equitable interests of beneficiaries under a settlement and all charges that would be registrable at the Land Charges Department if the land had been unregistered (*see* REGISTRATION OF ENCUMBRANCES). Minor interests are protected by registration of a notice, caution, inhibition, or restriction as appropriate.

minority *n.* The state of being an *infant (or minor). *Compare* MAJORITY.

minority clauses Clauses in treaties between states that make special provision for *ethnic minorities. For example, in the Greco-Bulgarian convention of 1919 there was a minority clause that allowed for free migration of minorities between the signatory powers.

minority protection Remedies evolved to safeguard a minority of company members from the abuse of *majority rule. They include *just and equitable winding-up, applying for relief on the basis of *unfair prejudice, bringing a *derivative action or a *representative action, and seeking an *investigation of the company.

minutes *pl. n.* Records of company business transacted at general meetings, board meetings, and meetings of managers. Registered companies are required to keep such records. Minutes of general meetings can be inspected by company members at the registered office.

miscarriage *n.* **1.** A failure of justice or a failure in the administration of justice. **2.** A spontaneous *abortion, i.e. one that is not induced.

mischief rule *See* INTERPRETATION OF STATUTES.

misconduct *n.* Incorrect or erroneous conduct. *See* WILFUL MISCONDUCT.

misdemeanour *n.* Formerly (i.e. before 1967), any of the less serious offences, as opposed to *felony.

misdescription *n.* A misleading or inaccurate physical or legal description of property in a contract for its sale. When a vendor cannot convey property corresponding to its description in the contract for sale, a breach of contract results, which at the very least gives the purchaser a right to damages.

If the misdescription is substantial (i.e. it is reasonable to suppose that it constitutes the basis for the purchaser entering into the contract in the first place), the vendor will be unable to enforce the contract against the purchaser. When there is an innocent misdescription, which is not substantial, the contract may be enforced by the vendor, but subject to a suitable reduction in the contractually agreed price, even if the purchaser would prefer to rescind the contract (*see* RESCISSION). Alternatively, the purchaser might prefer to compel the vendor to convey what title he can (despite the misdescription) and receive compensation in addition. If the misdescription operates in the purchaser's favour, the vendor has no right to claim any compensation from him.

Under the Property Misdescription Act 1991, *estate agents and property developers are prohibited from making false or misleading statements about property in the course of their business. Misdescription in this case relates to what purports to be fact and not to mere expressions of opinion. *Compare* MISREPRESENTATION.

misdirection *n.* An incorrect direction by a judge to a *jury on a matter of law. In such cases the Court of Appeal may quash the conviction.

misfeasance *n.* **1.** The negligent or otherwise improper performance of a lawful act. **2.** (in company law) An act by an officer of a company in the nature of a breach of trust or breach of duty, particularly relating to the company's assets. *Compare* MALFEASANCE; NONFEASANCE.

misfeasance summons An application to the court by a creditor, contributory, liquidator, or the official receiver during the course of winding up a company. The court is asked to examine the conduct of company officers and others who are suspected of a breach of a *fiduciary or other duty towards the company and it can order them to make restitution to the company.

misjoinder of parties An incorrect *joinder of parties in an action. In modern practice this does not cause the action to abate but it can be rectified by *amendment.

misleading advertising Advertising that deceives or is likely to deceive those to whom it is addressed or whom it reaches and, because of its deceptive nature, is likely to affect consumers' behaviour or injures or is likely to injure a competitor. EU directive 84/450 requires EU member states to harmonize laws in this area.

mispleading *n.* The omission of an essential allegation in a claim form or other statement of case. In modern practice, it can usually be rectified by *amendment.

misprision *n.* Failure to report an offence. The former crime of misprision of felony has now been replaced by the crime of *compounding an offence. However, the common-law offence of misprision of treason still exists; this occurs if a person knows or reasonably suspects that someone has committed treason but does not inform the proper authorities within a reasonable time. The punishment for this offence is forfeiture by the offender of all his property during his lifetime.

misrepresentation *n.* An untrue statement of fact, made by one party to the other in the course of negotiating a contract, that induces the other party to enter into the contract. The person making the misrepresentation is called the **representor**, and the person to whom it is made is the **representee**. A false statement of law, opinion, or intention does not constitute a misrepresentation; nor does a statement of fact known by the representee to be untrue. Moreover, unless the representee relies on the statement so that it becomes an **inducement** (though not necessarily the only inducement) to enter into the contract, it is not a misrepresentation. The remedies for misrepresentation vary according to the degree of culpability of the representor. If he is guilty of **fraudulent misrepresentation** (i.e. if he did not honestly believe in the truth of his statement, which is not the same as saying that he knew it to be false) the representee may, subject to certain limitations, set the contract aside by *rescission and may also sue for damages. If he is guilty of **negligent misrepresentation** (i.e. if he believed in his statement but had no reasonable grounds for doing so) the representee was formerly entitled only to rescission but may now (under the Misrepresentation Act 1967 or by an action in tort for negligence) also obtain *damages. If the representor has committed merely an **innocent misrepresentation** (one he reasonably believed to be true) the representee is restricted to rescission, subject to the discretion of the court under the 1967 Act to award him damages in lieu. A representee entitled to rescind a contract for misrepresentation may decide instead to *affirm it. *See also* MISDESCRIPTION; NONDISCLOSURE.

mistake *n.* A misunderstanding or erroneous belief about a matter of fact (**mistake of fact**) or a matter of law (**mistake of law**). In civil cases, mistake is particularly important in the law of contract. Mistakes of law have no effect on the validity of agreements, and neither do many mistakes of fact. When a mistake of fact does do so, it may render the agreement void under common-law rules (in which case it is referred to as an **operative mistake**) or it may make it voidable, i.e. liable, subject to certain limitations, to be set aside by *rescission under more lenient rules of equity.

When both parties to an agreement are under a misunderstanding, the mistake may be classified as either a **common mistake** (i.e. a single mistake shared by both) or a **mutual mistake** (i.e. each misunderstanding the other). In the case of common mistake, there is full *consensus ad idem* and the mistake renders the contract void only if it robs it of all substance. The principal (and almost the only) example is when the subject matter of the contract has, unknown to both parties, ceased to exist (**res extincta**). A common mistake about some particular attribute of the subject matter (e.g. that it is an original, not a copy) is not an operative mistake.

However, a common mistake relating to any really fundamental matter will render a contract voidable. In the case of mutual mistake there is no real **consensus**, but the contract is nevertheless valid if only one interpretation of what was agreed can be deduced from the parties' words and conduct. Otherwise, the mistake is operative and the contract void. When only one party to a contract is under a misunderstanding, his mistake may be called a **unilateral mistake** and it makes the contract void if it relates to the fundamental nature of the offer and the other party knew or ought to have known of it. Otherwise, the contract is valid so far as the law of mistake is concerned, though the circumstances may be such as to make it voidable for *misrepresentation.

A deed or other signed document (whether or not constituting a contract) that does not correctly record what both parties intended may be rectified by the courts. When one signatory to a document was fundamentally mistaken as to the character or effect of the transaction it embodies, he may (unless he was careless) plead his mistake as a defence to any action based on the document (*see* NON EST FACTUM).

In criminal cases, a mistake or accident may mean that a person lacked *mens rea. It has become clear in recent years that a person has a defence if he would have had a common-law defence, such as *consent, *provocation, or one of the *general defences, had the facts been as he mistakenly supposed them to be. If someone commits a crime in ignorance that the law forbids it, he is usually guilty (*ignorantia juris non excusat*: ignorance of the law is no excuse).

If a defendant makes a mistake as to the civil law that prevents him having the *mens rea* required to be guilty of the crime, he will normally be acquitted of the crime, even if his mistake is unreasonable (for example, if he damages someone else's property in the belief that it is his own, and this belief is caused by a mistake as to the law of property). *See also* GENERAL DEFENCES; INTOXICATION.

mistakes in judgment *See* SLIP RULE.

mistrial *n.* A trial that is vitiated by some fundamental defect.

mitigation *n.* **1.** Reduction in the severity of some penalty. Before *sentence is passed on someone convicted of a crime, the defence may make a plea in mitigation, putting forward reasons for making the sentence less severe than it might otherwise be. These might include personal or family circumstances of the offender, and the defence may also dispute facts raised by the prosecution to indicate aggravating circumstances. In raising mitigating factors, *hearsay evidence and documentary evidence of *character are accepted. **2.** Reduction in the loss or injury resulting from a tort or a breach of contract. The injured party is under a duty to take all reasonable steps to mitigate his loss when claiming *damages.

mixed action A form of court action combining a claim relating to real property with a claim for damages.

mixed fund A fund of money derived from the sale of both real and personal property.

mixed property *Property that has some of the attributes of both real and personal property. *Emblements are an example.

mock auction An auction during which (1) any lot is sold to someone at a price lower than his highest bid for it; (2) part of the price is repaid or credited to the bidder; (3) the right to bid is restricted to those who have bought or agreed to buy one or more articles; or (4) articles are given away or offered as gifts. Under the Mock Auction Act 1961 it is an offence to promote or conduct a mock auction of plate, plated articles, linen, china, glass, books, pictures, prints, furniture, jewellery, articles of household or personal use, ornaments, or any musical or scientific instrument.

molestation *n.* Behaviour that has the effect or intention of annoying or pestering one's spouse (or cohabitant) or children. Such an act need not involve violence or physical assault; harassment (for example by threatening letters or telephone calls) may constitute molestation. Under the Family Law Act 1996, spouses (and in some cases unmarried cohabitants) can apply for a court injunction to prevent molestation (*see* NONMOLESTATION ORDER). Magistrates' courts have similar powers under the 1978 Domestic Proceedings and Magistrates' Courts Act, but only if there is violence and only in relation to married couples. There are procedures for protecting children in an emergency (*see* EMERGENCY PROTECTION ORDER). *See also* BATTERED CHILD; BATTERED SPOUSE OR COHABITANT; STALKING.

money Bill A Bill that, in the opinion of the Speaker of the House of Commons, contains only provisions dealing with taxation, the Consolidated Fund, public money, the raising or replacement of loans by the state, and matters incidental to these subjects. Such a Bill can become an Act without the House of Lords' consent (*see* ACT OF PARLIAMENT).

money had and received A former ground for court action that occurred when the defendant was in possession of money that should have belonged to the claimant (for example, when money had been paid to an agent who then failed to pass it on to his principal).

money laundering Legitimizing money from organized or other crime by paying it through normal business channels. EU measures exist to control, on an EU-wide basis, the laundering of money, especially that resulting from organized crime.

moneylender *n.* A person whose business it is to lend money. The Moneylenders Acts 1900–27 contained provisions for the control of moneylenders, including the form of their contracts. Under the Acts, the term "moneylender" did not include pawnbrokers, friendly or building societies, corporate bodies with special powers to lend money, those carrying on a banking or insurance business, or businesses whose primary object is not the lending of money. The more extensive provisions of the Consumer Credit Act 1974 have replaced the provisions of the Moneylenders Acts.

monism *n.* The theory that national and international law form part of one legal structure, in which international law is supreme. It is opposed to **dualism**, which holds that they are separate systems operating in different fields.

monopoly *n.* A situation in which a substantial proportion of a particular type of business is transacted by a single enterprise or trader. The Fair Trading Act 1973 contains provisions assigning functions in respect of monopolies to the *Director General of Fair Trading and the Competition Commission. It defines a monopoly situation, in relation to the supply of goods and services and the export of goods, as one in which a single enterprise, connected group of companies, or trade association has one-quarter of the relevant business. When the Competition Commission finds that a monopoly situation exists and operates against the public interest, the Minister has powers to remedy or prevent the adverse effects. Sometimes monopolies involving more than one company (complex monopolies) are investigated. The Director General of Fair Trading may also investigate joint *abuses of a dominant position that breach Chapter II of the Competition Act 1998 and thus has a choice as to which provisions are used to investigate monopolies.

month *n.* A calendar month or a lunar month (28 days). The common law adopted the lunar month, but the Interpretation Act 1978 provides that the word is to be presumed to mean calendar month in Acts of Parliament, and the Law of Property Act 1925 provides similarly for deeds and other written documents.

moot *n.* A mock trial, often held in university law schools and at the Inns of Court, for students as practice for future advocacy. A hypothetical case is presented to students for preparation and then argued before the judge(s) at the moot. This practice originates in the formal moots held in the medieval Inns of Court, which were considered an essential part of legal education.

moral law The body of laws to which individuals feel themselves subject, often through their religious beliefs. *See also* CANON LAW; NATURAL LAW.

mortgage *n.* An interest in property created as a form of security for a loan or payment of a debt and terminated on payment of the loan or debt. The borrower, who offers the security, is the **mortgagor**; the lender, who provides the money, is the **mortgagee**. Virtually any property may be mortgaged (though land is the most common); exceptions include the salaries of public officials. The name is derived from Old French (literally: dead pledge), since at common law failure to repay on the due date of redemption (which in most mortgages is set very early) formerly resulted in the mortgagor losing all his rights over the property. By the rules of equity the mortgagor is now allowed to redeem his property at any time on payment of the loan together with interest and costs (*see* EQUITY OF REDEMPTION). The mortgagee has a right to take possession of the mortgaged property as soon as the mortgage is made, irrespective of whether the mortgagor has defaulted. However, this right (1) must only be used for the purpose of protecting or enforcing the security, (2) may be excluded by agreement, or (3) is subject to a power in the court to adjourn proceedings for possession, to suspend the execution of an order for possession, or to postpone the date for delivery of possession, where the mortgaged property is a dwelling house (Administration of Justice Act 1970 as amended). This right is normally used as a preliminary to an exercise of the mortgagee's power of sale. In face of continued nonpayment of the loan, the mortgagee may sell the mortgaged property under a *power of sale, appoint a *receiver, or obtain a decree of *foreclosure.

Under the Law of Property Act 1925 the only valid **legal mortgages** are (1) a lease subject to *cesser on redemption and (2) a deed expressed to be a charge by way of legal mortgage (*see* CHARGE). All other mortgages are equitable interests only (*see* EQUITABLE MORTGAGE). All mortgages of registered land are noted in the charges register on application by the mortgagee (*see* LAND REGISTRATION), and a *charge certificate is issued to him. When mortgaged land is unregistered, a first legal mortgagee keeps the title deeds. A subsequent legal mortgagee and any equitable mortgagee who does not have the title deeds should protect his interests by registration (*see* PUISNE MORTGAGE; REGISTRATION OF ENCUMBRANCES). *See also* PRIORITY OF MORTGAGES.

mortgage action A court action brought by a mortgagee for possession of the mortgaged property or payment of all money due to him, when the mortgagor has failed to pay the amounts due under the mortgage.

mortgagee *n. See* MORTGAGE.

mortgage interest relief Tax relief on the interest payments made to a lender on a loan for the purchase of the taxpayer's only or *main residence, which was available until 5 April 2000; after that date, the relief was withdrawn. It applied to the interest on a loan of up to £30,000; from 1998 until 5 April 2000 the rate of relief was 15%.

mortgagor *n.* *See* MORTGAGE.

motion *n.* Formerly, an application made orally and in open court to a judge for an order. This term has been rendered obsolete by the *Civil Procedure Rules; motions are now referred to as **applications**.

motive *n.* The purpose behind a course of action. Motive is not normally relevant in deciding guilt or innocence (for example, killing to save someone from suffering is still murder or manslaughter), although it may be of some relevance in the crime of *libel. Nor is a bad motive relevant in deciding legal guilt. However, a good motive may be invoked as a reason for mitigating a punishment upon conviction, and a bad motive may provide circumstantial evidence that the defendant committed the crime he is charged with.

motor car *See* MOTOR VEHICLE.

motor cycle *See* MOTOR VEHICLE.

motoring offences *See* OFFENCES RELATING TO ROAD TRAFFIC.

motor insurance *See* THIRD-PARTY INSURANCE.

Motor Insurers' Bureau A body set up by the insurance industry, by agreement with the Department of Transport. It provides cover if someone has been injured or killed in a motor accident and in respect of a liability required by the Road Traffic Act to be covered by a contract of insurance when either (1) a judgment against the party liable is unsatisfied, for example because the party is (in breach of the Road Traffic Act) uninsured, or (2) the wrongdoer cannot be identified.

motor vehicle For the purposes of the Road Traffic Acts, any mechanically propelled vehicle intended or adapted for use on the roads. This includes **motor cars** (vehicles of not more than 3 tonnes in unladen weight, designed to carry loads or up to seven passengers) and **motor cycles** (vehicles of not more than 8 cwt in unladen weight and having less than four wheels). A car from which the engine has been removed may still be considered to be mechanically propelled if the removal is temporary, but if so many parts have been removed that it cannot be restored to use at a reasonable expense, it ceases to be mechanically propelled. A dumper used for carrying materials at a building site is not intended for use on roads, even if it is in fact used on a road near the building site; and a go-kart is not intended nor adapted for use on the roads (even though it is capable of being used on the roads). *See also* CONVEYANCE.

motorway driving Contravention of the regulations relating to driving on a motorway, as outlined in the Highway Code, is an offence punishable by *endorsement (carrying 3 points under the *totting-up system) and discretionary *disqualification.

MOT test An annual test originally ordered by the Ministry of Transport (now Department of Transport, Local Government, and the Regions) to be carried out on all motor vehicles over a certain age to ensure that they comply with certain legal requirements relating to vehicle maintenance. The test covers brakes, steering, lights and indicators, windscreen wipers and washers, the exhaust system, horn, tyres (and to some extent, the wheels), bodywork and suspension (insofar as they affect the brakes and steering), and seat belts. It is an offence to put on the road a motor vehicle that has been registered for over three years (five years in Northern Ireland) without a valid test certificate. A certificate is issued for 12 months and must be renewed annually; a vehicle that is subject to a test cannot be licensed without a test certificate (*see* ROAD TAX). It is not an endorsable offence not to have an MOT certificate, but this may invalidate the motorist's insurance and result in a charge of *driving without insurance. An MOT certificate does not indicate that the vehicle is roadworthy in all respects and is not a defence to charges brought under the *vehicle construction and maintenance regulations.

movables *pl. n.* Tangible items of property other than land and goods fixed to the land (i.e. immovables).

MP (Member of Parliament) *See* HOUSE OF COMMONS.

MR *See* MASTER OF THE ROLLS.

multiple admissibility The principle of the law of evidence that if evidence is admissible for one purpose it may not be rejected solely because it is inadmissible for some other purpose. However, the *trier of fact may have to be directed not to consider the evidence when deciding those issues in respect of which it is inadmissible.

multiple agreement (under the Consumer Credit Act 1974) An agreement the terms of which are such that (1) part of it falls within one category of agreement mentioned in the Act and another part within a different category of agreement, which may or may not be mentioned in the Act; or (2) a part or the whole of it is placed within two or more categories of agreement mentioned in the Act. When part of an agreement falls within a category mentioned in the Act, that part is treated for the purposes of the Act as a separate agreement. When an agreement falls within two or more categories, it is treated as an agreement in each of the categories in question.

multi-track *n.* The track to which a civil case is allocated (*see* ALLOCATION) when the claim is more complex and/or for a higher amount (exceeding £15,000) than those catered for in the *fast track. With the exception of personal injury claims not exceeding £50,000, the jurisdiction for which is retained by the county court, these actions will be based in the High Court. Unlike the *small claims track and the fast track, the multi-track uses tools of *case management rather than standard procedure to process. Those tools include the use of *case management conferences and *pre-trial reviews.

municipal law The national, or internal, law of a state, as opposed to international law. *See also* DOCTRINE OF INCORPORATION; PRIVATE LAW; PUBLIC LAW.

muniments *pl. n.* Documents that prove a person's title to land. They include the relevant *title deeds, certificates of *official search, and other documents tracing ownership of the land through to the present owner.

munitions of war Vessels, aircraft, fighting vehicles, arms, ammunition, explosive devices, or any other articles, materials, or devices intended or adapted for use in war.

murder *n.* Homicide that is neither accidental nor lawful and does not fall into the categories of *manslaughter or *infanticide. The *mens rea* for murder is traditionally known as *malice aforethought and the punishment (since 1965) is *life imprisonment. Murder is subject to the special defences of *diminished responsibility, *suicide pact, and *provocation. Under the Crime (Sentences) Act 1997 a second conviction for attempted murder carries a mandatory sentence of life imprisonment (*see* REPEAT OFFENDER).

mute *adj. See* STANDING MUTE.

mutiny *n.* An offence against service law committed by any member of HM forces who combines with one or more other members (whether or not civilians are also involved) to overthrow or resist lawful authority in those forces or any forces cooperating with them. If a civilian is involved, his conduct will be a matter for the ordinary criminal law. The offence is also committed if the aim of the combination is to disobey lawful authority in a manner subversive of discipline, or for the purpose of avoiding any duty connected with operations against the enemy, or generally to impede the performance of any duty in HM forces or any cooperating forces.

mutual mistake *See* MISTAKE.

mutual wills Wills conferring reciprocal benefits, made by two or more persons who have agreed that the wills are not to be revoked. The court will enforce the agreement by declaring that the survivor holds the relevant property on *constructive trust to give effect to the mutual will. For example, H and W by agreement make wills leaving property to each other absolutely, each providing that if the other dies first the property goes instead to X. If after H's death W makes a fresh will in favour of Y, the court will on W's death nonetheless give effect to the interest left to X under the original mutual will. The fresh will is admitted to probate, but the *personal representatives of the survivor can only take the relevant property subject to a constructive trust in favour of X. The property that forms the subject matter of the trust is to be determined by construing the agreement contained in the mutual wills.

naked agreement *See* CONSIDERATION.

naked trust *See* BARE TRUST.

name *n. See* BUSINESS NAME; CHANGE OF NAME; COMPANY NAME; SURNAME.

name and arms clause A clause in a settlement providing that the beneficiary forfeits his entitlement unless he uses a specified surname and, if appropriate, coat of arms at all times. The clause is valid only if it is sufficiently precise.

National Assembly for Wales *See* WELSH ASSEMBLY.

national conditions of sale One of a number of sets of standard conditions of sale used by solicitors in drawing up closed contracts for the sale of land. Another set of conditions is made available by the Law Society. *Compare* OPEN CONTRACT; STATUTORY FORM OF CONDITIONS OF SALE.

National Crime Squad A body of police officers organized on a national basis to tackle serious and organized crime. It was set up under the Police Act 1997, in conjunction with the *Criminal Records Agency and the authorization of intrusive *surveillance operations.

National Health Service (NHS) A service established for England and Wales in 1948 as a result of the National Health Service Act 1946 and reorganized in 1974, 1982, 1990 (as a result of the National Health Service and Community Care Act 1990), and in 1999 (under the Health Act 1999). It is concerned with the provision of hospital, specialist, general practitioner (medical, dental, ophthalmic, and pharmaceutical), nursing, ambulance, and related services, under the ultimate responsibility of the Secretary of State for Health. The 1990 Act introduced major changes and divided the service into those bodies responsible for the acquisition of care (**contractors**) and those responsible for the provision of care (**providers**). In England the Health Service is administered by the National Health Service Executive headed by a Chief Executive, under which there are (since 31 March 1996) eight regional offices, which took over the functions of the **Regional Health Authorities** (RHAs), i.e. overall planning responsibility for their regions and allocation of resources to health authorities within these regions. In April 1996 the role of the contractors was taken over by new *Health Authorities, which assumed the functions of the **District Health Authorities** (DHAs), responsible for assessing and acquiring services required for their districts by awarding contracts to such providers as *NHS Trusts; and the **Family Health Service Authorities**, which awarded contracts for services provided by general practitioners, dentists, and pharmacists. An element of competition was introduced by the 1990 Act in that a DHA could place contracts for any, or all, of the health care required for its own district either with local services or with the services provided outside its area.

General practitioner services were reorganized in a similar way with some GPs (**fundholders**) holding their own budgets and having the power to purchase the services they required for their own patients from whichever provider gave them the service they needed. However, the Health Act 1999 ended GP fundholding and created *Primary Care Trusts. *See also* COMMISSION FOR HEALTH IMPROVEMENT.

national insurance A scheme of state-administered social security benefits (e.g. income support, incapacity benefit, and retirement pensions). These were inaugurated by the National Insurance Act 1946 and are now given effect by the Social Security Acts 1975–96. A separate industrial injuries insurance scheme was established by the National Insurance (Industrial Injuries) Act 1946, but the Social Security Acts now govern the payment of *industrial injuries disablement benefit. Entitlement to social security or disablement benefits is determined by adjudication officers; appeals from their decisions may be made to a *Social Security Appeal Tribunal.

nationality *n.* The state of being a citizen or subject of a particular country. *See* BRITISH CITIZENSHIP; BRITISH DEPENDENT TERRITORIES CITIZENSHIP; BRITISH OVERSEAS CITIZENSHIP; BRITISH SUBJECT; BRITISH NATIONAL (OVERSEAS).

nationalized industries Industries that have by statute been taken into public ownership as *corporations. They are administered by ministerially appointed boards (rather than by government departments). The minister controls and is accountable to Parliament for matters of general policy, but the day-to-day affairs of the industries are managed by the boards alone and are not subject to detailed parliamentary scrutiny. Nationalized industries in the UK have been progressively returned to the private sector through *privatization, mainly by being floated on the Stock Exchange as *public companies.

national treatment standard The doctrine that a state is only bound to treat aliens and their property in the same way as it would treat its own citizens. Opposed to the *international minimum standard, it is seen by its proponents (originally Latin American countries) as counteracting the attempts of economically and politically powerful Western states to use international law to impose their will on less well-developed states. Its effect, however, has been to expose foreign nationals to objectionable standards in states that regularly maltreat their own nationals.

natural child **1.** An illegitimate child (*see* ILLEGITIMACY). Until 1969 a gift by will to one's "children" was presumed to exclude natural (illegitimate) children, but there is now a presumption that it does include them. **2.** A child of one's body, as opposed to an adopted child.

naturalization *n.* The legal process by which a person acquires a new nationality. In the UK, *British citizenship or *British Dependent Territories citizenship is acquired by means of a certificate of naturalization. This is granted by the Secretary of State to an applicant who has satisfied statutory requirements as to residence and other matters and taken an *oath of allegiance.

natural justice Rules of fair play, originally developed by the courts of equity to control the decisions of inferior courts and then gradually extended (particularly in the 20th century) to apply equally to the decisions of administrative and domestic tribunals and of any authority exercising an *administrative power that affects a person's status, rights, or liabilities. Any decision reached in contravention of natural justice is void as *ultra vires. There are two principal rules. The first is the **rule against bias** (i.e. against departure from the standard of even-handed justice required of those who occupy judicial office) – **nemo judex in causa sua** (or **in propria causa**) (no man may be a judge in his own cause). This means that any decision, however fair it may seem, is invalid if made by a person with any financial or other interest in the outcome or any known bias that might have affected his impartiality. The second rule is known as **audi alteram partem** (hear the other side). It states that a decision cannot stand unless the person directly affected by it was given a fair opportunity both to state his case and to know and answer the other side's case.

natural law The permanent underlying basis of all law. The philosophers of ancient Greece, where the idea of natural law originated, considered that there was a kind of perfect justice given to man by nature and that man's laws should conform to this as closely as possible. Theories of natural law have been an important part of jurisprudence throughout legal history. Natural law is distinguished from **positive law**, which is the body of law imposed by the state. Natural law is both anterior and superior to positive law.

natural person A human being. *Compare* JURISTIC PERSON.

natural rights 1. (in *natural law) **a.** Rights conferred on all individuals by the natural law. **b.** The fundamental rights found in civilized nations to which all men are entitled without interference by the state. This concept of natural law was particularly popular in the 18th century. It has had great influence in the legal history of the USA, as seen, for example, in the Virginian Declaration of Rights: "All men are by nature equally free and independent and have certain inherent natural rights of which when they enter a society they cannot by any compact deprive or divest their posterity". *See also* HUMAN RIGHTS. **2.** (in land law) Rights automatically belonging to a landowner, violation of which constitutes an actionable *nuisance. The most obvious and important of these is the landowner's right to enjoy his land in its natural state and not to have support for it eroded by the activities of his neighbours (for example through excavation or quarrying operations). This right relates to the land rather than to buildings on it, although damages for infringing the natural right of support may reflect the damage done to buildings on the land affected by the neighbours' activities. A natural right to water may exist if it flows naturally through the landowner's property via a defined channel. *Compare* EASEMENT.

naval court A court formerly convened under the Merchant Shipping Act 1894 either by the captain of one of HM ships on foreign station or by a consular officer. Its purpose was to inquire into the abandonment or loss of any British ship, any complaint by an officer or seaman of such a ship, or any other matter requiring investigation in the interests of the owners of the ship or its cargo. It reported to the Department of Trade and Industry and had limited disciplinary powers. A naval court consisted of three to five members, each of whom was either a naval officer, the master of a British merchant ship, a consular officer, or a British merchant (each of the first three of these categories being represented if possible).

Inquiries into the fitness or conduct of an officer are now governed by the Merchant Shipping Act 1995, at the instigation of the Secretary of State. Inquiries are held in public and are conducted by a lawyer or judge, assisted by one or more assessors appointed by the Lord Chancellor. The person appointed to hear the inquiry is required to announce his decision at the end of the inquiry and to make a report to the Secretary of State. The inquiry may cancel or suspend any certificate of competence issued to the officer concerned, or censure him, if satisfied that he did not act to the standards required of him.

naval law *See* SERVICE LAW.

naval property Any chattel belonging to the Crown that is issued, or stored for the purpose of being issued when required, for naval purposes. *Compare* MILITARY STORES.

navigation *n.* **1.** The science of directing the course of a vessel or aircraft. Loss occasioned by **improper navigation** may arise even though a vessel is moored. **2.** A right to navigate inland waters.

necessaries *pl. n.* Goods or services suitable to the condition in life and actual requirements of a minor or a person subject to incapacity, e.g. essential clothing. Although such a person's legal *capacity to contract is limited, he must pay a reasonable price for necessaries sold and delivered to him.

necessary in a democratic society An expression set out in a number of the articles of the *European Convention on Human Rights: it makes that particular right a *qualified right and provides a signatory state with a defence of *proportionality.

necessity *n.* Pressure of circumstances compelling one to commit an illegal act. The extent to which English law accepts a defence of necessity to a criminal charge is unclear (*compare* DURESS; SELF-DEFENCE). There have, however, been acquittals on this basis when (1) a prisoner escaped from a burning gaol; and (2) the crew of a ship jettisoned the cargo (not belonging to them) to save the ship from sinking. The House of Lords has also recently ruled that a surgeon may have a defence of necessity if he operates in order to save life. Necessity is not, however, a defence to charges of theft or murder (for example when ship-wrecked victims kill and eat one of their number) and it is not usually a defence to driving offences. The definitions of some statutory offences incorporate such expressions as "unlawfully" or "without lawful authority or excuse" and so should admit necessity defences. Other statutory provisions (1) authorize police and fire officers, if necessary, to break into premises when a fire has broken out and do everything necessary to extinguish it; and (2) provide qualified exemption from compliance with traffic lights for fire engines, ambulances, and police vehicles.

Necessity is in some circumstances a defence to an action in tort, but it is probably limited to action taken to protect life or property in an emergency not caused by the defendant's negligence. The steps taken in the emergency must be reasonable.

negative clearance The procedure by which the European Commission determines that an agreement notified to it under the competition rules of the Treaty of Rome does not infringe the rules (*see* COMPETITION LAW). Alternatively, for agreements that infringe the rules, *block exemption may be granted. Most notifications contain an application for both negative clearance and, if the Commission determines that the rules apply, a block exemption.

negative pregnant An evasive reply to an allegation in a statement of case, which – while being a literal response – in fact evades the true matter at issue. For example, if A denies that he received £1000 from B, this is a negative pregnant if he in fact received a lesser amount and the matter at issue was that he received money from B. *Compare* AFFIRMATIVE PREGNANT.

negative resolution *See* DELEGATED LEGISLATION.

neglect *n.* It is a criminal offence for a parent or guardian to neglect their child in a way that is likely to cause unnecessary suffering or injury to health, when the parent is aware of (or reckless as to) the likely consequences of the neglect. Neglect may also be evidence of *negligence and may give rise to a charge of manslaughter if the neglected person dies.

negligence *n.* **1.** Carelessness amounting to the culpable breach of a duty: failure to do something that a reasonable man (i.e. an average responsible citizen) would do, or doing something that a reasonable man would not do. In cases of professional negligence, involving someone with a special skill, that person is expected to show the skill of an average member of his profession. Negligence may be an element in a few crimes, e.g. *careless and inconsiderate driving, and various regulatory offences, which are usually punished by fine. The main example of a serious crime that may be committed by negligence is *manslaughter (in one of its forms). When negligence is a basis of criminal liability, it is no defence to show that one was doing one's best if one's conduct still falls below that of the reasonable man in the circumstances. *See also* GROSS NEGLIGENCE. **2.** A tort consisting of the breach of a *duty of care resulting in damage to the claimant. Negligence in the sense of carelessness does not give rise to civil liability unless the defendant's failure to conform to the standards of the reasonable man was a breach of a duty of care owed to the claimant, which has caused damage to him. Negligence can be used to bring a civil action when there is no contract under which proceedings can be brought. Normally it is easier to sue for *breach of contract, but this is only possible when a contract exists. Generally, fewer heads of damage can be claimed in negligence than in breach of contract, but the rules limiting the time within which actions can be brought (*see* LIMITATION OF ACTIONS) may be more advantageous for actions in tort for negligence than for actions in contract. *See also* CONTRIBUTORY NEGLIGENCE; RES IPSA LOQUITUR.

negligent misstatement (negligent misrepresentation, careless statement) A false statement of fact made honestly but carelessly. A statement of opinion may be treated as a statement of fact if it carries the implication that the person making it has reasonable grounds for his opinion. A negligent misstatement is only actionable in tort if there has been breach of a duty to take care in making the statement that has caused damage to the claimant. There is no general *duty of care in making statements, particularly in relation to statements on financial matters. Responsibility for negligent misstatements is imposed only if they were made in circumstances that made it reasonable to rely on them. If a negligent misstatement induces the person to whom it was made to enter into a contract with the maker of the statement, the statement may be actionable as a term of the contract if the parties intended it to be a term or it may give rise to damages or *rescission under the Misrepresentation Act 1967 (*see also* MISREPRESENTATION).

negotiable instrument A document that constitutes an obligation to pay a sum of money and is transferable by delivery so that the holder for the time can sue upon it in his own name. The transferee can enforce the obligation even if the transferor's title is defective, provided that he accepted the document in good faith and for value and had no notice of the defect. The most important classes of negotiable instruments are *bills of exchange (including cheques) and *promissory notes.

negotiation *n.* (in international law) A diplomatic procedure by which representatives of states, either by direct personal contact or through correspondence, engage in discussing matters of mutual concern and attempt to resolve disputes that have arisen in relations between themselves.

negotiation of a bill The transfer of a *bill of exchange from one person to another so that the transferee becomes the holder. A bill payable to bearer is negotiated by *delivery; a bill payable to order is negotiated by the *endorsement of the holder completed by delivery. The issue of a bill to the payee is not a negotiation.

nemo dat quod non habet [Latin: no one can give what he has not got] The basic rule that a person who does not own property (e.g. a thief) cannot confer it on another except with the true owner's authority (i.e. as his agent). Exceptions to this rule include sales under statutory powers and cases in which the doctrine of *estoppel prevents the true owner from denying the authority of the seller to sell.

nemo debet bis vexari [Latin: no man ought to be twice vexed] No person should be twice sued or prosecuted upon the same set of facts if there has been a final decision of a competent court. The maxim reflects the policy underlying the doctrine of *estoppel *per rem judicatam* and *issue estoppel.

nemo est heres viventis [Latin: no one is the heir of a living person] A maxim stating that a person's *heir can be ascertained only at the time of his death, since until then his heir apparent may die or be disinherited. Thus an heir apparent has no legal or equitable interest in property he expects to inherit until it actually devolves upon him.

nemo judex in causa sua (nemo judex in propria causa) *See* NATURAL JUSTICE.

nemo tenetur seipsum accusare [Latin: no one is bound to incriminate himself] A maxim reflecting the policy underlying the *privilege against self-incrimination.

nervous shock A recognizable psychiatric illness caused by shock, as distinct from normal grief, sorrow, or anxiety. Those involved in an accident, who are known as **primary victims**, can recover damages for shock. Recovery by others (e.g. relatives of the accident victims), known as **secondary victims**, is strictly limited.

neutrality *n.* The legal status of a state that adopts a position of impartiality toward two other states who are at war with each other. The impartial state accords recognition of the state of belligerency between the two warring parties and this, in turn, creates rights and duties that fall upon all concerned.

neutralization *n.* The guarantee of the independence and political and territorial integrity of (usually) a small power by a collective agreement of great powers, subject to the condition that it will not take up arms against another state, except in self-defence, or enter into any treaty that may compromise its neutrality.

new trial (retrial) A second trial of a case ordered by an appellate court. In civil cases the Court of Appeal may order a new trial on grounds including misconduct by the judge (such as a serious misdirection), serious procedural irregularity, or (in rare cases) because fresh evidence has come to light. In criminal cases new trials are rarely ordered, but the former requirement that the appeal had to be based upon the admission of fresh evidence has been abolished. *See also* VENIRE DE NOVO.

next friend *See* LITIGATION FRIEND.

next of kin A person's closest blood relations. Parents and children (including those of unmarried parents) are treated as being closer than grandparents, grandchildren, or siblings.

NGO *See* NONGOVERNMENTAL ORGANIZATION.

NHS *See* NATIONAL HEALTH SERVICE.

NHS Trust A self-governing body within the *National Health Service that operates a local hospital. NHS Trusts, which are independent of *Health Authority control, have their own budgets and are responsible for their own policies and priorities.

nisi *adj.* [Latin] Not final or absolute. *See also* DECREE NISI.

no case to answer A submission by the defending party in a court action that the claimant's or prosecution's case is not sufficient for the defendant to need to make any reply, either because of insufficient legal grounds or because of insufficient factual evidence. If the submission succeeds, judgment is entered for the defence.

no-fault compensation A scheme based on the principle that injured persons should receive compensation for their injuries without having to prove fault against any individual. The term is American in origin, and in the USA and Canada it usually refers to compensation schemes for injuries occurring in highway accidents. New Zealand introduced a comprehensive no-fault compensation scheme for personal injuries caused by accident in 1974, which replaced actions in tort for personal injuries, but the scope of the original scheme has since been reduced. In the UK, industrial disablement benefit is a form of no-fault compensation.

noise *n. See* NUISANCE; NUISANCE NEIGHBOURS.

nolle prosequi [Latin: to be unwilling to prosecute] A procedure by which the *Attorney General may terminate criminal proceedings. The entry of a *nolle prosequi* automatically terminates criminal proceedings on *indictment, but the leave of the court is required in the case of a *summary trial. The procedure is most commonly employed when the accused cannot be produced in court to plead or stand his trial owing to physical or mental incapacity that is expected to be permanent. It is also sometimes used when the Attorney General considers that a prosecution is not in the public interest. His decision is not subject to any control by the courts. Unlike an acquittal, a *nolle prosequi* does not bar a further prosecution.

nominal capital *See* AUTHORIZED CAPITAL.

nominal damages A token sum of *damages awarded when a legal right has been infringed but no substantial loss has been caused.

nomination *n.* **1.** The naming of a person for a vacant post or office or as a candidate in a parliamentary or local-government election. **2.** The naming by a member of a friendly society of a person to take his interest in the society on his death, without the need for a formal will. The member must be 16 or over and the nomination must be made in writing; it may be revoked at any time by the member himself and is, in any event, revoked on his marriage.

nominee shareholder A company member who holds the shares registered in his name for the benefit of another. The identity of the person with the true interest may be subject to disclosure and to investigation under the Companies Act.

nonage *n.* The period during which someone is under the age of majority (18 years). *See* INFANT.

noncohabitation order An order made by magistrates relieving a wife of the duty of living with her husband. Since 1978 noncohabitation orders have been abolished, but orders made before 1978 may still be of relevance in *divorce proceedings.

noncommercial agreement A *consumer-credit agreement or a *consumer-hire agreement that is made by a creditor or owner but not in the course of a business carried on by him. Such an agreement is outside certain of the provisions of the Consumer Credit Act 1974.

noncontentious business Any business of a solicitor that is not *contentious business, i.e. it is business of a nonlitigious character.

nondisclosure *n.* **1. (concealment)** (in contract law) The failure by one party, during negotiations for a contract, to disclose to the other a fact known to him that would influence the other in deciding whether or not to enter into the contract. A full duty of disclosure exists only in the case of contracts *uberrimae fidei*, which are usually contracts of insurance. If the person to be insured tells an untruth, the contract will (like any other) be voidable for *misrepresentation; if this person also suppresses a material fact, it will be voidable for nondisclosure. In the case of other contracts, there is no general duty to volunteer information and mere silence cannot constitute misrepresentation. There is, however, a very limited duty of disclosure. A person who does volunteer information must not tell only a partial truth and must correct any statement that subsequently becomes to his knowledge untrue; breach of this duty will render the contract voidable for misrepresentation. **2.** (in court procedure) Failure of a party to include a document that should have been disclosed in his list of documents (*see* DISCLOSURE AND INSPECTION OF DOCUMENTS). The other party may seek an order for **specific disclosure** of the document or an order requiring the party making disclosure to verify his list of documents by *affidavit.

nondiscrimination notice Notice served by the Commission for Racial Equality or by the Equal Opportunities Commission requiring an offender who has practised illegal *racial discrimination or *sex discrimination not to commit such acts.

non est factum [Latin, from *non est factum suum*, it is not his deed] A plea that an agreement (originally a deed) mentioned in the statement of case was not the act of the defendant. It can be used as a defence to actions based on *mistakes in documents when the defendant was fundamentally mistaken as to the character or effect of the transaction embodied in the document.

nonfeasance *n.* Failure to perform an act required by law. Until 1961, a highway authority guilty of nonfeasance by failing to carry out repair and maintenance was not liable for injuries caused because of this. It was, however, liable for *misfeasance. The defence of nonfeasance was then abolished by statute, but an authority can plead instead the statutory defence that it took all reasonable care to secure that the highway was not dangerous.

nongovernmental organization (NGO) A private international organization that acts as a mechanism for cooperation among private national groups in both municipal and international affairs, particularly in economic, social, cultural, humanitarian, and technical fields. Under Article 71 of the United Nations Charter, the Economic and Social Council is empowered to make suitable arrangements for consultation with NGOs on matters within its competence.

nonjoinder *n.* A plea in *abatement alleging that the claimant had failed to join all necessary parties in the action. In modern practice this does not cause the action to abate but it can be rectified by *amendment.

nonjury list A list of cases for trial by judge alone in the High Court. *See also* LISTS.

nonmolestation order A wide-ranging order under the Family Law Act 1996 restraining a person (the respondent) from attacking or going near someone associated with the respondent (such as a cohabitant, spouse, or parent) or from otherwise doing what the court orders him not to do. *See also* BATTERED SPOUSE OR COHABITANT; MOLESTATION.

nonprovable debt A debt that cannot be claimed in the course of *bankruptcy proceedings. Examples are *statute-barred debts and debts that cannot be fixed or estimated. *Compare* PROVABLE DEBT.

nonresident parent A parent who is not living with his or her child and who may be liable to pay *child support maintenance. Nonresident parents were formerly known as **absent parents**.

nonsuit *n.* **1.** The withdrawal by a judge of a case from a jury with a verdict being entered in favour of the accused. **2.** Formerly, a claimant's withdrawal from a civil court action.

non-user *n.* The failure to exercise a right over land, which may be extinguished if the non-user continues for a sufficient period. *See* LIMITATION OF ACTIONS.

Northern Ireland Assembly A body established under the Northern Ireland Act 1998. It consists of 108 elected members and has limited primary legislative powers in such areas as agriculture, the environment, economic development, health, education, and social security. *See* DEVOLUTION.

notary (notary public) *n.* A legal practitioner, usually a solicitor, who attests or certifies deeds and other documents and notes or *protests dishonoured bills of exchange. **Ecclesiastical notaries** are usually diocesan registrars and the legal secretaries of bishops; **general notaries** may practise anywhere in England and Wales; and **district notaries** practise in a limited area. Diplomatic and consular officials may exercise notarial functions outside the UK.

not guilty **1.** A denial of the charges by an accused person in court. If there is more than one charge, the accused may plead guilty to some and not guilty to others. **2.** A *verdict finding that an accused person has not committed the offence with which he was charged. However, he may, at the same time, be found guilty of other offences. *See also* ACQUITTAL; INSANITY.

notice *n.* **1.** Knowledge of a fact. A person is said to have *actual notice of anything that he actually knows; *constructive notice of anything that he ought reasonably to know (for example, any fact that he would have discovered if he had made any inquiry that a reasonable man would have made); and *imputed notice of anything of which any agent of his has actual or constructive notice. **2.** (in employment law) Formal notification, given by either of the parties to a contract of employment, that the contract is to be terminated after a specified period. The period of notice to which each party is entitled is governed by the contract, subject to statutory minimum periods if the employee has been continuously employed in the business (*see* CONTINUOUS EMPLOYMENT) for more than four weeks. An employee who has been so employed for up to two years is entitled to a week's notice; one employed for a longer period is entitled to one week's notice for each year's continuous employment up to 12 years. Thus an employee who has been employed for 20 years must be given a statutory minimum of 12 weeks' notice, although his employment contract may entitle him to a longer period, which takes priority. An employee with four weeks' continuous employment must give at least one week's notice of his resignation. An employee whose conduct justifies immediate dismissal is treated as waiving his right to notice, as is an employer whose conduct amounts to *constructive dismissal. A fixed-term contract cannot be terminated by notice unless the contract expressly provides for this. **3.** (in land law) An entry against a registered title that may be lodged by a person with a right or interest in the land comprised in the title. The rights and interests that may be protected by a notice are listed in the Land Registration Act 1925, and a notice must always specify the right or interest it seeks to protect. A notice differs from a *caution or an *inhibition in that dealings with the land affected may still take place, but they will have effect subject to the right or interest protected by the notice. **4.** (in *Community legislation) A nonbinding document. Notices are often issued by the European Commission to explain further details of a competition regulation, for example in relation to exclusive distribution and purchasing agreements, cooperation agreements, subcontracting agreements, agency agreements, and the distinction between cooperative and concentrative *joint ventures. Notices are not binding on the Commission, whereas regulations are; however, in practice it would be very rare for the Commission to depart from policies set out in a notice.

notice of abandonment *See* ABANDONMENT; CONSTRUCTIVE TOTAL LOSS.

notice of discontinuance Notice served by a claimant (or by a defendant in respect of a *counterclaim) voluntarily giving up all or part of a claim. In general, a claimant may discontinue by filing a notice of discontinuance with the court and serving copies on all parties. Discontinuance does not require the permission of the court except in the following circumstances: (1) when an interim injunction has been granted; (2) when an undertaking to the court has been given; (3) when the claimant has received an interim payment; or (4) when there is more than one claimant.

notice of dishonour A notice that must be given by the holder of a *bill of exchange to the drawer and to each endorser when the bill has been dishonoured; any drawer or endorser to whom notice is not given is discharged. The notice must identify the bill and state that it has been dishonoured by nonacceptance or nonpayment. The notice must be given within a reasonable time of the *dishonour (to which strict rules apply). Certain excuses are recognized for failure to give notice or delay.

notice of intended prosecution A written notice issued to someone charged with any of certain specified driving offences stating that he or she will be prosecuted. These offences are: *speeding, *dangerous driving, *careless and inconsiderate driving, *ignoring traffic signals, and leaving a car in a dangerous position (*see* OBSTRUCTION). If the offender was not warned when he committed the offence that he might be prosecuted for it, he cannot normally be subsequently prosecuted unless he is served with either a summons or a notice of intended prosecution within 14 days of committing the offence. If he is prosecuted nonetheless, he may appeal against his conviction. If the notice was posted by registered or recorded mail so that it would normally have arrived within the 14 days, the motorist cannot plead that he did not receive it within that time. It is not necessary to serve a notice of intended prosecution when: (1) an accident happened at the time of the alleged offence owing to the presence on the road of the car involved in the alleged offence; (2) it was not possible to find out the name and address of the accused (or registered owner) in time; or (3) the motorist is charged with *causing death by dangerous or careless driving or *drunken driving.

notice to produce Notice by one party to a civil action requiring another to produce documents in his possession at the trial. If he fails to do so, *secondary evidence of the documents may be given. If there has been *disclosure and inspection of documents, the person making disclosure is deemed to be on notice to produce the documents that he stated were in his possession, custody, or power.

notice to quit The formal notification from a landlord to a tenant (or vice versa) terminating the tenancy on a specified date. The notice must be clear and unambiguous and it must terminate the tenancy in relation to the whole of the rented property: a notice to quit part of the property can be valid only if specifically allowed by the tenancy. When the tenant lives in the rented property, the notice to quit must be in a statutory form that tells the tenant his legal rights. Otherwise no particular form is required for a notice to quit.

The period of notice varies according to the kind of tenancy and any agreement between the parties. In the case of periodic tenancies for which no period has been agreed the following periods apply: a yearly or longer tenancy – six months; a monthly tenancy – one month; a quarterly tenancy – one quarter; a weekly tenancy – one week. The notice must be given so that it expires at the end of one of the periods of the tenancy, for example in a yearly tenancy beginning on 1 January, the notice must expire on 31 December. If tenants have statutory protection this can affect the length of the notice to quit. Thus residential tenants must be given at least four weeks' notice, tenants of *agricultural holdings must be given a year's notice, and tenants of *business tenancies are entitled to at least six months' notice. In these cases a tenant may be entitled to continue in occupation of the rented property even after the notice to quit has expired. If the landlord treats the tenancy as continuing after the notice to quit has expired, a new tenancy may be created.

notice to treat A notice required to be given, under the Compulsory Purchase Act 1965, by an acquiring authority to all persons interested in or having power to sell and convey or release land proposed to be compulsorily acquired (*see* COMPULSORY PURCHASE). The notice must give particulars of the land concerned, demand particulars of the recipient's estate and interest in the land and of his claim in respect of it, and state that the acquiring authority is willing to negotiate for the purchase of the land and regarding compensation payable for damage.

noting a bill *See* PROTEST.

not negotiable Words marked on a crossed cheque indicating that a transferee for value of the cheque gets no better title to it than his transferor had. Since the Cheques Act 1992 most banks have printed cheques that are not negotiable. A bill of exchange so marked is not transferable.

not proven A *verdict used in Scottish courts when the prosecution's case has not reached a sufficient standard of proof to establish the accused person's guilt, but there is some doubt about his innocence. The effect is the same as a not guilty verdict: the accused is released and cannot be tried again for the same offence.

nova causa interveniens *See* NOVUS ACTUS INTERVENIENS.

novation *n.* The substitution of a new contract for one already existing. The new contract may be between the same parties or it may involve the introduction of a new party, as in the case of the substitution of debtors. If A owes B £100 and B owes C £100, novation would occur if all three agreed that the existing debts were to be extinguished and that A is to pay C a new debt of £100. Novation should be distinguished from *assignment of a commercial agreement, in which no new agreement is needed and the benefit of a contract is transferred to the assignee.

novus actus interveniens (***nova causa interveniens***) [Latin: a new intervening act (or cause)] An act or event that breaks the causal connection between a wrong or crime committed by the defendant and subsequent happenings and therefore relieves the defendant from responsibility for these happenings. *See* CAUSATION.

no win, no fee *See* CONDITIONAL FEE AGREEMENT; MAINTENANCE AND CHAMPERTY.

nudum pactum [Latin: naked agreement] *See* CONSIDERATION.

nuisance *n.* An activity or state of affairs that interferes with the use or enjoyment of land or rights over land (**private nuisance**) or with the health, safety, or comfort of the public at large (**public nuisance**). Private nuisance is a tort, protecting occupiers of land from damage to the land, buildings, or vegetation or from unreasonable interference with their comfort or convenience by excessive noise, dust, fumes, smells, etc. An action is only available to persons who have property rights (e.g. owners, lessees) or exclusive occupation. Thus, for example, lodgers and members of a property owner's family cannot sue in private nuisance.

Physical damage is actionable when the damage is of a type that is reasonably foreseeable and provided it does not arise solely because the claimant has put his land to a hypersensitive use. Interference with comfort is actionable when it is considered unreasonable as judged by a number of factors, the most important of which is the nature of the locality. The main remedies are damages and an injunction. Alternatively there is a limited right to abate (i.e. remove) the nuisance.

Public nuisance is a crime. At common law it includes such activities as *obstruction of the highway, carrying on an offensive trade, and selling food unfit for human consumption. The Attorney General or a local authority may bring a civil action for an injunction on behalf of the public but a private citizen may obtain damages in tort only if he can prove some special damage over and above that suffered by the public at large.

Statutory nuisances are created by provisions dealing with noise, public health, and the prevention of pollution and permit a local authority to control neighbourhood nuisances by the issue of an *abatement notice.

The Protection from Harassment Act 1997 enables individuals to be prevented from harassing their neighbours (*see* NUISANCE NEIGHBOURS).

nuisance neighbours People who disturb the lives of those living nearby by interfering with their *quiet enjoyment of their homes. The Protection from Harassment Act 1997 provides enhanced protection for those suffering *nuisance (including noise) from their neighbours. Restraining orders can be obtained, which require the offender to do what the court orders (e.g. not to communicate, go near, or harass their neighbours); in some circumstances *eviction may be ordered. Offenders threatening violence can be jailed for up to five years and/or be subjected to an unlimited fine; even if the harassment does not give rise to fear for safety, the offender faces up to six months in jail and/or a fine of up to £5000.

nulla poena sine lege [Latin: no punishment without a law] The principle that a person can only be punished for a crime if the *punishment is prescribed by law. The punishment may be specified by a statute as a term of imprisonment or fine or it may be based on common-law principles. With the exception of treason and murder, for which the punishment is fixed, all statutory punishments are expressed in terms of the maximum possible punishment; judges have discretion to impose a lesser punishment according to the circumstances. At common law punishment is said to be **at large**, i.e. the amount of the fine or length of the prison sentence is entirely at the judge's discretion. In many cases, however, there are now statutes specifying the maximum punishment for common-law offences. Magistrates' courts are subject to shorter maxima than Crown courts; they are also usually subject to a minimum sentence of five days in cases of imprisonment.

nullity of marriage The invalidity of a marriage due to some defect existing at the time the marriage was celebrated (or, sometimes, arising afterwards). A marriage may be null in the sense that it is **void**, i.e. it was never in the eyes of the law a valid marriage (and the "spouses" are legally merely cohabitants). It may alternatively be **voidable**, i.e. valid until made void by a court decree of *annulment, which (since 1971) does not end the marriage retrospectively (so that, for example, the children of a marriage that is annulled will not be regarded as illegitimate). The form of decree, however, always states that the marriage "is and has been null and void". The main grounds for nullity are: close relationship, lack of age, lack of consent, and nonconsummation (*see* CONSUMMATION OF A MARRIAGE). When granting a decree of nullity the court has wide discretionary powers to make orders for *financial provision or *property adjustment. *See also* LEGITIMACY.

nullum crimen sine lege [Latin: no crime without a law] The principle that conduct does not constitute crime unless it has previously been declared to be so by the law; it is sometimes known as the **principle of legality**. Some serious offences are well-defined common-law offences (although the details relating to their definition may often be unclear until ruled upon by the judges); many regulatory offences (e.g. those involving road traffic and the manufacture of products) are constantly being created by statute. The principle is violated by the power occasionally attributed to judges to create new offences in order to punish morally harmful conduct (such as *conspiracy to outrage public decency).

nunc pro tunc [Latin: now instead of then] A phrase used of a judgment that is entered in such a way as to have legal effect from an earlier date.

nuncupative will An oral statement directing how property is to be distributed after death. Except in the case of *privileged wills and *donatio mortis causa*, such statements have no effect in English law.

oath *n.* A pronouncement swearing the truth of a statement or promise, usually by an appeal to God to witness its truth. An oath is required by law for various purposes, in particular for *affidavits and giving evidence in court. The usual **witness's oath** is: "I swear by Almighty God that the evidence which I shall give shall be the truth, the whole truth and nothing but the truth". Those who object to swearing an oath, on the grounds that to do so is contrary to their religious beliefs or that they have no religious beliefs, may instead *affirm.

oath of allegiance An oath to be faithful and bear true allegiance to the Crown. It is taken by members of both Houses at the opening of every new Parliament, by certain officers of the Crown on their appointment, and by those who become British citizens, British Dependent Territories citizens, British Overseas citizens or British subjects by registration, or British citizens or British Dependent Territories citizens by naturalization.

obiter dictum [Latin: a remark in passing] Something said by a judge while giving judgment that was not essential to the decision in the case. It does not form part of the *ratio decidendi* of the case and therefore creates no binding precedent, but may be cited as *persuasive authority in later cases.

objection in point of law A form of pleading by a defendant in his defence that raises an issue of law. When such an objection is raised the court may order the issue to be tried as a *preliminary point of law.

objection to indictment A procedure in which the accused in a *trial on indictment attempts to prove some objection to the indictment on legal grounds (e.g. that it contravenes, or fails to comply with, an enactment). The objection is raised by application to quash the indictment.

objects clause *See* MEMORANDUM OF ASSOCIATION; ULTRA VIRES.

objects of a power Persons in whose favour a *power of appointment may be exercised, i.e. potential appointees.

obligation *n.* **1.** A legal duty. **2.** A *bond by deed.

obliteration *n.* The deletion of words in a will. An obliteration is valid only if the words deleted are indecipherable or if the alteration is properly signed and witnessed.

obscene publications Material that tends to deprave or corrupt. Under the Obscene Publications Acts 1959 and 1964 it is an offence to publish an obscene article or to have an obscene article for publication for gain. For the purposes of the Acts, obscenity is not limited to pornographic or sexually corrupting material: a book advocating drug taking or violence, for instance, may be obscene. Whether or not particular material is obscene is a question of fact in each case, to be decided by the jury, and expert evidence is not usually permitted. Material that merely tends to shock or disgust is not obscene. The intention or motive of the author in writing or depicting the material is irrelevant.

"Publishing" an obscene article includes distributing, circulating, giving, hiring, or lending the article, offering it for sale or hire (the latter does not include displaying such material in a shop, which is merely an invitation to treat and not an offer), or transmitting it through the telephone system by means of a modem. An "article" may be material that is to be looked at or played over, rather than read, and can also include, for instance, a negative of a film or any article used to reproduce material to be read or looked at. This offence is one of *strict liability, but there is a defence of **lack of knowledge**, if the defendant can show he had not examined the article and had no reason to suspect that publishing it would constitute an offence. There is also a special defence of **public good**, which applies when the defendant shows that publication of the article was justified as being in the interests of science, literature, art, or learning. The offence of possessing an obscene article in the expectation that it will be published for financial gain is also subject to the defences of lack of knowledge and public good. If a magistrate suspects that obscene articles are kept in any premises for this purpose, he may issue a warrant authorizing the police to search for and seize the articles. If they prove to be obscene, the magistrate may order them to be forfeited.

The Acts do not apply to material published by means of television or broadcasting, but they do apply to cinema screening and theatre performances, subject to the rule that prosecutions in such cases require the consent of the Director of Public Prosecutions or the Attorney General, respectively. These offences, too, are subject to the public good defence.

There are also various special offences relating to obscenity, e.g. publishing obscene advertisements, sending unasked for material describing sexual techniques, or sending through the post any "indecent or obscene article" (the latter offence is limited to sexual obscenity, but also includes material that is merely indecent). It is an offence to take, make, distribute, or possess indecent photographs or pseudo-photographs of a child; a "pseudo-photograph" is an image, created by computer graphics or any other means, that resembles a photograph and can include electronically stored data that can be converted into such images. These offences are *arrestable offences, which may be tried either summarily or on *indictment and attract a sentence of up to six months' imprisonment and/or a fine on level 5.

obscene telephone calls It is a *summary offence to make an obscene, offensive, or annoying telephone call. The maximum punishment is three months' imprisonment and/or a *fine on level 5.

obstructing a police officer The offence of hindering a police officer who is in the course of doing his duty. "Obstruction" includes any intentional interference, e.g. by physical force, threats, telling lies or giving misleading information, refusing to cooperate in removing an obstruction, or warning a person who has committed a crime so that he can escape detection (e.g. warning a speeding driver that there is a police trap ahead). It is not, however, an offence merely not to answer, or to advise someone not to answer, police questions that he does not have to answer. A police officer is acting in the course of his duty if he is preventing or detecting crime (in particular, breaches of the peace) or obeying the orders of his superiors. However, he is not acting in the course of his duty when he is merely assisting the public in some way unconnected with crime. When the obstruction amounts to an *assault, the offence is punishable by imprisonment and/or a fine. One may be guilty of this offence even if the police officer was in plain clothes. There is no power of arrest unless accompanied by a breach of the peace.

obstruction n. The offence of causing or allowing a motor vehicle, trailer, or other object to stand on a road in such a way that it is likely to impede other road users or to use a vehicle on the road in a similar way (e.g. by driving unreasonably slowly). It is unnecessary to show that any other vehicle or person has in fact been obstructed. This offence is punishable by a fine. It is also an offence to leave a motor vehicle on a road in such a position or in such circumstances that it is likely to cause danger to other road users. This offence requires a *notice of intended prosecution and is punishable by a fine, *endorsement (which carries 3 penalty points under the *totting-up system), and discretionary *disqualification.

obstruction of recovery of premises *See* RECOVERY OF PREMISES.

occupation *n.* **1.** (in land law) The physical possession and control of land. Under the Land Registration Act 1925 the proprietary rights of a person in actual occupation may be an *overriding interest binding a purchaser of registered land, unless inquiry is made of that person and the rights are not disclosed. Under the Family Law Act 1996, spouses have rights of occupation in the *matrimonial home by virtue of marriage, which may be capable of protection as *land charges. **2.** (in international law) The act of taking control of territory belonging either to no one (**peaceful occupation**) or to a foreign state in the course of a war (**belligerent occupation**). Peaceful occupation is one of the methods of legally acquiring territory, provided the occupier can show a standard of control superior to that of any other claimant. Denmark acquired Greenland in this way, and the UK acquired Rockall. A belligerent occupant cannot acquire or annex the occupied territory during the course of the war. Certain provisions for the protection of enemy civilians in the Hague and Geneva Conventions are applied to those parts of the enemy territory that have been effectively occupied. A belligerent occupier must retain in force the ordinary penal laws and tribunals of the occupied power, but may alter them or impose new laws to ensure the security and orderly government of the occupying forces and administration. The government in exile is also regarded as continuing to represent the occupied state in international law without any special *recognition being necessary. *See also* CESSION; SUCCESSION.

occupation order Any of various orders under the Family Law Act 1996 relating to occupation of the *matrimonial home in cases of domestic violence. The orders can enforce the rights of co-owning spouses or spouses with *matrimonial home rights to occupy the home and provide for the exclusion of the respondent from the home or from any part of it. The orders can also extend similar rights to nonowning ex-spouses, whether or not they are actually in occupation, and also – under certain circumstances – to cohabitants or ex-cohabitants. *See also* BATTERED SPOUSE OR COHABITANT.

occupier *n.* A person in possession of land or buildings as owner, tenant, or trespasser. If he is a trespasser he may obtain a right to lawful occupation if the owner accepts money from him as rent, in which case a tenancy may be created, or through *adverse possession for a sufficient period.

occupier's liability The liability of an occupier of land or premises to persons on the land for the condition of the premises and things done there. The occupier for this purpose is the person or persons exercising control over the premises. At common law the extent of an occupier's liability varied according to whether the person on the land entered under a contract, as an *invitee, as a *licensee, or as a trespasser. The common law rules have been replaced by statutes. The English statutes distinguish between visitors and other persons on land. The Occupiers' Liability Act 1957 imposes on an occupier a *common duty of care to all his visitors (i.e. those who enter by his invitation or with his permission) to see that they will be reasonably safe in using the premises for the purpose for which they were invited or permitted to be there. Under the Occupiers' Liability Act 1984, an occupier only owes a duty to persons other than visitors (i.e. trespassers and persons who enter lawfully but without the occupier's permission) if the occupier is aware or has reasonable grounds to know of a danger on the premises and that a person may be in the vicinity of the danger and the risk is one against which he may reasonably be expected to offer some protection. The duty, if any, is confined to taking such care as is reasonable in all the circumstances to see that the danger does not cause death or personal injury to the person concerned. The duty may be discharged by taking such steps as are reasonable to give warning of the danger or to discourage persons from incurring the risk.

In Scotland, the Occupiers' Liability (Scotland) Act 1960 requires an occupier to show to *all* persons entering the premises such care as is reasonable in all the circumstances of the case.

occupying tenant A person in possession of premises in accordance with his rights under a lease or tenancy agreement, or as a *statutory tenant, assured agricultural occupier, or a *protected occupier, or under his rights as a tenant with a *restricted contract.

offence *n.* A *crime. The modern tendency is to refer to crimes as offences. Offences may be classified as *indictable or *summary and as *arrestable or nonarrestable.

offences against international law and order Crimes that affect the proper functioning of international society. Some authorities regard so-called international crimes as crimes of individuals that all or most states are bound by treaty to punish in accordance with national laws passed for that purpose. Examples of this type of crime are *piracy, *hijacking, and *war crimes. The International Law Commission has formulated Draft Articles on State Responsibility, which attempt to define international crimes for which individual states are liable. It gives as examples: (1) a serious breach of an international obligation essential to safeguard international peace (e.g. aggression) or peoples' rights to self-determination (e.g. colonial domination by force); (2) a widespread and serious breach of obligations essential to safeguard individuals (e.g. slavery, *genocide, or apartheid) or the environment (e.g. massive pollution).

offences against property Crimes that affect another person's rights of ownership (or in some cases possession or control). The main offences against property are *theft, offences of *deception and *making off without payment, *criminal damage, *arson, *forgery, and *forcible entry. Some offences against property, such as *burglary, *robbery, and *blackmail, may also contain elements of *offences against the person.

offences against public order Crimes that affect the smooth running of orderly society. The main offences against public order are *riot, *violent disorder, *affray, *threatening behaviour, stirring up *racial hatred, public *nuisance, and *obstruction of highways. *See also* RAVE; TRESPASS.

offences against the person Crimes that involve the use or threat of physical force against another person. The main offences against the person are *homicide, *infanticide, illegal *abortion, *causing death by dangerous driving, and *causing death by careless driving (fatal offences against the person); and *torture, *rape, *wounding, causing or inflicting *grievous bodily harm, *assault, aggravated assault, *battery, *kidnapping, and offences involving *indecency (nonfatal offences against the person). *See also* POISON.

offences against the state Crimes that affect the security of the state as a whole. The main offences against the state are *treason and *misprision of treason, *sedition (and incitement to *mutiny), offences involving *official secrets, and acts of *terrorism.

offences relating to road traffic Crimes that are associated with driving vehicles on public roads and related acts. The main offences in this category are *careless and inconsiderate driving, *causing death by careless driving, *dangerous driving, *causing death by dangerous driving, *drunken driving, *driving while disqualified, *driving without insurance, *driving without a licence, *speeding, *ignoring traffic signals, *parking offences, and *obstruction. Some road traffic offences require *notice of intended prosecution. Road traffic offences carry various penalties or combinations of penalties, such as fines, *endorsement of driving licence, *disqualification from driving, and in some circumstances imprisonment. The court may also make a *driving-test order. Many road traffic offences (especially the minor ones) are offences of *strict liability. *See also* DRIVING LICENCE; MOT TEST; ROAD TRAFFIC ACCIDENTS; ROAD TAX; SEAT BELT; VEHICLE CONSTRUCTION AND MAINTENANCE.

offences triable either way Crimes that may be tried either as an *indictable offence or a *summary offence. These include offences of deception, theft, bigamy, and sexual intercourse with a girl under the age of 16.

When an offence is triable either way, the magistrates' court must decide, on hearing the initial facts of the case, if it should be tried on indictment rather than summarily (for example, because it appears to be a serious case). Even if they decide that they can deal with the matter adequately themselves, they must give the defendant the choice of opting for trial upon indictment before a jury. There are three exceptional cases, however. (1) If the prosecution is being conducted by or on behalf of the Attorney General, Solicitor General, or Director of Public Prosecutions, and they apply for trial on indictment, the case must be tried on indictment. (2) If the case concerns criminal damage or any offences connected with criminal damage (except arson), and the damage appears to be less than £400, the case must be tried summarily. (3) If the defendant is a child or young person, he must be tried summarily unless: (a) he is charged with homicide; (b) he is charged jointly with someone over 17, and it would be better if they were tried together; or (c) he is aged between 14 and 17 and charged with an offence punishable by 14 years' imprisonment or more, and the court thinks that he should be sentenced to a long period of detention.

offender *n.* One who has committed a *crime. *See also* FIRST OFFENDER; FUGITIVE OFFENDER; JUVENILE OFFENDER; REPEAT OFFENDER.

offensive weapon Any object that is made, adapted, or intended to be used to cause physical injury to a person. Examples of objects made to cause injury are revolvers, coshes, and daggers; objects adapted to cause injury include bottles deliberately broken to attack someone with and sawn-off shotguns. In theory any object may be intended to be used to cause injury, but articles commonly intended for such use include sheath knives (or any household knife), pieces of wood, and stones.

It is an offence under the Prevention of Crime Act 1953 to have an offensive weapon in one's possession in a public place. This offence is punishable summarily by up to six months' imprisonment and/or a *fine at level 5 on the standard scale or on indictment with up to two years' imprisonment and/or a fine, and the court may order the weapon to be forfeited. There are special exceptions for those (such as soldiers or police officers) who carry offensive weapons in the course of duty and in cases of "reasonable excuse", but the defendant must prove that he comes within these categories. Self-defence is not usually a reasonable excuse unless there is an imminent and particular threat.

It is also an offence (finable only), under the Criminal Justice Act 1988, to possess in a public place a bladed or sharply pointed article (other than a folding penknife with a blade of three inches or less). Here, it is a defence to prove that the article was for use at work, for religious reasons (e.g. a Sikh's dagger), or part of a national costume, or that there was authority or good reason for its possession. The 1988 Act also gives the Home Secretary power to prohibit the manufacture, sale, hire, and importation of certain offensive weapons.

See also FIREARM; WEAPON OF OFFENCE; PROHIBITED WEAPON.

offer *n.* An indication of willingness to do or refrain from doing something that is capable of being converted by *acceptance into a legally binding *contract. It is made by an **offeror** to an **offeree** and is capable of acceptance only by an offeree who knows of its existence. Thus, a person giving information cannot claim a reward if he did not know that a reward was being offered. An offer must be distinguished from an **invitation to treat**, which is an invitation to others to make offers, as by displaying goods in a shop window; and a **declaration of intention**, which is a mere statement of intent to invite offers in the future, as by advertising an auction. *See also* LAPSE OF OFFER; REJECTION OF OFFER; REVOCATION OF OFFER.

office copy An exact copy of an official document, supplied and marked as such by the office that holds or issues the original. Office copies are generally admissible in evidence to the same extent as the original. Thus office copies of entries recorded at HM Land Registry are used in *conveyancing as evidence of title to registered land, and an office copy grant of probate may be used to prove an executor's right to receive or deal with the deceased's assets.

Office for the Supervision of Solicitors (OSS) The body that deals with complaints about solicitors; it was previously called the **Solicitors Complaints Bureau**.

Office of Fair Trading *See* DIRECTOR GENERAL OF FAIR TRADING.

Official Custodian for Charities A corporation sole created by the Charities Act 1960 for the purpose of acting as a custodian trustee of property held for charitable purposes. It is now governed by the Charities Act 1993 and is currently a member of the Charity Commission staff.

Official Journal (OJ) The official organ of the European Union, usually published every day and in each of the official languages of the EU. It is currently divided into two parts. One part (designated L) contains *Community legislation and bears references in the style "OJ [1997] L 23". The other (designated C) contains proposals of the European Commission, reports of proceedings in the European Parliament, notices concerning matters in the European Court, and other matters of general information; it carries references in the style "OJ [1997] C 23". There is a daily supplement containing publication of notices of public works and supply contracts and invitations to tender (*see* PUBLIC PROCUREMENT). The *OJ* can be bought from The Stationery Office and is published daily on the Internet.

Official Petitioner The *Director of Public Prosecutions when acting in respect of an application for a criminal bankruptcy order under the Powers of Criminal

Courts Act 1973. The power to issue such orders was abolished by the Criminal
Justice Act 1988.

official receiver The person appointed by the Department of Trade and Industry
who acts in *bankruptcy matters as interim receiver and manager of the estate of
the debtor, presides at the first meeting of creditors, and takes part in the debtor's
public examination. In the *compulsory winding-up of a company, he often becomes
*provisional liquidator when a winding-up order is made.

official referee Until 1972, a judicial officer of the *Supreme Court to whom
certain matters could be referred, usually cases involving prolonged examination of
accounts or large numbers of small items (such as building claims). The office was
abolished by the Courts Act 1971 but the functions previously discharged by official
referees can now be discharged by *circuit judges nominated by the Lord Chancellor
to take **official referees' business**. The official referee's court is now known as the
Technology and Construction Court and official referees as **judges of the
Technology and Construction Court**.

official search A search, in response to an applicant's *requisition, into the
registers of local land charges, the Land Charges Department, or HM Land Registry
(as appropriate) in order to disclose any registered matter relevant to the requisition.
A certificate is issued by the registrar giving details of encumbrances that the
search has revealed. In the case of the land charges register, a purchaser is not
bound by any encumbrance that a proper search fails to reveal, the official search
certificate being conclusive according to its tenor. If an entry is made in the land
charges register after the date of the certificate and before completion of the
purchase (other than in pursuance of a *priority notice entered on the register on
or before the date of the certificate), it will not affect the purchaser if the purchase
is completed within 15 working days after the issue of the certificate.
   In the case of registered land, a purchaser seeking to become the registered
proprietor is only bound by what is on the register and by *overriding interests.
When a purchaser has applied for an official search of the register, his subsequent
application to register the document effecting the purchase of the property
concerned takes precedence over any entry made by a third party in the register
during the priority period (30 days from the time the application for the search was
delivered). Should an official search fail to reveal a registered interest, the newly
registered owner is bound by that interest, but may be entitled to a statutory
idemnity. A local land charge search certificate is valid only at the time it is issued
and a purchaser is bound by any local charge registered subsequently. Since
December 1990 HM Land Registry has been open to public inspection: it is therefore
possible to discover, on payment of a fee, whether any specific property has been or
is about to be registered. The registers of local land charges and the Land Charges
Department are also open to public inspection.

official secrets For the purpose of the Official Secrets Acts 1911–89, information
that is categorized as a secret code or password or is intended to be (or might be)
useful to an enemy. It is an offence to make a sketch, plan, model, or note that
might be useful to an enemy. It is also an offence to obtain, record, or communicate
to anyone else a secret official code or password or any information or document
that is intended to be useful to an enemy. It is also an offence to enter, approach,
inspect, or pass over (e.g. in an aircraft) any prohibited place. Such places include
naval, military, or air-force establishments, national munitions factories or depots,
and any places belonging to or used by the Crown that an enemy would want to

know about. For all three offences the prosecution must prove that the act was done for a purpose that prejudices the safety or interests of the state. Even if no particular prejudicial act can be proved, someone may be convicted if it appears from the circumstances of the case, his conduct, or his known and proven character that his purpose was prejudicial to the interests of the state. There is also a presumption (which may be disproved by the defendant) that any act done within the scope of the three offences without lawful authority is prejudicial to the state's interests. All three offences are punishable by up to 14 years' imprisonment.

It is also an offence under the Official Secrets Act 1911, section 2, for the holder of a Crown office who has any document or information as a result of his position to pass it on to an unauthorized person, keep it, or use it in any other way that prejudices the state's interests. The information need not be secret or confidential and the defendant need not have realized that harm might result from his act. The offence is punishable by up to two years' imprisonment, and anyone who receives the information knowing or suspecting that it was given in breach of the Acts is liable to the same punishment. It is also an offence to attempt to commit, or incite, or aid and abet any of the above offences and to do any act of preparation for any of these offences. All such acts are subject to the same penalties as the offence they relate to. Thus, for example, buying paper in order to sketch a military installation is a preparatory act carrying a sentence of up to 14 years' imprisonment.

The Official Secrets Act 1989 replaces section 2 of the 1911 Act (above) with provisions protecting more limited classes of information from disclosure. A member or former member of the security and intelligence services, or a person notified that he is subject to this provision, commits an offence, punishable with up to two years' imprisonment and/or a fine, if without lawful authority he discloses or purports to disclose any information, document, or other article relating to security or intelligence. Similarly, Crown servants and "government contractors" are prohibited from making disclosures that damage security services' operations, endanger UK interests abroad, or result in the commission of an offence and from negligently failing to prevent such disclosures. Other offences relate to the disclosure by an ordinary citizen of protected information communicated in confidence by a Crown servant.

See also SABOTAGE; SPYING; TREASON.

Official Solicitor An officer of the Supreme Court who, when directed by the court, acts as *litigation friend (next friend) or childrens' guardian for those under a disability who have no one else to act for them; he may also be called upon to intervene and protect the interests of children. He can be appointed *judicial trustee in proceedings relating to disputed trusts.

OJ *See* OFFICIAL JOURNAL.

Old Bailey *See* CENTRAL CRIMINAL COURT.

oligopoly *n.* Control of a market by a small number of suppliers, which may or may not lead to the operation of a *cartel. *Compare* MONOPOLY.

Ombudsman *n. See* COMMISSIONS FOR LOCAL ADMINISTRATION; HOUSING OMBUDSMAN; LEGAL SERVICES OMBUDSMAN; PARLIAMENTARY COMMISSIONER FOR ADMINISTRATION. See also Appendix I.

omission *n.* A failure to act. It is not usually a crime to fail to act; for example, it is not usually a crime to stand by and watch a child who has fallen into a river drown. Sometimes, however, there is a duty on a person to act, either because of the terms of a contractual duty, or because he is a parent or guardian of a minor, or because he has voluntarily assumed a duty (e.g. looking after a disabled relative), or through a statutory imposition of such a duty. In such cases, omission may constitute a crime. Usually this will be a crime of *negligence (e.g. manslaughter, if the victim dies because of the defendant's omission); if it is a deliberate omission with a particular intention (e.g. the intention of starving someone to death) it will amount to murder. *See also* NEGLECT.

Similarly, there is no general liability in the law of tort for failing to act, but there are some situations where the law imposes a duty to take action to prevent harm to others. Thus occupiers of premises are under a duty to see that their visitors are reasonably safe (*see* OCCUPIER'S LIABILITY).

omnia praesumuntur rite et solemniter esse acta *See* PRESUMPTION.

onus of proof *See* BURDEN OF PROOF.

open contract A contract for the sale of land in which the only express terms are the identity of the parties, the property, and the price. An open contract is valid if it is in writing or, for contracts made before the Law of Property (Miscellaneous Provisions) Act 1989 came into force, it is evidenced by writing (*see* MEMORANDUM IN WRITING) or *part performance. Other necessary terms are implied, including: (1) a condition that the vendor must convey an unencumbered freehold title, although the purchaser is bound by any defect of which he knew and which cannot be removed; (2) the vendor must within a reasonable time produce at his own expense an abstract of title beginning with a *root of title at least 15 years old or, in the case of registered land, the documents specified by the Land Registration Act 1925; (3) a condition that the vendor will convey as *beneficial owner; (4) the purchaser must deliver any *requisitions on or objections to the title within a reasonable time after receiving the abstract; (5) the conveyance must be prepared by the purchaser at his own expense; (6) the vendor must give vacant possession on completion; (7) the transaction must be completed within a reasonable time: if it is not, the vendor is entitled to interest on the unpaid price and the purchaser to the income of the property from the time when completion should have occurred.

In the case of contracts made by correspondence, statutory conditions set out in regulations made under the Law of Property Act 1925 apply (*see* STATUTORY FORM OF CONDITIONS OF SALE). A vendor cannot insist on preparing the conveyance himself (a contractual term to this effect is void), but apart from this the implied and statutory conditions may be dispensed with, varied, or supplemented by agreement between the parties. In practice, the forms of contract generally used specify the parties' rights and obligations much more precisely.

opening speech **1.** A speech made by the prosecution counsel at the beginning of a criminal trial, briefly outlining the case against the accused and summarizing the evidence that the prosecution intends to call to prove its case. **2.** The speech made by counsel for the claimant at the beginning of a civil trial.

open procedure *See* PUBLIC PROCUREMENT.

open space An area in a *conservation area so designated by the Secretary of State for the Environment and consequently requiring "special attention" for planning purposes.

operative mistake *See* MISTAKE.

operative part *See* DEED.

operative words The part of a conveyance that effects the essence of the transaction; for example, the words "the Vendor hereby conveys Blackacre to the Purchaser in fee simple". No specific form of words is necessary provided that the intention is clear.

opinio juris [Latin, from *opinio juris sive necessitatis* (whether the opinion of law is compulsory)] An essential element of *custom, one of the four sources of *international law as outlined in the Statute of the *International Court of Justice. *Opinio juris* requires that custom should be regarded as state practice amounting to a legal obligation, which distinguishes it from mere usage.

opinion *n.* **1.** A judgment by the House of Lords. **2. (counsel's opinion)** A barrister's advice on a particular question. **3.** Advice on a case given by an *Advocate General before a final judgment of the *European Court of Justice.

opinion evidence Evidence of the opinions or beliefs of a witness, as opposed to evidence of facts about which he can give admissible evidence. At common law, opinion evidence is in general inadmissible but this rule is subject to many exceptions. Thus a nonexpert witness may testify as to age, speed of vehicles, handwriting, or identity. Expert witnesses (e.g. doctors) may give their opinions on any matter falling within their expertise. At common law, a witness could not give his opinion on an ultimate issue (i.e. the question that the court had to decide) but this rule, which was not very strictly applied in practice, was relaxed in respect of civil cases by the Civil Evidence Act 1972. *See also* HEARSAY EVIDENCE.

option *n.* A right to do or not to do something, usually within a specified time. An enforceable option may be acquired by contract (i.e. for consideration) or by deed to accept or reject an *offer within a specified period. An option to acquire land or an interest in it on specified terms will only bind third parties if it is registered (*see* REGISTRATION OF ENCUMBRANCES). If an option to buy does not specify the price it will only be valid if it specifies a means for determining the price, e.g. by a valuation to be made by a specified third party who is or will be under a duty to act. Thus an option to buy at a price to be agreed is void for uncertainty.

On the London *Stock Exchange, options to sell or to buy quoted securities are purchased for a certain sum of money, which is forfeited if they are not taken up. An option to sell is known as a **put option**, that to buy is a **call option**, and an option to either sell or buy is a **double option**. Under the Companies Act 1985, directors, shadow directors, and the spouses or children of either are prohibited from buying or selling options in the shares of their own company.

optional clause A clause of the Statute of the *International Court of Justice (Article 36(2)) that gives states the opportunity of signing a declaration by which they recognize as compulsory, in relation to any other state accepting the same obligation, the jurisdiction of the Court in all legal disputes concerning certain specified matters. Despite acceptance of the optional clause, it is common for states to append to their acceptance *reservations of their own making. These either concern specific topics that they will not allow the Court to settle or the reservations may, more sweepingly, exclude all matters that states consider to be within their domestic jurisdiction.

option to purchase A right to compel the owner of land to sell it to the option holder on agreed terms. The option constitutes an offer by its grantor that remains open in accordance with the terms of the option, enabling the grantee to accept it. This right binds third parties if entered as an *estate contract on the land charges register if the land is unregistered, or by the appropriate entry on the charges register in registered land. *See* REGISTRATION OF ENCUMBRANCES.

oral agreement A contract made by word of mouth, as opposed to one made in writing. *See also* IMPLIED CONTRACT.

oral evidence Spoken evidence given by a witness in court, usually on *oath. A witness's evidence must usually relate what he knows through the use of his own senses. However, under the Civil Evidence Act 1995 *hearsay evidence in civil cases is now permitted.

orality *n.* The principle that evidence must be given orally and subject to *cross-examination unless *affidavit evidence is admissible.

order *n.* **1.** A direction or command of a court. In this sense it is often used synonymously with *judgment. **2.** The document bearing the seal of the court recording its judgment in a case. **3.** A subdivision of the *Rules of the Supreme Court and the County Court Rules.

order for account An order in civil cases that the amount of money due from one party to another may be investigated. The order may be made before trial. Accounts are usually taken by a master or a referee and are most frequently ordered in partnership and trust matters.

order of discharge A court order resulting in the *discharge of a bankrupt.

Orders in Council Government orders of a legislative character made by the Crown and members of the Privy Council either under statutory powers conferred on Her Majesty in Council (*see* DELEGATED LEGISLATION; STATUTORY INSTRUMENT) or in exercise of the *royal prerogative. *Compare* ORDERS OF COUNCIL.

Orders of Council Orders of a legislative nature made by the Privy Council under statutory powers conferred on the Council alone. They relate mainly to the regulation of certain professions and professional bodies. *See* DELEGATED LEGISLATION. *Compare* ORDERS IN COUNCIL.

ordinance *n.* One of the forms taken by legislation under the *royal prerogative, normally legislation relating to UK dependencies.

ordinary resolution A decision reached by a simple majority (i.e. of more than 50%) of company members voting in person or by proxy. It is appropriate where no other type of resolution is expressly required by the Companies Acts or the *articles of association. *Compare* EXTRAORDINARY RESOLUTION; SPECIAL RESOLUTION.

ordinary share *See* SHARE.

original evidence **1.** Evidence of a statement made by a person other than the testifying witness, which is offered to prove that the statement was actually made rather than to prove its truth. Thus, if in an action for slander a witness testifies that he heard the defendant defame the claimant, his testimony is original evidence and not *hearsay evidence. **2.** *See* DIRECT EVIDENCE.

originating summons A form of originating *process in the High Court now rendered obsolete by the Civil Procedure Rules. Under the Rules, it has been replaced by the *Part 8 claim form.

origin system A system for protecting products in which each is identified by means of an **appellation of origin**, which is similar to a trade mark but may only be used for a product from a particular region. The regulations, which cover many products, were agreed in March 1996. The scheme stops manufacturers, etc., from other regions from using local names, such as Stilton cheese, Newcastle Brown Ale, and Jersey Royal potatoes.

OSS *See* OFFICE FOR THE SUPERVISION OF SOLICITORS.

ouster *n.* The act of wrongfully dispossessing someone of any kind of *hereditament, such as freehold property. *See* ADVERSE POSSESSION.

ouster of jurisdiction The exclusion of judicial proceedings in respect of any dispute. There is a presumption that statutes and other documents (e.g. contracts) do not oust the jurisdiction of the courts. *See* INTERPRETATION OF STATUTES.

outer Bar (utter Bar) Junior barristers, collectively, who sit outside the bar of the court, as opposed to *Queen's Counsel, who sit within it.

outraging public decency *See* CONSPIRACY.

outstanding term *See* SATISFIED TERM.

outworker *n. See* TELEWORKING.

overcrowding *n.* For statutory purposes a dwelling is overcrowded when two or more people of opposite sexes over the age of ten, and not married to one another or cohabiting, are obliged, because of lack of space, to sleep in the same room. There is also a test for overcrowding based on the number of people living in the dwelling compared with the number of rooms and the floor area of those rooms. Local authorities have a duty to prevent overcrowding and can take action against an owner-occupier, a landlord, or a tenant.

overreaching *n.* The process by which interests in land are converted on sale of the land into corresponding interests in the *capital money arising from the sale. Under the Settled Land Act 1925 the tenant for life always has the right to sell the settled land and overreach other interests, including interests in remainder and in reversion, with certain statutory exceptions (including the *principal mansion house).

Where land is held on a *trust of land, the law of Property Act 1925 provides that a purchaser of the land shall take free of the beneficiaries' interests, provided that the purchase money is paid to at least two trustees or a trust corporation. A mortgagee exercising his *power of sale is able to overreach the mortgagor's estate and *equity of redemption and convey the land free from the equitable right: the mortgagor's rights are transferred to the purchase money, the mortgagee being trustee of any such funds remaining after paying off the mortgage debt.

Overreaching in general affects only equitable rights.

overriding interests Certain rights and interests in registered land, listed in the Land Registration Act 1925, that cannot be protected by registration but, unless overreached, will bind the registered proprietor and any third party acquiring the land or any interest in it. The list includes legal *easements and *profits à prendre, rights of persons in actual occupation, rights acquired under the Limitation Acts (*see* LIMITATION OF ACTIONS), and leases granted for terms of up to 21 years.

overrule *vb.* To set aside the decision of a court in an earlier case. Because of the doctrine of *precedent, a court can generally only overrule decisions of courts lower than itself. The setting aside of the judgment of a lower court on appeal is called a **reversal**.

oversea company A *foreign company with an established place of business in Great Britain. Such companies are obliged to comply with certain formalities, such as filing their constitution or charter at the *Companies Registry and giving details of their directors and of who is authorized to accept service of legal proceedings and notices in the UK.

overseas divorce A divorce, annulment, or legal separation obtained overseas. There are different rules for the recognition of overseas divorces in the UK, according to whether or not they are obtained through judicial proceedings. An overseas divorce obtained through proceedings is recognized if: it is effective under the law of the country in which it was obtained; and either party to the marriage was habitually resident in, domiciled in, or a national of the country where it was obtained. An overseas divorce obtained otherwise than through proceedings is recognized if: it is effective under the law of the country where it was obtained; both parties were domiciled in that country, or one party was domiciled in that country and the other party was domiciled in another country that recognizes the divorce as valid; and neither party was habitually resident in the UK in the year preceding the divorce. *See also* EXTRAJUDICIAL DIVORCE.

owner-occupier *n.* A person who has legal ownership of a dwelling in which he lives or in which he lived before letting it on an *assured or *regulated tenancy. For statutory purposes, the term includes a tenant under a *long tenancy.

ownership *n.* The exclusive right to use, possess, and dispose of property, subject only to the rights of persons having a superior interest and to any restrictions on the owner's rights imposed by agreement with or by act of third parties or by operation of law. Ownership may be **corporeal**, i.e. of a material thing, which may itself be a *movable or an *immovable; or it may be **incorporeal**, i.e. of something intangible, such as of a copyright or patent. Ownership involves enjoyment of a number of rights over the property. The owner can alienate (i.e. sell or give away) some of these rights while still retaining others; for example, an owner of land may grant a right of way or a patent owner may grant a licence to manufacture the patented goods. Ownership may be held by different persons for different interests, for example when a freehold owner grants a lease or when land is settled on persons with interests in succession to one another (*see* SETTLED LAND). More than one person can own the same property at the same time. They may be either joint owners with a single title to the property (*see* JOINT TENANCY); or owners in common, each having a distinct title in the property that he can dispose of independently (*see* TENANCY IN COMMON).

A person may be both the legal and beneficial owner, or the legal ownership of property may be separate from the beneficial (equitable) ownership (i.e. the right to enjoy the property), as when a trustee owns the legal estate in land for the benefit of another.

A legally valid transaction may confer specific rights to use, possess, or deal with property without conferring ownership of it; for example, a contract may appoint a person as the owner's agent for the sale of specified land.

See also ESTATE.

P

P. Abbreviation for President (of the *Family Division of the High Court).

PACE Acronym for the Police and Criminal Evidence Act 1984.

pact *n. See* TREATY.

pacta sunt servanda [Latin] Agreements are to be kept; treaties should be observed. *Pacta sunt servanda* is the bedrock of the customary international law of treaties and, according to some authorities, the very foundation of international law. Without such an acceptance, treaties would become worthless.

pacta tertiis nec nocent nec prosunt [Latin] Treaties do not create either obligations or rights for third states without their consent.

paedophile *n.* A person who is sexually attracted to children (of either sex). Sexual activity with any children under the age of 16 is illegal. *See also* CHILD ABUSE; SEXUAL OFFENCE.

paid-up capital The amount actually paid to a company for shares allotted or issued to a shareholder. If a shareholder makes a full payment of the purchase price of the share, the amount received is referred to as **fully paid-up capital**. If the company permits the shareholder to make only partial payment of the total purchase price, such shares are referred to as **partly paid-up shares**, with the remaining balance recorded in the company's accounts as an amount that the company may *call upon in the future (**uncalled capital**).

pain and suffering The psychological consequences of personal injuries, in terms of pain, shock, consciousness that one's life expectancy has been shortened, embarrassment caused by disfigurement, etc. Damages are assessed on the extent to which the claimant actually experiences these feelings.

palatine courts Originally, courts of the counties palatine of Durham, Lancaster, and Chester. In modern times, only the Chancery courts of Durham and Lancaster survived, but their jurisdiction was transferred to the High Court by the Courts Act 1971. *See also* VICE CHANCELLOR.

Panel on Takeovers and Mergers *See* CITY CODE ON TAKEOVERS AND MERGERS.

paperless trading *See* ELECTRONIC DATA INTERCHANGE.

parallel import A product bought in one state and imported into another by the purchaser, often to take advantage of price differences between states; such products are also known as **grey market** goods. Parallel importation usually takes place outside supplier-authorized official distribution networks. Within the EU measures taken to prevent parallel imports in the Single Market will infringe *Article 81 of the Treaty of Rome (*see* EXPORT BANS). While it is permitted to restrict an exclusive distributor from soliciting sales outside his exclusive area, absolute territorial protection may not be given, either by contract terms or by conduct or oral arrangements.

paramount *adj.* (in land law) Superior; having or denoting a better right or title.

paramount clause *See* BILL OF LADING.

parcels *pl. n.* **1.** Plots of land. **2.** *See* DEED.

pardon *n.* The withdrawal of a sentence or punishment by the sovereign under the *prerogative of mercy. Once a pardon is granted, the accused cannot be tried and if he has already been convicted, he cannot be punished. The responsibility is upon him, however, to plead the pardon as a bar to prosecution or punishment; if he does not do so as soon as possible, he may be held to have waived it. A person may also be granted a **reprieve**, i.e. the temporary suspension of a punishment (for example, if he becomes insane after sentence is passed).

parent *n.* The mother or father of a child. The term also includes adoptive parents (*see* ADOPTION) but does not usually include *step-parents. At common law parents have **parental rights** over their children while they are minors, which include the right to physical control of the child, to control their education and determine their religion, to consent to medical treatment, to administer their property, to represent them in legal proceedings, and to discipline them reasonably. They also have **parental duties**, notably to maintain and educate their children, which can be legally enforced. Both parents exercise parental rights jointly, except in the case of illegitimate children, over whom the mother has exclusive parental rights unless the father has applied for *parental responsibility (he does, however, have a legal duty to maintain the child: *see* CHILD SUPPORT MAINTENANCE). Parental rights decline as the child grows older; in any dispute over their enforcement the *welfare of the child is the paramount consideration. *See also* PARENTS' LIABILITY; SECTION 8 ORDERS; SECTION 30 ORDER.

parental leave Time off work given to parents. The statutory provisions are contained in the Maternity and Parental Leave Regulations 1999, which set down key elements regarding such time off, although employers and employees are free to agree an improved contractual scheme.

In order to exercise the right to parental leave the employee must have been employed for a minimum of one year, must have or expect to have responsibility for the child, and must take any leave for the purpose of caring for the child. Up to 13 weeks' parental leave is available in respect of any individual child; it must be taken before the child is five years old. **Adoptive leave** (for employees who adopt a child) is available on the same basis, with the proviso that the leave must be taken within five years of the placement of the child (or before the child's 18th birthday, whichever is earlier). In the case of a disabled child, leave may be taken any time up to the child's 18th birthday; there are proposals to extend the period of this leave from 13 to 18 weeks.

In the absence of any contractual agreement on the operation of parental leave, the statutory provisions lay down default provisions. These state that leave must be taken in blocks of a week or more and that the maximum annual leave allowance is four weeks in respect of any individual child.

In order to exercise this right employees must give employers a minimum of 21 days' notice. Employers may postpone the leave but only if their business would be unduly disrupted. Fathers and prospective adoptive parents who want to guarantee that they can be present at the birth or placement of their child may book time off work without postponement. No notice is required to be given by employees returning to work, and on return employees are entitled to work in their same job.

Currently parental leave is unpaid, but this (and parental leave in general) is currently under review. However, from March 2003 working fathers are to receive the right to two weeks' paid paternity leave at the same flat rate as statutory maternity pay (*see* MATERNITY RIGHTS). Proposals are also underway to introduce paid adoptive leave as from 2003. In addition to the introduction of parental leave in 1999, provisions were introduced allowing for employees to take time off for domestic emergencies. Employees are entitled to a reasonable amount of unpaid time off in order to take action that is necessary in the following situations:

(1) To provide assistance on an occasion when a dependant falls ill, gives birth, or is injured or assaulted.

(2) To make arrangements for the provision of care for a dependant who is ill or injured, or in consequence of the death of a dependant.

(3) Because of the unexpected disruption or termination of arrangements for the care of a dependant.

(4) To deal with an incident that involves a child of the employee and occurs unexpectedly in a period during which an educational establishment the child attends is responsible for him.

parental order *See* SECTION 30 ORDER.

parental responsibility All the rights, duties, powers, and responsibilities that by law a parent of a child has in relation to the child and his or her property. The concept was introduced by the Children Act 1989, replacing *custody. Parental responsibility is automatically conferred on both parents if married, and on the mother alone if not. An unmarried father can acquire parental responsibility either by agreement with the mother or by applying to court for a *parental responsibility order. In determining whether to grant such an order the court must treat the child's welfare as its paramount consideration. Both parents retain parental responsibility on divorce. Other persons may acquire parental responsibility by virtue of being granted other orders. For example, anyone in whose favour a residence order (*see* SECTION 8 ORDERS) is made acquires parental responsibility for the duration of that order, and a *care order or an *emergency protection order confer parental responsibility on the relevant local authority. In all these cases, parental responsibility is shared with the parents. *See also* STEP-PARENT.

parental responsibility agreement A formal agreement between the mother and unmarried father of a child conferring *parental responsibility on the father. The agreement must be made on a set form, be signed and witnessed, and be registered in the Principal Registry of the Family Division in London. Once made, the agreement cannot be revoked by either party. Only a court may bring a parental responsibility agreement to an end – on the application of either party with parental responsibility or by the child himself if he has been given permission by the court to apply.

parental responsibility order An order made by a court conferring *parental responsibility on an unmarried father. In determining whether or not to make such an order, the court must treat the child's welfare as its paramount consideration. Courts will usually grant a parental responsibility order to a father who is able to demonstrate some degree of commitment and attachment to his child. A parental responsibility order may be revoked by a court.

parent company *See* SUBSIDIARY COMPANY.

parenting order An order, introduced by the Crime and Disorder Act 1998, that requires the parent or guardian of a child under the age of 16 to comply, for a period not exceeding 12 months, with such requirements as the court considers necessary for preventing offences being committed by this child. Parents whose children have been made the subject of a *child safety order may be required to attend courses that will assist them with their parenting skills. The rationale behind the introduction of such orders was that inadequate parental supervision is thought to be strongly associated with youth offending.

parents' liability Parents are not liable for their children's torts, but they may be liable for their own negligence in failing to supervise or train young children, where the absence of supervision or training has led a child to cause damage to others. In the case of older children, a parent can be vicariously liable for the torts of a child employed as a servant or agent on ordinary principles of *vicarious liability. There is no fixed age determining a child's liability for its own torts. A child may, however, be too young to form the intention necessary for a particular tort. In cases in which the negligence or contributory negligence of a child is in question, the test applied is whether the child's conduct measured up to the standard of care to be expected from an average child of that age.

Parents are not legally responsible for their children's crimes, although they may have to pay their *fines.

parent with care *See* CHILD SUPPORT MAINTENANCE.

parish *n.* A *local government area in England (outside Greater London) consisting of a division of a *district (though not all districts are so divided). All parishes have meetings and many have an elected parish council, which is a *local authority with a number of minor local governmental functions (e.g. the provision of allotments, bus shelters, and recreation grounds). A parish council may by resolution call its area a town, itself a town council, and its chairman the town mayor. The Local Government and Rating Act 1997 (effective from 19 May 1997) gives extra powers to parish councils in relation to rights of transport and crime prevention.

Paris Treaty The treaty, signed in Paris on 18 April 1951, that formed the *European Coal and Steel Community. Many of its provisions are similar to those of the later *Treaty of Rome, establishing the EEC, for example in the fields of *competition law and *state aid.

parking offences Offences relating to parking a motor vehicle. These include parking a vehicle within the limits of a pedestrian crossing or wherever signs or kerb markings indicate that parking is prohibited or restricted and failing to comply with the regulations associated with the use of parking meters. If the accused can show that road markings or signs indicating parking restrictions were absent or deficient, he may be acquitted. Parking offences are punishable by fine only; they are not subject to endorsement. *See also* OBSTRUCTION.

parlementaire *n.* [from French *parlementer*, to discuss terms; parley] An agent employed by a commander of a belligerent force in the field whose function is to go in person within the enemy lines for the purpose of communicating or negotiating openly and directly with the enemy commander.

Parliament *n.* The legislature of the UK, consisting of the sovereign, the House of Lords, and the House of Commons. Under the Parliament Act 1911, the maximum duration of any particular Parliament is five years, after which its functions expire. In practice, a Parliament's life always ends by its earlier **dissolution** by the sovereign under the *royal prerogative; this proclamation also summons its successor. The date of dissolution is chosen by the Prime Minister. The life of a Parliament is divided into sessions, normally of one year each, which are ended when Parliament is prorogued (also under the prerogative) by a royal commission. Each House divides a session into sittings, normally of a day's duration, which end when a motion for adjournment is passed. The functions of Parliament are the enactment of legislation (*see* ACT OF PARLIAMENT), the sanctioning of taxation and public expenditure, and the scrutiny and criticism of government policy and administration. *See also* SOVEREIGNTY OF PARLIAMENT.

Parliamentary Commissioner for Administration (Parliamentary Ombudsman) An independent official appointed under the Parliamentary Commissioner Act 1967 (as amended by the Parliamentary and Health Service Commissioners Act 1987) to investigate complaints by individuals or corporate bodies of injustice arising from maladministration by a government department or by certain nondepartmental public bodies, such as the Arts Council of England and the *Housing Corporation. Appointment of the Commissioner is by the Crown on the Prime Minister's advice. The Commissioner may investigate complaints only if they are submitted to him in writing through a Member of Parliament; investigation is entirely at his discretion. If he upholds a complaint and it is not remedied, he reports this to Parliament. Complaints of maladministration by devolved bodies in Wales and Scotland are investigated by the Welsh Administration Ombudsman and the Scottish Parliamentary Commissioner for Administration, respectively. *See also* HEALTH SERVICE COMMISSIONERS.

parliamentary committees *See* COMMITTEE OF THE WHOLE HOUSE; GRAND COMMITTEES, SCOTTISH AND WELSH; JOINT COMMITTEE ON STATUTORY INSTRUMENTS; STANDING COMMITTEE; SELECT COMMITTEE.

parliamentary counsel Civil servants (barristers or solicitors) who draft government Bills, government amendments to Bills, and any procedural motions required in connection with the passing of Bills. In 1996 proposals to contract out this activity to private practice lawyers were considered.

Parliamentary Ombudsman *See* PARLIAMENTARY COMMISSIONER FOR ADMINISTRATION.

parliamentary papers Papers published on the authority of either House of Parliament. They include Bills, the Official Reports of Parliamentary Debates (*see* HANSARD), and reports of parliamentary committees.

parliamentary privilege Special rights and immunities enjoyed by the Houses of Parliament and their members to enable them to carry out their functions effectively and without external interference. They are conferred mainly by the common law but partly by statute; they can be extended by statute but not by the resolution of either House.

The Commons have five main privileges. (1) The right of collective access to the sovereign through the Speaker. (2) The right of individual members to be free from civil (but not criminal) arrest. Since the abolition of imprisonment for debt, this privilege has been of only minor significance, but it would still shield a member against (for example) imprisonment for disobeying a court order in civil proceedings. (3) The individual right to freedom of speech. This substantial privilege means that a member cannot be made liable either civilly (e.g. for defamation) or criminally (e.g. for breach of the Official Secrets Acts) for anything said by him in the course of debates or other parliamentary proceedings. Under the Parliamentary Papers Act 1840 members are also not liable for statements repeated in reports published on the authority of the House. (4) The collective right to exclusive control of its own proceedings, so that it can (for example) exclude the public, prohibit reporting, and expel any member whom it may consider unfit to sit. (5) The collective right to punish for any **breach of privilege** or other **contempt**. Examples of breaches of privilege are initiating defamation proceedings in respect of privileged words and the reporting of secret proceedings. Other contempts include any conduct prejudicial to the proper functioning or dignity of the House, e.g. by refusing to give evidence to a committee, bribing members, or insulting the House. Members may be punished for contempt by expulsion, suspension, or imprisonment; others by reprimand or imprisonment. Imprisonment is terminated by prorogation. Whether or not particular conduct amounts to a contempt, and if so what punishment (if any) is appropriate, is considered by the Committee of Privileges, whose report the House is free to accept or reject after debate.

The privileges of the Lords are similar, except that members have an individual right of access to the sovereign and the House can fine for contempt and imprison for a fixed term, which is not affected by prorogation.

parol contract *See* SIMPLE CONTRACT.

parole (release on licence) *n.* The conditional *release of a prisoner from prison. Under the Criminal Justice Act 1991, anyone sentenced to imprisonment for between 12 months and 4 years must be released on licence after serving one-half of the sentence; those imprisoned for 4 years or more must be paroled after serving two-thirds of their sentence and may be considered for parole after serving half of the sentence. Local review committees in each area consider all cases and advise the Home Secretary, who may either release the prisoner himself or refer his case to the Parole Board. This Board includes a past or present judge, a psychiatrist, a person experienced in caring for discharged prisoners, and a person trained in the treatment of offenders. The Board considers reports and evidence relating to the prisoner (whom it may interview) and defines the conditions under which he may be released. Under the Crime (Sentences) Act 1997, the Parole Board (rather than the Home Secretary) has responsibility for the release of juveniles convicted of murder.

Parole remains in force until the prisoner would have served three-quarters of his sentence had he not been released. The Home Secretary may recall him to prison at any time, either on the recommendation of the Parole Board or whenever he thinks it necessary to do so without consulting the Board (but the prisoner has the right to appeal to the Parole Board).

If a prisoner on parole commits an offence during the period of his original sentence, he may have to serve any part of the original sentence still outstanding. In such cases limitations are imposed on his right to be considered again for parole.

parol evidence Evidence given orally, as opposed to *documentary evidence.

parol evidence rule The rule that parol evidence (i.e. oral evidence) cannot be given to contradict, alter, or vary a written document (such as a judicial record or a contract) unless there are allegations of fraud or mistake. In civil cases there is no longer a strict adherence to this rule.

parol lease A lease that is made either orally or in writing, but not by deed, and fulfils certain conditions. These are that it takes effect immediately it is made; it is for a period less than three years; and it is at the full market rent. *Periodic tenancies usually fulfil these conditions. Parol leases are the exception to the general rule that leases are not legally enforceable unless they are made by deed.

Part 8 claim form A form of originating *process used in cases in which the issues are likely to be ones of law or the interpretation of documents. It should not be used when disputed questions of fact are involved, for which proceedings begun by normal claim form are more appropriate. A Part 8 claim form must state that Part 8 of the Civil Procedure Rules applies and must set out the question the claimant wants the court to decide or the remedy that he seeks. Any evidence relied upon must be filed and served with the claim form. Part 8 claims are allocated as *multi-track proceedings.

Part 20 claim   A claim other than a claim by the claimant against the defendant. It includes (1) a *counterclaim by the defendant against the claimant; (2) a counterclaim by the defendant against a third party (i.e. a person who is not a party to the current proceedings), normally with the claimant; and (3) a claim by the defendant for an *indemnity or a *contribution from either a third party or from a party to the current proceedings. If the defendant to a claim alleges that a third party is liable to indemnify him or contribute to any judgment, or is someone that they seek to counterclaim against in addition to the claimant, he must bring that party into the proceedings by issuing a Part 20 claim form. Once done, the third party becomes known as the **Part 20 defendant**.

A defendant can issue a Part 20 claim form without requiring permission of the court if it is issued before or at the time of the filing of his defence. Directions in such a case will be dealt with as part of the normal system of *case management appropriate to the track to which the case has been allocated. If the time in which the defence must be filed has expired, permission is required from the court. This is normally sought by the use of an application notice filed at court and supported by evidence of reasons why the third party be introduced into the proceedings. If granted, the court will issue directions at that time. In any event, the court will consider further directions as to the future conduct of the proceedings when the time for filing the defence to the Part 20 claim by the third party or co-defendant has expired.

Part 36 offers and payments   Under the *Civil Procedure Rules, offers and payments made by parties in the pre-trial period in an attempt to encourage a settlement out of court. A **Part 36 payment** (formerly called **payment into court**) is made into the court; it can only be made once legal proceedings have started and only in respect of money claims. A **Part 36 offer** (formerly called a **Calderbank letter** or **offer**) can be made in the period before the start of proceedings or – in respect of nonmonetary claims – after proceedings have started. Both procedures place pressure on the other party to the litigation to settle.

In the case of a Part 36 payment, the other party is notified of the payment and that it may accept or reject the payment as a settlement. In the event of a rejection and the litigation proceeding to trial, the amount awarded is compared with the amount paid in. If the amount awarded is less than the sum previously paid into court, costs since the time of payment in will be awarded against the successful claimant. Part 36 offers have a similar purpose and effect in that the court will consider the contents of the offer when it considers the issue of costs, after finding liability and settling the amount of damages.

partial loss   (in marine insurance) Any loss of the subject matter of an insurance policy other than an *actual total loss or a *constructive total loss. In the case of a partial loss there is a lesser measure of indemnity than in the case of a total loss. *See also* AVERAGE.

partibility *n.* (of chattels) *See* PARTITION OF CHATTELS.

participator *n.* *See* CLOSE COMPANY.

particular average   *See* AVERAGE.

particular lien   *See* LIEN.

particulars *pl. n.* Details of an allegation of fact made in civil proceedings. Details of a claim (the **particulars of claim**) can be included in the *claim form or served separately on the defendant. When an allegation is ambiguous or pleaded in insufficient detail, the opposing party may make in writing (through the court) a **request for further information** (formerly called **request for further and better particulars**). The principal function of this procedure is to prevent *surprise.

parties *pl. n.* **1.** Persons who are involved together in some transaction, e.g. the parties to a deed or a contract. **2.** Persons who are involved together in litigation, either civil or criminal. *See also* JOINDER OF PARTIES.

partition *n.* **1.** The division of a territory into two or more units, each under a different government. **2.** The division of supreme power over a territory between different governments (e.g. federal and state). **3.** The formal separation, effected by deed, of land held in common ownership into parts, so that each co-owner takes his part solely, beneficially, and free from any rights of the others. Partition of land cannot be enforced without the consent of all the co-owners. **4.** The transfer to different companies of parts of a trade or undertaking (or two or more trades or undertakings) of a company. This is usually by means of a distribution agreement or a demerger under the Income and Corporation Taxes Act 1988. *Compare* PARTITION OF CHATTELS.

partition of chattels The division between co-owners of chattels held in undivided shares, so that each takes his part of the goods solely and absolutely. If chattels are **partible** (i.e. capable of being divided), the court may order partition under the Law of Property Act 1925 on the application of a co-owner.

partnership *n.* An association of two or more people formed for the purpose of carrying on a business with a view to profit. Partnerships are governed by the Partnership Act 1890. Unlike an incorporated *company, a partnership does not have a legal personality of its own and therefore partners are liable for the debts of the firm. On leaving the firm they remain liable for debts already incurred; they cease to be liable for future debts if proper notice of retirement has been published. A **limited partnership** is governed by the Limited Partnership Act 1907. It consists of **general partners**, who are fully liable for partnership debts, and **limited partners**, who are liable to the extent of their investment. Limited partners lose their limits of liability if they take part in management. A **partnership at will** is one for which no fixed duration has been agreed. Any partner may end the partnership at any time provided that he gives notice of his intention to do so to all the other partners, subject to any restriction in the partnership deed. *See also* LIMITED LIABILITY PARTNERSHIP.

part performance A doctrine of equity that a contract required to be evidenced in writing will still be enforceable even if it is not so evidenced provided that one of the parties does certain acts by which the contract is partly performed. For an act to bring the doctrine into play (i.e. a sufficient act of part performance) that act must be performed by the person alleging the contract to exist and must relate unequivocally to the contract; an example would be taking possession of property alleged to have been sold (under a contract entered into before 21 September 1989) to the person who takes possession. It is unclear whether mere payment of money is a sufficient act of part performance.

This doctrine applied primarily to contracts for the sale of land. However, such contracts entered into on or after 21 September 1989 are required, under the Law of Property (Miscellaneous Provisions) Act 1989, to be in writing (not merely evidenced in writing) if they are to be valid. Acts of part performance will not, as such, validate an unwritten land contract, although they may, in particular circumstances, give rise to a proprietary *estoppel or a *constructive trust.

party wall A wall or fence in premises that is shared with another owner or tenant in adjacent premises. The Party Wall Act 1996, which came into force on 1 July 1997, imposes obligations on owners carrying out works on party walls or fences. They must notify the adjoining owner or tenant in advance if they intend to repair a party wall or fence or build on a boundary; any damage that occurs as a result of the work must be repaired.

passing off Conducting one's business in such a way as to mislead the public into thinking that one's goods or services are those of another business. The commonest form of passing off is marketing goods with a design, packaging, or trade name that is very similar to that of someone else's goods. It is not necessary to prove an intention to deceive: innocent passing off is actionable.

passport *n.* A document, issued under the *royal prerogative by the Home Office through its executive agency the Passport Agency, that provides prima facie evidence of the holder's nationality. It is not required by law for leaving the UK, but it is required for entry into most other countries. Within the European Union, EU nationals are sent through quicker channels of entry although they are still subject to occasional passport checks, despite the Schengen Agreement reached by most EU states to abolish internal border checks, which came into force on 26 March 1995, and the creation of the *Single Market in the EU, which came into force on 1 January 1993. Concerns such as drug smuggling have made member states of the EU reluctant to abandon internal controls. Its issue is purely discretionary and the government may withdraw or revoke a passport at will. Under the Immigration Act 1988, a person seeking entry into the UK on the basis of his right of abode there must either produce an appropriate passport or a certificate showing such an entitlement, issued by or on behalf of the UK government. The British Visitor's Passport has been abolished and only a full British passport is adequate for foreign travel. Children need their own passports. However, children included on a parental passport before 5 October 1998 may continue to travel abroad on that passport either until reaching the age of 16 or until the passport is submitted for an amendment. The English courts have power to order the surrender of a foreign passport to protect the interest of children who might otherwise be removed unlawfully from the UK by a foreign parent. Similar powers to order surrender of a UK passport are contained in the Family Law Act 1986.

past consideration *See* CONSIDERATION.

pasture *n.* A *profit *à prendre* or *common conferring rights of grazing over another's land or on common land, which may be limited to particular types of animal, to fixed numbers of animals, or (in the case of a common) to as many animals as the land will support.

patent *n.* The grant of an exclusive right to exploit an invention. In the UK patents are granted by the Crown through the Patent Office, which is an executive agency of the Department of Trade and Industry. An applicant for a patent (usually the inventor or his employer) must show that the invention is new, is not obvious, and is capable of industrial application. An expert known as a **patent agent** often prepares the application, which must describe the invention in considerable detail. The Patent Office publishes these details if it grants a patent. A patent remains valid for 20 years from the date of application (the **priority date**) provided that the person to whom it has been granted (the **patentee**) continues to pay the appropriate fees. During this time, the patentee may assign his patent or grant licences to use it. Such transactions are registered in a public register at the Patent Office. If anyone infringes his monopoly, the patentee may sue for an *injunction and *damages or an *account of profits. However, a patent from the Patent Office gives exclusive rights in the UK only: the inventor must obtain a patent from the European Patent Office in Munich and patents in other foreign countries if he wishes to protect the invention elsewhere.

patent agent *See* PATENT.

patent ambiguity *See* AMBIGUITY.

patent defect *See* DEFECT.

patentee *n*. A person who has been granted a *patent.

Patents County Court A *county court designated by the Lord Chancellor under the Copyright, Design and Patents Act 1988 to exercise a special jurisdiction in cases relating to patents and designs. The Patents County Court provides a cheaper and quicker forum for patent and design cases than the *Patents Court of the High Court. Patents agents and solicitors, as well as barristers, have *rights of audience there.

Patents Court Collectively, the *Patents County Court and the **Patents Court of the High Court**. The latter forms part of the *Chancery Division of the High Court, having jurisdiction over matters arising under the Patents Acts 1949–77, the Registered Designs Acts 1949–61, and the Defence Contracts Act 1958, as well as the inherent jurisdiction of the High Court. Two *puisne judges of the Chancery Division with special experience of patent law are assigned to hear cases, but they will be assisted by special scientific advisers.

paternity leave *See* PARENTAL LEAVE.

patrial *n*. *See* IMMIGRATION.

pawn (pledge) *n*. An item of goods transferred by the owner (the **pawnor**) to another (the **pawnee**) as security for a debt. (The word is also used for the transfer itself.) A pawn involves a *bailment and the pawnor remains owner of the goods; the pawnee is liable for failure to take reasonable care of them. If the pawnor fails to repay the loan at the agreed time, the pawnee has the right at common law to sell the pawn; he must account to the pawnor for any surplus after discharging his debt. **Pawnbrokers** are dealers licensed to lend money at a specified rate of interest on the security of a pawn. Pawnbroking is regulated by provisions of the Consumer Credit Act 1974 (replacing the Pawnbrokers Acts 1872 and 1960) with regard to such matters as pawn receipts, rates of interest, redemption period and procedure, consequences of failure to redeem, and realization of the pawn. Under the Act, a pawn can be redeemed at any time within six months, or longer if agreed by both parties. At the end of the redemption period ownership of the pawn passes to the pawnbroker if the redemption period is six months and the value of the debt is £25 or less. If it is more than £25 the pawnbroker may sell the pawn after giving the pawnor notice, but the pawnor may still redeem the pawn at any time until it is sold. The pawnbroker must account to the pawnor for any surplus from the proceeds of sale after discharging his debt but he may claim any balance of the debt if the proceeds are insufficient.

Pay As You Earn (PAYE) A system for collecting *income tax in which the employer deducts tax direct from the employee's pay. The Inland Revenue gives every employee a code number, which the employer uses, together with tax tables, to work out how much tax to deduct (*see* PAYE WEEK NUMBER). The employer is then responsible for paying the tax to the Inland Revenue by the 19th day of each month.

PAYE *See* PAY AS YOU EARN.

PAYE week number One of a series of consecutive numbers given to successive seven-day periods within the tax year, used by employers in the calculation of tax due under *Pay As You Earn. Thus, Week 1 is the period 6–12 April inclusive, Week 2 is 13–19 April, and so on. The employer uses the week number in conjunction with the employee's tax code to determine his tax-free pay for the current tax year to date. This in turn is used to calculate the tax due. The week number relates to the period in which the pay day occurs, not necessarily the period in which the pay was earned.

payment by post The payment of a debt by the posting of notes, a cheque, or some other negotiable instrument. If the letter is lost in the post, the debt is not discharged unless the creditor has expressly or by implication requested payment by post and the debtor has sent a properly addressed letter.

payment in due course Payment made at or after the *maturity of a *bill of exchange to the holder of the bill by a payer in good faith and without notice that the holder's title to the bill is defective. A bill is discharged by payment in due course by or on behalf of the drawee or acceptor. When a bill is paid by the drawer or endorser it is not discharged and the party paying may have rights on it.

payment into court The payment by a defendant, into an account maintained by the court, of a sum in satisfaction of any or all of the claims made against him. Under the *Civil Procedure Rules, this is now referred to as **Part 36 payment**. *See* PART 36 OFFERS AND PAYMENTS.

payroll giving scheme A scheme for employees to give donations to charities by direct deduction from their pay. The employees receive tax relief on donations, and the government adds a further 10% to such gifts for three years from April 2000. The employer deducts the donation direct from the employee's wages or salary and pays it to the charity of the employee's choice through an agency.

pay statement *See* ITEMIZED PAY STATEMENT.

PC *See* PRIVY COUNCIL.

PCT *See* PRIMARY CARE TRUST.

peaceful assembly *See* FREEDOM OF ASSOCIATION.

peaceful enjoyment of possessions A right set out in Article 1 of the First Protocol to the European Convention on Human Rights and now part of UK law as a consequence of the *Human Rights Act 1998. This right is a *qualified right; as such, the public interest can be used to justify an interference with it providing that this is prescribed by law, designed for a legitimate purpose, and proportionate. Therefore the state may deprive individuals of their possessions and control to the use of property providing that this is prescribed by law, in the public interest, and proportionate.

pecuniary legacy *See* LEGACY.

penal notice *See* CONTEMPT OF COURT.

penal statute A statute that creates a criminal offence or provides for any penalty (e.g. a forfeiture) enforceable in civil proceedings. It is subject to strict construction (*see* INTERPRETATION OF STATUTES).

penalty *n*. **1.** A *punishment for a crime. A penalty must be clearly stated before it can be enforced. When statute creates an offence and specifies a penalty without saying how the offence is to be tried, there may be an implication that it is to be imposed by a magistrates' court. Article 7 of the European Convention on Human Rights forbids the use of retrospective criminal penalties, and this prohibition is now part of UK law as a consequence of the *Human Rights Act 1998. **2.** A sum specified in a contract as payable on its breach but not constituting a genuine estimate of the likely loss. *See* DAMAGES.

penalty points *See* TOTTING UP.

pendente lite [Latin] Until trial. When a will or the right to administer an estate is being disputed, the court may if necessary appoint an administrator *pendente lite* to deal with the estate until the proceedings have been resolved.

pending action Proceedings in court that relate to land or to some interest in it. The claimant should register the pending action as a land charge (*see* REGISTRATION OF ENCUMBRANCES) as soon as the proceedings begin. If he fails to do this a purchaser acquiring the land without knowing of the action will not be bound by the outcome.

pension *n*. Income paid to a person who has reached the state *retirement age (retirement pension) or who has retired from employment and benefits from a company or personal pension scheme. From April 2001 the state retirement pension was £75.50 per week for a single person and £115.90 for a married couple. The *State Earnings Related Pension Scheme (SERPS) can boost state pensions for employees with sufficient national insurance contributions. Those moving abroad receive only a frozen state pension. Contributions to a company pension scheme are made net of tax within Inland Revenue limits but only (for newer pensions) on income up to an earnings cap of £91,800 (in 2000–01). Employees may, up to that limit, pay up to 15% of their salary into a company pension scheme (including any *additional voluntary contributions) and may take a maximum pension of two-thirds their final salary on retirement. Maximum contributions for the self-employed and others in personal pension schemes are subject to the earnings cap for company pensions but vary according to age, ranging from 17.5% of net relevant earnings for those aged 35 or less at the beginning of the tax year to 40% for those aged 61 and over. Pensions paid are taxable in the hands of the recipient, although a proportion of the fund accumulated can be taken as a tax-free lump sum on retirement. The balance is used to purchase a compulsory *annuity. *See also* STAKEHOLDER PENSION.

pension earmarking A provision for financial relief on granting a divorce or judicial separation that, when the pension of one spouse (the main earner) becomes payable, part of its benefits will be paid to the other spouse. Thus on the death of the main earner, all payments will cease. *See also* PENSION SHARING ORDER.

pension sharing order An order that may be made by the court on granting a divorce, whereby the spouse with little or no pension either becomes a member of the main earner's pension scheme in her or his own right or, alternatively, receives a transfer of a designated percentage of this scheme into her or his own pension arrangement. Unlike *pension earmarking, pension sharing does not apply to *judicial separation.

PEP *See* PERSONAL EQUITY PLAN.

peppercorn rent An insignificant rent reserved for the purpose of showing that a lease or tenancy is granted for valuable *consideration.

per autre vie *See* ESTATE PUR AUTRE VIE.

per capita [Latin: by heads] For each person. Distribution of an estate or fund *per capita* is an equal distribution in the specified shares among all those entitled to it. *Compare* PER STIRPES.

per curiam (per cur.) [Latin] By the court. A proposition *per curiam* is one made by the judge (or, if there is more than one judge, assented to by all).

peremptory challenge *See* CHALLENGE TO JURY.

peremptory norm *See* JUS COGENS.

peremptory pleas *See* PLEAS IN BAR.

perfect and imperfect rights Legally recognized rights. Perfect rights are enforceable through court action but imperfect rights are not.

perfect trust *See* EXECUTED TRUST.

performance bond *See* BOND.

performance of contract The carrying out of obligations under a contract. Performance by both parties discharges the contract completely; performance by one party discharges him alone. The rules relating to performance distinguish between a **divisible contract** and an **indivisible** (or **entire**) **contract**. In a divisible contract the obligations of the parties are independent of each other, so that one party can demand performance by the other without rendering performance himself. Thus a landlord, though liable to be sued by his tenant for not carrying out a repairing covenant, is not prevented by his own default from enforcing the tenant's covenant to pay rent. Most contracts, however, are indivisible, i.e. the obligations of the parties are interdependent. Neither party can demand performance unless he himself either has performed or is ready and willing to do so. At common law, complete and precise performance was originally required, so that a party who rendered anything short of this (for example, a builder who carried out the contract work, but defectively in some respects) could recover nothing for his efforts. This extreme position was subsequently modified by the doctrine of **substantial performance**. A party who has substantially performed his obligations can now recover the contract price, reduced by damages awarded to the other party in respect of the defects.

    A **tender of performance** is the equivalent of performance, so that a seller who tenders the correct goods is discharged from the contract (and entitled to damages for breach) if the buyer rejects them. **Vicarious performance** (e.g. by a subcontractor) is good performance, except when personal performance is demanded by the contract. *See also* PART PERFORMANCE; SPECIFIC PERFORMANCE.

performers' rights The rights of performers, such as musicians, in the live performance of their works, to prevent others recording their performances. The rights are also infringed if anyone broadcasts a qualifying performance under the Copyright, Designs and Patents Act 1988 without consent or imports a recording of such a performance knowing that it was an illicit recording. The right is owned by the performer, although in commercial practice many performers enter into exclusive recording contracts in relation to their works, which give recording rights to a record company; in this case the company obtains *copyright in the sound recording and the performer loses his rights for the duration of the contract. The Copyright Term Directive 93/98 harmonized EU law in this area. Performers' rights must be protected under national law; the right must exist for 50 years from the end of the calendar year in which the performance takes place.

perils of the seas One of the heads of risk included in a marine insurance policy. It covers the insured against loss caused by fortuitous accidents or casualties of the seas, e.g. such events as unusual violence of wind or waves, striking submerged rocks, and collisions with other ships. The ordinary action of wind and waves in causing wear and tear is not, however, regarded as a peril of the seas.

per incuriam [Latin] Through lack of care. A decision of a court is made *per incuriam* if it fails to apply a relevant statutory provision or ignores a binding precedent. In criminal cases a decision made *per incuriam* will usually result in the conviction being quashed.

periodic tenancy A tenancy in which rent is payable at fixed intervals, usually weekly, monthly, quarterly, or yearly. The tenancy continues automatically from one period to another until terminated by *notice to quit. Periodic tenancies can be created by express agreement, orally or in writing. Alternatively they can be created by implication when rent is accepted by the owner of the land from the person who occupies it. This may arise, for example, when a tenant under a *fixed-term tenancy remains in possession at the end of his tenancy and the landlord continues to accept rent from him. The length of notice required to terminate the tenancy is usually the same as one of the periods of the tenancy.

perished goods Under the Sale of Goods Act 1979, goods under a contract of sale that have been either totally destroyed or so damaged that they no longer fit the contract description. The Act provides that a contract is void if it relates to specific goods that, unknown to the seller, have perished before it is made. If the goods perish after the contract is made, this event will make the contract void unless the risk has by then passed to the buyer (*see* TRANSFER OF RISK). These two propositions give statutory recognition to common-law rules relating to *mistake and *frustration of contract, respectively.

perjury *n.* The offence of giving false evidence or evidence that one does not believe to be true (even if it is in fact the truth). It is punishable by up to seven years' imprisonment and/or a fine. The offence may be committed by any witness who has taken the oath or affirmed, by the defendant at any stage of the trial, and by an interpreter. Perjury is only committed, however, in judicial proceedings, which include any proceedings before a court, tribunal, or someone with the power to hear evidence on oath (e.g. Commissioners of Income Tax hearing appeals against tax assessments). The evidence given must be relevant to the proceedings and must be given with knowledge that it is false or recklessly.

The Perjury Act 1911 also creates various offences related to perjury. These include making a **false statement** on oath in nonjudicial proceedings and making a false statement or declaration relating to marriage (e.g. to obtain a licence to marry or make an entry in a register of marriage) or to the registration of a birth or death. These offences are punishable by up to seven years' imprisonment on indictment. The offences of making a false statement in a statutory declaration or in any account, balance sheet, or document required to be made by Act of Parliament are punishable by up to two years' imprisonment.

See also SUBORNATION.

Permanent Court of Arbitration A standing panel of jurists established in 1900 under the 1899 *Hague Convention for the pacific settlement of disputes. Despite the name, it is neither permanent nor is it a court. Rather, it is a mechanism for promoting the creation of arbitration tribunals as required. Although resort to the Court is infrequent, it is by no means redundant: its facilities have been used, for example, by the Iran–United States Claims Tribunal, established in 1981.

permissive waste A kind of *waste that occurs when a tenant fails to maintain the property he leases and allows it to deteriorate.

per my et per tout [Norman French: by the half(?) and by all (the meaning of *my* is uncertain)] Denoting the unity of possession that is an essential characteristic of joint ownership of land. *See also* JOINT TENANCY.

perpetual injunction *See* INJUNCTION.

perpetual trusts *See* RULE AGAINST PERPETUAL TRUSTS.

perpetuating testimony A procedure for the recording of evidence in civil cases in which there is a danger that it might be lost (e.g. because of the death of a witness) before it can be used in a future action. It is rarely ordered.

perpetuity *n*. *See* RULE AGAINST PERPETUITIES.

per quod consortium amisit [Latin: by which he lost the benefit of her society] *See* CONSORTIUM.

per quod servitium amisit [Latin: by which he lost services] *See* LOSS OF SERVICES.

persistent offender Formerly, a person whose previous criminal record made him liable to be given an extended sentence of imprisonment. *Compare* REPEAT OFFENDER.

personal Act *See* ACT OF PARLIAMENT.

personal chattel *See* CHATTEL.

personal contract *See* DERECOGNITION.

personal-credit agreement An agreement made between an individual (the debtor) and any other person (the creditor) by which the creditor provides the debtor with credit of any amount. Personal-credit agreements (a concept under the Consumer Credit Act 1974) exclude loans, etc., to companies. *See also* CONSUMER-CREDIT AGREEMENT.

personal equity plan (PEP) A scheme to encourage individuals to invest in EU quoted companies and in qualifying equity-based investment trusts, which was introduced in January 1987. From 6 April 1999 no new subscriptions can be made to PEPs, but existing PEPs can continue after this date. The PEP is managed by an authorized investment manager; tax credits on dividends (paid before 5 April 2004) and income tax deducted at source are reclaimed by the manager. There were formerly two types of PEP, general and single-company, but in April 2001 this distinction was abolished. In addition, from 6 April 2001, the restriction of investments to EU companies is abolished, allowing investors to transfer their PEP funds to formerly "nonqualifying" companies. No income tax or capital gains tax is payable on income or gains generated by the PEP, unless interest of over £180 on cash deposited in the PEP is withdrawn in any one year. PEPs are being replaced by *Individual Savings Accounts (ISAs).

personal property (personalty) All *property that does not comprise land or incorporeal *hereditaments.

personal protection order An order formerly made under the Domestic Proceedings and Magistrates' Courts Act 1978 for the protection against violence of a spouse or a child of the family. Such protection is now provided by a *nonmolestation order under the Family Law Act 1996.

personal representative A person entitled to deal with a deceased person's estate in accordance with his will or under the rules relating to intestacy. Personal representatives include *executors and *administrators of all descriptions.

personal service The *service of a document in litigation effected by leaving a copy of the document with the person to be served. It is often wrongly supposed that it is necessary to touch the person to be served with the document, but it is in fact sufficient to leave it in his presence having informed him of its nature. Most documents required to be served personally can now be served by post.

personalty *n.* *See* PERSONAL PROPERTY.

personal union An arrangement in which two or more states share a single head of state. A personal union does not create a single international person; rather, each state retains its separate legal personality. For example, in 1603 James VI of Scotland became monarch of England (styled as James I) but continued to be monarch of Scotland (styled as James VI).

persona non grata [Latin: an unacceptable or unwelcome person] A *diplomatic agent who is unacceptable to the receiving state. The sending state should recall such an agent; if this fails to occur, the host state may ignore the presence of the agent or expel him from its territory.

per stirpes [Latin: by the roots] According to descent. When property in an estate or fund is distributed *per stirpes*, beneficiaries a generation removed from the primary class of beneficiaries receive between them the share attributable to their ancestor. For example, a will may leave property to A and B in equal shares with provision that if either predeceases the testator, the deceased beneficiary's children take his share in equal shares *per stirpes*. If, on the testator's death, both A and B have already died, A leaving two children and B three, A's children will each receive a quarter of the property, and B's children one-sixth each. *Compare* PER CAPITA.

persuading to murder The statutory offence, which is punishable by a maximum sentence of life imprisonment, of persuading or encouraging any person to murder anyone else. This offence is committed even by a foreigner temporarily in England who persuades someone to commit a murder abroad (such a person would not normally be guilty of *incitement), and thus applies to the activities of international terrorist organizations (*see* TERRORISM).

persuasive authority A decision or other pronouncement of law that, under the doctrine of *precedent, a court may but need not apply when deciding the case before it. Persuasive authorities include decisions of courts of equal or lesser standing, decisions of courts outside the English legal system (particularly, courts of Commonwealth countries having systems based on the common law), *obiter dicta*, and the opinions of eminent textbook writers.

perverse verdict A *verdict of a jury that is either entirely against the weight of the evidence or contrary to the judge's direction on a question of law.

perverting the course of justice Carrying out an act that tends or is intended to obstruct or defeat the administration of public justice. Common examples are inventing false evidence to mislead a court (in either civil or criminal proceedings) or an arbitration tribunal, making false statements to the police, stealing or destroying evidence, threatening witnesses, and attempting to influence jurors. The common-law offence of perverting the course of justice overlaps with certain forms of *contempt of court and with the separate offence of tampering with witnesses. It is not an offence, however, to offer money to someone to persuade him not to proceed with an action in the civil courts; nor is it an offence to offer to pay reasonable compensation to the victim of a crime, if he will agree not to take criminal proceedings. However, once he has made a statement to the police in connection with possible proceedings, it is an offence to attempt to induce him to withdraw or alter his statement.

petition *n.* A written application for a legal remedy or relief that is only available if statute or rules of procedure permit it. Examples are a petition for *divorce, a *bankruptcy petition, an *election petition, or a petition for winding up a company (*see* COMPULSORY WINDING-UP).

petition of right *See* CROWN PROCEEDINGS.

petroleum revenue tax A tax levied on the profits from sales of oil and gas extracted in the UK or on the continental shelf. The rate of tax (from 1 July 1993) is 50%, and the tax is abolished for new oilfields that get development consent on or after 16 March 1993.

petty sessions A court of summary jurisdiction now known as a *magistrates' court. The term was formerly used to denote a meeting of two or more *justices of the peace other than a general or *quarter sessions. A **petty-sessions area** is a geographical area for certain purposes of magistrates' court administration.

philanthropic purposes Purposes that are narrower than *benevolent purposes but wider than charitable purposes. *See* CHARITABLE TRUST.

picketing *n.* Attendance by employees and their trade union representatives at or near a place of work for the purpose of persuading others to work or not to work, or to exchange information, in contemplation or furtherance of a *trade dispute. There is no specific legal right to picket, nor any prohibition on picketing, but there is a concept of lawful picketing in the Trade Union and Labour Relations (Consolidation) Act 1992. Pickets have no immunity from prosecution for committing criminal offences and they have no right to compel others to stop or to listen to the pickets' views. However, employees and their trade union representatives picketing their own place of work are immune from civil legal action for inducing others to break commercial or employment contracts with the employer involved in the dispute. Such immunity extends to persons engaged in secondary picketing in certain circumstances. **Secondary picketing** occurs when the premises of an employer who is not an immediate party to the dispute are picketed. Persons picketing customers or suppliers of the employer in dispute have immunity, provided that they are likely to achieve their principal purpose of disrupting their own employer's trade with the employer in dispute. Thus in a dispute between an employer (A) and his workers, A's own employees may picket A's premises and employees of A's supplier (B) may picket B's premises (to prevent supplies reaching A), with the benefit of immunity from certain types of civil legal action.

When an employer tries to avoid the impact of the dispute by transferring business to his associated employer, the latter and his customers and suppliers may be picketed. Again, the pickets will have immunity if they are likely to achieve their principal purpose of disrupting the supply of goods or services transferred. All pickets lose their immunity if the action is taken without being first authorized by a ballot of the members of the union involved, or if the reason for the action is that the employer is employing a person who is not a trade union member.

"Flying pickets", who are neither employees nor trade union representatives of employees at the workplace picketed, have no immunity. The courts will grant injunctions to stop or prevent unlawful picketing. A *code of practice on picketing is published by the Department for Work and Pensions.

It is arguable that the incorporation of the European Convention on Human Rights into the English law via the *Human Rights Act 1998 will impact on the law affecting picketing. Article 10, the right of *freedom of expression, and Article 11, the right to freedom of peaceful assembly (*see* FREEDOM OF ASSOCIATION), could be used to challenge some of the existing restrictions laid down in Engish law. As picketing is a form of public demonstration (in an industrial context) the imposition of restrictions could raise the civil-liberties aspects of such restrictions sufficiently to amount to breaches of either or both of these Articles. The common law may therefore be compelled, in the fullness of time, to develop a peaceful right of assembly in respect to the public highway.

piracy *n.* **1. (piracy *jure gentium*)** Any illegal act of violence, detention, or robbery committed on a private ship for personal gain or revenge, against another ship, people, or property on the high seas. Piracy may also be committed on or against an aircraft. Piracy also includes operating a pirate ship or aircraft and inciting or assisting any other act of piracy. However, acts committed for political purposes are not piracy; nor are any acts committed by a warship or government ship or aircraft. Piracy is an international crime and all nations may exercise jurisdiction over pirates, regardless of the nationality of the ship or aircraft or the pirates. A ship or aircraft involved in piracy is also subject to seizure by any state. British courts have traditionally exercised such jurisdiction, and the power to do so is confirmed in the Tokyo Convention Act 1967.

English municipal law has created certain offences of piracy that are not covered by international law, but they are not subject to the jurisdiction of the English courts unless committed on board a British ship or within British territorial waters. Examples of such offences are revolt by the crew of a ship against their master and hijacking of the ship by the crew. These offences, if tried as piracy, are subject to life imprisonment (the death penalty for piracy accompanied by acts endangering life, or by an assault with intent to murder, has been abolished; *see* CAPITAL PUNISHMENT).

2. (in marine insurance) One of the risks covered by a marine insurance policy, which extends beyond the criminal offence to include a revolt by the crew or passengers and plundering generally.

3. Infringement of *copyright, *trade marks, or other *intellectual property rights. The owner's usual remedy is to obtain an *injunction to end the infringement, although piracy is often also a criminal offence.

piscary (fishery) *n.* A *profit *à prendre* or *common conferring the right to take fish from water on another's land.

place of safety order *See* EMERGENCY PROTECTION ORDER.

plaint *n.* Formerly, a statement in writing of a cause of action, used to initiate actions in the county courts. Under the Civil Procedure Rules, it has been replaced by the *claim form.

plaintiff *n. See* CLAIMANT.

planning permission *See* TOWN AND COUNTRY PLANNING.

plant *n. See* MACHINERY AND PLANT.

plc (public limited company) *See* LIMITED COMPANY; PUBLIC COMPANY.

plea *n.* **1.** A formal statement in court by or on behalf of an accused person as a response to the charge made against him. *See also* GUILTY; NOT GUILTY; PLEAS IN BAR. **2.** A defendant's answer to a claimant's declaration in an action at common law.

plea bargaining An agreement between the prosecution and the defence by which the accused changes his plea from not guilty to guilty in return for an offer by the prosecution (for example, to drop a more serious charge against the accused) or when the judge has informally let it be known that he will minimize the sentence if the accused pleads guilty. Any negotiations taking place between the judge and defence counsel must be in the presence of the prosecuting counsel: the accused is not a party to the negotiations. The accused must be allowed to make up his own mind freely about the proposals.

plead *vb.* To make a *plea.

pleading *n.* In colloquial usage, the claim form, defence, or any other document used in civil proceedings. The *Civil Procedure Rules have rendered this term obsolete, and it no longer has any formal meaning; pleadings are now called *statements of case. However, it continues to be used informally by both lawyers and lay people.

pleading guilty by post A procedure that allows a person to plead guilty to certain minor offences by letter without appearing at the court. The procedure applies only to *summary offences punishable with a maximum of three months' imprisonment. The accused may send details of any mitigating circumstances and these are read out to the court. The court cannot sentence a person who has pleaded guilty by post to imprisonment in his absence or disqualify him from driving without warning him of the possibility and giving him the opportunity to appear.

pleading in the alternative In civil cases, the process of including in a statement of case two or more inconsistent allegations and inviting the court to grant relief in respect of whichever allegation it finds to be well-founded.

pleas in bar (peremptory pleas) Pleas in *trials on indictment setting out some special ground for not proceeding with the indictment. There are four such pleas: *autrefois acquit, *autrefois convict, pardon, and special liability to repair a road or bridge.

plebiscite *n.* A public referendum or vote by the population of a territory to determine its choice of a sovereign or a *cession of territory to another state.

pledge *n. See* PAWN.

plene administravit [Latin: he has fully administered] The defence of a personal representative who has completed administration of a deceased's estate to a creditor's action to recover a debt of which he had no knowledge. Unless the creditor can prove that the personal representative still holds assets of the estate, he will obtain a judgment enforceable only against any such assets coming into the personal representative's hands in the future.

plough bote *See* ESTOVERS.

poaching *n.* Taking game without permission from private land or from land on which the killing of game is restricted. Wild animals cannot usually be stolen; there are, however, various statutory offences to cover poaching that do not amount to theft. For example, the Deer Act 1980 creates offences relating to taking, killing, or injuring deer or trespassing on land with the intention of committing any of these acts. Conviction may involve *forfeiture of the game taken or of the equipment and vehicles used in poaching. There are also special offences relating to taking or destroying fish in private waters or in waters with a private right of fishery. There is special legislation dealing with the poaching of endangered species.

poison *n.* A substance that, if ingested, is capable of endangering life or injuring health. It is an offence (punishable by up to five years' imprisonment) to cause someone to consume a poison or any other noxious substance (which can include drugs or alcohol administered in such quantities as to be harmful) with the intention of injuring or annoying them, even if no injury results. It is also an offence (punishable by up to ten years' imprisonment) to cause someone to consume such substances so that their life is endangered or they suffer grievous bodily harm as a result, even if this was not intended. Administering poison with the intention of killing someone or causing them serious harm may amount to an attempt to murder or to cause *grievous bodily harm. In both cases the attempt will be punishable with a maximum sentence of life imprisonment.

The sale of poisons is controlled by various statutes, principally the Medicines Act 1968 and Poisons Act 1972.

police authorities *See* POLICE FORCE.

Police Complaints Authority An independent body established under the Police and Criminal Evidence Act 1984 to supervise the investigation of complaints against the police. The Authority considers reports by chief constables on the results of such investigations and has power to direct that disciplinary charges be preferred. It may also direct that the charges be heard by a disciplinary tribunal consisting of the chief constable and two members of the Authority.

police court A *magistrates' court.

police force A body of police officers maintained for a police area by a police authority. In England and Wales there are five **police authorities** (Devon and Cornwall, Dyfed Powys, Greater Manchester, South Wales, and Thames Valley). London has the Metropolitan Police Authority, and Northern Ireland has the Police Authority for Northern Ireland. Police authorities consist of local councillors, magistrates, and independent members. They are responsible for maintaining adequate and efficient forces and (except in London), subject to the Home Secretary's approval, for appointing chief constables. (The London forces have Commissioners, and the appointment of the Commissioner of Police of the Metropolis is technically by the Crown.) Police authorities do not, however, exercise operational or managerial control, although they are responsible for ensuring that authorities comply with their statutory duties of *best value. Appointments to a police force, and the direction of its operations, are matters for the chief constable or Commissioner, and its detailed management is largely determined by regulations made by the Home Secretary.

police officer A person who, whatever his rank within a police force, holds the ancient office of **constable**, i.e. one who has undertaken to serve the Crown as an officer of the peace. His office is, in law, independent. He is not technically a Crown servant, since the Crown neither appoints him nor pays him, nor is he a local authority employee. *See* POLICE FORCE.

police protection order An order of the court enabling the police to remove a child to suitable accommodation if there is reasonable cause to believe that the child would otherwise be likely to suffer significant harm. No child may be kept in police protection for more than 72 hours and the police do not acquire *parental responsibility as a result of the order. *See also* SECTION 47 ENQUIRY.

political asylum Refuge granted to a person on political grounds. A person subject to UK immigration control (*see* IMMIGRATION) is allowed to enter and remain in the UK if he would be liable to persecution for reasons of race, religion, nationality, or political opinion if he was returned to the country from which he came. *See also* ASYLUM.

political offence An offence committed for a political purpose or inspired by a political motive, for which the alleged offender cannot be extradited (*see* EXTRADITION) or surrendered as a *fugitive offender. The act could be a combination of a politically motivated but criminally implemented act, or it may be more narrowly political, or it may be criminal activity that resulted from an attempt to escape a political system or discriminatory persecution. In all cases, however, the offence results from a dispute between the fugitive and the state that applies for extradition on some issue connected with the political control or government of the country.

poll tax *See* COMMUNITY CHARGE.

pollution *n.* Any action rendering the environment impure. Statutes relating wholly or partly to **air pollution** include the Clean Air Acts 1956 and 1968, the Health and Safety at Work Act 1974, the Control of Pollution Act 1974, the Environmental Protection Act 1990, and the Environment Act 1995, which control the emission of smoke into the atmosphere, the emission of noxious or offensive substances, and the composition of petrol and other fuels. **Water pollution** generally is governed by the Control of Pollution Act 1974 and the Environmental Protection Act 1990, under which it is an offence (among other things) to allow polluting matter to enter rivers or other inland waters or to impede their flow so as to aggravate pollution due to other causes. Control of pollution by oil is covered by the Prevention of Oil Pollution Act 1971. Pollution by the deposit of waste on land is governed primarily by the Control of Pollution Act 1974, which permits household, commercial, and industrial waste to be deposited only on licensed sites. Local authorities are required by the Act to collect and dispose of household waste free of charge; for the purposes of **refuse disposal** by their residents, they are also, by the Refuse Disposal (Amenity) Act 1978, obliged to provide free refuse dumps.

polygamy *n.* The practice of having more than one spouse. English law considers a marriage **actually polygamous** if there is in fact more than one spouse, and **potentially polygamous** if there is only one spouse but the marriage was contracted under a system of law that permits polygamy. No polygamous marriage may be validly contracted in England. If it is celebrated abroad, however, it will be recognized if at the time it was celebrated neither spouse was domiciled in England; if either spouse was at that time domiciled in England the marriage will be void. For the purposes of the Social Security Contributions and Benefits Act 1992 a polygamous marriage is to be treated as valid at any time while it is monogamous in fact.

port *n.* A place or town with access to the sea to which ships may conveniently come and at which they may load and unload. In charterparties and marine insurance policies, the word is construed in this commercial sense, as understood in the shipping business. For pilotage or revenue purposes, a port may extend over a larger geographical area than the commercial port.

portion *n.* Funds or other property given or left to a child by his parent or someone standing *in loco parentis* and intended to make permanent provision for him or to establish him in life (e.g. a sum provided to set the child up in business). Sums provided for the child's maintenance or education or to supplement his income do not qualify. A portion may be brought into *hotchpot and may be presumed to adeem a legacy (*see* ADEMPTION) unless there is evidence that the testator intended the portion to be disregarded on his death.

positive discrimination Actively favouring one sex or category of people over others because they are considered to be disadvantaged. Positive discrimination is usually illegal as it is in itself discrimination, but actions that encourage a particular group are permitted. Thus job advertisements which state that applications from women and ethnic minorities are welcome are legal, but choosing a candidate for a post solely on the grounds of racial origin or sex will not be permitted in most circumstances.

positive law *See* NATURAL LAW.

possession *n.* Actual control of property combined with the intention to use it, rightly or wrongly, as one's own. In the case of land, possession may be actual, when the owner has entered onto the land, or possession in law, when he has the right to enter but has not yet done so. Possession includes receipt of rent and profits, or the right to receive them. *See also* QUIET POSSESSION.

possessory lien *See* LIEN.

possessory title Ownership of land that can only be proved by evidence of the requisite period of *adverse possession or possession coupled with a defective documentary title. A proprietor of registered land having only possessory title is not protected against any adverse estate, interest, or right subsisting or capable of arising up to the time when the title was first registered.

possibility *n.* (in land law) An interest in land that depends on the occurrence of an uncertain future event. A **bare possibility**, such as a *spes successionis*, i.e. a person's expectation of inheriting land under the will of a testator who is still alive (i.e. depending on the testator dying without having revoked the will), confers no legal or equitable interest. A **possibility coupled with an interest** (e.g. B's rights under a conveyance "to A for life, and if C is living at A's death then to B") can be transferred by will or by deed. *See also* POSSIBILITY OF REVERTER; TENANT IN TAIL AFTER POSSIBILITY OF ISSUE EXTINCT.

possibility of reverter The interest of a person who has conveyed land to another until the occurrence of some specified event (which may never happen). The *determinable interest thus created will end automatically should this future event occur, and the legal estate will revert to the grantor. Thus, when A conveys land to B until he marries, A has a possibility of reverter when B marries (although if B dies unmarried, the possibility of reverter is lost). *See* SETTLED LAND.

post-mortem *n.* [Latin: after death] *See* AUTOPSY.

postnuptial settlement *See* MARRIAGE SETTLEMENT.

power *n.* A legal discretion (as opposed to a *duty) to carry out or refrain from carrying out any act. When powers affect the rights of others (e.g. the powers of *trustees and *administrative powers), their exercise can be challenged in the courts. An act that goes beyond the scope of a power as specified in the instrument creating it (e.g. a trust deed or statute) is invalid; so, too, is any act carried out in abuse of a power (e.g. when it is exercised after taking irrelevant considerations into account, for improper motives, or capriciously). *See also* ULTRA VIRES.

power in the nature of a trust *See* TRUST POWER.

power of appointment A right given to someone to dispose of property that is not his, within bounds established by the owner of the property (it is sometimes called a **mere** or **bare power**; *compare* TRUST POWER). The owner of the property (the **donor** of the power) gives a power to another (the **donee** of the power, or **appointor**) to appoint (give) the property to a person (the **appointee**) chosen by the appointor. The power may be **general** (under which an appointment may be made to anyone, including the donee or the appointor himself), **special** (an appointment may be made only within a class chosen by the donor), or **hybrid** (an appointment may be made to virtually anyone except a small class). The appointees have very limited rights – much more limited than those of beneficiaries under a trust. An appointment is void if it is made to someone not within the class chosen or if it is a *fraud on a power.

power of arrest (in cases of domestic violence) A power attached to, for example, a *nonmolestation order or an *occupation order, which enables a police constable to arrest without warrant a person whom he has reasonable cause for suspecting of being in breach of the order to which it is attached, even though that person might not be committing a criminal offence.

power of attorney (letter of attorney) A formal instrument by which one person empowers another to act on his behalf, either generally or in specific circumstances. A power to execute a *deed must itself be given by a deed.

power of sale 1. The right of a mortgagee to sell mortgaged property if the mortgagor has not repaid his loan by the contractual date of redemption. This power arises when the contractual date (stated in the mortgage document and usually very early in the period of the mortgage) has passed, but may only be exercised if interest due under the mortgage is two months in arrears, if there has been a breach of certain terms in the mortgage by the mortgagor, or if notice has been served on the mortgagor to repay the loan and the loan (or part of it) has not been repaid within three months of the notice. If the mortgagee sells the property under the power of sale, he owes a duty to the mortgagor to act with reasonable care and hold on trust any money surplus to that needed to pay his mortgage debt for the mortgagor's benefit. Certain types of mortgagee (such as building societies and local authorities) have a statutory duty to take care to obtain the best price that can reasonably be obtained through the exercise of the power of sale. **2.** The right of a *tenant for life under the Settled Land Act 1925 to sell the settled land for the best price in money that can be obtained. Such a sale *overreaches the interests of the subsequent beneficiaries.

power of search The legal right to search people or property. Private people have no powers of search, but various statutes, notably the Police and Criminal Evidence Act 1984, confer such powers on police or other officials, often on the authority of a **search warrant** issued by a magistrate or a High Court judge. The 1984 Act empowers the police to stop and search any person or vehicle found in a *public place for stolen or prohibited articles and to detain a person or vehicle for such a search. (An article is "prohibited" if it is either an *offensive weapon or made or adapted for use in connection with *burglary, *theft, taking a *conveyance, or obtaining property by *deception.) Before such a search the police officer must state his station and object. If out of uniform, he must produce evidence of his status. He must always give his grounds for the search if asked and must record details of it. A magistrate may issue a search warrant to an officer if he is satisfied that there are reasonable grounds for believing that a serious arrestable offence (*see* DETENTION) has been committed and material evidence is to be found on the premises. Under the Theft Act 1968, for example, police may obtain a warrant to search for stolen goods when there are reasonable grounds for believing that they are in someone's possession or on his premises. Under certain circumstances the police are given powers of search without requiring either a warrant or any superior authorization; for example, under the Misuse of Drugs Act 1971 (*see* CONTROLLED DRUGS) and the Terrorism Act 2000 (*see* TERRORISM). The police also have a general power, when arresting someone for an *arrestable offence, to enter and search any place in which the suspect is believed to be. Statutes sometimes give powers of search to public officials, e.g. customs officers, Department of Trade and Industry officials, or Inland Revenue officers.

Police powers of stop and search were extended under the Criminal Justice and Public Order Act 1994. Where a senior police officer reasonably believes that an incident involving serious violence may take place in his area he may issue an authorization (valid for 24 hours, extendable for up to 6 hours) for persons and vehicles (which can include caravans, ships, aircraft, and hovercraft and their passengers) to be stopped and searched if he thinks it expedient to do so to prevent violence. A constable in uniform may stop and search any person for the purpose of seeing whether that person is carrying an offensive weapon or an instrument that has a blade or a sharp point. Failure to stop is a *summary offence punishable by one month's imprisonment and/or a *fine on level 3. Failure to cooperate might amount to *obstructing a police officer in the execution of his duty. Similar powers are available to senior police officers to authorize searches for periods of 28 days to prevent acts of *terrorism connected with the affairs of Northern Ireland or international terrorism. Both failure to stop and wilful obstruction of a constable are *summary offences for the purpose of this power and are punishable by six months' imprisonment and/or a *fine on level 5.

practice *n.* **1.** The mode of proceeding to enforce a legal right. It is virtually synonymous with *procedure, but is sometimes used to denote informal rules of procedure as distinct from those derived from rules of court. **2.** A book on practice and procedure, such as the *Civil Procedure Rules.

Practice Directions Published statements, usually issued by the head of the court or division to which they relate, indicating the procedure to be followed in particular matters or the court's intended policy in certain cases. Unlike *rules of court, they have no statutory authority. They are normally published in the law reports. Masters' Practice Directions, issued by the Queen's Bench Masters, concern the administration of the *Queen's Bench Division.

practice master *See* CENTRAL OFFICE.

practising certificate An annual certificate issued by the *Law Society to a solicitor entitling him to practise. The fee chargeable includes the premium of an insurance policy indemnifying the solicitor against the consequences of professional negligence. Barristers obtain a practising certificate from the *Bar Council after they have successfully completed a twelve-month pupillage and have attended further education courses required by the Bar Council.

praecipe *n.* [Latin: command] **1.** A court document on which a party writes the particulars of a document that he wishes to have prepared or issued. In county court procedure, this document is now called a **request. 2.** Formerly, a writ requiring the sheriff to command the defendant either to do a certain thing or to show cause why he had not done it.

pre-action protocols Protocols introduced as a result of the recommendations of Lord Woolf's *Access to Justice* (Final Report) 1996 to speed up the early parts of the litigation process. Pre-action protocols encourage greater contact between the parties at the earliest possible opportunity in order to encourage better and earlier exchange of information with a view to fair and early settlement of claims. Two protocols only have been drawn up, one in clinical negligence actions and the other in personal injury actions. Pre-action protocols can be enforced by the court and are seen as an aspect of the courts' new responsibility of *case management under the *Civil Procedure Rules.

preamble *n.* The part of a statute that sets out its purposes and effects. It follows immediately after the long title and date of royal assent. Preambles are now virtually confined to statutes originating in private Bills.

precarious possession Possession of property at the will of another person.

precatory trust *See* PRECATORY WORDS.

precatory words Words that accompany a gift of property in a document, hoping, desiring, or requesting that the donee will dispose of the property in a particular way. It is often difficult to decide whether there is sufficient certainty of intention to create a trust (**precatory trust**) or whether the property is an absolute gift to the recipient. The courts have tended to construe gifts so as not to create a trust, unless there is no doubt that a trust was intended, although some recent cases have indicated a reversal of this trend, especially where the settlor has not taken legal advice.

precedent *n.* A judgment or decision of a court, normally recorded in a *law report, used as an authority for reaching the same decision in subsequent cases. In English law, judgments and decisions can represent **authoritative precedent** (which is generally binding and must be followed) or **persuasive precedent** (which need not be followed). It is that part of the judgment that represents the legal reasoning (or *ratio decidendi*) of a case that is binding, but only if the legal reasoning is from a superior court and, in general, from the same court in an earlier case. Accordingly, *ratio decidendis* of the *House of Lords are binding upon the *Court of Appeal and all lower courts and are normally followed by the House of Lords itself. The *ratio decidendis* of the Court of Appeal are binding on all lower courts and, subject to some exceptions, on the Court of Appeal itself. *Ratio decidendis* of the High Court are binding on inferior courts, but not on itself. The *ratio decidendis* of inferior courts do not create any binding precedent.

precept *n.* A lawful demand or direction, particularly a demand from a rating authority to another authority to levy rates for the benefit of the former. For example, a district council's rates include an amount that it collects as a result of a precept from its county council.

predatory pricing The practice, undertaken largely by dominant businesses, of pricing goods or services at such a low level that competitors are forced to leave the market. While small companies are entitled to price as they wish, provided this is not in collusion with other companies, dominant businesses must comply with *Article 82 of the Treaty of Rome and the Competition Act 1998; predatory pricing may be an *abuse of a dominant position contrary to these provisions. Companies can be fined for engaging in predatory pricing.

predecessor *n.* (in land law) A person through whom an owner's title to land is traced. Examples are a previous owner who sold, bequeathed, or settled the land and a mortgagee who exercised his power of sale.

pre-emption *n.* The right of first refusal to purchase land in the event that the grantor of the right should decide to sell. For example, if A makes a covenant that for five years he will not sell his land other than to B at £5000, A cannot be forced to sell (*compare* OPTION TO PURCHASE) but B's right of pre-emption prevents him from selling other than on the stated terms for five years. A right of pre-emption is valid only if it is sufficiently precise. There is some confusion with respect to registration of such a right: if it is capable of registration it will bind third parties only if registered (*see* REGISTRATION OF ENCUMBRANCES).

pre-emptive right **1.** The right of some shareholders under the Companies Act 1985 to be offered a proportion of certain classes of newly issued securities before they are offered to anyone else and upon terms at least as favourable. (*See also* RIGHTS ISSUE.) **2.** The right conferred by the articles of association upon shareholders in some private companies to be offered, on specified terms, first refusal of the shares of any shareholder wishing to transfer his holding.

preference *n.* **1.** The favouring by an insolvent debtor of a particular creditor (for example by paying one creditor in full when there is no prospect of paying the others). If the debtor subsequently becomes bankrupt (in the case of an individual) or goes into insolvent liquidation (in the case of a company), and was motivated by a desire to improve the position of the creditor, the court can order that the position be restored to what it would have been had that creditor not been given preference. The court can also make orders when the debtor has given property away or sold it at an undervalue. **2.** A floating *charge created within one year before the commencement of *winding-up in favour of an existing creditor. It is invalid if the company was insolvent at the time it was created unless the creditor provided some fresh benefit to the company at that time, e.g. by way of loan or goods supplied. If the charge was created in favour of a person connected with the company, the period is two years and it is not necessary to show that the company was insolvent at the time of its creation.

preference share *See* SHARE.

preferential debts The debts of a company on *winding-up or of an individual on bankruptcy that have priority over unsecured debts and those secured only by floating *charge. They are defined in the Insolvency Act 1986 and include various debts to government departments and to employees.

preferment *n.* **1.** The submission of a statement or information. **2.** The act of bringing a *bill of indictment before an appropriate court.

pregnancy *n.* (in employment law) *See* DISMISSAL; MATERNITY RIGHTS.

pregnancy *per alium* [Latin: by another] Pregnancy of a woman at the time of her marriage by someone other than her husband. If the husband was unaware of the true facts of the pregnancy, the marriage is voidable.

prehearing assessment *See* EMPLOYMENT TRIBUNAL.

pre-incorporation contract A contract purporting to be made by a person acting as agent for a company not yet formed. Under the Companies Act 1985, that person is personally liable on the contract.

prejudice *n.* Preconceived judgment. *See* UNFAIR PREJUDICE; WITHOUT PREJUDICE.

preliminary inquiries A set of inquiries presented by an intending purchaser of land or property to the intending vendor at an early stage in the transaction. Sometimes known as **precontract inquiries**, they relate to the state and condition of the property rather than to the title. Printed standard forms of inquiries are available. A vendor who gives false or misleading replies can be liable for misrepresentation, but a vendor's replies may be (and often are) noncommittal and evasive. Alternatively, a vendor may be required to complete a Seller's Property Information Form (*see* CONVEYANCING).

preliminary investigation (preliminary inquiry) The procedure in a magistrates' court to decide whether or not there is a sufficient case to commit an accused person for trial by the Crown Court. *See* COMMITTAL FOR TRIAL.

preliminary point of law A question of law ordered to be tried before the facts of the case are determined. Orders of this kind are normally made if the point of law will be decisive in the litigation or will result in a substantial saving of *costs.

premises *pl. n.* **1.** Land or buildings; a parcel of land. **2.** *See* DEED.

premium *n.* **1.** The sum payable (usually annually) by the insured to the insurer under a contract of *insurance. Since October 1994 household and motor insurance premiums have been subject to a duty known as **insurance premium tax** (5% in 2001). **2.** A lump sum that is sometimes paid by a tenant at the time of the grant, assignment, or renewal of his lease or tenancy. It was illegal to demand a premium in respect of a *protected tenancy but this does not apply to *assured tenancies. **3.** *See* CAPITAL.

prenuptial agreement An agreement entered into before marriage, usually to limit the claims one spouse can make on divorce from the other. Prenuptial agreements are common in the United States but are of dubious validity in the UK.

preparatory hearing A hearing before a judge of the Crown Court, before the jury are sworn, in a case of serious or complex fraud for the purpose of identifying issues likely to arise in the case and assisting in their comprehension and management. *See also* SERIOUS FRAUD OFFICE.

prerogative of mercy The power of the Crown, on the Home Secretary's advice, to pardon a criminal offence absolutely (and thereby relieving the defendant of all the consequences of conviction), to commute a sentence to a milder form, or to remit a sentence in part.

prerogative orders Orders issued by the High Court for the supervision of inferior courts, tribunals, and other bodies exercising judicial or quasi-judicial functions. They comprise *quashing orders, *mandatory orders, and *prohibition orders. Until 1938 they were **prerogative writs**, but since the Administration of Justice Act 1938 the only remaining prerogative writ is *habeas corpus.

prescribed by law A prerequisite for interference with any right in the European Convention of Human Rights: any such interference will be unlawful if it is not prescribed by law (or "in accordance with the law"). To be "prescribed by law" there must be a legal regime governing the interference in question. Moreover, that law must be both adequately accessible (in that citizens must be able to understand whether or not the law applies in a given case) and formulated with sufficient precision to enable citizens to regulate their conduct.

prescribed limit The maximum amount of alcohol a person is legally allowed to have in his blood if he is driving or in charge of a motor vehicle on a road or public place (*see* DRUNKEN DRIVING). The level is currently fixed at 80 milligrams of alcohol per 100 millilitres of blood.

prescription *n.* **1.** (in land law) The acquisition for the benefit of one's own land (the dominant tenement) of an *easement or *profit *à prendre* over another's land (the servient tenement) by uninterrupted use over a long period. A person claiming a right by prescription must show that his use did not have the servient owner's permission and was not kept secret or exercised by force. Under the Prescription Act 1832 most easements may be acquired by prescription over 20 years, the period being extended when the servient owner is under a disability (e.g. a child or person of unsound mind), although 40 years' use establishes an absolute and indefeasible right. The periods are 30 and 60 years in the case of profits. An absolute easement of light is acquired after 20 years' use. Rights can also be acquired at common law under the doctrine of *lost modern grant, or by proof of continuous use since time immemorial, i.e. since 1189. **2.** (in international law) The acquisition of title to territory through an uncontested exercise of sovereignty over an extended period of time. Prescription presupposes a prior sovereign authority whose control and administration over the territory in question has lapsed through (1) failure to occupy, (2) failure to administer, (3) abandonment or neglect, (4) a wrongful original claim, or (5) failure to contest a new claim.

presentment *n.* The act of presenting a *bill of exchange to the person upon whom it is drawn for his *acceptance or for payment. When a bill is payable after sight, presentment for acceptance is necessary in order to fix its *maturity. Bills must normally be presented for payment; otherwise the drawer and endorsers are discharged. There are rules as to the time and place of presentment.

presents *pl. n. See* DEED.

preserved county A *county that remains in existence for certain legal purposes, such as licensing legislation, although it has been abolished as a *local government area after local government reorganization. *See also* LOCAL GOVERNMENT COMMISSION FOR ENGLAND.

presiding judge A *puisne judge appointed by the Lord Chancellor to supervise the work of a circuit (*see* CIRCUIT SYSTEM). Each circuit has two presiding judges with the exception of the South-Eastern circuit, which has the Lord Chief Justice and two puisne judges. There is a Senior Presiding Judge for England and Wales.

pressing social need A concept that has been used by the European Court of Human Rights as the basis for assessing whether or not an interference with a *qualified right is necessary in a democratic society.

presumption *n.* A supposition that the law allows or requires to be made. Some presumptions relate to people, e.g. the presumption of innocence and of sanity (see entries below). Others concern events, e.g. the presumption of legality (***omnia***

praesumuntur rite et solemniter esse acta: all things are presumed to have been done correctly and solemnly). Most relate to the interpretation of written documents, particularly statutes (*see* INTERPRETATION OF STATUTES). Almost every presumption is a **rebuttable presumption**, i.e. it holds good only in the absence of contrary evidence. Thus, the presumption of innocence is destroyed by positive proof of guilt. An **irrebuttable presumption** is one that the law does not allow to be contradicted by evidence, as, for example, the presumption that a child below the age of 10 is incapable of committing a crime (*see* DOLI CAPAX). *See also* EQUITABLE PRESUMPTIONS.

presumption of advancement *See* ADVANCEMENT.

presumption of death A common-law presumption that someone has died. The presumption will be made if a spouse has been missing for at least seven years (with nothing to indicate that he or she is still alive) or by proof of other reasonable grounds (e.g. that the spouse was on a ship that sank). The courts are empowered to grant a decree of **presumption of death and dissolution of marriage**, enabling the other spouse to remarry; the remarriage will be valid even if the first spouse later reappears.

presumption of due execution If on the face of it a will appears to be duly executed, a court will not inquire further into the circumstances of its execution, but will presume that all formalities were properly observed, unless there is positive and reliable evidence to the contrary.

presumption of innocence The legal presumption that every person charged with a criminal offence is innocent until proved guilty. Although this is termed a "presumption" it is in fact a fundamental principle underlying the criminal law, which has been reinforced by the Human Rights Act 1998 (*see* FAIR TRIAL). *See* BURDEN OF PROOF.

presumption of legality *See* PRESUMPTION.

presumption of legitimacy *See* LEGITIMACY.

presumption of negligence *See* RES IPSA LOQUITUR.

presumption of sanity The legal presumption that every person charged with a criminal offence was sane (and therefore responsible in law) at the time he is alleged to have committed the crime. *See* INSANITY.

presumption of survivorship *See* COMMORIENTES.

presumptive evidence *See* PRIMA FACIE EVIDENCE.

pre-trial review A hearing for the preliminary consideration of an action or matter. The hearing is before a judge, who is required to consider the course of the proceedings and give all necessary directions for their future conduct. The judge also has power to enter judgment at the pre-trial review in some circumstances, e.g. if the defendant does not file a defence or appear at the hearing.

previous convictions (in the law of evidence) In general, evidence that a party or witness has been convicted of a criminal offence on some previous occasion is inadmissible in both civil and criminal cases as part of the opposing party's own case, unless it is admissible *similar-fact evidence or, in civil cases, unless it is relevant to any issue in the proceedings. However, a witness (other than an accused person) may be cross-examined about his previous convictions in order to impeach (discredit) him. Under the terms of the Criminal Evidence Act 1898, the accused may only be cross-examined about his previous convictions if (1) they are relevant to show that he is guilty of the offence with which he is charged (i.e. they would be admissible similar-fact evidence if they were tendered as part of the prosecution's own case); (2) the accused has attempted to establish his own good character or has cast imputations upon the character of the prosecutor or his witnesses; or (3) the accused has given evidence against any other person charged in the same proceedings. If a witness is asked about a previous conviction and denies the conviction, *evidence in rebuttal may be given. *See also* CREDIT.

previous statements (in the law of evidence) If a witness has on some previous occasion made a statement that is inconsistent with his present testimony, this may be put to him in *cross-examination in order to impeach (discredit) him; if he denies having made the statement, it may be proved by *secondary evidence. Evidence of the previous consistent statements of a witness is not in general admissible. It may, however, be given in order to rebut the suggestion that his present testimony is a recent fabrication or when it concerns the *complaint of the victim of a sexual offence. *See also* CREDIT.

price *n.* In a contract of sale, the money *consideration given in exchange for the transfer of ownership. In a contract of *sale of goods the price may be fixed by the contract, it may be left to be fixed in a manner agreed by the contract, or it may be determined by the course of dealing between the parties. If the price is not determined in any of the above ways, the buyer must pay a reasonable price. Under the Consumer Protection Act 1987, it is a criminal offence to give a misleading indication of the price of goods, services, accommodation, or facilities; for example, when the consumer might reasonably expect the price indicated to cover matters for which an additional charge is in fact made.

prima facie [from Latin *prima facies*, first appearance] At first appearance; on the face of things.

prima facie case A case that has been supported by sufficient evidence for it to be taken as proved in the absence of adequate evidence to the contrary.

prima facie evidence 1. (presumptive evidence) Evidence that is sufficient to discharge any evidential *burden of proof borne by a party and that may be sufficient to discharge the persuasive burden of proof if no evidence in rebuttal is tendered. **2.** Evidence of a fact that is of sufficient weight to justify a reasonable inference of its existence but does not amount to conclusive evidence of that fact.

Primary Care Trust (PCT) One of a group of bodies within the *National Health Service, established under the Health Act 1999 for providing, or arranging for the provision of, general medical services in local areas. Each PCT is established by an order made by the Secretary of State. PCTs replaced the GP fundholding system.

primary evidence Evidence, such as the original of a document, that by its nature does not suggest that better evidence is available. Even if an item of primary evidence is inadmissible (e.g. because it is the subject of a private *privilege), the same fact may, in most cases, be proved by *secondary evidence.

primary facts Facts found by the trial court to be established on the basis of the testimony of witnesses and the production of real or documentary evidence. Appellate courts are generally unwilling to change the trial court's findings concerning primary facts, but may reverse its decisions concerning the inferences to be drawn from them.

Prime Minister The head of the UK government, who is appointed by the Crown to select and preside over the *Cabinet and bears ultimate responsibility for the policy and machinery of government. The Prime Minister also advises the Crown on such matters as the dissolution of Parliament, the creation of peerages, and the making of senior appointments (e.g. the Ombudsman). Like the Cabinet, the office derives from *constitutional convention, which requires that the person appointed is the leader of the party with the greatest number of Members of Parliament.

principal *n.* **1.** (in criminal law) The person who actually carries out a crime. (Formerly, the actual perpetrator was known as the **principal in the first degree** and a person who aided and abetted was called **principal in the second degree**, but the former is now known as the principal and the latter as the secondary party.) A person can be a principal even if he does not carry out the act himself; for example, if he acts through an innocent agent, such as a child, or if he is legally responsible for the acts of another (e.g. because of *vicarious liability). *See also* ACCESSORY. **2.** (in the law of agency) The person on whose behalf an *agent acts. **3.** (in finance) The sum of money lent or invested, as distinguished from the interest.

principal mansion house The main house (other than a farmhouse or a house whose accompanying garden, park, and grounds occupy less than 25 acres) comprised in a settlement of land. Under the Settled Land Act 1925, if the terms of the settlement so provide, the tenant for life cannot sell the principal mansion house without the consent of the trustees or the court. Consent is necessary under a settlement made before 1926 unless its terms dispense with the requirement.

principle of legality *See* NULLUM CRIMEN SINE LEGE.

priority *n.* *See* PRIORITY OF ASSIGNMENT; PRIORITY OF MORTGAGES; PRIORITY OF TIME.

priority neighbourhood An area declared such by a housing authority, being broadly similar to a *housing action area. A priority neighbourhood is declared when it is not practicable either to constitute the area itself a housing action area or a general improvement area or to include it in one. Priority neighbourhoods are typically areas surrounding or adjoining housing action areas or general improvement areas.

priority notice **1.** A notice lodged at HM Land Registry that prevents, for 14 days, anyone other than the person lodging the notice from registering title to the land concerned or any dealing in it. Provided that he lodges his application for registration of his own title or dealing within the period of protection, he will not be bound by any other encumbrances lodged for registration before his own. In practice, dealings (i.e. transfers, mortgages, etc.) in land that is already registered are usually protected by the applicant's certificate of *official search rather than by separate registration of a priority notice. **2.** In the case of unregistered land, a notice lodged at the Land Charges Department of the intended registration of a charge. The priority notice is lodged at least 15 days before the intended charge is to take effect, and the subsequent registration of the charge will be effective from the time the charge was created, provided the application for registration is presented within 30 days after the priority notice. Thus when A is about to convey land to B, who is to give a restrictive covenant in A's favour, A may lodge a priority notice before completing the transaction and register the covenant afterwards. This will ensure that the covenant will bind any purchaser or mortgagee from B whose interest may arise before A can register the covenant as a charge.

priority of assignment The order in which two or more *assignments of a chose in action takes effect. This order is determined according to the date of receipt of the notice of assignment by the legal owner of the property assigned.

priority of mortgages The order in which two or more mortgages of the same property take effect. If there are several mortgages of the same property, and its value is less than the amount due on the mortgages, the respective claims of the mortgagees must be determined. Before 1926, priority often depended on the date order in which the mortgages were created. Since 1925 the order of priority in the case of *registered land is according to the date order in which the respective mortgages are registered. A first mortgagee of *unregistered land usually retains the title deeds and has priority over others except prior mortgages that are registered as a land charge in the Land Charges Registry. Otherwise the order is governed by the order of registration. Priority of equitable interests is determined by the date at which notice is received by the trustees. *See also* CONSOLIDATION OF MORTGAGES; TACKING.

priority of time When there are two or more competing equitable interests, the equitable maxim *qui prior est tempore potior est jure* (he who is earlier in time is stronger in law) applies. This means that the first in time prevails over the others. For example, where a property is subject to two mortgages, the one granted first has priority (*see* PRIORITY OF MORTGAGES). However, the priority can be affected by the existence of a purchaser for value without notice, fraud, estoppel, gross negligence, registration, and overreaching.

privacy *n.* The right to be left alone. The right to a private life as set out in Article 8 of the European Convention on Human Rights is now part of UK law as a consequence of the *Human Rights Act 1998. The right includes privacy of communications (telephone calls, correspondence, etc); privacy of the home and office; environmental protection; the protection of physical integrity; and protection from unjustified prosecution and conviction of those engaged in consensual nonviolent sexual activities. This right is a *qualified right; as such, the public interest can be used to justify an interference with it providing that this is prescribed by law, designed for a legitimate purpose, and proportionate. Public authorities have a limited but positive duty to protect privacy from interference by third parties.

private Act *See* ACT OF PARLIAMENT.

private Bill *See* BILL.

private carrier *See* CARRIER.

private company A residuary type of *registered company defined under the Companies Act 1985 as any company that is not a *public company. This form of company is prohibited from offering its shares to the public at large. Although not a strict requirement under the Act, it is common to find such companies placing restrictions on the *transfer of shares and confining them to other (often family) members. Unlike a public company, a private company can consist of only one *company member (**single-member company**), and many of the other restrictions that apply to public companies (such as those relating to *financial assistance) may be relaxed provided that the company complies with a specified procedure under the Act.

private defence Action taken in reasonable defence of one's person or property. It can be pleaded as a defence to an action in tort. The right of private defence includes the defence of one's family and, probably, of any other person from unlawful force.

private international law (conflict of laws) The part of the national law of a country that establishes rules for dealing with cases involving a foreign element (i.e. contact with some system of foreign law). For example, if a contract is made in England but is to be fulfilled abroad, it will be necessary to decide which law governs the validity of the contract. This is known as the question of **choice of law**. Generally, under the Rome Convention (1980; in force from 1 April 1991), the parties' choice of law in a written contract is respected; rules are set down in the Convention stating which laws apply if the parties to the contract have not made a choice. Sometimes the courts must also decide whether or not they have jurisdiction to hear the case and whether or not to recognize a *foreign judgment (such as a divorce obtained abroad).

Private international law must not be confused with public *international law.

private law The part of the law that deals with such aspects of relationships between individuals that are of no direct concern to the state. It includes the law of property and of trusts, family law, the law of contract, mercantile law, and the law of tort. *Compare* PUBLIC LAW.

private life *See* PRIVACY.

private member's Bill *See* BILL.

private nuisance *See* NUISANCE.

privatization *n.* A programme of denationalization – removing the provision of public utility services from the public sector into the private sector under the auspices of public companies with public shareholders. The shareholders may or may not include the government, but increasingly do not. *See also* NATIONALIZED INDUSTRIES.

privilege *n.* **1.** A special right or immunity in connection with legal proceedings conferred upon a person by virtue of his rank or office. For example, Members of Parliament enjoy certain privileges in relation to arrest, which, however, do not extend to arrest in connection with indictable offences (*see* PARLIAMENTARY PRIVILEGE). *See also* ABSOLUTE PRIVILEGE; QUALIFIED PRIVILEGE. **2.** (in the law of evidence) The right of a witness when testifying to refuse to answer certain types of question or of a party when disclosing documents (*see* DISCLOSURE AND INSPECTION OF DOCUMENTS) to refuse to produce certain types of document on the ground of some special interest recognized by law. Privileges are divided into two groups: **public-interest privilege** and **private privilege**. The Crown has always been able to claim public-interest privilege in relation to secrets of the state and other matters whose confidentiality is essential to the functioning of the public service (*see* CROWN PRIVILEGE). It is now recognized that a similar privilege may be claimed by private parties when some overriding public interest is involved. Private privileges include the **privilege against self-incrimination**, according to which a witness may not be asked a question the answer to which might tend to incriminate him; **legal professional privilege**, which protects confidential communications between lawyers and their clients and between lawyers and third parties with a view to advising their clients; and a privilege attaching to *without prejudice communications in the course of litigation. Under EU law there is no professional privilege between a lawyer working for a company and members of that company, only between a lawyer not employed by the company concerned and the company. *See also* MARITAL PRIVILEGES.

privileged communication **1.** A confidential official communication that may be withheld from production in court proceedings because disclosure of its contents would be against the public interest. **2.** A communication between parties in a confidential relationship, such as husband and wife or s solicitor and client, evidence of which may not be given without the consent of the party to whom the privilege belongs. Communications between patient and doctor are not privileged. **3.** (in the tort of *defamation) A communication protected by absolute or qualified privilege. No action for defamation may be brought for a communication that is protected by *absolute privilege. A communication covered by *qualified privilege is protected unle it was made maliciously.

privileged will A will that is valid even though it does not comply with the formal requirements of the Wills Act 1837 (e.g. in being written but not witnessed or in being oral) or is made by a minor. The right to make a privileged will is conferred by the 1837 Act (as extended by the Wills (Soldiers and Sailors) Act 1918) on any soldier in actual military service (a **soldier's will** or **military testament**) and any mariner or seaman at sea (a **mariner's will**). It also applies to airmen on actual military service and, on normal principles of statutory interpretation, to females as well as to males (for example, a female secretary aboard an ocean liner has been held to be a mariner at sea). **Actual military service** has been very widely interpreted. It is not confined to service as a combatant during time of war, but extends to service in any other capacity (e.g. as an auxiliary or a trainee) and to service when war is merely imminent. Service with an occupying force after a war is also included, as is service in support of the civil power against terrorists (e.g. in Northern Ireland). **At sea** has received a similarly wide interpretation. A member of the naval forces is treated as being at sea if he is in an equivalent position to a soldier or airman on actual military service (e.g. if he is on shore leave during wartime).

privilege of witness *See* PRIVILEGE.

privity *n.* The relationship that exists between people as a result of their participation in some transaction or event; for example, *privity of contract and *privity of estate.

privity of contract The relationship that exists between the parties to a contract. The common law doctrine of privity of contract established that only the parties to the contract, i.e. those that provided *consideration, could sue or be sued under the contract. Third parties could not derive rights from, nor have obligations imposed on them by, someone else's contract. This position has now been modified by the Contracts (Rights of Third Parties) Act 1999. By the provisions of the Act, a person can enforce a term of a contract to which he is not a party provided that the term purports to confer a benefit on him or the contract expressly provides for such enforcement.

privity of estate The relationship between landlord and tenant under the same lease; as long as the relationship subsists, the landlord and tenant may enforce their respective obligations against one another even though they were not original parties to the lease. Thus when A grants a lease to B who subsequently assigns his interest to C, while A conveys his reversion to D, D may enforce against C the tenant's covenants given by A although there is no contract between D and C. There is no privity between different leasehold estates. For example if A grants a lease to B who sublets to C, A cannot sue C to enforce positive obligations in either the lease or the sublease, although he may be able to enforce *restrictive covenants contained in the headlease, against C.

Privy Council (PC) A body, headed by the President of the Council, that formerly advised the Crown on government policy but has been superseded in that role by the *Cabinet. Its functions are now mainly formal (e.g. a few members are summoned to make *Orders in Council), but it has limited statutory powers of legislation (*see* ORDERS OF COUNCIL) and it also advises the sovereign, through committees, on certain judicial matters (*see* JUDICIAL COMMITTEE OF THE PRIVY COUNCIL) and other matters of a nonpolitical nature (e.g. the grant of university charters). There are about 350 Privy Counsellors, who include members of the royal family, all Cabinet ministers, the Speaker and other holders of high nonpolitical office, and persons honoured for public services. A Privy Counsellor is addressed as "Right Honourable".

prize court A municipal court that, in accordance with *international law, deals with questions relating to **prize**, i.e. ships, aircraft, or goods captured during wartime at sea or in port by the naval or air forces of a belligerent power. Prize law entitles the belligerent state to expropriate not only enemy vessels and goods but also neutral property suspected of carrying *contraband or running a *blockade. The Supreme Court of Judicature (Consolidation) Act 1925 constituted the High Court a prize court; jurisdiction in prize was vested in the Probate, Divorce and Admiralty Division until its transfer in 1970 to the Admiralty Court (part of the Queen's Bench Division). Prize appeals go to the Judicial Committee of the Privy Council.

probate *n.* A certificate issued by the Family Division of the High Court, on the application of *executors appointed by a will, to the effect that the will is valid and that the executors are authorized to administer the deceased's estate. When there is no apparent doubt about the will's validity, probate is granted in **common form** on the executors filing an *affidavit. Probate granted in common form can be revoked by the court at any time on the application of an interested party who proves that the will is invalid. When the will is disputed, probate in **solemn form** is granted, but only if the court decides that the will is valid after hearing the evidence on the disputed issues in a *probate action. All parties who knew of the probate action and of their interest in the estate are bound by the court's order, whether or not they were parties to the action.

probate action Proceedings in court to determine, for example, whether or not a disputed will is valid or to seek revocation of a previous grant of probate. Contentious probate business is dealt with by the Chancery Division of the High Court. A will may be challenged on the grounds that it was not properly executed (*see* EXECUTION OF WILL), that the testator lacked testamentary capacity, or that it has been revoked.

Probate, Divorce and Admiralty Division A division of the *High Court of Justice created by the Judicature Acts 1873–75 to take over the jurisdiction formerly exercised by the Court of Probate, the Court for Divorce and Matrimonial Causes, and the High Court of Admiralty. The Division was renamed the *Family Division by the Administration of Justice Act 1970: the Admiralty jurisdiction was transferred to the *Queen's Bench Division and the contentious probate jurisdiction to the *Chancery Division.

probation hostel Premises for the accommodation of persons who may be required to reside there by *community rehabilitation orders.

probation officer An officer whose duties include supervising persons bound by (for example) *community rehabilitation orders, *supervision orders, or *community punishment orders. A probation officer advises, assists, and befriends these and others (e.g. persons who have been released from prison or are on bail) and inquires into the circumstances of offenders in order to assist the court to determine how best to deal with them.

probation order *See* COMMUNITY REHABILITATION ORDER.

procedure *n.* (in court proceedings) The formal manner in which legal proceedings are conducted. *See also* ADJECTIVE LAW; PRACTICE; RULES OF COURT.

process *n.* **1.** (in court procedure) A document issued by a court to require the attendance of the parties or the performance of some initial step in the proceedings by a defendant. When it is used to initiate the proceedings it may be called the **originating process**. Most of the confusing process procedures have now been abolished and replaced under the *Civil Procedure Rules; proceedings are now usually initiated by the issue of a *claim form. **2.** *See* ABUSE OF PROCESS.

procès-verbal [French] An informal record or memorandum of international understandings arrived at in negotiations. It is frequently a preliminary step in concluding a *treaty.

procurator fiscal In Scotland, an officer of the sheriff court (roughly equivalent to the English county court). Appointed by the *Lord Advocate, he must be a qualified advocate or solicitor. His duties include initiating preliminary investigations into criminal cases in his district, taking written statements (precognitions) from witnesses, conducting the prosecution, and conducting inquiries into sudden or suspicious deaths.

Procurator General *See* TREASURY SOLICITOR.

procurement *n.* Persuading or inviting a woman to have sexual intercourse. The following are offences of procurement; the sexual intercourse sought may be marital intercourse. (1) Procuring a woman to have sexual intercourse with oneself or anyone else, anywhere in the world, by means of threats or false pretences. (2) Procuring a girl under the age of 21 to have sexual intercourse with a third person anywhere in the world. (3) Procuring a severely mentally retarded woman (who is incapable of guarding herself against exploitation) to have sexual intercourse anywhere in the world. These three offences are committed only if sexual intercourse takes place. (4) Procuring a woman to become a prostitute or to leave the UK with the intention that she should join or frequent a brothel. All these offences are punishable by up to two years' imprisonment.

procuring breach of contract (inducing breach of contract) The tort of intentionally persuading or inducing someone to break a contract made by him with a third party. It is actionable by the party who suffers loss from the breach. Thus a theatre manager may sue the person who induces a singer to break her contract to perform at his theatre. In some circumstances a defence of *justification is available. The tort also covers indirect procurement of breach of contract (i.e. by inducing persons not parties to the contract to procure the breach) and interference with the performance of a subsisting contract without actually causing a breach. These forms of the tort, however, are only actionable if unlawful means are used to procure the breach or interference. The operation of the tort in *trade disputes is limited by statute. *See also* INTERFERING WITH TRADE OR BUSINESS.

procuring disclosure of personal data An offence committed by someone who obtains personal information about an individual that is stored on a computer when he knows or believes that he is not a person to whom the data user is registered to disclose this data (*see* DATA PROTECTION). Other offences are committed when the data procured in this way is offered for sale or sold. In each case the offences were created by the Criminal Justice and Public Order Act 1994.

production of documents The act of a party in making available documents in his possession, custody, or power either for inspection by the other party (*see* DISCLOSURE AND INSPECTION OF DOCUMENTS) or for use as evidence at trial in accordance with a *notice to produce.

products liability The liability of manufacturers and other persons for defective products. Under the Consumer Protection Act 1987, passed to conform with the requirements of European Community law, the producer of a defective product that causes death or personal injury or damage to property is strictly liable for the damage. A claim may only be made for damage to property if the property was for private use or consumption and the value of the damage caused exceeds £275. A product is defective if its safety is not such as persons generally are entitled to expect. The persons liable for a defective product are: (1) the producer (i.e. the manufacturer, including producers of component parts and raw materials), (2) a person who holds himself out to be producer by putting his name or trade mark on the product, (3) a person who imports the product into the European Community, and (4) a supplier who fails, when reasonably requested to do so by the person injured, to identify the producer or importer of the product.

There are several defences to liability under the Act, e.g. *contributory negligence; that the defendant did not supply the product or did not supply it in the course of business; that the defect did not exist at the relevant time; and that the state of scientific and technical knowledge at the relevant time was not such that a producer of such products could be expected to have discovered the defect. Actions must be started within three years from the date when the claimant first had a cause of action or (if later) first knew or should have known the material facts, but not later than ten years from when the product was put into circulation. Liability under the Act may not be excluded by any contract or notice.

Compensation for defective products can also be obtained under the general principles of contract and tort. The purchaser of a defective product may sue the seller for *breach of contract in failing to supply a product that conforms to the contract (including its *implied conditions). An action in tort can be brought by anyone whose person or property is damaged by a defective product against the person whose *negligence caused the damage; this person may be the manufacturer or someone else, such as a distributor or a repairer.

profit-and-loss account A document presenting in summary form a true and fair view of the company's profit or loss as at the end of its financial year. It must show the items listed in one of the four formats set out in the Companies Act 1985. Its function is to show as profit or loss the difference between revenue generated and the expenditure incurred in the period covered by the account. *See also* ACCOUNTS.

profit à prendre The right to take soil, minerals, or produce (such as wood, turf, or fish) from another's land (the servient tenement) or to graze animals on it. It may exist as a legal or equitable interest. The right may be enjoyed exclusively by one person (a **several profit**) or by one person in common with others (a **common**). A profit may exist **in gross** (i.e. existing independently of any ownership of land by the person entitled) and may be exercisable without any limit on the amount of produce taken. It may be sold, bequeathed, or otherwise dealt with. Profits existing for the benefit of the owner's land (the dominant tenement) are generally exercisable only to the extent to which the dominant tenement can benefit. They may be *appurtenant, when the nature of the right depends on the terms of the grant; or *pur cause de vicinage* (Norman French: because of vicinity), in respect of cattle grazing the dominant tenement and straying onto the unfenced adjacent servient tenement. Profits may be created by express or implied grant or by statute; profits appurtenant may also arise by *prescription (or presumed grant). They may be extinguished (1) by an express release; (2) by the owner occupying the servient tenement; or (3) by implied release (e.g. through abandonment, which may be presumed through long *non-user, through changes to the dominant tenement that make enjoyment of the right unnecessary or impossible, or through an irreversible alteration of the servient tenement).

prohibited degrees of relationships Family relationships within which marriage is prohibited (and, if celebrated, is void) although sexual intercourse within such a relationship may not amount to *incest. A man, for example, may not marry his grandmother, aunt, or niece; a woman may not marry her grandfather, uncle, or nephew. Since 1986, there are fewer relationships of *affinity within which marriage is prohibited. For example, a man may now marry his mother-in-law provided his former wife and his former wife's father are both dead.

prohibited steps order *See* SECTION 8 ORDERS.

prohibited weapon A weapon suitable only for use by the armed forces and having no normal function in civilian life. Prohibited weapons include automatic firearms, weapons designed or adapted to discharge a poisonous liquid or gas, and ammunition containing poisonous substances. It is an offence (punishable with up to two years' imprisonment) to produce, sell, buy, or possess any prohibited weapon without the permission of the Defence Council. *See also* FIREARM; OFFENSIVE WEAPON.

prohibition notice A notice under the Health and Safety at Work Act 1974 specifying activities that, in the opinion of an inspector, involve a risk of serious personal injury and prohibiting them until specified safeguards have been adopted. *Compare* IMPROVEMENT NOTICE.

prohibition order A remedy in which the High Court orders an ecclesiastical or inferior court, tribunal, or administrative authority not to carry out an *ultra vires* act (for example, hearing a case that is outside its jurisdiction). It is available in cases in which, had the act been carried out, the remedy would have been a *quashing order and it is governed by broadly similar rules.

prohibitory injunction *See* INJUNCTION.

prolixity *n.* Excessive length or repetitiveness in statements of case, affidavits, or other documents. Modern rules of procedure discourage prolixity: prolix documents may be struck out or the costs of them disallowed.

promise *n.* An undertaking given by one person (the **promisor**) to another (the **promisee**) to do or refrain from doing something. It is legally binding only if contained in a *contract or made by *deed.

promissory estoppel *See* ESTOPPEL.

promissory note An unconditional promise in writing, made by one person to another and signed by the maker, engaging to pay a specified sum of money to (or to the order of) a specified person or to the bearer, either on demand or at a fixed or determinable future time. Promissory notes are *negotiable instruments and many of the provisions in the Bills of Exchange Act 1882 apply with necessary modifications to promissory notes. Promissory notes are not presented for acceptance and the party primarily liable is the maker of a note. A bank note is a promissory note issued by a bank; the sum of money mentioned on the note is payable to the bearer on demand.

promoter *n.* **1.** A person engaged in the formation or *flotation of a company. A promoter stands in a *fiduciary relationship to the company; his functions may include drafting a *prospectus, negotiating preliminary agreements, instructing solicitors, and obtaining directors. Solicitors, bankers, and other professionals involved in the company, but acting merely in their professional role, are not regarded as promoters. **2.** One who introduces a private *Bill.

proof *n.* **1.** The means by which the existence or nonexistence of a fact is established to the satisfaction of the court, including testimony, documentary evidence, presumptions, and judicial notice. Since most facts with which a court is concerned are not capable of being tested empirically, proof in the legal sense is quite different from proof in the context of mathematics or science. The uncorroborated evidence of one credible witness is sufficient proof for most purposes in the law. *See* STANDARD OF PROOF. **2.** (*Informal*) The written statement of a prospective witness obtained by a solicitor. A witness is said not to have **come up to proof** if he fails to testify in accordance with his proof.

proof beyond reasonable doubt The *standard of proof required in criminal proceedings. If the jury has any reasonable (even if unlikely) doubts about the guilt of the accused, it may not convict him. It is often paraphrased by the judge instructing the jury that they must be "satisfied so that they are sure" of the guilt of the accused. It is disputed whether this standard is ever applicable in civil proceedings (e.g. when there is an allegation of fraud): it is generally held that it is not. *See also* BURDEN OF PROOF.

proof of age The age of a person may be proved by *direct evidence, such as the testimony of someone present at the person's birth, and in some cases from his appearance. It is usually proved by producing a birth certificate, under the exception to the hearsay rule relating to statements in *public documents, and evidence that the person in question is the one referred to in the birth certificate.

proof of birth Birth is usually proved by the production of a birth certificate, which is admissible under the exception to the hearsay rule relating to statements in *public documents, coupled with evidence identifying the person in question with the person referred to in the birth certificate.

proof of handwriting Handwriting may be proved by the testimony of the person whose handwriting it is or by that of someone who saw him execute the document in question. It may also be proved by the opinion of someone familiar with the handwriting of the alleged writer or by comparison with a proved example of the writer's handwriting. Expert testimony is also admissible.

proof of marriage Legally valid evidence that a *marriage was celebrated. This will usually be shown by possession of a marriage certificate and proof of identity, but may also be shown by other forms of evidence.

proper law of a contract The system of law that is applied in *private international law to a contract with foreign elements. Which system governs the contract will depend on the intention of the parties to the contract, to be determined in each case by considering the terms of the contract, and all the surrounding facts. If the parties have expressly agreed which law should govern the contract, that law will normally be applied by virtue of the Rome Convention (1980; in force from 1 April 1991). If, as is usual, they have not expressly agreed, the courts try to infer their intention from all the circumstances; if it cannot be inferred, they will apply the system of law with which the contract has "its closest and most real connection". In the UK the Rome Convention is implemented by the Contracts Applicable Law Act 1990.

property *n.* Anything that can be owned. A distinction is made between **real property** (land and incorporeal *hereditaments) and **personal property** (all other kinds of property) and between **tangible property** (that which has a physical existence, e.g. chattels and land) and **intangible property** (*choses in action, including *intellectual property, and incorporeal hereditaments). For purposes of the law of *theft, property includes all real, personal, and intangible property, although land can only be stolen under certain specified conditions. For purposes of the law of *criminal damage, property does not include intangible property.

property adjustment order An order made by the court in proceedings for divorce, separation, or nullity that affects rights of ownership of property belonging to either spouse. Such orders include the transfer of property from one spouse to another, settling property for the benefit of the other spouse or children, varying marriage settlements, or extinguishing rights under such settlements. The courts have exceptionally wide discretion in making property adjustment orders, and each case will depend on its own facts. The general aim of the discretion, and factors to be considered, are identical with those listed in relation to *financial provision orders; two other factors to be considered are the need to provide adequate housing for both spouses, and especially for minor children, and the need to allow each spouse a share in the capital value of the family assets, especially the *matrimonial home. The courts have power to order the sale of the matrimonial home or to make the home subject to a deferred trust for sale, e.g. until the children grow up. As in the case of financial provision orders, the court must achieve a *clean break wherever possible. Property adjustment orders are often awarded in addition to financial provision orders and may only be made on or after the granting of the decree of divorce, separation, or nullity.

property in goods A right of *ownership in chattels.

property register *See* LAND REGISTRATION.

proponent *n.* The party who bears the evidential, and in some cases the persuasive, *burden of proof in relation to an issue in litigation.

proportionality *n.* **1.** A principle of the European Union ensuring that a legislative measure is introduced at EU level only when it is appropriate to have a measure at that level, and that when local legislation is all that is needed, this will be encouraged. *See also* SUBSIDIARITY. **2.** A central provision of the *European Convention on Human Rights. It applies particularly to the *qualified rights and where the expression "necessary in a democratic society" is contained within the article. Whether or not such a right has been violated will depend on whether the interference with the right is proportionate to the legitimate aim pursued by that interference. Thus even if a policy that interferes with a Convention right might be aimed at securing a legitimate purpose (e.g. the prevention of crime), this will not in itself justify the violation if the means adopted to secure the purpose are excessive in the circumstances.

propositus *n.* [Latin] **1.** The person immediately concerned with an issue. **2.** An ancestor through whom descent is traced. **3.** A testator when making his will.

propounder *n.* A person in a *probate action who claims that a disputed will is valid.

proprietary estoppel *See* ESTOPPEL.

proprietor *n.* One who owns land. In the case of registered land, the registered proprietor is the person entitled to the *legal estate and is recorded as such in the proprietorship register (*see* LAND REGISTRATION). The owners of equitable interests are protected by registration of their *minor interests in the appropriate manner.

proprietorship register *See* LAND REGISTRATION.

prorogation *n.* *See* PARLIAMENT.

proscribed organization An organization or association declared to be forbidden by the Home Secretary under the Terrorism Act 2000, because it appears to be concerned with terrorist activities (*see* TERRORISM).

prosecution *n.* The pursuit of legal proceedings, particularly criminal proceedings. (The term is also used for the party instituting the proceedings.) Criminal prosecutions on indictment are in the name of the Crown and summary prosecutions are in the name of an individual, usually a police officer, although a private individual may bring a prosecution (most private prosecutions are for assault). The *Attorney General can intervene in a private prosecution and either take it over or abandon it. Many government departments and other authorities have power to prosecute; for example, the Inland Revenue, the Department for Work and Pensions, and local authorities. Under the Prosecution of Offenders Act 1985, the duty of conducting prosecutions falls principally upon the *Crown Prosecution Service, which exercises the functions previously vested in the *Director of Public Prosecutions, its head. It also takes over the conduct of most proceedings instituted by the police. The *Attorney General's consent is required before prosecution for some offences, e.g. in cases involving official secrets.

prosecutor *n.* The person who institutes criminal proceedings on behalf of the Crown. *See* PROSECUTION.

prospectus *n.* A document inviting the public to invest in shares or debentures of a public company (*see* FLOTATION). The prospectus of a *listed company (called the **listing particulars**) must contain the information required by the Stock Exchange; the prospectus of an unlisted company must comply with the Financial Services Act 1986.

prostitution *n.* The offering of her body by a woman for sexual intercourse or other sexual activities in return for payment. Prostitution itself is not a crime, but various activities related to it are (*see* BROTHEL; KERB CRAWLING; LIVING ON IMMORAL EARNINGS; PROCUREMENT; SOLICITING). Advertising details of prostitutes may amount to a *conspiracy at common law or an *obscene publication. Certain offences concerned with brothels and living on immoral earnings also apply to male prostitution.

protected child A child whom someone wishes to adopt and over whom a local authority must exercise supervision. Under the 1976 Adoption Act, such supervision is only required when the child was not placed for adoption by an adoption agency; in agency cases, the agency itself will be responsible for supervision.

protected goods (under the Consumer Credit Act 1974) Goods that are the subject matter of a regulated *hire purchase or *conditional sale agreement of which the debtor is in breach, but under which he has already paid to the creditor one-third or more of the total price of the goods, which remain in the ownership of the creditor. The creditor may not recover possession of the goods except on an order of the court, which may allow the debtor further time to pay. The restriction does not apply if the debtor has terminated the agreement.

protected occupancy The right of an agricultural worker to occupy a *tied cottage with statutory protection similar to that of a *protected tenancy. Protected occupancies have been replaced by *assured agricultural occupancies by the Housing Act 1988, but protected occupancies already in existence continue to have the same protection as before.

protected person A head of state (or a member of a corporate head of state), head of government, or minister for foreign affairs, or any member of his family accompanying him; or a representative or official of a state or of an intergovernmental international organization who is entitled under international law to special protection from personal injury or any member of his family who is also a member of his household. The Internationally Protected Persons Act 1978 incorporates into English law the provisions of the 1974 New York Convention on Crimes against Internationally Protected Persons. The Act gives jurisdiction to English courts to try those charged with committing certain serious acts against protected persons (e.g. rape, assault, causing actual bodily harm, wounding or inflicting grievous bodily harm, kidnapping, and certain attacks on premises), even if the alleged acts were committed outside the UK. It also creates offences of threatening to commit any of the above acts anywhere in the world, and extends jurisdiction to various types of attempts and assistance. It is no defence to any of these offences that the defendant did not know that the victim was a protected person.

protected shorthold tenancy *See* ASSURED SHORTHOLD TENANCY.

protected site A site for which planning permission has been granted for one or more mobile homes to be set up.

protected state A state that, although nominally sovereign, is under the protection of another state. Usually the protected state allows the protector full control over its external affairs but retains control over its internal affairs. Examples are the Kingdom of Bhutan under the protection of India and the State of Brunei under British protection. A protected state is sometimes called a **protectorate**.

protected tenancy A contractual residential tenancy in which the tenant has the right to a *fair rent and *security of tenure. Protected tenancies have been replaced by *assured tenancies under the Housing Act 1988, but protected tenancies already in existence continue to have the same protection as before. To qualify as a protected tenancy, the premises must be let as a separate dwelling that is within certain rateable value limits and must have been created before the Housing Act 1988 came into force (15 January 1989). There are some exceptions, including lettings to students, holiday lettings, local authority housing, and lettings in which the rent includes payment for board or attendance. If a landlord wishes to terminate a protected tenancy he must first terminate the contractual tenancy in the usual way (*see* NOTICE TO QUIT). A *statutory tenancy then comes into existence and the landlord can obtain possession only by a court order. To do this he must have suitable grounds, such as nonpayment of rent, provision of suitable alternative accommodation for the tenant, or if the landlord needs the property for himself or one of his family to live in.

There were formerly two kinds of protected tenancy: controlled and regulated. All controlled tenancies have now been converted into *regulated tenancies. (*See* CONVERTED TENANCY.) **Furnished tenancies** have the same protection as unfurnished tenancies, but they are more likely to fall within one of the exceptions to protection. *See also* ASSURED SHORTHOLD TENANCY; SECURE TENANCY; RESTRICTED CONTRACT.

protection and indemnity association (or club) An association of shipowners formed to meet, out of funds contributed by its members, liabilities that arise from maritime activities and are not covered by insurance.

protectionism *n.* The practice of protecting states or EU interests by imposing trade barriers and customs duties to prevent imports from abroad. Protectionism is the opposite of free trade. As a party to the *General Agreement on Tariffs and Trade and the *World Trade Organization, the EU seeks to ensure free trade not only between the members of the EU and the *European Economic Area but also with other countries, although not to the same extent as within the EU.

protective award An award made by an employment tribunal ordering an employer to continue to pay wages for a "protection period" to employees who have been made redundant in breach of the consultation requirements laid down in the Trade Union and Labour Relations (Consolidation) Act 1992 (*see* REDUNDANCY). When an employer is proposing to dismiss as redundant 20 or more employees at one establishment within a period of 90 days or less, he must consult with appropriate representatives of the affected employees. Consultations must begin within good time, in any event 90 days before the first dismissal takes effect (if the employer is proposing to dismiss 100 or more employees within the 90 days) or at least 30 days beforehand (if the employer is proposing to dismiss between 20 and 99 employees). Failure to comply with these requirements gives a recognized trade union, an elected employee representative, or an affected employee a right to apply to an *employment tribunal. In the absence of special circumstances rendering it not reasonably practicable to comply with these requirements, the employment tribunal is empowered to make such a protective award. It has discretion regarding the duration of the protected period, subject to a maximum of 90 days. The Act gives the tribunal guidance that the protected period should be just and equitable in all the circumstances having regard to the seriousness of the employer's default. Each employee covered by the award is entitled to one week's pay for each week of the protected period. If the employer fails to make any or all of the payments due for this period, the individual employee may complain, within three months, to an employment tribunal, which may order payment.

protective trust (alimentary trust) A trust for a period no longer than the beneficiary's life, the period ending if certain events (commonly including the bankruptcy of the beneficiary) take place. At the occurrence of such an event, the income of the property is applied at the absolute discretion of the trustees for the beneficiary or his family, the beneficiary no longer having any right to receive the income himself.

protector of settlement The first person entitled, under a *strict settlement of land, to a life interest preceding the *entailed interest or (if there is no prior life interest) the settlor. Under the Fines and Recoveries Act 1833, a person entitled in *remainder to an entailed interest can only bar the entail completely, so as to create a fee simple in remainder, if the protector's consent is given by deed on or before execution of the disentailing deed. Without the protector's consent only the tenant in tail and his issue are barred; when they die out the land passes to the person next entitled in remainder or in reversion (in pre-1926 terminology, a **base fee**).

protest *n.* **1.** An express indication that an act is not to carry an implication that might otherwise attach to it. For example, when a payment is made **under protest**, the payer does not agree that he is liable for the payment. **2.** A procedure by which a *notary provides formal evidence of the *dishonour of a bill of exchange. When a *foreign bill has been dishonoured by nonacceptance or nonpayment it is handed to the notary, who usually presents it again. If it is still dishonoured, the notary attaches a slip showing the answer received and other particulars – a process called **noting**. The protest, in the form of a formal document, may then be drawn up at a later time.

protocol *n.* **1.** The original draft of a document. **2.** An international agreement of a less formal nature than a *treaty. It is often used to amend treaties. It may also be an instrument subsidiary or ancillary to a *convention, in which case it may deal with points of interpretation and reservations. **3.** A code of procedure. **4.** Minutes of a meeting setting out matters of agreement.

provable debt A debt in respect of which a creditor can claim a share of a bankrupt's assets. A provable debt must either be incurred by the bankrupt before a *bankruptcy order is made against him or arise after the order is made as a result of an obligation that existed beforehand. *Compare* NONPROVABLE DEBT.

proving a will Obtaining *probate of a will or *letters of administration *cum testamento annexo.*

provisional damages Damages given in personal injury cases when the injuries sustained may cause in the future some serious disease or other serious deterioration in the claimant's physical or mental condition. The court has the power to make an immediate award of damages on the basis of the claimant's present condition and order that he can come back within a specified time for a further award if the disease or condition develops.

provisional liquidator A person appointed by the court to conduct the *compulsory winding-up of a company pending the appointment of a *liquidator. Either the *official receiver or a qualified *insolvency practitioner may be appointed.

provisional orders Orders made by government ministers but requiring confirmation by Act of Parliament (a Provisional Order Confirmation Act) before becoming law. They do not, therefore, constitute *delegated legislation. Provisional orders were formerly used extensively, primarily to confer powers on local authorities, but have been largely superseded by *special procedure orders.

proviso *n.* A clause in a statute, deed, or other legal document introducing a qualification or condition to some other provision, frequently the one immediately preceding the proviso itself.

In criminal appellate procedure, **applying the proviso** occurs when the Court of Appeal uses the power conferred by the proviso to section 2 of the Criminal Appeal Act 1968. This empowers the court to dismiss an appeal if it considers that no miscarriage of justice has occurred, even though it believes that the point raised in the appeal might be decided in favour of the appellant.

provocation *n.* Conduct or words causing someone to lose his self-control. Provocation is not recognized as a *general defence to a criminal charge in English law, though what otherwise would have been murder may be reduced to manslaughter if provocation is shown (it is not, however, a defence to a charge of attempted murder).

The test for provocation is whether the acts or words involved did in fact make the defendant lose his self-control, and if so, whether they would also have made a reasonable man in the defendant's position do the same. This is a question of fact for the jury to decide in each case. A reasonable man for these purposes must be a person of the same sex and age as the defendant and sharing any characteristics of the defendant that might affect the seriousness of the provocation. For example, a sexually impotent defendant might be more easily provoked by taunts about his impotence than an ordinary man. The jury would therefore have to consider how a reasonable impotent man would have reacted. However, such characteristics as intoxication from alcohol or drugs cannot be attributed to the reasonable man. *See also* BATTERED SPOUSE OR COHABITANT.

proxy *n.* A person (not necessarily a company member) appointed by a company member to attend and vote instead of him at a company meeting. Directors often offer themselves as proxies by sending out proxy forms with the notice of the meeting. When this is done at company expense, forms must be sent to all company members alike. In the case of a *listed company, the form must enable members to direct the proxy whether to vote for or against the resolution; in other cases, it may specify that the proxy is to use his discretion. Usually a proxy can vote only upon a poll (*see* VOTING). In private companies the proxy can speak at the meeting.

psychopathic disorder For the purposes of the Mental Health Act 1983, a form of *mental disorder consisting of a persistent disorder or disability of mind (which may or may not include significant impairment of intelligence) that results in abnormally aggressive or seriously irresponsible conduct and requires, or is susceptible to, medical treatment.

Public Accounts Committee A nondepartmental select committee of the House of Commons, established in 1861 to examine government expenditure and report on any irregularity or other matter to which it considers that attention should be drawn. It has 15 members and its chairman is customarily a member of the Opposition.

public Act *See* ACT OF PARLIAMENT.

publication *n.* **1.** (in the law of *defamation) The communication of defamatory words to a person or persons other than the one defamed. In the English law of tort, publication to at least one other person must be proved. Communication between husband and wife does not amount to publication, but communication by the defendant to the spouse of the claimant is sufficient. Dictation of a defamatory statement to a secretary or typist is publication. Publication to persons other than the one defamed is not required in Scottish law or in criminal libel. **2.** (in copyright law) The issuing of reproductions of a work or edition to the public. Protection under the Copyright, Designs and Patents Act 1988 may depend on whether the work has been published. **3.** For the purposes of the Obscene Publications Acts, *see* OBSCENE PUBLICATIONS.

public Bill *See* BILL.

public body Any body, corporate or otherwise, that performs its duties and exercises its powers for the public benefit, as opposed to private gain. Under the Local Government Act 1972, public bodies include local authorities, trustees, commissioners, and those who have duties to provide cemetaries and markets and act for the improvement of any place, or who have powers to issue or levy *precepts.

public company A type of registered company that can offer its shares to the public (*compare* PRIVATE COMPANY). Its memorandum of association must state that it is a public company, that its name ends with the words "public limited company" (or plc), and that its *authorized capital is at least the authorized minimum (£50,000). It cannot do business until it has allotted shares with a nominal value corresponding with the authorized minimum. It cannot allot shares except upon payment of one-quarter of their nominal value plus any *share premium. £12,500 is therefore its minimum capital. It thus may not have much wealth or substance, although many assume the contrary. Under the Companies Act 1985 an undertaking to do work or perform services is not an acceptable *consideration for shares in a public company, and other non-cash considerations are subject to independent valuation and must be transferred to the company within five years of *allotment. *See also* FLOTATION; STOCK EXCHANGE.

public corporation A corporation established to perform a public function, frequently commercial but not necessarily so (it may be social, advisory, or of any other character). Thus bodies established to manage nationalized industries are public corporations, as are such bodies as English Nature. A public corporation is normally a **statutory corporation**, i.e. established by Act of Parliament; exceptions include the British Broadcasting Corporation, which was established by royal charter. The *privatization programme that has been in operation in the UK since the 1980s has reduced the number of public corporations as their functions have been taken over by public companies and the government has divested itself, either wholly or substantially, of the statutory and financial commitment to the provision of public utilities (such as telecommunications, water, electricity, and gas). As these corporations have been privatized, *regulatory agencies have been established as watchdog bodies.

public document A document concerned with a public matter, made under a public duty to inquire into all the circumstances recorded and meant for public inspection. Statements in public documents are admissible as an exception to the rule against *hearsay evidence.

public duties Certain public officers, including magistrates, councillors, school and college governors, and members of health authorities, are entitled under the Employment Rights Act 1996 to time off work to fulfil their official duties. An employee entitled to time off work for public duties does not have a statutory right to be paid for his periods of absence. No specific right to time off for jury service is given, but failure to attend jury service is contempt of court, therefore an implied right to time off probably exists.

public examination In *bankruptcy proceedings, an investigation into the conduct, dealings, and property of a debtor. It takes place in a court and the debtor is compelled to attend and answer questions on oath. The *official receiver has a discretion whether or not to apply to the court for a public examination after a bankruptcy order is made. He must apply (unless the court directs otherwise) if the creditors request it.

public general Act *See* ACT OF PARLIAMENT.

public good A special defence to some charges under the Obscene Publications Act. *See* OBSCENE PUBLICATIONS.

public house Under the Local Government Act 1966, any premises licensed for the sale of intoxicating liquor for consumption on the premises, this (apart from any ancillary or incidental trade or business) being the only trade carried on there.

public law The part of the law that deals with the constitution and functions of the organs of central and local government, the relationship between individuals and the state, and relationships between individuals that are of direct concern to the state. It includes constitutional law, administrative law, tax law, and criminal law. *Compare* PRIVATE LAW.

public limited company (plc) *See* LIMITED COMPANY; PUBLIC COMPANY.

public mischief Conduct damaging the interests of the community; for example, making bogus telephone calls to the police. Until 1975 this was regarded as a crime but it is now no longer so regarded, nor is conspiracy to effect a public mischief. There is, however, a special statutory offence of *wasting police time (but not, for example, the time of ambulancemen or firemen). *See also* BOMB HOAX; SENDING DISTRESSING LETTERS.

public morals The basic moral structure of society. Judges have occasionally said that they retain a general overriding discretion to punish as crimes behaviour that is destructive of public morals but it is not at all clear to what extent they should do so, although some crimes, such as incest, are presumably based on moral factors. The abolition of the crimes of homosexual conduct and suicide was based on the assumption that matters of morals that do not directly affect other people should not be the subject of criminal legislation. *See also* CORRUPTION OF PUBLIC MORALS.

public nuisance *See* NUISANCE.

public office Employment in the *Civil Service or in any other capacity in which remuneration is provided by Parliament or the Consolidated Fund. Public office also includes employment of an officer to whom the Overseas Service Act 1958 applies and employment funded by the Church Commissioners, the Agricultural Research Council, the Crown Estate Commissioners, and the Metropolitan Police Fund.

public or general rights *See* DECLARATION CONCERNING PUBLIC OR GENERAL RIGHTS.

public place A place to which the public has access. The main offences relating to public places are: (1) being found drunk or being drunk and disorderly in a public place; (2) carrying a *firearm, *offensive weapon, or bladed article in a public place; (3) *soliciting in a public place; and (4) displaying support for a *proscribed organization in a public place. *See also* OFFENCES AGAINST PUBLIC ORDER.

public policy The interests of the community. If a contract is (on common-law principles) contrary to public policy, this will normally make it an *illegal contract. In a few cases, however, such a contract is void but not illegal, and is treated slightly more leniently (for example, by *severance). Contracts that are illegal because they contravene public policy include any contract to commit a crime or a tort or to defraud the revenue, any contract that prejudices national safety or the administration of justice, and any *immoral contract. Contracts that are merely void include contracts in *restraint of trade and in *restraint of marriage and *marriage brokage contracts.

public procurement Obtaining goods or services for the use of the public sector.

Procurement in this sector is often formalized, and contracts for public works, supplies, or services, which can be large, are advertised for formal tender. In the 1970s the EU, finding that most public contracts in the EU were placed with local suppliers, issued directives requiring that large public supply and works contracts must be advertised throughout the EU and be open to all who meet the requirements set out in them. These directives have been amended and revised and now extend to cover services and utility contracts. Three alternative procedures for submitting tenders are set out in the directives; of these, the **open procedure** is generally regarded as the fairest and is the one that must most often be used. The basic principle for all three procedures is that if the value of a contract for public works, supplies, or services (or of a contract for utilities whether in the public sector or not) is over a certain minimum financial level, the contract must be advertised in the EU's *Official Journal* and suppliers from all EU states are entitled to put in tenders. The company winning the contract must be chosen fairly in accordance with formulae set down in the relevant directive. When the procedure is not followed, there is a right to claim damages under separate remedies directives.

public prosecutor *See* DIRECTOR OF PUBLIC PROSECUTIONS.

public trust A trust for the benefit of the public, which may or may not be a *charitable trust.

Public Trustee A public officer, appointed under the Public Trustee Act 1906, who is a *corporation sole and who may act as a *custodian trustee, a *judicial trustee, or an ordinary trustee. The Public Trustee cannot accept certain trusts, e.g. those exclusively for charitable or religious purposes, those governed by foreign law, or those involving the management of a business. He has a duty to administer small estates unless there is some good reason for his refusal.

puisne *adj.* [from Old French *puisné*, later born] Inferior; of lesser rank.

puisne judge Any ordinary judge of the High Court. Puisne judges are referred to as (for example) "Mr Justice Smith", even though they are knighted upon appointment. They must be barristers of at least ten years' standing.

puisne mortgage A legal mortgage of unregistered land in which the mortgagee does not keep the title deeds of the land as security. Usually a first mortgagee retains the deeds; thus subsequent mortgages will be puisne and should be protected by registration (*see* REGISTRATION OF ENCUMBRANCES).

punishment *n.* A penalty imposed on a defendant duly convicted of a crime by an authorized court. The punishment is declared in the *sentence of the court. The two basic principles governing punishment are *nullum crimen sine lege* and *nulla poena sine lege*. The powers of the court to punish offenders also depend on whether the crime is an *indictable offence or a *summary offence.

There are a number of different theories of punishment, and different aims and purposes underly the legal provisions of the English criminal system. The concept of **retribution** implies that a criminal merits his just punishment because he has done something morally or socially evil. Another aspect of retribution implies that the punishment should be related to the harm done by the crime, rather than to the moral guilt of the criminal. The utilitarian school, by contrast, believes that all punishment is evil, insofar as it adversely affects human happiness. It can only be justified, therefore, if it prevents greater unhappiness or harm. This is the basis of the theory of **deterrence**, in which the punishment is aimed at deterring the criminal from repeating his offences or deterring others from committing similar acts. Custodial sentences may be required to protect the public from further harm, particularly when the crimes involve violence. Sometimes these sentences are also justified as an expression of public condemnation and outrage. Recent thinking replaces the concept of retribution by the belief that sentences should be designed to assist in the rehabilitation of the criminal. To some extent these concepts are accepted in relation to young offenders, and are also reflected in the system of *parole (*see also* SPENT CONVICTION). Legislators and judges have to bear in mind these concepts in laying down and applying sentences. They must also be aware of society's need for a humane system of criminal justice.

Clearly the extent to which crimes should be punished without proof of *intention or *recklessness (e.g. crimes of *negligence and *strict liability) depends on which theory of punishment one adopts. Parliament has created a large number of so-called **regulatory offences** (e.g. road traffic offences and offences relating to production of food), which usually do not involve moral guilt and are often punished despite the absence of *mens rea*. It is also a matter of considerable controversy whether or not the criminal law should punish morally objectionable conduct that does not obviously harm anyone (e.g. obscene publications and various sex-related offences).

The European Convention on Human Rights (signed 1950) forbids the use of "inhuman or degrading" punishment; this prohibition is now part of UK law as a consequence of the *Human Rights Act 1998 (*see* DEGRADING TREATMENT OR PUNISHMENT; INHUMAN TREATMENT OR PUNISHMENT). Similarly, the prohibition on the use of **arbitrary punishment**, as set out in Article 7 of the Convention, is now incorporated into the Human Rights Act. This provision makes unlawful the use of criminal penalties that are not prescribed by law.

punitive damages *See* EXEMPLARY DAMAGES.

pur autre vie *See* ESTATE PUR AUTRE VIE.

pur cause de vicinage *See* PROFIT À PRENDRE; COMMON.

purchaser *n.* **1.** (in land law) Any person who acquires land otherwise than by mere operation of law. Thus a purchaser may be a mortgagee or one to whom land is given or bequeathed as well as one who buys land for money or other consideration. A tenant in tail (whose interest devolves upon him automatically on his ancestor's death) is not a purchaser, nor is one who acquires title by *adverse possession. **2.** A *buyer.

purchaser for value without notice One who acquires land either in return for money or other consideration having monetary value or under a marriage settlement and who does not know and has no reason to know of an encumbrance that adversely affects the land. Such a purchaser is not bound by certain equitable encumbrances, such as restrictive covenants created before 1926 or the rights of beneficiaries under a trust in unregistered land. However, in order to take free of encumbrances, such a purchaser must act in good faith (*bona fide*), and, in any event, most equitable encumbrances are capable of registration (*see* REGISTRATION OF ENCUMBRANCES) and a purchaser is deemed to know of any interest that is registered. Some encumbrances in registered land may be *overriding interests and will bind a purchaser whether he knows of them or not. Legal encumbrances (such as legal easements) always bind a purchaser of the land whether or not he knows of their existence.

purpose trust A trust that is not for the benefit of a human beneficiary and is not a *charitable trust. Such trusts are normally invalid as there is no one to enforce them; exceptions that are valid include trusts for the benefit of individual animals, for the maintenance of individual graves, and for the saying of masses. The courts, however, may be willing to construe what appears to be a purpose trust (e.g. a trust for a sports ground to be used by employees of a firm) as a trust for human beneficiaries, and thus valid.

putative father A man alleged to be the father of an illegitimate child. If the court accepts the mother's allegations, the man is declared the putative father and may be ordered to make periodical payments for the maintenance of the child by the Child Support Agency (*see* CHILD SUPPORT MAINTENANCE) or to pay a lump sum by the court. The putative father's name may also be entered on the child's birth certificate. *See also* ILLEGITIMACY.

Q

QBD *See* QUEEN'S BENCH DIVISION.

QC *See* QUEEN'S COUNSEL.

qualified acceptance An *acceptance of a bill of exchange that varies the effect of the bill as drawn; for example, either by making payment by the acceptor dependent on fulfilling a condition or by accepting to pay part only of the amount for which the bill is drawn (a **partial acceptance**). A qualified acceptance is distinguished from a **general acceptance**, which assents without qualification to the order of the drawer. The holder of a bill may refuse to take a qualified acceptance; if he does not obtain an unqualified acceptance he may treat the bill as dishonoured by nonacceptance. If a qualified acceptance is taken (subject to an exception as to partial acceptances) and the drawer or an endorser has not authorized the holder to take a qualified acceptance or does not subsequently assent to it, such drawer or endorser is discharged from his liability on the bill.

qualified privilege The defence that a statement cannot be made the subject of an action for *defamation because it was made on a privileged occasion and was not made maliciously, for an improper motive. Qualified privilege covers statements made fairly in situations in which there is a legal or moral obligation to give the information and the person to whom it is given has a corresponding duty or interest to receive it and when someone is acting in defence of his own property or reputation. Qualified privilege also covers fair and accurate reports of public meetings and various other public proceedings. The privilege attaching to professional communications between solicitor and client is probably qualified, rather than absolute. *Compare* ABSOLUTE PRIVILEGE.

qualified right A right set out in the European Convention on Human Rights that will only be violated if the interference with it is not proportionate (*see* PROPORTIONALITY). An interference with a qualified right that is not proportionate to the *legitimate aim being pursued will not be lawful. *Compare* ABSOLUTE RIGHT.

qualified title Ownership of a legal estate in registered land subject to some exception or qualification specified in the register. If, for example, X applies to register his title to land and there is some possibility that part of it may already have been sold to another person, X's title may be registered subject to the rights of anyone having a better title to that part. The state's guarantee of good title does not protect the proprietor in respect of the specified qualification. *Compare* ABSOLUTE TITLE.

qualifying child For the purposes of the Child Support Act 1991 (*see* CHILD SUPPORT MAINTENANCE), a child who is under the age of 16, or under the age of 19 and receiving full-time education, and who has not been married. This definition applies only to "natural" children (i.e. children of both parties) or adopted children; it does not include stepchildren. *See also* CHILD OF THE FAMILY.

qualifying distribution Formerly, a distribution of profits by a company on which *advance corporation tax had to be paid (*see also* IMPUTATION SYSTEM). Redeemable securities issued as a bonus were not treated as qualifying distribution.

quango *n.* quasi-autonomous non-governmental organization: a body appointed wholly or partly by the government (but not constituting a department of government) to perform some public function, normally administrative or advisory and frequently involving the distribution of public moneys. Examples are the Competition Commission and the Student Loans Company.

quantum *n.* (of damages) The amount of money awarded by way of damages.

quantum meruit *See* QUASI-CONTRACT.

quantum valebat [Latin: as much as it was worth] An action to claim the value of goods that were sold without any price having been fixed, when there was an implied promise to pay as much as they were worth.

quarantine *n.* A period of isolation of people or animals that have been in contact with a communicable disease. The period was originally 40 days (hence the name, which is derived from the Italian *quarantina*), but is now approximately the incubation period of the suspected disease. Quarantine is imposed, for example, by public health regulations relating to ships and aircraft or by orders made under the Animal Health Act 1981.

quarter days 25 March (**Lady Day**), 24 June (**Midsummer Day**), 29 September (**Michaelmas Day**), and 25 December (**Christmas Day**). Rents are sometimes made payable on these days.

quarter sessions Originally, a *court of record with quarterly meetings of the *justices of the peace for a county. City and borough quarter sessions were presided over by the recorder sitting alone. In modern times quarter sessions became a court for the trial of offences triable on indictment, other than those that had to be tried at *assizes. Quarter sessions were abolished by the Courts Act 1971 and their jurisdiction is now exercised by the *Crown Court.

quash *vb.* To invalidate a conviction made in an inferior court or to set aside a decision subject to judicial review. *See also* QUASHING ORDER.

quashing order A discretionary remedy, obtained by an application for *judicial review, in which the High Court orders decisions of inferior courts, tribunals, and administrative authorities to be brought before it and quashes them if they are *ultra vires* or show an *error on the face of the record. The claimant must apply for it within three months. As it is discretionary, a quashing order may be refused if alternative remedies exist. Originally called *certiorari*, it was renamed in 1999 under Part 54.1 (2)(d) of the Civil Procedure Rules.

quasi-contract *n.* A field of law covering cases in which one person has been unduly enriched at the expense of another and is under an obligation *quasi ex contractu* (as if from a contract) to make restitution to him. In many cases of quasi-contract, the defendant has received the benefit from the claimant himself. The claimant may have paid money to him under a mistake of fact, or under a void contract, or may have supplied services under the mistaken belief that he was contractually bound to do so. In that case, he is entitled to be paid a reasonable sum and is said to sue on a *quantum meruit* (as much as he deserved). Alternatively, the claimant may have been required to pay to a third party money for which the defendant was primarily liable. The defendant's receipt of the benefit need not necessarily, however, have been from the claimant. It is enough that it was at the latter's expense, and he may therefore be liable in quasi-contract for money paid to him by a third party on account of the claimant.

quasi-easement *n.* A right in the nature of an *easement enjoyed over a plot of land for the benefit of another plot owned by the same person: it would be an easement if the two plots of land were owned and occupied by different persons. If the second plot (the quasi-dominant tenement) is sold, the purchaser will acquire a full easement under the Law of Property Act 1925 provided the two parcels were occupied by different persons immediately before the sale. For example A, the owner of Blackacre and Whiteacre, lets Whiteacre to B, who uses a track across Blackacre. If A then sells the freehold estate in Whiteacre to B, B acquires an easement of way over the track. If the plots are not separately occupied an easement may still arise in favour of the purchaser of the quasi-dominant tenement if the easement claimed is permanent in nature, identifiable from inspection of the land, and used by the grantor (vendor) at the time of the conveyance for the benefit of the quasi-dominant tenement.

quasi-entail *n.* An equitable interest in land that is in the nature of an *entailed interest but subsists only during the life of a specified person. For example, if a life tenant A settles his life interest on B and the heirs of his body with remainder to C, B acquires a quasi-entail. The interests of B, his issue, and C all cease on A's death.

quasi-judicial *adj.* Describing a function that resembles the judicial function in that it involves deciding a dispute and ascertaining the facts and any relevant law, but differs in that it depends ultimately on the exercise of an executive discretion rather than the application of law.

queen *n.* **1.** The sovereign if female (*see* CROWN). **2.** The wife of the sovereign (**queen consort**). **3.** The widow of a sovereign (**queen dowager**).

Queen *n.* By the Royal Titles Act 1953, "Elizabeth II by the Grace of God of the United Kingdom of Great Britain and Northern Ireland and of Her other Realms and Territories Queen, Head of the Commonwealth, Defender of the Faith". The Act empowers Her Majesty to adopt by proclamation such other style and titles as she may think fit. *See also* CROWN.

Queen's Bench Division (QBD) The division of the *High Court of Justice whose principal business is the trial of civil actions based upon contract or tort. It also has important appellate functions in relation to appeals from *magistrates' courts and certain tribunals and exercises supervisory jurisdiction over all inferior courts. The *Admiralty Court and *Commercial Court are part of the QBD.

Queen's Bench Masters *See* MASTERS OF THE SUPREME COURT.

Queen's Counsel (QC) A senior *barrister of at least ten years' practice who has received a patent as "one of Her Majesty's counsel learned in the law". QCs are appointed on the recommendation of the Lord Chancellor and a list of new appointees is published annually on Maundy Thursday. In court they sit within the bar and wear silk gowns (hence they are also known informally as **silks**). If the monarch is a king these barristers are known as **King's Counsel (KC)**.

Queen's evidence Evidence given on behalf of the prosecution by an accused person who has confessed his own guilt and who then acts as a witness against his accomplices. Such evidence is generally considered less reliable than other evidence because the witness is likely to minimize his own role and exaggerate that of his accomplices. If it is not corroborated, the judge must warn the jury of the danger of convicting on the basis of this evidence alone. *See also* CORROBORATION.

Queen's Proctor A solicitor who, under the direction of the Attorney General, gives legal advice to the courts on difficult or disputed legal problems involving divorce and who intervenes, generally to prevent a divorce from being made absolute, in cases in which not all the material facts were before the court earlier. The office of Queen's Proctor is held by the *Treasury Solicitor.

Queen's Regulations *See* SERVICE LAW.

Queen's Speech (Speech from the Throne) A speech prepared by the government and read by the Queen to Parliament (assembled in the House of Lords) at the beginning of a parliamentary session. It outlines the government's principal legislative and policy proposals for the session.

que estate [Norman French: whose estate] A claim to have acquired by *prescription an easement or profit *à prendre* by virtue of the continuous use of the right both by the claimant and by those whose estate he has, i.e. those who owned the dominant tenement before him.

questioning of suspects *See* INTERROGATION; RIGHT OF SILENCE.

quia emptores [Latin: whereas purchasers (the first words of the preamble)] A statute of 1290 (still in force today) that forbids the creation of any new tenures (i.e. **subinfeudation**) other than by the Crown. Owners of land wishing to transfer the property may only do so by selling it, not by creating a new lord–tenant relationship. This is the basis of the modern system of conveying estates. The leasehold (or landlord and tenant) relationship fell outside the feudal system of tenures (only one of which effectively now remains, namely the freehold tenure of **socage**) and so can still be freely created as outside the scope of the statute. *See* FEUDAL SYSTEM.

quia timet [Latin: because he fears] A type of *injunction that is sought in order to restrain an anticipated wrong. The court will only grant such a remedy if the applicant can show that there is imminent danger of a substantial kind or that the injury, if it occurs, will be irreparable.

quicquid plantatur solo, solo cedit *See* FIXTURE.

quiet enjoyment One of the obligations of a landlord, which is implied in every *lease unless specifically excluded. It entitles the tenant to possess and enjoy the land he leases without interference from the landlord or anyone claiming rights through the landlord.

quiet possession Freedom from disturbance in the enjoyment of property. In contracts for the sale of goods, unless the seller makes it clear that he is contracting to transfer only the title that he or a third person has, there is an implied *warranty that the buyer will enjoy quiet possession of the goods. This warranty is broken not only if the seller and those claiming through him interfere with the buyer's quiet possession but also if the interference is by a third party claiming by virtue of a better title to the goods. The corresponding covenant upon the sale of land extends only to interferences by the seller and those claiming through him.

quit rent *See* RENTCHARGE.

quittance *n.* A document that acknowledges payment of a debt.

quorum *n.* **1.** The minimum number of people who must be present at a meeting in order for business to be transacted. The required number is usually laid down in the *articles of association, constitution, or rules of the company or other body concerned. *See also* GENERAL MEETING. **2.** Formerly, an indication in a Commission of the Peace of the particular justices (called **justices of the quorum**) required, at least one of whom had to be present in order for business to be done.

quota *n.* A limited quantity or number of goods or other items that are permitted by a state or body to be imported, exported, or manufactured. For example, in the fishing industry the EU sets national quotas for fishing catches (*see* COMMON FISHERIES POLICY). In the practice of "quota hopping", British vessels are bought by nationals of other EU states (especially Spain and the Netherlands) in order to qualify as UK-based and therefore acquire the catch quotas allocated to the UK in respect of those vessels. Attempts by the UK to prevent this practice have been held as unlawful by the European Court of Justice (*see* FISHERY LIMITS).

quotation *n.* A listing of a share price on the *Stock Exchange. A price may be obtained by accessing the **Stock Exchange Automated Quotations System** (**SEAQ**). A quotation can be cancelled or suspended if the company does not comply with the Rules of the Stock Exchange or if it becomes impossible to rely on market forces to arrive at a price for the securities (e.g. because of inaccurate accounts or manipulation of the market).

R

R. Abbreviation for *Rex* or *Regina* [Latin: King or Queen] Criminal prosecutions on indictment are brought in the name of the Crown, since a crime is viewed as a wrong against the public at large, or the state, represented by the monarch. Hence the formula *R.* v *Defendant* (the Crown versus the defendant).

Race Relations Board A body constituted to enforce the Race Relations Acts 1965 and 1968. These Acts have been replaced by the Race Relations Act 1976 and the Race Relations Board by the *Commission for Racial Equality.

racial discrimination Discrimination on the grounds of colour, race, nationality, or ethnic origins. It is dealt with by the Race Relations Acts of 1965, 1968, and 1976. The 1965 Act created an offence of incitement to *racial hatred and made racial discrimination illegal in public places. The 1968 Act prohibits discrimination in respect of goods, services, facilities, employment, accommodation, and advertisements. The 1976 Act prohibits indirect racial discrimination, as well as discrimination in clubs with more than 25 members. It also prohibits the types of discrimination dealt with by the 1975 Sex Discrimination Act (*see* SEX DISCRIMINATION). The Race Relations (Amendment) Act 2000 extends coverage of the 1976 Act by prohibiting racial discrimination in the functions of the police and other public authorities not previously covered by that Act. It also places a general duty on public authorities to eliminate discrimination and promote racial equality. The *Commission for Racial Equality has the power to conduct formal investigations into complaints. Individual complaints in the field of employment are dealt with by *employment tribunals; other complaints are dealt with in specified county courts.

racial harassment *See* RACIST ABUSE; THREATENING BEHAVIOUR.

racial hatred Hatred against a group of people because of their colour, race, nationality, or ethnic or national origins. Hatred against a religion is thus not directly covered (*see* BLASPHEMY). The Public Order Act 1986 contains six offences of stirring up racial hatred, which all require proof of words, behaviour, or material that are threatening, abusive, or insulting; there must be an *intention of stirring up racial hatred or the likelihood that this will happen. All offences are punishable with up to two years' imprisonment and/or a fine and require the Attorney General's consent before proceedings can be instituted.

The offences are as follows. (1) Using *threatening behaviour or words or displaying threatening written material. This offence may be committed in a public or private place, but it is a defence for the accused person to prove (*see* BURDEN OF PROOF) that he was inside a dwelling and had no reason to believe that his behaviour or display would be seen or heard by someone outside that or another dwelling. Even if the intention to stir up racial hatred is not proved, the accused can still be guilty of the offence if he is proved to have either intended his behaviour or material to be threatening or been aware that it might be so. The offence does not extend to behaviour or written material that is used solely for inclusion in a radio or television programme. A constable may *arrest without warrant anyone he reasonably suspects is committing this offence.

(2) Publishing or distributing to the public threatening written material. It is a

defence for the accused to prove that he was unaware of the material's contents and did not suspect that it was threatening.

(3) Presenting or directing the public performance of a play that involves the use of threatening words or behaviour. The actual performers do not commit or *aid and abet the offence, and recordings or broadcasts of plays can only involve the offence if outsiders attend. It is a defence for the accused to prove that he was unaware and had no reason to suspect that (a) the performance would involve use of the threatening words, or (b) the offending words were threatening, or (c) racial hatred would be likely to be stirred up during the performance.

(4) Distributing, showing, or playing a recording of visual images or sound to the public. It is a defence for the accused to prove that he was unaware of the recording's content and did not, and had no reason to, suspect that it was threatening.

(5) Providing, producing, or directing a radio or television programme involving threatening images or sounds. The offence is limited to broadcasts by satellite, community radio services, cable, pirate stations, and the like; it does not extend to BBC or IBA programmes. It is a defence if the accused can prove either of the following: (a) that he was unaware and had no reason to suspect that the offending material was threatening; or (b) that he was unaware and had no reason to suspect that (i) the programme would involve the offending material and that it was not reasonably practicable for him to remove the material or (ii) the programme would be broadcast or that racial hatred would be likely to be stirred up by it. Defence b(ii) is unavailable to those providing the broadcasting service. A broadcaster who uses the offending words can also commit the offence; defences (a) and b(ii) are available to him.

(6) Possessing threatening written material or a sound or visual recording with a view to its being distributed or broadcast, or (written material only) published, or (a recording only) shown or played. The offence does not extend to the BBC or IBA, and defence (a) above is available. The police are given entry and search powers in connection with the last offence.

Courts can order forfeiture of offending material after convictions.

The Protection from Harassment Act 1997 provides additional remedies for those harassed on racial grounds (*see* RACIST ABUSE); offenders may receive jail sentences of up to five years.

racist abuse Harassment of someone as a consequence of the harasser's biased views of that person's racial origins. The Protection from Harassment Act 1997 provides that offenders who make others fear for their safety can be jailed for up to five years and/or be subjected to an unlimited fine; even when the harassment does not give rise to fear for safety, the offender faces up to six months in jail and/or a fine of up to £5000.

rack rent The yearly amount of rent that a tenant could reasonably expect to pay on the open market; a rent representing the gross annual value of the holding. *Compare* GROUND RENT.

rape *n.* Sexual intercourse (vaginal or anal) with a woman or another man without their *consent, as a result of physical force or threats, or because the person was unconscious or asleep, or because consent as to the nature of the act was obtained through fraud. It is also rape if the person is mentally incapable of understanding what is being consenting to. The defendant must be proved to have known that the person did not consent or have been reckless as to consent. Indifference by the defendant to the question of consent would constitute recklessness. If, however, there is reasonable doubt as to whether he honestly believed that the person was consenting he will be entitled to be acquitted, even if his belief was unreasonable. The maximum penalty for rape or attempted rape is life imprisonment, but this is rarely imposed; however, the Crime (Sentences) Act 1997 provides for a mandatory sentence of life imprisonment for those convicted for a second time of rape or attempted rape (*see* REPEAT OFFENDER).

A husband can be convicted for raping his wife, and a boy under the age of 14 is guilty of rape if he has intercourse without consent (formerly, boys of this age were deemed incapable of rape even if intercourse had taken place). An unsuccessful rape can be treated as an *indecent assault or as an assault occasioning bodily harm or causing grievous bodily harm, depending on the circumstances (formerly, a rape by a boy was treated in this way). A woman can be charged with rape as an accessory.

rape offence Any one of the offences of rape, attempted rape, aiding, abetting, counselling, or procuring rape or attempted rape, incitement or conspiracy to rape, and burglary with intent to rape. In cases where the defendant to a rape offence pleads not guilty, the Sexual Offences (Amendment) Act 1976 limits the right to ask questions about the alleged victim's sexual experiences. It also prohibits (subject to special leave of the court) the reporting of details about the case that might enable members of the public to identify the woman. If such details are published, the publishers may be fined.

rapporteur *n.* An official of the European Parliament or of some other EU body whose job is to help discussions progress in connection with a particular matter and to prepare a report on it.

rates *pl. n.* Local taxes charged on property by local authorities to pay for the services they provide. The *community charge replaced domestic rates (i.e. those payable by private householders) in April 1990 in England and Wales (in 1989 in Scotland), but was itself replaced by the *council tax in April 1993. Owners of business and other nondomestic property remain liable to pay nondomestic rates based on a **Uniform Business Rate** (UBR), fixed by central government, and a local valuation of the property.

ratification *n.* **1.** Confirmation of an act. If, for example, X contracts with Y as agent for Z, but has in fact no authority to do so, Z may nevertheless adopt the contract by subsequent ratification. An unenforceable contract made with a minor can become enforceable if the minor ratifies the contract when he comes of age. **2.** (in international law) The approval of a *treaty, usually by the head of state (or by the head of state and legislature). This takes place when documents of ratification are either exchanged or deposited with a named depositary. Normally a treaty states expressly whether it will bind a party as soon as it is signed by that party's representative or whether it requires ratification. The Vienna Convention on Treaties (1969) provides that when a treaty does not specify whether or not ratification is required, reference will be made to the party's intention. Performance of a treaty may amount to implicit ratification. **3.** (in company law) A resolution of a general meeting sanctioning some irregularity in the running of a company. Some irregularities cannot be sanctioned, such as acts that are *ultra vires* or a *fraud on the minority.

ratio decidendi [Latin: the reason for deciding] The principle or principles of law on which the court reaches its decision. The *ratio* of the case has to be deduced from its facts, the reasons the court gave for reaching its decision, and the decision itself.

It is said to be the statement of law applied to the material facts. Only the *ratio* of a case is binding on inferior courts, by reason of the doctrine of *precedent.

rave *n.* An assembly, unlicensed by the local authority, of 100 or more people, partly or entirely in the open air, at which amplified music is played during the night and is likely to cause serious distress to local inhabitants. Under the Criminal Justice and Public Order Act 1994 a police officer of at least the rank of superintendent may issue directions to participants to leave if it is reasonably believed that two or more people are preparing for a rave or ten or more people are waiting for one to start or are already participating in an event that will attract 100 or more participants. A *summary offence is committed by anyone (excluding the occupier, a member of his family, and an employee or agent) who fails to leave as soon as reasonably practicable or who re-enters within seven days; it is punishable by up to three months' imprisonment and/or a fine on level 4. A uniformed police officer may arrest without warrant anyone refusing the leave. He may also stop and turn back within five miles of a rave anyone whom he believes to be travelling to the rave. Failure to comply is a summary offence punishable by a fine on level 3.

There are supplementary powers of entry for the purpose of clearing the land and seizing and removing vehicles and sound equipment. Any sound equipment under the control of a person convicted under these provisions may be made the subject of a *forfeiture order.

real *adj.* **1.** Relating to land. *See also* REAL ESTATE; REAL PROPERTY. **2.** Relating to a thing, rather than to a person. *See also* REAL EVIDENCE.

real estate Under the Administration of Estates Act 1925, all interests in land held by the deceased at death excluding interests in money charged on land.

real evidence Evidence in the form of material objects (e.g. weapons). When an object is admitted in evidence, it is usually marked as an *exhibit. Documents are not usually classified as real evidence, but may be treated as such if the physical characteristics of the document (rather than its content) are of significance. Some authorities include evidence of identification and the demeanour of witnesses within the classification of real evidence.

real property (realty) Land and incorporeal *hereditaments. *See* PROPERTY.

real security **1.** A mortgage. **2.** A *rentcharge secured on freehold land.

realty *n. See* REAL PROPERTY.

real union A treaty arrangement in which two or more states unite in order to make them one *international legal personality. A real union does not create a single state; each state can revive its own international personality should the real union be dissolved. An example of a real union was that between Sweden and Norway between 1814 and 1905.

reasonable doubt *See* PROOF BEYOND REASONABLE DOUBT.

reasonable financial provision The financial provision that the *dependants of a deceased person can reasonably expect to receive from his estate. If the deceased's will does not make such provision, or he dies intestate and the intestacy laws do not make such provision, the dependants may apply to the court for provision. A spouse is entitled to reasonable financial provision even if he or she already has enough resources for maintenance; in all other cases, reasonable financial provision comprises what is required for maintenance.

reasonable force At common law a person may use reasonable force in *self-defence and, in extreme circumstances, may be justified in killing an attacker. Reasonable force may be used in defending one's property, and if someone intrudes on one's property at night, one might be justified in treating this as a threat not merely to property, but to personal safety. An occupier of premises (even if he is not the owner) and possibly even a licensee (such as a lodger) may use reasonable force against a trespasser. The Criminal Law Act 1967 permits the use of reasonable force in order to prevent crime, to lawfully arrest a criminal or suspected criminal (or to help in arresting him), or to capture someone who has escaped from lawful detention. The Act extends to both police and private citizens. It is not altogether certain whether the statutory right includes the right to kill.

It is a statutory offence to set spring guns or mantraps, except in a private house between sunset and sunrise. One may use a dog in self-defence if this use is reasonable (*see* GUARD DOG).

If a person mistakenly thinks that he is entitled to use reasonable force when he is not, he will nonetheless be treated as if he was entitled to use such force, provided that the mistake he made was a reasonable one. It seems, however, that this does not apply if he made a mistake of law, rather than fact.

See also FORCIBLE ENTRY.

reasonable man An ordinary citizen, sometimes referred to as the "man on the Clapham omnibus". The standard of care in actions for *negligence is based on what a reasonable person might be expected to do considering the circumstances and the foreseeable consequences. The standard is not entirely uniform: a lower standard is expected of a child, but a higher standard is expected of someone, such as a doctor, who purports to possess a special skill.

rebuttable presumption *See* PRESUMPTION.

rebutter *n.* Formerly, a pleading served by a defendant in reply to the claimant's *surrejoinder. Such a pleading was very rare in modern practice and no longer exists under the *Civil Procedure Rules.

recall of witness The further examination of a witness after his evidence has been completed. The judge may permit the recall of a witness even after the close of a party's case to allow *evidence in rebuttal.

recaption *n.* The retaking of goods that have been wrongfully taken or are being wrongfully withheld. It is a form of *self-help.

receiver *n.* **1.** A person appointed by the court to preserve and protect property that is at risk, to enable another person to obtain the benefit of rights over the property or to obtain payment of a debt if the common-law remedy is inadequate. *See also* EQUITABLE EXECUTION. **2.** A person appointed under the terms of a *debenture or by the court to realize assets charged and apply the proceeds for the benefit of those entitled. Notice of appointment must be given to the Companies Registry and must appear upon business documents. The receiver may have power to manage the company. *See also* ADMINISTRATIVE RECEIVER; OFFICIAL RECEIVER.

receiving *n.* Acquiring exclusive control of stolen property or joint possession of it with the thief or another receiver. Thus if someone merely examines stolen goods in the presence of the thief, he is not guilty of receiving. Before 1968 this was an offence in itself, but it is now one form of the wider offence of *handling stolen goods.

receiving order Formerly, a court order made during the course of *bankruptcy proceedings that placed the debtor's property under the control of the *official receiver or of a *trustee in bankruptcy. *See* BANKRUPTCY ORDER.

reciprocity *n.* The principle that one will treat someone in a particular way if one is so treated by them. This is relevant under EU law in relation to agreements that the EU has with non-EU countries, particularly in relation to *public procurement and free trade.

recitals *pl. n. See* DEED.

recklessness *n.* A form of *mens rea* that amounts to less than *intention but more than *negligence. Many common-law offences can be committed either intentionally or recklessly, and it is now common for statutes to create offences of recklessness. Recklessness has normally been held to have a subjective meaning of being aware of the risk of a particular consequence arising from one's actions but deciding nonetheless to continue with one's actions and take the risk. However, the House of Lords has ruled that, in the context of *criminal damage, recklessness also has an objective meaning of giving no thought or being indifferent to an obvious risk. This definition makes the concept of recklessness far stricter and brings it very close to the traditional definition of negligence. In most cases the subjective definition applies to common-law offences and the objective definition to statutory offences. There are, however, dicta in the Court of Appeal applying the objective definition of recklessness to some common-law offences (e.g. rape).

recognition *n.* (in international law) **1.** The process by which one state declares that another political entity fulfils the conditions of statehood (*see* STATE) and that it is willing to deal with it as a member of the international community. Recognition usually takes place when a new state comes into being. Some authorities believe that recognition is constitutive, i.e. it is one of the conditions that create a state in international law (*see* CONSTITUTIVE THEORY). Most, however, regard it as being merely declaratory, i.e. an acceptance of a fact that already exists (*see* DECLARATORY THEORY). **2.** Acceptance of a government as the legal representative of the state. This may be *de facto* or *de jure*. The distinction is a fluid one, often involving a political element, since international law allows states discretion as to whether or not to accord recognition and of which kind. The according of recognition of either kind is usually an acknowledgment that the government recognized has effective control, but the decision to give merely *de facto* recognition may reflect a wish not to show approval of the nature of the government concerned (and at the same time to be able to continue to give *de jure* recognition to the ousted government). The significance of the distinction (which is of little legal consequence) therefore depends on the intention of the recognizing government. Recognition may be express or implied (for example, by entering into diplomatic relations with a new government). *See also* ESTRADA DOCTRINE; TOBAR DOCTRINE.

For purposes of English municipal law, the question of whether or not a state is recognized is sometimes relevant. Thus: (1) only a recognized state is entitled to *sovereign immunity from jurisdiction; (2) an unrecognized state cannot sue in English courts; and (3) when a foreign law is to be applied under the principles of *private international law, this can only be the law of a recognized state or subsidiary body set up by it. A Foreign and Commonwealth Office certificate stating that an entity is or is not recognized by the British government is usually taken as conclusive evidence in the courts. Since 1980 Britain has abandoned the practice of recognizing governments – only states are now the subject of express recognition.

recognition issue A trade dispute as to whether a particular trade union should be recognized by an employer as having the right to negotiate terms and conditions of employment on behalf of its members among the employer's workforce.

recognition procedure (in employment law) A statutory procedure introduced by the Employment Relations Act 1999 (operational from 6 June 2000) by which a trade union can secure the legal right to enter into *collective bargaining with an employer. As well as the benefit the trade union and its members secure from the fact of bargaining, a recognized trade union becomes entitled to all employment rights bestowed by employment legislation on recognized trade unions. The new procedure enables unions to seek statutory recognition for collective bargaining if they fail to secure a voluntary agreement with the employer concerned.

The statutory procedure is given in Schedule A1 of the Trade Union and Labour Relations (Consolidation) Act 1992. Statutory recognition can be requested by one or more independent trade unions, in the first instance from the employer. Such an approach (often with the assistance of *ACAS) may result in a voluntary agreement being made between the parties. Following a failure to arrive at a voluntary agreement a trade union may then refer the request to the *Central Arbitration Committee (CAC). If satisfied that the trade union has at least 10% membership among the group of workers it is seeking to represent, the CAC will then proceed to establish the viability of the union's request.

The CAC must satisfy itself that the proposed bargaining union is an appropriate unit and take into account such factors as the need for effective management, the relative views of the parties to the dispute, the existing national and local arrangements for bargaining, and the need to avoid fragmentation of existing bargaining units. Crucially the CAC must determine that the necessary support exists at the workplace for collective bargaining. In determining this issue a ballot may be held. However, if the CAC is satisfied that a majority of the workers in the unit are currently members of the applicant union, it may decide that a ballot is not needed. If a ballot is held (and it must be held if less than 50% of the workers are union members), the result must show that a majority of those voting support the union and that those voting in favour constitute at least 40% of the workers in the bargaining unit. The CAC then issues a declaration that the union is entitled to recognition on the basis either that a majority of the workers are union members or that a majority support collective bargaining. When this declaration has been made, the parties are given 30 days to negotiate a method of conducting collective bargaining. Failure to arrive at an agreement will result in a further reference to the CAC. If after a further period of arbitration no voluntary agreement can be reached by the parties, the CAC is empowered to specify a method for collective bargaining. This method then takes effect as a legally binding agreement between the parties.

The new statutory procedure also contains provisions for the derecognition of a trade union. Where recognition has been secured via the statutory route, distinct procedures are laid down for the removal of such recognition. Normally derecognition is not possible within the first three years of any award of recognition arising from a voluntary agreement. However, special procedures exist for cases in which the relevant employees fall below 21 in number, the employees request derecognition, the employer requests derecognition, and the union ceases to be independent.

recognizance *n.* An undertaking by an offender (or by sureties on his behalf) to forfeit a sum of money under certain conditions. Recognizances may be entered into to answer to judgment, i.e. to appear before the court for pronouncement of judgment on a specified date. This procedure may be appropriate if the accused wishes to appeal against conviction. Alternatively, recognizances may be used in addition to or in place of any other sentence or judgment, the offender being obligated to keep the peace and be of good behaviour. Magistrates have wide powers of binding over upon recognizances under the Statute of Westminster 1361 (which enacted into statute the laws of justices of the peace) and the Magistrates' Courts Act 1980; they may punish failure to comply with the order with imprisonment. *See* KEEPING THE PEACE.

reconciliation *n.* The coming together of estranged spouses. It is the general policy of the law to encourage reconciliation, and there are special organizations to help with this. Solicitors in divorce cases must certify whether or not they have discussed the possibility of reconciliation with their clients, and proceedings may be adjourned if the court feels there is a chance of reconciliation. When divorce cases are heard under the *special procedure the court will have no opportunity to judge whether there is a chance of reconciliation. If spouses have lived together for more than six months after separation in cases of divorce applications based on adultery, unreasonable behaviour, desertion, or separation, there is a presumption of law that they have become reconciled and a divorce is refused.

reconstruction of a company The transfer of the property of a registered company in a *voluntary winding-up to another company in exchange for shares in that company to be distributed among members of the company in liquidation. The liquidator effects the reconstruction with the authority of a *special resolution (members' voluntary winding-up) or the consent of the court or *liquidation committee (creditors' voluntary winding-up). A member who does not agree to the arrangement can require the liquidator to buy his shares. *See also* SCHEME OF ARRANGEMENT.

reconversion *n.* The imaginary process by which a fictional *conversion is considered not to have taken place: the property is reconverted in law to the state that, in fact, it has always held.

record *n.* The documents constituting an authentic account of the proceedings before a court, including the *claim form or other originating process, the statements of case, and the *judgment or order, but usually not the evidence tendered. The record of an inferior court is the only part of the proceedings that can be considered by the High Court when deciding whether to grant a *quashing order.

recorder *n.* **1.** A barrister or solicitor appointed as a part-time judge. Recorders agree to make themselves available regularly (unlike deputy judges, who are appointed *ad hoc*) and for at least four weeks a year. Recorders usually sit in the Crown Court but may sit in the county courts or the High Court. **2.** Formerly, a member of the Bar appointed to preside at City or borough *quarter sessions.

recovery *n.* Regaining possession of land from an unlawful occupier by proceedings in the High Court or a county court. *See* RECOVERY OF PREMISES.

recovery of costs *See* BILL OF COSTS.

recovery of premises The right to regain possession of property from which one has been unlawfully dispossessed (*see* FORCIBLE ENTRY) or the right of a court officer to enforce a judgment for this. It is a summary offence, punishable by up to six months' imprisonment and/or a *fine at level 5 on the standard scale, to resist or intentionally obstruct a court officer in the process of enforcing such a judgment, whether or not one knows that he is a court officer. There is, however, a specific defence if one can show that one believed that he was not a court officer. This offence covers most action taken by squatters to resist eviction, such as physical assaults, boarding up doors, or merely refusing to leave.

recreational charity A charity that provides facilities for leisure-time occupation in the interests of social welfare. After doubts expressed in the courts, Parliament confirmed in the Recreational Charities Act 1958 that these trusts were valid, as long as the facilities were provided with the aim of improving the conditions of life for those for whom they were primarily intended and were available to the public or a section of it.

rectification *n.* The correction of a document if it does not correctly express the common intention of the parties to it. Conveyances, leases, contracts, and certain registers of companies may be rectified on application to the court; the court exercises the jurisdiction to rectify with very great caution and only on the most cogent evidence. Parties to a document may, by agreement, rectify it without the court's consent, provided that the rights of third parties are not affected.

rectification of will Under the Administration of Justice Act 1982, a court has power to rectify a will that fails to carry out the intentions of the testator. However, this only arises when the court is satisfied that the failure was caused by clerical error or through a misunderstanding of the testator's instructions. An application for rectification should as a general rule be made within six months from the date on which *representation was first taken out.

reddendum *n.* The clause in a *lease that specifies the amount of the rent and when it should be paid.

redeemable share *See* SHARE.

redeem up, foreclose down A maxim applied in the context of *priority of mortgages. When there are successive mortgages of the same property, a mortgagee who is second or below in the order of priority may buy out (redeem) an earlier mortgagee. Any mortgagee may be redeemed by a mortgagee with a lower priority. If the matter is complicated and a court action is necessary, any person who might suffer in such an action must be made a party to it, i.e. the mortgagor and any mortgagees of lower priority to the mortgage being redeemed. Any person seeking to redeem by action must not only redeem any mortgages standing between him and the prior mortgage; he must also foreclose all subsequent mortgagees and the mortgagor. The principle does not apply to redemptions out of court.

redemption *n.* The return or repossession of property offered as security upon payment of a mortgage debt or a charge. The property may alternatively be conveyed by the mortgagee to a third party nominated by the mortgagor. *See* EQUITY OF REDEMPTION.

redress *n. See* REMEDY.

reduction of capital The reduction by a limited company of its share *capital. Under the Companies Act 1985 there are two principal methods by which this may be achieved. When the company has capital in excess of its needs it can extinguish or reduce the liability of its members on any uncalled capital or it can repay to them the nominal value of their shares. When the company has suffered losses it can cancel paid-up shares because they are unrepresented by available assets. The reduction, which requires a *special resolution, must be authorized by the articles of association and confirmed by the court. If a variation of *class rights is involved, the consent of the relevant class of shareholder is usually necessary. *See also* ALTERATION OF SHARE CAPITAL; AUTHORIZED CAPITAL.

redundancy *n.* **1.** (in employment law) The position of an employee who fills a job that no longer needs to be done. Under the Employment Rights Act 1996, dismissal for redundancy occurs when the reason is wholly or mainly that the employer has ceased or intends to cease carrying on the business in which the employee was employed, that he is transferring the business in which the employee works to another location, or that he needs fewer employees to carry out the work in the place in which the employee is employed. An employee dismissed in such circumstances is entitled to a statutory *redundancy payment if he has been continuously employed in the business (*see* CONTINUOUS EMPLOYMENT) for two years prior to the *effective date of termination of his employment, ignoring any period during which the employee was under the age of 18, and provided he is not over the age of 65. He may also be disqualified from receiving payment if the employer has offered him suitable alternative employment, starting within four weeks after his old employment ends, and the employee unreasonably refuses it. He may however try out alternative employment for up to four weeks without forfeiting his redundancy payment, if he decides not to accept this employment and his refusal is reasonable.

An employee who is laid off (i.e. not provided with work) or kept on short-time working, otherwise than as a result of industrial action, for four or more weeks continuously, or for six or more weeks (not more than three consecutively) in any 13-week period, may claim a redundancy payment in certain circumstances. He must give his employer at least the minimum required period of *notice terminating his employment, stating his intention to claim a redundancy payment. This notice must be given within four weeks after the end of the relevant period of lay-off or short-time working. However, the employer is not liable to give him a redundancy payment if he honours a written undertaking, given within seven days after receiving the employee's notice, to restore full-time working within four weeks after the employee's notice, for at least 13 weeks without interruption.

An employee who is dismissed for redundancy must be given reasonable time off during the notice period to seek other employment. If he is offered a new job starting before his notice expires, the employee may bring forward the termination of his old employment. However, the employer can challenge his right to a redundancy payment if he justifiably requires the employee to work for the full notice period. An employee forfeits his redundancy payment if, during the notice period, his employer justifiably dismisses him for misconduct other than strike action.

Disputes concerning redundancy and redundancy payments are determined by application to an *employment tribunal. The tribunal can also make a *protective award to employees on the application of an *independent trade union when the employer has failed to give sufficient notice of his intention to declare redundancies (*see* DISCLOSURE OF INFORMATION). *See also* COLLECTIVE REDUNDANCY.
2. (in statements of case) The inclusion of unnecessary or irrelevant material. The court may order redundant material in a statement of case to be struck out.

redundancy payment The sum that an employee dismissed because of *redundancy is entitled to receive from his employer under the Employment Rights Act 1996. The sum is the total of: (1) one and a half weeks' pay for each year of the employee's *continuous employment in which he was aged 41 or more; (2) one week's pay for each year's service between the ages of 22 and 41; and (3) half a week's pay for each year between the ages of 18 and 22. Continuous employment exceeding 20 years is ignored, and a maximum amount of weekly pay to be used in the calculation is prescribed by regulations made by the Secretary of State for Work and Pensions and reviewed annually. Employees under 18 or over 65 have no statutory right to a redundancy payment. The sum payable to employees between 64 and 65 years of age is reduced by one-twelfth for every complete month by which their age exceeds 64. Redundancy costs are met entirely by the employer, rebates from the Department for Work and Pensions having been abolished. An employer may be obliged under a collective agreement or individual employees' contracts of employment to pay sums in excess of the statutory requirement.

re-engagement order An order made by an *employment tribunal directing an employer who has been found to have unfairly dismissed an employee (*see* UNFAIR DISMISSAL) to provide him with comparable or other suitable employment in a post different from that from which he was dismissed (*compare* REINSTATEMENT ORDER). A re-engagement order might be made, for example, when the employee's former job no longer exists following a reorganization, but he could be similarly employed in a different post. The order is accompanied by the tribunal's directions specifying the nature and remuneration for the new employment, benefits that must be restored to the employee, and the date by which he is to be re-engaged. An employer cannot be forced to comply with the order; if he fails to do so the tribunal will award *compensation on the usual principles together with an additional sum.

re-entry *n.* Repossession by a landlord of land held under a lease when he effects *forfeiture. There are restrictions on re-entry without a court order. The normal method of enforcing a right of re-entry is therefore by issuing court proceedings for possession. *See also* EVICTION.

re-examination *n.* The questioning of a witness by the party who originally called him to testify, following the *cross-examination of the witness by the opposite party. *Leading questions may not be asked in re-examination. Re-examination must be confined to matters arising out of the cross-examination; new matter may only be introduced with the permission of the judge.

referee *n.* **1.** A person to whom a dispute is referred for an opinion. *See also* OFFICIAL REFEREE; REFERENCE. **2.** A person who provides a character reference for another.

reference *n.* **1.** The referral by a court of a case (or an issue arising in a case) to another court or an arbitrator (**referee**) for a decision or opinion. In the High Court any action or any question or issue of fact arising from it may be referred to an *official referee for trial. In the county courts, a case may be referred to the district judge for an opinion and report. Under the Treaty of Rome, a court may refer to the *European Court of Justice a question of Community law for a preliminary ruling and must do so if it is a court from which there is no appeal within the national system. **2.** (in succession) *See* INCORPORATION BY REFERENCE.

referential settlement A settlement incorporating by reference terms of an earlier settlement, either with or without variations. If the two settlements are inconsistent, a referential settlement may give rise to difficult questions relating to the precise meaning of the documents, when taken together.

reform *n. See* PUNISHMENT.

refreshing memory A procedure in which a witness may, while testifying, remind himself of events that he has forgotten by referring to a document that was made at the same time as the occurrence of the events in question and was accepted as accurate by the witness while the facts were fresh in his memory. At common law the document itself did not become evidence in the case, but it is now admissible in both civil and criminal cases.

refuse disposal *See* POLLUTION.

regent *n.* A person exercising all the royal functions while the sovereign is under 18 or totally incapacitated. Under the Regency Acts 1937 and 1953, the regent is the person next in line to the throne who is of age and is a commonwealth citizen domiciled in the UK. *Compare* COUNSELLORS OF STATE.

Regional Health Authorities *See* NATIONAL HEALTH SERVICE.

registered company A company incorporated by registration under the Companies Act 1985 (*see* REGISTRATION OF A COMPANY). There are several types of registered company (*see* LIMITED COMPANY; PRIVATE COMPANY; PUBLIC COMPANY; UNLIMITED COMPANY). *Compare* STATUTORY COMPANY.

registered design A design registered at the Designs Registry, which is part of the Patent Office (*see* PATENT). Registration gives monopoly rights over the outward appearance of an article, including its shape, configuration, pattern, or ornament, but not over the underlying idea. Works of sculpture, wall plaques, medals, and printed matter primarily of a literary or artistic character cannot be registered. *See* DESIGN RIGHT.

registered land Land to which the title in question is registered (*see* LAND REGISTRATION). Land subject to compulsory registration on dealing may be both registered and unregistered; for example, the freehold owner's title may not be registered if he acquired the land before compulsory registration was introduced in the area, but if he grants a lease for more than 21 years the tenant's leasehold title must be registered. Strictly, it is the legal estate or title that is registered, not the land itself. Since over 90% of all land in England and Wales is now registered, this is now the 'normal' way for ownership of land to be recorded, replacing title deeds.

registered office The official address of a registered company. It must be notified to the Companies Registry before *registration of the company and it must appear on company letter-heads and order forms. Documents may be served to a company's registered office and various registers and records may be inspected there.

register of members A record of the names, addresses, and shareholdings of members of a registered company, which is kept at the registered office or wherever it is compiled. The register must be kept open for public inspection (members free) for at least two hours daily; it may not be closed for longer than 30 days in any year.

registrar *n.* **1.** An official responsible for compiling and keeping a register, e.g. the Registrar of Companies. The office of Registrar of the Chancery Division of the High Court has now been abolished. **2.** In the *Court of Appeal, the officer (Registrar of Civil Appeals) responsible for superintending the prehearing stages of appeals in the Civil Division of the court. **3. (district registrar)** *See* DISTRICT JUDGE.

registration as citizen or subject A method by which certain persons can, either by right or at the Secretary of State's discretion, acquire *British citizenship, *British Dependent Territories citizenship, or *British Overseas citizenship or become *British Nationals (Overseas). Some people can also become *British subjects by registration. An *oath of allegiance must be taken by most adult applicants. *Compare* NATURALIZATION.

registration of a company The most usual method of forming an incorporated company (*see* INCORPORATION). Under the Companies Act 1985 the following documents must be delivered with the appropriate fee to the *Companies Registry: the *memorandum of association signed by at least two company members, *articles of association (if any), statements relating to the directors, secretary, and the *registered office, and a statutory declaration that the Companies Act has been complied with. The Registrar will then enter the company's name in the *companies register and issue a *certificate of incorporation.

registration of birth The recording of a birth by a Registrar of Births and Deaths under the Births and Deaths Registration Act 1953. Information for this purpose must be supplied to him within 42 days of the birth by a parent of the child, the occupier of the premises in which the birth takes place, a person present at the birth, or a person having charge of the child. The informant must supply details of the date and place of birth, the name and sex of the child, and its parentage, which are entered on the **birth certificate**; an unmarried father's name may be included on the birth certificate in certain circumstances. A birth certificate may be obtained from the Registrar, the Superintendent Registrar, or the General Register Office; a short form of the certificate, relating to the child's name, sex, and date of birth but not parentage, may also be obtained (*see* ILLEGITIMACY). Children may consult the birth register to discover who their registered parents are and adopted children over the age of 18 have a right to see their original birth certificate. *See also* HUMAN FERTILIZATION AND EMBRYOLOGY AUTHORITY.

registration of commons *See* COMMON LAND.

registration of death The recording of a death by the Registrar of Births and Deaths under the Births and Deaths Registration Act 1953. This must take place within five days of the death or, if written notice of the death is given to the Registrar within that period, within 14 days. It may be effected by any relative of the deceased present at the death or during the last illness, by any other relative, by any person present at the death, or by the occupier or any inmate of the premises on which the death occurred. The informant must supply details of the date and place of death, the name, sex, address, and occupation of the deceased, and the cause of death. A **death certificate** may be obtained from the Registrar, the Superintendent Registrar, or the General Register Office.

registration of encumbrances Registration of *land charges and other interests affecting the rights of landowners. If registered, these charges are binding on third parties who acquire the land affected or any interest in it. If not registered, however, they will not bind most third parties and thus lose their effectiveness as interests or rights of occupation in the land itself. A person contemplating buying or taking an interest (e.g. a mortgage) in land should therefore search the relevant registers to ensure that there are no charges registered that would influence him against proceeding. The registers are therefore always searched in any *conveyancing transaction by the purchaser or his solicitor. There are four relevant registers.

(1) **Local land charges**, arising in favour of a local authority from the exercise of its statutory powers, are recorded in a **local land charges register** maintained by the authority concerned in relation both to registered and unregistered titles. Examples

include rights to the repayment of improvement grants, compulsory purchase and smoke control orders, and planning decisions affecting the development or use of premises. Local land charges do not appear in any national register.

(2) When the title to land is registered (*see* LAND REGISTRATION), encumbrances other than local land charges can be protected by registration of the appropriate entry in the charges register of the title at the Land Registry. This may be as a *minor interest, protected by a *notice or by a *restriction or *caution. Some encumbrances also rank as *overriding interests and so do not require registration.

(3) In the case of *unregistered land, registers are maintained by the *Land Charges Department of the following types of interest recorded against the names of persons owning land.

(a) Land charges, comprising **Class A**: certain statutory charges registered on the application of the chargee; **Class B**: similar charges registered automatically; **Class C**: (i) *puisne mortgages, (ii) *limited owners' charges, (iii) *general equitable charges, and (iv) *estate contracts; **Class D**: (i) Inland Revenue charges for *inheritance tax, (ii) *restrictive covenants created after 1925 and affecting freehold land, and (iii) equitable *easements created after 1925; **Class E**: annuities created before 1926 and registered after 1925; and **Class F**: spouses' rights of occupation under the Family Law Act 1996.

(b) *Pending actions relating to land or any interest in it, and petitions for *bankruptcy.

(c) Writs or orders of the court imposing a charge on, or appointing a receiver or sequestrator of, land, and all *bankruptcy orders.

(d) *Deeds of arrangement affecting land.

Land charges remain registered until discharged by the chargee or the court. Registration of pending actions, writs and orders, and deeds of arrangement must be renewed every five years.

(4) A floating charge on the assets (including land) of a limited company and any other charge on a company's land that was created before 1970 for securing money need only be registered at the Companies Registry, under the Companies Act 1985. A fixed charge on a company's land created after 1969 should be registered both at the Companies Registry and the Land Charges Department (or charges register of the registered title as appropriate).

Although a chargee is protected by registration against all persons acquiring any interest in the land affected, the Law of Property Act 1969 provides that a purchaser is bound only by registered charges of which he knew or ought to have known when the contract was made. Thus if the purchaser discovers an undisclosed registered charge before completing the contract, he may rescind or pursue other contractual remedies against his vendor as the circumstances allow. If he completes the transaction, however, he will be bound by the charge.

registration of marriage The official recording of details relating to a marriage after it has been solemnized. (It is not to be confused with registration of notice of an intended marriage.) The details usually registered include the names, ages, occupations, and addresses of the parties, names and occupations of their fathers, and place of solemnization of the marriage. Certified copies of the details may be issued on request.

registration of merchant ships *See* SHIP.

registration of title *See* LAND REGISTRATION.

regular forces Generally, the armed forces of the Crown other than *reserve forces or auxiliary forces.

regulated agreement Any *consumer-credit agreement or *consumer-hire agreement under the Consumer Credit Act 1974, other than one specifically exempted by the Act. Exempted agreements include debtor-creditor-supplier agreements secured by a land mortgage, in which the creditor is a local authority or building society who finances the purchase of that land or the provision of dwellings on the land, and *debtor-creditor agreements secured by a land mortgage. The Act also enables the Secretary of State to exempt other consumer-credit agreements in which the number of payments to be made by the debtor does not exceed a specified number, the rate of the total charge for credit does not exceed a specified rate, or the agreement has a connection with a country outside the UK.

regulated mortgage A legal *mortgage (usually predating 8 December 1965) of land that is subject to a *regulated tenancy binding on the mortgagee. The Rent Act 1977 (Part X) provides relief to mortgagors under regulated mortgages in certain cases of hardship.

regulated tenancy A *protected tenancy or a *statutory tenancy. It is a protected tenancy until the contractual element is terminated, when it becomes a statutory tenancy. Regulated tenancies have been replaced by *assured tenancies by the Housing Act 1988.

regulations of the EU See COMMUNITY LEGISLATION.

regulatory agency Any of the nonministerial government departments with statutory duties of control over privatized industries. Each of the statutes that provided for the *privatization of services formerly provided by public corporations also made provision for the establishment of a regulatory agency for the service in question; these agencies include the Office of Telecommunications (Oftel), the Office of Gas and Electricity Markets (Ofgem), the Office of Water Services (Ofwat), the Office for Standards in Education (Ofsted), and the Office of the National Lottery (Oflot).

rehabilitation n. See PUNISHMENT; SPENT CONVICTION.

rehabilitation order An order relating to a building acquired by a local housing authority before 2 December 1974 in a *clearance area that is, in the housing authority's opinion, capable of being improved so as to be available for use as a dwelling for 15 years. Under a rehabilitation order, the authority's duty to demolish the building is replaced by one to improve it or ensure that it is improved.

rehearing n. **1.** A second hearing of a case already adjudicated upon, e.g. an *appeal to the Crown Court from conviction by a magistrates' court. All the evidence is heard again and either side may introduce fresh evidence without leave. **2.** The hearing of an appeal by the *Court of Appeal, in which the Court will consider all the evidence presented to the trial court (if it is relevant to the appeal) by reading the verbatim transcript of the trial; it will not usually permit fresh evidence to be given. The Court of Appeal will usually not disturb the trial judge's findings on *primary facts, as opposed to the inferences to be drawn from those facts.

Reid test See LAY DAYS.

reinstatement order An order made by an *employment tribunal directing an employer who has been found to have unfairly dismissed an employee (see UNFAIR

DISMISSAL) to restore him to his former job (*compare* RE-ENGAGEMENT ORDER). The employee is to be treated as if he had not been dismissed and is therefore entitled to recover any benefits (such as arrears of pay) that he has lost during his period of unemployment. However, pay in lieu of notice, *ex gratia* payments by the employer, state unemployment or supplementary benefits, and other sums he has received because of his dismissal or any subsequent unemployment will be taken into account. An employer cannot be forced to comply with an order for reinstatement; if he fails to do so, *compensation will be awarded to the employee on the usual principles together with an additional sum.

reinsurance *n.* The procedure in which an insurer insures himself with another insurer against some or all of his liability for a risk that he has himself underwritten in an earlier *insurance contract. Reinsurance is undertaken when the potential loss attached to the risk is too great for the insurer to bear alone. A valid contract of insurance gives the insurer an *insurable interest to support a reinsurance.

rejection of offer The refusal of an *offer by the offeree. Once an offer has been rejected, it cannot subsequently be accepted by the offeree. A counter-offer ranks as a rejection, but a mere inquiry as to the possibility of varying some term does not. *See also* LAPSE OF OFFER; REVOCATION OF OFFER.

rejoinder *n.* Formerly, a pleading served by a defendant in answer to the claimant's *reply. Such a pleading could only be served with the court's permission.

relation back The treating of an act or event as having legal effect from a date earlier than that on which it actually takes place. Thus a grant of *probate relates back to the date of the testator's death.

relator *n.* A person at whose request an action is brought by the *Attorney General to enforce some public right. Although the relator is not the claimant, he is liable for the *costs of the proceedings. The Attorney General must consent to the issue of the originating process and his discretion in deciding whether or not to sue on behalf of the relator is absolute and cannot be reviewed by the court.

release *n.* **1.** The renunciation of a right of legal action against another. The fact that a release has been granted should be specifically pleaded as a defence if the person who granted it subsequently initiates court proceedings. **2.** Any document by which one person discharges another from any claim with respect to a particular matter. **3.** The freeing of a person formerly detained, either upon *discharge when sentencing him or at the end of a prison sentence. The early release of prisoners is subject to *parole, but the Home Secretary has a duty to release unconditionally anyone sentenced to less than 12 months' imprisonment after half of the sentence has been served. Other conditions for the early release of prisoners are specified in the Criminal Justice Act 1991.

release on licence *See* PAROLE.

relevance (relevancy) *n.* (in the law of evidence) The relationship between two facts that renders one probable from the existence of the other, either taken by itself or in connection with other facts. Although most relevant facts are admissible in evidence, relevance is not the same as *admissibility, since even relevant evidence must be excluded if it falls within one of the *exclusionary rules. If no exclusionary rule is involved, all facts that have logical relevance to a fact in issue may be proved even though they are not in issue themselves.

relevant evidence *See* RELEVANCE.

relevant facts *See* RELEVANCE.

relevant transfer A situation that may arise when a business or part of a business (the transferor) changes ownership and staff transfer to the new owner (the transferee). If the change of ownership falls within the scope of the Transfer of Undertakings Protection of Employment Regulations 1981 (**TUPE**), then there is an automatic transfer of an employee's contract of employment. TUPE was the UK government's response to EC Directive 77/187, known as the Acquired Rights Directive, the main objective of which was to safeguard employees' rights in the event of a change of employer. Employees are protected via TUPE where there is a relevant transfer. This, however, is not always a straightforward issue to determine. Because the Acquired Rights Directive is very wide in its scope, both the European Court and national courts have taken a wide view of what situations amount to a relevant transfer. The situations in which a relevant transfer has been held to operate are numerous. The simplest situation is where one company acquires another and staff transfer. More complex situations include contracting out services, the transfer of contracts and franchises, and the transfer of leases. TUPE operates in each of these situations if staff have followed the transfer or have lost employment as a consequence.

There are a number of important issues to note where a relevant transfer occurs. First there is an automatic transfer of the transferor's rights and obligations arising from the employment relationship they have with their staff. Because of this the employee's terms and conditions (with very limited exceptions in the area of pension rights) must be maintained by the new employer (the transferee). Secondly, a relevant transfer cannot be the basis for dismissal unless an employee can be shown to have been dismissed for economic reasons or as a result of technical reorganization. Where an employee, being aware of a proposed transfer, informs either the transferor or the transferee that he objects to the transfer, his transfer does not take effect and his contract of employment is terminated, but he has no claim for unfair dismissal. If a dismissal occurs as a direct result of the transfer this is automatically unfair. If an employer seeks to argue a dismissal was for an economic, technical, or organizational reason, it is not automatically unfair but it can be depending on the employer's procedure.

Finally, TUPE puts in place the need for a consultative process to ensure the free exchange of information between the transferee, the transferor, and the staff who may be affected. The transferor has a duty to inform and consult with a recognized independent trade union when any of its members may be affected by the transfer. The employer must inform union representatives in writing, long enough before the relevant transfer to enable consultations to take place, of the fact that a transfer is to take place; when this is to occur and the reasons for it; the legal, economic, and social implications of the transfer for the affected employees; and the measures the employer is to take (if any) in relation to those employees. If there are no employee representatives, information must be given to all employees. The transferee has a duty to provide the transferor with sufficient information to enable him to give these facts. During consultations the employer has a duty to consider any representations made by trade union or staff representatives and reply to them; if he rejects them he is obliged to give his reasons for doing so. If any employer fails to inform or consult, a complaint may be presented to an employment tribunal within three months of the completion of the relevant transfer. The employer can argue that his failure to perform a particular duty was due to special circumstances but that he took all reasonably practicable steps to inform and consult. Although this is a potential defence, tribunals interpret it very narrowly. Insolvency does not amount to special circumstances. If the complaint is upheld, the tribunal can order the employer to pay appropriate compensation not exceeding 13 weeks' pay for the employee(s) in question.

The scope of the Acquired Rights Directive has now been expanded; consequent modifications to TUPE are currently under discussion. Changes include a discretion for EU member states to extend the protection of national law to require transferees to provide equivalent pensions, and for contractual terms to be varied when a transfer is coincidental with insolvency proceedings and when the variation in a contract of employment is to ensure continuation of the organization. It will also be possible for employee representatives to negotiate changes in contractual terms following the transfer of an important business. There are new provisions dealing with employee representation as well as amendments to the procedures for information and consultation.

relief *n.* **1.** *See* REMEDY. **2.** A tax concession; for example, a personal allowance (*see* INCOME TAX) or roll-over relief (*see* CAPITAL GAINS TAX). **3.** Payment by a feudal tenant following succession to him of land after the death of the former tenant.

relief from forfeiture A discretionary power of the courts to restore a lease to a tenant when the landlord claims or has exercised his right of *forfeiture.

remainder *n.* An interest in land that comes into effect in possession only when a prior interest ends. For example if A settles land on B for life then on C in fee simple, C's interest is in remainder until B dies. All interests in remainder are necessarily equitable (*see* FEE SIMPLE ABSOLUTE IN POSSESSION). A settlement may create several successive remainders; for example, a settlement on A for life, remainder to B for life, remainder to C in tail, remainder to D in fee simple. B, C, and D are called **remaindermen**. There can be no remainder after a fee simple. *See also* REVERSION.

remainderman *n.* *See* REMAINDER.

remand *vb.* To commit an accused person to custody or release him on *bail during an adjournment. After arrest a suspect is normally kept at the police station until he is brought before the magistrates. If the offence with which he is charged is triable summarily or is an indictable offence that is being tried summarily (*see* OFFENCES TRIABLE EITHER WAY), the court may adjourn the case and remand the accused. If the offence is being tried on indictment, the court may likewise adjourn the case and remand the accused before inquiring into the offence as examining justices. Remand in custody has traditionally been made for no more than eight clear days, excluding the day on which the accused was remanded and the day on which he is to appear again before the court (the "eight-day rule"). If the accused had to be remanded for more than eight days, he was normally released on bail unless there was some special reason why bail should be refused. However, the court could remand a suspect for a further period (or any number of further periods) of eight days after the end of the original remand order. If the period of time spent on remand became excessive, the accused could apply for bail. However, following claims that eight-day remand hearings served no useful purpose and wasted prison service resources, the Home Secretary was empowered in 1988 to provide remand periods not exceeding 28 days for accused persons aged 17 or over, in particular areas or classes of case. The abolition of the eight-day rule was extended, by the Criminal Procedure and Investigations Act 1996, to those under 17 for offences alleged to have been committed on or after 1 February 1997. A remand order may also be made upon adjournment of a trial at any stage, at the request of either the prosecution or the defence, or after conviction, if the court wishes to obtain a report before sentencing. Bail must normally be granted, however, when remanding for reports.

Upon remand the suspect is sent to the local prison. *Juvenile offenders may be remanded instead to local authority accommodation. Under the Criminal Justice and Public Order Act 1994, the court may remand a juvenile offender to secure accommodation in a *community home or a registered children's home, provided the charge or conviction is for a violent or sexual attack, the offence is one for which an adult could be imprisoned for at least 14 years, or there is a recent history of absconding and the charge or conviction relates to an imprisonable offence committed while remanded to the local authority. As a result of major amendments to the Children and Young Persons Act 1969, the minimum age for being remanded to secure accommodation has been reduced to 12.

remedial constructive trust *See* CONSTRUCTIVE TRUST.

remedy (redress, relief) *n.* Any of the methods available at law for the enforcement, protection, or recovery of rights or for obtaining redress for their infringement. A **civil remedy** may be granted by a court to a party to a civil action. It may include the common law remedy of *damages and/or the *equitable remedies of *quantum meruit* (*see* QUASI-CONTRACT), *injunction, decree of *specific performance, or *declaration.

remission *n.* Cancellation of part of a prison sentence. Formerly, a prisoner could earn remission of one-third of his sentence by good behaviour in prison and was released upon remission without any conditions. However, a prisoner serving an *extended sentence, or a prisoner serving more than 18 months' imprisonment, who was under the age of 21 when sentenced, could only be released on licence (*see* PAROLE). Remission of a sentence for good conduct was abolished by the Criminal Justice Act 1991, which specifies the conditions now required for the early release of prisoners.

remoteness of damage The extent to which a defendant is liable for the consequences of his wrongful act or omission. In contract, the defendant compensates for damage only if it was within his **reasonable contemplation**. He is presumed to have contemplated (and is therefore liable for) damage likely to result from the breach according to the usual course of events. Unusual damage resulting from special circumstances is regarded as within his contemplation only if a reasonable man, knowing what he knew or ought to have known, would have thought it liable to result.

In tort there is no single test to determine whether or not damage is too remote. In actions for *negligence and other forms of liability based on fault, the defendant is responsible only for damage of the type he should have foreseen, but if damage of that type is foreseeable, it is no defence that the extent of the resulting damage is greater than could have been expected. In torts of *strict liability, the defendant may be liable even for unforeseeable damage. Thus the keeper of an animal belonging to a dangerous species is liable for any damage it causes, whether foreseeable or not.

removal of action The transfer of a High Court action from a district registry to London (or vice versa) or of a county court action to the High Court (or vice versa).

renewal of lease The grant of a fresh *lease on similar terms to those of a pre-existing lease between the same parties. A lease sometimes contains a clause that gives the lessee an option to renew the lease when it expires. If the renewal is to be on the same terms, including the option to renew, the lease is known as a **perpetually renewable lease**; by statute, however, it is instead deemed to be a lease for 2000 years.

renouncing probate An executor's refusal, after the testator's death and in signed writing filed at a probate registry, to accept the office of executor. In such circumstances the person who would be entitled on intestacy to apply for letters of administration may apply for a grant of *letters of administration *cum testamento annexo.*

rent *n.* Payment by a tenant to his landlord under the terms of a *lease or *tenancy agreement. The obligation to pay rent is implied in all leases. If the tenant fails to pay his rent, the landlord can levy *distress for rent, take action for *forfeiture of the lease, or bring a court action against the tenant to claim the rent due. The manner and time of payment is as specified in the lease or tenancy agreement. If there is no express provision, rent should be paid to the landlord or his agent at the end of each *rental period or, in the case of a *fixed term, at the end of each year. The tenant can only deduct from the rent amounts that the lease or tenancy agreement allows. If the parties wish, the rent need not be paid in money: it may be in the form of service to the landlord or payment in kind. However, the amount of rent must be certain or capable of being ascertained. *See also* FAIR RENT.

rental period A period in a lease or tenancy for which the tenant must make a payment of rent. In the absence of agreement, this is yearly in the case of a *fixed term. For other periods, *see* PERIODIC TENANCY.

rent assessment committee A committee that decides any dispute concerning the amount of a *fair rent determined by a rent officer for a tenancy of a dwelling-house under the Rent Act 1977 (where it still applies). A rent assessment committee may also, on application by a tenant, determine whether a proposed increase in rent for an *assured tenancy (under the Housing Act 1988) is what the landlord could obtain on the open market and, if not, it may fix what this should be. Committees' members are drawn from panels appointed by the Secretary of State and the Lord Chancellor, and they are under the supervision of the Council on Tribunals. *See also* RENT TRIBUNAL.

rent book A book or other document used to record rent paid and other tenancy details. A landlord must give his tenant a rent book when there is a weekly tenancy of residential property unless a substantial proportion of the rent is payment for board.

rentcharge *n.* A periodic payment of money charged on land, but excluding rent payable under a lease or tenancy and sums payable as interest. Depending on the manner in which the rentcharge arose, it may be called a **chief rent** or **fee farm rent**, but the effect is similar. A rentcharge owned on terms equivalent to a fee simple absolute in possession or term of years absolute can be a legal interest in land, but one subsisting on other terms (e.g. for life) is an equitable interest, registrable as a *general equitable charge. If the rent falls into arrears, the owner of the rentcharge may (on 40 days' arrears) enter the land and take its income until the debt is paid or lease the land to trustees who have powers to raise the money. On 21 days' arrears, he may enter the land and seize the debtor's goods as security for the rent (*see* DISTRESS). In general, a deed creating a rentcharge also reserves to its owner the right to forfeit the debtor's interest in the land if the rent is not paid. The Law of Property (Amendment) Act 1926 provides that freehold land subject to a rentcharge owner's right of forfeiture (a right of re-entry) can still qualify as a fee simple absolute in possession.

A rentcharge may also be secured on another rentcharge, rather than directly on land. For example, A grants a rentcharge (R1) over his land of £50 a year to B, who grants a rentcharge (R2) secured on R1 of £25 a year to C. If B is more than 21 days in arrear, C may appoint a receiver to collect the £50 from A and to pay C his £25 plus the expenses of the recovery, and account to B for any surplus.

The Rentcharges Act 1977 prohibits the creation of new rentcharges after 21 August 1977, except for (1) certain charges, usually in favour of the landowner's family, the effect of which is to make the land subject to a *trust of land; and (2) **estate rentcharges**. The latter are usually reserved by a developer selling plots on an estate subject to covenants given by the purchasers to protect the character of the estate; they entitle the owner of the rentcharge to enforce the purchasers' covenants even after all the plots have been sold off.

rent officer An official appointed by central government who determines *fair rents and keeps a register of all fair rents in his local area. Under the Housing Act 1988, rent officers are given additional functions relating to housing benefit and rent allowance subsidy.

rent rebate A rent subsidy paid by local authorities to their own needy tenants, as part of *housing benefit. The conditions vary from one local authority to another.

rent registration 1. The registration by a rent officer of a *fair rent determined by himself or a rent assessment committee under the Rent Act 1977. This procedure is now abolished except for rents already so fixed. **2.** The registration by a local authority of a *restricted contract rent determined by a rent tribunal or rent assessment committee. Since the passing of the Housing Act 1988, rents of new tenancies are not registered.

rent service 1. Any rent payable where a landlord and tenant relationship exists. **2.** Originally, a rent payable to a feudal lord.

rent tribunal A tribunal to whom the determination of the rent properly payable under a *restricted contract may be referred. Rent tribunals also have power to grant limited security of tenure, but only if the contract was made before the commencement of the Housing Act 1980. Until that Act they were distinctly constituted bodies, but their functions are now carried out by *rent assessment committees sitting as rent tribunals. No new restricted contracts can be made since the passing of the Housing Act 1988.

renvoi *n.* [French: sending back] The doctrine whereby the courts of one country in certain circumstances apply the law of another country in resolving a legal dispute. A problem arises in private international law when one country's rule as to conflict of law refers a case to the law of a foreign country, and the law of that country refers the case either back to the law of the first country (**remission**) or to the law of a third country (**transmission**). For example, under English conflict rules, if a person dies intestate, the succession to his personal property is governed by the law of the country in which he is domiciled. Under Italian conflict rules, however, succession to personal property in such cases is governed by the law of the intestater's nationality. Thus if an English national dies intestate while domiciled in Italy, a *renvoi* problem will arise – English law will refer the matter to the law of his domicile (i.e. Italian law) and Italian law would refer the matter to the law of his nationality (i.e. English law).

repairs *pl. n.* (in landlord and tenant law) *See* COVENANT TO REPAIR.

reparations *pl. n.* (in international law) **1.** Compensation for injuries or international torts (breaches of international obligations). Whenever possible, international courts or arbitration tribunals will rule that reparations be made by means of restitution in kind; if this is not possible, compensation is by payment of a sum equivalent to the value of restitution in kind. The aim of reparations is to eradicate the consequences of the illegal act. It is not clear, however, whether there is an obligation to make reparations for all breaches of international law. **2.** Payments made by a defeated state to the conquering state to compensate for damage suffered by the victor.

repatriation *n.* A person's voluntary return from a foreign country to that of which he is a national. *Compare* DEPORTATION.

repeal *n.* The total or partial revocation of a statute by one passed subsequently. A statute is normally repealed by express words, but if provisions of a later statute are inconsistent with those of an earlier one this will imply that Parliament intended a repeal. Repeal does not affect any transaction that has been completed under the repealed statute.

repeat offender An offender who commits the same offence on more than one occasion. Under the Crime (Sentences) Act 1997, from 1999 those convicted for a third time for dealing in hard drugs or for burglary face minimum *sentences of seven and three years, respectively, unless the judge finds that this is unjust. The Act also provides for a mandatory life sentence for those convicted for a second time of rape or attempted rape, manslaughter, attempted murder, wounding with intent to do grievous bodily harm, robbery with a firearm, or possession of a firearm with intent to endanger life. In exceptional circumstances the judge may choose not to impose the mandatory sentence on such an offender but must provide a full explanation as to why this has not been done.

replevin *n.* A procedure to recover goods that have been taken out of the claimant's possession (usually by way of distress for unpaid rent), the effect of which is to restore them to the claimant provisionally, pending the outcome of an action to determine the rights of the parties.

reply *n.* A statement of case served by the claimant in a civil action in answer to the *defence. It is often contained in the same document as a defence to a *counterclaim.

repossession *n.* (of mortgaged property) The right of a mortgagee to obtain vacant possession of the property occupied by a mortgagor, in accordance with the terms of the mortgage. All mortgagees have a right to possession of the property from the time the mortgage is granted unless they have contracted out of the right. It is, however, unusual for a mortgagee to exercise such a right unless the mortgagor has defaulted in some way. *See also* MORTGAGE; POWER OF SALE.

representation *n.* **1.** The state of being represented, e.g. by an elected representative in the House of Commons (*see also* PARLIAMENT), by a defending counsel in court, or by an agent acting on behalf of his principal. **2.** (in succession) Taking the place of another. The court grants to executors or administrators the right to represent the deceased, i.e. to collect, sell, and transfer the deceased's assets (in accordance with the will or intestacy rules) as if they were the owners. Under the Wills Act 1837 a *devise or *legacy in favour of a child or remoter descendant of the testator who predeceases him leaving descendants of his own does not lapse but is inherited by those surviving descendants, who therefore represent their deceased ancestor (*see* PER STIRPES). **3.** (in contract law) A statement. A person who has been induced to enter into a contract on the basis of a statement that is untrue or misrepresents a material fact may sue for damages or for rescission of the contract (*see* MISREPRESENTATION). Under the Consumer Credit Act 1974 a representation includes a *condition, *warranty, or any other statement or undertaking, either oral or in writing. Many contracts exclude all prior representations from terms of the contract, although in consumer contracts such an exclusion may be void if unfair.

representative action An action brought by or against one or more persons as representative(s) of a larger group. All the persons represented must have the same interest in the proceedings, and therefore a representative action cannot generally be brought if each member of the group has a separate claim for damages. Judgment in a representative action is binding upon all the persons represented. Such actions are not normally possible under English law, although they are common in the United States. An example of a representative action is one brought by company members on behalf of themselves and other members against the company in respect of a wrong done to them by it (e.g. a denial of their voting or class rights embodied in the articles of association or an *ultra vires* act). *Compare* DERIVATIVE ACTION; GROUP ACTION.

reprisals *pl. n.* Retaliatory measures taken by one state against another to settle a dispute occasioned by the other's illegal or unjustified conduct. Reprisals include boycotts, *embargoes, and limited military action. A military reprisal, if otherwise than for the purpose of lawful self-defence under Article 51 of the United Nations Charter, is now illegal under international law.

republication of will The re-execution with proper formalities of an existing will, or of a *codicil to it that contains some reference to the will, which has the effect of confirming that will. When republished, the will takes effect as if made at the date of republication. A republication may have the effect of validating an unattested alteration made to the will before its re-execution or the execution of the confirmatory codicil. *Compare* REVIVAL OF WILL.

repudiation *n.* (in contract law) **1.** An anticipatory *breach of contract. **2.** A minor's disclaimer of a contract that is voidable because of his minority (*see* CAPACITY TO CONTRACT; RESCISSION).

repugnancy *n.* Contradiction or inconsistency in the terms of a document. Generally the court construes documents to give effect to the parties' primary intention (the **main purpose rule**). If this cannot be established and the document's provisions are directly contradictory, the court treats the later provision as effective in the case of a will and the earlier one in the case of a deed. Thus a transfer of property to A and B "as beneficial joint tenants in equal shares" confers a *joint tenancy unless it was effected by will, when it will be treated as conferring a *tenancy in common in equal shares.

reputation *n.* The estimation in which a person is generally held. *See* CHARACTER; DEFAMATION.

reputed ownership Goods that at the beginning of the bankruptcy of a trader are in his possession with the consent of the true owner and in circumstances suggesting that the bankrupt is the owner are said to be in the bankrupt's reputed ownership. Such goods are treated as the bankrupt's own goods and are therefore available for distribution to his creditors.

request for further information *See* INTERROGATORY; PARTICULARS.

requisition *n.* **1.** (in land law) An application to HM Land Registry, the Land Charges Department, or a local authority for a certificate of *official search to reveal whether or not land is affected by encumbrances. **2.** (in *conveyancing) A request by an intending purchaser or mortgagee arising from the *abstract of title supplied by the owner. For example if an abstracted deed shows that the land is affected by encumbrances contained in an earlier deed that has not been abstracted, the purchaser will raise a requisition demanding proper evidence of the encumbrances. **3.** (in military law) The compulsory acquisition of property for use by the armed forces. The Army Act 1955 and the Air Force Act 1955, for example, contain provisions that, if brought into force by a government order made in the public interest, enable commanding officers to issue requisitioning orders authorizing the acquisition (in return for payment and compensation for damage) of vehicles, horses' food, and stores.

reregistration *n.* The procedure enabling a registered company to change its status, e.g. from limited to unlimited or from public to private (or, in either case, vice versa).

resale *n.* *See* RIGHT OF RESALE.

resale price maintenance The fixing by a supplier of the price at which his goods may be sold by others. This may be attempted by contractual arrangements or by nonlegal means, such as blacklisting by trade associations. Resale price maintenance is now prohibited by the Competition Act 1998 and Article 81 of the Treaty of Rome. Provisions in contracts of sale between suppliers and dealers fixing minimum prices are void, and it is illegal to withhold supplies on the grounds of adverse pricing. Fines of 10% of turnover can be imposed for breach of these provisions. Formerly, resale price maintenance was permitted for books and certain nonprescription drugs, but even these exceptions have now been declared illegal.

rescission *n.* The setting aside of a *voidable contract, which is thereby treated as if it had never existed. Rescission is an irrevocable step and can be effected by any clear indication of intention to be no longer bound by the contract; this intention must be either communicated to the other party or publicly evidenced in some way. Rescission can also be effected by a formal action (a remedy developed by the courts of equity). There are limits on the right of rescission. It cannot be exercised unless *restitutio in integrum* is possible, i.e. unless it is possible to restore both parties to their original positions, and it cannot be exercised if this would involve upsetting rights acquired by third parties. Thus, a buyer of goods cannot rescind if he cannot return the goods, and a seller of goods cannot rescind if they have been resold to a third party.

The setting aside of a proprietary contract by a minor is normally called **repudiation** rather than rescission, but there is no distinction in substance. The treating of a contract as discharged by breach (*see* BREACH OF CONTRACT) is frequently, but misleadingly, called rescission. It does not operate retrospectively and is permissible whether or not *restitutio* is possible.

rescue *n.* **1.** Action to save people or property from danger. There is no general duty to rescue people or property from danger, though a master of a ship is bound by statute to render assistance to people in danger at sea. Voluntary attempts to rescue people in danger are encouraged by the law. Someone injured in such a rescue attempt may recover damages from the person whose negligence created the danger. The rescuer is not regarded as having assumed the risk of being injured and courts are reluctant to find that his injuries were due to *contributory negligence. Attempts to rescue property may not be treated so sympathetically. **2.** The forcible removal of a person in the custody of the law, which is a criminal offence. **3.** The recovery of property that has been taken by way of *distress. If the distress was unlawful, the owner is entitled to recover it.

resealed probate A grant of *probate issued in one country and approved (and sealed again) by the court of another, giving the executor authority to deal with the testator's property in that second country.

reservation *n.* **1.** (in international law) A unilateral statement made by a state, when signing, ratifying, accepting, approving, or acceding to a treaty, in order to exclude or modify the legal effect of certain provisions of the treaty in their application to that state. This device is used by signatory states to exempt particular policies from challenge. The UK has made one reservation in relation to the *right to education in Article 2 of the First Protocol to the European Convention on Human Rights. The *Human Rights Act 1998 also excludes public authorities from duties under Article 2 where this reservation applies. **2.** (in land law) The creation of an easement or other right in a conveyance of land that is for the benefit of land retained by the vendor or transferor. For example, if A is selling Blackacre but requires a right of way over it for access to land he is retaining, the conveyance of Blackacre to the purchaser will reserve the right of way for the benefit of A's retained land. Such a reservation may be implied in circumstances of necessity. *See* EASEMENT OF NECESSITY.

reservation of title *See* RETENTION OF TITLE.

reserve capital *See* AUTHORIZED CAPITAL.

reserve forces Forces not in active service. They include the Army Reserve, the Territorial Army, the Air Force Reserve, the Royal Auxiliary Air Force, the Royal Naval Reserve, the Royal Naval Special Reserve, and the Royal Marines Reserve. The Reserve Forces Act 1996 provides a new power allowing call-out of reserve forces for humanitarian disaster relief and operations and introduced two new categories of reserve. The **high readiness reserve** will consist of about 3000 volunteers who have agreed, with their employers' consent, to accept increased liability for being called out. These volunteers will be people with special skills, such as linguists and public information specialists. The **sponsored reserve** will undertake some support tasks currently restricted to regular personnel. The legislation also makes provision to allow reservists to volunteer to undertake productive tasks other than training without being called out. There are powers to increase the military pay of reservists called out for operations if this pay is less than their civilian pay would be. There are also powers to pay employers for additional costs when the reservists are called out. A **Reserve Forces Appeal Tribunal**, set up under the 1996 Act, hears appeals from reservists and employers who are dissatisfied.

res extincta [Latin] Matter that has ceased to exist. *See* MISTAKE.

res gestae [Latin: things done] The events with which the court is concerned or others contemporaneous with them. In the law of evidence, *res gestae* denotes: (1) a rule of relevance according to which events forming part of the *res gestae* are admissible; (2) an exception to the rule against *hearsay evidence under which statements forming part of the *res gestae* are admissible, for example if they accompany and explain some relevant act or relate to the declarant's contemporaneous state of mind or his contemporaneous physical sensations.

residence *n.* **1.** The place in which a person has his home. The term has been defined in various ways for different purposes in Acts of Parliament. For example, the Income and Corporation Taxes Act 1988 provides that, for the purposes of tax, a person is resident in the UK even if he has left the UK for occasional residence abroad. Temporary residents are chargeable to tax in the UK if they stay in the UK for a period (or periods adding up to) six months in any year. It is possible to be a resident of more than one country at the same time. *See also* DOMICILE; HABITUAL RESIDENCE; MAIN RESIDENCE. **2.** In the case of a *company not incorporated in the United Kingdom, the country in which central management and control is located; companies incorporated in the United Kingdom are deemed to reside there irrespective of the location of central management and control. Residence determines the company's liability to *corporation tax.

residence order *See* SECTION 8 ORDERS.

residential occupier A person who is living in a property as a result of his contractual rights, his statutory rights, his rights under a rule of law, or because other people are restricted by law from removing him. It is an offence to force a residential occupier to leave the property without complying with the proper procedure. *See* ADVERSE OCCUPATION; EVICTION; FORCIBLE ENTRY; HARASSMENT OF OCCUPIER.

residuary devise *See* DEVISE.

residuary estate (residue) The property comprising a deceased person's estate after payment of his debts, funeral expenses, costs of administration of the estate, and all specific (and demonstrative) bequests and devises. If a will does not dispose of the whole of a testator's property, the residue passes to those entitled under the rules applying on *intestacy.

residuary legacy *See* LEGACY.

residue *n.* *See* RESIDUARY ESTATE.

res ipsa loquitur [Latin: the thing speaks for itself] A principle often applied in the law of tort of *negligence. If an accident has occurred of a kind that usually only happens if someone has been negligent, and the state of affairs that produced the accident was under the control of the defendant, it may be presumed in the absence of evidence that the accident was caused by the defendant's negligence.

resisting arrest Taking any action to prevent one's arrest. A person may use *reasonable force to resist an illegal arrest. If he resists a legal arrest, however, he lays himself open to a charge of assaulting or *obstructing a police officer in the course of his duty. The fact that the police officer was in plain clothes is no defence to such a charge. The House of Lords has ruled that it is the right and duty of every citizen to take reasonable steps to prevent a breach of the peace by detaining the offender. The offender therefore has no right to resist such an arrest on the grounds of *self-defence; if he uses force to do so, he may be guilty of an assault.

res judicata [Latin: a matter that has been decided] The principle that when a matter has been finally adjudicated upon by a court of competent jurisdiction it may not be reopened or challenged by the original parties or their successors in interest. It is also known as **action estoppel**. It does not preclude an appeal or a challenge to the jurisdiction of the court. Its justification is the need for finality in litigation. *See also* ESTOPPEL.

resolution *n.* **1.** A decision reached by a majority of the members at a company meeting. *See* ELECTIVE RESOLUTION; EXTRAORDINARY RESOLUTION; ORDINARY RESOLUTION;

SPECIAL RESOLUTION; WRITTEN RESOLUTION. **2.** The decision of a meeting of any other assembly, such as the *United Nations. Such a resolution, strictly speaking, has no binding effect on either the Security Council or the United Nations as a whole.

respondeat superior [Latin: let the principal answer] The doctrine by which an employer is responsible for certain wrongs committed by his employee in the course of his employment. *See* VICARIOUS LIABILITY.

respondent *n.* The defending party in an appeal or petition to the courts. *Compare* DEFENDANT.

respondentia *n. See* HYPOTHECATION.

restitutio in integrum [Latin] Restoration to the original position. *See* DAMAGES; RESCISSION.

restitution *n.* The return of property to the owner or person entitled to possession. If one person has unjustifiably received either property or money from another, he has an obligation to restore it to the rightful owner in order that he should not be unjustly enriched or retain an unjustified advantage. This obligation exists when, for example, goods or money have been transferred under compulsion (duress), under mistake, or under a transaction that fails because of illegality, lack of formality, or for any other reason or when the person who has taken the property has acquired a benefit through his actions without justification.

In certain circumstances the courts may make a **restitution order** in respect of property. Under the Theft Act 1968, if someone is convicted of any offence relating to stolen goods the court may order that the stolen goods or their proceeds should be restored to the person entitled to recover them. The court will only exercise this power, however, in clear cases that do not involve disputed questions of fact or law. Under the Police (Property) Act 1897, magistrates' courts are empowered to make a restitution order in favour of a person who is apparently the owner of property that has been obtained by the police in connection with any crime, even when no charge can be brought or the goods are seized under a search warrant. If the owner cannot be found, the court may make any order it thinks fit (usually an order for sale by auction). The police have no power to retain property lawfully seized merely because they think the court will probably make a restitution order.

restraint of marriage A condition in a contract or other disposition intended to prevent someone from marrying. Such conditions are usually (unless they are very limited) void, as they are considered to be against *public policy.

restraint of trade A contractual term that limits a person's right to exercise his trade or carry on his business. An example is a term in an employment contract or partnership agreement prohibiting a party from engaging in a similar business for a specified period after the relationship ends. Such a term is void unless the party relying on it shows that it does not offend *public policy; it must also be reasonable as between the parties. Many such terms are reasonable and therefore valid. *See also* GARDEN LEAVE CLAUSE.

restraint on alienation Provisions in a grant or conveyance of land that purport to prevent the owner from disposing of it. Restraints of an absolute nature are generally void. Partial restraints on alienation may be upheld by the courts.

restraints of princes (in marine insurance) Political or executive acts causing loss or damage, as distinct from such acts as riots or ordinary judicial processes. Such acts, more common in time of war, need not be done by officials of governments, but may be done by individuals exhorted or compelled to them by the states of which they are nationals.

restricted contract For the purposes of the Rent Act 1977, a contract granting someone the right to occupy a dwelling for a rent that includes payment for the use of furniture or for services. A contract creating a *regulated tenancy is not, however, a restricted contract. No new restricted contracts can be made since the Housing Act 1988 came into force. However, the occupant may qualify for *security of tenure as an *assured tenant.

restricted-use credit agreement (under the Consumer Credit Act 1974) A regulated *consumer-credit agreement that either (1) finances a transaction (which may or may not form part of the agreement) between the debtor and the creditor, e.g. a purchase of goods; (2) finances a transaction between the debtor and a person (the supplier) other than the creditor; or (3) refinances any existing indebtedness of the debtor's, to either the creditor or another person.

restriction *n.* (in land law) A limitation of the right of a registered proprietor to deal with the land or charge in a registered title. For instance, a beneficiary may enter a restriction against his trustees if the trust provides that the land may not be sold without the beneficiary's consent. A restriction may also be entered by, or with the concurrence of, the registered proprietor, and there are cases in which the Chief Land Registrar is obliged to enter a restriction (for example, when persons are registered as joint proprietors, and the survivor will not have power to give a valid receipt for *capital money arising on a disposition of the land).

restriction order An order placing special restrictions (for a specified period or without limit of time) on the discharge from hospital of a person detained there by a *hospital order. It may be made by the Crown Court (but not a magistrates' court) when this appears necessary for the public protection, and its principal effects are that discharge may be authorized only by the Home Secretary and may be subject to conditions (e.g. subsequent supervision by a mental welfare officer).

restrictive covenant An obligation created by *deed that curtails the rights of an owner of land; for example, a covenant not to use the land for the purposes of any business. A covenant imposing a positive obligation on the landowner (the covenantor), for example to repair fences, is not a restrictive covenant. Third parties who acquire freehold land affected by a restrictive covenant will be bound by it if it is registered (*see* REGISTRATION OF ENCUMBRANCES) or, in the case of covenants created before 1926, if they are aware or ought to be aware of it (*see* CONSTRUCTIVE NOTICE). The covenant may also be enforceable by successors of the original beneficiary (the covenantee) if it was annexed to (i.e. expressly taken for the benefit of) the covenantee's land or if the benefit of it was expressly assigned. Section 78(1) of the Law of Property Act 1925 has been interpreted as providing a form of statutory annexation. Thus, unless there is an express stipulation to the contrary, all covenants shall be deemed binding on successors to the original covenantee. The benefit of a covenant will not be annexed, however, if the covenantee's land is not actually capable of benefiting from the covenant; for example, if it is too far away to be affected. Restrictive covenants contained in leases are not registrable but are nevertheless generally enforceable between third parties (*see* COVENANT RUNNING WITH THE LAND). *See also* BUILDING SCHEME.

restrictive endorsement An *endorsement that prohibits the further negotiation (transfer) of a *bill of exchange (for example, "Pay X only") or states that it is a mere authority to deal with the bill as thereby directed and not a transfer of ownership of the bill (for example, "Pay X or order for collection"). A restrictive endorsement gives the endorsee the right to receive payment of the bill and to sue any party to it that his endorser could have sued, but gives him no power to transfer his rights as endorsee unless it expressly authorizes him to do so.

Restrictive Practices Court A superior *court of record created by the Restrictive Trade Practices Act 1956. Its jurisdiction was to determine matters arising under the legislation controlling *restrictive trade practices and *resale price maintenance, principally determining whether or not restrictive agreements registered with the *Director General of Fair Trading were contrary to the public interest. It was abolished under the Competition Act 1998 and its functions taken over by the Office of Fair Trading.

restrictive trade practices Arrangements in industry designed to maintain high prices or earnings or to exclude outsiders from a trade or profession. Examples include *resale price maintenance contracts, agreements between manufacturers to restrict output so that demand remains unsatisfied and a high price is maintained, similar agreements concerning the provision of services, and rules restricting entry to a trade or profession. Under the Competition Act 1998, certain types of restrictive agreement are presumed to be against the public interest (and therefore void) unless they are first registered with the *Director General of Fair Trading and then justified to the Office of Fair Trading (OFT). The OFT can declare whether or not an agreement is contrary to the public interest and make orders restraining the parties from giving effect to it and from making a new similar agreement. It can also decide whether or not goods of any particular class should be exempt from the statutory prohibition on resale price maintenance.

Agreements that are important to the national economy or hold down prices may be exempted by the Secretary of State. The provision of certain services (including legal, dental, educational, surveying, and medical and related services) are exempt under the Act, as are ministers of religion and certain exclusive dealings and intellectual property agreements.

resulting trust A trust arising by operation of law and in some cases based on the unexpressed but presumed intention of the settlor. When the beneficial interest of a trust is not completely disposed of, the undisposed interest results (i.e. goes back) to the settlor or to his estate. A resulting trust is also created when purchased property is transferred to someone other than the person who provides the price (compare ADVANCEMENT); it may also arise when property is transferred voluntarily. Resulting trusts may be regarded either as similar to *implied trusts or as a category of them. There is sometimes no clear distinction between a resulting trust and a *constructive trust, and the courts sometimes appear to use the terms interchangeably.

resulting use (implied use) A *use that arose when legal ownership (seisin) was transferred, but the transferor did not state for whose use (benefit) the property was to be: the benefit of the property therefore still belonged to the transferor.

retention of title (reservation of title) A stipulation on a contract of sale that the right of ownership of the goods shall not pass to the buyer until the buyer has paid the seller in full or has discharged all liabilities owing to the seller. It is also known as a **Romalpa clause**, from the case *Aluminium Industrie BV v Romalpa Aluminium Ltd* (1976).

retirement age (in the state pension scheme) The age at which an individual can start to receive a state retirement *pension. The state retirement age for men in the

UK is currently 65 and for women 60. However, the government is harmonizing retirement ages at 65 for both men and women, in order to comply with EU law on *equal pay.

retirement of jury The withdrawal of the *jury from the court at the end of the trial so that they may decide on their verdict in private. The jury members are not allowed contact with the public until they reach (or fail to reach) a verdict. They may not afterwards disclose the content of their discussions in reaching a verdict.

retirement of trustees A right of trustees to be released from their trusteeship. Originally trustees were not allowed to retire, but retirement is now possible subject to certain safeguards. Under the Trusts of Land and Appointment of Trustees Act 1996, when there is no person nominated to appoint new trustees in the trust instrument and the beneficiaries are of full age, sound mind, and absolutely entitled, the beneficiaries may give a written direction to the trustees to retire from the trust.

retorsion (retortion) *n.* A lawful means of retaliation by one state against another. It is usually provoked by an equally lawful, but discourteous, act of the other state, such as trade discrimination measures that single out foreign nationals or by hostile propaganda produced via government-controlled sources of information. *See also* REPRISALS; SANCTION; SELF-HELP.

retour sans protêt [French: return without protest] A direction on a *bill of exchange to the effect that the bill should be returned without *protest if it is dishonoured.

retrial *n. See* NEW TRIAL.

retribution *n. See* PUNISHMENT.

retrospective legislation (retroactive legislation) Legislation that operates on matters taking place before its enactment, e.g. by penalizing conduct that was lawful when it occurred. There is a presumption that statutes are not intended to have retroactive effect unless they merely change legal procedure (*see* INTERPRETATION OF STATUTES).

retrospective penalties *See* PENALTY.

return *n.* **1.** A formal document, such as an *annual return or the document giving particulars of shares allotted and to whom (**return of the allotment**), which must be delivered to the Companies Registry within one month of *allotment. **2.** The official result of the votes cast in an election.

return day The day specified in a summons for the hearing of the summons.

returning officer Under the Representation of the People Act 1983, a person – generally the sheriff of a county or chairman of a district or London borough council – designated by an order made by the Secretary of State to be responsible for the conduct of parliamentary elections.

revenue statute An Act of Parliament concerning taxation.

reversal of judgment The alteration of a *judgment on appeal, either wholly or in part.

reversion (reverter) *n.* The interest in land of a person (called the **reversioner**) who has granted some lesser interest than his own to another but has not disposed of the whole of his own interest. For example, if A grants land to B for life, A has an interest in reversion, since the land reverts to him on B's death. Similarly, a person who lets or sublets land to another retains an interest in reversion. The reversionary interest of a lessor can subsist as a legal estate, but the reversion after any other interest than a lease is necessarily an equitable interest.

reversionary lease Any lease for a term beginning at a future date. However, under the Law of Property Act 1925 a lease granted at a rent or for a capital sum is void if it is to take effect more than 21 years after it is executed.

reverter *n. See* REVERSION.

reverter of sites Reversion of land donated for charitable purposes to the donor or his successors in title when the land ceases to be used for the specified purposes. Many of these donations occurred under 19th-century statutes to enable voluntary schools, libraries, museums, and churches and chapels to be established. Since that time, many of these charitable purposes have ceased, and it has often proved difficult to trace the beneficial owners entitled to the reverter. Under the Reverter of Sites Act 1987, when a charitable purpose comes to an end, the trustees holding the land are given a right to manage it and keep it in repair. If the beneficial owner remains unidentifiable, the land can be sold and the proceeds used for charitable purposes.

revival of will The re-execution with proper formalities of a will that has been revoked other than by destruction, or the execution of a *codicil to it, showing the testator's intention that the will should be effective notwithstanding the earlier revocation. Under the Wills Act 1837 these are the only ways in which a will that has been revoked can be revived. A revived will operates as if executed at the time of its revival. *Compare* REPUBLICATION OF WILL.

revocation of offer The withdrawal of an *offer by the offeror so that it can no longer be accepted. Revocation takes effect as soon as it is known to the offeree (from whatever source); offers can be revoked at any time before acceptance unless they are coupled with an *option. *See also* LAPSE OF OFFER; REJECTION OF OFFER.

revocation of probate The cancellation by the court of a grant of probate that was obtained by fraud or mistake. The revocation does not affect those who have purchased assets of the estate from the executors before the revocation.

revocation of will The cancellation of a will. The testator may revoke his will by destroying it with that intention or by making a new will inconsistent with the original. A will is automatically revoked by the testator's valid marriage, unless it appears from the will that at the time it was made the testator was expecting to marry a particular person and that he intended his will not to be revoked by the marriage. A particular disposition in a will may similarly take effect in spite of the marriage. The dissolution of a marriage does not revoke a will but the Wills Act 1837 provides that in the event of divorce or annulment any devise or bequest to a former spouse lapses in the absence of contrary intention in the will.

right *n.* **1.** Title to or an interest in any property. **2.** Any other interest or privilege recognized and protected by law. **3.** Freedom to exercise any power conferred by law. *See also* HUMAN RIGHTS; NATURAL RIGHTS.

right of abode *See* IMMIGRATION.

right of action **1.** The right to take a particular case to court (*see* CLAIM). **2.** A chose in action (*see* CHOSE).

right of audience The right of an *advocate to be heard in legal proceedings. Barristers have the right of audience in the Crown Court, High Court, Court of Appeal, and House of Lords. Solicitors have a limited right of audience in some Crown Court centres specified by the Lord Chancellor. In the county courts and magistrates' courts both barristers and solicitors can appear. Many administrative tribunals have no rules concerning rights of audience and a party may be represented by any person he chooses.

right of common *See* COMMON.

right of establishment The right under the Treaty of Rome of a national of a member state of the European Community to engage in and manage businesses in any other member state.

right of light An *easement giving the owner of a dominant tenement the right to the access across the servient tenement of a sufficient quantity of light for the ordinary purposes to which the dominant tenement may be put. No easement can be acquired for a greater amount of light than is necessary for such purposes. *See* ANCIENT LIGHTS.

right of re-entry *See* RE-ENTRY.

right of resale The right that the seller in a contract of sale has to resell if the buyer does not pay the price as agreed. When the goods are perishable or the *unpaid seller gives notice to the buyer of his intention to resell, and the buyer does not pay the price within a reasonable time, if the seller is in possession of the goods he may resell them and recover from the first buyer damages for any loss.

right of silence The right of someone charged with an offence or being tried on a criminal charge not to make any statement or give any evidence. Often cited as a prime example of the fairness of the English criminal system, being intended to protect the innocent, it was also criticized as unduly hampering the conviction of the guilty and has therefore been modified. If a suspect fails to mention something at the time of his arrest or charge that is later relied on in his defence, this may result in a court at a subsequent trial drawing such inferences as appear proper (*see* CAUTION). Sometimes, however, statute obliges him to answer, as in certain fraud investigations by the *Serious Fraud Office (although this has been held contrary to the European Convention on Human Rights).

Failure of an accused aged 14 or over to give evidence in his own defence or refusal to answer questions without good cause will also allow such inferences to be drawn. Inferences may also be drawn from a suspect's failure to account for any object, mark, or substance found on his person, in his clothing or footwear, or otherwise in his possession at the time of arrest. The police officer must reasonably believe that such items are attributable to an offence and inform the suspect accordingly. Inferences may also be drawn from a suspect's failure to account for his presence at a particular place.

right of support **1.** An *easement conferring on the owner of the dominant tenement the right to have buildings on his land supported by those on the servient tenement. For example, houses forming a semidetached pair are likely to have mutual rights of support. **2.** For the right to preserve support for land in its natural state, *see* NATURAL RIGHTS.

right of survivorship (*jus accrescendi*) The right of a joint owner of property to acquire absolute ownership of the entire property on the death of the other owner(s). *See* JOINT TENANCY.

right of water 1. An *easement conferring on the owner of a *dominant tenement rights in connection with water, such as the rights to take water or to discharge water onto another's land, or a right to enter another's land to open sluice gates in order to prevent flooding of the dominant tenement. **2.** A *natural right to use water flowing through a channel on one's land.

right of way The right to pass over another's land. It may exist as a public right exercisable by anyone; as an *easement for the benefit of a particular piece of land; or as a *licence, purely personal to the person to whom it is granted.

rights issue A method of raising share *capital for a company from existing members rather than from the public at large. Members are given a right to acquire further shares, usually in proportion to their existing holding and at a price below the market value of existing shares. This right may be sold (**renounced**) to a third party. *See also* PRE-EMPTIVE RIGHT.

right to air The right to a flow of air over land or buildings from neighbouring premises. It may be enjoyed on any terms agreed by personal arrangement between neighbouring landowners, but can only exist as an *easement if the right can be sufficiently defined. Thus an easement for the flow of air through a specific ventilation passage may exist, but a right to a general flow of air over the chimneys of a house does not qualify as an easement so is not an interest in the land itself.

right to begin The right of a party at trial to present his case to the court first (i.e. to **open the case**) by making the opening speech and presenting his evidence. The right to begin usually belongs to the party who carries the persuasive *burden of proof. Thus, in a criminal case the prosecution always has the right to begin; in civil cases the claimant normally begins, but the defendant may do so when he has the burden of proving all issues.

right to buy *See* SECURE TENANCY.

right to education A right set out in Article 2 of the First Protocol to the European Convention on Human Rights and now part of UK law as a consequence of the *Human Rights Act 1998. It is limited to primary and secondary education and does not create a duty to fund or subsidize private education. The right includes a duty to respect the religious and philosophical convictions of the parents regardless of whether or not the child is in the state sector.

right to life A right set out in Article 2 of the European Convention on Human Rights and now part of UK law as a consequence of the *Human Rights Act 1998. The right to life does not make the use of the death sentence unlawful (*but see* CAPITAL PUNISHMENT). Article 2 makes unlawful the use of lethal force where the use of force was greater than that which was absolutely necessary (this is a higher test than imposed by section 3 of the Criminal Law Act 1967). The right to life also imposes a duty on public authorities to take reasonable measures to protect life from threats from third parties. Article 2 also imposes a duty to ensure that any investigation of a death caused by a public body is independent and effective.

right to marry A right set out in Article 12 of the European Convention on Human Rights and now part of UK law as a consequence of the *Human Rights Act. The right is not a particularly strong one; it only exists subject to the national laws governing the exercise of this right.

riot *n.* An offence committed when 12 or more persons, present together, intentionally use or threaten unlawful violence (*see* VIOLENT DISORDER) for a common purpose. The collective conduct must be such as would have caused a reasonable person to fear for his safety, though no-one else need be present. A person is only guilty of riot if he intended to use violence or was aware that his conduct might be violent. The offence of riot is found in the Public Order Act 1986, though it can be committed in private as well as in public places. It replaces the common-law offence of riot and is punishable with up to ten years' imprisonment and/or a fine. Under the Riot (Damages) Act 1886, when property has been destroyed, damaged, or stolen in the course of a tumultuous riot, the owner is entitled to compensation out of public funds. *See also* AFFRAY.

road *n.* For purposes of offences relating to road traffic, any *highway or other route to which the general public has access. A road must be a route leading from one place to another, and this is always a question of fact. It may include a hotel forecourt, a road privately owned but to which the public has access, or a bridge over which a road passes, but a car park is usually not regarded as a road. Some traffic offences are defined to cover roads and "other public places".

road rage Aggressive behaviour while driving motor vehicles on roads. Although there is no specific road rage offence, such behaviour may involve breach of other laws. If the aggressor causes injury he may face a conviction for *dangerous driving or for some other similar offence.

road tax A tax (formally called **vehicle excise duty**) that must be paid in respect of any mechanically propelled vehicle used, parked, or kept on a public road. It is an offence to fail to pay it. Electrically propelled vehicles and invalid vehicles do not have to be taxed, and no tax is required when a motorist is driving to and from a prearranged *MOT test. It is also an offence to fail to display a tax disc showing that the vehicle has been taxed, unless one has applied for a new disc before the old one expired and it is within 14 days from the date of expiry. The tax disc must be displayed on the nearside lower corner of the windscreen. Failure to pay road tax or display the tax disc is punishable by fine, but is not subject to endorsement.

road traffic accidents If an accident has been caused by the presence of a motor vehicle on a road and results in injury to anyone or damage to anyone else's vehicle or to property on the road or neighbouring land (e.g. someone's garden wall), it is an offence for the driver of the vehicle not to stop, unless he can show that he did not know that the accident happened. It is also an offence to refuse to give one's name and address to anyone who reasonably requires it (e.g. a police officer or another driver or pedestrian involved in the accident), unless one reports the accident to the police as soon as possible (not later than 24 hours after it occurred). If a person has been injured in a road accident, it is an offence not to produce one's certificate of insurance (*see* THIRD-PARTY INSURANCE) for a police officer or anyone else with reasonable grounds for asking for it, unless one reports the accident to the police not later than 24 hours after it occurred and, at the same time or within five days, produces the certificate of insurance at any police station one specifies. *See also* ACCIDENT RECORD BOOK.

Failure to stop after an accident or give particulars is an endorsable offence (carrying 5–10 penalty points under the *totting-up system) and is subject to a *fine at level 5 on the standard scale and to discretionary *disqualification.

robbery *n.* The offence of using force against any person, or putting them in fear of being subjected to force, in order to commit a theft, either before the theft or during the course of it. It is also robbery to threaten to use physical force in these circumstances, even if the person threatened is not frightened by the threats. The degree of force required is a question of fact in each case to be decided by the jury; nudging someone so that he loses his balance may constitute sufficient force. The force must, however, be directed against the person, rather than his property. Robbery and assaults with intent to rob are punishable by a maximum sentence of life imprisonment.

rogatory letter *See* LETTER OF REQUEST.

rolled-up plea A form of the defence of *fair comment in an action for defamation. If the words complained of contain a mixture of statements of fact and comment, the defendant may plead that "the said words in so far as they consist of allegations of fact are true in substance and in fact, and in so far as they consist of expressions of opinion they are fair comments made in good faith and without malice upon the said facts, which are a matter of public interest". The defendant must give particulars of which words he alleges are statements of fact and of the circumstances he relies on to show that the words are true.

Romalpa clause *See* RETENTION OF TITLE.

Rome Treaty *See* TREATY OF ROME.

root of title The document from which an owner of unregistered land traces his ownership. A good root must be at least 15 years old, deal with the whole legal and beneficial ownership of the land, describe it sufficiently to identify it, and cast no doubt on the title. A vendor must supply and the purchaser must accept such a root unless their contract provides otherwise.

rout *n.* An old public-order offence approximating to *riot.

royal assent The agreement of the Crown, given under the *royal prerogative and signified either by the sovereign in person or by royal commissioners, that converts a Bill into an *Act of Parliament or gives a Measure (*see* CHURCH OF ENGLAND) the force of an Act. It is the duty of the Clerk of the Parliaments to endorse the date on which it was given immediately after the long title.

royal prerogative The special rights, powers, and immunities to which the Crown alone is entitled under the common law. Most prerogative acts are now performed by the government on behalf of the Crown. Some, however, are performed by the sovereign in person on the advice of the government (e.g. the dissolution of Parliament) or as required by constitutional convention (e.g. the appointment of a Prime Minister). A few prerogative acts (e.g. the granting of certain honours, such as the Order of the Garter) are performed in accordance with the sovereign's personal wishes.

The Crown has limited powers of legislating under the prerogative, principally as respects the civil service and UK dependent territories. It does so by Order in Council, ordinance, letters patent, or royal warrant. The dissolution and prorogation of Parliament and the granting of the royal assent to Bills take place under the prerogative. Originally the fountain of justice from which the first courts of law sprang, the Crown still exercises (through the Home Secretary) the *prerogative of mercy and retains the right (through the Attorney General) to stop a prosecution by entering a *nolle prosequi. In foreign affairs, the sovereign declares war, makes peace and international treaties, and issues passports under the prerogative. Many appointments (e.g. the higher judiciary, archbishops, and diocesan bishops) are made under the prerogative, and a variety of honours, including new hereditary peerages, are conferred by the Crown as the fountain of honour. The sovereign is head of the armed forces, and, although much of the law governing these is now statutory, their disposition generally remains a matter for the prerogative. There is a prerogative power, subject to the payment of compensation, to expropriate or requisition private property in times of war or apprehended war. Miscellaneous prerogative rights include the rights to *treasure trove and to *bona vacantia*. An important immunity of the sovereign is the prerogative of perfection. The common-law maxim that "the King can do no wrong" resulted in the complete immunity of the sovereign personally from all civil and criminal proceedings for anything that he or she might do. This personal immunity remains, but actions may now be brought against the Crown under the Crown Proceedings Act 1947 (*see* CROWN PROCEEDINGS).

If a statute confers on the Crown powers that duplicate prerogative powers, the latter are suspended during the existence of the statute unless it either abolishes them or preserves them as alternative powers.

royal proclamation A document by which the sovereign exercises certain prerogative powers (e.g. the summoning and dissolution of Parliament) and certain legislative powers conferred on her by statute (e.g. the declaration of a state of emergency; *see* EMERGENCY POWERS).

royal title *See* QUEEN.

royalty *n.* A sum payable for the right to use someone else's property for the purpose of gain. Royalties are paid on *wasting assets, which have a limited lifespan. For example, the royalty paid by a licensee to mine someone's land is a fixed sum per tonne of the mineral he extracts, and an author's royalty is similarly determined by the total number of his books the publisher sells. Royalties are paid generally for the licensing of *intellectual property.

RSC *See* RULES OF THE SUPREME COURT.

rule against bias *See* NATURAL JUSTICE.

rule against double portions A rule designed to ensure, as far as possible, equality between children entitled under a settlement and under a will, both made by the same person. Thus if a father promises to pay substantial sums of money to certain of his children to advance them and at his death the money has not been paid, but the children (together with others) are entitled to legacies under his will, the payment of the legacies and the moneys due under the settlement will be considered together. Thus if an advancement of £10,000 and a legacy of £5000 are due to one son and a legacy of £10,000 is due to another son, the first son will not receive his legacy, to ensure equality between the children. *See* HOTCHPOT.

rule against inalienability A rule that prevents property from being rendered incapable of transfer within the perpetuity period, i.e. a life presently existing plus a period of 21 years. A gift that prevents transfer within this period is void. The rule is similar to the *rule against perpetual trusts.

rule against perpetual trusts The rule that prohibits noncharitable trusts from lasting beyond the perpetuity period, i.e. a lifetime presently existing plus a period of 21 years. A trust that may last beyond that period is void. *Compare* RULE AGAINST INALIENABILITY; RULE AGAINST PERPETUITIES.

rule against perpetuities (rule against remoteness of future vesting) A rule developed by the *common law to enable a court to declare void any future or postponed interest in property that might possibly vest (i.e. become enjoyable as of right) outside the **perpetuity period**. This comprises (1) the lifetimes of persons mentioned (or mentioned by implication) in the disposition who are alive at that time and whose existence governs the timing of the vesting of the future interest (the relevant **lives in being**), plus (2) 21 years, plus (3) (in the case of a posthumous beneficiary) any actual period of gestation. The period runs from the date of execution of the deed or, if the disposition is contained in a will, from the death of the testator. The purpose of the rule is to prevent land being tied up for an indefinite period, which would hinder its ultimate disposal.

The common law rules relating to perpetuities have been supplemented (though not replaced) by the Perpetuities and Accumulations Act 1964. When a disposition would otherwise be void under the common law rules, the Act allows a period in which one can **wait and see** whether the interest will in fact vest within the perpetuity period; only if it becomes clear that it cannot do so will the disposition be void. For these purposes, the perpetuity period is varied in that the Act provides a new list of lives in being (the **statutory lives in being**). The Act also provides for a fixed perpetuity period unrelated to lives.

rule against remoteness of future vesting *See* RULE AGAINST PERPETUITIES.

rule in *Saunders* v *Vautier* [from the case *Saunders* v *Vautier* (1841)] A rule under which the beneficiaries of a trust, if of full age (18), sound mind, and between them wholly entitled to the trust property, may direct the trustees to end the trust and transfer the trust property to themselves as beneficiaries absolutely.

rule of law 1. The supremacy of law. **2.** A feature attributed to the UK constitution by Professor Dicey (*Law of the Constitution*, 1885). It embodied three concepts: the absolute predominance of regular law, so that the government has no arbitrary authority over the citizen; the equal subjection of all (including officials) to the ordinary law administered by the ordinary courts; and the fact that the citizen's personal freedoms are formulated and protected by the ordinary law rather than by abstract constitutional declarations.

rules of court Rules regulating the practice and procedure of a court, usually made by a rule committee acting under a statutory power. *See also* CIVIL PROCEDURE RULES; CROWN COURT RULES.

Rules of the Supreme Court (RSC) Formerly, rules governing the practice and procedure of the *Supreme Court of Judicature. The rules were made under a statutory power by the **Supreme Court Rule Committee**, a body appointed by the *Lord Chancellor and comprising himself, the *Master of the Rolls, the heads of the Divisions of the High Court, and four practitioners. The Rules were revoked in 1999 by the *Civil Procedure Rules, which have re-enacted some of the rules of the RSC.

running-account credit (under the Consumer Credit Act 1974) A facility under a *personal-credit agreement that enables a debtor to receive periodically from the creditor or a third party cash, goods or services to an amount or value that does not exceed the *credit limit (if any), taking into account payments made by or to the credit of the debtor. Examples are bank overdrafts and credit cards. The credit provided will be taken not to exceed £25,000 and the agreement will be a consumer-credit agreement if the credit limit does not exceed £25,000. The Act specifies three situations in which running-account credit will not exceed £25,000 in cases in which there is no credit limit or, if there is, it exceeds £25,000.

running days *See* LAY DAYS.

running with the land *See* COVENANT RUNNING WITH THE LAND.

Rylands v Fletcher, rule in A principle of strict liability for dangerous things accumulated on land that escape from the land and cause damage. It was first stated in the case *Rylands* v *Fletcher* (1868), in which the defendant had a reservoir built on his land that caused flooding of the claimant's mine. The accumulation of dangerous things must constitute a non-natural use of the land. A use is non-natural in modern law if it is a special use creating an abnormal risk of damage. The occupier of the land is liable for damage caused by an escape if the damage is of a kind that is a reasonably foreseeable consequence of the escape, subject to the defences of common benefit, act of a stranger, statutory authority, consent of the claimant, default of the claimant, or act of God.

S

s. (*pl.* **ss.**) The recognized abbreviation used in citing a particular section of a statute, as in "s. 4", "ss. 70–73".

Sabbath *n. See* SUNDAY TRADING.

sabotage *n.* Damage to or destruction of property, especially the property of an employer during a strike or of the state for political reasons. Sabotage as such is not an offence, although it may be treated as *criminal damage. The courts have, however, interpreted the phrase "prohibited place" in the Official Secrets Act 1911 to bring sabotage against the state within the scope of that Act, even though it is clear that Parliament's intention was only to prohibit spying. *See* OFFICIAL SECRETS.

safe haven A zone of territory within a sovereign state demarcated by the United Nations (or other international organization) as a refuge to which a persecuted *ethnic minority can choose to retire. While within such a zone the ethnic minority is afforded military protection by the body that established the zone. The international community set up safe havens in Iraq and the former Yugoslavia in response to acts of systematic persecution carried out by the government of the sovereign state concerned against part of its own population. *See also* HUMANITARIAN INTERVENTION.

safety at work Every employer has a common-law duty to take reasonable care for his employees' health, safety, and welfare at work: he may be sued in the courts for damages if an employee is injured through the employer's negligence or failure to observe the safety regulations. The employer cannot contract out of this liability and, under the Employers' Liability (Compulsory Insurance) Act 1969, must insure against his liability for employees' injuries and diseases sustained or contracted at work. The Health and Safety at Work Act 1974 further requires employers to ensure, as far as is reasonably practicable, that their working methods, equipment, premises, and environment are safe and to give such training, information, and supervision as will ensure their employees' health and safety (*see* HEALTH AND SAFETY COMMISSION). Anyone employing more than five persons must maintain a written statement of his general policy concerning his employees' health and safety (dealing, for example, with safety rules and protective clothing) and must keep them informed of it. He must also give relevant information to the *safety representatives of his employees' trade unions and establish a *safety committee where appropriate.

The Employment Act 1989 contains legislation for the protection of female workers. It is prohibited to employ women in a factory within four weeks of childbirth; to employ women in a range of processes involving lead or lead compounds; and to employ women in a range of processes in the pottery industry. There are also restrictions on women working on ships and aeroplanes during pregnancy.

Employees also have a duty to take reasonable care for their own health and safety, for example by complying with safety regulations and using protective equipment supplied to them. Employers and employees who fail to comply with the requirements of the Health and Safety at Work Act 1974 face prosecution in the criminal courts. An employee dismissed for health and safety reasons is under certain circumstances regarded as having been unfairly dismissed. It is also regarded as automatically unfair to select an employee for redundancy on certain grounds connected with health and safety.

safety committee A committee that, under the Health and Safety at Work Act 1974, an employer must establish within three months after a written request from at least two employees' *safety representatives. The employer must consult with the safety representatives as to the composition of the committee and must also display a notice in his premises informing his employees of its composition and the workplaces it covers. The *code of practice published by the Health and Safety Commission suggests that safety committees' responsibilities should include monitoring accidents and disease occurring in the workplace and developing improved safety rules and systems of work and training of employees with regard to safety.

safety representatives Employees appointed by trade unions to represent the interests of their colleagues regarding their health, safety, and welfare at work. Regulations made under the Health and Safety at Work Act 1974 give a trade union recognized as having negotiating rights on behalf of a group or class of employees the right to appoint at least one of those employees as a safety representative. The representatives' statutory powers include the investigation of accidents and industrial diseases occurring at the workplace and inspection of the premises to determine their causes. The employer must allow them time off work with pay to train for and perform their duties and to attend meetings of *safety committees. *See also* DISCLOSURE OF INFORMATION.

sale *n.* A contract involving the *sale of goods or a similar contract involving the transfer of land.

sale by description A contract of sale of goods containing words identifying its subject matter, e.g. 1000 tonnes of Western White Wheat. Even when the subject matter of the contract is physically ascertained at the time of contracting, e.g. a particular motor car, the contract may contain words of description or identification. The goods delivered must match their description in the contract; otherwise the seller is in breach of an *implied condition of the contract and the buyer, if he acts promptly, may reject the goods.

sale by sample A contract of sale of goods made on the basis that the bulk of goods to be delivered to the buyer will match a sample submitted by the seller. If the bulk does not match the sample the seller is in breach of an *implied condition of the contract and the buyer may reject the goods. The seller must give the buyer a reasonable opportunity of comparing the bulk with the sample and the goods must be free from any defect making them unmerchantable that would not be apparent on reasonable examination of the sample.

sale of goods A contract by which a seller transfers or agrees to transfer the ownership of goods to a buyer in exchange for a money price. If ownership is to pass at a future time the contract is called an **agreement to sell**. The contract, which need not be in writing, may contain *express terms. Terms may also be implied by law (*see also* IMPLIED CONDITION); for example, that the seller has a right to sell, that the goods correspond with the description under which they are sold, and that the goods are of *satisfactory quality and are reasonably fit for the buyer's purpose. Unless the parties agree otherwise the seller must hand over the goods in exchange for the price and the buyer must pay the price in exchange for the goods. Much of the law governing the sale of goods is codified in the Sale of Goods Act 1979.

sale on approval *See* SALE OR RETURN.

sale or return (sale on approval) The delivery of goods to a person on terms
that allow him to keep the goods for a time before he decides whether or not to buy
them. Unless otherwise agreed, such a person becomes the owner if he signifies his
approval of the goods or carries out any other act adopting the transaction. He will
also become the owner if he retains the goods beyond the time fixed for their
return, or, if no time has been fixed, beyond a reasonable time.

salvage *n.* The service rendered by a person who saves or helps to save maritime
property. Salvage may be the subject of an express agreement. In the absence of any
agreement, a salvor is entitled by law to an award (also known as salvage), which is
assessed by the court and payable out of the salvaged property, if he shows that the
property was in real danger and that he acted with some skill and in a purely
voluntary capacity. The award can also take account of the saving of life, but this
alone gives no claim to an award as there is no property saved out of which
payment can be ordered. The rules apply equally to aircraft. However, no award of
salvage may be made unless the ship or aircraft is on or over the sea or tidal waters.
Property saved in a nontidal river cannot be subject to a salvage claim.

salvage of trust property A power that existed before 1926 for the court to
authorize a payment for preserving (or salvaging) trust property (e.g. repairing
buildings) even though the document creating the trust did not permit such
payment. A wider power was given by statute in 1925, under which the court can
authorize any transaction that is expedient.

sanction *n.* **1.** A *punishment for a crime. *See* NULLA POENA SINE LEGE. **2.** A measure
taken against a state to compel it to obey international law or to punish it for a
breach of international law. It is often said that international law is deficient
because it lacks the power to impose sanctions or even to compel states to accept
the jurisdiction of courts (*see* INTERNATIONAL COURT OF JUSTICE). There are, however,
certain sanctions that can be applied. A state may, in certain cases, use force in self-
defence, or as a sanction against an act of aggression, or as a reprisal (for example,
by expropriating property belonging to citizens of a country that had previously
carried out unlawful acts of expropriation). It may also act by way of *retorsion.
There are also certain powers of sanction available under the United Nations system,
such as economic (and, at least in theory, military) sanctions, although the powers of
the Security Council to impose sanctions are subject to veto. *See also* ANGARY.

Sanderson order *See* BULLOCK ORDER.

sanity *n.* *See* PRESUMPTION OF SANITY.

***sans recours* (without recourse to me)** A stipulation that the drawer or an
endorser of a *bill of exchange may add to his signature, thus repudiating his
liability to the holder. If the bill is dishonoured, the holder has no recourse to the
drawer or endorser who has made such a stipulation.

SARs (Substantial Acquisition Rules) Rules, administered by the Panel on
Takeovers and Mergers, governing the acquisition of substantial shareholdings in
public companies. *See* CITY CODE ON TAKEOVERS AND MERGERS; CONCERT PARTY; DAWN
RAID.

satisfaction *n.* **1.** The fulfilment of a claim. *See also* ACCORD AND SATISFACTION.
2. A doctrine of equity under which an obligation is discharged by payment,
performance, or some similar act. The doctrine applies when the acts of a settlor

are unclear. If the settlor discharges his obligation by an act different from that required, the obligation is said to be satisfied provided that the act he does is a sufficient substitute for the act he is charged to do. Thus if he owes a debt and leaves a legacy of the same or a greater amount to the creditor, the creditor is satisfied. Closely analogous to satisfaction are cases in which payment of a legacy is satisfied by payment of a *portion and one legacy is satisfied by payment of another (*see* ADEMPTION); in these cases, however, there is no prior obligation owed by the settlor.

satisfactory quality An *implied condition that goods sold in the course of business will meet the standard that a reasonable person would regard as satisfactory. In assessing this, account is taken of any description of the goods, the price (if relevant), and all other circumstances. The quality of goods includes their state and condition, taking account of their fitness for purpose, appearance and finish, freedom from minor defects, safety, and durability. Most commercial agreements exclude the implied conditions and replace them with express *warranties, although unreasonable exclusions in standard-form contracts, even between two businesses, may be void under the law relating to *unfair contract terms. Satisfactory quality replaced the term **merchantable quality** by the Sale and Supply of Goods Act 1994, with effect from 3 January 1995.

satisfied term The expired period of an interest in land for a term of years created for a specific purpose that has been fulfilled. For example, when land under a *strict settlement is assigned to trustees for a term of years on trust to raise capital sums for members of the settlor's family, the term is satisfied when the sums have been raised. Under the Law of Property Act 1925, the estate or interest in the land ceases when the purpose is fulfilled. A term of years that has not expired although the purpose for which it was created has been fulfilled is called an **outstanding term**.

Saunders v Vautier See RULE IN SAUNDERS V VAUTIER.

scandalous statement A statement that is irrelevant and abusive. When such a statement appears in statements of case or in an affidavit the court or a judge may order it to be struck out.

schedule *n.* An appendix to an Act of Parliament or other legislation that deals with points of detail supplementary to the main part.

scheme *n.* A document, normally approved by the court, that contains provisions for the management or distribution of property or for resolving a dispute concerning allegedly conflicting rights. For example, the court or the *Charity Commissioners may approve a scheme for the management of a charitable trust.

scheme of arrangement **1.** An agreement between a debtor and his creditors to arrange the debtor's affairs to satisfy the creditors. The debtor usually agrees to such an arrangement in order to avoid *bankruptcy. If the arrangement is agreed when no *bankruptcy order has been made, it is governed primarily by the ordinary law of contract. However, if it is for the benefit of the debtor's creditors generally, or if the debtor is insolvent and it is for the benefit of at least three of his creditors, it is a *deed of arrangement and subject to statutory control unless it is a voluntary arrangement. An arrangement agreed after a bankruptcy order has been made is governed by the statutory provisions relating to bankruptcy (*see* VOLUNTARY ARRANGEMENT). **2.** An agreement between a company and its creditors or members when the company is in financial difficulties or to effect a *takeover. It must be approved by a majority in number (holding 75% in value) of those creditors or members at separate meetings and sanctioned by the court. All creditors or members involved in the scheme are bound by it, although the court can make special provision for those who dissent (Companies Act 1985). Agreements with company creditors can often be more conveniently concluded by *voluntary arrangement under the Insolvency Act 1986.

Schengen Agreement The agreement between most member states of the European Union (but not the UK) to abolish internal border controls. It came into force on 26 March 1995. *See also* PASSPORT.

scienter rule *See* CLASSIFICATION OF ANIMALS.

Scottish Parliament A body established by the Scotland Act 1998 (and operative from July 1999), having 129 elected members (**Members of the Scottish Parliament; MSPs**) and possessing limited primary legislative powers over such matters as health, school education, and forestry, as defined within the Act. It may alter the basic rate of income tax in Scotland by up to three pence in the pound. The **Scottish Executive** (the devolved government of Scotland) is formed by the party or parties with the majority of seats in the Parliament. *See* DEVOLUTION.

Scott Schedule A document used in *official referee's business for giving *particulars when the claim is in respect of a large number of individual items (e.g. a landlord's claim for dilapidations). The Scott Schedule is divided into columns providing for (1) the consecutive numbering of the items; (2) the full description of each item; (3) the contention of each party against each item as to liability or amount; and (4) a column for the use of the court. It is named after a former official referee.

scuttling *n.* Sinking a ship (particularly with a view to making a fraudulent insurance claim) by making or opening holes in its hull to allow the entry of water.

seal *n.* Wax impressed with a design and attached to any document as a sign of its authenticity; alternatively, an adhesive wafer or anything else intended to serve the purpose of a seal may be used. Under the terms of the Law of Property (Miscellaneous Provisions) Act 1989, *deeds no longer require a seal in order to be validly executed.

SEAQ (Stock Exchange Automated Quotations System) *See* QUOTATION.

search **1.** *vb.* To examine the registers maintained by HM Land Registry, the Land Charges Department, or the registers of local land charges during an *official search. **2.** *n. See* POWER OF SEARCH.

search before Crown Court The searching of a person on the order of the Crown Court when that person has been ordered by the court to pay a fine or to pay money for some other reason (e.g. forfeiture of a *recognizance). Any money found on the person can be used towards payment of the sum due, any excess being returned.

search of ship The right that a belligerent power has during wartime, under public international law, to search any ship of a neutral power on the high seas in order to discover whether it is carrying *contraband.

search order An order made by the High Court (usually the Chancery Division) requiring a defendant to permit a claimant or his representatives to enter the defendant's premises to inspect or take away material evidence that the defendant might wish to remove or destroy in order to frustrate the claimant's claim, or to force a defendant to answer certain questions. Formerly (until 1999) known as an **Anton Piller order**, from the case *Anton Piller KG* v *Manufacturing Processes* (1976), the order is commonly used in cases where the copyright of video films or tapes or computer software is alleged to have been infringed. By statute the *privilege against self-incrimination does not apply.

search warrant *See* POWER OF SEARCH.

seat belt A belt fitted in a motor vehicle, designed to restrict the forward movement of a driver or front-seat passenger in the event of an accident. All passenger vehicles with seating for fewer than 13 passengers and most four-wheeled goods vehicles registered after 1 January 1965 must comply with statutory regulations governing seat belts, although the details of these regulations vary according to the date when the vehicle was first registered. It is compulsory for all drivers and front-seat passengers in cars registered after 1964, light vans registered after 1966, and three-wheeler vehicles registered after 1969 to wear seat belts at all times when the vehicle is moving, and for back-seat passengers to wear seat belts when these are fitted, subject to certain exceptions. These exceptions are: (1) drivers carrying out any manoeuvre that includes reversing (passengers must still wear their seat belts during such manoeuvres); (2) drivers making local delivery or collection rounds in specially adapted vehicles (e.g. milkmen in milk vans); (3) anyone whose seat belt has become faulty during the drive or who has already arranged to have a faulty belt repaired; (4) anyone whose belt has locked on a steep hill; (5) anyone supervising a learner who is reversing; (6) certain categories of people with a special exemption certificate on medical grounds.

Any front-seat passenger over the age of 14 is responsible for wearing his own seat belt, but the driver of the car is responsible for ensuring that front-seat passengers under the age of 14 wear a seat belt. Children under the age of one must wear an approved child restraint. Over the age of one they can wear an adult seat belt, preferably with an approved booster cushion to raise them to a suitable height. Alternatively they can sit in the back seat fitted with an approved restraint. When more passengers are carried than there are seat belts available, the passengers who do not have seat belts do not break the law by not being restrained. Thus in a four-seater car with a fifth passenger sitting in the middle of the back seat, the middle back passenger does not break the law by being unrestrained.

Failure to wear a seat belt carries a *fine at level 2 on the standard scale and may also be regarded as *contributory negligence in a claim for injuries sustained in a road traffic accident, leading to a reduction in damages.

sea waybill A receipt for goods that contains or evidences the contract for the carriage of goods by sea and also identifies the person to whom delivery of the goods is to be made by the carrier in accordance with that contract. A sea waybill is not a *bill of lading: it is commonly used in container transport and, unlike a bill of lading, does not have to be produced at the port of discharge in order to obtain delivery.

seaworthy *adj.* **1.** Having at the start of a voyage the degree of fitness (as respects the ship, her crew, and her equipment) for that particular voyage that a careful owner might be expected to require of his ship. **2.** The suitability of a particular ship to carry a particular cargo. Obligations relating to seaworthiness are implied by law in charterparties and imposed by the Hague Rules in bills of lading. A marine insurance policy incorporates by statute a warranty that the insured ship is seaworthy.

secession *n.* The action of breaking away or formally withdrawing from an alliance, a federation, a political or religious organization, etc. An example of secession is the attempted withdrawal of the Confederate States from the United States in the War of Secession (1861–65).

secondary evidence Evidence that by its nature suggests the existence of better evidence and might be rejected if that better evidence is available (e.g. a copy of a document). Secondary evidence is generally admissible if the absence of the *primary evidence is explained.

secondary party An *accessory to a crime.

secondary use *See* SHIFTING USE.

Secretary of State *See* MINISTER.

secret profits Profits made by an *agent during the course of his agency without the knowledge or authorization of his principal. The principal may require the agent to account for secret profits.

secret trust A trust whose existence is not revealed in the document transferring the property to the person who is to be the trustee. It arises when a testator (or more rarely a settlor) gives property to someone on that person's express or implied promise to hold the property on trust for a third party. On the face of the document the transaction appears to be an outright gift, and the existence of a trust is not apparent. Such trusts are sometimes called **fully secret trusts**, to distinguish them from *half-secret trusts, but the term secret trust is sometimes used for both. Doctrinal difficulties have arisen with secret trusts because they appear to allow a will to be altered indirectly without the need to comply with the formalities of the Wills Act 1837, and their theoretical basis is unclear. Some recent cases have suggested that there is no conflict with the Wills Act, since the trust operates ordinary equitable jurisdiction.

section 8 orders Court orders under the Children Act 1989 that settle practical details concerning the child's care and upbringing in any family proceedings in which the child's welfare is a matter for consideration (such as matrimonial, wardship, or adoption proceedings). Section 8 orders, which replace the old access, custody, and care and control orders, include residence, contact, prohibited steps, and specific issues orders. A **residence order** settles arrangements about where a child is to live. Such an order is typically made when parents live apart and cannot agree where the child is to live. Residence orders may also be made in respect of nonparents: in such a case, the order would confer parental responsibility on those in whose favour the order is made. A **contact order** defines the extent and nature of the contact the child is to have with other individuals. A contact order cannot be made in favour of a local authority or while the child is in care. A **prohibited steps order** prohibits certain specified steps (for example, taking a child abroad) being taken without the consent of the court and can be made against anyone regardless of whether he or she has parental responsibility for the child. A **specific issue order** deals with any specific issues concerning the child's upbringing, such as education or medical treatment.

Section 8 orders are only necessary when there is a dispute between the parents or others in relation to a child and are usually only made in respect of children up to the age of 16. In determining whether or not to make such an order, the court must treat the child's welfare as paramount.

section 30 order (parental order) An order of the court made under section 30 of the Human Fertilization and Embryology Act 1990, which provides for a child to be treated in law as the child of the parties to a marriage if the child has been carried by a woman other than the wife as a result of *human assisted reproduction. Application must be made within six months of the child's birth and the child's home must be with the husband and wife at the time of the application.

section 37 investigation An investigation of a child's circumstances ordered by the court to be carried out by a local authority when the court has cause for serious concern about the child's upbringing. The order may be made in any *family proceedings, for example when an application for a residence or contact order is being made by a parent (*see* SECTION 8 ORDERS). The local authority carrying out the investigation must consider whether it should apply for a *care order or a *supervision order or assistance for the child or its family or take any other action with respect to the child.

section 47 enquiry An enquiry carried out by a local authority in order to enable it to decide whether or not it should take any action to safeguard and promote the welfare of a particular child. The local authority is under a duty to carry out such an investigation if it has reasonable cause to suspect that a child is suffering or likely to suffer significant harm, or is the subject of an *emergency protection order, or is in police protection (*see* POLICE PROTECTION ORDER). As a result of its enquiries a local authority might decide that no action is required; alternatively, it may decide that the family in question is in need of support and provide the appropriate services, or it may apply for an emergency protection order, a *care order, a *supervision order, or a *child assessment order. If, in the course of its enquiries, a local authority is denied access to a child, it should immediately apply to court for an emergency protection order.

sector theory A proposed basis for national claims to sovereignty over both the Arctic and Antarctica. The sector theory delineates a meridian line from the pole to the farthest extremity of the contiguous state's land mass. All territory within that sector is thereupon purported to be under the sovereignty of the claimant state. It should be noted that this theory is not universally recognized as the sole basis for claiming territory in these regions.

secure accommodation order An order that allows a local authority to restrict the liberty of a child whom it is looking after by placing him in secure accommodation. Under the Children Act 1989 such orders may only be sought in respect of a child who has a history of absconding from unsecure accommodation and who, if he does abscond, is likely to suffer significant harm.

secured creditor A person who holds some security, such as a mortgage, for money he has lent. If the debtor becomes bankrupt the creditor has a choice. He may surrender his security and claim the amount of the debt from the bankrupt's assets; he may realize or evaluate the security and claim any balance of the debt in excess of the value of the security; or he may rely on the security and not make any claim in the bankruptcy proceedings. *Compare* UNSECURED CREDITOR.

secure tenancy A residential tenancy in which the tenant has statutory protection if he occupies the rented property as his home. It applies only if there is a certain kind of landlord, such as a local authority, the *Housing Corporation, or a *housing action trust. Certain tenants are excluded from protection; these include students, the occupants of almshouses, licensed premises, and accommodation for the homeless, and those renting accommodation on long leases or who have a *service tenancy.

If a secure tenancy is for a fixed term, the tenancy continues at the end of the term as a *periodic tenancy. A landlord can only terminate a secure tenancy by serving a notice on the tenant in a special statutory form and can only obtain possession with the tenant's consent or, if this is refused, by a court order. An order is granted only if the landlord has statutory grounds similar to those required in the case of an *assured tenancy. When the holder of a secure tenancy dies, his spouse or a member of his family who has lived with him for the past 12 months can succeed him as tenant. Under certain conditions, secure tenants have a right to buy their rented property, at a discount on the market value of the property, and with their landlord supplying a mortgage. The Housing Act 1988 contains provisions for the transfer of public-sector housing to the private sector and to housing action trusts. *See also* INTRODUCTORY TENANCY.

secure training order *See* JUVENILE OFFENDER.

securities *pl. n.* Loosely, *stocks, *shares, *debentures, *bonds, or any other rights to receive dividends or interest. Strictly, the term should only be used for rights backed by some sort of security, as in the case of debentures.

Securities and Investment Board (SIB) The agency set up under the Financial Services Act 1986 to ensure that those who are engaged in investment business (including dealing in, arranging deals in, and managing investments and also giving investment advice) are honest, competent, and solvent. It is an offence, unless exempt, to carry on investment business without SIB authorization (which may be obtained directly or via membership of a recognized *self-regulatory organization or professional body). Those in contravention may be unable to enforce transactions, and investors who suffer loss may be entitled to compensation. The composition of the Board must reflect a proper balance between the interests of those who carry on investment business and the interests of the public.

Security Council (of the UN) *See* UNITED NATIONS.

security for costs A sum payable by a claimant to a civil action as a condition of being permitted to continue with the action. The court has discretion as to whether or not to order security for costs and may exercise it only in four circumstances: (1) when the claimant is ordinarily resident out of the area of the jurisdiction; (2) when the claimant is suing on behalf of someone who will be unable to pay the defendant's costs if ordered to do so; (3) when the claimaint's address is dishonestly not stated or incorrectly stated on the originating process; or (4) the claimant has changed his address during the course of the proceedings in order to evade the consequences of the litigation. A defendant may not be ordered to give security for costs. When security is ordered the claimant is usually ordered to pay a sum into court.

security of tenure Statutory protection given to tenants that restricts landlords' rights to obtain possession. The conditions for obtaining possession vary according to the kind of tenancy, but a court order is usually required. *See* AGRICULTURAL HOLDING; ASSURED AGRICULTURAL OCCUPANCY; ASSURED SHORTHOLD TENANCY; ASSURED TENANCY; BUSINESS TENANCY; LONG TENANCY; PROTECTED TENANCY; PROTECTED OCCUPANCY; SECURE TENANCY; STATUTORY TENANCY.

sedition *n.* The speaking or writing of words that are likely to incite ordinary people to public disorder or insurrection. Sedition is a common-law offence (known as **seditious libel** if the words are written) if it is committed with the intention of (1) arousing hatred, contempt, or disaffection against the sovereign or her successors (but not the monarchy as such), the government of the UK, or either House of Parliament or the administration of justice; (2) encouraging any change of the law by unlawful means; or (3) raising discontent among Her Majesty's subjects or promoting ill-will and hostility between different classes of subjects. There must be an intention to achieve these consequences by violence and disorder. An agreement to carry out an act to further any of these intentions is a criminal *conspiracy.

seduction *n.* **1.** Enticement to have sexual intercourse. Until 1971 parents could sue a seducer for loss of services of their child, but this has now been abolished. It is an offence for a parent to cause or encourage the seduction of a daughter under the age of 16, the *age of consent. **2.** The offence under the Incitement to Disaffection Act 1934 of maliciously and advisedly endeavouring to persuade any member of HM forces to abandon his duty or allegiance to the Crown.

seisin *n.* Possession of a freehold estate in land. Historically, availability of certain remedies for a landowner depended on being able to show seisin. In modern times it is unnecessary to distinguish between seisin and possession, the latter being the basis of most remedies available to a landowner. *See also* UNITY OF SEISIN.

select committee A committee appointed by either House of Parliament or both Houses jointly to investigate and report on a matter of interest to them in the performance of their functions. Examples are the committees of the Commons that examine government expenditure or the activities of government departments and the nationalized industries, and the *Joint Committee on Statutory Instruments.

self-assessment *n.* A system enabling taxpayers to assess their own tax liabilities for the year. Modified tax forms, introduced with effect from the tax year 1996–97, contain an optional self-assessment section. Individuals who do not want to assess their own tax must complete the return with details of their taxable income, etc., and return it by 30 September in order for the Inland Revenue to calculate the tax due. Taxpayers who opt for self-assessment must fill in the relevant section and return their tax forms by 31 January. There are automatic penalties for late returns. Self-assessment mainly affects company directors, employees paying tax at the higher rate of 40%, and the self-employed.

self-build society A *housing association whose object is to provide, for sale to or occupation by its members, dwellings built or improved principally by their own labour.

self-defence *n.* **1.** A defence at common law to charges of *offences against the person (including homicide) when *reasonable force is used to defend oneself, or one's family, or anyone else against attack or threatened attack. The scope of the defence often overlaps with the statutory right to use reasonable force to prevent a crime, but also extends to cases in which the statutory right is inapplicable (for example, when the attacker is for some reason not guilty of a crime). There is no rule of law that a person must retreat before acting in self-defence. If a person acting in self-defence mistakenly uses more force than was necessary in the circumstances and kills his attacker, he has no defence of self-defence (since the force was not reasonable) and the killing will therefore amount to murder, unless he can show that there was also *provocation. However, in deciding whether the force used was justified or reasonably thought to be justified, the jury must bear in mind the difficulty of quickly assessing the correct amount of force to be used. *See also* GENERAL DEFENCES. **2.** One of the very few bases for a legal use of force under international law. Under *Chapter VII (Article 51) of the United Nations Charter, the inherent right of self-defence is preserved. Reference to "inherent right" has promoted the belief that the pre-Charter right of self-defence in customary international law is specifically preserved by the Charter. However, the pre-existing right is arguably wider in scope than that allowed for by the terms of Article 51 and may arguably also allow for anticipatory self-defence. *See also* SELF-HELP; USE OF FORCE.

self-determination *n.* (in international law) The right of a people living within a non-self-governing territory to choose for themselves the political and legal status of that territory. They may choose independence and the formation of a separate state, integration into another state, or association with an independent state, with autonomy in internal affairs. The systems of *mandates and trusteeship marked a step towards recognizing a legal right of self-determination, but it is not yet completely recognized as a legal norm. It is probably illegal for another state to intervene against a liberation movement and it may be legal to give assistance to such a movement. *See also* ERGA OMNES obligations.

self-employed *adj.* In business on one's own account, i.e. not engaged as an employee under a *contract of employment. Statutory employment provisions do not apply to the self-employed. A self-employed person may nevertheless be the employer of others.

self-help *n.* **1.** Action taken by a person to whom a wrong has been done to protect his rights without recourse to the courts. Self-help is permitted in certain torts, such as *trespass and *nuisance. A trespasser may be evicted provided only reasonable force is used. A nuisance may be abated (*see* ABATEMENT). *See also* RECAPTION. **2.** Independent and self-directed action taken by an injured state against the transgressing state in order to gain redress. Until the middle of the 20th century the right of self-help was claimed by states as one of the essential attributes of *sovereignty. In the absence of an international executive agency, an injured state undertook on its own account the defence of the claim it was making. Forcible measures falling short of war might prove sufficient; failing these, war might be resorted to as the ultimate means of self-help. Since self-help was regarded at international law as a legal remedy, the results secured by it were recognized by the international community as a final settlement of the case. Since the establishment of the United Nations, self-help with regard to *use of force can only be legal in so far as it forms part of a legitimate claim to *self-defence. The remaining forms of self-help are countermeasures, such as *retorsion and *reprisals.

self-regulatory organization (SRO) A body whose members carry on investment business and regulate their own conduct. When its rules and practices ensure that its members are fit and proper persons, it may be recognized by the *Securities and Investment Board; its members then become authorized under the Financial Services Act 1986.

seller *n.* The party to a contract of *sale of goods who transfers or agrees to transfer ownership of the goods to the buyer. The term may also be used in the context of the transfer of the ownership of land, but a seller of land is more usually called a **vendor.**

Seller's Property Information Form *See* CONVEYANCING.

semiconductor topography Etching on a computer chip otherwise known as a **mask work** or **right**: an *intellectual property right protecting the layout of a semiconductor chip or integrated circuit. Such rights are protected in the EU under directive 87/54.

semi-secret trust *See* HALF-SECRET TRUST.

sending distressing letters The finable offence, under the Malicious Communications Act 1988, of sending to someone a letter or some other article that conveys an indecent or grossly offensive message, a threat, or information that is false and known or believed by the sender to be false. Sending an indecent or grossly offensive article is similarly punishable. The sender must have aimed to cause distress or anxiety. If the material contains a threat, there is a defence similar to that available on a *blackmail charge.

sentence *n.* The judgment of a court stating the *punishment to be imposed on a defendant who has pleaded guilty to a crime or been found guilty by the jury. Before the sentence is imposed, the prosecution must present the judge with the accused's *antecedents and the defence may then make a plea in *mitigation of the sentence. If the probation officer wishes to make a report, this should be done before the defence makes its plea in mitigation (*see* SOCIAL INQUIRY REPORT). The judge may also obtain reports from nonlegal specialists (medical experts or social workers) on the mental, physical, social, or personal circumstances of the accused; if such reports are not immediately available, he may adjourn the case (and remand the accused) until they are obtained. Reports are desirable when the sentence may involve a *community rehabilitation order or when the defendant is facing his first prison sentence. The court must have reports before making a *community punishment order, when the offender is under 21 years old, or before attaching conditions for medical treatment to a community rehabilitation order. A report is no longer required when an adult is being sentenced to custody.

Sentence must be pronounced in open court by the presiding judge and is almost always pronounced in the presence of the accused. The sentence may be altered (or rescinded) within 28 days by the trial court, and the Crown Court also has a further (common-law) power to postpone sentence for more than 28 days when circumstances require this (e.g. when disqualifying from driving under the *totting-up provisions, if the driving licence is not available). There is a power to postpone sentence for up to six months (*see* DEFERRED SENTENCE).

Courts have very wide discretionary powers of sentencing in all crimes (except murder and treason). The penalties prescribed by law are maximum penalties, to be imposed in the most serious cases, and the judge must decide what is the appropriate sentence in each case. However, the Crime (Sentences) Act 1997 introduces automatic minimum sentences for second-time violent offenders (*see* REPEAT OFFENDER) and for persistent burglars (*see* BURGLARY) and dealers in hard drugs (*see* CONTROLLED DRUGS). Judges may give a lesser sentence for burglary and drug dealing if the court considers the minimum would be unjust in all the circumstances. *See also* CUSTODY.

Apart from imprisonment (which may be a *concurrent sentence or a *suspended sentence) and *fines, the courts can impose community rehabilitation orders, community punishment orders, *curfew orders, confiscation orders, and *hospital orders, as well as an absolute or conditional *discharge. (For the sentencing of young offenders, *see* JUVENILE OFFENDER.) Magistrates' courts have less extensive powers of sentencing, but may sometimes, upon convicting an offender, remit him to the Crown Court for sentence (e.g. when he has been tried summarily for an offence triable either way). They are not empowered to sentence first offenders to imprisonment unless satisfied there is no other appropriate way of dealing with them. There is usually a right of appeal against sentence to the *Court of Appeal. The *Attorney General may refer cases to the Court of Appeal (with its permission) when Crown Court sentences appear unduly lenient. The Court of Appeal may then quash the sentence and substitute any sentence that they think appropriate and that the Crown Court had power to pass. *See also* NULLA POENA SINE LEGE.

separate trials *See* JOINDER OF DEFENDANTS.

separation *n*. *See* JUDICIAL SEPARATION ORDER; LIVING APART.

separation agreement An agreement between husband and wife releasing each other from the duty to cohabit. Such an agreement will only be valid (subject to the ordinary rules of the law of contract) if the marriage has already broken down; it will be void (contrary to public policy) if they enter into it to provide for the contingency that the marriage may break down at some future date. Separation agreements often contain further clauses (such as nonmolestation clauses, maintenance clauses, *dum casta* clauses) or an agreement not to bring other matrimonial proceedings based on past conduct ("*Rose* v *Rose* clauses"). Under the Family Law Act 1996 such orders will not be granted unless the interests of the children are settled first. A spouse may also relinquish his rights or powers in relation to his children, but the court has an overriding discretion not to enforce such provisions if they are not for the children's benefit. A separation agreement in writing may be a *maintenance agreement and governed by the Matrimonial Causes Act 1973.

separation of powers The doctrine that the liberty of the individual is secure only if the three primary functions of the state (legislative, executive, and judicial) are exercised by distinct and independent organs. It was propounded by Montesquieu (*De l'Esprit des Lois*, 1748), who regarded it as a feature of the UK constitution. In fact, however, while the judiciary is largely independent, the legislature and the executive depend on one another and their members overlap. The doctrine had a great influence over the form adopted for the constitution of the USA and many other countries.

separation order *See* JUDICIAL SEPARATION ORDER.

sequestration *n*. A court order in the form of a writ to (usually four) commissioners (**sequestrators**), ordering them to seize control of a person's property. The order may be made against someone who is in *contempt of court because he has not complied with a court order (such as an injunction). The property is detained until he complies with the order.

Serious Fraud Office (SFO) A body established in 1987 to be responsible for investigating and prosecuting serious or complex frauds. The *Attorney General appoints and superintends its director. The director is empowered to investigate any suspected offence that appears to involve serious fraud and may employ any suitable person to help in the investigation. Serious and complex fraud cases can go straight to the Crown Court without *committal for trial. That court can hold *preparatory hearings to clarify issues for the jury and settle points of law.

SERPS *See* STATE EARNINGS RELATED PENSION SCHEME.

servant *n.* An *employee.

service *n.* **1.** The delivery of any document relating to court proceedings. Service may be made by physically handing the document to the person concerned (*see* PERSONAL SERVICE) or it may be delivered to the *address for service supplied by that person (*see also* SUBSTITUTED SERVICE). Once the document has been formally issued by the court, it must be served within 12 months (or, in the case of claim forms, four months) unless the court allows this period to be extended. In the case of certain motoring offences, such as speeding and careless and inconsiderate driving, the police must serve a summons within 14 days unless the accused was warned at the time of the offence that he might be prosecuted or unless they serve a *notice of intended prosecution within 14 days. **2. (contract of service)** *See* CONTRACT OF EMPLOYMENT.

service court A court with jurisdiction over service personnel, who are subject to the services' discipline Acts, which are renewed every five years. *See also* SERVICE LAW.

service law The law that regulates the conduct of members of the armed forces. It consists of **naval law**, **military law**, and **air-force law** (military law is the branch relating to the army, but the expression is frequently used to describe all three branches). Its primary sources are the Naval Discipline Act 1957, the Army Act 1955, and the Air Force Act 1955; supplementary sources are Admiralty Instructions and the **Queen's Regulations** both for the Army and for the Royal Air Force. The three Acts concerned require annual renewal. Every fifth year an Armed Forces Act enables them to continue in force for one year and provides that for each of the following four years they may be continued in force by an Order in Council that has been approved by resolution of each House of Parliament (the last such Act was the Armed Forces Act 2001, which applies from 11 May 2001). The purpose of this procedure (which did not apply to the Naval Discipline Act 1957 until this was provided by the Armed Forces Act 1971) is to ensure that Parliament has an annual opportunity of debating matters relating to the armed forces.

Service law is a specialized code of criminal law. Its essential concern is the maintenance of discipline and it embodies a variety of offences (including *desertion, malingering, and insubordination) that have no counterpart in the ordinary criminal law. Since 1 April 1997 it has been an offence against service law to refuse to take a service compulsory drug test; in addition, the service authorities have been empowered to take fingerprints or DNA samples from those convicted of service offences, for criminal records purposes. Commanding officers have powers of dealing with minor offences summarily and, with effect from 2 October 2000, a member of the armed forces may appeal against the commanding officer's finding and/or award to a **Summary Appeal Court**. The Summary Appeal Court, consisting of a judge advocate and two officers, may uphold, quash, or vary the commanding officer's finding or award. But the tribunals primarily responsible for the trial and punishment of offences are the *courts martial. Service law applies to a member of the armed forces wherever he may be. In the UK he is subject both to service law and to the ordinary criminal law. When he is not in the UK, the ordinary criminal law does not in general apply to him; the relevant Acts therefore provide that it is an offence under service law for any serviceman to do anything that constitutes an offence under the ordinary criminal law. The effect of this general provision is to create, in the case of a member of the armed forces who is in the UK, a duality of offences. If, for example, a soldier in the UK steals, he commits an offence against both the ordinary criminal law and service law. He cannot, however, be punished under both.

Although service law applies primarily to members of the armed forces, certain classes of civilians are also subject to it. These include civilians employed outside the UK within the limits of the command of any officer commanding a body of the regular forces and the families of members of the armed forces residing with them outside the UK. The inclusion of the latter has had the effect of extending the jurisdiction of courts martial to cases with which they are manifestly not equipped to deal. This has led to the establishment of *standing civilian courts.

service out of the jurisdiction *Service of a claim form or other originating *process outside England and Wales. Permission of the court is required, which will only be granted in a limited number of situations specified by *rules of court. In general, some particular connection must be shown between the defendant or the subject matter of the proceedings and the jurisdiction of the English courts. If the defendant is domiciled in a member state of the EU, the Civil Jurisdiction and Judgments Act 1982 normally requires him to be sued in the courts of his domicile, but the court's permission is not required to serve originating process against such a defendant in respect of cases where the English courts have jurisdiction.

service tenancy A tenancy in which the landlord is also the tenant's employer and the premises were let as a condition of that employment. Although such a tenancy may be an *assured tenancy, the landlord can apply to the county court for possession when he ceases to employ the tenant. The court has a discretion whether or not to grant possession in this case.

servient tenement Land that is subject to an encumbrance, such as an easement, profit à *prendre*, or restrictive covenant, created for the benefit of other land, called the **dominant tenement**.

servitude *n.* A restriction upon the exercise of a state's sovereignty over its territory. For example, in 1856 Russia agreed by treaty not to fortify its own islands in the mouth of the Gulf of Bothnia.

set-off *n.* **1.** A monetary cross-claim that is also a defence to the claim made in the action by the claimant. In modern practice, any claim by a defendant to a sum of money (whether of an ascertained amount or not) that is also used as a defence may be set off against the claimant's claim. The importance of the distinction between a set-off and a *counterclaim arises principally in relation to *costs when both parties are successful. If the defendant's plea is a set-off, the claimant will recover the amount of his claim less the amount set off, and in the county court, the costs will normally be calculated in relation to the net sum recovered. If the defendant's plea is a counterclaim, the claimant will recover the costs of the claim and the defendant the costs of the counterclaim, subject to the court's overriding discretion as to costs. **2.** The deduction of monies owed against sums due to be paid. Many commercial contracts lawfully contain a clause prohibiting set-offs or counterclaims. However, in the absence of such a clause the right to set off sums in this way is permitted.

setting aside An order of a court cancelling or making void some other order or *judgment or some step taken by a party in the action.

setting down for trial Formerly, the final stage of the interlocutory (interim) proceedings in an action begun by writ in the High Court. Under the *Civil Procedure Rules, this is now dealt with through the procedure for *allocation for trial.

settled *adj.* Ordinarily resident in the UK and not subject under immigration law to any restriction on length of stay there. *See* BRITISH CITIZENSHIP; IMMIGRATION.

settled land Land that is the subject of a *settlement under the Settled Land Act 1925, i.e. land in which two or more beneficial interests exist in succession to one another or land that is subject to certain other fetters on the owner's powers. No such settlements can be created after 1996; most of the arrangements described below can now exist as *trusts of land with the exception of *entailed interests, which can no longer be created. Existing settlements continue until coming naturally to an end. The categories were as follows. (1) Land held in trust for any persons by way of succession; for example, in trust for A for life then B for life then C in fee simple. (2) Entailed interests. (3) Land owned subject to a *gift over on a specified event. (4) Land owned for a *determinable interest. (5) Land conveyed to a person under 18 years (a minor cannot own or convey a legal estate in land). (6) Land in which a future interest may come into possession on a specified event. For example, when land is left to A and B provided they respectively attain the age of 18, the elder is absolutely entitled to a half share on reaching 18 but may become entitled to the whole of the land absolutely if the younger dies during minority. (7) Land charged voluntarily (i.e. without *consideration) or in consideration of marriage or by way of family arrangement with payment of any rentcharge or capital sum; for example, when the owner charges his land with payment of income to his wife during her life or widowhood.

A settlement made during the life of the settlor was effected by a **trust instrument** and a **vesting deed**. The trust instrument declared the beneficial interests in the land and appointed two or more individuals, or a trust corporation (e.g. a bank), as **trustees of the settlement** (*see* SETTLED LAND ACT TRUSTEES). The vesting deed transferred the legal estate in the settled land to the immediate beneficiary; it also had to identify the trustees of the settlement. A will that effected a settlement constituted the trust instrument; the legal estate devolved upon the testator's personal representatives on trust to vest it, by deed or *assent, in the immediate beneficiary. When the legal estate could not be transferred to the immediate beneficiary (e.g. because he was under 18), it had to be vested in a *statutory owner.

The purpose of the Act was to balance the protection of beneficiaries with future interests against the principle that the person immediately entitled in possession should not be prevented by the existence of future interests from prudently managing and dealing with the land. Thus the Act conferred on the immediate beneficiary powers to sell the land at the best price reasonably obtainable, to exchange it for other land, and to grant certain leases (up to 50 years, or 100 years for mining, or 999 years for building or forestry). These transactions *overreached the interests of the subsequent beneficiaries, who acquired corresponding interests in the capital money or income arising from them. The immediate beneficiary could also mortgage the land to raise money to pay off other encumbrances, to give equality of value on an exchange, and to pay for certain improvements. He could insist that the cost of certain improvements (such as rebuilding the *principal mansion house and installation of drainage and electricity) be paid out of capital. His statutory powers could be extended by the terms of the settlement but could not be excluded or restricted. The Act imposed on the immediate beneficiary, in exercising these powers, the duties of a trustee for all parties having a beneficial interest in the land. The beneficiary thus had a dual role. When the immediate beneficiary sold or otherwise disposed of settled land, the vesting deed formed the basis of his title. The purchaser was not concerned with the interests of beneficiaries whose rights are overreached (*see* CURTAIN PROVISIONS) but had to pay the price to the trustees of the settlement or, at the direction of the immediate beneficiary (the tenant for life or the person exercising the powers of the tenant for life), into court.

Settled Land Act trustees (trustees of the settlement) Two or more individuals or a trust corporation (such as a bank) who are trustees of *settled land. Their primary function is to receive *capital money arising on a sale or other disposition of the land by the immediate beneficiary and to hold it in trust for those entitled under the settlement. Their consent is also necessary before the immediate beneficiary can validly exercise certain of his statutory powers; for example, to sell the *principal mansion house or timber cut from the land if the settlement so requires or to vary rights (such as easements) over other land that benefit the settled land.

The trustees are generally appointed by the trust instrument but must be named in the vesting deed. If no trustees are appointed, the Settled Land Act 1925 provides that they will be either (1) trustees having a power of sale of other land comprised in the settlement and held on similar trusts; (2) trustees having a future power of sale of the settled land; (3) persons appointed by the beneficiaries if they are of full age and entitled to dispose of the whole settled estate; or (4) the settlor's personal representatives, when the settlement is effected by will. Trustees can also be appointed by the court.

settlement *n.* A disposition of land or other property, made by deed, will, or very rarely by statute (as in the Duke of Marlborough Annuity Act 1706), under which trusts are created by the *settlor designating the beneficiaries and the terms on which they are to take the property. Settlements are of many different kinds; for example, *marriage settlements, *strict settlements, *voluntary settlements, and, particularly, settlements under the Settled Land Act 1925 (*see* SETTLED LAND). All settlements of land now take effect (since 1997) as *trusts of land.

settlement of action The voluntary conclusion of civil litigation by agreement of the parties. Settlement may be made at any time and is usually followed by the claimant filing a *notice of discontinuance. No particular formality must be followed, but if money is claimed by a party under a disability (e.g. a minor or a mental patient), a settlement is not valid (in so far as it relates to his claim) without the approval of the court. *See also* STRUCTURED SETTLEMENT; TOMLIN ORDER.

settlor *n.* A person who creates a *settlement. In a broad sense the term includes testators; in a more restricted sense it signifies one who settles property during his life.

several *adj.* Separate (in contrast to 'joint'), as in *joint and several, *several tenancy.

several tenancy Ownership of land by one person absolutely, not jointly or in common with another. *Compare* JOINT TENANCY; TENANCY IN COMMON.

severance *n.* **1.** The conversion of an equitable *joint tenancy in land into a *tenancy in common. Severance may be effected, for example, by mutual agreement of the joint tenants, by the bankruptcy of one of them, by sale of the land or of one joint tenant's interest, or by written notice to the other joint tenants. It is not possible to sever a legal joint tenancy, since a tenancy in common cannot exist as a legal estate. Any words in a conveyance of land to two or more people that show an intention that they take separate shares will be construed as **words of severance** creating an equitable tenancy in common, rather than a joint tenancy. **2.** The separation of the good parts of a contract from the bad, which are rejected. The doctrine of severance applies to any contract which contains clauses that are void by statute or common law, or even, in some cases, illegal, provided there are no *public policy grounds against severing (see VOID CONTRACT). The courts will, if possible, save the contract from total invalidity by severing the offending part and the rest of the contract will stand under what is known as the "blue pencil" test. When little remains after severance, the whole contract terminates. Many commercial contracts contain a clause stating that void provisions may be severed. **3.** An order amending an *indictment so that the accused is tried separately on any count or counts of the indictment.

severance pay Money to which an employee is entitled at common law upon the termination of his contract of employment; for example, pay in lieu of notice, when he is dismissed with inadequate notice or none. An employee dismissed before the expiry of a fixed-term contract can claim damages in the courts to compensate him for the loss of pay he would have earned during the rest of the term, unless he was dismissed for a breach of contract entitling the employer to dismiss him. *See also* REDUNDANCY PAYMENT; UNFAIR DISMISSAL; WRONGFUL DISMISSAL.

severe disablement allowance A noncontributory tax-free benefit formerly payable to those unable to work due to long-term sickness or disablement and who had not enough national insurance contributions to claim *incapacity benefit. The claimant had to show that he had been continuously incapable of work for the preceding 28 weeks. This benefit has been abolished by the Welfare Reform and Pensions Act 1999 and no new claims can be made.

severe mental impairment *See* ARRESTED DEVELOPMENT.

sex change A change in a person's sexual characteristics, usually by means of surgical operation and hormone treatment. For the purposes of marriage, the law does not recognize the validity of such a change; sex is deemed to be determined at birth and cannot be changed. For the purposes of employment, however, English law now recognizes the validity of a sex change (*see* GENDER REASSIGNMENT). *See also* TRANSSEXUAL.

sex discrimination Discrimination on the ground of sex under either the Sex Discrimination Act or the Equal Pay Act. The Sex Discrimination Act has a wider definition of sex than the Equal Pay Act in that it includes within its scope discrimination on grounds of transsexualism (*see* GENDER REASSIGNMENT) and (probably) sexual orientation. The Equal Pay Act 1970 forbids having different terms for men and women in their contracts of employment (*see also* EQUAL PAY). The Sex Discrimination Act 1975 (as amended by the Sex Discrimination Act 1986) goes further, prohibiting discrimination when offering a contract of employment and before entering into such a contract. It also prohibits discrimination in employment on the grounds of marital status and discrimination in partnerships with six or more partners, trade unions, qualifying or authorizing bodies, vocational training, and education. The Act provides for special exceptions; for example, when male or female characteristics are a genuine requirement of the job. It is also unlawful to victimize someone who has complained of illegal discrimination. The Act covers both direct and indirect discrimination. The latter includes making conditions that apply to both sexes but in such a way that, for instance, the proportion of women who can fulfil the conditions is considerably less than men. An example would be insisting on a record of continuous service for promotion, which is far more difficult for women to satisfy because of pregnancy and motherhood. The Acts are reviewed by the *Equal Opportunities Commission and enforced by *employment tribunals.

Restrictions preventing women from working where they wish, including the right to work underground, were removed by the Employment Act 1989.

sex offenders *See* SEXUAL OFFENCE.

sexual intercourse The penetration of the vagina by the penis. For the purposes of sexual offences involving intercourse, penetration need only be slight and rupture of the hymen or ejaculation is not required. *See also* UNLAWFUL SEXUAL INTERCOURSE.

sexual offence Any crime that involves sexual intercourse or any other sexual act. The main crimes in this category are *rape, *buggery, *incest, *indecent assault, *indecent exposure, *gross indecency, and *abduction (*see also* CHILD ABUSE). The Sex Offenders Act 1997 created a national register of sex offenders; the names of those convicted of any of a range of sexual offences are entered in this register. Under the 1997 Act, sex offenders are obliged to tell police every time they move; those failing to register a change of address within 14 days may be jailed for up to six months and ordered to pay a fine of up to £5000. Under the Crime and Disorder Act 1998, convicted sex offenders are subject to supervision on release for up to ten years.

SFO *See* SERIOUS FRAUD OFFICE.

shadow director A person who is not a director of a company but who gives instructions (rather than professional advice) upon which the directors are accustomed to act. Certain statutory provisions (for example, those relating to put and call *options) apply to both shadow directors and directors proper.

sham marriage A marriage entered into for some ulterior motive, without the intention of cohabiting with the other party. Such marriages will usually nonetheless be deemed valid, unless one of the parties (e.g. a person trying to escape extradition) deceives the other party as to his identity or the marriage is entered into to escape a threat to life, limb, or liberty (e.g. to enable a person imprisoned under harsh conditions to leave his or her country) or to escape imprisonment.

sham plea *See* FALSE PLEA.

share *n.* A unit that measures the holder's interest in and liability to a company. Because an incorporated *company is in law a separate entity from the company membership, it is possible to divide and sell that entity in specified units (*see* (NOMINAL) CAPITAL). In the case of a company limited by shares (*see* LIMITED COMPANY) the liability of shareholders is confined to the purchase price of the shares. Once purchased, these units of the company become intangible property in their own right and can be bought and sold as an activity distinct from the trading activities of the company in question. While the company is a going concern, shares carry rights in relation to voting and sharing profits (*see* DIVIDEND). When a *limited company is wound up the shareholders have rights to share in the assets after debts have been paid. If there are no such assets shareholders lose the amount of their investment but are not liable for the company's debts (see FRAUDULENT TRADING; WRONGFUL TRADING).

Preference shares usually carry a right to a fixed percentage dividend, e.g. 10% of the nominal value (see AUTHORIZED CAPITAL), before ordinary shareholders receive anything and holders also have the right to the return of the nominal value of their shares before ordinary shareholders (but after creditors). Holders of **participating preference shares** have further rights to share surplus profits or assets with the ordinary shareholders. Preference shares are generally **cumulative**, i.e. if no dividend is declared in one year, holders are entitled to arrears when eventually one is paid. Usually preference shareholders can vote only when their *class rights are being varied.

Ordinary shares constitute the risk capital (also called equity capital), as they carry no prior rights in relation to dividends or return of nominal value. However, the rights they do carry are unlimited in extent: if the company is successful, the ordinary shareholders are not restricted to a fixed dividend (unlike the preference shareholders) and the high yield upon their shares will cause these to increase in value. Similarly, if there are surplus assets on a winding-up, the ordinary shareholders will take what is left after the preference shareholders have been satisfied. Because ordinary shareholders carry the risk of the enterprise, they generally have full voting rights in a *general meeting (though some companies issue nonvoting ordinary shares to raise additional capital without diluting the control of the company).

Redeemable shares are issued subject to the proviso that they will or may be bought back (at the option of the shareholder or the company) by the company. They cannot be bought back unless fully paid-up and then only out of profits (see CAPITAL REDEMPTION RESERVE) or the proceeds of a fresh issue of shares made for the purpose.

A **golden share** enables the holder, usually the government, to outvote all other shareholders on certain types of company resolution.

share capital *See* CAPITAL.

share certificate A document issued by a company evidencing that a named person is a company member and stating the number of shares registered in his name and the extent to which they are paid up (see CALL). A company can be precluded by *estoppel from denying its accuracy. The certificate must normally be produced on a *transfer of shares. *Compare* SHARE WARRANT.

share premium The amount by which the price at which a share was issued exceeds its nominal value (see AUTHORIZED CAPITAL). Share premiums must be credited by the company to a **share premium account**, which is subject to the rules relating to *reduction of capital and can only be used for certain purposes, e.g. paying up bonus shares (see BONUS ISSUE).

share transfer A document transferring registered shares, i.e. shares for which a *share certificate has been issued, usually on a **stock transfer form**. A share transfer in proper form must usually be delivered to the company before it places the transferee's name on the register of members (Stock Transfer Act 1963). *See also* TRANSFER OF SHARES.

share warrant A document issued by a company certifying that the bearer is entitled to the shares specified in it. The name of the bearer will not appear on the register of members until he surrenders the warrant to the company in return for *transfer of the shares, but he may be regarded as a company member under the provisions of the articles of association. The company is contractually bound to recognize the bearer as shareholder. *Compare* SHARE CERTIFICATE.

sheriff *n.* The principal officer of the Crown in a county. In relation to the administration of justice, his (or her) functions (in practice discharged by the under-sheriff) include the execution of *process issuing from criminal courts, levying forfeiture of *recognizances, and the *enforcement of judgments of the High Court by writs of *fieri facias*, possession, and delivery.

sheriff's interpleader *See* INTERPLEADER.

shifting use (secondary use) Formerly, a *use that operated to terminate a preceding use. For example, if property was given to X to the use of A, but then to the use of B when C paid £100 to D, B had a shifting use, which arose when C made the specified payment.

ship *n.* For the purposes of the Merchant Shipping Act 1894 (which provides among other things for the registration of British ships), any vessel used in navigation and not propelled by oars. The officially required registration of ships is set out in the Merchant Shipping (Registration, etc.) Act 1993; a central register of British ships is kept. For the purposes of ownership, a British ship is notionally divided into 64 shares. Each share may be in different ownership, but no share may be in the ownership of an alien or a foreign company. Co-owners will commonly appoint a **ship's husband** or managing owner to manage the ship. The definition of "British ship" in the Merchant Shipping Act 1988, in relation to fishing rights, has been challenged under EU law (*see* FISHERY LIMITS; QUOTA).

shipwreck *n.* *See* WRECK.

shock *n.* *See* NERVOUS SHOCK.

shoplifting *n.* Dishonestly removing goods from a shop without paying for them. Shoplifters could be charged with *making off without payment under the Theft Act 1978, but it is more usual to charge them with *theft under the Theft Act 1968. It is not legally necessary to remove the goods from the shop precincts in order to be guilty of shoplifting, but in practice it is advisable to wait until the accused has left the shop before stopping him, as it is then easier to prove the intention to steal (*see also* ARREST). A cashier in the shop who deliberately rings up a lower price than the true price may be guilty of aiding and abetting theft.

short cause list A list of cases for hearing for which the trial is expected to last less than four hours.

short committal *See* COMMITTAL FOR TRIAL.

short notice A lesser period of notice of a company meeting than that required by law. In the case of an *annual general meeting it may be agreed by all members entitled to attend and vote at it; for other meetings 95% of the shareholders must agree. There are strict requirements for the details to be given for short notice and service of the notice.

short title *See* ACT OF PARLIAMENT.

SIB *See* SECURITIES AND INVESTMENT BOARD.

sickness benefit A former state benefit payable for 28 weeks to those who did not qualify for *statutory sick pay. It was replaced by *incapacity benefit in April 1995.

sic utere tuo ut alienum non laedas [Latin] Use your own property in such a way that you do not injure other people's: a maxim often used in cases of nuisance. It is misleading, since only an unreasonable interference with a neighbour's property is actionable as a nuisance.

signature of treaty The formal and official affixing of names to the text of a *treaty by the representatives of the negotiating states, either as a means of expressing the definitive consent of the state to be bound by the terms of the treaty or as an expression of provisional consent subject to *ratification, acceptance, or approval.

signature of will *See* EXECUTION OF WILL.

silence *n. See* RIGHT OF SILENCE.

silk *n. See* QUEEN'S COUNSEL.

similar-fact evidence Evidence that a party, especially the accused, has on previous occasions misconducted himself in a way similar to the misconduct being alleged against him in the proceedings before the court. The evidence frequently takes the form of a *previous conviction. In general, the prosecution may not offer similar-fact evidence as part of its case unless it can be shown to be relevant to an issue before the jury, for example by rebutting some defence advanced by the accused. Thus, if a person charged with fraud contends that he was honestly mistaken, the fact that he has committed similar frauds on previous occasions may be admissible. The judge may in his discretion exclude otherwise admissible similar-fact evidence under section 78 of the Police and Criminal Evidence Act 1984 if he considers that it would have an adverse effect on the fairness of the proceedings.

simple contract (parol contract) Any *contract other than one made by *deed.

simple trust *See* BARE TRUST.

sine die [Latin] Without a date. To adjourn a case *sine die* is to adjourn it without setting a date for a future hearing.

single administrative document (SAD) A single document declaring an import into an EU state. This is an improvement on the system it replaced, in which many documents were required before a product could be imported into the EU.

Single European Act The legislation passed in 1986 in the European Community (in force from 1 July 1987) that committed all member states to an integrated method of trading with no frontiers between countries by 31 December 1992. It was the first Act to amend the principles of the Treaty of Rome. In practice, some of its terms on harmonization, such as the insurance market, have taken considerably longer to implement. The main creation of the Single European Act is the *Single Market for trading in goods and services within the EU.

Single Market The concept that underlies trading in the European Union, as codified in the *Single European Act 1986. The Single Market came into force on 1 January 1993 with between 90% and 95% of the necessary legislation enacted by all member countries. The measures covered by the legislation include: the elimination of frontier controls (the full measures have been repeatedly delayed); the acceptance throughout the market of professional qualifications; the acceptance of national standards for product harmonization; open tendering for public supply contracts; the free movement of capital between states; a reduction of state aid for certain industries; and the harmonization of VAT and excise duties throughout the market.

single-member company *See* PRIVATE COMPANY.

single-union agreement A collective agreement within a company or establishment that recognizes only one *independent trade union for the purposes of *collective bargaining. The selection of the union to be recognized for this purpose is frequently now based on the so-called *beauty competition. This agreement does not restrict the rights of individual employees to belong to a union of their choice or not to belong to a union. However, their only access to collective bargaining is through the single union.

sittings *pl. n.* (in the *Supreme Court) The four periods of the legal year during which the full range of judicial business is transacted. The sittings are Michaelmas, Hilary, Easter, and Trinity. Sittings were substituted for *terms by the Judicature Act 1873. *See also* VACATIONS.

slander *n.* A defamatory statement made by such means as spoken words or gestures, i.e. not in permanent form. Generally slander is only actionable on proof that its publication has caused special damage (actual financial or material loss), not merely loss of reputation. Proof of special damage is not necessary when the slander implies the commission of a criminal offence punishable by imprisonment, infection with a contagious disease, unchastity in a woman, or is calculated to disparage a person in his office, business, trade, or profession. *See* DEFAMATION.

slander of goods (disparagement of goods) A false statement, made maliciously, that disparages the quality of goods manufactured and sold by the claimant. It is a form of the tort of *malicious falsehood. In order to be actionable, the statement must allege some specific defect in the claimant's goods. A mere assertion by a rival trader that his goods are better is not sufficient, even if the claim was false and malicious.

slander of title A false statement, made maliciously, that impugns a vendor's title to sell property. It is a form of the tort of *malicious falsehood.

slavery *n.* The prohibition on slavery or forced labour as set out in Article 4 of the European Convention on Human Rights is now part of UK law as a consequence of the *Human Rights Act 1998. There are exceptions to this prohibition for prisoners, military service, normal civic obligations, and in emergencies.

slip rule The rule permitting the correction of clerical mistakes arising from any accidental slip or omission in judgments or orders. Such errors can be corrected at any time by the court on application without an appeal.

small agreement **1.** (under the Consumer Credit Act 1974) A regulated *consumer-credit agreement for credit not exceeding £50, other than a hire-purchase or conditional-sale agreement, or a regulated *consumer-hire agreement that does not require the hirer to make payments exceeding £50. In both cases the agreement is either unsecured or secured by a guarantee or indemnity only. Some small agreements are outside certain provisions of the Act. **2.** (under the Competition Act 1998) An agreement in which the parties are exempt from the imposition of penalties (fines) for anticompetitive practices. Section 39 of the Act provides the exemption, and the Competition Act 1998 (Small Agreements and

Conduct of Minor Significance) Regulations 2000 defines an anticompetitive agreement as "small" when both parties to it have a total turnover of under £20M. However, no exemption applies for a price-fixing agreement. Moreover, small agreements are not exempt from other provisions of the 1998 Act, and thus restrictive clauses in them may still be void.

small claims track The track to which a civil case is allocated when the claim is for an amount of no more than £5000 (*see* ALLOCATION). Before the introduction of the *Civil Procedure Rules in 1999, small claims were automatically referred to arbitration. However, a small claims hearing retains most of the aspects of the former procedure: the hearing is informal and in public, is based on a paper adjudication with the parties' consent, and there are generally no experts and no costs.

Despite the limit of £5000, with the approval of the court parties may consent to use the small claims track even if their claim value exceeds £5000.

SMEs Small and medium enterprises: businesses having fewer than 500 employees and a share capital or business capital of less than 75M euros. SMEs are encouraged by the European Commission through various aid programmes.

smuggling *n.* The offence of importing or exporting specified goods that are subject to customs or excise duties without having paid the requisite duties. Smuggled goods are liable to confiscation and the smuggler is liable to pay treble their value or a sum laid down by the law (whichever is the greater); offenders may alternatively, or additionally, receive a term of imprisonment.

Social Chapter The section of the Treaty of Rome (European Community Treaty; Articles 117–121) that reflects the agreement of member states with respect to the social policies issues of the European Union. The objectives of the Social Chapter are to promote employment, improve living and working conditions, establish dialogue between management and workers by means of works councils, implement proper social protection, and develop human resources with a view to lasting high employment. The social provisions include unpaid *parental leave for new parents and the principle of *equal pay for male and female workers for equal work. The British government finally agreed to the incorporation of these social aims and objectives into the main body of the founding Community Treaty in 1997 with the signing of the *Amsterdam Treaty. This has led to the adoption of a number of measures, including the implementation of unpaid parental leave and *European Works Councils and new rights for part-time workers (who are now entitled to be treated no less favourably than comparable full-time workers in their contractual terms and conditions).

social fund A fund established under the Social Security Act 1986 to meet special needs of individuals who are entitled to benefit from it (e.g. by cold-weather payments). It is under the control of the Social Fund Commissioner, who appoints social fund officers to administer it and reports to the Secretary of State for Work and Pensions (formerly Social Security). Cold-weather payments are paid (to those entitled) for any consecutive seven-day period when the temperature averages 0° C or below. Other benefits from the social fund include interest-free budgeting loans and crisis loans, maternity and funeral payments, and community-care grants. Loans are repayable by deductions from social security benefits received by the loan recipients or their partners.

social inquiry report A report prepared by a probation officer and made to a criminal court to assist it in deciding what *sentence to impose on a convicted person. The report gives details of the person's background, family, home circumstances, relationships, attitudes, job situation, and prospects. It is based on interviews with the accused person and his family and friends. The report gives the probation officer's opinion on the suitability of particular kinds of sentence; for example, how well the accused would be likely to respond to an order for community service.

social policy rule *See* INTERPRETATION OF STATUTES.

Social Security Appeal Tribunal A tribunal that hears appeals from decisions by adjudication officers on claims for social security benefits (*see* NATIONAL INSURANCE). Such tribunals are subject to the supervision of the *Council on Tribunals; appeal against their decisions on a point of law can be made to a **Social Security Commissioner**.

sodomy *n. See* BUGGERY.

soft law (in international law) Guidelines of behaviour, such as those provided by treaties not yet in force, resolutions of the United Nations, or international conferences, that are not binding in themselves but are more than mere statements of political aspiration (they fall into a legal/political limbo between these two states). Soft law contrasts with **hard law**, i.e. those legal obligations, found either in *treaties or customary international law (*see* CUSTOM), that are binding in and of themselves.

software *n.* Computer programs, which are protected by *copyright under the Copyright, Designs and Patents Act 1988. EU Directive 91/250 on the legal protection of computer programs provides that all member states must protect computer programs by copyright law. The directive also provides a right to make back-up copies of software and a very limited *decompilation right. A right to repair is also included, unless a software licence prohibits this. The UK implemented the directive by the Copyright (Computer Programs) Regulations 1992.

soldier's will *See* PRIVILEGED WILL.

solemn form *See* PROBATE.

sole solicitor A solicitor who is the sole principal of a practice, rather than one who practises in partnership with others.

soliciting *n.* **1.** The offence by a prostitute of attempting to obtain prospective clients in a street or public place. It is punishable by a *fine at level 2 on the standard scale on a first conviction and at level 3 on a subsequent conviction. Any act committed by the prostitute (even smiling provocatively) may constitute soliciting, but an advertisement inviting men to visit her is not soliciting. "Street" is widely defined to include roads, lanes, bridges, courtyards, alleyways, passages, etc., open to the public, as well as doorways and entrances of houses on the street, and ground adjoining and open to the street. If a prostitute in a private house attracts the attention of men in the street (for example by tapping on the window and inviting them in, or even merely by sitting at the window illuminated by a red light), this may be considered soliciting "in a street". **2.** The offence by a man of persistently accosting a woman in a public place for the purpose of prostitution (*see also* KERB CRAWLING) or persistently accosting anybody in a public place for immoral purposes. "Persistently" requires either a number of single invitations to different people or more than one invitation to the same person.

solicitor *n.* A legal practitioner admitted to practice under the provisions of the

Solicitors Act 1974. Solicitors normally take a three-year law degree at university, then a one-year legal practice course and examination at a law college, followed by two years as an employee under a training contract (previously called **articles of clerkship**), after which they are admitted as solicitors. Those taking a nonlaw degree spend two years at law college, taking a common professional examination in the first year. Practising solicitors must possess a *practising certificate. Solicitors form much the larger part of the English legal profession (*compare* BARRISTER), undertaking the general aspects of giving legal advice and conducting legal proceedings. They have *rights of audience in the lower courts but may not act as advocates in the Supreme Court (except in chambers) or the House of Lords unless they have acquired a relevant *advocacy qualification under the terms of the Courts and Legal Services Act 1990. A solicitor may be sued for professional negligence and owes the duties of a *fiduciary to his client; these include the duty to preserve the confidentiality of the client's affairs.

solicitor and own client basis of costs A basis of *assessment of costs on which is calculated the sum that a privately represented client must pay his own solicitor. On this basis, all costs are allowed provided that they are of a reasonable amount and have not been unreasonably incurred.

Solicitor General A law officer of the Crown immediately subordinate to the *Attorney General. The Solicitor General is usually a Member of Parliament of the ruling party. He acts as deputy to the Attorney General and may exercise any power vested by statute in the latter (unless the statute otherwise provides) if the office of Attorney General is vacant or the Attorney General is unable to act through illness or has authorized him to act.

Solicitors' Disciplinary Tribunal A tribunal established under the Solicitors Act 1974 for hearing applications and complaints against solicitors. It has the power to strike the name of a solicitor off the roll and to restore the name of a solicitor previously struck off, suspend a solicitor from practice, and order the payment of a penalty. The members of the tribunal are practising solicitors of not less than ten years' standing and some lay members. They are appointed by the *Master of the Rolls. Appeals from decisions of the tribunal can be brought to the High Court of the Master of the Rolls. *See also* OFFICE FOR THE SUPERVISION OF SOLICITORS.

solicitor's lien The right of a solicitor to retain papers or property of his client as security for the payment of his costs. There are two types of lien: a retaining lien, i.e. a right to retain property already in his possession until he has been paid costs due to him; and a lien on property recovered or preserved, i.e. a right to ask the court to direct that personal property recovered under a judgment obtained by his exertions stand as security for his costs of the recovery. By statute the second type of lien has been extended to confer upon the court the power to make a *charging order over real and personal property recovered or preserved in proceedings by the solicitor.

Solicitors Practice Rules Rules, made by the Council of the *Law Society with the agreement of the *Master of the Rolls, for regulating the professional practice, conduct, and discipline of solicitors. The power to make the rules is conferred by the Solicitors Act 1974.

sovereign *n. See* CROWN.

sovereign immunity The exemption of the sovereign or other head of a foreign state and foreign governmental departments from the jurisdiction of the English courts. The principles governing this exemption are now contained in the State Immunity Act 1978 and are consistent with the European Convention on State Immunity. The immunity granted is no longer absolute; it is subject to numerous exceptions outlined in the Act. Subject to modifications, the Diplomatic Privileges Act 1964 extends to foreign sovereigns the same privileges and immunities as are granted to heads of diplomatic missions. It is now clear under English law that such immunity does not apply to former heads of state who are alleged to have committed crimes against humanity.

sovereignty *n.* Supreme authority in a state. In any state sovereignty is vested in the institution, person, or body having the ultimate authority to impose law on everyone else in the state and the power to alter any pre-existing law. How and by whom the authority is exercised varies according to the political nature of the state. In many countries the executive, legislative, and judicial powers of sovereignty are exercised by different bodies. One of these bodies may in fact retain sovereignty by having ultimate control over the others. But in some countries, such as the USA, the powers are carefully balanced by a constitution. In the UK sovereignty is vested in Parliament (*see* SOVEREIGNTY OF PARLIAMENT).

In international law, it is an essential aspect of sovereignty that all states should have supreme control over their internal affairs, subject to the recognized limitations imposed by international law. These limitations include, in particular, the international law of *human rights and the rules forbidding the use of force. However, no state or international organization may intervene in matters that fall within the domestic jurisdiction of another state. The concept of state sovereignty was outlined, among other things, in a declaration on Principles of International Law (Resolution 2625), proclaimed by the General Assembly of the United Nations in 1970.

sovereignty of Parliament The constitutional principle that the legislative competence of Parliament is unlimited. No court in the UK can question its power to enact any law that it pleases. In practice, however, Parliament does not assume unlimited authority; it can legislate only for territories that are recognized by international law to be within its competence, i.e. the UK, the Channel Islands and the Isle of Man, and UK dependencies. The *Welsh Assembly, *Scottish Parliament, and *Northern Ireland Assembly have devolved power in certain areas.

SPC *See* SUMMONS PRODUCTION CENTRE.

Speaker *n. See* HOUSE OF COMMONS; LORD CHANCELLOR.

special administration *See* LIMITED ADMINISTRATION.

special agent *See* AGENT.

special business Business that can only be transacted at a general meeting if its general nature has been specified in the notice convening the meeting. *See* ANNUAL GENERAL MEETING; EXTRAORDINARY GENERAL MEETING.

special case **1.** A statement of facts agreed by the parties to a civil action and directed by the court to be tried at a different time from that of the trial of the action. It may raise issues of fact or law and should be signed by counsel if settled by him. **2.** Formerly, a statement of the findings of an arbitrator, submitted for the opinion of the High Court. This procedure has now been replaced by a form of *appeal on a question of law only.

special damages *See* GENERAL AND SPECIAL DAMAGES.

special defences *See* GENERAL DEFENCES.

special endorsement *See* ENDORSEMENT.

special hospital A hospital (e.g. Broadmoor or Rampton) controlled and managed by the Home Secretary for persons suffering from *mental disorder who require detention under special security conditions, because of their dangerous, violent, or criminal propensities.

speciality *n.* The principle that the state requesting the *extradition of a fugitive from another state must, in order for the request to succeed, specify the crime for which the accused is to be extradited. Further, the requesting state must only try the individual for the crime specified in the extradition request. *See also* DOUBLE CRIMINALITY.

special notice The 28 days' notice that is required to be given to a registered company of an intention to propose certain resolutions at a *general meeting of the company. These resolutions are: (1) appointing or removing an auditor; (2) removing a director before his term of office expires or appointing a new director to replace him at the same meeting; and (3) appointing or approving the appointment of a director over the age of 70. The company must then give 21 days' notice of the meeting to the members. *See* SHORT NOTICE.

special parliamentary procedure *See* SPECIAL PROCEDURE ORDERS.

special plea A *plea in bar of arraignment, e.g. *autrefois acquit* or *autrefois convict*.

special power *See* POWER OF APPOINTMENT.

special procedure (in divorce proceedings) A speedy, simple, and cheap procedure for uncontested divorce cases introduced in the mid-1970s. A district judge scrutinizes the divorce application and, if satisfied that the ground is made out, issues a certificate to that effect. The divorce is then formally granted in open court; neither party need appear. The introduction of the special procedure revolutionized divorce law and is now used in the majority of cases.

special procedure material Jounalistic and other confidential material acquired or created in the course of a trade, business, profession, or unpaid office. Under the Police and Criminal Evidence Act 1984, *warrants to search for such material can only be obtained by following a special procedure and require the authority of a *circuit judge.

special procedure orders A form of *delegated legislation consisting of orders made by government ministers under powers that are expressed in the enabling statute to be exercisable by order subject to **special parliamentary procedure**. The Statutory Orders (Special Procedure) Act 1945 then applies, and, after a local inquiry is held, the order must be laid before Parliament and petitions for its annulment or amendment may be presented. Special procedure orders, which have largely replaced provisional orders, are used primarily to confer powers on local authorities. The *compulsory purchase of land must also in certain cases (e.g. land owned by local authorities or the National Trust) be effected by a special procedure order.

special resolution A decision reached by a majority of not less than 75% of company members voting in person or by proxy at a general meeting. At least 21 days' notice must be given of the meeting.

special trust *See* ACTIVE TRUST.

specialty *n. See* DEED.

special verdict **1.** A verdict of not guilty by reason of *insanity. **2.** A verdict on particular questions of fact, without a general conclusion (in criminal cases) as to guilt or (in civil cases) in favour of the claimant or the defendant. The judge asks the jury their opinion on the facts, but decides the general question himself. Such verdicts in criminal cases are very rare. *Compare* GENERAL VERDICT.

specification *n.* **1.** (in *patent law) A document that must be lodged with an application for a patent for an invention. It must contain a description of the invention, a claim defining the matter for which the applicant seeks protection, and any drawing referred to in the description or claim. **2.** A general document in which a commercial buyer or seller describes goods to be bought or sold. It is sometimes incorporated into the contract by reference.

specific delivery *See* WRIT OF DELIVERY.

specific devise *See* DEVISE.

specific directions *See* COMMUNITY LEGAL SERVICE.

specific goods Goods specifically identified at the time a contract of sale is made, e.g. a named car with a specified registration number. If the subject matter is not so identified, the contract is for the sale of *unascertained goods. In a contract for the sale of specific goods the seller is bound to deliver the identified goods and no others.

specific intent *See* INTENTION.

specific issue order *See* SECTION 8 ORDERS.

specific legacy *See* LEGACY.

specific performance A court order to a person to fulfil his obligations under a contract. For example, when contracts have been exchanged for the sale of a house, the court may order a reluctant seller to complete the sale. The remedy is a discretionary one and is not available in certain cases; for example, for the enforcement of a contract of employment or when the payment of damages would be a sufficient remedy.

specimen of blood A specimen of blood for analysis, used as an alternative to a *specimen of breath in cases involving *drunken driving. A police officer may require a specimen of blood if he reasonably believes that he cannot demand a breath specimen for medical reasons, if an approved and reliable device for taking a breath specimen is unavailable or cannot be used, or if the defendant is suspected of being unfit to drive and a doctor believes that his condition is due to a drug. A police officer may also ask for a blood specimen if the suspect is in hospital (subject to the consent of the doctor treating him). A suspect may be asked to give a blood specimen under these conditions even if he has already given a breath specimen.

A blood specimen may only be taken with the defendant's consent and by a medical practitioner, otherwise it cannot be used as evidence in any proceedings. It must be analysed by a qualified analyst, who must sign a certificate stating how much alcohol he found. The suspect may ask to be given half the specimen for his own analysis, which may be used to contradict the prosecution's evidence; if he has asked for but was not given half of the sample, the other half may not be used in evidence against him. A *specimen of urine may sometimes be taken as an alternative to a blood specimen.

In all other respects the law relating to blood specimens is the same as that relating to breath specimens.

specimen of breath A specimen of breath for analysis taken from a person suspected of *drunken driving. It is this specimen that usually forms the evidence for a prosecution and conviction for offences of drunken driving and should not be confused with the preliminary *breath test. The specimen may be required whenever the police are investigating any of these offences, but only if the suspect is at the police station. Usually he will have been brought to the station under arrest as a result of a positive breath test or refusal to undergo such a test. It is an offence not to provide a specimen without a reasonable excuse, and the police officer should warn a suspect of this when asking for the specimen. This offence is punishable by fine or imprisonment, endorsement (which carries 10 penalty points under the *totting-up system), and discretionary disqualification (in cases of being in charge of a vehicle) or compulsory disqualification (in cases of driving or attempting to drive).

The suspect must give two breath specimens, which should be measured by means of an approved electronic device (not the *breathalyser used for the preliminary breath test) that automatically prints out the level of alcohol in the breath. A print-out of the lower of the two readings is used as evidence in a subsequent trial, together with a signed certificate by a police officer that it refers to the defendant's specimen given at the stated time. The defendant must be given a copy of these documents at least seven days before his trial, and he may serve notice not later than three days before the trial that he requires the police officer who signed it to attend the hearing. At his trial, a defendant may bring evidence to show that he drank more alcohol between the time of the alleged offence and giving the specimen and that this accounted for his exceeding the prescribed limit. It is an offence, however, to deliberately drink more alcohol in order to make it difficult to prove his guilt.

Once a suspect has given a specimen he is free to leave the police station, but the police may detain him if they reasonably suspect that he is likely to continue driving with an excess alcohol level or while unfit to drive. Under certain circumstances the suspect can provide either a *specimen of blood or a *specimen of urine instead of a breath specimen. If the breath specimen records a reading of more than 35 but less than 50 micrograms of alcohol per 100 ml of breath (and prosecution is intended), the suspect is entitled to ask that it should be replaced by a blood or urine specimen.

specimen of urine A specimen of urine for analysis, used as an alternative to a *specimen of breath in cases involving *drunken driving. A specimen of urine may be required when there are objections to taking a breath specimen and when a medical practitioner thinks that a *specimen of blood should not be taken for medical reasons. A urine specimen must be provided within one hour after it has been asked for; two specimens are asked for, and it is the second specimen that is used as evidence in a subsequent trial. In all other respects the law relating to urine specimens is the same as the law relating to blood and breath specimens.

speeding *n.* Driving a motor vehicle at a speed in excess of that permitted. All vehicles adapted to carry more than seven passengers (apart from the driver) and all goods vehicles are restricted at all times to a maximum speed of 40 mph (unless they weigh less than 30 cwt unladen, in which case the maximum speed is 50 mph). Invalid carriages are restricted to 20 mph. Goods vehicles exceeding 3 tons unladen are restricted on motorways to 60 mph. Other vehicles are subject to speed limits determined by the class of road, unless road signs specifically indicate otherwise (i.e. 30 mph for restricted roads; 60 mph for single carriageways; 70 mph for dual carriageways and motorways).

The penalty for speeding is a fine, *endorsement (carrying 3 penalty points under the *totting-up system), and discretionary *disqualification. A person cannot be convicted of a speeding offence on the evidence of one witness alone, but the evidence of a single police officer reading his speedometer may be enough to secure a conviction. Speeding may itself be evidence of *careless and inconsiderate driving or *dangerous driving, but it is an offence in its own right even if it caused no danger and the driver was not in any way at fault. Speeding offences are subject to the requirement of a *notice of intended prosecution.

spent conviction A conviction that, after a specified number of years known as the **rehabilitation period**, may in all subsequent civil proceedings be treated as if it had never existed. The length of the rehabilitation period depends on the gravity of the offence, and some convictions are not subject to rehabilitation (e.g. when the sentence was life imprisonment). Dismissal from a job on the grounds of an undisclosed spent conviction may amount to *unfair dismissal. Similarly, to deny that one has been convicted if the conviction is spent does not amount to *perjury or *deception. Malicious publication of statements about a person's spent convictions can make the publisher liable for defamation, even if the statements are true. The provisions relating to spent convictions do not apply in criminal proceedings, but counsel and the court should, as far as possible, avoid referring to a spent conviction and references to it in open court may only be made with express leave of the judge in the interests of justice. A spent conviction in a record should be marked as such. *See also* CRIMINAL RECORDS AGENCY.

spes successionis [Latin: hope of succeeding] *See* POSSIBILITY.

split order Formerly, an order for custody of a child made by divorce courts, granting legal custody to one parent and care and control to the other. It was made obsolete by the Children Act 1989. *See* PARENTAL RESPONSIBILITY; SECTION 8 ORDERS.

split trial A trial in the *High Court (or, exceptionally, in the county courts) in which the issues of liability and amount of damages are tried separately.

springing use Formerly, a *use that arose on the occurrence of a future event. If property was given to X to the use of A when A married, A had a springing use that arose on his marriage.

spying (espionage) *n.* Obtaining or passing on to an enemy information that might prejudice the safety or interests of the state or be useful to an enemy. *See* OFFICIAL SECRETS.

squatter *n.* A person unlawfully occupying land. *See* ADVERSE OCCUPATION; ADVERSE POSSESSION; TRESPASS.

squatter's title *See* ADVERSE POSSESSION.

S1 Statement *See* WRITTEN STATEMENT OF TERMS OF EMPLOYMENT.

stag *n.* A speculator who applies for a new issue of securities in a public company with the intention of making a quick profit by reselling them if they increase in value within a few days of issue. This will only occur if the issue is oversubscribed, i.e. if there are more applicants for shares than there are shares available.

stakeholder pension A new type of low-cost pension, available from 6 April

2001. Employers with five or more employees may have to make a stakeholder pension available to their staff. Employers can choose to do this from 6 April 2001, and they must do this by 8 October 2001. Stakeholder pensions are also available from authorized financial institutions, such as insurance companies, banks, and building societies. Stakeholder pension providers can only charge a maximum of 1% of the value of the pension fund each year to manage the fund, plus costs and charges (such as stamp duty). Any extra services and any extra charges not provided for by law, such as advice on choosing a pension or life assurance cover, must be optional. All stakeholder schemes will accept contributions of as little as £20, payable weekly, monthly, or at less regular intervals. The scheme must be run by trustees or by an authorized stakeholder manager.

stakeholder's interpleader *See* INTERPLEADER.

stalking Persistent threatening behaviour by one person against another. The Protection from Harassment Act 1997 creates two offences relating to stalking. If the harasser's behaviour makes the victim fear for his or her safety, the maximum penalty is five years' imprisonment and/or an unlimited fine. When the behaviour does not lead to a fear of violence but does cause distress, the maximum penalty is six months in prison and/or a fine of up to £5000. The behaviour must have taken place on more than one occasion and the prosecution must show that a reasonable person would realize that the behaviour would have the effect of causing the victim to fear violence or feel harassed. Both offences are immediately arrestable without a warrant, and the police have power to search the harasser's property. The courts may make a restraining order immediately after convicting a person of either of the two offences. In Scotland the common law has always provided protection against stalking through the offence of breach of the peace. *See also* MOLESTATION.

stamp duty A tax payable on certain legal documents specified by statute. It can take the form either of a fixed duty, in which the same amount is payable on all documents of the same kind, or an *ad valorem* duty, when the amount of duty varies according to the value of the transaction effected by the document. Documents that are insufficiently or improperly stamped cannot be admitted as evidence in civil proceedings and they are therefore legally unenforceable. Documents must be sent for stamping within certain time limits to avoid incurring penalties. Stamp duty is controlled by the Inland Revenue. Stamp duty is payable on all transfers of land at 0% up to and including a value of £60,000; 1% if the value of the transfer is over £60,000 but not more than £250,000, 3% on transfers over £250,000 but less than £500,000, and 4% above £500,000. The rates on other types of property, including leases and stocks and shares, also vary with the value.

standard basis (of assessment of costs) *See* COSTS.

standard-form contract A commercial contract (e.g. a routine contract of carriage or insurance) that is concluded on terms issued by the offeror in standard form and allows for no effective negotiation. In French law such a contract is known as a ***contrat d'adhésion***.

standard investment criteria *See* GENERAL POWER OF INVESTMENT.

standard of proof The degree of proof required for any fact in issue in litigation, which is established by assessing the evidence relevant to it. In criminal cases the standard is *proof beyond reasonable doubt (*see also* BURDEN OF PROOF); in civil cases (including divorce petitions) the standard is proof on a balance of probabilities.

standing civilian court A court, provided for by the Armed Forces Act 1976, for the trial outside the UK of lesser offences committed by certain civilians, e.g. the families of servicemen (*see* SERVICE LAW). The Secretary of State for Defence (with the approval of the Lord Chancellor) specifies which areas such courts serve and draws up panels of serving officers and civilians to sit as assessors. The Lord Chancellor appoints legally qualified persons to act as magistrates in the courts.

standing committee A committee of the House of Commons appointed to take the committee stage of public Bills allotted to it by the government. There are about 8 such committees (the number varies according to need), each consisting of between 16 and 50 members who are nominated by a Committee of Selection to reflect the political composition of the House as a whole. *Compare* COMMITTEE OF THE WHOLE HOUSE.

standing mute The refusal of the defendant in a trial on indictment to plead to the indictment. A jury, drawn from any 12 people who happen to be present, must be empanelled to say whether the defendant is **mute of malice** (i.e. is wilfully refusing to plead) or is **mute by visitation of God** (i.e. is suffering from some physical or mental impairment that is preventing him from pleading). None of the jurors may be challenged by the defendant. If the verdict of the jury is mute of malice, a plea of *not guilty is entered; if mute by visitation of God, the jury must consider whether the defendant is *unfit to plead.

A person who is merely deaf and dumb may plead to an indictment through an interpreter. *See also* UNFIT TO PLEAD.

stare decisis [Latin: to stand by things decided] A maxim expressing the underlying basis of the doctrine of *precedent, i.e. that it is necessary to abide by former precedents when the same points arise again in litigation.

state *n.* A sovereign and independent entity capable of entering into relations with other states (*compare* PROTECTED STATE) and enjoying *international legal personality. To qualify as a state, the entity must have: (1) a permanent population (although, as in the case of the Vatican or Nauru, this may be very small); (2) a defined territory over which it exercises authority (although its borders, as in the case of Israel, need not be defined or undisputed); (3) an effective government. There are currently over 180 states. When a new state comes into existence, it is automatically bound by the principles of international law.

For some purposes, entities that do not normally qualify as fully fledged states may nonetheless be treated as such. Liechtenstein, for example, was refused admission as a state to the League of Nations (and did not become a member of the United Nations until 1990), but is a party to the Statute of the International Court of Justice, which is only open to states. *See also* BOUNDARY; JURISDICTION.

state aid Government assistance, often to local businesses, which is usually of a financial nature and discriminates against businesses trying to compete with them. Articles 87–89 of the *Treaty of Rome and provisions in the *Paris Treaty regulate the granting of such aid. Article 87 prohibits state aid, but the EU may approve certain types of state aid that are beneficial. About 30 cases a year are challenged by the European Commission under these provisions.

State Earnings Related Pension Scheme (SERPS) A scheme run by the UK government to provide a pension for employees in addition to the state retirement *pension. Contributions are made through national insurance payments. Those wishing to contract out of SERPS may subscribe to a personal pension scheme. SERPS is expected to be reformed in September 2002, to provide more generous benefits for certain groups, such as the disabled. This will be called the **State Second Pension**.

statement of affairs 1. A document that must be prepared by a debtor after a *bankruptcy order has been made against him except when the bankruptcy order was made on his own petition or when the court excuses him. It gives details of his assets, debts and liabilities, the names and addresses of his creditors, and what securities they hold. The debtor must send the statement to the official receiver, and the creditors are entitled to inspect it. A debtor who wrongly fails to submit a statement of affairs is guilty of *contempt of court. *See also* BANKRUPTCY. **2.** *See* VOLUNTARY WINDING-UP.

statement of arrangement for children A statement of proposed arrangements for the children of divorcing parents, which must be filed before a divorce is granted. The statement must be scrutinized by the court, which may make certain orders in respect of the children.

statement of case A formal written statement in a civil action served by each party on the other, containing the *allegations of fact that the party proposes to prove at trial (but not the evidence by which they are to be proved) and stating the remedy (if any) that the party claims in the action. Before the introduction of the *Civil Procedure Rules in 1999, statements of case were called **pleadings**. Statements of case include *claim forms, *particulars of claim, *defences, *counterclaims, and replies to defences. All statements must include a *Statement of Truth. Statements of case must contain only **material facts**, i.e. those facts essential to the party's claim or defence, and not the subordinate facts that are the means of proving them. It is customary to include the inferences of law that the party claims are to be drawn from the facts stated, although this is not essential. Allegations of law as such (legal arguments) are not permitted. Since the purpose of statements of case is to define clearly the issues in the action and to give the parties notice of the other side's case, sufficient details must be given of each allegation.

statement of claim Formerly, a pleading served by the claimant in an action begun by writ of summons in the High Court. Under the *Civil Procedure Rules, statements of claim are now known as *particulars of claim.

Statement of Objections A document issued by the European Commission setting out the case against a business that has infringed the rules of competition law under *Articles 81 and 82 of the Treaty of Rome. The statement will set a reasonable time limit for a reply, which can be extended (about 2–3 months is the usual period initially given).

statement of reasons for dismissal A written notice of the reasons for an employee's dismissal or for the nonrenewal of a fixed-term contract. Under the terms of the Employment Rights Act 1996, a dismissed employee having one year's *continuous employment may demand such a statement from his employer and may complain to an employment tribunal if the statement is refused or not provided within 14 days. If an employee is dismissed during her pregnancy or after the birth of her child in circumstances in which her maternity leave period ends by reason of the dismissal, the employee is entitled to such a statement without making any request and irrespective of the period of continuous employment (*see* MATERNITY RIGHTS).

Statement of Truth (in civil proceedings) A statement made by a party (or his authorized agent, e.g. lawyer) that he believes the content of the document in which the Statement of Truth appears is true. The requirement of the Statement of Truth was the result of the *Civil Procedure Rules and seeks to avoid the need to swear affidavits in support of various statements made during a claim. Statements of Truth are required in *statements of case, witness statements, and experts' reports. The deliberate provision of false information in a Statement of Truth is a contempt of court.

statements of standard accounting practice (SSAP) Statements published by the Accounting Standards Board that define the principles on which a company's assets and liabilities should be valued and its profits and losses computed.

state of emergency *See* EMERGENCY POWERS.

state responsibility The obligation of a state to make reparation arising from a failure to comply with a legal obligation under international law. *See also* ESPOUSAL OF CLAIM.

State Second Pension *See* STATE EARNINGS RELATED PENSION SCHEME.

Stationery Office, The (tSO) The privatized body that, on 1 October 1996, took over the functions of *Her Majesty's Stationery Office (HMSO) in selling government and related legislative material. All Acts of Parliament and government regulations can be purchased from tSO. HMSO remains in public ownership; its functions include administration of Crown and Parliamentary copyright through its Copyright Unit.

status *n.* A person's legal standing or capacity. The term derives from Roman law, in which it referred to a person's freedom, citizenship, and family rights. Status is an index to legal rights and duties, powers, and disabilities.

statute *n. See* ACT OF PARLIAMENT.

statute-barred debt A debt that has not been recovered within the period allowed by the legislation relating to *limitation of actions. Such a debt can no longer be recovered by action. The limitation period for debts due on promises made by deed is 12 years from the date the debt became due. For other debts the limitation period is six years from the date the debt became due. However, in certain contracts of loan that do not provide for repayment of the debt by a fixed date and in which repayment is not conditional on a demand by the creditor, the six-year period will not start to run until the creditor makes a demand in writing for repayment of the debt.

statute book The entire body of existing statutes.

statute law The body of law contained in Acts of Parliament. *Compare* CASE LAW.

statutorily protected tenancy A tenancy that has *security of tenure and, in some cases, statutory control of rent.

statutory assignment *See* ASSIGNMENT.

statutory company A *company incorporated by the promotion of a private Act of Parliament. *Compare* REGISTERED COMPANY.

statutory corporation *See* PUBLIC CORPORATION.

statutory declaration A *declaration made in a prescribed form before a justice of the peace, notary public, or other person authorized to administer an oath. Statutory declarations are used in extrajudicial proceedings and not in court, but have similar effects to declarations made on oath.

statutory demand A standard form used for the enforcement of debts. It typically sets out a demand by a creditor to a debtor to honour payment of an amount owing. The amount may be due immediately or at a future date (if the creditor has reasonable grounds for believing that it will not be paid at this date). The demand will also specify a period of three weeks for repayment or other satisfactory solution. Failure to comply with the demand by the debtor will be evidence of an inability by the debtor to pay creditors and can be used to support a *compulsory winding-up petition.

Statutory Form of Conditions of Sale Standard terms of contract for the sale and purchase of land, published by the Lord Chancellor under the Law of Property Act 1925. They cover, for example, the vendor's obligations in proving his title to the land, the completion of the transaction, and the payment of interest by the purchaser if he fails to complete on the due date. The Statutory Form applies automatically to contracts made by correspondence subject to any express agreement between the parties, and any valid contract for the sale and purchase of land may be expressed to incorporate the Statutory Form.

statutory instrument Any *delegated legislation (not including subdelegated legislation) to which the Statutory Instruments Act 1946 applies. This includes (1) delegation made under powers conferred by an Act passed after 1947, either on the Crown or on a government minister, and expressed by that Act to be exercisable by Order in Council in the former case or by statutory instrument in the latter; or (2) delegation made after 1947 under powers conferred by an earlier Act and formerly governed by the Rules Publication Act 1893 (which was replaced by the 1946 Act and provided for the publication of delegated legislation to which it applied in an official series known as **statutory rules and orders**). Regulations or orders made before the 1946 Act came into force may still be statutory instruments if the power they exercise was a power to make statutory rules within the meaning of pre-existing legislation, which was duly conferred on a rule-making authority under that legislation.

The 1946 Act relates in part to the publicity to be given to statutory instruments, requiring them to be numbered, printed, and published by the Queen's printer. They are numbered consecutively for each calendar year in the order in which the printer receives them; for example, the first statutory instrument to be received in 1993 would be cited as "S.I. 1993 No. 1". Moreover, as a modification of the rule *ignorantia juris non excusat* (ignorance of the law is no excuse), the Act makes nonpublication a defence to proceedings for contravening a statutory instrument unless other adequate steps had been taken to bring it to the public notice. The Act is also concerned with certain aspects of parliamentary control. It standardizes negative resolution procedure for statutory instruments by providing that, if the enabling statute simply makes them subject to annulment by resolution of either House of Parliament, they are to be laid before Parliament for 40 days and liable to annulment during that period. It further provides that any statutory instrument required to be laid (either because of that rule or because the enabling statute expressly says so) must be laid before becoming operative unless there is good reason to the contrary (in which case, an explanation must be given to the Lord Chancellor and the Speaker). *See also* JOINT COMMITTEE ON STATUTORY INSTRUMENTS.

statutory interpretation *See* INTERPRETATION OF STATUTES.

statutory lives in being *See* RULE AGAINST PERPETUITIES.

statutory maternity pay *See* MATERNITY RIGHTS.

statutory owner A person having the powers of an immediate beneficiary of *settled land, where the beneficiary himself is under 18 or there is no immediate beneficiary (for example, in a discretionary settlement in which no beneficiary has been appointed). The statutory owner is either the person of full age on whom the powers are conferred by the settlement; the trustees of the settlement (*see* SETTLED LAND ACT TRUSTEES); or, in a settlement made by will on a beneficiary under 18, the testator's personal representatives until a vesting instrument has been effected.

statutory periodic tenancy A *periodic tenancy that comes into operation on the expiration of an *assured tenancy for a *fixed term unless that tenancy is terminated by a court order or *surrender of the tenancy. The statutory periodic tenancy is on the same terms as the fixed term tenancy before it expired, except for the condition for terminating the tenancy at the end of the term. However, the landlord or tenant can apply to a *rent assessment committee to vary the terms of the tenancy. *See also* ASSURED SHORTHOLD TENANCY.

statutory rules and orders *See* STATUTORY INSTRUMENT.

statutory sick pay (SSP) Weekly payments by employers to employees unable to work because of sickness; it is payable, after the first three days of sickness, for a period of up to 28 weeks, after which employees can claim *incapacity benefit. Employees who do not qualify for SSP include those with fixed contracts of no more than three months and recipients of any social security benefits during the previous eight weeks. Formerly all employers were entitled to an 80% reimbursement for SSP by the government, and smaller companies were entitled to full reimbursement after the first six weeks of each SSP claim. However, this position has been gradually altered since 1994. Currently in most cases no recoupment will be possible. The only exception is where an employer pays out, in any income-tax month, SSP exceeding 13% of his liability to pay national insurance contributions in that month. In such circumstances that excess can be recouped.

statutory tenancy A tenancy that comes into existence when the contractual element of a *protected tenancy is terminated and the former protected tenant continues to live in the property (a company cannot be a statutory tenant). A statutory tenancy continues only for as long as the tenant lives in the property (therefore it will end if the tenant attempts to sublet). When the tenant dies, however, the statutory tenancy can be transmitted to his spouse if she was living in the dwelling immediately before the tenant's death. If there is no spouse, the tenancy can be transferred to another member of the tenant's family who was living with him for the previous two years. This is known as a **statutory tenancy by succession**. The terms of a statutory tenancy are, in general, the same as those of the original contractual tenancy. If there is no provision for notice in the original tenancy, the tenant must give three months notice to terminate his tenancy. A landlord can terminate a statutory tenancy only by obtaining a court order for possession. Statutory tenancies are being phased out as no new protected tenancies can be created after the Housing Act 1988. *See* ASSURED TENANCY.

statutory trust Until 1997, a trust created by statute when land was held by trustees on trust pending its sale (*see* TRUST FOR SALE). Any income from the land prior to its sale and the proceeds of sale itself was held in trust by the trustees. Unless there was a contrary intention, the trustees had the right, at their discretion, to postpone sale. Since 1997, statutory trusts have been replaced by *trusts of land governed by the Trusts of Land and Appointment of Trustees Act 1996.

stay of execution An order suspending the *execution of the order of a court. In the High Court a stay of execution by writ of *fieri facias* may be granted subject to the condition that the debtor pays the judgment debt by specified instalments (unlike the county courts, the High Court has no other power to order the payment of judgment debts by instalments).

stay of proceedings An order by the court suspending proceedings, usually because of some misconduct by the claimant (e.g. in a claim for damages for personal injury, unreasonably refusing to attend for medical examination by a doctor nominated by the defendant).

step-parent *n.* A person who is married to the father or mother of a child but is not the natural parent of the child. A step-parent has no automatic legal status in relation to his or her step-children, but will usually qualify to apply, as of right, for a *section 8 order in respect of the child by virtue of being married to the child's natural parent. Step-parents may acquire *parental responsibility either by applying to court for a residence order (which automatically confers parental responsibility) or by applying to adopt the child together with the child's natural parent. There is, however, a policy of discouraging step-parent adoption since the effect will be to irrevocably sever the child's legal ties with its other natural parent.

stipendiary magistrate *See* DISTRICT JUDGE (MAGISTRATES' COURT).

stock *n.* **1.** A fixed-interest loan raised by the government or a local authority. **2.** Shares in a registered company that have been converted into a single holding with a nominal value equal to that of the total of the shares. For example, a holder of 100 shares of £1 each will have £100 stock after conversion. **3.** *See* LOAN CAPITAL.

Stock Exchange The International Stock Exchange of the UK and the Republic of Ireland Ltd: the body responsible for regulating the issue and marketing of company securities. Admission to the **Listed Market** must be sponsored by a member of the Stock Exchange and is available only to shares of large public companies that have published *accounts for the three years preceding the application and that have satisfied the listing rules (the *Yellow Book*). These rules ensure that sufficient information is supplied, both on admission and subsequently, to enable investors to assess the merits of the shares. Admission to the **Alternative Investment Market** (**AIM**) is available to smaller companies who meet the statutory requirements. Deals in listed shares will usually be arranged through a member of the Stock Exchange acting as a market intermediary and taking a commission. Some market intermediaries specialize in particular securities; intermediaries who arrange deals in these securities are called **matching brokers**; intermediaries who will themselves buy or sell the securities are called **market makers**, and the prices they quote are **quotations**.

stock transfer form *See* SHARE TRANSFER.

stop notice 1. A court procedure available to protect those who have an interest in shares but have not been registered as company members. The notice prevents the company from registering a transfer of the shares or paying a dividend upon them without informing the server of the notice. **2.** A notice served by a local planning authority when they consider that any activity specified in an *enforcement notice should be prevented before the time for compliance given by that notice. It takes effect on a date specified therein, which is 3 to 28 days after service, and a site notice may be posted, drawing attention to its provisions.

stoppage *in transitu* A remedy available to an *unpaid seller of goods when the buyer has become insolvent and the goods are still in course of transit. If the seller gives notice of stoppage to the carrier or other bailee of the goods, he is entitled to have them redelivered to him and may then retain possession of them until the price is paid or tendered. If the right is not exercised, the goods will fall into the insolvent buyer's estate and go towards satisfying his creditors generally.

stowaway *n.* A person who secretes himself upon a ship and goes to sea. This is a criminal offence under the Merchant Shipping Act 1894.

street offence Any offence relating to the use of public streets. Examples are *obstruction, failing to obey police regulations about movement of traffic or pedestrians, *kerb crawling, and *soliciting.

strict construction *See* INTERPRETATION OF STATUTES.

strict liability **1.** (in criminal law) Liability for a crime that is imposed without the necessity of proving *mens rea* with respect to one or more of the elements of the crime. There are few crimes of strict liability at common law but such crimes are often created by statute, particularly to control or regulate daily activities; examples include offences relating to the production and marketing of food and *offences relating to road traffic. The usual penalty for crimes of strict liability is a fine. Most crimes of strict liability do, however, require *mens rea* in respect of at least some of the elements of the crime. In some cases statute provides for strict liability, but then allows a defence if the accused can prove (*see* BURDEN OF PROOF) that he had no reason to know of or suspect certain facts, so that, in effect, the crime becomes one of *negligence. *Automatism is a defence to all crimes, including crimes of strict liability. **2.** (in tort) Liability for a wrong that is imposed without the claimant having to prove that the defendant was at fault. Strict liability is exceptional in the law of tort, but is imposed for torts involving dangerous animals (*see* CLASSIFICATION OF ANIMALS) and dangerous things (the rule in *Rylands* v *Fletcher*), *conversion, *defamation, *products liability, and some cases of *breach of statutory duty. It is no defence in these torts that the defendant took reasonable care to prevent damage, but various other defences are admitted.

strict settlement A trust conferring beneficial interests in land that render it *settled land, governed by the Settled Land Act 1925. Generally the purpose of a strict settlement is to create successive interests that will keep the land in the settlor's family. The usual form of marriage settlement gave a life interest to the husband with remainder (after provisions for the wife during widowhood and for younger children of the marriage) to the first and other sons in *tail, a further remainder to any daughters as tenants in common in tail, and a final remainder to the husband in fee simple. The beneficiaries under a strict settlement have equitable interests in the land. Since 1997, such settlements exist as a TRUST OF LAND.

strike *n.* A cessation of work or refusal to work by employees acting together in connection with a *trade dispute to secure better terms and conditions of employment for themselves and/or other workers. A trade union cannot call its members out on strike unless it has held a secret ballot and the majority agree to the action. Under terms of the Trade Union and Labour Relations (Consolidation) Act 1992 trade union ballots for industrial action must be fully postal and, if a ballot involves 50 or more members, it must be subject to independent scrutiny. Seven days' notice of the union's intention to ballot its members on industrial action must be given to the employer and the union must provide the employer with details of the ballot result and give him at least seven days' written notice of those members it intends to call out on strike. A strike ballot remains effective for four weeks. This period may be extended to eight weeks if the union and employer agree. The Trade Union and Labour Relations (Consolidation) Act 1992 provides for a "Citizen's Right" for any individual to sue the union if he is deprived (or likely to be deprived) of any goods or services because of unlawfully organized industrial action. Until recently a claimant suing under the "Citizen's Right" provision could seek financial assistance from the Commissioner for Protection Against Unlawful Action, but this office was abolished by the Employment Relations Act 1999. The functions of the Commissioner have been transferred to the *Certification Officer.

striking off **1.** The removal of a solicitor's name from the roll of solicitors of the Supreme Court, either at his request or for misconduct. **2.** A similar procedure in other professions (e.g. the erasure of a doctor's name from the register of general medical practitioners). **3.** The removal of a limited company from the companies register, often because it has failed to file accounts.

structured settlement A form of *settlement of action used in cases of serious personal injuries in which it is agreed that the injured person will receive, in addition to a lump sum for losses already suffered, further payments on a periodic basis to cover future needs. The periodic payments are funded by an annuity purchased by the defendant and can be index-linked to provide for inflation.

structure plan A written statement formulating a local planning authority's policy on development and land use, including environmental improvement and traffic management policy.

subdelegated legislation Legislation made under powers conferred by *delegated legislation or by subdelegated legislation itself (in which case it is technically sub-subdelegated legislation). Subdelegated legislation is quite common (as when the parent Act authorizes a minister to make regulations and these in turn authorize others to make orders), but sub-subdelegated legislation is rare (though examples have existed in wartime); the chain has not in practice been further extended. Subdelegated legislation is not subject to any form of parliamentary control but it is subject to judicial control by means of the doctrine of *ultra vires*.

subject to contract *See* ACCEPTANCE.

***sub judice* rule** **1.** A rule limiting comment and disclosure relating to judicial proceedings, in order not to prejudge the issue or influence the jury. *See* CONTEMPT OF COURT. **2.** A parliamentary practice in which the Speaker prevents any reference in questions or debates to matters pending decision in court proceedings (civil or criminal). In the case of civil proceedings, he has power to waive the rule if a matter of national interest is involved.

sublease (subtenancy, underlease) *n.* A *lease granted by a person who is himself a lessee of the same property. The sublease must be shorter than the main lease. Thus a lessee with a lease for 10 years can grant a sublease for a period up to 10 years less one day. The formalities for creating and terminating a sublease are the same as those for a lease. There is often a covenant in a lease prohibiting subletting. If a lessee sublets in breach of the covenant the sublease will be valid, but the landlord may have a right of *forfeiture of the lease. In some cases the lease specifies that the lessee may only sublet with the landlord's consent. In this case, the landlord may not withhold his consent unreasonably and he cannot charge a fee for giving his consent unless there is express provision for this in the lease. If the main lease is forfeited, any sublease automatically comes to an end. However, the surrender of a lease does not affect any sublease.

subletting *n.* The granting of a *sublease.

submortgage *n.* A mortgage of a mortgage. A **submortgagor** is a person who holds a mortgage over another's land and charges that mortgage as security for a debt he owes to a third party (the **submortgagee**). If the submortgagor defaults, the submortgagee may sell the mortgage (but not the land) and recover the debt from the proceeds.

subordinate legislation *See* DELEGATED LEGISLATION.

subornation *n.* Procuring another to commit an offence. Normally subornation is included in the offence of aiding, abetting, or procuring (*see* ACCESSORY), but there is a special statutory offence of **subornation of perjury**.

subpoena *n. See* WITNESS SUMMONS.

subrogation *n.* The substitution of one person for another so that the person substituted succeeds to the rights of the other. Thus an insurer who indemnifies his insured against the loss of goods may be subrogated to the insured person's rights against a third party whose negligence caused the loss.

subscribing witness A person who signs a written document as an attesting witness to the signature of another.

subsidiarity *n.* A principle of the European Union, introduced by Article 3A of the *Maastricht Treaty, ensuring that in areas which do not fall within the exclusive competence of the EU, it shall not take action unless the objectives of the proposed action cannot be adequately achieved by individual member states. Thus it provides for legislation at national level when EU measures are not required.

subsidiary company A company controlled by another company, its **holding** (or **parent**) **company**. For general purposes, such control is established when the holding company has a majority of the voting rights attached to its shares (either by virtue of its ownership of those shares or because of an agreement with other shareholders) or the right to appoint or remove a majority of its board of directors. If company A controls company B, which itself controls company C, then company C is the subsidiary of both company B and company A. For the purposes of *group accounts, a wider definition applies: the subsidiary need not be incorporated (*see* COMPANY) and control can also be established in other ways, e.g. when the holding company has the right, under the subsidiary's *articles or *memorandum of association, to exercise a dominant influence over it.

Substantial Acquisition Rules *See* SARS.

substantial damages *See* DAMAGES.

substantial performance *See* PERFORMANCE OF CONTRACT.

substantive law The part of the law that deals with rights, duties, and all other matters that are not matters purely of practice and procedure. *Compare* ADJECTIVE LAW.

substituted service The service of documents in civil litigation other than by *personal service or (when postal service is permitted) by post. An order of the court is required for substituted service, and the application for it must be supported by an *affidavit. It may take the form of service by letter, advertisement, or any other method likely to bring the proceedings to the attention of the defendant. Substituted service has all the effects of personal service. It is often sought against defendants who are deliberately evading personal service.

substitutional legacy A legacy that passes to descendants of a beneficiary who is named in a will if this beneficiary has predeceased the testator. *See also* REPRESENTATION.

subtenancy *n.* *See* SUBLEASE.

subtenant *n.* A tenant who holds a *sublease.

sub-trust (derivative trust) *n.* A trust created out of a trust. If A has an interest under a trust and declares himself trustee of the interest for B and C, B and C have interests under a subtrust as far as the original settlor is concerned.

succession *n.* **1.** The law and procedures under which beneficiaries become entitled to property under a testator's will or on intestacy. **2.** (in international law) The transfer of sovereignty over a territorial entity from one subject of international law (i.e. one state) to another. As a result of succession, an existing state becomes totally extinguished (as when Tanganyika and Zanzibar ceased to exist in 1964 on the formation of Tanzania) or a state transfers part of its territory to another state.

sue *vb.* To make a claim for a remedy in the civil courts by issuing court proceedings.

sufferance *n.* *See* TENANCY AT SUFFERANCE.

suicide *n.* The act of killing oneself intentionally. Since 1961 suicide itself is not a crime, but there is a special statutory crime (punishable by up to 14 years' imprisonment) of aiding, abetting, counselling, or procuring a suicide. In practice very few prosecutions are brought for this offence. Doing nothing to stop someone else from committing suicide is not abetting it, but euthanasia (mercy killing) in the form of giving assistance to the sufferer (rather than actually killing him) may amount to aiding. When two people agree that one of them shall kill the other and then commit suicide (a **suicide pact**), the one who does the killing is guilty, if he survives, not of murder but of manslaughter.

sui generis [Latin: of its own kind] Forming a class of its own; unique.

sui juris [Latin: of his own right] Describing the status of a person who is of full age and capacity. *Compare* ALIENI JURIS.

suit *n.* A court claim. The term is commonly used for any court proceedings although originally it denoted a suit in equity as opposed to an action at law. When a case is referred to as (for example) "Jones at the suit of Smith" (or "Jones a.t.s. Smith") Jones is the defendant in an action brought by Smith.

summary conviction A *conviction in a magistrates' court. The magistrates are the judges of both fact and law and must either convict the accused or dismiss the case. The usual form of words for a conviction is "We find the case proved", and a conviction may be returned on a simple majority verdict. Under the Magistrates' Courts Act 1980, the magistrates may remand the accused for a medical examination if they are satisfied that he has committed the act he is charged with, but are in doubt as to his mental condition and whether or not to make a hospital order. Such a finding has the force of a conviction for purposes of the accused's right to be granted bail.

summary financial statement A statement providing financial information about a company that is derived from its annual *accounts. *Listed companies may opt to supply this abbreviated form of the accounts to their members in place of the full accounts, but only if the members do not object.

summary judgment A procedure enabling a claimant in an action for debt or damages in the High Court to obtain judgment without the defendant being permitted to defend the action. It can be used in most actions except when these include a claim for *libel, *slander, *malicious prosecution, or *false imprisonment or an allegation of *fraud. Summary judgment will be entered on behalf of a claimant in those situations in which the court is satisfied that there is no real possibility of the defendant successfully defending himself against the claim. The procedure may also be invoked by the defendant in those situations in which it is accepted by the court that there is no real possibility of the claim succeeding.

summary offence An offence that can only be tried summarily, i.e. before magistrates. Most minor offences (e.g. common assault and battery) are summary. Prosecutions for all summary offences must be started within six months of the commission of the offence, unless statute expressly provides to the contrary. *Compare* INDICTABLE OFFENCE; OFFENCES TRIABLE EITHER WAY.

summary trial Trial by magistrates without a jury. All summary offences are tried in this way, as well as some *offences triable either way. The main procedural principles followed in *trial on indictment also apply to summary trial, but there are some differences of which the most important are as follows. (1) The accused does not usually have to be present at the hearing. (2) Objections cannot usually be made either to information laid before the magistrates or to a summons or warrant served on the defendant on the grounds of "defects of substance or form" (unless they are fundamental defects). (3) In the case of summary offences, the accused may send in a written plea of guilty, together with a statement of mitigation, and the case may then be tried without the prosecution or defence appearing.

summing up A judge's speech at the end of a trial by *jury, in which he explains to the jury what its functions are, directs the members of the jury on any relevant points of law, and summarizes all the evidence that has been given in the trial.

summons *n.* A court order to an individual to appear in court at a specified place and time. The term is used in criminal cases for appearance at a magistrates' court. Before the introduction of the *Civil Procedure Rules in 1999, it was used in civil cases for hearings in the county court and applications to a judge sitting in chambers about procedural matters prior to the court hearing. Such orders are now made by **application notice**. *See also* WITNESS SUMMONS.

Summons Production Centre (SPC) An organization within the administrative structure of the *county courts system for the production of summonses issued by large-scale users of the county court, particularly public utilities. It is located in Northampton.

Sunday trading The opening of shops for trading on a Sunday, which is governed by the Sunday Trading Act 1994 as consolidated in the Employment Rights Act 1996. Small shops may open at will on a Sunday. The 1994 Act repealed the Shops Act 1950, which prohibited large shops from Sunday trading. Large shops with a floor area over 280 square metres may now open on Sunday if notice is given to the local authority, provided that they open for no more than six hours beginning no earlier than 10.00 a.m. and ending no later than 6.00 p.m. These rules do not include Easter Sunday or Christmas Day when it falls on a Sunday. Local authorities may keep registers of large shops open for Sunday trading; these are open to inspection. Certain large shops can open on a Sunday without the need to register, including farm shops, off-licences, motor and cycle suppliers, pharmacies, airport shops, shops at railway stations, motorway service areas, petrol-filling stations, shops supplying ships or aircrafts, stores selling at exhibitions, and shops occupied by people who observe the Jewish Sabbath (Saturday). Fines can be levied for breach of the requirements. The Act also controls noisy unloading on a Sunday.

Shopworkers who were taken on before 25 August 1994 (other than those employed for Sunday working only), and those who were taken on after that date who are not required by their contracts to work on Sundays, have a legal right to refuse to work on Sundays unless they have agreed to do so (for example, by signing an "opting-in notice").

superior court Any of the higher courts of the legal system, whose jurisdiction is not limited, for example, by geography or by value of the subject matter of the claim and whose decisions have weight as *precedents. In English law, the superior courts are the *House of Lords, the *Court of Appeal, the *High Court, and the *Crown Court, together with the *Judicial Committee of the Privy Council. Decisions of superior courts are not subject to judicial review by the High Court. *Compare* INFERIOR COURT.

superior orders A plea that certain conduct does not constitute a crime because it was committed in obedience to the orders of a superior (usually a superior officer in the armed forces). It could arise, for example, on the unjustified shooting of a rioter when the military are restoring order. UK law does not recognize the plea as a defence in itself. If an order is unlawful, a soldier's duty is to disobey it. If, however, an unlawful order is not manifestly so, the plea could be raised as establishing that the soldier did not have the necessary *mens rea*.

supervision order 1. An order of the court placing a child under the supervision of a local authority or a probation officer whose duty it is to advise and assist the child. The court can make a supervision order only if certain *threshold criteria are satisfied. A supervisor may have wide powers, for example to ensure that the child lives as directed or attends specified activities; in addition, the supervisor may apply for an **education supervision order** if the child is of compulsory school age and not receiving adequate education. A supervision order does not confer *parental responsibility and initially lasts only for one year with a possible extension for up to a maximum of three years. *Compare* CARE ORDER. **2.** *See* SUSPENDED SENTENCE.

support funding *See* COMMUNITY LEGAL SERVICE.

suppression of documents The dishonest destruction, hiding, or defacing of any valuable security (i.e. almost any document creating, extinguishing, or transferring a right in money or property), will or similar document, or any original document (but not a copy) belonging to or filed in any court or governmental department. If done with the purpose of gaining as a result, or causing loss to someone else, it is an offence punishable by up to seven years' imprisonment. *See also* FORGERY.

supra protest *See* ACCEPTANCE SUPRA PROTEST.

supremacy *n.* The prevalence of one law or document over another that conflicts with it. Within the European Union, EU law prevails over national law; there are many instances of national law being overturned by the *European Court of Justice when a member state has ignored provisions of the Treaty of Rome. However, in certain areas, for example competition law, national laws may be permitted when they are stricter than provisions in EU law.

Supreme Court of Judicature A court created by the Judicature Acts 1873–75 to take over the jurisdiction of all the higher courts, other than the House of Lords, existing at that time. It does not sit as a single court but comprises the *High Court of Justice, the *Court of Appeal, and the *Crown Court. Its practice and procedure are regulated by the *Civil Procedure Rules.

Supreme Court Rule Committee *See* RULES OF THE SUPREME COURT.

surety *n.* **1.** Security in the form of money to be forfeited upon nonappearance in court, offered either by the defendant himself or by other people of suitable financial resources, character, and relationship to the defendant. **2.** Any person who offers security for another. *See* BAIL; RECOGNIZANCE.

surname *n.* A family name. Upon marriage a wife is entitled to take her husband's surname (and title or rank) and to continue using it after his death or divorce (unless she uses it for fraudulent purposes), although she is not obliged to do so. A legitimate child, by custom, takes the name of his father and an illegitimate child that of his mother (although the father's name may be entered on the birth registration if both parents agree or an affiliation order names the man as the putative father). Upon adoption a child automatically takes the name of his adoptive parents. *See also* CHANGE OF NAME.

surprise *n.* (in court procedure) An unexpected event that causes a party to be put at some disadvantage in litigation. Many rules of pre-trial procedure are designed to prevent surprise; for example, any matter that might otherwise take the opposite party by surprise must be specifically pleaded, and there are rules concerning the exchange of the reports of expert witnesses. Surprise is an argument often put forward by parties seeking to resist amendments of statements of case and other documents; if justifiably raised at trial, it may result in an adjournment being offered to the disadvantaged party.

surrebutter *n.* Formerly, a pleading served by a claimant in reply to the defendant's *rebutter. Such a pleading was very rare in modern practice and no longer exists under the *Civil Procedure Rules.

surrejoinder *n.* Formerly, a pleading served by a claimant in answer to the defendant's *rejoinder. Such a pleading was very rare in modern practice and no longer exists under the *Civil Procedure Rules.

surrender of tenancy The termination of a *lease, which occurs when a tenant gives up his interest to his landlord. Surrender can be express or implied. Express surrender is usually in the form of a deed. When the lease is for less than three years, no deed is needed provided that the tenant signs a written agreement to surrender. Implied surrender occurs when the actions of both parties show that they consider the lease to be at an end; for example, when the tenant gives up possession and the landlord reoccupies the property.

surrender to custody To give oneself into the custody of the court or police at an appointed time and place. It is the primary condition of all releases on *bail to surrender to custody; in order to achieve this, the court may attach conditions to the bail, such as the provision of a *surety or restrictions on movement. Failure to surrender to custody is an offence (*see* ABSCONDING). The police may arrest without warrant anyone whom they reasonably believe is not going to surrender to custody or anyone whom they have been informed by a surety (who wishes to be relieved of his undertaking) is not going to surrender.

surrogacy *n.* The role of a woman (a **surrogate mother**) who is commissioned to bear a child by a married couple unable to have children themselves. The pregnancy is usually initiated through artificial insemination of the surrogate mother by the husband, although sometimes the wife's eggs are used; in this case the surrogate has no genetic relationship to the child, being simply a host for the embryo. The Surrogacy Arrangements Act 1985 prohibits commercial agencies from engaging women to act as surrogate mothers. Breach of the prohibition is punishable with a fine of up to £2000 or three months' imprisonment. Surrogate mothers and commissioning parents are exempt from liability. Advertising surrogacy services is punishable with a similar maximum fine. *See also* SECTION 30 ORDER.

surveillance *n.* Keeping watch on a suspect. The Police Act 1997 provides a formal system for authorization of intrusive surveillance operations by chief police officers. A team of independent commissioners oversees the arrangements and investigates complaints. Police and customs officials are also required to seek prior approval from a commissioner for authorizations in particularly sensitive cases – such as those involving legal *privilege, for example – except in cases of emergency. *See also* ELECTRONIC SURVEILLANCE.

survival of cause of action on death At common law all causes of action in personal actions (i.e. contract and tort) died with the person in whom they were vested (*actio personalis moritur cum persona*). By statute, however, all such causes of actions, except for defamation and claims for certain types of loss, survive against or for the benefit of the deceased. *See also* FATAL ACCIDENTS.

survivorship *n. See* COMMORIENTES; RIGHT OF SURVIVORSHIP.

sus law The law that formerly empowered the police to arrest any reputed thief or suspected person found loitering with intent to commit an arrestable offence. This law caused much public concern and was abolished by the Criminal Attempts Act 1981. *See* INTERFERING WITH VEHICLES.

suspended sentence A prison sentence that does not take effect immediately. When a person is sentenced to imprisonment for less than two years, the court may, in exceptional circumstances, order that he should not actually be imprisoned unless he commits another offence within a specified operational period of between one and two years. If the suspended sentence is for a prison term of more than six months, the court may also make a **suspended sentence supervision order**, placing the offender under the care of a probation officer. If the offender fails to comply with the terms of such an order he is liable to a fine.

Formerly, when an offender had been sentenced to a term of imprisonment of more than three months but less than two years, and the court felt that it would not be right to suspend the whole of the sentence, it could instead make an order for a **partially suspended sentence**, under which the offender served part of the sentence. Partially suspended sentences were abolished by the Criminal Justice Act 1991.

symbolic delivery *See* DELIVERY.

synallagmatic contract *See* BILATERAL CONTRACT.

synod *n.* A deliberative assembly of the clergy. *See* CHURCH OF ENGLAND.

Table A Model *articles of association that apply to companies limited by shares unless other articles excluding or modifying them are delivered to the Companies Registry when the company is registered. The company is subject to the Table A in force at the time it was registered. **Tables B, C, D, E,** and **F** specify forms of *memorandum of association and *articles of association to be adopted by particular types of company.

tacking *n.* Before 1926, the right of a mortgagee who made a second advance to the mortgagor to attach his second advance to the first one so that it had priority over the claims of any intervening mortgagee, provided that he has received no notice of any intervening mortgage. This exception to the rules relating to *priority of mortgages was abolished in 1925.

tail *n.* An *entailed interest.

tail general An *entailed interest under which the class of descendants who can succeed to the land is not limited to the issue of a specified spouse of the first tenant in tail. *Compare* TAIL SPECIAL.

tail male An *entailed interest under which only male descendants of the original tenant in tail can succeed to the land. If the male line dies out, the land goes to the person next entitled in *remainder or in *reversion. The interest may be general or special: *see* TAIL GENERAL; TAIL SPECIAL.

tail special An *entailed interest under which only the descendants of the first tenant in tail and a specified spouse can succeed to the land; for example, when land is settled on "John and the heirs of his body begotten on Mary". *Compare* TAIL GENERAL.

takeover *n.* The acquisition of control by one company over another, usually smaller, company (the **target company**). This is usually achieved (1) by buying shares in the target company with the agreement of all its members (if they are few) or of only its *controllers; (2) by purchases on the *Stock Exchange; or (3) by means of a *takeover bid. *Compare* MERGER. *See also* CITY CODE ON TAKEOVERS AND MERGERS; CONCERT PARTY; DAWN RAID.

takeover bid A technique for effecting a *takeover or a *merger. The bidder makes an offer to the members of the target company to acquire their shares (either for cash or in exchange for shares in the bidding company) in the hope of receiving sufficient acceptances to obtain voting control of the target company. Unless there is a *scheme of arrangement – and providing that the court does not order otherwise – if members holding not less than 90% in value of the shares involved in the bid accept the offer, the bidding company can compulsorily acquire the shares of the remaining members.

taking at sea A risk commonly covered in policies of marine insurance, which includes seizure or capture of a vessel by enemies or pirates.

talaq *n.* An Islamic divorce, usually effected by a triple declaration ("I divorce you") by the husband to the wife in front of witnesses. In some Moslem countries this may be done informally; in other countries it must be pronounced before an authorized officer of the court. It may also be effected by a written **talaqnama**. *See also* EXTRAJUDICIAL DIVORCE.

tangible property *Property that has a physical existence, e.g. chattels and land but not *choses in action nor incorporeal *hereditaments (which are **intangible property**).

tax *n.* A compulsory contribution to the state's funds. It is levied either directly on the taxpayer by means of *income tax, *capital gains tax, *inheritance tax, and *corporation tax; or indirectly through tax on purchases of goods and services (*see* VALUE-ADDED TAX) and through various kinds of duty, e.g. *road tax, *stamp duty, and duties on betting and gaming.

taxable person *See* VALUE-ADDED TAX.

taxable supply *See* VALUE-ADDED TAX.

taxation of costs *See* ASSESSMENT OF COSTS.

tax avoidance The lawful arrangement or planning of one's affairs so as to reduce liability to tax. *Compare* TAX EVASION.

tax evasion Any illegal action taken to avoid the lawful assessment of taxes; for example, by concealing or failing to declare income. *Compare* TAX AVOIDANCE.

Tax Exempt Special Savings Account (Tessa) A savings account, introduced with effect from January 1991, that is exempt from *income tax and *capital gains tax. The exemption is limited to an amount of £9000 in total, and there is a limit of £3000 on investments in the first year and £1800 in each subsequent year (the maximum of £1800 can only be invested in the fifth year if a reduced amount was invested in one of the previous years). Savers with a matured Tessa could invest all the capital (i.e. up to £9000) from this account in a new Tessa during the first year, provided the new account was opened within six months of the maturity date of the old Tessa. There are restrictions on permissible withdrawals from the account. No new Tessas can be opened after 5 April 1999, but existing Tessas continue until maturity; the capital of a matured Tessa can be transferred to an *Individual Savings Account (ISA) without affecting the annual ISA allowance, provided that this is done within six months of the maturity date of the Tessa.

taxing master *See* COSTS OFFICER.

taxing statute An Act of Parliament that imposes tax. Any ambiguity is construed in favour of the taxpayer (*see* INTERPRETATION OF STATUTES).

tax point The date on which a taxable supply becomes liable for *value-added tax. The rate of tax chargeable on the supply is the rate in force at the tax point, and the supply must be accounted for in the tax period in which the tax point occurs. If the supply is a straightforward sale of goods, the tax point is normally the date on which the customer takes possession of the goods. For the supply of services, the tax point is normally the date on which the service is completed. In the case of hirings, rentals, continuous or metered supplies (e.g. electricity), and supplies that are subject to progress payments, the tax point is either the date on which an invoice is issued or the date on which payment is received, whichever is earlier. If the supplier issues a tax invoice, this must show the tax point.

tax year (fiscal year) The year of assessment for *income tax and *capital gains tax purposes. It runs from 6 April to 5 April in the following year. *See also* FINANCIAL YEAR.

Technology and Construction Court *See* OFFICIAL REFEREE.

technology transfer The licensing of *intellectual property. EU regulation 240/96 provides *block exemption from *Article 81 (competition law) for certain categories of patent and *knowhow licence (and also for trade mark, design, copyright, and other intellectual property licences that are ancillary to a patent or knowhow licence). The regulation, which replaced earlier legislation on 1 April 1996, applies to new licences entered into after that date and sets out those provisions in licensing agreements that are permitted, those that are exempted, and those that are prohibited (blacklisted), the presence of which prevents the exemption from applying. The regulation also provides that agreements that do not contain blacklisted provisions but otherwise do not come within the regulation may be notified to the Commission for individual exemption; if no objection is raised by the Commission within four months, the agreement may be deemed acceptable (this is called the **opposition procedure**).

telephone tapping Secretly listening to telephone conversations by interfering with the line. It is illegal except when authorized by the Home Secretary. *See also* ELECTRONIC SURVEILLANCE.

teleworking *n.* A form of employment in which employees use information technology to enable them to work mainly from home. The advantages to the employer are the elimination of transport problems, reduction in office overheads, and increased flexibility. Teleworkers are distinguished from **outworkers** in that the former are engaged in white-collar work, as opposed to the manual tasks performed by poorly paid female outworkers.

tenancy *n.* Broadly, the interest of one who holds land by any right or title. The term is often used in a more restricted sense, however, for the arrangement in which the owner (the *landlord) allows another person (the tenant) to take possession of the land for an agreed period, usually in return for rent. There are many ways of establishing a tenancy, from a formal *lease by deed to an informal verbal arrangement. The latter is legally binding on the parties if it satisfies the requirements for an *agreement for a lease. A tenancy can also come into existence through statute law (*see* STATUTORY PERIODIC TENANCY).

The different kinds of tenancy are: tenancy for a *fixed term, *joint tenancy, *periodic tenancy, *tenancy at sufferance, *tenancy at will, *tenancy by estoppel, and *tenancy in common. The terms and conditions of tenancies vary considerably according to the kind of tenancy and the wishes of the parties. There are many statutory controls which affect tenancies, particularly in relation to *security of tenure and rent. *See also* ASSURED TENANCY.

tenancy at sufferance A tenancy that arises when a tenant is *holding over and the landlord has not indicated whether or not he agrees to the tenant's continued occupation. If the landlord gives his express agreement, the tenancy becomes a *tenancy at will.

tenancy at will A tenancy that can be terminated by the landlord or the tenant at any time. A tenancy at will usually arises by implication, when the owner of land allows a person to occupy it although he has no *fixed term, *periodic tenancy, or *licence (for example, when a landlord agrees to the tenant *holding over). More rarely, a tenancy at will may be created by express agreement. If the landlord starts to accept rent on a regular basis, an ordinary *periodic tenancy is created. A tenant who holds over after a fixed-term *assured tenancy expires may have a *statutory periodic tenancy. A tenancy at will of business premises does not have the statutory protection given to a *business tenancy. In the case of residential premises, however, the usual statutory protection from *eviction will apply. A tenancy at will can be terminated by the landlord demanding possession or if either he or the tenant dies or parts with his interest in the land.

tenancy by estoppel A tenancy that exists despite the fact that the person who granted it had no legal right to do so. Such a tenancy is binding on the landlord and tenant but not on anyone else. If the landlord subsequently acquires the right to grant the tenancy, it automatically becomes a full legal tenancy.

tenancy for years A tenancy for a *fixed term.

tenancy from year to year A yearly *periodic tenancy.

tenancy in common Equitable ownership of land by two or more persons in equal or unequal *undivided shares. Each co-owner may sell or dispose of his share by will, and a share does not pass automatically by the right of survivorship on the death of a co-owner but forms part of his estate (*compare* JOINT TENANCY). Under the Law of Property Act 1925 the legal estate is held by the co-owners as joint tenants on trust for themselves as equitable tenants in common, and a *trust of land is implied.

tenant *n.* A person who is granted a *lease or a *tenancy. A tenant need not be an individual; for example, a company can be a tenant.

tenantable repair The maintenance of a property in a condition fit for letting to a tenant. The phrase is sometimes used in a *covenant to repair. The use of the word "tenantable" has no significant effect on the parties' usual obligations under the covenant.

tenant for life (life tenant) A person owning land for an equitable interest that subsists for the whole of his life but terminates on his death (*see also* LIFE INTEREST). The statutory powers of a tenant for life are laid down by the Settled Land Act 1925 (*see* SETTLED LAND). *See also* TRUST OF LAND.

tenant in tail A person entitled in possession or on the death of his ancestor to an *entailed interest.

tenant in tail after possibility of issue extinct The interest of an original tenant in *tail special when the specified spouse has died and there are no heirs entitled to succeed to the entailed interest. The tenant in tail retains his powers under the Settled Land Act 1925 (*see* SETTLED LAND) but cannot bar the entail (*see* ENTAILED INTEREST). This position cannot arise when the land is held in tail general, since while the tenant in tail lives there is always a possibility he may have children by another wife.

tenant *pur autre vie* *See* ESTATE PUR AUTRE VIE.

tenant's fixtures Fixtures attached to rented property by a tenant that the tenant is entitled to remove at the end of the tenancy. These are: *trade fixtures, ornamental and domestic fixtures (such as blinds and mirrors) whose removal does no serious damage, and (subject to certain statutory rules) agricultural fixtures. Tenants are not entitled to remove any other fixtures.

tender *n.* **1.** An offer to supply (or to purchase) goods or services. Normally a tender must be accepted to create a contract, except when the invitation to tender states unequivocally that the lowest (or highest) tender will be accepted. If the tender is to supply goods as required by the other party, it may be a standing offer and creates contracts as and when particular orders are placed. Whether or not the tenderer can withdraw from supplying future orders depends upon the terms of the tender, in particular whether the tenderer binds himself (for consideration) to execute all orders. **2.** An offer of performance, acceptance of which requires the concurrence of the other party, e.g. the tender of the price of goods by a buyer to a seller.

tender before action (tender before claim) A *defence to a claim for a debt or liquidated demand alleging that the defendant offered to pay the sum claimed before the claimant began his action. In order to rely upon this defence the defendant must pay the sum tendered into court and give notice of the payment to the claimant. *See also* PART 36 OFFERS AND PAYMENTS.

tender offer An offer of a company's securities to the public (*see* FLOTATION) at a uniform price (above a specified minimum) that is determined by the bids received and ensures that all the securities are taken up.

tenure *n.* Under the *feudal system, the relationship between lord and tenant, which determined the conditions under which the land was held. Today the term is used to indicate the nature of a legal estate in land, i.e. freehold or leasehold. The only tenurial relationship of practical significance in modern law is that of landlord and tenant (or leasehold). *See also* SECURITY OF TENURE.

term *n.* **1.** Originally, any of four periods of the year during which judicial business had to be transacted. For this purpose terms were abolished by the Judicature Acts 1873–75, and the legal year is now divided into *sittings and *vacations. In the *Inns of Court the year is still divided into terms that have the same names as the court sittings but are shorter. A student **keeps term** as part of the qualification for call to the Bar by dining in his Inn on a specified number of occasions during the term. **2.** Any provision forming part of a contract. A term may be either a *condition, a warranty, or an *innominate term, depending on its importance, and either an *express term or an *implied term, depending on its form. **3.** The duration of a leasehold interest in land. *See* TERM OF YEARS.

term for years *See* TERM OF YEARS.

term of years (term for years) An interest in land that subsists for or by reference to some specified period of time. It includes interests subsisting for less than a year (e.g. a lease for six months) and periodic tenancies (e.g. a weekly, monthly, or yearly tenancy determinable by notice to quit). It can also include time-share agreements, e.g. of one specified week in each of a number of years. The commencement date and maximum duration of the term must be identifiable before the lease takes effect. *See also* TERM OF YEARS ABSOLUTE.

term of years absolute A leasehold estate in land: a *term of years that may or may not be brought to an end by notice, forfeiture, or any other event except the death of any person. Thus a lease "to X for 25 years if Y shall so long live" is not a valid term of years absolute. Under the Law of Property Act 1925 a term of years absolute can exist as a *legal estate provided it is created in the required manner, i.e. by deed in the case of a term of three years or more.

terra nullius *See* DISCOVERY.

territoriality *n.* (in international law) The principle that states should not exercise their jurisdiction outside the area of their territory. They are entitled, however, to exercise jurisdiction within their territory over acts committed by their citizens outside their territory, and all states have jurisdiction over *offences against international law and order. The territory of a state for purposes of jurisdiction includes its ships and aeroplanes. A state may exercise jurisdiction over crimes that are either originated within its territory but completed outside or originated outside its territory and completed inside.

territorial limits The geographical limits within which an Act of Parliament operates, which include, in the UK, the territorial sea up to the 12-mile limit. The limits are restricted by international law (*see* SOVEREIGNTY OF PARLIAMENT).

territorial waters The band of sea between the limit of the *internal waters of a state (*see* BASELINE) and the *high seas, over which the state has certain specified rights. These rights are governed by a 1958 Geneva Convention, which is taken to represent the position under customary international law. New rules were proposed in a 1982 United Nations Convention on the Law of the Sea (*see* LAW OF THE SEA). A coastal state exercises sovereignty over its territorial waters, which includes, in particular, the following. (1) An exclusive right to fish and to exploit the resources of the seabed and subsoil of the seabed and exclusive use of the airspace above the territorial sea. (2) The exclusive right to use the territorial waters to transport people and goods from one part of the state to another. (3) The right to enact laws concerning navigation, immigration, customs dues, and health, which bind all foreign ships. (4) The right to ask a warship that ignores navigation regulations to leave the territorial waters. (5) Certain powers of arrest over merchant ships and people on board and jurisdiction to try crimes committed on board such ships within the territorial waters. (6) The right to exclude fighting in the territorial waters during a war in which the coastal state is neutral. All foreign ships, however, have a right of **innocent passage** through the territorial sea, i.e. the right to pass through, provided they do not prejudice the peace, security, or good order of the coastal state (submarines must navigate on the surface). *See also* HOT PURSUIT, RIGHT OF.

The extent of the territorial sea is usually measured from the low-tide mark on the shore, but in estuaries and small bays it is measured from a **closing line** between two points on the shore, which delimits the state's internal waters. The width of the territorial sea is a matter of dispute in international law. Traditionally it has been fixed at 3 nautical miles (*see* CANNON-SHOT RULE), but many states have claimed 12 miles or more, and this will probably become the normal width. The Territorial Sea Act 1987 fixes the territorial waters of the UK at 12 nautical miles. Beyond the territorial sea, states have a **contiguous zone**, not exceeding 24 nautical miles, in which they may exercise jurisdiction over certain infringements of their customs, fiscal, immigration, or sanitary regulations. In recent years many states (including the UK) have also claimed **exclusive fishery zones** extending 200 miles beyond the low-tide mark. The UK is subject to the EU's *Common Fisheries Policy in relation to fishing. *See also* EXCLUSIVE ECONOMIC ZONE.

terrorism *n.* The use or threat of violence for political ends, including putting the public in fear. The Terrorism Act 2000 has abolished all the previous statutory provisions relating to terrorism, apart from a number of specific provisions that continue to exist under the Northern Ireland (Emergency Provisions) Act 1996, the Terrorism (Temporary Provisions) Act 1989, and the Criminal Justice (Terrorism and Conspiracy) Act 1998. The Terrorism Act 2000 defines terrorism in section 1 as (a) the use or threat of action that involves serious violence against a person or serious damage to property, endangers a person's life, creates a serious risk to the health or safety of the public or a section of the public, or is designed to interfere with or disrupt an electronic system, or (b) the use or threat of violence designed to influence the government or intimidate the public or a section of the public: in both cases the use or threat of such action or violence is made for the purpose of advancing a political, religious, or ideological cause. The Act also provides that the action referred to includes that taken within as well as outside the United Kingdom. The Act contains provisions that allow for certain organizations to be declared as **proscribed organizations**. It then becomes an offence to be a member of such an organization. The Act also contains detailed provisions as to property defined as being "terrorist property" and the forfeiture of such property. There are detailed provisions relating to the investigation of terrorist activities that grant the police and security services special and extra powers. These include special powers to stop and search, detain, and interrogate those suspected of involvement in terrorist activities.

The Act was a further attempt at bringing UK legislation into line with the 1977 European Convention on the Suppression of Terrorism. This was needed in order to ensure that persons within the UK who were suspected of terrorist activity in other parts of Europe could be successfully extradited to face trial in those other states. Much of the legislation is directed at the situation in Northern Ireland. However, this is likely to change as the focus now shifts to dealing with international terrorism.

Tessa *n. See* TAX EXEMPT SPECIAL SAVINGS ACCOUNT.

testament *n.* A *will. Strictly speaking, a testament is a will dealing only with the testator's personal property, not his land.

testamentary capacity The ability to make a legally valid will. Persons under 18 years (apart from members of the armed forces on active service – *see* PRIVILEGED WILL) and mental patients do not have testamentary capacity. The testator must, at the time he makes his will, understand the nature of the document, the property of which he is disposing, the persons who have a natural claim to provision from his estate, and the manner in which he provides for his estate to be distributed.

testamentary expenses Costs incurred by a deceased's personal representatives in administering his estate.

testamentary freedom The principle that a person is free to dispose of his property by will in whatever manner he chooses. This freedom is restricted by the Inheritance (Provision for Family and Dependants) Act 1975, which allows members of a deceased person's family or his dependants to apply to the court for provision from his estate if his will does not adequately provide for them.

testamentary guardian A person appointed by will to be the *guardian of a child under 18.

testamentary intention The principle that a person's will must reflect his true wishes. Thus a will executed as a result of coercion, fraud, or undue influence will be set aside by the court.

testamentary trust A trust contained in a will.

testate *adj.* Having left, at one's death, a legally valid will.

testator *n.* A person who makes a will.

testatum *n. See* DEED.

test case A case brought to test a principle of law that, once established, can be applied in other cases. Thus when there are a number of claimants with similar claims, a test case may be brought by one of them, after which the remainder of the claims can be settled out of court on the same basis. *Compare* REPRESENTATIVE ACTION.

testimonium *n.* *See* DEED.

testimony (testimonial evidence) *n.* A statement of a witness in court, usually on oath, offered as evidence of the truth of what is stated.

textbooks *pl. n.* Textbooks are sometimes cited in court to assist in the interpretation of the law. They have no authority as a source of law but merely provide an expert opinion as to the current state of the law. There was formerly a convention that only the works of dead authors could be cited, but modern practice also allows citation of living authors. The **Books of Authority**, i.e. the works of Glanvil, Bracton, Littleton, Coke, and Blackstone, are treated as having the same authority as cases of the same period.

thalweg, rule of the [from German: downway] The rule for determining the BOUNDARY line between two states that are separated by a navigable river containing a newly formed island. According to this rule, the boundary line moves with the centre of the navigable channel, i.e. it is delineated as being the centre of the course with the strongest current, so that the newly formed island must lie on one side of it or the other. On non-navigable rivers, however, the middle line of the river will mark the boundary between the two states between which it flows. Thus, a newly formed island might well fall partly on one side of the boundary line and partly on the other. *See also* ACCRETION; AVULSION.

theft *n.* The dishonest appropriation of property belonging to someone else with the intention of keeping it permanently (*see* DISHONESTY). "Appropriation" is defined in the Theft Act 1968 as the assumption of the rights of the owner of the property and includes any act showing that one is treating the property as one's own, which need not necessarily involve taking it away. For example, switching price tags from one item to another in a shop to enable one to buy goods at a lower price could amount to an appropriation, as could purporting to sell someone else's property. If a person acquires property without stealing it, but later decides to keep the property unlawfully, he may be regarded as having appropriated it. For example, if A lends his golf clubs to B for a week and B subsequently decides to keep the clubs or sell them, this indicates that B has assumed the rights of the owner unlawfully. "Property" includes all tangible and intangible objects and choses in action (e.g. bank balances) but there are special rules in the Theft Act 1968 governing land and wild plants and animals (*see* POACHING). Property belongs to anyone who either owns it or has physical possession or control of it. The Act expressly states that a person is not dishonest if he believes (even if unreasonably) that he is legally entitled to appropriate the property or that the owner would consent or could not be discovered by taking reasonable steps. The punishment for theft is up to ten years' imprisonment.

Under the Theft Act 1978, obtaining goods or services without paying for them is now covered by the offence of *making off without payment (*see also* SHOPLIFTING). Cases in which property is obtained by deception are usually dealt with as *deception offences. Theft involving the use of force may amount to *robbery. *See also* BURGLARY; CONVEYANCE.

thing *n.* *See* CHOSE.

third-party insurance Insurance against risks to people other than those that are parties to the policy. It is illegal to use, or allow anyone else to use, a motor vehicle on a road unless there is a valid insurance policy covering death, physical injury, or damage caused by the use of the vehicle in Great Britain. It also covers any liability resulting from the use of a vehicle (or a trailer) that is compulsorily insurable in EU countries. The policy is only considered valid when a certificate of insurance has been issued.

There is a duty upon anyone driving a motor vehicle to give his name and address and that of the car owner and to produce the certificate of insurance whenever asked to do so by a police officer. He may, however, produce it within five days at any police station he specifies at the time he was asked to produce it. There is also a duty to give details of one's insurance to any person making a claim against it or to any chief police officer who is checking whether the legal requirements of insurance are complied with. Breach of any of these duties is punishable by fine. *See also* DRIVING WITHOUT INSURANCE.

third-party proceedings Proceedings brought by a defendant to a civil action against a person not already a party to the action. Under the *Civil Procedure Rules such proceedings are now known as *Part 20 claims.

threat *n.* The expression of an intention to harm someone with the object of forcing them to do something. A threat (or **menace**), or the action of threatening someone (*see* INTIMIDATION), is an ingredient of many crimes. *See* BLACKMAIL; BOMB HOAX; CRIMINAL DAMAGE; DURESS; FORCIBLE ENTRY; INTIMIDATION; RACIAL HATRED; RAPE; SENDING DISTRESSING LETTERS; THREATENING BEHAVIOUR; VIOLENT DISORDER.

threatening behaviour It is an offence, punishable with up to six months' imprisonment and/or a fine, to use towards another person threatening, abusive, or insulting words or behaviour. It is a similar offence to distribute or display anything that is threatening, abusive, or insulting. In both cases it must be proved either that the accused person had the specific intent (*see* INTOXICATION) to cause the other person to believe that immediate unlawful violence would be used against him or, simply, that the threatened person was likely to believe that violence would be used against him. A constable may *arrest without warrant anyone he reasonably suspects is committing either of these offences.

It is also an offence, punishable with a fine, to use threatening or disorderly behaviour, or to display anything that is threatening, abusive, or insulting, within the hearing or sight of anyone likely to be harassed, alarmed, or distressed by it. Here, it is a defence if the accused person proves (*see* BURDEN OF PROOF) either that he had no reason to believe that there was anyone within hearing or sight who was likely to be harassed, alarmed, or distressed, or that he was inside a dwelling (any living accommodation, including a hotel bedroom) and had no reason to believe that the behaviour or display would be heard or seen by someone outside, or that his conduct was reasonable. A constable may *arrest without warrant anyone he reasonably suspects of committing this offence if, after warning him to stop, the person repeats the offence.

All these offences were introduced by the Public Order Act 1986 to replace similar offences; they may be committed in private as well as public places unless the behaviour or display took place inside a dwelling. A further offence of intentionally causing harassment (primarily aimed at racial harassment) was introduced by the Criminal Justice and Public Order Act 1994; it is punishable by a fine and/or six months' imprisonment. *See also* RACIAL HATRED; RACIST ABUSE; STALKING; VIOLENT DISORDER.

three certainties *See* TRUST.

three-tier system A system for allocating cases between *Crown Court centres. First-tier centres deal with both criminal and High Court civil cases and are served by High Court *puisne judges, *circuit judges, and *recorders. Second-tier centres deal only with criminal cases, but are served by the same kinds of judge as first-tier centres. Third-tier centres deal only with criminal cases and are served by circuit judges and recorders only.

threshold criteria The minimum preconditions that must be met before the court is able to make a care or supervision order. These are set out in the Children Act 1989 and are that the child is suffering or likely to suffer significant harm either caused by the care or lack of care given to it by its parents or because the child is beyond parental control. *See also* CARE ORDER; SUPERVISION ORDER.

tidal waters Under the Merchant Shipping Act 1894, any part of the sea and of a river within the ebb and flow of the tide at ordinary spring tides, excluding harbours.

tied cottage A dwelling provided for the tenant of a *service tenancy, usually in relation to agricultural workers' accommodation. *See also* AGRICULTURAL DWELLING-HOUSE ADVISORY COMMITTEE; ASSURED AGRICULTURAL OCCUPANCY.

time charter *See* CHARTERPARTY.

time immemorial *See* LEGAL MEMORY.

time policy A marine insurance policy that covers a ship against risks arising in the course of any voyage during a specified period. It differs from a **voyage policy**, covering risks arising in a specified voyage of any duration. A policy may, however, be **mixed**, i.e. restricted in cover as to both time and voyage. *See also* DEVIATION.

time provisions in contracts Provisions in contracts that relate to the time within which acts are to be performed. The question often arises whether or not a time provision constitutes a *condition of the contract. If it does, it is said that time is **of the essence**. In general, time is of the essence only if the contract says so or if an intention that it should be so is to be inferred from the nature of the transaction or the circumstances surrounding it. Most suppliers' contracts, however, include an express term that time is not of the essence.

title *n.* **1.** A person's right of *ownership of property. Someone with a **good title** has adequate evidence to establish his right. *See* ABSOLUTE TITLE; QUALIFIED TITLE; TITLE DEEDS. **2.** The heading of an *Act of Parliament, which may be a **long title** or a **short title**. **3.** The name of a particular court action, which is derived from the heading of the originating *process that initiated it.

title deeds Documents that prove a person's ownership of land and the terms on which he owns it. In the case of unregistered land they consist of all *conveyances, *mortgages, and other documents tracing ownership of the land back to a good *root of title at least 15 years old. Title deeds to registered land are the land certificate or charge certificate (*see* LAND REGISTRATION).

Tobar doctrine The doctrine that *recognition of a government should only be granted if that administration came to power by legitimate democratic means. Named after its creator, the Ecuadorian Minister of Foreign Relations, it was first adopted by five Central American states in 1907 and embodied in a treaty. After later US approval, the doctrine became known as the **Wilsonian policy**. Although it had the laudable aim of trying to maintain stability in a notoriously unstable part of the world, the doctrine has been applied inconsistently; since the end of World War II, the USA and many other states have favoured the more pragmatic *Estrada doctrine.

TOLATA (TLATA) Acronym for the Trusts of Land and Appointment of Trustees Act 1996. *See* TRUST OF LAND.

Tomlin order A form of order used to give effect to a compromise of litigation in the High Court. It is based on a *Practice Direction issued by Mr Justice Tomlin in 1927. The order is made by consent of the parties and states that on terms agreed between them (which are scheduled to the order) all further proceedings are to be stayed except for the purpose of putting the agreed terms into effect.

tools of trade A workman's tools, which he is entitled to keep if he is made bankrupt. They include all tools, books, vehicles, and other items of equipment necessary for the bankrupt's personal use in his employment, business, or vocation.

tort *n.* [Old French: harm, wrong; from Latin *tortus*, twisted or crooked] A wrongful act or omission for which *damages can be obtained in a civil court by the person wronged, other than a wrong that is only a *breach of contract. The law of tort is mainly concerned with providing compensation for personal injury and property damage caused by *negligence. It also protects other interests, however, such as reputation (*see* DEFAMATION), personal freedom (*see* ASSAULT; FALSE IMPRISONMENT), title to property (*see* CONVERSION; TRESPASS), enjoyment of property (*see* NUISANCE), and commercial interests (*see* INTIMIDATION; CONSPIRACY; PASSING OFF). It must usually be shown that the wrong was done intentionally or negligently, but there are some torts of *strict liability. Most torts are actionable only if they have caused damage, but torts whose main function is to protect rights rather than to compensate for damage (such as trespass) are actionable without proof of damage. The person principally liable is the one who committed the tort (the **tortfeasor**) but under the rules of *vicarious liability one may be liable for a tort committed by another person. The main remedy for a tort is an action for damages, but in some cases an *injunction can be obtained to prevent repetition of the injury. Other remedies are *self-help and orders for specific restitution of property.

Some torts are also breaches of contract. Negligent driving by a taxi-driver that causes injury to his passenger is both the tort of negligence and breach of the contract to carry the passenger safely to his destination. The passenger may sue either in tort or for breach of contract, or both. Many torts are also crimes. Assault is both a crime and a tort. *Dangerous driving is a crime and may give rise to an action in tort if it causes injury to another person. The crime is prosecuted by agents of the state in the name of the Crown. It is left to the injured person to seek compensation from the wrongdoer by means of an action in tort.

tortfeasor *n.* One who commits a *tort. *See also* JOINT TORTFEASORS.

tortious *adj.* Having the nature of a *tort; wrongful.

torture *n.* Under section 134 of the Criminal Justice Act 1988, the offence committed by a public official (or someone with the official's acquiescence) of intentionally inflicting severe physical or mental suffering on any person anywhere in the world. It carries a maximum sentence of life imprisonment. Under this Act, the accused had a defence if he proved that his conduct was legally authorized, justified, or excusable. However, the prohibition on torture as set out in Article 3 of the European Convention on Human Rights is now part of UK law as a consequence of the *Human Rights Act. This right is an *absolute right, and torture can never be justified as being in the public interest, no matter how great that public interest might be. Public authorities have a limited but positive duty to protect this right from interference by third parties.

total loss (in marine insurance) *See* ACTUAL TOTAL LOSS; CONSTRUCTIVE TOTAL LOSS. *Compare* PARTIAL LOSS.

totting up The system under which offences endorsed on a driving licence are added up to empower the courts to order *disqualification from driving. Until 1 November 1982, certain road offences (listed in a Schedule to the Road Traffic Act 1972) were totted up if, within three years before committing the latest offence, the accused had been convicted and had his licence endorsed on two occasions. Since that date the system has been altered. All traffic offences that are subject to compulsory or discretionary disqualification are now assigned a number of **penalty points** (reflecting the gravity of the offence). When a person is convicted of any of these offences, and his licence is endorsed but he is not disqualified, the endorsement states the number of points for that offence. If he is disqualified for the offence, the penalty points that would normally apply to that offence are not endorsed. When the penalty points endorsed within the past three years – together with the points acquired on the latest offence – amount to 12 or more, the court must order disqualification for a minimum of six months, but the points applying to the latest offence are not endorsed. If the accused has already been disqualified within the three years before the latest endorsable conviction, the minimum disqualification is for one year; if he has been disqualified more than once, the minimum is two years. Mitigating circumstances are still permitted (to prevent disqualification or shorten the period), but only upon proof of exceptional hardship. When several offences are committed together, the licence is only endorsed with the points relating to the gravest offence. If a person is disqualified under this system, all previous points are eliminated, and he gets back a clean licence after disqualification. Under the Road Traffic (New Drivers) Act 1995, with effect from 1 June 1997, if a driver is convicted of an endorsable offence and accumulates 6 or more penalty points within two years of passing a driving test, his licence is revoked and he must retake the test. Penalty points for the most important offences are as follows.

3–11 points – any offence involving obligatory disqualification for which disqualification was not ordered because of special reasons or mitigating circumstances.

10 points – being in charge when unfit or with excess alcohol in the body (*see* DRUNKEN DRIVING); failing to provide a *specimen of breath.

5–10 points – failing to stop after a *road traffic accident; failing to report an accident.

3–9 points – *careless and inconsiderate driving.

8 points – taking a *conveyance.

6–8 points – *driving without insurance.

7 points – *driving while disqualified.

4 points – failing to provide a specimen for a preliminary *breath test.

3 points – *speeding (if a fixed penalty); leaving a car in a dangerous position (*see* OBSTRUCTION).

2 points – *driving without a licence; driving under age.

All endorsements on the licence before 1 November 1982 count as 3 points.

touting *n.* Seeking business by approaching potential customers. Under the Criminal Justice and Public Order Act 1994 it is a summary offence (punishable by a fine) for unauthorized persons to offer or display for sale, in a public place, a ticket for a designated football match or other sporting event for which more than 6000 tickets are issued. Similarly, it is a summary offence (punishable by a fine) for taxi operators to solicit persons to hire vehicles to carry them as passengers unless they are licensed operators within an authorized scheme that permits such soliciting. Both offences are *arrestable offences.

town and country planning A system of controlling the use of land administered by **local planning authorities** under the Town and Country Planning Act 1990, which is subject to supervisory powers of the Secretary of State. These authorities include both county and district councils (or unitary authorities) and also, in Greater London, the London borough councils and the Court of Common Council of the City. The background to control is the **development plan**. Councils formulate and keep under review structure plans of general policy for their areas, and the other authorities maintain local plans of detailed policy for theirs. The structure plan and local plan for an area constitute its development plan. The machinery of control is **planning permission**, without which no *development of land may take place. The Secretary of State has granted permission for certain classes of development ("permitted development") by a general development order applicable throughout England and Wales; permission may be granted for particular cases by special development orders. In all other cases permission is a matter for local planning authorities (normally at district or borough level), with a right of appeal to the Secretary of State against its refusal or against conditions attached to it. The implementation of control is by local planning authorities, primarily by serving an *enforcement notice.

town clerk The office held by the head of the permanent staff (normally a qualified solicitor) of some local authorities. Under the Local Government Act 1972, the office ceased to be obligatory and most authorities now appoint a chief executive instead.

tracing trust property (following trust property) The right of a beneficiary under a *fiduciary relationship to recover trust property or its value if it is wrongfully disposed of by the fiduciary. The right exists against anyone except a person who has purchased the trust property without notice of the fiduciary obligation; a beneficiary may, for example, recover the property from a trustee who has mixed trust property with his own funds, or from a person to whom the property has wrongly been given.

track (in civil proceedings) See ALLOCATION; CASE MANAGEMENT.

trade description Any direct or indirect indication of certain characteristics of goods or of any part of them, such as their quantity, size, fitness for their purpose, time or place of origin, method of manufacture or processing, and price. Under the Trade Descriptions Act 1968, it is a criminal offence to apply a trade description to goods that is false or to supply or offer to supply any goods to which such a description is applied (*see* FALSE TRADE DESCRIPTION).

trade dispute Any dispute between workers and their own employer relating to one or more of the following: (1) terms and conditions of employment; (2) the engagement or nonengagement, suspension, or dismissal of any employee; (3) allocation of duties between employees; (4) disciplinary matters; (5) trade union membership or nonmembership; (6) facilities for trade union officials; and (7) negotiating machinery and the recognition of trade unions' negotiating rights on behalf of employees. Under terms of the Trade Union and Labour Relations

(Consolidation) Act 1992, a person cannot be sued in *tort for an act that is committed in contemplation or furtherance of a trade dispute on the grounds that it induces or threatens any breach or interference with the performance of a contract. Generally such immunity extends only to the acts of employees against their own employer. Secondary industrial action may be unlawful when it is directed against an employer who is neither a party to the dispute nor the customer or supplier of the employer in dispute (*see also* PICKETING). Moreover, there is no immunity in respect of action taken to enforce a *closed-shop agreement.

The 1992 Act gives similar immunity to trade unions for their acts committed in contemplation or furtherance of a trade dispute provided the act concerned is authorized by a majority vote in favour of the action in a secret ballot of the union's members. A trade union member can obtain a court order preventing industrial action being taken if it has not been authorized by a ballot. When the immunity does not apply, a union is only liable in respect of action that has been authorized or endorsed by a responsible person (which includes the principal executive committee, general secretary, president, paid officials, or committees to whom they report). The president, general secretary, or principal executive committee may repudiate such authorization or endorsement provided they act promptly and notify the person giving the authorization or endorsement in writing and without delay.

When a trade union's immunity does not apply and it is ordered to pay damages (other than for causing personal injury or for breach of duty concerning the ownership control or use of property, or for *products liability under the Consumer Protection Act 1987), the amount awarded may not exceed specified limits. These range from £10,000 for a union with under 5000 members to £250,000 for a union with 100 000 or more members, and the limits may be varied by statutory instrument. Payment of damages awarded against a trade union or employers' association may not be enforced against certain protected property, including its political and pension funds and the personal assets of its trustees, members, or paid officials, as distinct from assets they hold for the union's or association's purposes.

trade fixture A fixture attached to rented premises by a tenant for the purpose of his trade or business. A tenant can remove trade fixtures at any time during his tenancy, as well as at the end of it. *See also* TENANT'S FIXTURES.

trade mark A distinctive symbol that identifies particular products of a trader to the general public. The symbol may consist of a device, words, or a combination of these. A trader may register his trade mark at the Register of Trade Marks, which is at the Patent Office (*see* PATENT). He then enjoys the exclusive right to use the trade mark in connection with the goods for which it was registered. Any person or firm that has a trade connection with the goods may register a trade mark. For example, he may be the manufacturer, a dealer, importer, or retailer. Under the Trade Marks Act 1994 (and EU directive 89/104), registration is initially for ten years; it is then renewable. Trade marks can be registered for ever. However, the right to remain on the register may be lost if the trade mark is not used or is misused. The owner of a trade mark may assign it or allow others to use it. If anyone uses a registered trade mark without the owner's permission, or uses a mark that is likely to be confused with a registered trade mark, the owner can sue for an *injunction and *damages or an *account of profits. Unregistered marks are protected by *passing off. Since 1 April 1996 *Community Trade Marks can now be obtained. These are cheaper than trade marks obtained by registration in several individual EU states. Trade marks are an example of *intellectual property.

trade mark at common law A *trade mark that is not registered in the Register of Trade Marks but is identified with particular goods through established use. The trade mark's owner may bring an action for *passing off in the case of infringement.

trade secret Some process or product belonging to a business, disclosure of which would harm the business's interests. The courts will generally grant injunctions to prohibit any threatened disclosure of trade secrets by employees, former employees, and others to whom the secrets have been disclosed in confidence. There is a relationship of trust and confidence between employer and employee that may be destroyed if the employee discloses a trade secret, providing a reason for dismissal; such a dismissal may be fair if the procedure adopted complies with the necessary requirements. *See* RESTRAINT OF TRADE; UNFAIR DISMISSAL.

trade union An organization whose members are wholly or mainly workers and whose principal purposes include the regulation of relations between workers and employers or employers' associations. Unions' affairs are regulated by the Trade Union and Labour Relations (Consolidation) Act 1992. This provides that: secret ballots must be held for election of unions' executive committees and before any industrial action backed by the union (*see* STRIKE); union funds cannot be used to indemnify individuals for fines imposed by a court for a criminal offence or contempt of court; and unions' accounting records must be open to inspection by their members, who can challenge any unlawful use of the funds through the courts. There is a right for trade union members not to be unjustifiably disciplined by their union (for example for failing to take industrial action). A member can apply to an *employment tribunal for a declaration that he has been unjustifiably disciplined. The employment tribunal can award compensation if the claim is upheld. Trade-union members seeking to enforce their union membership rights can obtain advice and financial and legal assistance from the *Certification Officer, as the successor of the now abolished position of Commissioner for the Rights of Trade Union Members.

trade union official An officer of a trade union (or of a branch or section of it) or a person elected or appointed in accordance with the union's rules to represent a group of its members. An employee who is a trade-union official is entitled to time off work, paid at his normal rate, for certain purposes. These must be official union duties concerning industrial relations between his employer and any associated employer and their employees or training approved by the Trades Union Congress and relevant to his union duties.

trading stamps Stamps bought from a trading-stamp company by a retailer and given to his customers when they purchase goods. The customer obtains stamps in proportion to the goods purchased, and when he has collected enough stamps he can exchange them for goods from the trading-stamp company. The issue of trading stamps is regulated by the Trading Stamp Act 1964. Each stamp must be clearly marked with a monetary value and the name of the issuing company. The retailer aims to cover the cost of the stamps by profits from the increased custom he hopes they will attract.

traffic offences *See* OFFENCES RELATING TO ROAD TRAFFIC.

transfer *n.* (in land law) A deed by which ownership of registered land is conveyed. *See also* CONVEYANCING.

transfer of action *See* REMOVAL OF ACTION.

transfer of risk The passing from the seller of property to the buyer of the incidence of the loss if the property is damaged or destroyed. The Sale of Goods Act 1979 provides that, unless it is otherwise agreed, goods remain at the seller's risk until ownership passes to the buyer. After that they are at the buyer's risk, whether or not delivery has been made.

transfer of shares A transaction resulting in a change of share ownership. It usually involves (1) a contract to sell the shares; (2) their transfer by delivery of a *share warrant or execution of a *share transfer; and (3) entry of the transferee's name on the register of members of the company. Shares in private companies and partly paid shares may be subject to restrictions on transfer. *See also* TRANSMISSION OF SHARES.

transfer of undertakings *See* RELEVANT TRANSFER.

transferred malice *See* MALICE.

transformation *n.* (in international law) *See* DOCTRINE OF INCORPORATION.

transmission of shares A transfer of shares that occurs automatically, by operation of law, upon bankruptcy (from the bankrupt to his trustee in bankruptcy) or upon death (to the personal representatives of the deceased). The transferees do not become company members until the company enters their names upon the register of members; in the meantime they are unable to attend or vote at company meetings. *See also* TRANSFER OF SHARES.

transnational corporation An enterprise consisting of commercial entities in more than one state that are linked by ownership or otherwise. Transnational corporations operate in such a way that they exercise a uniform, cohesive, and common policy in order to further their economic interests. This policy can allow them to wield significant influence over the activities of those states in which they carry out their commercial activities, i.e. by exerting pressure over the direction of domestic policy of the host states.

transparency *n.* An essential condition for those operating in a market, which ensures that the rules to which they are subject are made obvious. Generally, it ensures that the reasons behind measures and the applicable regulations are clear to all, so that all are treated fairly.

transsexual *n.* A person who firmly believes he or she belongs to the sex opposite to his or her gender at birth; transsexuals may undergo surgery and drug treatment to alter the external appearance of their bodies to conform with their view of themselves (*see* SEX CHANGE). Under English law, for the purposes of marriage transsexuals are regarded as belonging to the sex determined at their birth and registered on their birth certificates. For the purposes of employment, however, the law now recognizes the validity of sex changes in transsexuals (*see* GENDER REASSIGNMENT).

travaux préparatoires [French] Preparatory works that form a background to the enactment of legislation; for example, recommendations of Royal Commissions and consultative documents published by the government. They may not be used by the courts as an aid to interpreting the legislation. *See* INTERPRETATION OF STATUTES.

traverse 1. *vb.* To deny an allegation of fact made in the claim form or defence. **2.** *n.* The denial itself.

treachery *n.* Conduct that assists an enemy. This was defined under the Treachery Act 1940 as an offence relating to World War II, which was punishable by death. There is now, however, no specific crime of treachery: acts of this sort are usually dealt with under the Official Secrets Acts (*see* OFFICIAL SECRETS) or, in some cases, as *treason.

treason *n.* Conduct comprising a breach of allegiance owed to the sovereign or the state. Under the Treason Act 1351, high treason included violating the king's wife, eldest unmarried daughter, or wife of the king's eldest son; openly attempting to prevent the heir to the throne from succeeding; and killing the chancellor or any judge while performing their duties. Treason was redefined by the Treason Act 1795 and the principal forms now include: (1) compassing the death or serious injury of the sovereign or his (or her) spouse or eldest son; (2) levying war against the sovereign in his (or her) realm, which includes any insurrection against the authority of the sovereign or of the government that goes beyond *riot or *violent disorder; (3) giving aid or comfort to the sovereign's enemies in wartime. The penalty for treason (fixed by law) was formerly death but is now life imprisonment.

treasure trove Formerly, items of gold and silver found in a concealed place, having been hidden by an owner who was untraceable. Under medieval law they belonged to the Crown, but only if it could be proved at a coroner's inquest that the owner had intended to retrieve the items and had not merely abandoned them. If the items were lost or abandoned, the finder acquired a right to possess them. The Treasure Act 1996 (in force from September 1997) altered the law in this field; the Act and the Code of Practice made under it apply only to England, Wales, and Northern Ireland. The definition of treasure now includes any object at least 300 years old and containing more than 5% precious metal (excluding single coins). The Crown is now entitled to receive *all* treasure and will pay a reward to the finder. The Act creates a new offence of failing to report the discovery of treasure, with a maximum penalty of a £5000 fine or three months' imprisonment (or both). The Code of Practice sets out guidelines on such matters as which objects should be reported; how finders can seek advice from museums and archaeologists in the event of a large find; government policy on the payment of *ex gratia* rewards, including rewards to landowners and rewards for finds resulting from trespass; and policy and procedures for reaching valuations, including the commissioning of reports from independent experts and provisions for finders to submit their own valuations.

Treasury Counsel Treasury Counsel to the Crown at the Central Criminal Court: a group of barristers, nominated by the Attorney General, who receive briefs from the *Director of Public Prosecutions to appear for the prosecution in trials at the *Central Criminal Court (Old Bailey). There are six Senior Counsel (who, despite the name, are not Queen's Counsel) and ten Junior Counsel.

Treasury Solicitor (HM Procurator General and Treasury Solicitor) A solicitor who advises the Treasury on legal matters, instructs parliamentary counsel on Bills, instructs counsel to appear on behalf of the Crown in civil cases involving Treasury issues, and acts as *Queen's Proctor. Between 1883 and 1908 the office was combined with that of *Director of Public Prosecutions. The Treasury Solicitor's Department is the largest division of the Government Legal Service; the Treasury Solicitor is the head of this service.

treaty *n.* An international agreement in writing between two states (a **bilateral treaty**) or a number of states (a **multilateral treaty**). Such agreements can also be known as *conventions, **pacts**, *protocols, *final acts, **arrangements**, and **general acts**. Treaties are binding in international law and constitute the equivalent of the municipal-law contract, conveyance, or legislation. Some treaties create law only for those states that are parties to them, some codify pre-existing customary international law, and some propound rules that eventually develop into customary international law, binding upon all states (e.g. the Genocide Convention). Federal states, colonial states, and public international organizations are sometimes also able to enter into treaty obligations. The Vienna Convention on the Law of Treaties (1969) defines in detail the rules relating to inter state treaties and is itself generally considered to declare or develop customary international law in this area. Treaties are normally concluded by the process of *ratification. *See also* HIGH CONTRACTING PARTIES; RESERVATION; SIGNATURE OF TREATY.

In England the power to make or enter into treaties belongs to the monarch, acting on the advice of government ministers, but a treaty does not become part of English municipal law until brought into force by an Act of Parliament.

Treaty of Paris *See* PARIS TREATY.

Treaty of Rome The treaty founding the European Economic Community (now known as the ^European Community) and the European Atomic Energy Community (*see also* EUROPEAN UNION). The treaty was signed in Rome on 25 March 1957 by its founder members, i.e. Belgium, West Germany, France, Italy, Luxembourg, and the Netherlands. It has since been amended (*see* SINGLE EUROPEAN ACT; AMSTERDAM TREATY) and is now known as the **European Community Treaty** (Treaty Establishing the European Community as Amended by Subsequent Treaties).

Treaty on European Union *See* MAASTRICHT TREATY.

tree preservation order An order made by a local planning authority (*see* TOWN AND COUNTRY PLANNING) prohibiting, in the interests of amenity, the felling of a tree (or trees) without its consent. *See also* CONSERVATION AREA.

trespass *n.* A wrongful direct interference with another person or with his possession of land or goods. In the middle ages, any wrongful act was called a trespass, but only some trespasses, such as trespass by force and arms (*vi et armis*), were dealt with in the King's Courts. The distinguishing feature of trespass in modern law is that it is a direct and immediate interference with person or property, such as striking a person, entering his land, or taking away his goods without his consent. Indirect or consequential injury, such as leaving an unlit hole into which someone falls, is not trespass. Trespass is actionable *per se*, i.e. the act of trespass is itself a *tort and it is not necessary to prove that it has caused actual damage.

There are three kinds of trespass: to the person, to goods, and to land. **Trespass to the person** may be intentional or negligent, but since negligent physical injuries are remedied by an action for *negligence, the action for trespass to the person is now only brought for intentional acts, in the form of actions for *assault, *battery, and *false imprisonment. **Trespass to goods** includes touching, moving, or carrying them away (*de bonis asportatis*). It may be intentional or negligent, but *inevitable accident is a defence. **Trespass to land** usually takes the form of entering it without permission. It is no defence to show that the trespass was innocent (e.g. that the trespasser honestly believed that the land belonged to him). Trespass to land or goods is a wrong to possession rather than to ownership. Thus a tenant of rented property, for example, has the right to sue for trespass to that property. Trespass to land is a tort but not normally a crime: the notice "Trespassers will be prosecuted" is therefore usually misleading.

However, trespass may sometimes constitute a crime. Thus squatters may be guilty of a crime (*see* ADVERSE OCCUPATION); it is a crime to trespass on diplomatic or consular premises or premises similarly protected by immunity; and it is a crime to enter and remain on any premises as a trespasser with a *weapon of offence for which one has no authority or reasonable excuse, or to be on any premises, land, or water as a trespasser with a *firearm for which one has no reasonable excuse. The Criminal Justice and Public Order Act 1994 created the offences of aggravated trespass and collective trespass. The summary offence of **aggravated trespass** occurs when a trespasser in the open air seeks to intimidate, obstruct, or disrupt a lawful activity, such as hunting; an offender can be arrested and failure to leave the land on the direction of a senior police officer is also an offence. **Collective trespass** occurs when two or more people are trespassing with the purpose of residing on land belonging to another person. The police have powers to direct collective trespassers to leave if they have caused damage, used threatening or abusive words towards the occupier, or brought six or more vehicles (which may be caravans) onto the land (*see also* UNAUTHORIZED CAMPING). Failure to leave or re-entry within three months is a summary offence for which a uniformed police officer has a power of arrest. Both collective and aggravated trespass are punishable by a fine and/or three months' imprisonment. *See also* AIRSPACE; BURGLARY; TRESPASSORY ASSEMBLY.

trespass *ab initio* [Latin: trespass from the beginning] A form of trespass that occurs when a person enters land with authority given by law, e.g. to arrest a criminal or search for stolen goods, and subsequently commits an act that is an abuse of that authority. The authority is cancelled retrospectively and the entry is deemed to have been a trespass from the beginning.

trespass by relation A form of trespass based on the legal fiction that a person's actual possession of land dates from the moment he became entitled to possession. It arose from the rule that only the possessor of land can sue for trespass to it. When someone entitled to immediate possession of land enters into possession of it at some later date, his possession is deemed to relate back to the moment he became entitled to it to enable him to sue for acts of trespass committed in the intervening period.

trespassory assembly An assembly of more than 20 people in the open air on land to which the public has no right, or a limited right, of access, when the occupier has not consented to the event and it is likely to result in serious disruption to the life of the community or significant damage to land, monuments, or buildings of historical, architectural, archaeological, or scientific importance. A chief office of police may apply to prohibit such an assembly if he reasonably believes it is going to be held. Knowingly organizing or inciting a trespassory assembly are *summary offences punishable by a *fine on level 4 and/or three months' imprisonment; knowingly taking part attracts a fine on level 3. A uniformed police officer has powers of arrest for these offences as well as a power to stop people proceeding to such an assembly.

trial *n.* The hearing of a civil or criminal case before a court of competent jurisdiction. Trials must, with rare exceptions (*see* IN CAMERA), be held in public. At the trial all issues of law and fact arising in the case will be determined. *See also* SUMMARY TRIAL; TRIAL ON INDICTMENT.

trial at bar   *Trial on indictment before three or more judges of the *Queen's Bench Division and a jury: formerly used for the trial of criminal cases of exceptional public importance. The last such trial was that of Sir Roger Casement for treason in 1916 and the procedure was abolished by the Courts Act 1971.

trial on indictment   The trial of a person charged with an *indictable offence, which is by jury in the *Crown Court. The *indictment is read out to the accused at the start of the trial. There are a number of differences between trial on indictment and *summary trial (i.e. by magistrates). The courts have power to impose greater penalties on indictment and there is no time limit before which indictable offences must be tried (most summary offences must be tried within six months).

tribunal *n.*   *See* ADMINISTRATIVE TRIBUNAL; DOMESTIC TRIBUNAL; TRIBUNAL OF INQUIRY.

tribunal of inquiry   A tribunal appointed under the Tribunals of Inquiry (Evidence) Act 1921 to investigate a matter of public importance. The Act provides machinery for the thorough examination of any matter (e.g. a national disaster or alleged corruption in government) that is a source of public disquiet but is not the subject of ordinary proceedings in the ordinary courts. A tribunal is appointed on resolutions of both Houses of Parliament, its chairman is normally a senior judge, and it has all the powers of the High Court concerning the summoning and examination of witnesses and the production of documents.

trier of fact   A member of a court who has the duty to decide questions of fact. In criminal trials on indictment and civil trials with a jury, the jury is the trier of fact; in civil trials by judge alone and in summary trials, the judge and magistrates, respectively, decide all issues both of law and fact.

TRIPS   The Agreement on Trade Related Aspects of Intellectual Property Rights 1994: the international agreement on *intellectual property rights that arose from the Uruguay Round of the *General Agreement on Tariffs and Trade (*see* WORLD TRADE ORGANIZATION). It is designed to reduce distortions and impediments to international trade while taking account of the need to promote effective protection of intellectual property rights. It also aims to ensure that measures to enforce these rights do not themselves become barriers to legitimate trade. TRIPS sets out how participating nations will protect intellectual property rights: for copyright they should comply with some provisions of the *Berne Convention; computer programs and databases will also be protected by copyright. Trade marks and patents should be protected in accordance with the Paris Convention for the Protection of Intellectual Property (1971), with additional protection for designs and the layout of integrated circuits. Developed countries were given until 1 January 1996 to bring their legislation into conformity with TRIPS. Developing countries were given until 2000, and the least developed countries an additional six years.

trover *n.*   The original form of the modern action in tort for *conversion of goods. Trover was based on a fictitious allegation that the claimant had lost the goods and the defendant found them and converted them to his own use. The old form of action has disappeared, but its name is still sometimes used as a synonym for conversion.

trust *n.*   **1.** An arrangement in which a *settlor transfers property to one or more *trustees, who will hold it for the benefit of one or more persons (the **beneficiaries** or *cestuis que trust*, who may include the trustee(s) or the settlor) who are entitled to enforce the trust, if necessary by action in court. The trust, recognized originally in Chancery, is based on confidence and developed from the *use; it has been described as the most important contribution of English *equity to jurisprudence. The beneficiary has rights against the trustee and may also have rights over the property in the hands of others (*see* TRACING TRUST PROPERTY). When a sole beneficiary is 18 or over, sane, and entitled to all the trust property, he may require the trustees to transfer that property to him; this applies equally when all the beneficiaries are 18 or over, sane, and likewise entitled. For a trust to exist, the **three certainties** must be present: certainty of intention (i.e. to create a trust), certainty of subject matter (the property in the trust), and certainty of objects (those who will or may benefit under the trust).

There are few formal technical requirements necessary for the creation of a trust, except where land is concerned, though express trusts are usually found in professionally drafted documents. Trusts are also commonly used to protect an individual's (or company's) ownership of property, when it is feared that the possessor of the property may become insolvent. *See* ACTIVE TRUST; CHARITABLE TRUST; DISCRETIONARY TRUST; EXECUTED TRUST; EXPRESS TRUST; IMPLIED TRUST; PROTECTIVE TRUST; SECRET TRUST; STATUTORY TRUST.

2. (in the National Health Service) *See* NHS TRUST; PRIMARY CARE TRUST.

trust corporation The *Public Trustee or a corporation either appointed by the court to act as trustee or automatically entitled to do so because it is incorporated in the UK and has issued capital of at least £250,000 of which at least £100,000 has been paid up in cash. A trust corporation may exercise all the powers that would otherwise require two trustees (e.g. selling land). The clearing banks and others have subsidiary companies that are trust corporations.

trustee *n.* A person having a nominal title to property that he holds for the benefit of one or more others, the beneficiaries (*see* TRUST). Trustees may be individuals or corporate bodies (*see* TRUST CORPORATION) and can include such specialists as *judicial trustees, *custodian trustees, and the *Public Trustee. A trustee must show a high standard of care towards his beneficiaries, must not allow his interests to conflict with those of his beneficiaries, and must not profit from his trust. He is not usually entitled to remuneration although he may recover expenses necessarily incurred (*see* CHARGING CLAUSE). Trustees may refuse their office, retire, or resign, but they remain liable for acts carried out during their trusteeship. The power to appoint replacement trustees is usually given either to the beneficiaries or to the remaining trustees; in default the court will appoint replacement trustees. Trustees have a wide range of powers and duties, including a duty to act equally between the beneficiaries and a power to advance money to them (*see* ADVANCEMENT). In the exercise of their duties they are answerable to the court.

trustee *de son tort* [from Latin: of his own wrongdoing] A person unconnected with a trust who takes upon himself to act as a trustee. He is thereafter liable as if he had been appointed a trustee.

trustee in bankruptcy A person in whom the property of a bankrupt is vested for the benefit of the bankrupt's creditors. The trustee in bankruptcy must collect the bankrupt's assets, sell them, and distribute the proceeds among those with valid claims against the bankrupt. Some claims (e.g. by the Inland Revenue) take preference over others.

trustee investments *See* AUTHORIZED INVESTMENTS.

trusteeship *n. See* TRUST TERRITORY.

trustees of land The trustees of a *trust of land.

trustees of the settlement *See* SETTLED LAND ACT TRUSTEES.

trust for sale A trust in which the trustees have an obligation to sell the property and hold the proceeds of sale in trust for the beneficiaries. Such a trust used to be imposed by statute in situations in which land is owned by two or more persons jointly or as tenants in common. Since 1997, all such trusts, including those already in existence in 1997, have become *trusts of land. Under the Administration of Estates Act 1925, an intestate's estate is held by his administrators on trust for sale. If his property includes land, this will now be a trust of land. Trusts for sale may be expressly created, but if the property of the trust includes land, it will be a trust of land, and a power to postpone sale will be implied.

trust instrument A deed under which property is vested in trustees upon trust to apply it for the benefit of the beneficiaries specified in the deed. In the case of *settled land, the trust instrument appoints the trustees of the settlement, sets out the interests to which the beneficiaries are entitled and any powers conferred in extension of those contained in the Settled Land Act 1925, and bears any *ad valorem* stamp duty payable in respect of the settlement. A will admitted to probate may also act as a trust instrument.

trust of land Any trust of property that consists of or includes land. These trusts were introduced by the Trusts of Land and Appointment of Trustees Act 1996 (TOLATA). Since 1997, where land is owned by more than one person or by a number of persons in succession, a trust of land will be imposed. In this respect the trust of land replaces both statutory *trusts for sale and Settled Land Act settlements (*see* SETTLED LAND). Land in co-ownership must be held by trustees of land, of which there must be not more than four individuals, or a trust corporation. Often, the trustees and the beneficiaries are the same people; for example, a husband and wife who own their home jointly will usually be both trustees and beneficiaries of the trust of land. The point of imposing such a trust is to allow *overreaching to take place on a sale or other disposition of the property. The trustees of land have all the powers of a beneficial (outright) owner, but have duties to consult the beneficiaries and manage the land for their benefit. The beneficiaries have the right to occupy the land if it is suitable for that purpose. *See also* JOINT TENANCY; TENANCY IN COMMON.

trust power (power in the nature of a trust) A *power of appointment held by trustees. The trustees are bound to consider whether or not to exercise the power, which donees of a mere power are not obliged to do, and to that extent objects of a trust power have rights similar to, but perhaps weaker than, those of beneficiaries under a trust.

trust property Property subject to a *trust, normally held by trustees (it may include trust documents, which affect the trust). If trust property is wrongfully disposed of, it may be recovered by the beneficiaries (*see* TRACING TRUST PROPERTY).

trust territory Any of the territories formerly under a League of Nations *mandate, which after 1945 were placed under the **trusteeship** of the United Nations until ready for independence. All trust territories are now independent states.

tSO *See* STATIONERY OFFICE, THE.

TUPE Transfer of Undertakings (Protection of Employment) Regulations 1981. *See* RELEVANT TRANSFER.

turbary *n.* A *profit *à prendre* or *common conferring the right to take peat or turf from another's land, for use as fuel.

turning Queen's evidence *See* QUEEN'S EVIDENCE.

turpis causa [Latin] A disreputable cause. *See* EX TURPI CAUSA NON ORITUR ACTIO; ILLEGAL CONTRACT.

twin-track planning *See* CONCURRENT PLANNING.

two-counsel rule A rule of etiquette of the Bar that required junior counsel to be instructed to assist Queen's Counsel when the latter appeared in court or in chambers. This rule has now been abolished, but two counsel are often instructed when the weight of the case justifies it.

uberrimae fidei [Latin: of the utmost good faith] Describing a class of contracts in which one party has a preliminary duty to disclose material facts relevant to the subject matter to the other party. *Nondisclosure makes the contract voidable (*see* VOIDABLE CONTRACT). Examples of this class are *insurance contracts, in which knowledge of many material facts is confined to the party seeking insurance.

UBR Uniform Business Rate. *See* RATES.

ulterior intent An element of the *mens rea* for certain crimes that requires an intention to bring about a consequence beyond the criminal act (*see* ACTUS REUS) itself. Crimes of ulterior consent include burglary with intent (*see* BURGLARY) and *wounding with intent. In the former, the ulterior intent is the intention to commit one of four crimes (theft, causing grievous bodily harm, rape, or causing criminal damage) having entered the building as a trespasser (the *actus reus*).

ultra vires [Latin: beyond the powers] Describing an act by a public authority, company, or other body that goes beyond the limits of the powers conferred on it. *Ultra vires* acts are invalid (*compare* INTRA VIRES). The *ultra vires* doctrine applies to all powers, whether created by statute or by a private document or agreement (such as a trust deed or contract of agency). In the field of public (especially administrative) law it governs the validity of all *delegated and *subdelegated legislation. This is *ultra vires* not only if it contains provisions not authorized by the enabling power but also if it does not comply with any procedural requirements regulating the exercise of the power. Subdelegated legislation that is within the terms of the delegated legislation authorizing it may still be invalid if the power to make that legislation did not include the power to subdelegate (*see* DELEGATUS NON POTEST DELEGARE). The individual can normally establish the invalidity of delegated or subdelegated legislation by raising the point as a defence in proceedings against him for contravening it. The doctrine also governs the validity of decisions made by inferior courts or administrative or domestic tribunals and the validity of the exercise of any *administrative power. The decision of a court or tribunal is *ultra vires* if it exceeds jurisdiction, contravenes procedural requirements, or disregards the rules of natural justice (the power conferring jurisdiction being construed as requiring the observance of these). The exercise of an administrative power is *ultra vires* not only if unauthorized in substance, but equally if (for example) it is procedurally irregular, improperly motivated, or in breach of the rules of natural justice. The remedies available for this second aspect of the doctrine are *quashing orders, *prohibition orders, *declaration, and *injunction (the first two of these are public remedies, not available against decisions of domestic tribunals whose jurisdiction is based solely on contract).

Acts by a registered company are *ultra vires* if they exceed the objects clause of the *memorandum of association. A company member can restrain such acts prior to performance; thereafter they are treated as valid (though they may be a breach of directors' duties). Section 35 of the Companies Act 1985 (as amended in 1989) made it much harder to challenge *ultra vires* acts of a company.

umpire *n. See* ARBITRATION.

UN *See* UNITED NATIONS.

unascertained goods Goods that are not specifically identified at the time a contract of sale is made. For example, in a contract for the sale of 1000 tonnes of soya bean meal, the seller may deliver any 1000 tonnes that answer the contract description. When the correct quantity has been set aside for delivery to the buyer, the goods are described as **ascertained**. Ownership does not pass to the buyer until the goods have been ascertained. *Compare* SPECIFIC GOODS.

unauthorized camping The summary offence of camping in vehicles on land without the consent of the occupier, or on land forming part of a highway, or on any other unoccupied land and failing to comply with a direction to leave by the local authority. It is also an offence to re-enter the land within three months. The local authority may direct the removal of vehicles or any other property; it may also apply to a magistrates' court for an order authorizing removal. A vehicle does not have to be fit for use on the roads and includes any body or chassis, with or without wheels, and any caravan. Both the offences are punishable by a *fine on level 3. Defences of illness, mechanical breakdown, or immediate emergency may be available. Local authorities may establish caravan sites for *gipsies but are no longer under a duty to do so. *See also* TRESPASS.

unchastity *n. See* IMPUTATION OF UNCHASTITY.

UNCID Uniform Rules of Conduct for Interchange of Trade Data by Teletransmission: a set of rules for *electronic data interchange that were drawn up by the International Chamber of Commerce in 1988. These rules can be incorporated into contracts if the parties wish to do so.

uncollected goods *See* DISPOSAL OF UNCOLLECTED GOODS.

unconditional surrender *See* CAPITULATION.

unconscionable bargain *See* CATCHING BARGAIN.

undefended cause **1.** A court action in which the defendant: (1) fails to acknowledge service of the claim form; (2) fails to enter a defence; or (3) fails to appear, or be represented, at the hearing of the case despite the fact that he has received notice of it. If the defendant fails to defend the action, the claimant may obtain early judgment against him by filing with the court a request for judgment. In cases where the defendant has failed to file either an acknowledgment of service or a defence within the 14 days permitted to do so from the date of service of the claim form and the particulars of claim on the defendant, a request for judgment in *default can be made. If an acknowledgment of service was filed but a defence was not, judgment cannot be requested until the expiry of 28 days from the date of the service of the particulars of claim. Given that there has been no investigation into the merits of the case when a court enters judgment in default (it being a purely administrative process), the courts have wide powers, at the request of the defendant, to cancel any judgment entered in default (*see* SETTING ASIDE). **2.** An application for divorce, nullity, or separation not contested by the respondent. This may be because: (1) the respondent declares he does not intend to contest the divorce; (2) he gives notice of his intention to defend but fails to file an answer within the time allowed; (3) he files no answer at all; or (4) the answer filed has been struck out.

underlease *n. See* SUBLEASE.

undertaking *n.* **1.** A promise, especially in legal proceedings, that creates an obligation. A solicitor who breaks such a promise will be in breach of disciplinary rules. **2.** A business, such as a company, partnership, or sole trader. *Article 81 of the Treaty of Rome applies to agreements between undertakings. EU case law has established that some state bodies of a trading nature, as well as charities and trade associations, may under certain circumstances be classed as undertakings.

underwriter *n.* **1.** A member of an insurance company or a *Lloyd's syndicate who decides whether or not to accept a particular risk for a specified premium. In general, the public only deal with underwriters through a broker. **2.** An individual, finance company, or issuing house who undertakes for a commission to acquire a specified number of shares in a company if those shares are not taken up by the public during a *flotation.

In both cases the underwriter may relieve himself of part of his liability by effecting similar arrangements with **subunderwriters**.

undischarged bankrupt A person who has been made bankrupt and who has not yet received an order of discharge from the court. Such a person is disqualified from holding certain offices, which include justice of the peace, councillor, and Member of Parliament. He must not obtain credit for more than £250 without informing the creditor that he is an undischarged bankrupt, and he must not carry on a business without disclosing the name under which he was made bankrupt to those who deal with him. *See also* BANKRUPTCY.

undisclosed principal *See* AGENT.

undivided shares The equitable interests in land owned by tenants in common. Each co-owner has a specified (but not necessarily equal) share in the property, which he may dispose of separately from the others. Such shares are held under a *trust of land. *See also* TENANCY IN COMMON.

undue influence Influence that prevents someone from exercising an independent judgment with respect to any transaction. A contract or gift procured by the exercise of undue influence is liable to be set aside by the courts. The exercise of undue influence must normally be proved affirmatively – it must be shown that there is a dealing or transaction in which an unfair advantage has been taken of another person. In the case of certain relationships (for example, between parent and child, husband and wife, doctor and patient, solicitor and client) undue influence is presumed to be exercised in the absence of evidence to the contrary, and banks should advise spouses to seek independent legal advice before mortgaging the family home at the behest of the other spouse for business loans.

unemployment benefit A former benefit paid under the Social Security Act 1975 as amended by the Social Security Act 1986 to an unemployed person satisfying certain conditions. From 7 October 1996 it was replaced by the *jobseeker's allowance.

unenforceable contract A contract that, although valid, cannot be enforced by action because it is neither **evidenced in writing** nor (when this is a permissible alternative) supported by a sufficient act of *part performance. Two classes of contracts are involved – guarantees, and contracts for the sale of land entered into before 21 September 1989. By the Statute of Frauds 1677 (in the case of guarantees) and the Law of Property Act 1925 (for land contracts), no contract of either class is enforceable unless its existence and its terms are evidenced by some written note or memorandum signed by the defendant or his agent. By the equitable doctrine of part performance, a land contract entered into before 21 September 1989 (but not a guarantee) can be enforced if, alternatively, the claimant has carried out some act that can be taken as evidencing the existence of the contract. Note that land contracts entered into on or after 21 September 1989 will not even be valid unless they are in writing; the requirement of writing is no longer merely an evidential one.

unenforceable trust A trust that is valid but cannot be directly enforced by a beneficiary. *See* PURPOSE TRUST.

unfair consumer practices *See* CONSUMER PROTECTION.

unfair contract terms Contractual terms relating to the exclusion or restriction of a person's liability that, under the Unfair Contract Terms Act 1977 and Unfair Terms in Consumer Contracts Regulations 1999, are either ineffective or effective only so far as is reasonable. *See* EXCLUSION AND RESTRICTION OF NEGLIGENCE LIABILITY; EXEMPTION CLAUSE; INTERNATIONAL SUPPLY CONTRACT.

unfair dismissal The dismissal of an employee that an employment tribunal finds is unfair. Under the Employment Rights Act 1996 employees have the right not to be unfairly dismissed, provided they have served the required period of *continuous employment and are not over 65 or the normal retirement age for an employee in that particular job. However, employees dismissed for an *inadmissible reason have this right whatever their age or length of service. An employee who considers he has been unfairly dismissed can apply within three months after the *effective date of termination of his employment contract to an employment tribunal for *reinstatement, *re-engagement, or *compensation. The tribunal will make an award unless the employer can show that the principal reason for the dismissal was the employee's incapability, lack of qualifications, or conduct; redundancy; the fact that it would be illegal to continue employing him; or some other substantial reason. The tribunal must also decide that the employer acted unreasonably in dismissing the employee.

The statutory protection does not apply to the following: (1) employees ordinarily working outside Great Britain; (2) a person employed by his spouse; (3) members of the police and armed forces; (4) the crews of fishing vessels in certain circumstances; and (5) workers who, at the time of their dismissal, are taking industrial action that has lasted more than eight weeks.

unfair prejudice Unfair conduct on the part of those entrusted to run and control a company in respect of (usually minority) *company members. Any member affected may apply to the court under the Companies Act 1985, and the court is empowered under the Act to make such order as it thinks fit. Commonly, the unfair conduct consists of actions having the effect of seriously diminishing the value of the complainant's shareholding. In this instance the usual remedy sought is for the purchase of the complainant's shares at a fair price. *See also* MINORITY PROTECTION.

unfavourable witness An *adverse witness who is not *hostile towards the party who called him to testify. An unfavourable witness may not be cross-examined by that party.

unfitness or incompetence *See* IMPUTATION OF UNFITNESS OR INCOMPETENCE.

unfit to plead Describing an accused person who is under a disability (e.g. mental incapacity) that would constitute a bar to his being tried. When the question of fitness to plead arises (e.g. when the defendant is *standing mute by visitation of God), a jury is empanelled to determine the question of the accused's fitness; if they find him under disability the court must order that the accused be admitted to a hospital specified by the Secretary of State. The court may postpone consideration of the question of the accused's fitness to plead until the defence case is opened so that (for example) the strength of the prosecution case may be tested. The procedure is governed by the Criminal Procedure (Insanity) Act 1964.

Uniform Business Rate (UBR) *See* RATES.

unilateral contract A contract in which one party (the promisor) undertakes to do or refrain from doing something if the other party (the promisee) does or refrains from doing something, but the promisee does not undertake to do or refrain from doing that thing. An example of a unilateral contract is one in which the promisor offers a reward for the giving of information. *Compare* BILATERAL CONTRACT.

unilateral discharge *See* ACCORD AND SATISFACTION.

unilateral mistake *See* MISTAKE.

unincorporated body An association that has no legal personality distinct from those of its members (*compare* CORPORATION). Examples of unincorporated bodies are *partnerships and *clubs.

union membership agreement *See* CLOSED-SHOP AGREEMENT.

unitary authority An all-purpose *local authority created under the Local Government Act 1992 and subsequent legislation to replace the two-tier system of local government by *county and *district councils. Unitary authorities were established in Wales (and Scotland) in April 1996 and in certain nonmetropolitan counties in England between 1996 and 1998; single-tier authorities also administer *Greater London and the former metropolitan county areas (since 1986) and the Isle of Wight (since 1995). *See also* LOCAL GOVERNMENT COMMISSION FOR ENGLAND.

United Nations (UN) An international organization, based in New York and Geneva, set up by the United Nations Charter in 1945 to replace the League of Nations. The main aims of the UN are: (1) to maintain international peace and security and to bring about settlement of international disputes by peaceful means; (2) to develop friendly relations among nations; and (3) to achieve international cooperation in solving international problems of an economic or cultural nature and in promoting respect for human rights. The Charter sets out certain fundamental principles, which include the undertaking to refrain from using or threatening force against the territory or political independence of any state.

   The Charter established six principal organs, of which the most important are the General Assembly, the Security Council, the Economic and Social Council, and the *International Court of Justice. The **General Assembly** is the debating forum of the UN, consisting of all the member states; it can pass resolutions, but these are not legally binding upon member states. The **Security Council** has five permanent members (China, France, Russia, the UK, and the USA), and ten temporary members elected for two-year periods. Its resolutions are binding on member states, but each permanent member has the right to veto a resolution. It is empowered, under certain conditions, to make recommendations and take measures to maintain the peace, including the establishment of peacekeeping military forces in sensitive areas.

   The United Nations has lost credibility as an international legal organization because it has often been divided upon issues on the basis of political (rather than legal) factors or has passed resolutions of a political nature. Nevertheless it remains important as the only world organization (almost all independent states are members of the UN) and as a forum for discussion and development of international law.

In certain policy areas the United Nations operates through subsidiary organs; for example, the United Nations High Commissioner for Refugees (UNHCR) and the United Nations Children's Fund (UNICEF).

Uniting for Peace Resolution A resolution passed by the General Assembly (GA) of the *United Nations in 1950 in which the GA assumed the authority to determine what constituted a threat to the peace, a breach of the peace, or an act of aggression. In the event of any of these occurring, the GA resolved to invite member states to take collective action, including the use of armed force. It is highly doubtful that this attempt by the General Assembly to usurp the role of the Security Council has any legal authority to allow it to act in this way. It has been seen more as a declaration of the frustration of the nonaligned countries at the superpower stalemate that previously existed in the Security Council.

unit trust A *trust enabling small investors to buy interests in a diversity of companies and other investments. These investments are held by trustees (responsible for holding the investments and collecting and distributing income), who enter into a trust deed with the managers of the fund (who select, buy, and sell the investments). The managers sell units to investors, who thus acquire an interest in the fund proportionate to their investment. There is a service charge that provides the remuneration of the managers. Unit trusts are subject to regulation and supervision by the Department of Trade and Industry.

unity of personality Formerly, the common-law doctrine that husband and wife were one person in the eyes of the law. This doctrine has now been almost entirely abolished. However, the court still has jurisdiction to stay proceedings in tort brought by one spouse against another if there will be no substantial benefit from it; a husband and wife may not be convicted of criminal conspiracy together with each other (unless a third person is involved); and there are certain limitations on criminal proceedings in relation to theft of property belonging to one's spouse.

unity of seisin The ownership of two plots of land by the same person. Easements and other rights over a *servient tenement for the benefit of a *dominant tenement are extinguished if both tenements come into the same ownership.

unjust enrichment *See* QUASI-CONTRACT.

unlawful assembly *See* VIOLENT DISORDER.

unlawful possession of drugs *See* CONTROLLED DRUGS.

unlawful sexual intercourse Sexual intercourse that occurs in any of the *sexual offences involving intercourse, including intercourse with a girl under the age of 16 or a mentally defective woman. In this context "unlawful" implies extramarital intercourse.

unlawful trust *See* VOID TRUST.

unlawful wounding *Wounding or *wounding with intent that is not justified by, for example, self-defence or by statutory powers given to the police to arrest criminals.

unless order An order of the court instructing a party to comply with directions specified in the order and also stating the consequences of noncompliance with the order within a specified time. Any sanction for noncompliance attaching to such an order must be proportionate to the request being ordered.

unlimited company A type of *registered company whose members have an unlimited liability. Thus on winding-up, the company can make demands upon its members until it has sufficient funds to meet the creditors' claims. The risk that members of unlimited companies assume is balanced by certain advantages: an unlimited company (unless it is a parent or subsidiary of a limited company) does not have to deliver its *accounts to the Companies Registry and it has more freedom to deal with its capital than a limited company. Unlimited companies may be formed with an *authorized capital, thus enabling them to issue shares and raise working capital, but members' liability is not limited to the nominal value of these shares.

unliquidated damages *See* DAMAGES.

unnatural offence *Buggery. Other "unnatural" forms of intercourse, however, are not included in the term.

unopposed proceedings Proceedings in which any person entitled to oppose fails to take any step (or any further step) in the proceedings, having been given an opportunity to do so. Unopposed proceedings often end in a judgment in *default but may not do so in proceedings in which the remedy claimed can only be obtained by some judicial determination, e.g. in *undefended causes in divorce proceedings.

unpaid seller A seller of goods who has not been paid in full for them or who has received a cheque or other *negotiable instrument that has not been honoured. Although ownership of the goods may have passed to the buyer, an unpaid seller has certain rights against the goods themselves. Under the Sale of Goods Act 1979, these rights are: (1) a possessory *lien (particular, not general); (2) a right of *stoppage *in transitu*; and (3) a *right of resale.

unpaid vendor's lien An equitable right arising in favour of a vendor of land against the purchaser (and those taking title through him as *volunteers) if the vendor has given *possession of the land to the purchaser before receiving the whole of the purchase price. This form of *lien gives the vendor no right to possession of the land but entitles him to seek a court order for the sale of the property to ensure that he is paid the money owing by the purchaser.

unreasonable behaviour Behaviour of a respondent that may be evidence that a marriage has broken down irretrievably, entitling the petitioner to a *divorce. Such conduct need not be unreasonable in itself – the real test is whether it is reasonable to expect the petitioner to continue living with the respondent, taking into account the behaviour of both parties and their particular personalities and characteristics. The behaviour may be "positive" (for example, persistent drunkenness, violence, or obsessive conduct) or "negative" (for example, neglect or indifference); a petition may succeed even if the respondent is not responsible for the behaviour, due (for example) to an illness.

unregistered company A *company that is incorporated otherwise than by registration under the Companies Acts. Unregistered companies, which include *statutory companies and *foreign companies, are subject to some provisions of the Companies Act 1985.

unregistered land Land to which the title in question is not registered at HM Land Registry. The majority of land has already become registered as the system of land registration now demands the compulsory registration of all land on transfer. *Compare* REGISTERED LAND. *See also* REGISTRATION OF ENCUMBRANCES.

unsecured creditor A person who has lent money without obtaining any security. *Compare* SECURED CREDITOR.

unsolicited goods Goods sent to someone (other than a trader) who has not asked for them to be sent. It is not in itself an offence to send unsolicited goods (except for matter describing human sexual techniques or advertisements for such matter), but it is a criminal offence to demand payment for them. A person who receives unsolicited goods is an involuntary bailee of them (*see* BAILMENT) and may not destroy or damage them. If he disposes of them, he might be guilty of theft. Statute, however, permits him to treat them as his own property after six months (or 30 days if he has asked the sender to take them back).

unsworn evidence Evidence given by a child under the age of 14 in a criminal case in accordance with the provisions of the Youth Justice and Criminal Evidence Act 1999. The child must be sufficiently intelligent to justify the reception of his evidence and understand the duty of speaking the truth. Formerly, the child's evidence had to be supported by some *corroboration, but this requirement has now been abolished.

unsworn statement A statement made from the dock by an accused person while not on oath. The evidentiary effect of such a statement was much disputed, but the right to make one, which had been preserved when the accused was made a competent witness by the Criminal Evidence Act 1898, was abolished by the Criminal Justice Act 1982.

uplift *n.* The amount by which a solicitor is allowed to increase a claim for *costs above the basic charge for the work involved. *See also* CONDITIONAL FEE AGREEMENT.

urine specimen *See* SPECIMEN OF URINE.

usage *n.* A long-established and well-known practice in a particular market or trade. It may affect the interpretation of, and the nature of *implied terms in, a contract made in that market or trade.

use *n.* [possibly from Latin: *opus*, benefit] Formerly, a right, recognized only in Chancery, of a beneficiary (the **cestui que use**) against the legal owner of land. The medieval common law recognized only legal rights, which were often restricted in nature, but the Chancery protected those to whose use or benefit land was given, although they were not the legal owners. If A held property to the use of B, A was the legal owner (**feoffee to uses**) and B was the beneficiary (*cestui que use*). Uses gave flexibility and helped the evasion of feudal incidents (the medieval equivalent of tax liability). In 1535 the Statute of Uses executed the use, i.e. converted the rights of a *cestui que use* to legal rights, but the statute proved ineffective (*see* USE UPON A USE); it was repealed and uses were abolished in 1925.

use and occupation Possession and/or use of land by a person in unlawful occupation of it. A person claiming to recover possession of the land by proceedings in court can also claim a money sum to compensate him for the defendant's unlawful use and occupation.

use classes *See* DEVELOPMENT.

use of force The use of offensive military action, whether amounting to war or not, is prohibited under Article 2(4) of the United Nations Charter. The only exceptions to this strict rule are as follows: (1) when the use of force is by way of an *enforcement action (Article 39 within *Chapter VII of the UN Charter); (2) when force is used for the purposes of *self-defence under Chapter VII (Article 51); and (3) controversially, when a state uses force for the purposes of self-defence under customary international law (arguably preserved by Article 51). Resort to force upon any other basis is illegal under international law.

user *n.* The use or enjoyment of property.

use upon a use Formerly, a right recognized by the Chancery after the Statute of Uses 1535 (*see* USE). In a situation in which A held property to the use of (i.e. for the benefit of) B, who held to the use of C, the Statute made B the legal owner but did not affect the second use to C (the use upon a use), who remained entitled to the benefit. The second use eventually developed into the *trust.

usual covenants The covenants that a good conveyancing practitioner would insert in a *lease. When an *agreement for a lease does not specify the terms of the lease, there is a term implied in the agreement that the lease will contain the usual covenants. The following are generally accepted as usual: by the landlord, a covenant for *quiet enjoyment; by the tenant, to pay rent, to pay tenants' rates and taxes, to keep the premises in repair, and to allow the landlord to enter to see the state of repair. There is also a condition for *re-entry for nonpayment of rent. Whether or not any other covenant is usual is a matter of evidence.

uti possidetis [Latin: as you possess] A principle usually applied in international law to the delineation of borders. When a colony gains independence, the colonial boundaries are accepted as the boundaries of the newly independent state. This practice, first adopted for the sake of expediency by the Spanish American colonies when they declared independence, has since been employed elsewhere in the world following the withdrawal of empire.

The principle of *uti possidetis* is also applied to the status of movable public property of belligerent states. Unless a peace treaty provides to the contrary, each party will retain such property as was in its possession on the day the hostilities ceased.

utter Bar *See* OUTER BAR.

V

vacantia bona *See* BONA VACANTIA.

vacant possession The exclusive use of land, to which a purchaser is entitled on completion of the transaction unless he has contracted to buy subject to another's right of occupation.

vacations *pl. n.* The periods between the end of any of the *sittings of the Supreme Court and the beginning of the next sitting, i.e. the *Long Vacation, Christmas Vacation, Easter Vacation, and Whitsun Vacation.

vaccine damage payment A tax-free lump-sum payment made, under the Vaccine Damage Payments Act 1979, in compensation for severe disablement caused by a vaccine administered under the British government's vaccination programme.

vagrant *n.* A person classified under the Vagrancy Act 1824 as an "idle and disorderly person", a "rogue and vagabond", or an "incorrigible rogue". The first of these groups includes pedlars who trade without a licence, prostitutes who behave indecently in a public place, and those who beg in a public place. Rogues and vagabonds include those with a second conviction for being idle and disorderly, those who collect charity under false pretences, and tramps who do not make use of available places of shelter. Incorrigible rogues include those with a second conviction for being rogues and vagabonds. Vagrants are usually liable to imprisonment for between one month and one year, depending on which class they fall under, although beggars and tramps sleeping rough are liable only to fines. The Act also provides for various powers to search them or their property.

valuable consideration *See* CONSIDERATION.

value *n.* Valuable *consideration.

value-added tax (VAT) A tax payable on a wide range of supplies of goods and services by way of business. As well as straightforward sales, **taxable supplies** include hirings, rentals, the granting of rights, and the distribution of promotional gifts. VAT is also payable on imports. The amount of tax payable is a percentage of the value of the supply (at present 17.5% except for domestic fuel, which is charged at 8%) and the liability for the tax arises at the time of the supply (*see* TAX POINT). Any person, firm, or organization that makes regular taxable supplies above a certain annual value (£54,000 since 1 April 2001) must register with the Customs and Excise, who administer the tax. A registered person (known as a **taxable person**) must collect from his customers the tax due on the supplies that he makes. This is known as his **output tax**. He pays the tax to the Customs and Excise on a periodic basis (usually quarterly), but in doing so he may reclaim any VAT that he has himself paid in the course of his business (his **input tax**). The entire tax is therefore borne by the ultimate consumer. VAT came into force on 1 April 1973, replacing purchase tax and selective employment tax. *See also* EXEMPT SUPPLY; ZERO-RATED SUPPLY.

valued policy An insurance policy that specifies the value of the property insured as agreed between the parties. A policy is not valued merely because it specifies an amount as the sum insured, for that is no more than an estimate of value by the person insured. The essence of a valued policy is that it is based on an agreed valuation, which is conclusive; the insured will recover its full amount even if this exceeds the actual value of the property at the time of loss.

value received Words that may appear on a *bill of exchange indicating either that value has been received by the drawer from the payee or by the acceptor from the drawer. Such words are not necessary; every party whose signature appears on a bill is presumed, unless the contrary is proved, to have become a party for value.

vandalism *n.* Defacing or damaging property. There is no offence of vandalism as such, but it will usually constitute an offence of *criminal damage.

variance *n.* A discrepancy between a statement in the statements of case or between a statement in these documents and the evidence adduced in support of it at trial. In modern practice, it can be rectified by *amendment.

variation of trust A trustee is normally obliged to carry out a trust according to its precise terms; if he fails to do so, he is liable to be sued by his beneficiaries. There are, however, circumstances (both under the court's own jurisdiction and by statute) in which a trust may be varied, and a wide discretion is given to the court, under the Variation of Trusts Act 1958, to vary a trust, provided (usually) that the variation is for the benefit of those on whose behalf the court is acting.

VAT *See* VALUE-ADDED TAX.

VC *See* VICE CHANCELLOR.

VCT *See* VENTURE CAPITAL TRUST.

VDU *See* VISUAL DISPLAY UNIT.

vehicle *n.* *See* MOTOR VEHICLE.

vehicle construction and maintenance There are detailed rules governing the manufacture and subsequent maintenance of motor vehicles, failure to comply with which may constitute a criminal offence. The main rules deal with such matters as the brakes and steering system, mirrors, windscreen wipers and washers, petrol tanks, door hinges and latches, silencers, pollution prevention, indicators, speedometers, lights, and tyres. There are also regulations governing the use of a motor vehicle. Breach of the regulations relating to brakes, steering system, or tyres or breach of any of the regulations relating to construction, maintenance, or use in a manner that causes or is likely to cause danger is an offence punishable by *endorsement (and carrying 3 penalty points under the *totting-up system) and discretionary disqualification. Other breaches are subject to fines but not to endorsement. There are also special offences relating to the sale or attempted sale of vehicles whose use on the roads would be a breach of the regulations, to the fitting of parts to a vehicle in such a way that its subsequent use would be in breach of the regulations, and to selling or supplying parts whose fitting would cause the vehicle's subsequent use to be in breach of the regulations. These offences do not apply, however, if the defendant proves that the vehicle was sold for export or that he reasonably believed that it would not be used in Britain in an unlawful condition. *See also* MOT TEST.

vehicle insurance *See* THIRD-PARTY INSURANCE; DRIVING WITHOUT INSURANCE.

vehicle interference *See* INTERFERING WITH VEHICLES.

vendor *n.* A seller, particularly one who sells land.

vendor and purchaser summons A procedure enabling parties to a contract for the sale of land, who disagree on a matter that prevents completion of the contract, to apply to a judge in chambers for a ruling. It is often employed to resolve questions of interpretation of terms of the contract.

venereal disease Any infectious disease transmitted through sexual contact (such as HIV infection, syphilis, or gonorrhoea). If a spouse at the time of marriage was, unknown to his (or her) partner, suffering from a venereal disease this constitutes a ground for annulment of the marriage. Evidence of a venereal disease contracted since the marriage, when neither partner was previously suffering from it, may be prima facie evidence of adultery.

venire de novo [Latin: to come anew] An order made by the Court of Appeal (Criminal Division) annulling a trial on indictment and ordering a *new trial on the ground of some fundamental flaw in the proceedings (e.g. failure to obtain a necessary consent to the institution of proceedings). Originally, it was a writ (**_venire facias de novo juratores_**) addressed to the sheriff, ordering him to cause new jurors to try the case afresh.

venture capital trust (VCT) An *investment company listed on the London Stock Exchange that specializes in investing in companies of the same kind as those that can qualify under the *Enterprise Investment Scheme. This enables individuals to spread the risk over a number of qualifying companies. The investor buys shares in the VCT, and fund managers invest the money raised in trading companies; the profits are paid out as dividends. The investor is entitled to relief from income tax and capital gains tax.

verbals _pl. n._ Any remarks that an accused person has made in the presence of the police. These are written down by the police and may be read out as evidence at the trial. _See also_ CAUTION.

verdict _n._ **1.** A *jury's finding on the matters referred to it in a criminal or civil trial. The jury is asked to give its decision to the court separately for each of the questions it was asked to consider (for example, when there are several charges on the *indictment). The reply is usually given by the foreman. A jury reaches its verdict in secret and no subsequent inquiry can be made as to how it was reached. The jury must try to reach a unanimous verdict but a *majority verdict is accepted in certain circumstances. If the jury cannot agree a verdict at all they are discharged and there is a new trial. Verdicts are either *general or *special. The usual form of verdict is general (such as a finding of *guilty or *not guilty); special verdicts are exceptional. A jury may decide that the accused is not guilty of the offence charged but guilty of some lesser offence (_see_ ALTERNATIVE VERDICT). _See also_ PERVERSE VERDICT. **2.** The finding of a coroner's inquest. _See_ INQUISITION.

vertical agreements Agreements between businesses at different levels of trade; for example, agreements between suppliers and distributors or between wholesalers and retailers (_compare_ HORIZONTAL AGREEMENTS). Both EU regulation 2790/99 and the UK Competition Act 1998 (Land and Vertical Agreements Exclusion) Order 2000 exempt certain vertical agreements from the competition rules. The EU exemption applies provided that clauses from a list of banned clauses are not included in the agreement concerned and a 30% market share threshold is not exceeded. Many vertical agreements benefit from *block exemption protection.

vest _vb._ **1.** To confer legal ownership of land on someone. **2.** To confer legal rights on someone.

vested in interest Indicating a present right to a future interest in property. For example, if property is left by will "to A for life, remainder to A's first son", A being childless at the testator's death, A's first son's right to the property is vested in interest as soon as he is born and his interest is a **vested remainder**. *Compare* VESTED IN POSSESSION.

vested in possession Indicating an immediate right to the enjoyment of an interest in property. *Compare* VESTED IN INTEREST.

vested remainder *See* VESTED IN INTEREST.

vested rights Rights that have accrued to a person, as opposed to rights that he may or may not acquire. There is a presumption that Acts of Parliament are not intended to interfere with vested rights, particularly without payment of compensation. *See* INTERPRETATION OF STATUTES.

vesting assent A document that transfers ownership of *settled land from personal representatives of a deceased tenant for life or statutory owner to the beneficiary entitled to it under the settlement. The assent must be signed by the personal representatives but need not be executed as a deed and it should contain the same information required to be included in a vesting deed by the Settled Land Act 1925.

vesting declaration A statement in a deed appointing new trustees that the trust property is to vest in them, i.e. be in their possession.

vesting deed *See* SETTLED LAND.

vesting order An order of the High Court creating or transferring a legal estate in land. Such an order may be made, for example, when an equitable mortgagee exercises his power of sale: the court may make an order vesting the land in the purchaser.

veto *n.* **1.** (in international law) The power given to any permanent member of the Security Council of the *United Nations to refuse to agree to any nonprocedural proposal (there is no such power in relation to procedural matters) and thereby defeat it. An abstention is not equivalent to a veto. The President of the Security Council has power to determine which questions are nonprocedural. The General Assembly of the UN passed a *Uniting for Peace Resolution in 1950, providing for the Assembly to take over some of the functions of the Security Council when the Council's work has been paralysed by use of the veto. This resolution, however, was only a political gesture and failed to overcome the veto power. **2.** (in EU law) **a.** The power of a member state in the *Council of the European Union to block legislation when a unanimous decision in favour of a measure is required. Although much EU legislation only requires a qualified majority decision of the Council, unanimity votes are required in such areas as taxation, budgets, foreign policy, and the admission of new member states. **b.** The power of the *European Parliament to reject legislation proposed by the Commission by means of the *codecision procedure.

vexatious action An action brought for the purpose of annoying the opponent and with no reasonable prospect of success. A **vexatious litigant** is a person who regularly brings such actions. The actions may be struck out and the court may order, on an application made by the Attorney General, that no legal proceedings may be begun or continued by the vexatious litigant without the leave of the court.

vicarious liability (vicarious responsibility) Legal liability imposed on one person for torts or crimes committed by another (usually an employee but sometimes an *independent contractor or agent), although the person made vicariously liable is not personally at fault. An employer is vicariously liable for torts committed by his employees when he has authorized or ratified them or when the tort was committed in the course of the employees' work. Thus negligent driving by someone employed as a driver is a tort committed in the course of his employment, but if the driver were to assault a passing pedestrian for motives of private revenge, the assault would not be connected with his job and his employer would not be liable. The purpose of the doctrine of vicarious liability is to ensure that an employer pays the costs of damage caused by his business operations. His vicarious liability, however, is in addition to the liability of the employee, who remains personally liable for his own torts. The person injured by the tort may sue either or both of them, but will generally prefer to sue the employer.

Vicarious criminal liability may effectively be imposed by statute on an employer for certain offences committed by an employee in relation to his employment. Thus it has been held that an employer is guilty of selling unfit food under the Food Act 1984 when his employee does the physical act of selling (the employee is also guilty, though in practice is rarely prosecuted). Likewise, an employer may be guilty of supplying goods under a false trade description when it is his employee who actually delivers them. For an offence that normally requires *mens rea*, an employer will only be vicariously liable if the offence relates to licensing laws. For example, if a licensee has delegated the entire management of his licensed premises to another person, and that person has committed the offence with the necessary *mens rea*, the licensee will be vicariously liable.

Vicarious liability for crimes may be imposed in certain other circumstances. The registered owner of a vehicle, for example, is expressly made liable by statute for fixed-penalty and excess parking charges, even if the fault for the offence was not his. If the offence is a regulatory offence of *strict liability, the courts often also impose vicarious liability if the offence is defined in the statute in a way that makes this possible.

vicarious performance *See* PERFORMANCE OF CONTRACT.

vicarious responsibility *See* VICARIOUS LIABILITY.

Vice Chancellor (VC) 1. A judge who is vice president of the *Chancery Division of the High Court (the *Lord Chancellor is the president but in practice rarely, if ever, sits in the Division). The Vice Chancellor is by statute responsible to the Lord Chancellor for the organization and management of the business of the Division and is *ex officio* a member of the *Court of Appeal. **2.** Formerly, a judge of the *palatine courts. The title is still held by the judge assigned to exercise Chancery jurisdiction in Lancashire.

victim *n.* (in human rights law) A person who is actually and directly affected by an act or omission that is incompatible with the European Convention on Human Rights, or a person who is at risk of being directly affected. Only victims have a right to take proceedings. *See* HUMAN RIGHTS ACT.

video evidence Evidence from witnesses provided on video, either through live video link or prerecorded. For civil cases, a Video-conferencing Protocol issued by the Bar Council sets out the requirements for the use of video-conferencing equipment in the High Court. Oral evidence of an overseas witness, for example, may be recorded on video tape or provided through a live link, although its acceptance is at the discretion of the court. For example, if cross-examination is needed, a video recording would not suffice, whereas a live link might. The Video Recordings Act

1993 and the Criminal Justice Act 1988 (as amended by the Criminal Justice Act 1991) set out the law on the use of videos in evidence. There are special rules for children giving video evidence. A child of under 14 may give evidence by video link in cases involving sex offences or assault against children, but the judge has a discretion to determine whether a child may be too young to give good evidence. When prerecorded child statements are used in evidence, the interview from which the recording is made must last no longer than one hour and no leading questions may be asked. However, evidence in the form of a video recording cannot be subject to cross-examination and does not carry the weight of live testimony.

video recordings (in evidence) *See* VIDEO EVIDENCE.

vi et armis [Latin: by force and arms] The allegation in medieval pleading that a trespass had been committed with force and therefore was a matter for the King's Courts because it involved a breach of the peace. The term survived as a formal requirement of pleading until 1852. *See* TRESPASS.

view *n.* (in court proceedings) The inspection by a judge, or judge and jury, of any place or thing with respect to which any question arises in the course of litigation, including if necessary places or things outside the jurisdiction of the court. A view is part of the evidence in the case and the judge should not hold a private view of a public place in the absence of the parties. The judge has discretion to decide whether or not to hold a view; he may decide to do so even if the parties are opposed.

vinculo matrimonii *See* A VINCULO MATRIMONII.

vindictive damages *See* EXEMPLARY DAMAGES.

violence for securing entry *See* FORCIBLE ENTRY.

violent disorder An offence committed when three or more persons, present together, use or threaten unlawful violence. The collective conduct must be such as would have caused a reasonable person to fear for his safety, though no-one else need be present. "Violence" includes violent conduct towards property as well as persons and extends to conduct causing or intended to cause injury or damage. It therefore includes throwing a missile at someone though it does not hit him or falls short. The offence is found in the Public Order Act 1986, though it can be committed in private as well as in public places. It replaces the common-law offence of **unlawful assembly** and is punishable with up to five years' imprisonment and/or a fine. Violent disorder differs from *riot in the smaller minimum number of participants, the absence of need to prove community of purpose, and a lesser maximum punishment. However, both are *arrestable offences. As with *affray, a person is only guilty if he intended to use or threaten violence or was aware that his conduct might be violent or threaten violence. For this purpose, an intoxicated person is taken to be aware of what a sober person would have been aware. If the police fear that a violent event may take place they may now exercise stop-and-search powers (*see* POWER OF SEARCH).

It is also an offence, punishable with six months' imprisonment and/or a fine, to do any of the following, without legal authority, in order to compel a person to do (or not to do) something he has a right to do (or not to do): use violence towards or intimidate that person, his wife, or children or injure his property; persistently follow him; hide his property or hinder his use of it; watch or beset him or his place of residence, work, or business; or follow him with two or more others in a disorderly manner in a street or road. This offence is aimed mainly at disorderly *picketing. However, it is lawful to watch or beset a place (other than a residence) for the sole purpose of peacefully obtaining or communicating information or peacefully persuading any person to work or not to work.

visiting forces Commonwealth forces stationed in the UK and any other forces from abroad designated by Order in Council, including their civilian components. The Visiting Forces Act 1952 empowers the service courts of such forces to exercise jurisdiction over their members according to their national law (but not to carry out the death penalty). It exempts their members from trial by UK criminal courts in the case of offences committed on duty, against other members, or against the property of the force or other members. The Income and Corporation Taxes Act 1988 confers certain exemptions from UK taxation on members of visiting forces.

visitor *n.* **1.** A person appointed to visit and inspect an institution and, in particular, to inquire into internal irregularities. Many universities have a visitor (frequently the Crown), and judges are visitors of the Inns of Court. Boards of Visitors, appointed for prisons by the Home Secretary, act as disciplinary tribunals for breaches of the Prison Rules. A Lord Chancellor's Visitor is appointed under the Mental Health Act 1983 to visit patients and inquire into their ability to manage their affairs. **2.** A person who enters land or premises at the invitation or with the permission of the occupier. *See* OCCUPIER'S LIABILITY.

visual display unit (VDU) A computer screen. The EU's visual display screen directive on health and safety and the visual display units (computer screens) directive 90/270 protects employees by setting out requirements for such matters as risk assessments of computers used at work and by providing for free sight tests and footstools for staff and regular breaks from VDU work.

void *adj.* Having no legal effect.

voidable *adj.* Capable of being avoided (set aside).

voidable contract A contract that, though valid when made, is liable to be subsequently set aside (*compare* VOID CONTRACT). Voidable contracts may arise through *misrepresentation, some instances of *mistake, *nondisclosure, and duress (*see* ECONOMIC DURESS; UNDUE INFLUENCE). Certain proprietary contracts entered into by minors are also voidable (*see* CAPACITY TO CONTRACT). The setting aside of a voidable contract is effected by *rescission.

voidable marriage *See* NULLITY OF MARRIAGE.

voidable trust A trust that can be set aside, e.g. a trust created by an *infant. It may be repudiated by the infant on his attaining majority (18) or shortly thereafter; if the trust is not repudiated, it becomes valid and binding. A trust may also be set aside if it is made as a result of fraud, duress, or undue influence.

void contract A contract that has no legal force from the moment of its making (*compare* VOIDABLE CONTRACT). Void contracts occur when there is lack of *capacity to contract and by the operation in some instances of the doctrine of *mistake. An *illegal contract is void. In addition, certain contracts (e.g. *gaming and wagering contracts) are declared void but not illegal by statute, and certain contracts that are at common law contrary to *public policy are merely void but not illegal. Under UK and EU *competition law on restrictive trade practices, clauses infringing those laws are void but usually the rest of the contract continues. Contracts that are void or, in certain cases, illegal may be saved by *severance.

void marriage *See* NULLITY OF MARRIAGE.

void trust (unlawful trust) A trust that it is against the policy of the law to enforce. Such trusts include those that offend the *rule against perpetuities or the *rule against inalienability or that are contrary to public policy. If a trust is void, the property in the trust will normally be held on *resulting trust for the settlor or his estate.

voir dire (voire dire) [Norman French: to speak the truth] **1.** The preliminary examination by a judge of a witness to determine his competence or of a juror to determine his qualification for jury service. **2.** An inquiry conducted by the judge in the absence of the jury into the admissibility of an item of evidence (e.g. a *confession). It is sometimes called a **trial within a trial**. **3.** Formerly, a special oath taken by witnesses called to testify on the *voir dire*.

volenti non fit injuria [Latin: no wrong is done to one who consents] The defence that the claimant consented to the injury or (more usually) to the risk of being injured. Knowledge of the risk of injury is not sufficient; there must also be (even if only by implication) full and free consent to bear the risk. A claimant who has assumed the risk of injury has no action if the injury occurs. The scope of the defence is limited by statute in cases involving business liability and public and private transport.

voluntary *adj*. Without valuable *consideration.

voluntary accommodation Accommodation provided by a local authority for children whose parents are temporarily unable to look after them or for children who have been abandoned. (It is important to distinguish between a child who is being accommodated by a local authority and a child who is the subject of a *care order.) The purpose of a local authority in supplying accommodation is to support *children in need and their families; it is not a means for the local authority to gain control of the child against the parents' wishes. The local authority does not acquire *parental responsibility for a child who is accommodated; parents with parental responsibility must consent to their child being accommodated and may remove the child without notice and without the consent of the local authority (before 1989 it was necessary to give 28 days' notice before removing the child from voluntary care). If a child is the subject of a care order the local authority acquires parental responsibility for that child and may act against the parents' wishes.

voluntary arrangement **1.** An agreement between a debtor and his creditors concerning the payment of his debts under the provisions of the Insolvency Act 1986. It takes the form of either a *scheme of arrangement or a *composition. It can be made either before bankruptcy proceedings are initiated or between an *undischarged bankrupt and his creditors. The court makes an order, called an **interim order**, to protect the debtor from bankruptcy and other court proceedings while an agreement is worked out. The debtor presents his proposals to a creditors' meeting to which all his creditors must be invited. If the meeting agrees with the debtor's proposals, the **approved voluntary arrangement** becomes binding on all the debtor's creditors, whether or not they attended the meeting. The approved voluntary arrangement does not have to be registered as a *deed of arrangement. The meeting's decision is reported to the court, which may discharge the interim order if no agreement has been reached. An *insolvency practitioner (the **supervisor**) is appointed to supervise the carrying out of an approved voluntary arrangement. He may petition for a *bankruptcy order if the debtor fails to comply with the terms of the arrangement. **2.** A similar agreement between a company in financial difficulties and its creditors. Under the Insolvency Act 1986 it must be approved by meetings of both the company and the creditors; if it affects the priority of *preferential debts, the consent of the preferential creditors is required. If the arrangement is approved it becomes binding from the date of the creditors' meeting; there is no interim order. It is supervised by a **nominee**, who must be a qualified *insolvency practitioner. An *administration order may be granted to assist the conclusion of a voluntary arrangement.

voluntary bill procedure A procedure enabling the prosecution to apply to a judge of the High Court to obtain consent for preferring a *bill of indictment against a defendant. This procedure is usually used when a magistrates' court has held committal proceedings but has refused to commit the defendant for trial on indictment.

voluntary confession See CONFESSION.

voluntary conveyance See VOLUNTARY DISPOSITION.

voluntary disposition A conveyance or other transfer of ownership of land, made otherwise than for valuable *consideration. Under the Law of Property Act 1925, a voluntary disposition made with intent to defraud a purchaser can be set aside at the instigation of the purchaser.

voluntary liquidation See VOLUNTARY WINDING-UP.

voluntary settlement A *settlement made without valuable *consideration. For any voluntary settlement to be enforced, a trust must be executed, i.e. completed; hence the maxim "equity will not assist a volunteer".

voluntary waste A kind of *waste that occurs when a tenant takes positive action that damages the land he leases.

voluntary winding-up (voluntary liquidation) A *winding-up procedure initiated by a special or extraordinary resolution of the company. In a **members' voluntary winding-up**, the directors must make a statutory **declaration of solvency** within the five weeks preceding the resolution. This declaration states that the directors have investigated the affairs of the company and are of the opinion that the company will be able to pay its debts in full within a specified period, not exceeding 12 months from the date of the resolution. The liquidator is appointed by the company members. A **creditors' voluntary winding-up** arises when no declaration of solvency has been made or when the liquidator in a members' voluntary winding-up disagrees with the forecast made by the directors. In these circumstances the company must hold a meeting of its creditors and lay before it a **statement of affairs** disclosing its assets and liabilities. A *liquidator may be nominated by the company and by the creditors; the creditors' nominee is preferred unless the court orders otherwise. If the company nominee acts as liquidator prior to the creditors' meeting he can only exercise his powers with the consent of the court. The creditors can also appoint a *liquidation committee.

In both types of voluntary winding-up the powers of the directors are restricted after the resolution for voluntary winding-up has been passed and they cease when a liquidator has been appointed.

volunteer *n.* A person who, in relation to any transaction, has not given valuable *consideration.

voting *n.* **1.** (in a registered company) The process of casting a vote on a motion proposed at a company meeting. Initially the vote is taken upon a show of hands, i.e. each company member present in person has one vote. If the result is disputed, it is usually possible for the chairman or members (present in person or by *proxy) to demand a **poll**, in which votes are cast (in person or by proxy) in accordance with the number and class of *shares held. Particulars of these voting rights are usually stated in the memorandum or articles of association. The chairman usually has a casting vote in the event of an equality of votes. Members may agree among themselves how they will cast their votes in relation to particular types of resolution (**voting agreement**). **2.** (in a parliamentary or local-government election) *See* ELECTION.

voyage charter *See* CHARTERPARTY.

voyage policy *See* TIME POLICY.

wagering contract *See* GAMING CONTRACT.

wages council A statutory body empowered by the Wages Act 1986 to prescribe minimum rates of pay in a particular industry. The wages orders made by wages councils did not apply to employees under the age of 21. Each council consisted of representatives of employers and employees in the industry concerned and independent members. Councils were usually established for industries in which employees' collective bargaining power was comparatively weak.

The Wages Act 1986 abolished the power to create new wages councils, and the Trade Union Reform and Employment Rights Act 1993 repealed Part II of the Wages Act 1986, thereby abolishing the remaining 26 wages councils and also the requirement to pay statutory minimum remuneration in certain sectors of industry. *See also* MINIMUM WAGE.

wait and see principle *See* RULE AGAINST PERPETUITIES.

waiver *n.* **1.** The act of abandoning or refraining from asserting a legal right. **2.** The instrument that declares the act of waiving. **3.** Variation of a contract.

waiver of privilege *See* ABSOLUTE PRIVILEGE.

waiver of tort Giving up the right to sue for damages for a tort in favour of some other remedy, e.g. a restitution action for money that the tortfeasor has made from the tort.

war *n.* The legal state of affairs that exists when states use force to vindicate rights or settle disputes between themselves. States can engage in hostilities (e.g. reprisals) without being in a technical state of war, and they can be in a state of war without much fighting taking place. At common law a state of war could not exist until there had been a formal declaration of war or commencement of hostilities by the Crown. The legal condition of war automatically terminates diplomatic relations and certain types of treaties between the participants. Normal intercourse and commerce between British subjects and those of a power with which the Crown is at war are prohibited.

In the Kellogg–Briand Pact (also known as the Pact of Paris) of 1928, the contracting parties renounced war as an instrument of national policy and undertook to settle their disputes by peaceful means. The United Nations Charter declares that all parties to it "shall refrain...from the threat or use of force against the territorial integrity or political independence of any state" or in a manner inconsistent with the Charter, and this is commonly accepted as an accurate statement of customary international law. Nonetheless it appears that states still retain a right of *self-defence, at least if they have been the victims of armed attack and until the Security Council can act. The Security Council is also authorized to use force (or to call upon states to do so) under certain circumstances in order to protect the peace, although in practice this power has not been invoked (*see* USE OF FORCE). The right of self-defence includes a collective right to assist other states acting in self-defence.

The Hague Conventions and Geneva Conventions provide rules governing the conduct of wars and stating the rights and duties of both combatants and noncombatants during war. However, they do not deal with all aspects of warfare or all types of war. There have also been various specific conventions governing particular issues, including a 1972 convention on the use or possession of bacteriological and toxic weapons, a 1976 convention on the military use of environmental modification techniques, and a 1981 convention and three protocols on cruel or indiscriminate non-nuclear weapons. Civil wars are not usually illegal from the point of view of international law, but it is uncertain whether or not other states may legally help either the insurgents or the established authorities (*see* BELLIGERENT COMMUNITIES, RECOGNITION OF; INSURGENCY). The 1977 First and Second Protocols to the Geneva Conventions of 1949, respectively, extend some of the laws of war to civil wars and wars of national liberation (*see* SELF-DETERMINATION).

See also AGGRESSION; HUMANITARIAN INTERVENTION; MARTENS CLAUSE; OCCUPATION; OFFENCES AGAINST INTERNATIONAL LAW AND ORDER; WAR CRIMES.

war crimes Any violation of the laws or customs of war amounting to a criminal act. According to the Charter of the Nuremberg International Military Tribunal of 1946, war crimes include murder, ill-treatment, or deportation of civilian populations, murder or ill-treatment of prisoners of war, killing hostages, plundering property, and wanton destruction of population centres or devastation that is not justified by military necessity. The Nuremberg Tribunal also defined a new category of **crimes against humanity**, consisting essentially of murder, extermination, enslavement, deportation, and other inhumane acts committed against any civilian population before or during World War II and persecution on political, racial, or religious grounds (but only if the persecution is connected with war crimes or crimes against peace); these acts are crimes against humanity whether or not they violate the domestic law of the country where the crime was committed. It is now arguable that this definition is of general application and is wider than that of war crimes. In consequence, the prohibition of crimes against humanity denies the right of any state to treat its citizens as it pleases. This has had major implications for the relationship between state *sovereignty and *humanitarian intervention.

The Tribunal also created a third category of **crimes against peace**, i.e. planning, preparing, or waging a war of aggression or a war in violation of international treaties. It is generally considered that these definitions now form part of customary international law.

War crimes tribunals were established at the end of World War II with jurisdiction to try and punish those who allegedly committed war crimes while acting in the interests of the European Axis countries or Japan. More recently, under *Chapter VII of the UN Charter, the UN Security Council has set up *ad hoc* war crimes tribunals in relation to the conflicts in the former Yugoslavia (1993) and Rwanda (1994). *See also* INTERNATIONAL CRIMINAL COURT.

The War Crimes Act 1991 gives jurisdiction to UK courts to try those charged with war crimes committed in German-held territory during World War II, irrespective of the accused's nationality at the time. Prosecutions may be brought with the consent of the Attorney General for *homicide offences.

ward of court **1.** A minor under the care of a *guardian (appointed by the parents or the court), who exercises rights and duties over the child subject to the general control and discretion of the court. **2.** A minor in respect of whom a *wardship order has been made and over whom the court exercises parental rights and duties. A child becomes a ward of court when a wardship order is made and remains a ward until he reaches the age of 18 or the court orders that he should cease to be a ward. Any child who is actually in England or Wales (or ordinarily resident in England or Wales) may be made a ward of court, even though he is neither domiciled there nor a British subject. Marriage of a ward does not necessarily terminate the wardship.

wardship *n.* The jurisdiction of the High Court to make a child a *ward of court and assume responsibility for its welfare. The jurisdiction is almost unlimited, although subject to consideration of the child's welfare and, to some extent, the rights of other persons and the public interest. The court exercises detailed control of the ward: it may appoint the Official Solicitor to act as his children's guardian and may order either parent to make periodical payments for his maintenance. Wardship proceedings are heard in private and the usual rules of evidence may be relaxed (e.g. in respect of hearsay evidence). The court may enforce its orders by injunction; breach of this or tampering with the ward may constitute contempt of court.

Wardship proceedings are usually used (1) when there is a dispute between estranged parents but no divorce proceedings have been started; (2) when a foster parent or potential adopter wishes to prevent relatives interfering with the child or when a third party wishes to remove the child from parents who are considered unfit to have parental responsibility; (3) when a child has been "kidnapped" by a parent; (4) to exercise control over a wayward child; and (5) to control medical treatment, such as sterilization, even when this is contrary to the wishes of the child. Any person who can establish a proper interest in the child may apply for wardship (including the child himself), but the Children Act 1989 restricts the right of local authorities to use wardship proceedings. It also repeals the court's power to commit a ward to the care or supervision of a local authority. Since the Children Act came into force use of wardship may be limited as the court may prefer to make a *section 8 order instead.

war injuries It is normal in the UK on the outbreak of war to enact provisions (e.g. the Personal Injuries (Emergency Powers) Act 1939) excluding civil liability for injuries caused by the discharge of missiles, the use of weapons, explosives, etc.

warned list *See* CAUSE LIST.

warning of caveat A notice given to a person who has entered a *caveat warning him to appear and state what his interest is.

warrant *n.* **1.** A document authorizing some action, especially the payment of money. A **warehouse** (or **wharfinger's**) **warrant** is issued when goods are taken into a public warehouse and must be produced when they are removed. This document is negotiable and transferable by endorsement. *See also* ENFORCEMENT OF JUDGMENT; SHARE WARRANT. **2.** A written document issued by a magistrate for the *arrest of a person or the search of his property (*see* POWER OF SEARCH). When a suspect has fled abroad and there is an extradition treaty covering the offence he is suspected of, the magistrate who has jurisdiction over the place in which the offence was allegedly committed may issue an arrest warrant to enable the Director of Public Prosecutions and the Home Secretary to extradite the suspect. *See also* GENERAL WARRANT.

warrant backed for bail *See* BACKED FOR BAIL.

warranty *n.* **1.** (in contract law) A term or promise in a contract, breach of which will entitle the innocent party to damages but not to treat the contract as discharged by breach. *Compare* CONDITION. *See also* INNOMINATE TERMS. **2.** (in insurance law) A promise by the insured, breach of which will entitle the insurer to treat the contract as discharged by breach. The word therefore has the same meaning as *condition in the general law of contract. **3.** Loosely, a manufacturer's written promise as to the extent he will repair, replace, or otherwise compensate for defective goods; a *guarantee.

war risks Under the Marine and Aviation Insurance (War Risks) Act 1952, risks arising from hostilities, rebellion, revolution, and civil war or from civil strife resulting from such events.

waste *n.* **1.** Any alteration of tenanted property that is caused by the tenant's action or neglect. It includes damage, deterioration, and improvement (*see* AMELIORATING WASTE; EQUITABLE WASTE; PERMISSIVE WASTE; VOLUNTARY WASTE). Landlords can take action against tenants who cause waste (*see* IMPEACHABLE WASTE). The extent of a tenant's liability varies according to the kind of tenancy. Most tenants are liable for equitable and voluntary waste. *Fixed-term tenants are also liable for permissive waste, as are yearly *periodic tenants (but only to the extent that they must keep the premises wind- and water-tight). A *tenant for life under a *settlement is prima facie liable for ameliorating waste, rarely liable for permissive waste, and usually liable for voluntary and equitable waste (unless exempted or made "unimpeachable of waste" by the terms of the settlement). **2.** *See* POLLUTION.

wasted costs order An order for *costs made against the legal or other representative of a party on the ground that they were incurred by any improper, unreasonable, or negligent act or omission of the representative or his employee.

wasting assets Property forming part of a deceased's estate and having a reducing value (e.g. a leasehold interest in land). Unless the will directs otherwise, the personal representatives have a duty to sell such assets.

wasting police time An offence committed by someone who causes wasteful employment of the police by making a false report about an offence or by implying that a person or property is in danger or that he has information relevant to a police inquiry. The consent of the Director of Public Prosecutions is required for prosecutions for this offence, which is punishable by a fine and/or imprisonment.

water *n.* *See* RIGHT OF WATER.

water pollution *See* POLLUTION.

waybill *n.* *See* SEA WAYBILL.

weapon of offence Any *offensive weapon or any article made, adapted, or intended for incapacitating someone (e.g. a rope to tie someone with or pepper to make him sneeze). There are special offences of aggravated *burglary and of *trespass with a weapon of offence. *See also* FIREARM.

wear and tear *See* FAIR WEAR AND TEAR.

weekly tenancy A weekly *periodic tenancy.

welfare law Law enacted to give effect to society's responsibility for the well-being of individuals. It relates to such matters as social security (*see* NATIONAL INSURANCE) and income support, employment protection, health and safety at work, and housing. Most of the services available to individuals under welfare law are covered by the Department for Work and Pensions (formerly Social Security).

welfare of the child The wellbeing of a child must be the paramount consideration of the court in all proceedings concerning the child's upbringing. Under the Children Act 1989, any delay in determining the question of upbringing is deemed likely to prejudice the welfare of the child. However, a court will only make an order concerning a child if it considers that this is the only means of ensuring the child's welfare. In adoption proceedings the welfare of the child is the first, but not necessarily the paramount, consideration of the court, although this is currently under review (*see* ADOPTION).

Welsh Assembly The National Assembly for Wales, a body established by the Government of Wales Act 1998. The Assembly has 60 elected salaried members. It does not have legislative or taxing powers, exercising instead a diverse range of functions, such as housing, education, economic development, and flood defence. In operation from 1999, the Assembly has taken over many of the powers and responsibilities of the Secretary of State for Wales. *See* DEVOLUTION.

Welsh company A *registered company whose memorandum of association states that its registered office is situated in Wales. Welsh companies may lodge documents at the Companies Registry in Welsh and may adopt in their name the Welsh equivalents for "limited" (cyfyngedig) and "public limited company" (cwmni cyfyngedig cyhoeddus, or c.c.c.). An English translation must be provided.

wharf *n.* Under the Merchant Shipping Act 1894, any premises (including quays and docks) in or upon which goods landed from ships may be lawfully placed.

whistle-blowing *n.* The disclosure by an employee of information regarding his employer's business. In certain circumstances (with respect to disclosures of wrongdoing by the employer) employees are given legal protection from retaliation by the employer. The Public Interest Disclosure Act 1998 protects employees from dismissal, or subjection to any detriment, with respect to certain types of disclosures. Contractual provisions attempting to oust the operation of the Act (e.g. the use of 'gagging clauses' in an employment contract) are rendered void by the Act.

Qualifying disclosures must be made in good faith and must pertain to any of the following: (1) criminal offences; (2) the breach of a legal obligation; (3) a miscarriage of justice; (4) a danger to the health or safety of any individual; (5) damage to the environment; (6) deliberate covering up of information tending to show any of the above matters. Qualifying disclosures may be made to the employer or (by means of internal procedures) to a legal adviser, a minister of the Crown, or a prescribed regulator. If an employee is unable to make disclosures to any of these named persons, or fears retaliation in making such disclosures, then wider disclosure may be made (as long as this is not for personal gain). Wider disclosure could be, for example, to the police, the media, a Member of Parliament, or a non-prescribed regulator. Workers and employees who are dismissed or subjected to a detriment as a result of making a qualifying disclosure to an appropriate recipient can, within three months of such action, make a complaint to an employment tribunal.

white paper *See* COMMAND PAPERS.

whole blood *See* CONSANGUINITY.

widow's benefit A benefit formerly payable to widows. In April 2001 it was renamed *bereavement benefit and now applies equally to men and women.

wife's services *See* CONSORTIUM.

wild animals *See* CLASSIFICATION OF ANIMALS; DANGEROUS ANIMALS; POACHING.

wilful *adj.* Deliberate; intended: usually used of wrongful actions in which the conduct is intended and executed by a free agent.

wilful default The failure of a person to do what he should do, either intentionally or through recklessness; for example, nonappearance at court.

wilful misconduct Intentionally doing something that is wrong, or wrongfully omitting to do something, or doing something or omitting to do something that shows reckless indifference as to what the consequences may be.

wilful neglect Deliberate or intentional failure to perform a duty.

wilful neglect to maintain *See* FAILURE TO MAINTAIN.

wilful refusal to consummate The unjustified decision not to consummate a marriage, which may be grounds for annulment of the marriage. There will be no wilful refusal if the unwillingness to consummate is temporary, due to shyness, or due to some physical abnormality that cannot be safely corrected by surgical means. *See also* CONSUMMATION OF A MARRIAGE.

will *n.* A document by which a person (called the **testator**) appoints *executors to administer his estate after his death, and directs the manner in which it is to be distributed to the beneficiaries he specifies. To be valid, the will must comply with the formal requirements of the Wills Act 1837 (*see* EXECUTION OF WILL) and the testator must have *testamentary capacity when the will is made. A will can be amended by the execution of a *codicil or a duly executed alteration. It can be revoked by the testator destroying it with that intention, or making another will. It may be revoked in part through partial destruction (with the necessary intent), *obliteration of words (rendering them indecipherable) or through signed and attested alterations (such as scoring out words). It is automatically revoked if the testator marries except where at the time it was made the testator was expecting to marry a particular person and he intended his will to survive the act of marriage. *See also* INTERPRETATION OF WILLS; JOINT WILL; MUTUAL WILLS; NUNCUPATIVE WILL; PRIVILEGED WILL; REVOCATION OF WILL.

winding-up (liquidation) A procedure by which a company can be dissolved. It may be instigated by members or creditors of the company (*see* VOLUNTARY WINDING-UP) or by order of the court (*see* COMPULSORY WINDING-UP). In both cases the process involves the appointment of a *liquidator to assume control of the company from its directors. He collects the assets, pays debts, and distributes any surplus to company members in accordance with their rights.

with costs A phrase appended to the order of a court that has the effect of awarding the *costs of the proceedings to the successful party.

withdrawal of defence A procedure enabling a defendant in an action in the High Court to serve a notice on the claimant indicating that he is not proceeding with his defence or with part of it. The defendant is then in *default of defence and the claimant may proceed to judgment by application.

withdrawal of issue from jury A procedure enabling a judge, who is not satisfied that there is sufficient evidence to discharge the evidential *burden of proof borne by a party, to discharge the jury and enter judgment for the opponent if the issue is decisive of the litigation. If the issue is not decisive of the litigation as a whole, he may direct the jury to find against that party in respect of that issue.

without notice application A procedure in civil litigation by which one party may apply for an order of court to be made without the other party being aware of it. An example may occur when one party wishes to freeze the assets of the other party. Secrecy is essential to avoid the other party having the opportunity to dispose of the assets. In cases of this sort it is possible for a without notice application to be made for a *search order or a *freezing injunction.

without prejudice A phrase used to enable parties to negotiate settlement of a claim without implying any admission of liability. Letters and other documents headed "without prejudice" cannot be adduced as evidence in any court action without the consent of both parties. However, they may be relevant when costs are discussed in courts – thus the phrase "without prejudice save as to costs" is often added on settlement correspondence. Whether or not a discussion or letter is "without prejudice" and therefore cannot be disclosed to the court depends on whether it was a genuine attempt to settle a dispute, not whether the words "without prejudice" were written on a letter or said in a meeting. The reason such discussions are kept secret from the court is that the courts are keen to encourage settlement of disputes without recourse to the courts, and if settlement discussions could be disclosed it may deter people from settling disputes.

without recourse to me *See* SANS RECOURS.

witness *n.* **1.** A person who observes the signing of a legal document in case it is subsequently necessary to verify the authenticity of the signature. He adds his own signature to the document as a witness. Many legal documents are only valid if properly witnessed (*see* DEED; WILL). **2.** A person who gives *evidence. In court, witnesses are required either to give evidence on *oath or to *affirm that their evidence is true. Most people are qualified to give evidence in any case (*see* COMPETENCE) but there are certain exceptions; for example, when the judge considers the witness mentally unfit to give evidence. In civil cases a child who is too young to understand the nature of an oath is not a competent witness, although in criminal cases a young child may be allowed to give *unsworn evidence. There is no minimum age below which a child cannot give evidence, but the judge has a discretion to determine whether or not a child is too young to be a competent witness. Most competent witnesses can be compelled to give evidence (a witness who refuses to answer is in *contempt of court) but again there are exceptions. For example, a witness cannot be compelled to answer a question that may *incriminate him. A witness's evidence is usually given orally in open court. However in certain circumstances evidence is allowed by *affidavit (*see* COMMISSION) or by video link (*see* VIDEO EVIDENCE). The evidence of certain witnesses is considered to be unreliable and requires *corroboration. The Criminal Procedure and Investigations Act 1996 set out new procedures for the issue of *witness summonses in summary cases and new rules on formalities in witness statements (effective from 1 April 1997). *See also* ADVERSE WITNESS; HOSTILE WITNESS; ZEALOUS WITNESS; INTERFERING WITH WITNESSES; PERJURY; QUEEN'S EVIDENCE.

witnessing part *See* DEED.

witness's oath *See* OATH.

witness summons An order to a person to appear in court on a certain day to give evidence. Before the introduction of the Civil Procedure Rules in 1999, this order was known as a **subpoena**. The party calling the witness must pay his reasonable expenses. A witness who fails to comply with the order is in *contempt of court. The order is made under penalty of fine or imprisonment for default. There are two kinds of witness summons: a summons requiring a person to give evidence (formerly called a **subpoena *ad testificandum***); and a summons requiring him to produce particular documents that are required as evidence (formerly called a **subpoena *duces tecum***).

women employees *See* EQUALITY CLAUSE; EQUAL PAY; MATERNITY RIGHTS; SAFETY AT WORK; SEX DISCRIMINATION.

words of art Words whose legal interpretation has been fixed so that the legal effect of their use is known.

words of limitation Words in a conveyance of land that define the interest transferred; for example, "in fee simple".

words of procreation The words in a settlement of land that created an *entailed interest. Unless the land was expressly settled on the beneficiary "and the heirs of his body" or "in tail", an entailed interest would not result.

words of purchase The words in a conveyance of land that identify the person to whom the property is transferred.

words of severance *See* SEVERANCE.

work done and materials supplied, contract for A contract the substance of which is that skill and labour must be exercised in carrying out the contract, in addition to supplying the materials used in the work. Examples are contracts by an artist to paint a portrait and by a builder to fit double glazing. Such a contract is distinct from a contract of sale of goods, in which the substance of the contract is a product to be sold.

worker *n.* An *employee.

work-in *n.* Industrial action in which employees occupy their workplace against the will of their employer and continue working. Generally such action constitutes *trespass, and the employer can apply to the court for an order that the employees restore possession of the premises to him.

working day 1. For banking and financial purposes, any day other than Saturday, Sunday, and *bank holidays. *See also* SUNDAY TRADING. **2.** (of a court) Any day other than Sunday or holidays, called a ***dies juridicus***. A day on which no legal business can be carried on is called a ***dies non***.

working families tax credit An income-related benefit payable under the Tax Credits Act 1999 to persons responsible for children, whose income and savings are below a prescribed amount, but who are in remunerative work. Administered by the Inland Revenue rather than the Benefits Agency, it replaced **family credit** from 5 October 1999.

working hours The EU Working Time Directive (93/104) of 1993 required all member states to limit the working week of employees to 48 hours (except when employees have agreed otherwise). The provisions of this Directive were enacted by the British government in the Working Time Regulations 1998. Key elements of the Regulations require a maximum working week of 48 hours, daily rest breaks, weekly rest periods, and annual paid leave of four weeks in each holiday year. The Regulations also contain protections with respect to night working. They are enforced by the Health and Safety Executive.

World Bank *See* INTERNATIONAL BANK FOR RECONSTRUCTION AND DEVELOPMENT.

World Trade Organization (WTO) An international trade organization formed under the *General Agreement on Tariffs and Trade (GATT) to replace GATT and implement measures agreed at the Uruguay Round (1994) by 2002. It began operating on 1 January 1995. The WTO's aims are to continue the work of GATT in agreeing international trading rules and furthering the liberalization of international trade. The WTO extends its jurisdiction into such aspects of trading as intellectual property rights (*see* TRIPS). WTO rules are very important in international trade contracts. The highest authority of the WTO is the Ministerial Conference, held at least every two years. By 30 November 2000 the WTO had 140 member states and a further 29 governments had applied to join.

wounding *n.* Breaking the continuity of the skin or of a membrane (such as that lining the cheeks or lips). Scratching, bruising, burning, or breaking a bone without tearing the skin do not constitute wounding. **Malicious wounding** is an offence punishable by up to five years' imprisonment. It requires an intention to cause some physical harm (not necessarily a wound) or foresight of the risk of causing physical harm. A person is not guilty of this offence if he intended only to frighten his victim but in fact accidentally wounded him, although he would be guilty of *assault or *battery.

wounding with intent The aggravated *assault of a person with the intention of causing *grievous bodily harm (even if grievous harm does not in fact result) or *wounding with the intention of resisting a lawful arrest. Wounding with intent carries a maximum sentence of life imprisonment; a second conviction for wounding with intent to do grievous bodily harm carries a mandatory life sentence (*see* REPEAT OFFENDER). *See also* ULTERIOR INTENT.

wreck *n.* **1. (shipwreck)** The destruction of a ship at sea, as by foundering in a storm or being driven onto rocks. **2.** The remains of a wrecked ship. **3.** Goods cast up by the sea from a wrecked ship.

writ *n.* An order issued by a court in the sovereign's name that directs some act or forebearance. Originally, a writ was an instrument under seal bearing some command of the sovereign.

writ of delivery A *writ of execution to enforce a judgment for delivery of goods. It directs the *sheriff to seize the goods and deliver them to the claimant or to recover their assessed value. If the writ does not offer the defendant the option of retaining the goods by paying their assessed value, it is known as a **writ of specific delivery**.

writ of execution A writ used in the *enforcement of a judgment. It may be a writ of *fieri facias, a *writ of possession, a *writ of delivery, a writ of *sequestration, or any further writ in aid of any of these writs.

writ of possession A writ directing the *sheriff to enter upon land to give vacant possession to the claimant. It is used to enforce judgments for the possession of land.

writ of summons Formerly, a writ by which an action was commenced in the High Court. Civil proceedings in the High Court are now initiated through a *claim form.

written resolution A *resolution signed by all company members and treated as effective even though it is not passed at a properly convened company meeting. Under the Companies Act 1985 *private companies can, in some circumstances, pass

resolutions in this way; other companies may have power to do so under their
*articles of association.

written statement of terms of employment A statement in writing that an
employer must give to certain employees under the terms of the Employment
Rights Act 1996, which aims to comply with the EU Proof of Employment
Relationship Directive. Not later than two months after the beginning of
employment, the employer must give to every employee who works for eight or
more hours a week a written statement (known as an **SI Statement**) setting out the
following information: (1) the names of employer and employee; (2) the date
employment began; (3) the date when the employee's continuous employment began;
(4) the scale or rate of remuneration or method of calculating remuneration; (5) the
intervals at which remuneration is paid; (6) the hours of work; (7) the holiday
entitlement (which must be sufficiently specific to allow the employee's holiday
entitlement to be precisely calculated); (8) the procedure to be adopted in the event
of incapacity for work as a result of sickness or injury (including sick pay
provisions, if any); (9) pensions and pension schemes; (10) the length of notice the
employee is obliged to give and entitled to receive to terminate the contract; (11) the
title of the job the employee is employed to do or, as an alternative to the job title, a
brief description of the work; (12) if the employment is not intended to be
permanent, the period for which it is expected to continue or, if it is for a fixed
term, the date it is intended to end; (13) either the place of work or, if the employee
is required to work at various places, an indication that this is the case; (14) any
collective bargaining agreements that directly affect the terms and conditions of
employment. If the employee is required to work outside the UK for more than one
month there is a requirement for additional information to be given relating to the
length of the period of this employment, the currency in which remuneration is to
be paid in that period, details of additional remuneration or benefits connected with
working outside the UK, and the repatriation arrangements.

If any amendment is made to these terms after the statement has been (or should
have been) issued, the employer must give the employee a written statement setting
out the details of the change not later than one month after the change has been
made. Failure to comply with the requirements set out above gives the employee the
right to complain to an *employment tribunal at any time during the currency of
the employment, or within three months of the employment coming to an end. The
written statement, although providing evidence of the terms of employment, is not
itself the *contract of employment.

wrong *n.* An illegal or immoral act. A distinction must be drawn between moral
wrongs and legal wrongs. Some moral wrongs, such as murder or theft, are also
crimes punishable by law. But many moral offences are not legal wrongs and some
technical legal offences, such as parking offences, are not generally regarded as
morally blameworthy. Legal wrongs may be criminal or civil. *Crimes are offences
against society as a whole, not merely against the victim of the crime. Civil wrongs,
such as *torts, *breaches of contract, and interferences with property rights, are
wrongs to the individuals affected.

wrongful dismissal The termination of an employee's contract of employment
in a manner that is not in accordance with that contract. Thus when an employee is
dismissed without the notice to which he is entitled (in circumstances that do not
justify summary dismissal) or when the employer prematurely terminates the
employee's fixed-term contract, the employee is entitled to claim damages in the
courts or an employment tribunal at common law for wrongful dismissal. The

court's jurisdiction concerns only the parties' contractual rights and not their statutory rights under the employment protection legislation (*compare* UNFAIR DISMISSAL). If a breach of statutory rights arises, an employee may also bring a claim for unfair dismissal. However, this must be done before an employment tribunal.

wrongful interference with goods Under the Torts (Interference with Goods) Act 1977, any of various torts to goods. It includes *conversion, *trespass to goods, negligence so far as it results in damage to goods or to an interest in goods, and any other tort (except *detinue, which is abolished by the Act) that results in damage to goods or an interest in goods.

wrongful trading Carrying on business knowing that the company has no reasonable prospect of avoiding an insolvent *winding-up. Such knowledge may be implied if a reasonably diligent person would have realized the position. Directors responsible may be ordered to contribute to the assets of the company when the winding-up occurs unless they can prove that, after acquiring the relevant knowledge, they endeavoured to minimize loss to the company's creditors, e.g. by initiating a winding-up or *administration order. *See also* FRAUDULENT TRADING.

WTO *See* WORLD TRADE ORGANIZATION.

year and thereafter from year to year Words sometimes used in a tenancy agreement, the effect of which is that the tenant has a *fixed-term tenancy for the first year, followed by a yearly *periodic tenancy.

Year Books *See* LAW REPORTS.

yearly tenancy A yearly *periodic tenancy.

Yellow Book *See* STOCK EXCHANGE.

yielding and paying Words that usually introduce the clause in a *lease that specifies the rent. *See also* REDDENDUM.

York–Antwerp rules *See* AVERAGE.

young offender *See* JUVENILE OFFENDER.

young offender institution *See* DETENTION IN A YOUNG OFFENDER INSTITUTION.

young workers *See* CHILD EMPLOYEE.

youth court A *magistrates' court exercising jurisdiction over crimes committed by *juvenile offenders and other matters relating to children under 18. It was formerly called a **juvenile court**. The court consists of either three lay *magistrates (at least one of whom should normally be a man and one a woman) or a single *district judge (magistrates' court) (normally accompanied by a lay magistrate of the opposite sex). All these magistrates are selected from the **youth court panel**, whose members are thought to be specially qualified to deal with juveniles and who have received additional training for this purpose. The proceedings of the court are not open to the general public, access being very restricted and determined by the Children and Young Persons Act 1933, section 42 (as amended) and by the Home Office and Lord Chancellor's Department Joint Circular on access to youth courts in June 1998. The press may not publish the identity of any juvenile concerned in the court's proceedings unless the court or the Home Secretary so orders, although reporting restrictions are lifted on conviction. Court proceedings are generally more informal than in the magistrates' court for adult offenders, and hearings can be heard in locations other than other court buildings, although generally they will be in existing magistrates' courts. There is a restriction in the timing of a youth court sitting in that it is not permitted within one hour either side of another court sitting. The Narey Report (Home Office 1997) recommended that this restriction be abolished in favour of separate waiting areas for youths and adults accused, to prevent the mixing of the two types of offender.

youth custody *See* DETENTION IN A YOUNG OFFENDER INSTITUTION.

Z

zealous witness A *witness who displays undue favouritism towards one party in the case.

zebra crossing A road crossing for pedestrians, identified by studs and alternating black and white stripes on the carriageway and lighted yellow globes (normally flashing) at each end. Pedestrians take precedence over vehicles on crossings uncontrolled by police or traffic wardens, and it is an offence for vehicles to wait or overtake within their limits.

zero-rated supply A supply that is within the scope of *value-added tax but is charged at a nil rate. Examples are food (excluding restaurant and take-away meals), books and journals, and children's clothes; all exports are also zero-rated. Unlike *exempt supplies, zero-rated supplies count towards the turnover limit above which registration for VAT is compulsory, and any input tax relating to them may be reclaimed by the registered trader.

Appendix I. Useful Addresses

ACAS – *See* Advisory, Conciliation and Arbitration Service

Adoption Contact Register
General Register Office
Adoptions Section
Smedley Hydro
Trafalgar Road
Southport
Merseyside
PR8 2HH
Tel 0151 471 4830
Web www.adoptions@ons.gov.uk

ADR Group (Alternative Dispute Resolution)
Grove House
Grove Road
Redland
Bristol
BS6 6UN
Tel 0117 946 7180
Web www.adrgoup.co.uk

Advertising Standards Authority
2 Torrington Place
London
WC1E 7HW
Tel 020 7580 5555
Web www.asa.org.uk

Advisory, Conciliation and Arbitration Service (ACAS)
Brandon House
180 Borough High Street
London
SE1 1LW
Tel 020 7396 5100
Web www.acas.org.uk

Association of British Insurers
51 Gresham Street
London
EC2V 7HQ
Tel 020 7600 3333
Web www.abi.org.uk

Bar Council – *See* General Council of the Bar

British Agencies for Adoption and Fostering (BAAF)
Skyline House
200 Union Street
London
SE1 0LX
Tel 020 7593 2000
Web www.baaf.org.uk

Business Software Alliance (BSA)
79 Knightsbridge
London
SW1X 7RB
0800 510510
Web www.bsa.org.uk

Centre for Effective Dispute Resolution (CEDR)
Princes House
95 Gresham Street
London
EC2V 7NA
Tel 020 7600 0500
Web www.cedr.co.uk

Chartered Institute of Patent Agents
Staple Inn Buildings
High Holborn
London
WC1V 7PZ
Tel 020 7405 9450
Web www.cipa.org.uk

Child Support Agency
PO Box 55
Brierley Hill
West Midlands
DY5 1YL
Enquiry Line 08457 133133
Web www.dss.gov.uk/csa

Community Trade Mark Office
Office for Harmonization in the Internal Market
(Trade Marks and Designs)
Avenida de Aguilera, 20
E-03080 Alicante
Spain
Tel 00 34 965 139 100
Web www.oami.eu.int

Companies House
Crown Way
Cardiff
CF14 3UZ
Tel 0870 333 3636
Web www.companieshouse.gov.uk

Consumers' Association (CA)
2 Marylebone Road
London
NW1 4DX
Tel 0207 770 7000
Web www.which@which.net

The Court Service
(*For information on jury service*)
Southside
105 Victoria Street
London
SW1E 6QT
Tel 020 7210 2266
Web www.courtservice.gov.uk

Criminal Injuries Compensation
  Authority (CICA)
Morley House
26–30 Holborn Viaduct
London
EC1A 2JQ
Tel 020 7842
Web www.cica.gov.uk

Department for Education and Skills
  (DfES)
Sanctuary Buildings
Great Smith Street
Westminster
London
SW1P 3BT
Tel 0870 000 2288
Web www.dfes.gov.uk

Department of Health
Richmond House
Whitehall
London
SW1A 2NL
Tel 020 7210 4850
Web www.doh.gov.uk

Department of Trade and Industry
1 Victoria Street
London

SW1H 0ET
Tel 020 7215 5000
Web www.dti.gov.uk

Design Council
34 Bow Street
London
WC2E 7DL
Tel 020 7420 5200
Web www.design-council.org.uk

Employment Tribunals – Central Office
19–29 Woburn Place
London
WC1H 0LU
Tel 020 7273 3000
Web www.employmenttribunals.
  gov.uk

Equal Opportunities Commission
Arndale House
Arndale Centre
Manchester
M4 3EQ
Tel 0161 833 9244
Web www.eoc.org.uk

European Commission (Commission of
  the European Communities)
200 Rue de la Loi
B-1049 Brussels
Belgium
Tel 00 322 299 1111
London 0171 973 1992
Web www.europa.int/comm

European Commission of Human
  Rights
Secretary of the Commission
Conseil de L'Europe
F-67075 Strasbourg Cedex
France
Tel 00 33 88 41 2000
Fax 00 33 88 41 2792
Web www.humanrights.coe.int

European Patent Office
Erhardstrasse 27
D-80331 Munich
Germany
Tel 00 49 89 23990
Fax 00 49 89 2399 4465
Web www.european-patent-office.org

European Trade Mark Office
Avenida de Aguilera, 20
E-03080 Alicante
Spain
Tel 00 34 965 139 100
Fax 00 34 965 131 344
Web www.oami.eu.int

Federation Against Software Theft
(FAST)
Clivemont House
54 Clivemont Road
Maidenhead
Berkshire
SL6 7BS
Tel 01628 622121
Web www.fast.org.uk

The General Council of the Bar of
England and Wales (Bar Council)
3 Bedford Row
London
WC1R 4DB
Tel 020 7242 0082
Web www.barcouncil.org.uk

General Register Office (GRO)
(*For information on birth, marriage, and
death certificates*)
Office for National Statistics
Smedley Hydro
Trafalgar Road
Southport
PR8 2HH
Tel 0870 243 7788
Web www.statistics.gov.uk

The General Register Office for Scotland
New Register House
3 West Register Street
Edinburgh
EH1 3YT
Tel 0131 334 0380
Web www.gro-scotland.gov.uk

Health and Safety Executive
Rose Court, Ground Floor North
2 Southwark Bridge
London
SE1 9HS
Tel 020 7717 6000
Web www.hse.gov.uk

Her Majesty's Stationery Office
(*For administration of Crown copyright*)
The Copyright Unit
St Clements House
2–16 Colegate
Norwich
NR3 1BQ
Tel 01603 621000
Fax 01603 723000
Web www.hmso.gov.uk

Home Office
50 Queen Anne's Gate
London
SW1H 9AT
Tel 020 7273 4000
Web www.homeoffice.gov.uk

Housing Corporation
149 Tottenham Court Road
London
W1T 7BN
Tel 020 7393 2000
Web www.housingcorp.gov.uk

Information Commissioner's Office
Wycliffe House
Water Lane
Wilmslow
Cheshire
SK9 5AF
Tel 01625 545700
Web www.dataprotection.gov.uk

Inland Revenue
National Contributions Office
Benton Park View
Longbenton
Newcastle upon Tyne
NE98 1ZZ
Tel 0191 213 5000
Web www.inlandrevenue.gov.uk

Inland Revenue Stamp Office
South-West Wing
Bush House
Strand
London
WC2B 4QN
Tel 020 7438 7252
Web www.inlandrevenue.gov.uk/so

Institute of Chartered Accountants in
England and Wales
Chartered Accounts' Hall
PO Box 433
Moorgate Place
London
EC2P 2BJ
Tel 020 7920 8100
Web www.icaew.co.uk

Institute of Trade Mark Agents
Fourth Floor
Canterbury House
2–6 Sydenham Road
Croydon
CR0 9XE
Tel 020 8686 2052
Web www.itma.org.uk

Law Centres Federation
Duchess House
18–19 Warren Street
London
W1T 5LR
Tel 020 7387 8570
Web www.lawcentres.org.uk

Law Commission
Conquest House
37–38 John Street
Theobalds Road
London
WC1N 2BQ
Tel 020 7453 1220
Web www.lawcom.gov.uk

Law Society of England and Wales
113 Chancery Lane
London
WC2A 1PL
Tel 020 7242 1222
Web www.lawsoc.org.uk

Law Society of Northern Ireland
Law Society House
98 Victoria Street
Belfast
BT1 3JZ
Tel 02890 231614
Web www.lawsoc-ni.org.uk

Law Society of Scotland
26 Drumsheugh Gardens

Edinburgh
EH3 7YR
Tel 0131 226 7411
Web www.lawscot.org.uk

Legal Services Commission
85 Gray's Inn Road
London
WC1X 8TX
Tel 020 7759 0000
Web www.legalservices.gov.uk

National Consumer Council
20 Grosvenor Gardens
London
SW1W 0DH
Tel 020 7730 3469
Web www.ncc.org.uk

Northern Ireland Office
Block B
Castle Buildings
Belfast
BT4 3SG
Tel 0208 900700
Web www.nio.gov.uk
and
11 Millbank
London
SW1P 4PN
Tel 020 7210 3000

Office for Standards in Education
(Ofsted)
Alexandra House
33 Kingsway
London
WC2B 6SE
Tel 020 7421 6800
Web www.ofsted.gov.uk

Office for the Supervision of
Solicitors
Victoria Court
8 Dormer Place
Leamington Spa
Warwickshire
CV32 5AE
Tel 01926 8220082
Web www.oss.lawsociety.org.uk

Office of Fair Trading
Fleetbank House

2-6 Salisbury Square
London
EC4Y 8JX
Tel 020 7211 8000
Web www.oft.gov.uk

Office of Gas and Electricity Markets
   (Ofgem)
9 Millbank
London
SW1P 3GE
Tel 020 7901 7000
Web www.ofgem.gov.uk

Office of the National Lottery (Oflot)
2 Monck Street
London
SW1P 2BQ
Tel 08457 125596
Web www.natlotcomm.gov.uk

Office of Telecommunications (Oftel)
50 Ludgate Hill
London
EC4M 7JJ
Tel 020 7634 8700
Web www.oftel.gov.uk

Office of Water Services (Ofwat)
Centre City Tower
7 Hill Street
Birmingham
B5 4UA
Tel 0121 625 1300
Web www.ofwat.gov.uk

Ombudsmen

Estate Agents Ombudsmen
Beckett House
Fourbridge Street
Salisbury
SP1 2LX
Tel 01722 333306
Web www.oea.co.uk

Financial Ombudsman Service
South Quay Plaza
183 Marsh Wall
London
E14 9SR
Tel 0845 080 1800
Web www.financial-ombudsman.org.uk

Independent Housing Ombudsman
Norman House
105–109 Strand
London
WC2R 0AA
Tel 020 7836 3630
Web www.ihos.org.uk

Office of the Legal Services
   Ombudsman
22 Oxford Court
Oxford Street
Manchester
M2 3WQ
Tel 0161 839 7262
Web www.olso.org

Commission for Local Administration
   in England
Local Government Ombudsman
21 Queen Anne's Gate
London
SW1H 9BU
Tel 020 7915 3210
Web www.lgo.org.uk

Commission for Local Administration
   in Wales
Local Government Ombudsman for
   Wales
Derwen House
Court Road
Bridgend
CF31 1BN
Tel 01656 661325
Web www.ombudsman-wales.org

The Parliamentary and Health Service
   Ombudsman
Millbank Tower
Millbank
London
SW1P 4QP
Tel 0845 015 4033
Web www.ombudsman.org.uk

The Pensions Ombudsman
11 Belgrave Road
London
SW1V 1RB
Tel 020 7834 9144
Web www.pensions-ombudsman.
   org.uk

UK Passport Agency
Clive House
70 Petty France
London
SW1H 9HD
Tel 0171 799 2728
Web www.ukpa.gov.uk

Patent Office, Designs Office and Trade
  Marks Office
Concept House
Cardiff Road
Newport
South Wales
NP10 8QQ
Tel 08459 500505
Fax 01633 813600
Web www.patent.gov.uk

Police Complaints Authority
10 Great George Street
London
SW1P 3AE
Tel 020 7273 6450
Web www.pca.gov.uk

Principal Registry (Family Division)
(*For information on wills and
  divorce*)
Somerset House
London
WC2R 1LP
Tel 0207 947 6000
Web www.courtservice.gov.uk

Scotland Office
1 Melville Crescent
Edinburgh
EH3 7HW
Tel 0131 244 9010
Web www.scottishsecretary.co.uk

  and

Dover House
Whitehall
London
SW1A 2AU
Tel 020 7270 6754

Solicitors Directory Listing of Experts
Chambers and Partners' Directory
Chambers & Partners
Saville House
23 Long Lane
London
EC1A 9HL
Tel 020 7606 1300
Fax 020 7600 3191
Web www.chambersandpartners.com

The Solicitors' Disciplinary Tribunal
Gate House
1 Farringdon Street
London EC4
Tel 020 7329 4808

The Stationery Office (tSO)
St. Crispins
Duke Street
Norwich
NR3 1PD
Tel 01603 622211
For sale of statutory material:
Orders – Tel 020 7242 6393
Web www.clicktso.com

United Nations
Centre for Human Rights
8–14 Avenue de la Paix
1211 Geneva 10
Switzerland
00 41 22 917 9000
Web www.unog.ch

The Wales Office
Cathays Park
Cardiff
CF10 3NQ
Tel 029 20 825111
Web www.ossw.wales.gov.uk

  and

Office of the Secretary of State for
  Wales
Gwydyr House
Whitehall
London
SW1A 2ER
Tel 0207 270 3000

Appendix II. Directorates General of the European Commission

DGI	External Relations: Commercial Policy and Relations with North America, the Far East, Australia, and New Zealand
DGIA	External Relations: Europe and the New Independent States, Common Foreign and Security Policy, and External Missions
DGIB	External Relations: Southern Mediterranean, Middle and Near East, Latin America, South and South-East Asia, and North-South Cooperation
DGII	Economic and Financial Affairs
DGIII	Industry
DGIV	Competition
DGV	Employment, Industrial Relations, and Social Affairs
DGVI	Agriculture
DGVII	Transport
DGVIII	Development
DGIX	Personnel and Administration
DGX	Information, Communication, Culture, Audiovisual
DGXI	Environment, Nuclear Safety, and Civil Protection
DGXII	Science, Research, and Development
DGXIII	Telecommunications, Information Market, and Exploitation of Research
DGXIV	Fisheries
DGXV	Internal Market and Financial Services
DGXVI	Regional Policies and Cohesion
DGXVII	Energy
DGXIX	Budgets
DGXXI	Customs and Indirect Taxation
DGXXII	Education, Training, and Youth
DGXXIII	Enterprise Policy, Distributive Trades, Tourism, and Cooperatives
DGXXIV	Consumer Policy and Consumer Health Protection